MW01044618

COMMUNICATION
AND
GROUP
DECISION MAKING

SECOND EDITION

For Ann, Karla, Kristy, and Tyler
&
For Lisa and Sam. . . .
The group members who mean the most to us.

COMMUNICATION
AND
GROUP
DECISION MAKING

SECOND EDITION

RANDY Y. HIROKAWA
MARSHALL SCOTT POOLE

SAGE Publications
International Educational and Professional Publisher
Thousand Oaks   London   New Delhi

For information address:

SAGE Publications, Inc.
2455 Teller Road
Thousand Oaks, California 91320
E-mail: order@sagepub.com

SAGE Publications Ltd.
6 Bonhill Street
London EC2A 4PU
United Kingdom

SAGE Publications India Pvt. Ltd.
M-32 Market
Greater Kailash I
New Delhi 110 048 India

Printed in the United States of America

Library of Congress Cataloging-in-Publication Data

Communication and group decision making / [edited by]
  Randy Y. Hirokawa and Marshall Scott Poole.—2nd ed.
     p.   cm.
  Includes bibliographical references and index.
  ISBN 0-7619-0461-1 (alk. paper).—ISBN 0-7619-0462-X
(pbk.: alk. paper).
     1. Decision-making, Group. 2. Communication in management.
  I. Hirokawa, Randy Y. II. Poole, Marshall Scott, 1951-
HD30.23.C65   1996
658.4'036—dc20   96-4514

This book is printed on alkaline paper.

96 97 98 99 10 9 8 7 6 5 4 3 2 1

Sage Production Editor: Gillian Dickens   Sage Typesetter: Marion Warren

Contents

PART I: INTRODUCTION

1. Introduction: Communication and Group Decision Making   3
   Marshall Scott Poole and Randy Y. Hirokawa

2. Remembering and "Re-Membering": A History of
   Theory and Research on Communication and
   Group Decision Making   19
   Lawrence R. Frey

PART II: THEORIES

3. Functional Theory and Communication in
   Decision-Making and Problem-Solving Groups:
   An Expanded View   55
   Dennis S. Gouran and Randy Y. Hirokawa

4. Symbolic Convergence Theory and Communication
   in Group Decision Making   81
   Ernest G. Bormann

5. The Structuration of Group Decisions   114
   Marshall Scott Poole, David R. Seibold,
   and Robert D. McPhee

6. Bona Fide Groups: An Alternative Perspective for
   Communication and Small Group Decision Making   147
   Linda L. Putnam and Cynthia Stohl

7. Small Group Communication May Not Influence
   Decision Making: An Amplification of Socio-Egocentric
   Theory   179
   Dean E. Hewes

PART III: PROCESSES

8. Developmental Processes in Group Decision Making   215
   Marshall Scott Poole and Carolyn L. Baldwin

9. Communication and Influence in Group
   Decision Making   242
   David R. Seibold, Renée A. Meyers, and Sunwolf

10. Communication and Group Decision-Making
    Effectiveness   269
    Randy Y. Hirokawa, Larry Erbert, and Anthony Hurst

11. Leadership Skills and the Dialectics of Leadership
    in Group Decision Making   301
    J. Kevin Barge

PART IV: PROCEDURES

12. Procedures for Enhancing Group Decision Making   345
    Susan Jarboe

13. Procedural Influence on Group Decision Making:
    The Case of Straw Polls—Observation and Simulation   384
    James H. Davis, Lorne Hulbert, and Wing Tung Au

14. New Communication Technologies for Group
    Decision Making: Toward an Integrative Framework   426
    Poppy Lauretta McLeod

    Index   463

    About the Contributors   483

INTRODUCTION

Introduction
Communication and Group Decision Making

MARSHALL SCOTT POOLE
RANDY Y. HIROKAWA

The great mystery of all conduct is social conduct. I have had to study it all my life, but I cannot pretend to understand it. I may seem to know a man through and through, and still I would not want to say the first thing about what he will do in a group.

—Anonymous

A committee is a cul-de-sac down which promising young ideas are lured and then quietly strangled.

—Anonymous

There is a world of difference between making a decision alone and making a group decision. The unique chemistry of social interaction can distill the best that each member has to offer, creating a resonance of ideas and a synthesis of viewpoints. A different chemistry can stop the reaction and contaminate the product. The catalyst for such social chemistry is communication. It is the medium for the coordination and control of group activities, member socialization, group integration, and conflict management, among other functions.

As important as group communication processes are, they have proven elusive and difficult to understand. In part, this is because they are truly complex. The interaction of multiple parties subject to manifold psychological, social, and contextual influences is one of the most difficult objects of study in the human sciences. The type of theory necessary to make sense of processes differs from those commonly found in the social sciences. Rather than explaining dependent variables as a function of input variables, theories of process must account for the generative mechanisms that produce the interaction sequences and temporal processes that lead to various "outcomes" (Harré & Secord, 1973; Van de Ven & Poole, 1995). Theories of process are more like stories or narratives than traditional X-causes-Y explanations.

As a result of these complexities, theories of group communication have been relatively slow in coming. In the first edition of this book, along with other commentators of the early 1980s, we lamented the lack of theory in the area. As the present edition shows, a number of strong theoretical frameworks have developed over the past 15 years, along with considerable empirical evidence. At the time of this writing, at least two additional perspectives, an encompassing framework by Cragan, Shields, and Wright (1994) and the naturalistic perspective on groups (Frey, 1994b), are in the early stages of development. We hope there will be chapters on these in the next edition.

This book advances a unique perspective on group decision making that is complementary to approaches taken in management, psychology, and sociology. The chapters are distinctive, both in their explicit focus on communication processes and in their location in a unique intellectual tradition. The field of speech communication has its roots in the humanistic discipline of rhetoric, with its dual concern for the critical study of speech and writing and for the pragmatics of effective communication. These emphases interact to produce pragmatically tempered theories. Because these theories focus on discourse, they tend to place greater emphasis on processes and skills than on inputs such as structures and traits. An additional leavening is the traditional rhetorical concern with larger philosophical issues. Communication scholarship has emphasized the careful analysis of theoretical assumptions and the importance of linking findings to overarching theoretical frameworks. A particularly important theoretical problem relevant to communication is the nature of meaning and how to arrive at full and rigorous interpretations of discourse. This combination of tendencies has produced a unique approach and problem focus, one that we believe fills an important niche in the study of group dynamics.

Another contribution of the field of communication to the study of groups has been in the development and refinement of methods for the study of interaction processes. Research on interaction poses methodological problems sufficient to give even the most energetic and skillful researchers pause. Outstanding among them are the interpretive problems of determining the meaning or function of communicative acts, the difficulties in sorting out group and individual sources of influence, and the logistical problems involved in dealing with the large masses of data generated by various observational techniques. Group communication researchers have tackled these problems with a wide array of approaches, some borrowed and improved, and some developed within the field. Communication researchers have developed a number of useful and interesting coding systems, such as Gouran's (1969) system for the classification of orientation statements, Leathers's (1969) process disruption coding system, Fisher's (1970) decision proposal coding system and social information processing coding system (Fisher, Drecksel, & Werbel, 1978), Poole's (Poole & Roth, 1989a) system for coding group work climate and conflict, and Hirokawa's functional coding system (Hirokawa & Rost, 1992). Along with these have come theories and techniques for the assessment of reliability and validity of coding schemes and interpretations (Folger, Hewes, & Poole, 1984; Poole, Folger, & Hewes, 1987). Qualitative approaches have also been employed (see Frey, 1994a, 1995), including ethnography of communication (Phillipsen, 1977), discourse analysis (Geist & Chandler, 1984), and rhetorical criticism (Chesebro, Cragan, & McCullough, 1973). Techniques for analysis of interaction processes have been developed and refined, including flexible phase mapping (Holmes & Poole, 1991; Poole & Holmes, 1995), Markov and semi-Markov models (Hewes, 1980; Hewes, Planalp, & Streibel, 1980), and fuzzy-set models for consensus measurement (Spillman, Bezdek, & Spillman, 1979).

This volume takes stock of recent developments in group communication research. Each chapter pulls together a body of literature and advances an integrative framework for its particular area. The volume is divided into four parts. Part I gives an introduction to the topic of communication and group decision making. In this first chapter, we will consider some critical issues for theory and research. Chapter 2, by Lawrence Frey, presents a brief history of the area. Part II presents five theoretical perspectives on group communication and decision making: the functional approach (Chapter 3), symbolic convergence theory (Chapter 4), theory of structuration (Chapter 5), the bona fide group perspective (Chapter 6), and a socio-egocentric model of group decision making (Chapter 7). Part III is concerned with critical processes in group decision making. Chapter 8 presents theory and evidence on developmental processes in group decision making. The focus of Chapter 9 is communicative influence in decision making. Chapter 10 reviews the influence of communication on decision-making effectiveness. Chapter 11 concludes this section with a discussion of leadership communication and its role in group decision making. Part IV focuses on procedures and techniques for aiding group decision making. Chapters 12 and 13 are concerned with various types of procedures and their benefits and costs for decision-making groups. Chapter 14 presents an integrative theoretical framework for understanding how computerized group support systems affect decision making.

The remainder of this first chapter is divided into two sections. First, we discuss two general perspectives on the role of communication in group decision making. Then we consider some general issues that we believe are important to further advances in research on communication and group decision making.

Theoretical Perspectives on Group Decision Making

We can distinguish two views of how communication influences group decision making. Communication can be studied as the *medium* of group interaction, and thereby the channel for the effects of various factors on group decision processes and outcomes. In addition, communication can be viewed as *constitutive* of group decisions—as the means for creating the social reality in which a decision is constructed. In this view, communication is the very substance of decision making, rather than merely a channel.

COMMUNICATION AS A MEDIUM FOR DECISION MAKING

To regard communication as a medium is to place the main emphasis on factors or processes other than communication per se in the explanation of decisions. Two types of factors are invoked to explain decision behavior and outcomes: (a) factors describing the inputs into and context of the decision, such as group size, group composition, members' preferences, or task type; (b) factors determining the nature of interaction processes, such as group polarization or leadership style. Decision processes and outcomes are treated as dependent variables, determined by the two sets of factors.

According to this view, communication serves as a medium for the influence of input or contextual factors on group processes. To give one example, group size has been found to be negatively correlated with average member input. It therefore is presumed to influence the communication medium, the amount of critical discussion that ideas receive and, through this, decision quality (Shaw, 1981, chap. 6). In similar fashion, members' knowledge determines the expressed pool of ideas and thereby influences and limits group solutions (Davis, 1969). Exogenous factors—in this case, group size and range of knowledge—are the focus of interest, and communication is by and large simply a channel for their effects.

As a medium, communication can exert its own distorting or biasing effects on decisions, as in the case of groupthink (Janis, 1972). These effects are often converted into variables in their own right, however—causes acting parallel to or interacting with exogenous factors. Ultimately they too can be shown to depend on exogenous conditions. In general, the tendency of mediational research is to regard communication as a substrate that transmits the effects of exogenous factors that do most of the explanatory work.

This view is important because it recognizes the instrumentality of communication. As a primary tool of social action, communication mediates the effects of traits, knowledge, preferences, task characteristics, and scores of other influences on decision making. It is important to understand the nature of this mediation—which is often not at all simple—if we are to understand group decision making. Like all tools, communication can shape both the user and the forces applied.

COMMUNICATION AND THE CONSTITUTION OF DECISIONS

Though studies that regard communication as a medium are more common, we can also focus on the role of communication in the constitution of decisions. Communication constitutes decisions in at least two senses: (a) Through communication the form and content of decisions are worked out. Decisions can be viewed as emerging texts or developing ideas, and we can trace the communicative processes of accumulation, deletion, elaboration, and alteration of premises. (b) At a more fundamental level, decisions are social products embedded in "social reality." Communication processes are the primary means through which social realities are created and sustained, and therefore are the prerequisites for making decisions. Studies of this grounding have focused on, among other things, the role of communication in creating shared realities (Bormann, Chapter 4, this volume), the enactment and use of structures in interaction (Poole, Seibold, & McPhee, Chapter 5, this volume), boundary setting (Putnam & Stohl, Chapter 6, this volume), and leadership as a mediational process (Barge, Chapter 11, this volume).

Studies of communication as a constitutive force necessarily have interpretive components, because they are concerned with social reality as experienced by participants. However, this does not rule out causal components in explanation; some studies also attempt to trace the effects of exogenous factors on interpretive and constitutive processes (and, in turn, the social constitution or mediation of these exogenous factors). Poole and McPhee (1994) describe this mode of explanation as *dialectical*.

The constitutive perspective is important because it considers the active role of communication in creating and sustaining social practices. It regards decision making as an inherently problematic phenomenon. It asserts that, at base, decision making depends on the skills of members and on the constitutive power of language and social action.

RELATIONSHIP OF MEDIUM AND CONSTITUTIVE VIEWS

The foregoing discussion suggests that any perspective that regards communication as constitutive also treats it as a medium. It is as a medium for other factors that the constitutive force of communication comes into play. However, the converse is not true. Perspectives that regard communication only as a medium disregard social construction. Although the majority of empirical studies have and continue to focus on communication as a medium, the constitutive viewpoint is gaining currency. Several of the theories in Part II and most of the chapters in Parts III and IV directly address the constitutive role of communication.

As both types of group communication theories evolve, we believe it is important that they tackle several key issues. Some of these are addressed in the next section.

Directions, Problems, Opportunities

Growth of our knowledge has the unexpected benefit of making us aware of what we do *not* know. As research advances, unresolved issues and unquestioned assumptions come into sharper focus. These can be viewed as gaps or shortcomings, but we believe it is more productive to view them as opportunities for ambitious scholars to make a contribution. At least five challenges confront group decision-making research at present.

WHAT, EXACTLY, IS A DECISION?

Judging by most accounts, defining a decision is fairly straightforward. Decisions are assumed to be discrete events, clearly distinguishable from other group activities. This reflects the commonsense assumptions of researchers who are themselves everyday decision makers. Decision makers often can identify discrete decision points and feel a sense of completion at making a decision. These boundaries are not always as clear as they seem at first, however, and there is not always agreement on what events are involved in a given decision. Definitions of decision-making episodes are ambiguous in several respects.

Almost every decision involves a series of activities and choices nested in choices of wider scope, rather than a single simple choice. Should investigators aim for the "least divisible unit," treating each choice in the series as if it were a decision in its own right, or should they consider only the larger decision and treat smaller-grained choices as "subcomponents"? Unfortunately, there are no clear guidelines for separating "major" decisions from "minor" ones. As Simon (1976) observed, every choice is embedded in a means-ends hierarchy in which it serves both as a means for a larger choice and as the end of more restricted choices. For any decision we study, we can always second-guess ourselves, either by going up the hierarchy to find a "more significant" decision, or by going down to find a "more basic" decision. This problem is particularly acute in studies of decisions in the field of communications. For example, Poole (Poole & Roth, 1989a, 1989b) analyzed decisions drawn from a set of government committee meetings. The complexity of their task forced the committees to subdivide their deliberations, which made it extremely difficult to decide whether the subcomponents (each of which was quite complicated) or the larger issues defined by the committees' agendas should be used as the unit of analysis. One way of resolving this issue might have been to have the participants define meaningful decision units, but this, too, would be problematic if there were disagreements.

Defining the beginning and the end of a decision process is also difficult. Does a decision begin when the group states a goal or problem, when it first becomes aware of an issue, or when a single member recognizes a need? Does it end when the choice is made, after the "integration" period, or when the group explicitly takes up another issue? Setting temporal boundaries is complicated still further by the fact that discussions and negotiations that influence the decision often occur outside the meeting itself. Should these be included as part of the decision, or only as they figure in actual group meetings?

Tackling these issues is essential for studies of natural groups, but it is also important for laboratory research. To be able to create valid simulations of decisions, researchers need guidelines regarding the steps their tasks must include, the nature of the context they must set up, and what they must require subjects to do.

DECISION MAKING IS NOT ALL A GROUP DOES

Related to this is another issue: Groups do more than make decisions. Decision making is but one practice suspended in a web of other practices, including information sharing, socializing, relating to people and groups external to the group, educating new members, defining roles and status in the group, meeting rituals such as reading the minutes, and the physical activities and work the group must perform. The relationship of these practices to decisions is complicated: When the group appears to be making a decision, members may have other goals or interests in mind, and when they are engaged in other activities, members may be tacitly working on the decision. March and Olsen (1976) catalog numerous other "nondecision" functions that decisions may serve, including justifying procedures, defining virtue and truth, distributing glory or blame, reaffirming trust, expressing and discovering interests, fulfilling role expectations, and "having a good time." For many decisions, prudent choice may be of secondary interest, overshadowed by other concerns.

How do we situate decision making in this web of other practices? One response is to continue to focus on the strand of decision behavior that winds through meetings and to determine how the many other activities influence decision making (see, e.g., March & Olsen, 1976). Others have advocated placing less emphasis on the study of decision making per se, focusing instead on other aspects of group life (see, e.g., Frey, 1994a, 1995). Decision making could still be studied but only as it figures in other group phenomena, such as the provision of social support or teamwork. Whatever the resolution, it is important to acknowledge that groups do much more than make decisions and that these other practices are vital to the group as well. This implies, in turn, that we must broaden our conceptualization of communicative functions in groups.

WHAT FUNCTIONS DOES COMMUNICATION SERVE IN GROUPS?

The heart of any process-oriented theory of decision making is a conception of how communication enters into group activity. We have distinguished two general viewpoints—the mediational and the constitutive perspectives. At a more specific level it is necessary to consider the particular functions that communication serves in decision making. The work of Bales (1950, 1953) and of Carter, Haythorn, Meirowitz, and Lanzetta (1951) pioneered functional analysis of group interaction. Communication researchers have advanced other functional systems (e.g., Fisher, 1970; Gouran, 1969; Gouran & Hirokawa, 1983; Mabry, 1975).

Among the functions considered by group communication researchers are: (a) social information processing functions, which involve the analysis and combination of information, as well as the generation, elaboration, and evaluation of ideas; (b) analytic functions, which involve the analysis of circumstances and contingencies surrounding the choice-making situation; (c) procedural functions, encompassing the establishment and maintenance of procedures and rules for arriving at a decision; (d) goal-related functions, which pertain to the establishment and monitoring of group goals and values; (e) synergistic functions, involving the coordination and motivation of group members; and (f) rhetorical functions, such as persuasion, social influence, leadership, and visioning.

Street and Cappella (1985) edited a volume outlining a general functional approach to communication. They identified several additional functions that might be considered by group communication researchers, including the maintenance of coherence in discourse, dominance and control, and the management of interpersonal intimacy.

One way to work out the communicative implications of the intertwining group activities discussed above would be to develop models of how the various communicative functions relate to one another. Do some functions serve as bases or necessary conditions for others? Are some functional realms largely independent of each other? Do some functions reinforce or interfere with the operation of others? Bales (1953) and Mabry (1975) can serve as excellent models for this sort of theoretical work. Both specify critical functions, their underlying dimensions, and a model of functional relationships linked to Parson's general theory of society.

It is also important to consider the question of what such functions represent. In most cases, researchers identify communicative functions and simply assert that they are there. However, many regard members' perceptions of understandings of discourse as important. In such cases it seems important to assess whether researcher-identified functions match members' perceptions or interpretations. Work on the validation of coding systems (Folger et al., 1984; Poole et al., 1987) provides theories and methods for assessing this match.

PROBLEMS WITH EXOGENOUS VARIABLES

A number of models or typologies of variables that shape group processes have been advanced (e.g., Cragan et al., 1994; Hare, 1976; McGrath, 1984; McGrath & Altman, 1966; Shaw, 1981). All seem to have one thing in common: their almost stunning complexity. Dozens of determinants are listed, and other than gathering them under general categories, such as "task structure" or "environment," these frameworks do not lend much structure to their lists. It is critical that we master this mess and prioritize the variables that influence group interaction in terms of relative strength or importance. Not every variable is equal in terms of impact on decision making.

Meta-analysis is one strategy that seems likely to help. We already know from literature reviews that task is a strong determinant of group processes (Bochner, 1974; McGrath, 1984). A recent meta-analysis (Mullen & Copper, 1994) has shown group cohesiveness to have definite effects on group performance. As more and more studies are conducted, more meta-analyses can be performed, and the relative impact of input variables can be assessed and graded.

But no matter how many meta-analyses are conducted, nothing can substitute for the development of sound theories that focus on the input-process-output relationship. The introduction to the first edition recommended the development of contingency theories, and we still believe this is important. A contingency theory of group decision making is premised on the assumption that group outcomes are a function of the match between (a) the demands placed on the group and the resources provided it, and (b) the communicative processes the group enacts to meet these demands and deploy its resources. If the group process is appropriate for the demands and resources, positive outcomes will ensue, but if it is not, negative outcomes will result.

Developing a contingency theory requires us to determine which exogenous variables adequately represent key demands and resources. Variables such as task complexity, time pressure, and conflict potential are examples of "demand" variables, whereas group composition and cohesiveness exemplify "resource" variables. Once a set of such variables has been identified, communicative processes that might respond to them must be characterized. Variables such as conflict management style and fulfillment of critical decision functions, as well as profiles of specific types of communication acts (e.g., orientation) can be used to characterize these processes. Then the degree of match between exogenous and process variables must be determined. This requires the theorist to work out which processes are useful responses to the exogenous contingencies. With these three pieces of the puzzle in place, evaluation of the theory can proceed.

No complete contingency theory of group decision making has been advanced. Gladstein (1984) worked toward a contingency theory of group performance. McGrath (1984) and Hirokawa (1990) have presented analyses of the effects of task contingencies on group outcomes. Poole and Roth (1989a, 1989b; see also Poole & Baldwin, Chapter 8, this volume) tested a partial contingency theory of decision development. McGrath's (1991) time-interaction-performance (TIP) theory also presents a partial contingency theory. Progress has been made but there is a great need for more work in this arena.

Beyond the need for theory development, there is another troubling issue—many key exogenous variables have not been clearly conceptualized or defined. Task, one of the most important input variables, continues to defy comprehensive analyses. Starting with work by Hackman (1969) and Shaw (1973), extending to that of McGrath (1984), several sets of dimensions and typologies of group tasks have been presented. However, none has proven completely satisfactory. McGrath (1984) attempts to synthesize previous efforts in his task circumplex, but his typology is really only practicable for clearly defined experimental tasks. It breaks down when applied to tasks of real groups, which generally combine elements of two or more of his eight quadrants. Group composition is also an ill-defined variable. Although the importance of group composition in terms of skill, intellect, needs, and other variables is widely acknowledged, there are no general theories of how composition affects work. Generally it is assumed that the more of a good characteristic the group has, the better. In the case of some individual traits, such as dogmatism, however, having only one person high in this trait can have considerable effects on the group. Different types of composition effects need to be sorted out.

In short, a major task for future group communication research is to clarify the tangle of exogenous variables. If this can be accomplished, it will facilitate development of improved models of the input-process-output chain.

OUTCOMES

Most group communication research is concerned with the bottom line, the impact of communication processes on outcomes such as decision quality, member satisfaction, commitment to the decision, and member motivation. However, incorporating outcomes into group communication research is not as straightforward as it seems. Although reliable and valid measures of attitudes such as satisfaction, commitment, and motivation have been developed, these data are sometimes analyzed inappropriately. Because the responses of members of the same group are not independent, it is not appropriate to include each individual response in statistical analyses without blocking for or controlling for group membership. Techniques for multilevel analysis that incorporate both group and individual effects are described by Anderson and Ager (1978) and by Dansereau and Markham (1987).

Things are not at all straightforward in the assessment of the key outcome variable, decision quality. Much progress has been made in understanding the role of communication in effective decision making (see Hirokawa, Erbert, & Hurst, Chapter 10, this volume). However, the construct of decision quality is problematic. It is difficult to measure for tasks that do not have a correct answer, which includes the majority of real-world tasks. A solution judged to be effective in the short run may prove disastrous over the long run. A decision effective from the perspective of one party may be disadvantageous for other parties. Moreover, most quality assessment assumes that groups are working on the same task. Although this is generally true for experimental tasks, it is not so for field observation, which often samples groups working on disparate tasks. Though some very good studies of decision quality have been conducted, this construct still needs theoretical and operational polishing.

For all outcome constructs there is an additional complication. We generally treat outcomes as though they happen at the end of a simple decision process. However, most process theorists would argue that there is a recursive relationship such that outcomes "loop back" to influence group processes and some exogenous variables. For example, the outcomes of a prior decision may affect the group's level of aspiration and cohesiveness, which in turn influence the current decision process. Members' dissatisfaction with the decision process for one decision may change their behavior in future decision episodes. Moreover, outcomes do not simply emerge at the end of a decision. Members are experiencing satisfaction, judging the quality of the emerging decision, and assessing their own commitment to it as the decision is being made. Outcomes may therefore be reconceptualized as dynamic variables that influence the system via feedback loops throughout the decision process. The conceptual and statistical measures needed to incorporate this into our theories will prove challenging for future group communication scholars.

Conclusion

Group communication research has made much progress over the past 10 years and is poised to make even greater strides in the future. This is a propitious time for research on group communication and interaction in general. The upswing of interest in communication that we noted in the first edition has swelled in the ensuing 10 years. This makes the present a good time for increasing the linkage of group communication research with other traditions to forge a broader, more complete study of group processes.

References

Anderson, L. R., & Ager, J. W. (1978). Analysis of variance in small group research. *Personality and Social Psychology Bulletin, 4*, 341-345.

Bales, R. F. (1950). *Interaction process analysis: A method for studying small groups.* Reading, MA: Addison-Wesley.

Bales, R. F. (1953). The equilibrium problem in small groups. In T. Parsons, E. A. Shils, & R. F. Bales (Eds.), *Working papers in the theory of action* (pp. 111-161). New York: Free Press.

Bochner, A. P. (1974). Task and instrumentation variables as factor jeopardizing the validity of published group communication research, 1970-71. *Speech Monographs, 41*, 169-174.

Carter, L. F., Haythorn, W., Meirowitz, B., & Lanzetta, J. (1951). The relation of categorizations and ratings in the observation of group behavior. *Human Relations, 4*, 239-254.

Chesebro, J. W., Cragan, J. F., & McCullough, P. (1973). The small group techniques of the radical revolutionary: A synthetic study of consciousness raising. *Communication Monographs, 40*, 136-146.

Cragan, J. F., Shields, D. C., & Wright, D. W. (1994). *A unified theory of small group communication: Accounting for paradigms, theories, processes, skills, and outcomes.* Unpublished manuscript, Illinois State University, Normal.

Dansereau, F., & Markham, S. E. (1987). Levels of analysis in personnel and human resources management. In K. Rowland & G. Ferris (Eds.), *Research in personnel and human resources management* (pp. 1-50). Greenwich, CT: JAI.

Davis, J. H. (1969). *Group performance.* Reading, MA: Addison-Wesley.

Fisher, B. A. (1970). Decision emergence: Phases in group decision-making. *Speech Monographs, 37,* 53-66.

Fisher, B. A., Drecksel, G. L., & Werbel, W. (1978). Social information processing analysis (SIPA): Coding ongoing human communication. *Small Group Behavior, 10,* 3-21.

Folger, J. P., Hewes, D. E., & Poole, M. S. (1984). Coding social interaction. In B. Dervin & M. Voight (Eds.), *Progress in the communication sciences* (Vol. 4, pp. 115-161). Norwood, NJ: Ablex.

Frey, L. R. (Ed.). (1994a). *Group communication in context: Studies of natural groups.* Hillsdale, NJ: Lawrence Erlbaum.

Frey, L. R. (1994b). The naturalistic paradigm: Studying small groups in the postmodern era. *Small Group Research, 25,* 551-577.

Frey, L. R. (Ed.). (1995). *Innovations in group facilitation: Application in natural settings.* Creskill, NJ: Hampton Press.

Geist, P., & Chandler, T. (1984). Account analysis of influence in group decision-making. *Communication Monographs, 51,* 67-78.

Gladstein, D. L. (1984). Groups in context: A model of task group effectiveness. *Administrative Science Quarterly, 29,* 499-517.

Gouran, D. S. (1969). Variables related to consensus in group discussions of questions of policy. *Speech Monographs, 36,* 387-391.

Gouran, D. S., & Hirokawa, R. Y. (1983). The role of communication in decision-making groups: A functional perspective. In M. S. Mander (Ed.), *Communications in transition* (pp. 166-185). New York: Praeger.

Hackman, J. R. (1969). Toward understanding the role of tasks in behavioral research. *Acta Psychologica, 31,* 97-128.

Hare, A. P. (1976). *Handbook of small group research* (2nd ed.). New York: Free Press.

Harré, R., & Secord, P. F. (1973). *The explanation of social behavior.* Totowa, NJ: Littlefield, Adams.

Hewes, D. E. (1980). Stochastic modelling of communication processes. In P. R. Monge & J. N. Cappella (Eds.), *Multivariate techniques in human communication research* (pp. 393-427). New York: Academic Press.

Hewes, D. E., Planalp, S., & Streibel, M. (1980). Analyzing social interaction: Some excruciating models and exhilarating results. In D. Nimmo (Ed.), *Communication yearbook 4* (pp. 123-144). New Brunswick, NJ: ICA-Transaction Books.

Hirokawa, R. Y. (1990). The role of communication in group decision-making efficacy: Task-contingency perspective. *Small Group Research, 21,* 190-204.

Hirokawa, R. Y., & Rost, K. M. (1992). Effective group decision-making in organizations: A field test of vigilant interaction theory. *Management Communication Quarterly, 5,* 267-288.

Holmes, M., & Poole, M. S. (1991). The longitudinal analysis of interaction. In B. Montgomery & S. Duck (Eds.), *Studying interpersonal interaction* (pp. 286-302). New York: Guilford.

Janis, I. L. (1972). *Victims of groupthink: Psychological studies of foreign policy decisions and fiascoes.* Boston: Houghton-Mifflin.

Leathers, D. G. (1969). Process disruption and measurement in small group communication. *Quarterly Journal of Speech, 55,* 287-300.

Mabry, E. A. (1975). An exploratory analysis of a developmental model for task-oriented small groups. *Human Communication Research, 2,* 66-74.

March, J., & Olsen, J. P. (1976). *Ambiguity and choice in organizations.* Oslo, Norway: Universitetsforlaget.

McGrath, J. E. (1984). *Groups: Interaction and performance.* Englewood Cliffs, NJ: Prentice Hall.

McGrath, J. E. (1991). Time, interaction, and performance (TIP): A theory of groups. *Small Group Research, 22,* 147-174.

McGrath, J. E., & Altman, I. (1966). *Small group research: A synthesis and critique of the field.* New York: Holt, Rinehart & Winston.

Mullen, B., & Copper, C. (1994). The relationship between group cohesiveness and performance: An integration. *Psychological Bulletin, 115,* 210-227.

Phillipsen, G. (1977). Linearity of research design in ethnographic studies of speaking. *Communication Quarterly, 25,* 42-50.

Poole, M. S., Folger, J. P., & Hewes, D. E. (1987). Methods of interaction analysis. In G. R. Miller & M. Roloff (Eds.), *Explorations in interpersonal communication* (2nd ed.) (pp. 220-256). Newbury Park, CA: Sage.

Poole, M. S., & Holmes, M. E. (1995). Decision development in computer-assisted group decision making. *Human Communication Research, 22,* 90-127.

Poole, M. S., & McPhee, R. D. (1994). Methodology in interpersonal communication research. In M. Knapp & G. R. Miller (Eds.), *Handbook of interpersonal communication* (2nd ed., pp. 42-100). Thousand Oaks, CA: Sage.

Poole, M. S., & Roth, J. (1989a). Decision development in small groups IV: A typology of decision paths. *Human Communication Research, 15,* 323-356.

Poole, M. S., & Roth, J. (1989b). Decision development in small groups V: Test of a contingency model. *Human Communication Research, 15,* 549-589.

Shaw, M. E. (1973). Scaling group tasks: A method for the dimensional analysis. *JSAS Catalog of Selected Documents in Psychology, 3,* 8.

Shaw, M. E. (1981). *Group dynamics: The psychology of small group behavior* (3rd ed.). New York: McGraw-Hill.

Simon, H. A. (1976). *Administrative behavior: A study of the decision-making process in administrative organization* (3rd ed.). New York: Free Press.

Spillman, B., Bezdek, J., & Spillman, R. (1979). Development of an instrument for the dynamic measurement of consensus. *Communication Monographs, 46,* 1-12.

Street, R. L., & Cappella, J. H. (Eds.). (1985). *Sequence and pattern in communication behaviour.* London: Edward Arnold.

Van de Ven, A. H., & Poole, M. S. (1995). Explaining development and change in organizations. *Academy of Management Review, 20,* 510-540.

Remembering and "Re-Membering"
A History of Theory and Research on Communication and Group Decision Making

LAWRENCE R. FREY

A morsel of genuine history is a thing so rare as to be always valuable.
—*Thomas Jefferson*

Most real-life groups are embedded within a history that constitutes and continually is reconstituted by their communication practices and decision-making outcomes. This shared history, constructed socially over time through language, arguments, stories, and symbols, represents a "deep structure" that influences the "surface structure" of a group's interactional patterns and decision making. Anyone who has heard the argument, "That's not how we've done it in the past," understands the significant impact that history can have on group behavior.

Theory and research on communication and group decision making are also embedded within a historical context. Over the past 70 years, the study of communication in general, and its relationship to group decision making in particular, has evolved from a seed to a tree with firmly planted roots.

This chapter reconstructs a history of theory and research on the relationship between communication and group decision making. The purpose of this reconstruction is to provide a ground for understanding where we have come from and where we are heading. History is not just a description of what occurred; more important, it provides a basis for making claims about the current status of group communication research and the most profitable directions for future research. On a more pragmatic note, this historical account serves as an introduction to the chapters in this text, which unpack what is touched on or only hinted at in this chapter.

Every history, however, is a *constructed* history—it is as much a social and political act as it is a "fact." This review is no exception, and its boundary conditions are as follows. First, this review focuses only on the relationship between communication and group decision making, exploring how communication is related to effective and ineffective group decision making. Second, this history is divided into relatively arbitrary eras of study to help bracket the research, even though there is an ebb and flow to this history that gets lost in any such category system. Third, this history would indeed be impoverished were it not for the histories that have come before. The author is deeply indebted, and the reader is referred, to previous reviews and critiques of group communication research.[1] Their insights have significantly shaped this history; indeed, this chapter might best be regarded as a *meta-history*, a history of these histories.

The Early Years: 1920-1945

> If [group] discussion is the fundamental and essential factor in democracy
> . . . then its technique must be mastered by the average citizen and its
> philosophy must be inculcated in the habits and attitudes of all people.
> (Johnson, 1939, p. 440)

Contemporary reviews typically argue that group communication as a field of study did not begin in any substantial way until the 1950s. Though this may be true from a disciplinary perspective, the seeds for the boom in group research from 1945 to 1970 were planted in the first half of the 20th century. Dashiell (1935) identified 15 studies published between 1924 and 1934 that bear directly on group discussion, and Dickens and Heffernan (1949) found 28 studies between 1934 and 1946. A review of this literature reveals three major lines of study that were converging on the importance of group discussion and that had significant implications for understanding group decision making.

The first group of founders were social psychologists who demonstrated the superiority of group discussion over individuals, primarily for answering questions of fact. Groups were found to be superior both quantitatively (i.e., speed of decision making) and qualitatively (i.e., correctness of decision) when compared to the average individual working alone (e.g., Marston, 1924; Barton, 1926; Watson, 1928; Shaw, 1932). The superiority of group discussion was due to the effects discussion had on attitude change (e.g., Jenness, 1932; Des Jarlais, 1943). Dickens and Heffernan (1949) concluded that these studies established a clear and important relationship between group discussion and decision outcomes: "After [group] discussion, judgments tend to improve in accuracy and correctness" (p. 26).

A second group in the speech field adapted philosopher John Dewey's (1910, 1933) work on human thought patterns to group discussion. In 1910, Dewey proposed the "reflective thinking" process, a five-step, cognitive pattern people use to solve complex problems: "(1) a felt difficulty; (2) its location and definition; (3) suggestion of possible solution; (4) development by reasoning of the bearing of the suggestions; (5) further observation and experiment leading to its acceptance or rejection; that is, the conclusion of belief or disbelief" (p. 72). During the 1920s and 1930s, the reflective thinking process was adopted as a model for democratic group decision making by textbook writers (e.g., Sheffield, 1926; Baird, 1927; Elliot, 1927; McBurney & Hance, 1939). With the exception of Carr's (1929) finding that group discussion was characterized qualitatively by these reflective thinking steps and Johnson's (1943) instrument for measuring the process, empirical research on promoting effective group decision making by using reflective thinking did not occur until later. The impact of Dewey's ideas on group communication and decision-making research, however, cannot be underestimated.

The third group consisted of sociologists and psychologists who gathered quantitative data about whether and how discussion functioned within groups to promote thinking and what factors made a discussion successful. They developed observational instruments to measure group interaction, discussion, and planning (e.g., Carr, 1930; Wrightstone, 1934; Newsletter, 1937; Sanderson, 1938; Miller, 1939;

Chapple, 1940, 1942). Miller's (1939) observational scheme, for example, documented the positive effects of group discussion on thinking processes by showing that 42% of members' contributions were either questions, reasoning from premises, or supported opinions. These instruments laid the groundwork for the group interaction observational schemes that were to dominate the 1950s and 1960s.

Although research on group discussion and its effects was in its infancy during this era, and often overlooked the characteristics of the discussion process in favor of examining the outcomes produced by discussion, the value of studying communication and group decision making was firmly established. And, as Dickens and Heffernan (1949) acknowledged, the lead in group research during this period shifted from psychology to the field of speech.

The Grand Old Days: 1945-1970

> Group discussion, as an object of study, presents as varied and complex a phenomenon as appears on the human scene. (Black, 1955, p. 15)

Small group theory and research flourished between 1945 and 1970, especially in the United States. This growth was due, in part, to the profound effects of World War II. People were appalled by Hitler's atrocities, and group research was seen as a promising way to prevent such events from recurring.

First, and foremost, this period was characterized by grand theories of small group behavior. These theories, or at least their applications to group behavior, sought to explain the influence of environmental forces on people's behavior, the nature of group interaction, and the relationship between group processes and outcomes. Two theories in particular deserve a special place in the annals of history: field theory and interaction theory.

FIELD THEORY

Kurt Lewin (1947a, 1947b, 1947c, 1948, 1951) adapted some of the principles from physics to explain individual and group behavior. His *field theory* argued that individuals live in a subjective "life-space" (a field) in which they are motivated by personal needs and goals. Sharing their life-space with others in a group makes them interdependent, thereby transforming a collection of individuals into a group.

This common life-space is created and sustained by *group cohesion,* the attraction members have toward a group and their commitment to work together toward a common goal. Researchers began to view member interdependence and group cohesion as resulting from communication, which, in turn, enhanced group decision making. Research revealed, for example, that both the quantity and quality of interactions helped produce group cohesion (Lott & Lott, 1961; Moran, 1966), and that group cohesion led to more active information gathering as well as more argumentative discussions (Back, 1951). Research also demonstrated that cohesion enhanced task accomplishment. Cohesive groups had members who had a greater desire to work together, were more satisfied with their task accomplishment, and were more productive in accomplishing the task (Schachter, Ellertson, McBride, & Gregory, 1951; Exline, 1957).

Field theory also claimed that developing interdependence and group cohesion involved constantly balancing three often conflicting factors that are present in a group situation: individual members' needs, the group's collective goals, and the constraints and demands imposed by the external environment. This last factor led to research on *communication networks,* "the arrangement (or pattern) of communication channels among the members of a group" (Shaw, 1981, p. 453). To study these issues, researchers imposed structures and networks (such as the wheel, circle, chain, or "Y") that restricted who could communicate, usually via written means, with whom, and then examined the effects on leadership emergence, organizational development, member relations, and problem-solving efficiency. Although some differences in group problem solving were found among these networks, later studies showed that with practice each network was as effective as the others.

Finally, field theory argued that individual and group actions "locomote" or move a group toward or away from group goals. The most important person who locomotes a group is the leader, and field theory had a profound effect on the study of *leadership.* Leadership theory started foregrounding the effects of leaders' communication behavior on group decision making. For example, *style theory* claimed that three leadership communication styles—democratic, authoritarian, and laissez-faire—produced differences in group behavior, including both the quantity and quality of task output, whereas *functional theory* claimed that leadership results whenever members perform behaviors that locomote a group toward accomplishing its task (see Barge, Chapter 11, this volume).

INTERACTION THEORY

Robert Freed Bales (1950a, 1952, 1953, 1959) was interested in understanding small groups as microcosms of larger social organizations, and how social systems adapt and change. His *equilibrium theory* argued that groups are in the constant process of managing external pressures (emanating from the larger system in which they are embedded) and internal pressures (those resulting from interaction among group members). Groups meeting over time thus strive to establish an equilibrium, a balance, between external and internal forces. However, whereas field theory focused primarily on the effects of the external environment on groups, Bales focused on the internal forces that shape group interaction; hence, his theory became known as *interaction theory*.

To study group interaction, Bales (1950a, 1950b, 1968, 1970) developed what has now become his legacy, the *Interaction Process Analysis* (IPA) observational scheme for coding behaviors enacted during group discussion. The IPA classified the function (not the content) of a communication act (defined as any meaningful unit that was the equivalent of a single simple sentence) into 12 categories (6 socioemotional and 6 task categories).

By analyzing the quality of group solutions, Bales identified the relative percentage that effective groups (and individual members) should spend on each communication unit and the specific problems that result from an imbalance, or lack of equilibrium, in complementary categories (e.g., problems of decision result from an imbalance in the number of "agree" and "disagree" units). Bales was thus one of the first researchers to study empirically the relationship between communication and effective group decision making.

Interaction theory also led to questions about *developmental processes,* the naturally occurring phases by which groups solve problems and make decisions (see Poole & Baldwin, Chapter 8, this volume). *Linear models,* whereby groups move through the same sequence of phases for each decision, became *the* dominant model for explaining group development and the difference between effective and ineffective decision making (e.g., Bales & Strodtbeck, 1951; Tuckman, 1965). Simply put, groups that followed the model were effective and those that didn't were not. Scheidel and Crowell (1964, 1966), however, proposed a *spiral model* of group development based on their finding that groups did not proceed from idea to idea in a step-by-step manner but instead often looked back and discussed a particular idea throughout their meetings. Fisher (1970) later synthesized these two models in an analysis of verbal interactions about decision proposals in groups that reach consensus, finding four phases as well as spiralling processes whereby a particular proposal was developed and tested throughout the course of a group's development.

All these models assumed that the qualitative differences between phases were the types of verbal behaviors members enacted. Researchers' methods for studying group discourse, however, changed radically during this period. Bales's IPA scheme coded each communication act as divorced from past and future acts, but Scheidel and Crowell looked at the *sequential* structure of discussion by analyzing *interacts*—how one communication act led to another. They found a number of patterned interacts, such as idea proposals being followed mostly by clarification statements. Their research thus provided the first true analysis of *interaction* within decision-making group discussions.

Another important question raised by interaction theory concerned communication differences between *consensus* and *nonconsensus* groups. Gouran (1969), for example, found that consensus groups were characterized by more orientation statements than nonconsensus groups. There was an interesting downside, however, to too much consensus and group cohesion. Stoner (1961, cited in Wallach, Kogan, & Bem, 1962) discovered that groups often make more daring decisions after discussing a problem than was indicated by individual members' prediscussion choices, a tendency that became known as "risky shift." Subsequent researchers also discovered a "cautious shift" whereby groups make more cautious decisions than their individual members would make had the group discussion not occurred. Many explanations were offered, but the crucial point was that these *choice shifts* occurred *because* of group discussion.

One answer to understanding how communication affected faulty decision making (such as extreme choice shifts) was to examine the *causes of breakdowns* in group discussion. Leistner (1952), for example, found that discussion broke down because of fallacious reasoning, the difficulty of attaining reflective thinking, language problems, and the inability to resolve conflict. Stageberg (1952) argued that single words (those that are incomplete, equivocal, relative, emotive, classifiers, fictions, or projective adjectives) often were the major obstacle to effective group discussion. Black (1955), however, was the first to approach group discussion from a *rhetorical perspective,* showing that breakdowns in group discussion have their sources in misused rhetorical principles, such as examples and enthymemes. Leathers (1969) later found that disruptions were most often caused by five types of contributions: high-level abstractions, low-level abstractions, unequivocal personal commitments, implicit inferences, and facetious interpolations. This rhetorical approach, although virtually ignored during this era, would later serve as an important foundation for explaining the relationship between argumentation and group decision making (see Alderton & Frey, 1986; Seibold, Meyers, & Sunwolf, Chapter 9, this volume).

Interaction theory truly had a profound effect on the study of group behavior. Most important, it shifted researchers' attention from external constraints imposed on groups to the internal processes that characterize group discussion and decision making.

SUMMARY

From 1945 until 1970, group communication theory and research flourished. This wealth of knowledge showed that group discussion was indeed an incredibly complex phenomenon. The value of a communication approach was also apparent: Understanding group decision making meant examining the communication processes that characterized effective and ineffective groups. A communication perspective of group decision making was thus firmly in place by the end of this era.

The Decade of Discontent: 1970-1980

The absence of progress in advancing group communication theory appears to stem from the conceptual barrenness in research on groups. This barrenness, in turn, derives from a preoccupation with designs that dictate questions as opposed to questions that dictate designs. (Cragan & Wright, 1980, p. 199)

Every discipline has its growing pains, and the communication discipline certainly experienced them during the 1970s. Scholars throughout the discipline questioned the assumptive bases and the traditional theoretical and methodological taken-for-granteds in the study of communication phenomena (see Benson & Pearce, 1977; Cronkhite & Liska, 1977). The study of group communication certainly was not immune. Group communication scholars experienced an epistemic crisis concerning the criteria appropriate for apprehending the proverbial elephant. Articles by Bormann (1970), Gouran (1970, 1973), Mortensen (1970), Fisher (1971), Fisher and Hawes (1971), Larson (1971), and Bochner (1974) at the beginning of the 1970s, and those by Becker (1980), Bormann (1980), and Cragan and Wright (1980) at the beginning of the 1980s, ranged from accusations, admonishments, and caveats to rules and prescriptions for the salvation of group communication research.

Embedded within these critiques, however, was a set of epistemic criteria that constituted a substantive body of knowledge about how group communication research should be conducted. This set of criteria addressed three interrelated concerns: (a) the relationship between theory and research; (b) the appropriate content of research, or what constitutes evidence; and (c) the methodological procedures that should guide research.

THE ROLE OF THEORY IN GROUP COMMUNICATION RESEARCH

One persistent theme running throughout these critiques was the lack of a theoretical base for group communication research. Gouran (1970) was one of the first to point out that researchers devoted more attention to using sophisticated statistical procedures than to asking important questions. Mortensen (1970) argued that "the 'disjointed and incoherent' tenor of much group research is evident in the very absence of an underlying theoretical framework for the enormous body of literature published" (p. 304). Group communication research was seen as being characterized by a "variable-analytic" approach, and if a science of group communication was forthcoming, it had to be based on theoretical underpinnings.

Some theories of group behavior were offered during this period. Fisher and Hawes's (1971) *interact system model,* an inductive methodology for studying group communication acts and interacts that could potentially lead to *grounded theory* (Glaser & Strauss, 1967), did spawn a lot of the Markov work done in later studies (e.g., Ellis & Fisher, 1975), but its impact was more limited than would have been expected when first published. One problem was that researchers were told to look for patterns but given few other guidelines. Categories that give rise to patterns must come from theory, and none were provided. Another problem was the lack of an explanation for why the interact system operates as it does. There is no explanatory power in simply listing temporal relations without showing causality, which cannot be inferred inductively but must be worked out theoretically.

Janis (1972) also extended the work done on risky and cautious shifts during the 1960s, introducing a theory that outlined the antecedent conditions that give rise to *groupthink,* "a mode of thinking that people engage in when they are deeply involved in a cohesive in-group, when the members' striving for unanimity overrides their motivation to realistically appraise alternative courses of action" (Janis, 1982, p. 9). Courtright (1978) showed subsequently in a laboratory investigation that the presence or absence of disagreement (conflict or hostility) among group members was the best discriminator between groupthink and non-groupthink groups.

Janis and Mann (1977) later developed a theory that tied effective and ineffective group decision making to how well group members consider relevant information in relation to the choices available to them. Cline and Cline (1979) provided some empirical evidence for this theory, showing that information-giving statements occurred substantially more often and that agreeing, disagreeing, and information-requesting statements occurred less frequently than expected by chance in risky-shift and cautious-shift group discussions. Janis and Mann (1977) argued that group members needed to be "vigilant" in processing information to avoid making faulty decisions.

Group communication researchers on the whole, however, did not engage much in theory development and testing. This era was characterized by a lack of substantive theoretical positions regarding either group communication in general or its relationship to decision making.

THE CONTENT OF GROUP COMMUNICATION RESEARCH

The second concern about the content of group communication research grew out of the general movement within the Speech Communication discipline to consider the appropriate range of its explanatory
shell. In 1969, the New Orleans Conference called for restricting the field
to "the variables involved directly in communicative exchange" (Kibler
& Barker, 1969, p. 33), and this prescription was taken to heart by group
communication scholars. No longer was any study about small groups
deemed relevant, or provided constitutive form, under the umbrella of
communication study.

Scholars agreed that research should focus on task groups, and three
general criteria were advanced about the appropriate content of task-
group communication research. First, researchers were urged to study
actual messages exchanged between group members. Second, researchers
should examine *how messages affect group products*. Yet as Gouran (1970)
pointed out, "There appears to be no working consensus among small
group researchers about the outcomes of interpersonal interaction
which are most in need of study" (p. 217). Fisher and Hawes (1971)
encouraged researchers to study group development, and Gouran
(1973) suggested four outcomes: consensus, effectiveness, satisfaction,
and cohesiveness. Third, researchers were urged to study how significant *input variables* (typically psychological or situational constraints)
affect group communication and group outcomes.

In spite of the lack of theory, group communication research certainly
flourished during this era. Cragan and Wright (1980) report that there
were 114 group studies published in communication journals during
the 1970s. Gouran, Hirokawa, McGee, and Miller (1994) classify these
studies with respect to process-oriented versus outcome-oriented research.

Process-oriented researchers studied the communication processes by
which decisions and solutions to problems develop. Many continued
the task of developing *observational coding schemes* to describe group
discourse (e.g., Fisher, 1970; Stech, 1970; Bodaken, Lashbrook, & Champagne, 1971; McCroskey & Wright, 1971; Gouran & Baird, 1972; Mabry,
1975; Gouran, Brown, & Henry, 1978; Leathers, 1979). Others focused
on the *distributional and sequential communication structures* that characterize decision-making groups, finding differences between problem-

solving and informal groups (Gouran & Baird, 1972) and between cooperative and competitive group discussions (Baird, 1974). Other researchers continued looking for communication behaviors that could differentiate *group developmental stages*. For example, Ellis and Fisher (1975), using Fisher and Hawes's (1971) interact system model, found three phases of conflict present throughout the interactions of groups that achieved consensus: interpersonal conflict, confrontation, and substantive conflict.

Outcome-oriented researchers, on the other hand, studied the effects of communication on group decision making. One line of research investigated how to improve idea generation and decision making by using *group discussion facilitation procedures* (see Frey, 1995; Jarboe, Chapter 12, this volume). Nelson, Petelle, and Monroe (1974), for example, found that groups that used a topical system as part of their brainstorming process maximized both the quantity and quality of ideas generated. A second line of research continued to investigate communication as related to *group consensus*. Gouran's (1969) finding that orientation statements were related to consensus was verified under controlled conditions by both Kline (1972) and Knutson (1972). Finally, some researchers assessed directly how group communication affected *decision quality*. Leathers (1972), for example, manipulated experimentally the interactional features of problem-solving groups (one was disrupted by confederates, another developed naturally, and a third was facilitated by confederates), and had judges rate the quality of feedback in the group and the quality of the group solution. Groups experiencing high-quality communication did produce higher-quality solutions than groups experiencing medium- or low-quality communication. Gouran et al. (1978) later found that the perceived quality of decision-making group discussions could be accounted for by a small number of communication behaviors: goal directness, relevance of issues, amplifications, evenness of participation, documentation, examination of issues, handling of issues, interpersonal relations, and leadership functions. However, not all research showed the positive effects of communication on decision quality. Bell (1979), for example, found no differences in the correctness of solutions between high-substantive and low-substantive group discussions.

These research studies, though lacking theoretical grounding, did clarify the communication that characterizes task groups and how it affects group decision making. The work started by these process-oriented and outcome-oriented researchers also led to the major theories advanced during the 1980s.

METHODOLOGICAL PROCEDURES IN GROUP COMMUNICATION RESEARCH

The third concern was with the methodological procedures most appropriate for studying the proposed content criteria. Although many research studies were conducted during the 1970s, there was deep dissatisfaction with the way the research was done. This concern centered on three broad methodological needs.

First, scholars questioned whether the most appropriate laboratory research designs were being used. They argued that researchers should employ process models and reject input-output models (Bormann, 1970; Fisher, 1971; Gouran, 1973); use multivariate instead of bivariate designs (Gouran, 1973); differentiate the types of tasks employed (Bochner, 1974); use group instead of individual tasks and not use tasks with known outcomes (Bormann, 1970; Fisher, 1971); and assess elements over time (Bormann, 1970; Fisher, 1971).

Second, critics called for using more robust methodological procedures for studying group interaction. This meant studying message intensity, salience, and modes (Mortensen, 1970); distinguishing between the function and property of communication (Gouran, 1973); studying sequential and contingent relationships among units of communication (Gouran, 1973) through the study of interacts and double interacts (Fisher, 1971; Fisher & Hawes, 1971); and reporting reliability findings for both acts and categories (Bochner, 1974).

The third criticism concerned the lack of generalizability of the research. Greater generalizability would occur when researchers studied groups rather than collectivities of individuals (Fisher, 1971); observed established groups outside of the laboratory setting (Bormann, 1970, 1980; Fisher, 1971; Becker, 1980); duplicated real-life situations in the laboratory (Fisher, 1971); studied "creative groups" (such as those that create ad campaigns, theater productions, etc.; Becker, 1980); used qualitative research methods (Bormann, 1980); and replicated research findings (Bormann, 1980; Cragan & Wright, 1980).

SUMMARY

The 1970s truly were a period of deep discontent with the field of communication in general and the study of group communication in particular. Although group communication research certainly flourished, as measured by the sheer number of studies conducted, critics found this research generally to be atheoretical and less than methodologically sound.

Even though this was a bleak period in the history of group communication research, it did inspire a newfound interest in theory and more informed, programmatic research during the 1980s. Like the conflict stage that was shown to characterize the development of decision-making groups as they attempted to solve their tasks, so too was this conflict period necessary for moving forward in the study of communication and group decision making.

The Infusion of Theory: 1980-1990

> Inquiry [during the 1980s] has moved out of the more or less exploratory, atheoretical, unfocused mode and now exhibits the influence of . . . reasonably clear, well-developed, and theoretically grounded orientations, with communication as the central concern. (Gouran, Hirokawa, McGee, & Miller, 1994, p. 258)

The critiques during the 1970s certainly did not stop researchers from studying group communication during the 1980s; quite the contrary, the criticisms and suggestions inspired new ways of studying the effects of communication on group decision making. Most significant was the theoretically charged nature of the research. Frey (1988) reports that 72% of group communication research published between 1980 and 1988 was based on an explicit theoretical base. Three theories in particular, as well as several theory-driven research paths, infused group communication research.

THE FUNCTIONAL APPROACH

The central premise of the *functional approach* is that effective group decision making requires the satisfaction of fundamental tasks or requirements, called *functional prerequisites,* and that communication is the means by which these critical requirements are satisfied (see Gouran & Hirokawa, Chapter 3, this volume; Hirokawa, Erbert, & Hurst, Chapter 10, this volume; Hirokawa & Scheerhorn, 1986). Hirokawa (1983) initially hypothesized five functions for effective group decision making: (a) establishment of operating procedures; (b) analysis of the problem; (c) generation of alternative solutions; (d) establishment of evaluation criteria; and (e) evaluation of operating procedures. His study showed, however, that only two, analyzing the group problem and establishing operating procedures, were related (positively and negatively, respectively) to problem-solving effectiveness. Hirokawa (1985) later suggested four critical functions:

> (1) thorough and accurate understanding of the choice-making situation; (2) identification of a range of realistic alternative courses of action; (3) thorough and accurate assessment of the positive qualities or consequences associated with alternative choices; and (4) thorough and accurate assessment of the negative qualities or consequences associated with alternative choices. (p. 212)

Decision quality was related most to meeting the first and fourth functions, and achieving these critical functions was a better predictor of decision-making effectiveness than the discussion procedure used to reach the decision (reflective-thinking, ideal-solution, single-question, or free discussion format). Hirokawa (1988) and Hirokawa and Rost (1992) later provided additional support for the theory, showing in both a laboratory study as well as a field study of established organizational groups, respectively, that high-quality groups did fulfill these four functions.

The functional perspective speaks directly to the relationship between communication and group decision making, claiming that communication that helps meet these functions promotes effective group decision making, whereas faulty communication and a lack of vigilance produce low-quality decisions. Nonetheless, the functional perspective has its critics (see Billingsley, 1993; Stohl & Holmes, 1993; Wyatt, 1993). First, critics question the assumptions on which the theory is based: Decision making as a rational process is countered by the argument that rationality is limited or bounded (e.g., by time constraints, by amount of information available) and that viewing decision quality as an objective characteristic ignores those cases in which the quality of outcomes is indeterminate. Second, the role of communication in groups in this theory is restricted to task accomplishment and ignores the socioemotional communication that characterizes group life and its effects on group decision making. Third, the scope conditions of the theory (e.g., tasks must be within members' intellectual ability, relevant information is available) may be true only for zero-history, laboratory decision-making groups. In the real world, where groups are embedded within systems, tasks beyond members' intellectual abilities, for example, often are imposed.

The functional perspective may be an incomplete picture of communication and group decision making. There can be no doubt, however, that this theory has had a profound impact on theorizing about communication and group decision making that has helped produce a substantial body of empirical research testing that relationship.

THE STRUCTURATIONAL APPROACH

The *theory of structuration*, based on the work of Anthony Giddens (1976, 1979, 1984), seeks to understand group interaction by accounting for both individual and systemic processes, how institutions affect group interaction, and how groups mediate the dialectic of stability and change (see Poole, Seibold, & McPhee, 1985, 1986, Chapter 5, this volume). The theory differentiates *systems*, observable patterns of relationships among individuals or collectives, from *structures*, rules and resources involved in the production and reproduction of social systems. Structuration, then, is "the process of producing and reproducing social systems through members' applications of generative rules and resources (structures)" (Poole et al., 1986, pp. 245-246).

As members interact in a group, they appropriate from social institutions the rules and resources that they use to reach decisions. The rules and resources, however, are also outcomes because by invoking them in practice, they are reaffirmed and reproduced. They may, of course, also change as members use them. Studying group decision making from a structurational perspective, therefore, entails examining the way rules and resources are used in practice and the way such practices reproduce these structures.

Group research from a structurational perspective has had two primary foci: the development of group decisions and argumentation in groups. With regard to *group development*, Poole (1981, 1983a, 1983b) and Poole and Roth (1989a, 1989b) offer impressive support for a *multiple sequence model* that rejects group development as a linear, unitary sequence of distinct phases and views groups as working concurrently on three interlocking "activity tracks": task-process activities (used to manage the task), relational activities (used to manage interpersonal relations), and topical focus (issues of concern to a group; see Poole & Baldwin, Chapter 8, this volume). These activities, moreover, often are interrupted by "breakpoints," intermittent causal processes that mark the development of a new track or trajectory for a group, such as delays and disruptions, or even agenda-setting and procedural statements (Fisher & Stutman, 1987). Group development might proceed in several alternative sequences depending on how these tracks are managed and what breakpoints occur. This research thus examines how different activities enter into the structuration of decision processes in the evolution of group decision making.

The second path explores *group argument*. From a structurational perspective, arguments are both systems (observable interactional patterns) and structures (rules and resources that enable argument) that are structurated in interaction (see Seibold & Meyers, 1986; Meyers & Seibold, 1990a, 1990b; Seibold, Meyers, & Sunwolf, Chapter 9, this volume). Group argument, then, is "the production of *interactive messages* by *social arguers* in group *discussion*. These messages are patterned, rule governed, and collaboratively produced" (Meyers & Seibold, 1990a, p. 287). Researchers currently are attempting to explain the way in which argument both creates decisions and, in the process, is reaffirmed as the means by which decisions are to be reached. Meyers and Seibold's (1990a) research, for example, shows how group argument, in spite of being based on disagreement, is characterized by convergence-producing activity with the ultimate purpose of moving a group toward consensus.

The structurational approach is a substantive theory with which scholars have only begun to paint a picture of group interaction. At its core is a view of communication as both the process by which groups make decisions and the product that is reproduced every time a group decision is made. The next step in developing the theory is to increase its predictive ability by articulating the rules and social practices that make some choices more likely than others. Otherwise, as Gouran (1990) claims, "The principal value of the structurational perspective may be reduced to providing post hoc explanations of specific instances of decision-making activity" (p. 318).

SYMBOLIC CONVERGENCE THEORY

Symbolic convergence theory, developed by Ernest Bormann (1972, 1982, 1983, 1986, Chapter 4, this volume) describes the communication process by which group members come to share a common social reality. Symbolic convergence is achieved by people sharing *fantasies,* "the creative and imaginative shared interpretation of events that fulfills a group psychological or rhetorical need" (Bormann, 1986, p. 221). When a number of these shared fantasy themes demonstrate similar scenarios, they form a *fantasy type.* Group members then integrate these shared fantasy themes and types into a unified *rhetorical vision* that gives them a broader view of things.

Most symbolic convergence research to date has attempted to document the presence of a shared group consciousness and the reasons why members are predisposed to share some fantasies and reject others (usually because of members' psychological predispositions and/or rhetorical skills, and common group concerns). Symbolic convergence, however, is useful for explaining how specific decisions receive the support of group members through the sharing of fantasies about the way a group processes information, what constitutes good evidence, the best ways to make decisions, and the best ways to cope with changing circumstances. Ball (1990), for example, showed how fantasies shared in President Kennedy's inner circle led to involvement in the Diem Coup.

Symbolic convergence theory is a rhetorical approach that explains the communication process by which group members come to share a common vision and make a collective decision. Though the theory has received only limited empirical testing, its foregrounding of group discourse as the means by which symbolic convergence occurs provides a potentially powerful explanation of the effects of communication on group decision making.

OTHER THEORY-DRIVEN RESEARCH DIRECTIONS

Although these three theories received the most attention during the 1980s, there were other research studies that investigated communication and group decision making. Once again, the distinguishing characteristic of this research, in contrast to research conducted during the 1970s, was the use of theory as a guiding light.

Perhaps the best example of how theory informed research during this era was the study of social-influence processes in groups. A number of researchers adopted *persuasive arguments theory* as an explanation for choice shifts (see Alderton & Frey, 1986; Seibold & Meyers, 1986; Seibold et al., Chapter 9, this volume). According to this theory, groups shift because members predominately forward persuasive arguments favoring the direction of the shift; research during the 1980s generally supported this position. Cline and Cline (1980) also provided evidence for a diffusion of responsibility theory for explaining differences between risky- and cautious-shift groups, and Alderton and Frey (1983) used O'Keefe's (1977) distinction between argument$_1$ (argument as act) and argument$_2$ (argument as process) to show that reactions to arguments explained choice shifts better than did arguments per se.

A variety of theories were also used by group communication researchers. Alderton (1980), for example, used attribution theory to examine communication and group decision making, whereas Donohue, Hawes, and Mabee (1981) adopted a structural-functional approach and used Markov analysis to explain how communication holds a group together. Tompkins and Cheney (1983) and Geist and Chandler (1984) used Harré and Secord's (1973) theory of social behavior to analyze accounts of how group decisions are made within organizations. Canary, Brossman, and Seibold (1987) used argumentation theory to differentiate consensus and dissensus groups, while Beatty (1989) employed an input-output model to study how decision-rule orientation affects group consensus. Jarboe (1988) tested the ability of three theoretical models to account for the relationships among discussion procedure, topic and solution multiplicity, group productivity, and member satisfaction. Even the applied use of group facilitation techniques received a boost from theory with Bales and Cohen's (1979) theory-driven observational system, called SYMLOG (System for the Multiple Level Observation of Groups), which was used as an intervention tool by Schantz (1986) in a work group where a suspected drug addict was inhibiting the group's productivity, and by Boethius (1987) to diagnose unification and polarization in administrative teams.

SUMMARY

The 1980s were an important time for theory and research on group communication and decision-making effectiveness. Though the sheer number of group communication studies published in the journals decreased during this era (96 articles were reported by Cragan & Wright, 1990) as compared with the 1970s, the quality of the research increased significantly because of the infusion of theory. Important questions were now tied to testing and generating theories, with a substantial decrease in the number of variable-analytic studies. As Cragan and Wright (1990) concluded, "It's difficult to believe that small group communication research was so theory-barren in the 1970s when one considers how theory-rich it was in the 1980s" (p. 226).

The Future Is Now: Communication and Group Decision Making at the Crossroads

> The failure to attract more group communication researchers stems from the current generation's inability to generate the social prerequisites for a thriving research community. For the most part, group communication research has failed to inspire the imagination, to pose puzzles that are really interesting, and to link its studies to pressing social questions. (Poole, 1990, p. 241)

At first glance, the state of knowledge about communication and group decision making seems healthy. The 1980s saw a return to grand theories and research informed by some of the criticisms offered during the 1970s. There are, however, cracks in this research that suggest deeper and more fundamental problems in the study of communication and group decision making.

First, the explanatory power of the theories advanced during the 1980s is limited at the present time. One reason is that there are only a few researchers who have applied a theory across a number of studies (such as Hirokawa's studies using the functional perspective). Most of the remaining studies are one-shot, theory-based research; more programmatic research programs that investigate a particular theory are needed. Equally important, only a few researchers have pitted competing theories against one another. Future research about the effects of communication on group decision making would benefit from direct comparisons among competing theoretical positions.

Second, although every article published during the 1980s was concerned with group communication behavior, there is little agreement regarding which type of communication is most important to study. The communication behavior investigated is so diverse as to be impossible to categorize, and there are only a few researchers who have studied the same behavior across different studies. A common research perspective that prioritizes the communication behaviors that are most important to study is needed.

Researchers must also be more vigilant in developing and reporting the use of communication coding schemes. Researchers typically devote more attention to advancing reliability than validity claims, and the sheer diversity of the content of communication that is being coded suggests that researchers need to justify the validity of the communication behavior they study. They must also provide as much information as possible about the reliability of these coding schemes. Frey (1988), for example, found that 29% of the studies published between 1980 and 1988 reported reliability for the entire scheme, 29% reported reliability for individual acts, 25% reported reliability for categories, and only 17% reported reliability for both acts and categories. Researchers also need to develop more process-oriented observational schemes that code interacts and double interacts. The majority of these coding schemes (74%) focused on isolated acts, ignoring communication as interaction.

Third, there are still serious concerns about the methodological procedures used to study communication and group decision making. Frey (1988) found that 64% of the studies assessed zero-history groups, 72% used students, 60% took place in a laboratory (50% of "field" research studied groups created for classroom purposes), and 72% observed a group only once (for groups observed more often, the mean number of observations was only 2.75). In a review of research published during the 1990s in *Small Group Research*, Frey (1994) found that 66% used students and 67% studied groups in a laboratory setting or classroom. Most researchers thus still study a single meeting of zero-history, college student groups in the laboratory or classroom.

The problem with studying such groups, as pointed out in the beginning of this chapter, is that real-life groups are embedded within a context that influences their communication and decision making. Barge and Keyton's (1994) analysis of the discourse of the meetings of a city council, for example, offers empirical evidence of the effects of the historical context by showing how group members used their shared history as an argument for influencing and justifying the procedures they employed and the decisions they made. Research on zero-history laboratory groups is decontextual, making it impossible to assess how group members use history, or any contextual variable, to influence their discussions and decision making.

One cure often cited is for researchers to move from the laboratory into the highly contextualized world of real groups. Putnam and Stohl (1990), however, argue that it is not enough to study natural groups; researchers should study *bona fide groups*, those that have stable yet permeable boundaries and are interdependent with other groups in their immediate context. This embeddedness and the movement that occurs among groups have important consequences for group discussion and decision making.

Studying bona fide groups, however, is not enough. Researchers must also expand the scope of the "decision-making groups" they study as well as the communication behavior that gets counted as contributing to group decision making. Most research uses the organizational work group as its exemplar (see Putnam & Stohl, Chapter 6, this volume), which has embedded within it ideological values and political positions that theorists, researchers, and practitioners privilege. Frey (1992, 1994), for example, contends that researchers have been co-opted by organizations (perhaps because of the lure of easy consulting money), and that group decision making within this context serves primarily to promote management's philosophy of "bottom-line" profits. Wyatt (1993), in a feminist critique of the literature, uses economic theory to explain why researchers privilege groups in the work context and devalue other types of groups: Work done in task groups (usually by men and emphasizing decision and policy making) represents "productive" labor, whereas work done in nontask groups (most often groups that include an increased number of women and focus on interpersonal issues) represents "reproductive" labor ("women's work"). This distinction between productive and reproductive labor mirrors the way men traditionally separate work life from home and social life (see Oakley, 1974). Given this focus on task groups, the communication that gets seen as contributing to group decision making is quite clear: The important task talk is separated from the relatively inconsequential socioemotional talk. This separation can be traced back to Bales (1953), who argued that although groups must satisfy both task and socioemotional needs, getting tasks accomplished often works against being able to maintain positive interpersonal relationships (see Gouran, Hirokawa, McGee, & Miller, 1994). What gets valued, consequently, is a particular type of discourse associated with male talk: linear, propositional, task-oriented statements. Women's talk, which does not necessarily take this form (e.g., sharing personal stories), becomes, by definition, of secondary importance to making decisions (see Meyers & Brashers, 1994). This depriviteging is further exacerbated when one considers that the vast majority of tasks given to laboratory groups to solve (composed primarily of white, middle-class males, or embedded within an educational system that favors them) are those upon which men generally do well (such as mathematical problems); hence, "there is little or no research on problem solving in interpersonal communication, where women's linguistic and relationship skills might be more relevant" (Wyatt, 1993, p. 59). Frey's (1988) review of the group literature supports this contention, as less than 5% of the studies were concerned with tasks other than decision making (such as social-support tasks).

Researchers, therefore, must expand the range of groups and the communication behavior they study. Researchers have virtually ignored such groups as families, support groups, children's groups, church groups, deviant or fringe groups (such as gangs), and many more. Researchers have also ignored how communication is used to make important decisions that help create and sustain group identity, socialize new members, provide social support, develop high-quality interpersonal relationships, and make changes in group processes.

Even the study of communication within traditional decision-making groups needs to be reconsidered. Hewes (1986; Chapter 7, this volume) argues that we do not yet have adequate evidence that communication even affects group decision making, and offers an alternative theory, a socio-egocentric model in which noninteractive inputs determine decision outputs. Scheerhorn, Geist, and Teboul (1994) believe that researchers are not focusing on the most salient communication, as there is a sizable incongruity between the communication that occurs in natural decision-making groups and the representation of that communication in the group literature. Their content analysis of the research published between 1982 and 1991, based almost exclusively on zero-history laboratory groups, showed that group communication is dominated by decision-making episodes. Their analysis of six ongoing, natural decision-making groups, however, showed that information dissemination was the primary episode, followed distantly by coordination/organization and decision-making episodes. The value of studying these previously snubbed episodes, and the rich research questions they suggest, will become apparent as researchers leave the friendly confines of the laboratory and study real decision-making groups.

Finally, innovations and changes in the real world are bound to have important consequences on the study of communication and group decision making. For example, as computer networking becomes more prevalent, some interesting questions arise about the microlevel effects of this medium on communication and group decision making (see McLeod, Chapter 14, this volume). Computerized group decision support systems (GDSSs) act as a facilitation technique that influences how groups structure their activities. Brashers, Adkins, and Meyers (1994), for example, found that GDSSs impact the critical discussion of arguments in ways different from face-to-face groups, whereas Poole, DeSanctis, Kirsch, and Jackson (1995) report that different appropriations of GDSS features influence the quality of team efforts. Though we know little about computerized group meetings, they promise to change the way in which group members communicate and make decisions.

Another important question concerns the effects of cultural diversity on group communication and decision making. As the workplace becomes more diverse, cultural differences (in power distance, uncertainty reduction, individualism, and masculinity, for example) are bound to affect group communication and decision making (see Bantz, 1993). Multiculturalism promises to have a significant impact on theories and research about communication and group decision making.

These philosophical, conceptual, methodological, technological, and cultural challenges do not invalidate the theory and research we have come to cherish; their value lies in opening up promising avenues for increasing the quality and generalizability of group communication research. In today's multicultural world, scholars are being asked to construct theories and conduct research in ways that are open to more voices and methods in the hopes of generating the social prerequisites for a thriving research community.

Conclusion

The study of group communication in general, and its relationship to decision making in particular, has scaled many heights and traversed many valleys—from the beginnings of this research, to the boom of the 1950s and 1960s, to the dissatisfaction of the 1970s, to the return to grand theories in the 1980s, to the critiques that only now are emerging. The style of writing used throughout this review mirrors intentionally the understanding and outlook present within each of these periods: The earliest research was descriptive, seeking ways of articulating the emerging field of group communication and, usually only indirectly, its relationship to group decision making; the second period forged ahead enthusiastically with theory and research with great hope of solving virtually all social problems; the third period was a dark and critical disillusionment with the "paradigm of unfulfilled promise" (Gouran, 1985); the fourth period was an enthusiastic return to grand theories and research informed by some critical issues raised during the previous period; and the present period finds us questioning the ideological/axiological, epistemological, metatheoretical, and methodological assumptions that inform the study of communication and group decision making.

The study of communication and group decision making has grown tremendously over the past 70 years. Today, philosophy, theory, and research about this relationship is more complex, informed, diverse, sensitive, and inclusive than ever, and promises to be even more so in the future. Understanding our historical roots can only help promote growth, for, to turn a phrase: Those who don't remember history and use it to "re-member" and move forward are bound to repeat it.

Note

1. See Dashiell (1935), Timmons (1941), Dickens and Heffernan (1949), Keltner (1960, 1961), Bormann (1970, 1980), Gouran (1970, 1973, 1985, 1988), Mortensen (1970), Fisher (1971), Fisher and Hawes (1971), Larson (1971), Becker (1980), Cragan and Wright (1980, 1990), Hirokawa (1982), Gouran and Fisher (1984), Frey (1988, 1995), Gouran and Hirokawa (1988), Poole (1990), Putnam and Stohl (1990), Gouran, Hirokawa, Julian, and Leatham (1993), and Gouran, Hirokawa, McGee, and Miller (1994). (Note: Throughout this chapter cites are arranged chronologically to indicate the historical development of theory and research.)

References

Alderton, S. (1980). Attributions of responsibility for socially deviant behavior in decision-making discussions as a function of situation and locus of control of attributor. *Central States Speech Journal, 31*, 117-127.

Alderton, S. M., & Frey, L. R. (1983). Effects of reactions to arguments on group outcome: The case of group polarization. *Central States Speech Journal, 34*, 88-95.

Alderton, S. M., & Frey, L. R. (1986). Argumentation in small group decision-making. In R. Y. Hirokawa & M. S. Poole (Eds.), *Communication and group decision-making* (1st ed., pp. 157-174). Beverly Hills, CA: Sage.

Back, K. W. (1951). Influence through social communication. *Journal of Abnormal and Social Psychology, 46*, 9-23.

Baird, A. C. (1927). *Public discussion and debate*. Boston: Ginn.

Baird, J. E., Jr. (1974). A comparison of distributional and sequential structure in cooperative and competitive group discussions. *Speech Monographs, 41*, 226-232.

Bales, R. F. (1950a). *Interaction process analysis: A method for the study of small groups*. Cambridge, MA: Addison-Wesley.

Bales, R. F. (1950b). A set of categories for the analysis of small group interaction. *American Sociological Review, 15*, 257-263.

Bales, R. F. (1952). Some uniformities of behavior in small social systems. In G. E. Swanson, T. H. Newcomb, & E. L. Hartley (Eds.), *Readings in social psychology* (pp. 146-159). New York: Holt.

Bales, R. F. (1953). The equilibrium problem in small groups. In T. Parsons, R. F. Bales, & E. A. Shils (Eds.), *Working papers in the theory of action* (pp. 111-161). Glencoe, IL: Free Press.

Bales, R. F. (1959). small group theory and research. In R. K. Merton, L. Broom, & L. S. Cottrell, Jr. (Eds.), *Sociology today: Problems and prospects* (pp. 293-305). New York: Basic Books.

Bales, R. F. (1968). Interaction process analysis. In D. L. Sills (Ed.), *International encyclopedia of the social sciences* (Vol. 7, pp. 465-471). New York: Macmillan/Free Press.

Bales, R. F. (1970). *Personality and interpersonal behavior*. New York: Holt, Rinehart & Winston.

Bales, R. F., & Cohen, S. P. (1979). *SYMLOG: A system for the multiple level observation of groups*. New York: Free Press.

Bales, R. F., & Strodtbeck, F. L. (1951). Phases in group problem solving. *Journal of Abnormal and Social Psychology, 46*, 485-495.

Ball, M. A. (1990). A case study of the Kennedy administration's decision-making concerning the Diem coup of November, 1963. *Western Journal of Speech Communication*, 54, 557-574.

Bantz, C. R. (1993). Cultural diversity and group cross-cultural team research. *Journal of Applied Communication Research*, 21, 1-20.

Barge, J. K., & Keyton, J. (1994). Contextualizing power and social influence in groups. In L. R. Frey (Ed.), *Group communication in context: Studies of natural groups* (pp. 85-105). Hillsdale, NJ: Lawrence Erlbaum.

Barton, W. A., Jr. (1926). The effect of group activity and individual effort in developing ability to solve problems in first year algebra. *Educational Administration and Supervision*, 12, 412-518.

Beatty, M. J. (1989). Group members' decision rule orientations and consensus. *Human Communication Research*, 16, 279-296.

Becker, S. L. (1980). Directions of small group research for the 1980's. *Central States Speech Journal*, 31, 221-224.

Bell, M. A. (1979). The effects of substantive and affective verbal conflict on the quality of decisions of small problem solving groups. *Central States Speech Journal*, 30, 75-82.

Benson, T., & Pearce, W. B. (Eds.). (1977). Alternative theoretical bases for the study of human communication: A symposium. *Communication Quarterly*, 25, 3-73.

Billingsley, J. M. (1993). An evaluation of the functional perspective in small group communication. In S. A. Deetz (Ed.), *Communication yearbook 16* (pp. 615-622). Newbury Park, CA: Sage.

Black, E. B. (1955). Considerations of the rhetorical causes of breakdown in discussion. *Speech Monographs*, 22, 15-19.

Bochner, A. P. (1974). Task and instrumentation variables as factors jeopardizing the validity of published group communication research, 1970-71. *Communication Monographs*, 41, 169-178.

Bodaken, E. M., Lashbrook, W. B., & Champagne, M. (1971). PROANA: A computerized technique for the analysis of small group interaction. *Western Speech*, 35, 112-115.

Boethius, S. B. (1987). The view from the middle: Perceiving patterns of interaction in middle management groups. *International Journal of Small Group Research*, 3, 1-15.

Bormann, E. G. (1970). The paradox and promise of small group research. *Speech Monographs*, 41, 169-178.

Bormann, E. G. (1972). Fantasy and rhetorical vision: The rhetorical criticism of social reality. *Quarterly Journal of Speech*, 58, 396-407.

Bormann, E. G. (1980). The paradox and promise of small group communication revisited. *Central States Speech Journal*, 31, 214-220.

Bormann, E. G. (1982). Colloquy I. Fantasy and rhetorical vision: Ten years later. *Quarterly Journal of Speech*, 58, 396-407.

Bormann, E. G. (1983). The symbolic convergence theory of communication and the creation, raising, and sustaining of public consciousness. In J. I. Sisco (Ed.), *The Jensen lectures: Contemporary communication studies* (pp. 71-90). Tampa: University of South Florida, Department of Communication.

Bormann, E. G. (1986). Symbolic convergence theory and communication in group decision-making. In R. Y. Hirokawa & M. S. Poole (Eds.), *Communication and group decision-making* (1st ed., pp. 219-236). Beverly Hills, CA: Sage.

Brashers, D. E., Adkins, M., & Meyers, R. A. (1994). Argumentation and computer-mediated group decision making. In L. R. Frey (Ed.), *Group communication in context: Studies of natural groups* (pp. 263-282). Hillsdale, NJ: Lawrence Erlbaum.

Canary, D. J., Brossman, B. G., & Seibold, D. R. (1987). Argument structures in decision-making groups. *Southern Speech Communication Journal, 53,* 18-37.

Carr, L. J. (1929). Experimental sociology: A preliminary note on theory and method. *Social Forces, 8,* 63-74.

Carr, L. J. (1930). Experimentation in face-to-face interaction. *Public American Sociological Society Papers, 24,* 174-176.

Chapple, E. D. (1940). Measuring human relations: An introduction to the study of interaction of individuals. *Genetic Psychology Monographs, 22,* 3-147.

Chapple, E. D. (1942). The measurement of interpersonal behavior. *Transactions of the New York Academy of Science, 4,* 222-233.

Cline, R. J., & Cline, T. R. (1980). A structural analysis of risky-shift and cautious-shift discussions: The diffusion of responsibility theory. *Communication Quarterly, 28,* 26-36.

Cline, T. R., & Cline, R. J. (1979). Risky and cautious decision shifts in small groups. *Southern Speech Communication Journal, 44,* 252-263.

Courtright, J. A. (1978). A laboratory investigation of groupthink. *Communication Monographs, 45,* 229-246.

Cragan, J. F., & Wright, D. W. (1980). Small group communication research of the 1970s: A synthesis and critique. *Central States Speech Journal, 31,* 197-213.

Cragan, J. F., & Wright, D. W. (1990). Small group communication research of the 1980s: A synthesis and critique. *Communication Studies, 41,* 212-236.

Cronkhite, G., & Liska, J. (Eds.). (1977). What criteria should be used to judge the admissibility of evidence to support theoretical propositions in communication research? *Western Journal of Speech Communication, 41,* 3-65.

Dashiell, J. F. (1935). Experimental studies of the influence of social situations on the behavior of individual human adults. In C. Murchison (Ed.), *Handbook of social psychology* (pp. 1097-1158). Worchester, MA: Clark University Press.

Des Jarlais, R. W. (1943). A measurement of participants' change of opinion during group discussion. *Speech Abstracts, 3,* 37.

Dewey, J. (1910). *How we think.* Boston: D. C. Heath.

Dewey, J. (1933). *How we think: A restatement of the relation of reflective thinking to the educative process* (2nd ed.). Boston: D. C. Heath.

Dickens, M., & Heffernan, M. (1949). Experimental research in group discussion. *Quarterly Journal of Speech, 35,* 23-29.

Donohue, W. A., Hawes, L. C., & Mabee, T. (1981). Testing a structural-functional model of group decision-making using Markov analysis. *Human Communication Research, 7,* 133-146.

Elliot, H. S. (1927). *The why and how of group discussion.* New York: Association Press.

Ellis, D. G., & Fisher, B. A. (1975). Phases of conflict in small group development: A Markov analysis. *Human Communication Research, 1,* 195-212.

Exline, R. V. (1957). Group climate as a factor in the relevance and accuracy of social perception. *Journal of Abnormal and Social Psychology, 55,* 382-388.

Fisher, B. A. (1970). Decision emergence: Phases in group decision-making. *Speech Monographs, 37,* 53-66.

Fisher, B. A. (1971). Communication research and the task-oriented group. *Journal of Communication, 21,* 136-149.

Fisher, B. A., & Hawes, L. (1971). An interact system model: Generating a grounded theory of small groups. *Quarterly Journal of Speech, 57,* 444-453.

Fisher, B. A., & Stutman, R. K. (1987). An assessment of group trajectories: Analyzing developmental breakpoints. *Communication Quarterly, 35,* 105-124.

Frey, L. R. (1988, November). *Meeting the challenges posed during the 70s: A critical review of small group research during the 80s.* Paper presented at the meeting of the Speech Communication Association, New Orleans.

Frey, L. R. (1992, November). *The state of the field: Setting the agenda for qualitative communication research on naturalistic groups.* Paper presented at the meeting of the Speech Communication Association, Chicago.

Frey, L. R. (1994). The naturalistic paradigm: Studying small groups in the postmodern era. *Small Group Research, 25,* 551-577.

Frey, L. R. (1995). Introduction: Applied communication research on group facilitation in natural settings. In L. R. Frey (Ed.), *Innovation in group facilitation: Applications in natural settings* (pp. 1-23). Cresskill, NJ: Hampton Press.

Geist, P., & Chandler, T. (1984). Account analysis of influence in group decision-making. *Communication Monographs, 51,* 67-78.

Giddens, A. (1976). *New rules of sociological method.* New York: Basic Books.

Giddens, A. (1979). *Central problems in social theory: Action, structure, and contradiction in social analysis.* Berkeley: University of California Press.

Giddens, A. (1984). *The constitution of society: Outline of the theory of structuration.* Berkeley: University of California Press.

Glaser, B. G., & Strauss, A. L. (1967). *The discovery of grounded theory: Strategies for qualitative research.* Chicago: Aldine.

Gouran, D. S. (1969). Variables related to consensus in group discussions of questions of policy. *Speech Monographs, 36,* 387-391.

Gouran, D. S. (1970). Response to "The paradox and promise of small group research." *Speech Monographs, 37,* 217-218.

Gouran, D. S. (1973). Group communication: Perspectives and priorities for future research. *Quarterly Journal of Speech, 58,* 22-29.

Gouran, D. S. (1985). The paradigm of unfulfilled promise: A critical examination of the history of research on small groups in speech communication. In T. W. Benson (Ed.), *Speech communication in the 20th century* (pp. 90-108). Carbondale: Southern Illinois University Press.

Gouran, D. S. (1988). Group decision making: An approach to integrative research. In C. H. Tardy (Ed.), *A handbook for the study of human communication* (pp. 247-267). Norwood, NJ: Ablex.

Gouran, D. S. (1990). Exploring the predictive potential of structuration theory. In J. A. Anderson (Ed.), *Communication yearbook 13* (pp. 313-322). Newbury Park, CA: Sage.

Gouran, D. S., & Baird, J. E., Jr. (1972). An analysis of distributional and sequential structure in problem-solving and informal group discussions. *Speech Monographs, 39,* 18-22.

Gouran, D. S., Brown, C. R., & Henry, D. R. (1978). Behavioral correlates of perceptions of quality in decision-making discussions. *Communication Monographs, 45,* 51-63.

Gouran, D. S., & Fisher, B. A. (1984). The functions of human communication in the formation, maintenance, and performance of small groups. In C. C. Arnold & J. W. Bowers (Eds.), *Handbook of rhetorical and communication theory* (pp. 622-658). Boston: Allyn & Bacon.

Gouran, D. S., & Hirokawa, R. Y. (1988, November). *Small group communication in the 1980s.* Paper presented at the meeting of the Speech Communication Association, New Orleans, LA.

Gouran, D. S., Hirokawa, R. Y., Julian, K. M., & Leatham, G. B. (1993). The evolution and current status of the functional perspective on communication in decision-making and problem-solving groups: A critical analysis. In S. A. Deetz (Ed.), *Communication yearbook 16* (pp. 573-600). Newbury Park, CA: Sage.

Gouran, D. S., Hirokawa, R. Y., McGee, M. C., & Miller, L. L. (1994). Communication in groups: Research trends and theoretical perspectives. In F. Casmir (Ed.), *Building communication theory: A socio/cultural approach* (pp. 241-268). Hillsdale, NJ: Lawrence Erlbaum.

Harré, R., & Secord, P. F. (1973). *The explanation of social behavior.* Totowa, NJ: Littlefield, Adams.

Hewes, D. E. (1986). A socio-egocentric model of group decision-making. In R. Y. Hirokawa & M. S. Poole (Eds.), *Communication and group decision-making* (1st ed., pp. 265-291). Beverly Hills, CA: Sage.

Hirokawa, R. Y. (1982). Group communication and problem-solving effectiveness I: A critical review of inconsistent findings. *Communication Quarterly, 30,* 134-141.

Hirokawa, R. Y. (1983). Group communication and problem-solving effectiveness II: An exploratory investigation of procedural functions. *Western Journal of Speech Communication, 47,* 59-74.

Hirokawa, R. Y. (1985). Discussion procedures and decision-making performance: A test of a functional perspective. *Human Communication Research, 12,* 203-224.

Hirokawa, R. Y. (1988). Group communication and decision-making performance: A continued test of the functional perspective. *Human Communication Research, 14,* 487-515.

Hirokawa, R. Y., & Rost, K. M. (1992). Effective group decision making in organizations: A field test of the vigilant interaction theory. *Management Communication Quarterly, 5,* 267-288.

Hirokawa, R. Y., & Scheerhorn, D. R. (1986). Communication in faulty group decision-making. In R. Y. Hirokawa & M. S. Poole (Eds.), *Communication and group decision-making* (1st ed., pp. 63-80). Beverly Hills, CA: Sage.

Janis, I. L. (1972). *Victims of groupthink: A psychological study of foreign policy decisions and fiascoes.* Boston: Houghton Mifflin.

Janis, I. L. (1982). *Groupthink: Psychological studies of policy decisions and fiascoes* (2nd ed.). Boston: Houghton Mifflin.

Janis, I. L., & Mann, L. (1977). *Decision making: A psychological analysis of conflict, choice, and commitment.* New York: Free Press.

Jarboe, S. (1988). A comparison of input-output, process-output, and input-process-output models of small group problem-solving effectiveness. *Communication Monographs, 55,* 121-142.

Jenness, A. (1932). The role of discussion in changing opinion regarding a matter of fact. *Journal of Abnormal and Social Psychology, 27,* 29-34, 279-296.

Johnson, A. (1939). Teaching the fundamentals of speech through group discussion. *Quarterly Journal of Speech, 25,* 440-447.

Johnson, A. (1943). An experimental study in the analysis and measurement of reflective thinking. *Speech Monographs, 10,* 83-96.

Keltner, J. W. (1960). Communication in discussion and group processes: Some research trends of the decade 1950-1959. Part I. *Journal of Communication, 10,* 195-204.

Keltner, J. W. (1961). Communication in discussion and group processes: Some research trends of the decade 1950-1959. Part II. *Journal of Communication, 11,* 27-33.

Kibler, R. J., & Barker, L. L. (Eds.). (1969). *Conceptual frontiers in speech-communication.* New York: Speech Association of America.

Kline, J. A. (1972). Orientation and group consensus. *Communication Studies, 23,* 44-47.

Knutson, T. J. (1972). An experimental study of the effects of orientation behavior on small group consensus. *Speech Monographs, 39,* 159-165.

Larson, C. E. (1971). Speech communication research on small groups. *Speech Teacher, 20,* 89-107.

Leathers, D. G. (1969). Process disruption and measurement in small group communication. *Quarterly Journal of Speech, 55,* 287-300.

Leathers, D. G. (1972). Quality of group communication as a determinant of group product. *Speech Monographs, 39,* 166-173.

Leathers, D. G. (1979). Informational potential of the nonverbal and verbal components of feedback responses. *Southern Speech Communication Journal, 44,* 331-354.

Leistner, C. A. (1952). Discussion breakdown. *Southern Communication Journal, 17,* 278-285.

Lewin, K. (1947a). Frontiers in group dynamics: Concept, method, and reality in social science: Social equilibria and social change. *Human Relations, 1,* 5-41.

Lewin, K. (1947b). Frontiers in group dynamics: 2. Channels of group life; social planning and action research. *Human Relations, 1,* 143-153.

Lewin, K. (1947c). Group decision and social change. In T. M. Newcomb & E. L. Hartley (Eds.), *Readings in social psychology* (pp. 330-344). New York: Holt.

Lewin, K. (1948). *Resolving social conflicts: Selected papers on group dynamics.* New York: Harper.

Lewin, K. (1951). *Field theory in social science.* New York: Harper.

Lott, A. J., & Lott, B. E. (1961). Group cohesiveness, communication level, and conformity. *Journal of Abnormal and Social Psychology, 62,* 408-412.

Mabry, E. A. (1975). An instrument for assessing content themes in group interaction. *Communication Monographs, 42,* 291-297.

Marston, W. M. (1924). Studies in testimony. *Journal of Criminal Law & Criminology, 15,* 5-31.

McBurney, J. H., & Hance, K. G. (1939). *The principles and methods of discussion.* New York: Harper & Brothers.

McCroskey, J. C., & Wright, D. W. (1971). The development of an instrument for measuring interaction behavior in small groups. *Speech Monographs, 38,* 335-340.

Meyers, R. A., & Brashers, D. E. (1994). Expanding the boundaries of small group communication research: Exploring a feminist perspective. *Communication Studies, 45,* 65-85.

Meyers, R. A., & Seibold, D. R. (1990a). Perspectives on group argument: A critical review of persuasive arguments theory and an alternative structurational view. In J. A. Anderson (Ed.), *Communication yearbook 13* (pp. 268-302). Newbury Park, CA: Sage.

Meyers, R. A., & Seibold, D. R. (1990b). Persuasive arguments and group influence: Research evidence and strategic implications. In M. J. Cody & M. L. McLaughlin (Eds.), *The psychology of tactical communication* (pp. 136-159). Clevedon, UK: Multilingual Matters.

Miller, D. C. (1939). An experiment in the measurement of social interaction in group discussion. *American Sociological Review, 4,* 241-251.

Moran, G. (1966). Dyadic attraction and orientational consensus. *Journal of Personality and Social Psychology, 4,* 94-99.

Mortensen, C. D. (1970). The state of small group research. *Quarterly Journal of Speech, 56,* 304-309.

Nelson, W., Petelle, J. L., & Monroe, C. (1974). A revised strategy for idea generation in small group decision making. *Speech Teacher, 23,* 191-196.

Newsletter, W. I. (1937). An experiment in the defining and measuring of group adjustment. *American Sociological Review, 2*, 230-236.

Oakley, A. (1974). *The sociology of housework.* New York: Pantheon.

O'Keefe, D. J. (1977). Two concepts of argument. *Journal of the American Forensic Association, 13*, 121-128.

Poole, M. S. (1981). Decision development in small groups I: A comparison of two models. *Communication Monographs, 48*, 1-24.

Poole, M. S. (1983a). Decision development in small groups II: A study of multiple sequences in decision making. *Communication Monographs, 50*, 206-232.

Poole, M. S. (1983b). Decision development in small groups III: A multiple sequence model of group decision development. *Communication Monographs, 50*, 321-341.

Poole, M. S. (1990). Do we have any theories of group communication? *Communication Studies, 41*, 237-247.

Poole, M. S., DeSanctis, G., Kirsch, L., & Jackson, M. (1995). Group decision support systems as facilitators of quality team efforts. In L. R. Frey (Ed.), *Innovations in group facilitation techniques: Applications in natural settings* (pp. 299-320). Cresskill, NJ: Hampton Press.

Poole, M. S., & Roth, J. (1989a). Decision development in small groups IV: A typology of group decision paths. *Human Communication Research, 15*, 323-356.

Poole, M. S., & Roth, J. (1989b). Decision development in small groups V: Test of a contingency model. *Human Communication Research, 15*, 549-589.

Poole, M. S., Seibold, D. R., & McPhee, R. D. (1985). Group decision-making as a structurational process. *Quarterly Journal of Speech, 71*, 74-102.

Poole, M. S., Seibold, D. R., & McPhee, R. D. (1986). A structurational approach to theory-building in group decision-making research. In R. Y. Hirokawa & M. S. Poole (Eds.), *Communication and group decision-making* (1st ed., pp. 237-264). Beverly Hills, CA: Sage.

Putnam, L. L., & Stohl, C. (1990). Bona fide groups: A reconceptualization of groups in context. *Communication Studies, 41*, 248-265.

Sanderson, D. (1938). Group description. *Social Forces, 16*, 309-319.

Schachter, S., Ellertson, N., McBride, D., & Gregory, D. (1951). An experimental study of cohesiveness and productivity. *Human Relations, 4*, 229-238.

Schantz, D. (1986). The use of SYMLOG as a diagnostic tool in drug-related problems on the job. *International Journal of Small Group Research, 2*, 219-224.

Scheerhorn, D., Geist, P., & Teboul, JC. B. (1994). Beyond decision making in decision-making groups: Implications for the study of group communication. In L. R. Frey (Ed.), *Group communication in context: Studies of natural groups* (pp. 247-262). Hillsdale, NJ: Lawrence Erlbaum.

Scheidel, T. M., & Crowell, L. (1964). Idea development in small discussion groups. *Quarterly Journal of Speech, 50*, 140-145.

Scheidel, T. M., & Crowell, L. (1966). Feedback in small group communication. *Quarterly Journal of Speech, 52*, 273-278.

Seibold, D. R., & Meyers, R. A. (1986). Communication and influence in group decision-making. In R. Y. Hirokawa & M. S. Poole (Eds.), *Communication and group decision-making* (1st ed., pp. 133-155). Beverly Hills, CA: Sage.

Shaw, M. E. (1932). A comparison of individuals and small groups in the rational solution of complex problems. *American Journal of Psychology, 44*, 491-504.

Shaw, M. E. (1981). *Group dynamics: The psychology of small group behavior* (3rd ed.). New York: McGraw-Hill.

Sheffield, A. D. (1926). *Creative discussion: A statement of method for leaders and members of discussion groups and conferences* (3rd ed.). New York: American Press.

Stageberg, N. C. (1952). Obstacle-words in group conference. *Journal of Communication, 2,* 82-87.

Stech, E. L. (1970). An analysis of interaction structure in the discussion of a ranking task. *Speech Monographs, 37,* 249-256.

Stohl, C., & Holmes, M. E. (1993). A functional perspective for bona fide groups. In S. A. Deetz (Ed.), *Communication yearbook 16* (pp. 601-614). Newbury Park, CA: Sage.

Stoner, J. A. F. (1961). *A comparison of individual and group decisions involving risk.* Unpublished master's thesis, Massachusetts Institute of Technology, Cambridge.

Timmons, W. M. (1941). Discussion, debating, and research. *Quarterly Journal of Speech, 27,* 415-421.

Tompkins, P. K., & Cheney, G. (1983). The uses of account analysis: A study of organizational decision-making and identification. In L. L. Putnam & M. E. Paconowsky (Eds.), *Communication and organizations: An interpretive approach* (pp. 123-146). Beverly Hills, CA: Sage.

Tuckman, B. W. (1965). Developmental sequence in small groups. *Psychological Bulletin, 64,* 384-399.

Wallach, M. A., Kogan, N., & Bem, D. J. (1962). Group influence on individual risk taking. *Journal of Abnormal and Social Psychology, 65,* 75-86.

Watson, G. B. (1928). Do groups think more efficiently than individuals? *Journal of Abnormal and Social Psychology, 23,* 328-336.

Wrightstone, J. W. (1934). An instrument for measuring group discussion and planning. *Journal of Educational Research, 27,* 641-650.

Wyatt, N. (1993). Organizing and relating: Feminist critique of small group communication. In S. P. Brown & N. Wyatt (Eds.), *Transforming visions: Feminist critiques in communication studies* (pp. 51-86). Cresskill, NJ: Hampton Press.

THEORIES

Functional Theory and Communication in Decision-Making and Problem-Solving Groups

An Expanded View

DENNIS S. GOURAN
RANDY Y. HIROKAWA

During the past quarter century, research on communication in decision-making and problem-solving groups has contributed to the emergence of what was first formally recognized in 1983 as the "functional perspective" (see Gouran & Hirokawa, 1983). From this perspective, communication is the instrument by which members of groups, with varying degrees of success, reach decisions and generate solutions to problems. Crucial to successful decision making and problem solving in groups is the extent to which members' interaction ensures that particular requirements of their tasks are being fulfilled. These requirements are ones that, in principle, relate directly to the appropriateness of the choices groups make. If they are not adequately addressed, the chances of the group's making a good decision or identifying an effective solution to a problem are diminished.

In recent essays, Gouran, Hirokawa, Julian, and Leatham (1993) and Gouran, Hirokawa, McGee, and Miller (1994) have identified the origins of the functional perspective, the general propositions to which it has led, the ways in which interaction contributes to the outcomes groups achieve, and the philosophical foundations on which inquiry emanating from the perspective rests. The focus in these discussions has been on task-related requirements. As Irving Janis (1989) has so aptly noted, however, decision making and problem solving are activities that groups frequently perform under the influence of powerful social influences that can and do interfere with the ability of participants to satisfy the essential requirements of a decision-making or problem-solving task.

Despite acknowledgments of problems arising in the social domain of group interaction and of observations concerning how one might respond to them (see, e.g., Gouran, 1992; Gouran & Hirokawa, 1986), the functional perspective at its current stage of evolution, at best, insufficiently accommodates environmental factors that bear on how well or poorly communication serves to ensure that fundamental requirements are met. A major purpose of this chapter is to explore ways in which social constraints can, and often do, affect task-related interaction in groups and, hence, the extent to which members are able to satisfy requirements, as well as the likelihood of their achieving desired outcomes. In addition, the chapter examines ways in which communication may function to minimize the impact of these constraints. Such an exploration will advance the functional perspective and expand the range of situations in group interaction to which it can usefully apply.

The Current Status of Functional Theory

In their recent essay, Gouran et al. (1993) argue that the probability of an appropriate choice in a decision-making or problem-solving discussion depends on whether interaction assists members

1. to show correct understanding of the issues to be resolved;
2. to determine the minimal characteristics any alternative, to be acceptable, must possess;
3. to identify a relevant and realistic set of alternatives;

4. to examine carefully the alternatives in relationship to each previously agreed-upon characteristic of an acceptable choice; and

5. to select the alternative that analysis reveals to be the most likely to have desired characteristics. (p. 580)

Seven assumptions underlie this set of propositions. To the extent that the conditions assumed are inapplicable in specific instances, the likelihood of a group's being able to fulfill the requirements suggested by the propositions is severely limited. The assumptions are as follows:

1. The members of a decision-making or problem-solving group are motivated to make an appropriate choice.
2. The choice confronted is nonobvious.
3. The collective resources of the group in respect to the particular task exceed those of individual members.
4. The requisites of the task are specifiable.
5. Relevant information is available to the members or can be acquired.
6. The task is within the intellectual capabilities of the members to perform.
7. Communication is instrumental. (Gouran et al., 1993, p. 579)

To date, a number of empirical and laboratory investigations have provided partial support for the functional perspective (e.g., Cragan & Wright, 1993; Hirokawa, 1980, 1982, 1983a, 1983b, 1985, 1987, 1988; Hirokawa, Ice, & Cook, 1988; Hirokawa & Johnston, 1989; Hirokawa & McLeod, 1993; Hirokawa, Oetzel, Aleman, & Elston, 1991; Hirokawa & Rost, 1990; Nakanishi, 1990; Papa & Graham, 1990; Propp & Nelson, 1994). In addition, case studies of instances of failed group decisions have established evidence of deficiencies in respect to one or more of the propositions identified above (e.g., Gouran, 1984, 1987, 1990; Gouran, Hirokawa, & Martz, 1986; Hirokawa, Gouran, & Martz, 1988; Martz, 1986; Mason, 1984; McKinney, 1985). Hirokawa (1982) and Gouran (1991) summarize still other evidence supportive of the basic tenets of functional theory.

Deficiencies

Despite evidence of the kind noted, inconsistency remains a problem in tests and applications of functional theory. Those investigating communication in groups have not found uniformly that groups showing attention to the requirements of their task make more appropriate decisions than groups displaying relative inattention to them.

An explanation for this is suggested by the manner in which researchers have determined whether or not task requirements have been satisfied. Typically, they have done so on the basis of frequency counts, as suggested by decisions of trained leaders or by global judgments of raters. In the first instance, if a particular utterance appears to be consistent with the general description of a given task requirement provided by the investigator, the act is credited with serving the corresponding function (see, e.g., Hirokawa & Pace, 1983). In the second instance, raters render general judgments of the extent to which communication appears to be serving task-related functions (e.g., Gouran, Brown, & Henry, 1978).

In neither case above is a qualitative evaluation rendered. Coders and raters have not been asked to assess how well communicative acts have served the functions posed by task requirements, and to which they ostensibly correspond. However, there is nothing in the theory as such that would take investigators in this direction. In short, the theory is insufficiently sensitive to aspects of communication that determine the likelihood that it will have desired effects. One may better appreciate the importance of this shortcoming with the aid of some specific examples.

Suppose that a group of presidential advisers was discussing possible candidates for an appointment to a top-level position, and a powerful member observed that any nominee, to be acceptable, would have to show evidence of competence, intelligence, and a history of public service—not unreasonable criteria. On the surface, communication would seem to be addressing the requirement of determining the minimal characteristics that seriously considered alternatives (in this case, nominees) must possess. As a result, such a contribution would be counted as serving a positive function.

What is not in evidence in this example is how well the act is serving the function noted in the context of the particular issues being addressed. Competence, intelligence, and prior service alone might be insufficient to ensure that one would perform well in the position of interest, but deference to the powerful group member has unduly restricted the range of criteria utilized. Inattention to other relevant considerations could lead to an unfortunate choice. Incidentally, this appears to be precisely what happened in the early stages of the Clinton administration, with the embarrassing consequence that several of his initial appointees soon had to be replaced (Drew, 1994). In this case, prior acquaintance with the president or his wife appeared to be the dominant criterion.

As another illustration, consider a group that is nearing the end of its deliberations and is examining alternatives in relationship to its previously determined list of criteria. A simple declaration by a group member that a particular alternative satisfies the criteria would be taken as evidence of communication's functioning in accordance with the requirements of the group's task. What it takes to establish that an alternative satisfies a criterion or set of criteria, however, usually entails a good deal more than a person's opinion.

Though the utterance in question qualifies as serving the function of fulfilling an important task requirement, at a qualitative level it has not done so very well. Clearly, the form of an utterance is not the best index of its value in assuring that a group is meeting task requirements.

In both of these examples, the groups involved would be more apt to make a poor decision than a good one, yet in the absence of any direct evaluation of the extent to which communication serves its functions well, the behaviors identified would be viewed as consistent with the specifications of the theory. We think it important to note here that most of the inconsistency in past research has been associated with groups whose communicative behavior appears to be serving necessary task-related functions, not the reverse. In other words, we do not find much evidence of groups that are completely inattentive to task functions reaching good decisions. The problem, then, appears to rest with inadequate bases for determining what constitutes satisfaction of task requirements.

This examination suggests a need for some refinements in functional theory if its predictive validity and explanatory utility are to be better established. In particular, the theory should be modified to allow for differences in the functional impact of communication on how well the members of a group engage task requirements that are essential to making appropriate choices. Achieving this requires some additional assumptions and propositions. Before we introduce these, however, we believe that it is necessary that one first understand factors that contribute to less-than-adequate fulfillment of task requirements. The recent work of Irving Janis (1989) on the impact of social constraints is particularly instructive in this regard.

Constraints on Effective Decision Making

As a result of years of study of decision-making processes and considerable consulting experience in government agencies and other organizations, Janis (1989) identified numerous sources of frequently negative influence on the performance of groups. He refers to these sources of influence as "constraints" and has grouped them under the following three headings: cognitive, affiliative, and egocentric.

COGNITIVE CONSTRAINTS

Cognitive constraints come into play when the members of a group confront a task for which little information is available, time is sharply limited, and/or the matter to be resolved is beyond the level of complexity they ordinarily face. For instance, a sudden downturn in the economy might cause many prospective college students to decide to defer further education. In such a case, college and university officials would be faced with an unexpected set of problems concerning how to manage a shortfall in tuition income. The ripple effect of this type of situation would be far-reaching and could have significant implications for numerous aspects of day-to-day operations.

Under circumstances of the kind noted, group members, according to Janis, may resort to analogies or fall back on standard operating procedures in making choices, rather than deal with the problem confronted in its own terms. As a result, they take considerable risk of not developing a proper understanding of the issue to be resolved or of not finding adequate means for dealing with it.

The Ford administration's response to rumors of an incipient swine flu epidemic in the mid-1970s is a case in point (Neustadt & May, 1986). A program of inoculation was put into effect for what turned out not to be a serious threat. Not only was the program unnecessary, its implementation actually led to illness among some of these who received the vaccine developed to combat the anticipated but nonexistent epidemic.

AFFILIATIVE CONSTRAINTS

Affiliative constraints are apt to arise under conditions in which relationships among members of a group are a dominant concern and in which members fear either deterioration in such relationships or undue influence from one or more individuals whose thinking is not always in line with majority sentiments. The common tendency to exert pressure on deviant group members and the consequent shifting that accompanies such pressure to ensure that the group will be of one mind illustrate this situation well (Aronson, 1980).

Most of us have found ourselves at one time or another regretting not having spoken out when the other members of a group have gone in a direction we think unwise because we did not wish to disturb the apparent unity of the group, only to discover later that others were harboring the same doubts. This phenomenon, often referred to as "pluralistic ignorance" (Schanck, 1932), was vividly described by Harvey (1974) in recounting an incident in which an entire family took a trip the members individually had no interest in taking.

EGOCENTRIC CONSTRAINTS

Egocentric constraints are likely when at least one member of a group has a highly pronounced need for control or is otherwise driven by personal motivations. As more than one observer has noted, former President Richard Nixon was ultimately responsible for his own political undoing in the Watergate case because of his inability to permit normal investigative processes to move forward in regard to the break-in at the Democratic National Headquarters. Instead, his need for control dominated discussions among members of his inner circle and culminated in the fateful decision to engage in a cover-up (see, e.g., Chesin, 1973; Lukas, 1973; Wicker, 1990).

Signs That Social Constraints Are Present and Exerting Influence

When any of the previously mentioned constraints becomes dominant, the interests of effective decision making and problem solving are apt to be ill served unless action is taken. A significant obstacle to such action, however, is the fact that cognitive, affiliative, and egocentric constraints are not always clearly evident to those who are succumbing to their influence. Despite this feature of the various categories being considered, overt signs often appear in the patterns of interaction that occur among the members of decision-making and problem-solving groups. An important step for the further development and advancement of functional theory, therefore, is identification of the sorts of indicators that typically accompany the emergence of cognitive, affiliative, and egocentric constraints.

It is beyond the scope of our discussion to undertake an exhaustive examination of all of the ways in which cognitive, affiliative, and egocentric constraints are reflected in group interaction. Rather, our purpose is to illustrate some possibilities that may foster more systematic investigations and cataloging of signs. The following observations, therefore, are intended more as a stimulus for inquiry than as an elaboration of constraint/interaction relationships.

SIGNS OF COGNITIVE CONSTRAINTS

As we mentioned earlier, when a group is performing under the influence of a cognitive constraint, the task before it usually is one for which information is limited, time pressures are substantial, the issues are excessively complex, or any combination of these. Indicative of the presence of such constraints are direct and indirect acknowledgments; for example, "How do they expect us to deal with this problem in only two weeks?" (*direct acknowledgment*), and, "Here we go again—another case of hurry up and wait" (*indirect acknowledgment*). To the degree that others in the group are reinforcing such observations, one can more easily assume that a cognitive constraint has taken hold, or at least is well along in the process.

Another indicator of the presence of cognitive constraints is the *sense of urgency* the members of a group display in respect to making a choice as opposed to examining the problem or issue at hand. If completion of the task appears to be more important than understanding what the task requires to produce a desired outcome, group members could well be displaying their underlying uncertainty or feelings of being overwhelmed by the task. Reluctance to move to the point of choice could also be symptomatic of such states.

Janis and Mann (1977) refer to the former tendency as "hypervigilance" and to the latter as "defensive avoidance." If relevant signs are present, one would be well advised to see if the rush to judgment or the apparent reluctance to choose is accompanied by legitimate concerns before concluding that a cognitive constraint is exerting an unhealthy influence on the process. On the other hand, one should not be too conservative in this respect, lest an actual constraint take hold and do irreparable damage.

Finally, the *types of proposals* group members introduce may signify the presence of one or more cognitive constraints. If proposals appear to be reliant on precedents or on what others have done in similar situations, without any corresponding examination of the merits of such actions in relation to the present situation, one has a reasonably good clue that either expediency or avoidance is driving the interaction. Such proposals may further indicate that participants are feeling uncomfortable about their ability to deal with the task they have been asked to perform.

SIGNS OF AFFILIATIVE CONSTRAINTS

Because affiliative constraints arise in relation to concerns about the interpersonal relationships among the members of a decision-making or problem-solving group, utterances reflecting such concerns provide useful insights into the probable presence of this type of constraint. In situations involving a desire by some group members to avoid impairing relationships with other members, one might anticipate observing a rather *uneven distribution of interaction.* Rather than risk possible rejection, some participants will withhold their input. Moreover, when they do contribute, they are likely to refrain from making substantive comments and, instead, will reinforce the judgments expressed by more active and, apparently, influential members whom they fear or otherwise prefer not to antagonize (see, e.g., Courtright, 1978). Such individuals also frequently exhibit a *heightened susceptibility to pressure for uniformity* exerted by the majority. Participants who retreat easily from positions they have advanced or who tend to qualify what they have to say with expressions of doubt often make clear an uncritical willingness to conform to majority sentiment.

Affiliative constraints, of course, are not always the result of fear of sanction or reprisal. Often the culture of a group has evolved in such a way that achieving consensus, rather than making the best possible choice, is the norm. Asch (1956) noted such a tendency even in newly formed groups whose members had no special allegiance to either the group as a whole or to any particular members. In more well-established groups, interaction may be characterized by a good deal of *friendliness* and *attempts to maintain a climate of camaraderie*. If a participant is likely to become unhappy about a given choice, from the perspective of the other members it may be preferable to turn to other alternatives in the interest of keeping the peace.

When members appear to be overly concerned with individual needs for inclusion (Schutz, 1958), one can be reasonably confident that an affiliative constraint is driving the decision-making or problem-solving process. *Sustained efforts to placate disgruntled members* or *to ensure that diverse opinions are accommodated in the choice made* are often indicative of the dominance of an affiliative constraint. Attempts to bring opinion deviants into line may also signify the presence of this type of constraint.

SIGNS OF EGOCENTRIC CONSTRAINTS

Behavior reflective of the operation of egocentric constraints can take a variety of forms, some of which are subtle and others of which are fairly conspicuous. Regardless of the form, what egocentrically governed behavior typically reveals is a *win-lose orientation*. Among those members of a group whose preoccupation is to gain acceptance of the choices they favor, one can expect to observe an *imbalance in the examination of information and positions* on issues. The tendency among egocentrically driven participants is to *bolster preferred alternatives and the evidence supportive of them* (Janis & Mann, 1977) while simultaneously being *overly critical of competing ideas*.

Even when a person under the influence of an egocentric constraint prefaces his or her comments with such a seemingly dispassionate or conciliatory sentiment as, "I can see that," "but" (a reason or reasons for disagreeing) almost inevitably follows. When emotional commitment is high for such an individual, moreover, interaction with others is often characterized by a *high level of defensiveness* (Gibb, 1961).

Egocentric constraints are not always the product of commitment to preferred alternatives. In some instances, the task-related issues being discussed are irrelevant. Much more important to some group members is the need to prevail. For them, prevailing may even be the paramount concern. Interaction provides an opportunity to reinforce one's self-image and indulge one's desires for control. Rather than addressing matters of substance, this type of participant is much more likely to *dwell on past achievements* and *to remind other group members of his or her self-identified (or otherwise acknowledged) capabilities and skills.*

Observations along the lines of, "Please, don't question me, I know what I am talking about," or "I have been dealing with this kind of problem for over ten years," permeate the contributions of the egocentrically motivated individual. Such a participant may *eschew expression of personal interest or gain* and instead frame arguments in terms of "the principle of the thing." He or she will, moreover, frequently leave the impression that disagreeing or questioning on the part of others is personally insulting.

An Expanded Role for Communication

To date, the functional perspective has exhibited concern primarily with whether or not communication serves to promote fulfillment of specific task requirements. As we earlier suggested, however, the question of how well it serves such functions has been a matter of considerable neglect. In particular, scholars have neglected social influences that limit the extent to which members of groups are attentive to fundamental requirements. Although some of the proponents of this perspective have acknowledged problems in the social and relational domains that act as constraints on the ways in which communication functions in relation to basic task requirements (e.g., Gouran, 1982; Gouran & Hirokawa, 1986; Hirokawa & Scheerhorn, 1986) and have even suggested means for minimizing their impact, they have not dealt with constraints in any systematic way.

One of the important contributions of Janis's (1989) constraints model has been to provide a structure and typology that allow for a more disciplined explanation of how communication fits within the functional perspective. What remains is the need to expand the perspective in light of the set of constraints Janis has identified and the additional functions they imply. Such expansion may lead to an increase in the predictive validity and explanatory utility of the theory. It should also lead to the development of more carefully designed and analyzed investigations of the communication/outcome relationship in decision-making and problem-solving discussions and, thereby, reduce the inconsistency that characterizes much of the extant research.

From the previous discussion of the three categories of constraints that can and do influence how well the members of a group can satisfy the requisites of their task, it should be clear that recognition and accurate interpretation of relevant signs are only starting points. It should also be clear that each type of constraint poses different types of problems for successful performance, even if the consequence is ultimately the same, that is, a failure to deal effectively with the issues involved in making decisions and generating solutions to problems.

Cognitive constraints relate to perceived deficiencies in the resources (information, time, and skills necessary for performing the task) available to group members. When present, they lead to superficiality in the analysis of issues and alternatives a group may be considering. In some instances they may even sharply limit the number of alternatives a group is willing to consider. Affiliative constraints contribute to preoccupations with relationships and the well-being of the group. As a result, they can shift the focus of inquiry from making the best choice to the accommodation of differences in point of view. The Clinton administration suffered from this problem in a number of decisions during its first 2 years (Drew, 1994). Egocentric constraints derive from the personal needs of the members (typically needs concerned with control). Such constraints are productive of conflict, the culmination of which is often acquiescence rather than informed choice.

The force and, ultimately, the influence any given type of constraint will exert on the performance of a group depend on whether steps have been taken to prevent, if possible, its intrusion; how quickly it is recognized; and how appropriately communication functions to address and to counteract any deleterious effects it might be having. Left unattended, any of the three types of constraints we have been discussing is likely to gather momentum and eventually dominate interaction in potentially injurious ways. As a result, it is important to respond to the emergence of cognitive, affiliative, and egocentric constraints in their incipient stages. Otherwise, they are more apt to become highly problematic.

One might think of early response to the emergence of social constraints as a necessary, but not sufficient, condition for ensuring that the substantive requirements of a decision-making or problem-solving task are fulfilled. As, if not more, important is how directly responsive interaction is to the difficulty or difficulties posed by a particular constraint. If strategic choices are inappropriate, too indirect, or peripheral, the effect may be exacerbation of the problem, as in the case of psychological reactance (see Brehm, 1966). Group members may become entrenched in positions to which they are not initially all that strongly committed. This appears to have been what occurred in the Watergate cover-up (Wicker, 1990). In other instances, the failure to deal with a constraint early on might even lead to the introduction of yet another debilitating constraint. For example, efforts by some group members to appease a controlling individual in the interest of maintaining group harmony could easily create conflicts with others and prompt in them a desire to exercise control. In these sorts of situations, the interests of informed choice are not likely to be served very well.

Learning to interpret the signs of cognitive, affiliative, and egocentric constraints can be of value in dealing with the timing of responses to the problems to which they are contributing. Determining what is the best strategic choice, however, is a different matter. Unfortunately, communication scholars have not focused much attention on the nexus of strategic responses to the types of problems we have been discussing, largely because they have not been accustomed to viewing decision-making and problem-solving processes in terms of the social constraints acting on them (see, e.g., Hirokawa, 1983b, 1988; Hirokawa, Ice, & Cook, 1988; Jarboe, 1988; Pyron, 1964; Pyron & Sharp, 1963). At least, they have not considered them from the sort of perspective an organized structure, such as the one developed and promulgated by Janis (1989), provides.

Following is an effort to identify some general considerations that can clarify and guide the communicative interventions open to members of groups that are falling victim to cognitive, affiliative, and egocentric constraints. Our observations are necessarily speculative, but we trust that they provide a basis for further systematic inquiry and research, having as their aim establishment of the comparative merits of different strategic approaches to problems that interfere with a group's ability to satisfy the fundamental requirements of its task.

Considerations Involving Communicative Interventions as Responses to Cognitive, Affiliative, and Egocentric Constraints

We begin with an acknowledgment that in most, if not all, instances cognitive, affiliative, and egocentric constraints are likely to be present. The question is not whether their emergence can be completely prevented, but instead whether the negative aspects of their impact on the process of making informed choices can be minimized. To think otherwise would be unrealistic and counter to our understanding of normal human tendencies. The principle of management rather than of elimination, therefore, underlies all of the considerations we introduce below in our discussion of strategic responses to cognitive, affiliative, and egocentric constraints that, if left unchecked, will exert an unhealthy influence on a group's performance of its task.

RESPONDING TO COGNITIVE CONSTRAINTS

Because cognitive constraints relate to perceptions of the adequacy of resources for making decisions or finding solutions to problems, the members of a group, you will recall, are apt to look for evidence of what others, or they themselves, have done in apparently and roughly comparable situations. Dawes (1994) has noted this tendency among clinical psychologists and psychotherapists in their diagnoses of problems and recommendations for treatment. They are frequently guilty of selective recall and, as a result, misdiagnose psychological states or develop questionable approaches to dealing with clients.

When the signs of cognitive constraints that point group members toward past actions and standard operating procedures begin to surface, it may be a good idea to acknowledge the similarity of the present situation to others rather than to deny it, but also to make a conscious effort to look for differences. Rarely are two situations so alike that what applies to one necessarily applies to the other. Had decision makers in the 1960s not been so convinced that the conflict between North and South Vietnam represented the same kind of aggression that led to

World War II, American involvement might have taken quite a different turn (Dawes, 1988). By reminding group members of the dangers in analogizing and by attempting to identify what is unique about the present situation, one can help to overcome predispositions to reach premature conclusions about which, among a set of alternatives, best addresses the issue or problem at hand and to avoid excessive reliance on "tried and true" solutions.

Another way in which one can attempt to minimize the influence of a cognitive constraint is to ask at the outset what deficiencies in resources (e.g., information, time, and expertise) the participants perceive and to assess what realistic possibilities exist for overcoming these deficiencies. The anxiety that leads to a reliance on shortcuts is often a product of misperception and underestimation of group members' capacity for accomplishing their task.

By deliberately making resources an object of discussion, a participant can help to create a climate in which accurate assessment and stock taking are possible. Taking account of resources by posing such question as, "What do we know?", "What do we need to know?", and, "How can we find out what we need to know?", can do much to set a tone that enables group members to proceed in a methodical way when they move to other aspects of a task, for instance, determining the nature of the problem to be resolved or assessing the merits of alternative solutions.

Yet another strategy for minimizing negative intrusive influence of cognitive constraints is to make salient the possible costs associated with choosing unwisely or inappropriately. Under conditions in which the costs of being wrong can be substantial, one has greater incentive to avoid mistakes or errors in judgment. The Federal Reserve Board, for example, might be less prone to raise the prime interest rate to prevent the economy from overheating on the grounds that this solution has worked in the past if one were to establish a reasonable probability that under current circumstances the measure could reduce consumer demand to the point that strong recessionary influences would come into play, substantially limit tax revenues, and further increase an already unacceptable deficit situation.

Cost-benefit analysis has long been recognized as an important aspect of effective decision making (Bazerman & Neale, 1992). Unfortunately, the manner in which some groups engage in it is perfunctory and reduces merely to a listing of possibilities. To be effective, cost-benefit analysis requires relevant information and an ability to draw accurate inferences from it. In the absence of such factors, it becomes little more than an exercise in form.

None of these considerations or the general strategies they suggest, of course, will necessarily ensure that a group will choose intelligently. Their value lies in shifting a frame of reference from which group members are inclined to rely nonreflectively on actions taken in analogous situations to one more conducive to innovation and discovery. With such a shift may follow a more cautious and deliberate approach to the matters in need of resolution and greater attention to specific task requirements.

RESPONDING TO AFFILIATIVE CONSTRAINTS

Because a group itself is often important to the individuals who comprise it, some of them will be motivated to maintain as harmonious an atmosphere as possible. As we have noted earlier, however, when this motivation is dominant, the satisfaction of task requirements may suffer. If a group's main concern is either to achieve unity or to accommodate the interests of its members and to maximize their satisfaction, following a less-than-vigilant path in a decision-making or problem-solving discussion is not especially problematic. In many situations, however, making a good decision (i.e., one that has desired consequences in relation to the issues it addresses) or generating an effective solution to a problem is the outcome of interest. When this is the case, promoting unity and/or group well-being at the expense of sound decision-making or problem-solving procedures is problematic.

To minimize possibilities for displacement of the motive of making the best possible choice, one is well advised to cultivate the habit of securing at the outset of a decision-making or problem-solving discussion agreement among the participants about precisely what it is they are attempting to accomplish. This could entail the negotiation of a definition of an acceptable choice as one that is warranted on the basis of criteria that are independent of the personal preferences of the members or the perceived need of the group to present a united front. If the members openly commit themselves to making the best possible choice, then, as in other cases involving public commitment, they have a greater likelihood of remaining consistent (Festinger, 1957).

Further contributing to minimization of the ill effects of affiliative constraints are conscious efforts to separate issues from personalities. Members of groups often refrain from being critical of others' input because they wish to avoid hurting feelings or taking the risk of retaliation. Withholding input, however, is not the answer. Inhibited communication can result in less-than-optimum choices, both in the context of mixed-motive interactions, such as negotiations (Fisher & Ury, 1981), and in so-called single-motive interactions of the type we have been discussing (Folger, Poole, & Stutman, 1993). Unfortunately, those who are not reluctant to express their views, or who somehow overcome their reluctance, sometimes elicit the very reactions they would like to avoid by appearing to personalize issues or to be attacking those to whom they are directing their comments.

Making clear that one is questioning ideas rather than attacking the source of them can do much to maintain a congenial climate while allowing for necessary input (Fisher & Ury, 1981). As in the case of clarifying what the group is supposed to be accomplishing, attempting to establish a climate in which ideas can be separated from personalities may require early discussion, the aim of which is to remind group members that the merits of ideas have to be examined critically and that such efforts should neither be personal in nature nor interpreted in that way.

In addition to what can be done at the outset of a discussion to reduce tendencies to promote unity and harmony at the expense of informed choice, a participant who sees the former tendency emerging in the course of interaction might make overt calls for disagreement. Janis (1982) goes so far as to recommend the regular appointment of individuals to the role of devil's advocate. Although we are not convinced of the need for so formal a mechanism, the principle behind it is sensible. By asking for expressions of disagreement, or at least evaluative assessments of ideational input that may be lacking in merit, one makes clear that personal considerations are not at issue and that the determination of utility is.

As with cost-benefit analysis, it is important that calls for disagreement be genuine, not merely perfunctory. Lyndon Johnson ostensibly wanted to hear all sides of his policy in Vietnam until someone actually expressed an opposing view (Kearns, 1976). He even took to referring to his press secretary, Bill Moyers, as "Mr. Stop the Bombing" (Janis, 1972, p. 120). Moyers eventually resigned his position rather than continue to be an object of derision and humiliation.

Consistent with our discussion of cognitive constraints, the approaches described above for minimizing the deleterious effects of affiliative constraints carry no guarantee of success. Yet taking these approaches can lead to a reduction in the concerns that often inhibit group members' willingness to focus on task-related matters in the manner they should. The critical assessment of ideas and information need not disturb the cohesiveness of a group if the parties to a decision-making or problem-solving discussion make clear that the focus of their disagreements, judgments, doubts, and questions is substantive. Establishing such a focus can even lead to increased cohesiveness and facilitate consensus, as Guetzkow and Gyr (1954) discovered in their study of substantive and affective conflict in decision-making conferences in the business realm.

RESPONDING TO EGOCENTRIC CONSTRAINTS

We indicated earlier that egocentric constraints are reflective of individual group members' desires or needs for control. So pronounced are these needs in some instances that significant amounts of discussion, even entire phases, are devoted to negotiating and establishing the decision-making rights of members and the authority structure of groups (see Bales & Strodtbeck, 1951; Ellis & Fisher, 1975; Fisher, 1970). In addition, because such constraints relate to desires to control outcomes, participants may be more consciously aware of their presence than they are of either cognitive or affiliative constraints. As a result, egocentric constraints are often more resistant to counteractive influence than are the other two types. The situation is not hopeless, however, as we shall attempt to establish.

Individuals with high needs for control stand either in symmetrical or asymmetrical relationship to other group members. When the relationships are symmetrical—that is, no party has more power than other parties—the successful exercise of influence depends on willing compliance of the target(s). Heightening awareness of the nature of the relationships through such comments as, "We all have a stake in the outcome," "We need everyone's best thinking on this issue," or "If we cannot reach consensus, we will have to decide by majority vote," serves notice to the controlling type of individual that others in the group are not going to knuckle under simply because someone wants to prevail and that they understand their rights as group members.

In being thus aware, participants are more likely to require of would-be sources of influence the same attention to the demands of the task expected of everyone else. This assumes, of course, that at least some members of the group understand and appreciate the requisites of the task and the obligations they impose for informed, thoughtful deliberation.

More problematic to the interests of informed choice are situations in which egocentric constraints arise as the result of needs for influence or control of one or more members whose relationships to others in respect to power are asymmetrical. Under these conditions, less powerful group members are prone to assess the possible consequences of resistance and suppress concerns they may have both about what more powerful ones are saying and how they are going about trying to gain concurrence. Fears of reprisal are often legitimate; however, one may still have some latitude within which to address the problem.

Instead of being directly confrontational, a group participant might attempt to engage a more powerful and controlling individual in self-reflection and examination by raising such questions as, "Could you share a little more of the thinking behind your position?", "Do we have sufficient evidence to draw that conclusion?", "Might it not be a good idea to suspend judgment until we have considered the other options?", "What reservations do you have about going ahead with this plan?", or "What do the people in _____ (some unit or agency) have to say about this idea?" In shifting the focus to self-examination, the individual attempting to gain acceptance of his or her position may become more aware of deficiencies in that position or, at least, be less insistent in promoting it.

One should not presume that those who seek to control outcomes are necessarily incapable of informed thought or good judgment. The critical issue is whether or not they are behaving in a manner that is consistent with acknowledged principles of effective choice. When they are not, the sorts of strategies we have been describing can help to overcome or, at least, reduce the problems created by egocentric constraints. Should they prove ineffectual, then one may have to become more confrontational and be prepared to accept the consequences. Our effort has been to show that going to this extreme may not be necessary and that one should consider possibilities short of it that could still have the desired consequences. At least, we feel that one should undertake such measures first.

Modifications

In view of the deficiencies of functional theory at its present stage and the implications of the preceding discussion of the social constraints, several modifications appear to be warranted. To the assumptions underlying the theory, we would add three. First, one or more of the members of the group must be capable of recognizing and interpreting the signs of unwanted cognitive, affiliative, and egocentric constraints. Second, the members are aware of how well interaction is serving to satisfy fundamental task requirements. Third, members will take steps to minimize and counteract sources of influence that limit prospects for fulfilling fundamental task requirements.

As in the case with the other seven assumptions, if these additional ones are not tenable, one has less reason to expect that a group will make the most appropriate choice. An inability to recognize the signs of cognitive, affiliative, and egocentric constraints makes it more likely that the emergence of any one type will become dominant and influence, in potentially injurious ways, the choice a group makes. Similarly, if the members are unaware of qualitative differences in how well communication is serving necessary functions, the chances for achieving the desired outcome may be sharply reduced. Recognizing potentially or actually problematic situations, of course, is not sufficient for overcoming them. Such situations require response—hence, our third additional assumption.

The original seven assumptions have a systematic order, such that if any one of them does not obtain, it matters much less if the ones that follow do. Within such a hierarchical structure, our first additional assumption logically precedes the present assumption #7, that is, that communication is instrumental. The remaining two logically follow it. So conceived, the revised list of assumptions is as follows:

1. The members of a decision-making or problem-solving group are motivated to make an appropriate choice.
2. The choice confronted is nonobvious.
3. The collective resources of the group in respect to the particular task exceed those of individual members.
4. The requisites of the task are specifiable.
5. Relevant information is available to the members or can be acquired.
6. The task is within the intellectual capabilities of the members to perform.
7. One or more of the members of the group must be capable of recognizing and interpreting the signs of unwanted cognitive, affiliative, and egocentric constraints.
8. Communication is instrumental.
9. Members are aware of how well interaction is serving to satisfy fundamental task requirements.
10. Members will take steps to minimize and counteract sources of influence that limit prospects for adequately fulfilling fundamental task requirements.

The material we have introduced in this chapter also suggests some expansion in the general propositions that comprise functional theory. The original five propositions we now view as relating to fundamental task requirements. They are fundamental in the sense that a failure to satisfy each renders an appropriate choice unlikely. To these, we would add several other propositions concerning preventive and corrective measures that an effective group would take in the interest of minimizing the intrusiveness of cognitive, affiliative, and egocentric constraints that otherwise may limit the ability of members to satisfy the more basic and essential requirements of their task.

These additional propositions are not direct extensions of existing evidence. Rather, they derive from the general implications we have drawn from the discussion of constraints and possible strategic response to them. Their largely hypothetical character, we hope, will stimulate further inquiry and provide greater guidance for researchers interested in the communication/decisional outcome relationship.

At the base of much of our discussion is the need for groups to be alert to potential difficulties and to take steps to minimize the chances for their having major impact. Accordingly, we would add as propositions to the theoretical framework that the members of a group (a) make clear their interest in arriving at the best possible decision, (b) identify the resources necessary for making such a decision, (c) recognize possible obstacles to be confronted, (d) specify the procedures to be followed, and (e) establish the ground rules for interaction.

As preventive measures, such initial actions, in principle, will facilitate satisfaction of the five fundamental task requirements on which the theory originally focused. We realize that such measures may not suffice, however. As a result, we believe it important to add propositions that refer to corrective actions. A proposition suggested by the considerations we have introduced is that the members of a group, when necessary, will employ appropriate interventions for overcoming cognitive, affiliative, and egocentric constraints that are interfering with the satisfaction of fundamental task requirements. In addition, that they will review the process by which the group comes to a decision and, if indicated, reconsider the choice (even to the point of starting over).

The combination of preventive and counteractive measures suggested by the inclusion of these additional propositions emphasizes the qualitative dimension of interaction. These measures also expand the scope of functions communication serves. Performance of these functions, however, does not ensure that a group will succeed in making an appropriate choice. Divorced from the fundamental requirements of the task, communication serving such functions has limited significance. We, therefore, view the new propositions as ancillary to the remaining and most basic general proposition.

With the addition of the propositions discussed above, we now treat the five original ones as subcategories of a larger general proposition. The rephrasing, we trust, makes clear that communication must address fundamental task requirements, but that this is not its exclusive role. The revised version of the propositions central to the functional perspective, then, holds that the likelihood of a group's making an appropriate choice is at a maximum under conditions in which members

1. make clear their interest in arriving at the best possible decision;
2. identify the resources necessary for making such a decision;
3. recognize possible obstacles to be confronted;
4. specify the procedures to be followed;
5. establish ground rules for interaction;
6. attempt to satisfy fundamental task requirements by
   a. showing correct understanding of the issue to be resolved;

b. determining the minimal characteristics any alternative, to be acceptable, must possess;

c. identifying a relevant and realistic set of alternatives;

d. examining carefully the alternatives in relationship to each previously agreed-upon characteristic of an acceptable choice; and

e. selecting the alternative that analysis reveals to be most likely to have the desired characteristics;

7. employ appropriate interventions for overcoming cognitive, affiliative, and egocentric constraints that are interfering with the satisfaction of fundamental task requirements; and

8. review the process by which the group comes to a decision and, if indicated, reconsider judgments reached (even to the point of starting over).

Conclusion

In identifying some of the ways in which members of decision-making and problem-solving groups understand the requirements for making appropriate decisions and generating effective solutions to problems, we have also established the basis for a research agenda. Whether our suspicions concerning how an expanded role for communication in the performance of decision-making and problem-solving tasks will be confirmed remains to be determined. In revising functional theory in the ways outlined in this chapter, however, our hope is that we have provided sufficient grounds to move forward with the sorts of inquiries that not only will contribute to advancements and refinements in the functional perspective on communication in decision-making and problem-solving groups, but that, in longer range, will prove to have practical value as well.

References

Aronson, E. (1980). *The social animal* (3rd ed.). San Francisco: Freeman.

Asch, S. E. (1956). Studies of independence and conformity: A minority of one against a unanimous majority. *Psychological Monographs, 70*(Whole 416).

Bales, R. F., & Strodtbeck, F. L. (1951). Phases in group problem-solving. *Journal of Abnormal and Social Psychology, 46*, 485-495.

Bazerman, M. H., & Neale, M. A. (1992). *Negotiating rationally*. New York: Free Press.

Brehm, J. W. (1966). *A theory of psychological reactance*. New York: Academic Press.

Chesin, E. S. (1973). *President Nixon's psychiatric profile*. New York: Berkeley Publishing.

Courtright, J. A. (1978). A laboratory investigation of groupthink. *Communication Monographs, 45*, 229-246.

Cragan, J. F., & Wright, D. W. (1993). The functional theory of small group decision-making: A replication. *Journal of Social Behavior and Personality, 8*, 165-174.

Dawes, R. M. (1988). *Rational choice in an uncertain world*. San Diego, CA: Harcourt Brace Jovanovich.

Dawes, R. M. (1994). *House of cards: Psychology and psychotherapy built on myth*. New York: Free Press.

Drew, E. (1994). *On the edge: The Clinton presidency*. New York: Simon & Schuster.

Ellis, D. G., & Fisher, B. A. (1975). Phases of conflict in small group development: A Markov analysis. *Human Communication Research, 1*, 195-212.

Festinger, L. (1957). *A theory of cognitive dissonance*. Stanford, CA: Stanford University Press.

Fisher, B. A. (1970). Decision emergence: Phases in group decision-making. *Speech Monographs, 37*, 53-66.

Fisher, R., & Ury, W. (1981). *Getting to yes*. Boston: Houghton Mifflin.

Folger, J. P., Poole, M. S., & Stutman, R. K. (1993). *Working through conflict* (2nd ed.). New York: HarperCollins.

Gibb, J. R. (1961). Defensive communication. *Journal of Communication, 11*, 141-148.

Gouran, D. S. (1968). Group decision making: An approach to integrative research. In C. H. Tardy (Ed.), *A handbook for the study of communication* (pp. 247-268). Norwood, NJ: Ablex.

Gouran, D. S. (1982). *Making decisions in groups: Choices and consequences*. Glenview, IL: Scott, Foresman.

Gouran, D. S. (1984). Communicative influences related to the Watergate coverup: The failure of collective judgment. *Central States Speech Journal, 35*, 260-268.

Gouran, D. S. (1987). The failure of argument in decisions leading to the "Challenger disaster": A two-level analysis. In J. W. Wenzel (Ed.), *Argument and critical practices: Proceedings of the Fifth SCA/AFA Conference on Argumentation* (pp. 439-448). Annandale, VA: Speech Communication Association.

Gouran, D. S. (1990). Factors affecting the decision-making process in the Attorney General's Commission on Pornography: A case study of unwarranted collective judgment. In R. S. Rodgers (Ed.), *Free speech yearbook 28* (pp. 104-119). Carbondale: Southern Illinois University Press.

Gouran, D. S. (1991). Rational approaches to decision-making and problem-solving discussion. *Quarterly Journal of Speech, 77*, 343-358.

Gouran, D. S. (1992). Principles of counteractive influence in decision-making and problem-solving groups. In R. S. Cathcart & L. A. Samovar (Eds.), *Small group communication: A reader* (6th ed., pp. 221-235). Dubuque, IA: William C. Brown.

Gouran, D. S., Brown, C. R., & Henry, D. R. (1978). Behavioral correlates of perceptions of quality in decision-making discussions. *Communication Monographs, 45*, 51-63.

Gouran, D. S., & Hirokawa, R. Y. (1983). The role of communication in decision-making groups: A functional perspective. In M. S. Mander (Ed.), *Communications in transition* (pp. 168-185). New York: Praeger.

Gouran, D. S., & Hirokawa, R. Y. (1986). Counteractive functions of communication in effective group decision-making. In R. Y. Hirokawa & M. S. Poole (Eds.), *Communication and group decision-making* (pp. 81-90). Beverly Hills, CA: Sage.

Gouran, D. S., Hirokawa, R. Y., Julian, K. M., & Leatham, G. B. (1993). The evolution and current status of the functional perspective on communication in decision-making and problem-solving groups. In S. A. Deetz (Ed.), *Communication yearbook 16* (pp. 573-600). Newbury Park, CA: Sage.

Gouran, D. S., Hirokawa, R. Y., & Martz, A. E. (1986). A critical analysis of factors related to decisional processes involved in the Challenger disaster. *Central States Speech Journal, 37,* 119-135.

Gouran, D. S., Hirokawa, R. Y., McGee, M. C., & Miller, L. L. (1994). Communication in groups: Research trends and theoretical perspectives. In F. L. Casmir (Ed.), *Building communication theories: A socio/cultural approach* (pp. 241-268). Hillsdale, NJ: Lawrence Erlbaum.

Guetzkow, H., & Gyr, J. R. (1954). An analysis of conflict in decision making groups. *Human Relations, 7,* 367-382.

Harvey, J. B. (1974). The Abilene paradox: The management of agreement. *Organizational Dynamics, 3,* 63-80.

Hirokawa, R. Y. (1980). *A function-oriented analysis of small group interaction within effective and ineffective decision-making groups: An exploratory investigation.* Unpublished doctoral dissertation, University of Washington, Seattle.

Hirokawa, R. Y. (1982). Group communication and problem-solving effectiveness I: A critical review of inconsistent findings. *Communication Quarterly, 30,* 134-141.

Hirokawa, R. Y. (1983a). Communication and problem-solving effectiveness II: An exploratory investigation of procedural functions. *Western Journal of Speech Communication, 47,* 59-74.

Hirokawa, R. Y. (1983b). A descriptive investigation of the possible communication-based reasons for effective and ineffective group decision making. *Communication Monographs, 50,* 363-379.

Hirokawa, R. Y. (1985). Discussion procedures and decision-making performance: A test of a functional perspective. *Human Communication Research, 12,* 203-224.

Hirokawa, R. Y. (1987). Why informed groups make faulty decisions: An investigation of possible interaction-based explanations. *Small Group Behavior, 18,* 3-29.

Hirokawa, R. Y. (1988). Group communication and decision-making performance: A continued test of the functional perspective. *Human Communication Research, 14,* 487-515.

Hirokawa, R. Y., Gouran, D. S., & Martz, A. E. (1988). Understanding the sources of faulty group decision making: A lesson from the Challenger disaster. *Small Group Behavior, 19,* 411-433.

Hirokawa, R. Y., Ice, R., & Cook, J. (1988). Preference for procedural order, discussion structure, and group decision performance. *Communication Quarterly, 36,* 217-226.

Hirokawa, R. Y., & Johnston, D. D. (1989). Toward a general theory of group decision making: Development of an integrated model. *Small Group Behavior, 20,* 500-524.

Hirokawa, R. Y., & McLeod, P. L. (1993, November). *Communication, decision development, and decision quality in small groups: An integration of two approaches.* Paper presented at the annual meeting of the Speech Communication Association, Miami Beach.

Hirokawa, R. Y., Oetzel, J., Aleman, C., & Elston, S. (1991). *The effects of evaluation clarity and bias on the relationship between vigilant interaction and decision-making efficacy.* Unpublished manuscript, University of Iowa, Iowa City.

Hirokawa, R. Y., & Pace, R. C. (1983). A descriptive investigation of the possible communication-based reasons for effective and ineffective group decision-making. *Communication Monographs, 50,* 363-379.

Hirokawa, R. Y., & Rost, K. M. (1990, November). *Going from the little aquarium to the big ocean: Field test of the group interaction-performance relationship.* Paper presented at the annual meeting of the Speech Communication Association, Chicago.

Hirokawa, R. Y., & Scheerhorn, D. R. (1986). Communication in faulty group decision-making. In R. Y. Hirokawa & M. S. Poole (Eds.), *Communication and group decision-making* (pp. 63-80). Beverly Hills, CA: Sage.

Janis, I. L. (1972). *Victims of groupthink: Psychological studies of foreign policy decisions and fiascoes*. Boston: Houghton Mifflin.

Janis, I. L. (1982). *Groupthink* (2nd ed.). Boston: Houghton Mifflin.

Janis, I. L. (1989). *Crucial decisions: Leadership in policy making and crisis management*. New York: Free Press.

Janis, I. L., & Mann, L. (1977). *Decision making: A psychological analysis of conflict, choice, and commitment*. New York: Free Press.

Jarboe, S. (1988). A comparison of input-output, process-output, and input-process-output models of small group problem-solving effectiveness. *Communication Monographs, 55*, 122-142.

Kearns, D. (1976). *Lyndon Johnson and the American dream*. New York: Harper & Row.

Lukas, A. J. (1973). *Nightmare: The underside of the Nixon years*. New York: Viking.

Martz, A. E. (1986). *An investigation of the functions of communication in the production and acceptance of unwarranted inferences by members of decision-making groups*. Unpublished master's thesis, Pennsylvania State University, University Park.

Mason, G. E. (1984). *An empirical investigation of inferential and related communication processes distinguishing between effective and ineffective decision-making groups*. Unpublished doctoral dissertation, Indiana University, Bloomington.

McKinney, B. C. (1985). *Decision-making in the President's Commission on the Assassination of President Kennedy: A descriptive analysis employing Irving Janis's groupthink hypothesis*. Unpublished doctoral dissertation, Pennsylvania State University, University Park.

Nakanishi, M. (1990, November). *Group communication and decision-making effectiveness: A test of the functional perspective*. Paper presented at the annual meeting of the Speech Communication Association, Chicago.

Neustadt, R. E., & May, E. R. (1986). *Thinking in time: The uses of history for decision makers*. New York: Free Press.

Papa, M. J., & Graham, E. E. (1990, November). *A test of the ecological validity of the functional communicative perspective of small group decision-making*. Paper presented at the annual meeting of the Speech Communication Association, Chicago.

Propp, K. M., & Nelson, D. (1994, April). *Decision-making performance in naturalistic groups: A test of the ecological validity of the functional perspective*. Paper presented at the annual meeting of the Central States Communication Association, Oklahoma City, OK.

Pyron, H. C. (1964). An experimental study of the role of reflective thinking and performance in business and professional conferences and discussions. *Speech Monographs, 31*, 157-161.

Pyron, H. C., & Sharp, H., Jr. (1963). A quantitative study of reflective thinking and performance in problem-solving discussion. *Journal of Communication, 13*, 157-161.

Schanck, R. L. (1932). A study of a community and its groups and institutions conceived of as behaviors of individuals. *Psychological Monographs, 43*(Whole No. 195).

Schutz, W. C. (1958). *FIRO: A three-dimensional theory of interpersonal behavior*. New York: Holt, Rinehart & Winston.

Wicker, T. (1990). *One of us: Richard Nixon and the American dream*. New York: Random House.

Symbolic Convergence Theory and Communication in Group Decision Making

ERNEST G. BORMANN

The symbolic convergence theory of communication is a general theory that accounts for the appearance of a group consciousness, with its implied shared emotions, motives, and meanings. Although the theory has application to many communication contexts, small group communication scholars made the preliminary studies from which the theory evolved and it is particularly applicable to the study of small group communication.

In this chapter I will apply the symbolic convergence theory to the communication associated with group decision making. To lay the groundwork for explaining group decision making in terms of the theory, I will first discuss how the symbolic convergence theory of communication explains the creation and development of special communication theories and of a more specific group culture, and then indicate how that evolving culture interacts with the task dimension to shape the communication processes of decision making.

The Nature of Communication Theory

Scholars discussing communication theory and using the term *theory* in their studies and works often mean different things (Bormann, 1989). At least five important meanings should be distinguished to avoid confusion when presenting a theoretical chapter.

I will mention three important meanings of *theory* that are nonetheless beyond the focus of this chapter to clarify my two focal concerns. In the first sense, *theory* refers to abstract statements and concepts unrelated to practice. This use of the term *theory* is often pejorative as in the phrase, "That is all very well in theory but it would never work in practice." A second meaning of *theory* refers to a general explanation of communication that is as yet untested. What *theory* means in this instance is that I have a hunch or hypothesis that the connection exists but I have no solid evidence that that is the case. The third meaning for *theory* refers to a stipulated and conjectured body of assumed principles, axioms, and postulates belonging to a subject field. The procedure is to develop a series of stipulated features, relationships, and generalizations about communication much as one might develop mathematical postulates. Taking the assumptions as a basis, scholars then exegetically expand on them by armchair speculation to posit new concepts and connections. Having developed a coherent and plausible body of assumptions, scholars often take the next legitimate step and test the assumptions of the third kind of theory in the laboratory or field. However, scholars sometimes begin to write as though the assumptions they started with have now become empirically validated foundation terms and relationships. They treat their theory as though it had metamorphosed into the crucial fifth meaning of the term *theory* explained below.

Two meanings for the term *theory* are central to my analysis. The first that is of concern refers to a particular conception or view of how to communicate and the methods for doing so. This meaning of theory is closely tied to the practice of communication. Craig (1989) has characterized this sort of theory as viewing communication as a practical discipline. He notes, "As a practical discipline, our essential purpose is to cultivate communicative *praxis*, or practical art, through critical study" (pp. 97-98). I shall argue that included in such formulations are integrated accounts that provide a philosophical rationale for communication practices, an ideal model of good communication practices, and how-to advice on becoming a good communicator.

The last meaning for the term *theory* refers to a consistent and coherent group of general propositions used as explanations for a class of phenomena. This last meaning differs from the practice-oriented notion of theory in that it denotes a more or less verified or established explanation accounting for known facts or phenomena. The final meaning for theory is not only denotively clear in specifying the essential criteria required to be considered a member of the class but it is rhetorically a prestigious concept among scholars and intellectuals. For many intellectual communities, the term *theory*, when used in this last sense, denotes one of the highest forms of intellectual activity and a solid path to knowledge. The term connotes science and the scientific in all of its forms. Because of the honorific nature of the term many in the academic community will be tempted to use the term for mental constructions such as hypotheses, conjectures, principles, and practices (the second and third meanings for the term) to give these thought structures added standing in the scholarly community. In the remainder of the chapter I will use the term *theory* only for the fourth and fifth meanings outlined above.

To distinguish between the fourth and fifth meanings, I will characterize those rule-governed and conventional thought structures closely tied to communication practices (the fourth meaning of the term) as *special theories* and those verified, consistent, and coherent thought structures composed of general propositions used as explanations for a class of phenomena as *general theories*.

SPECIAL COMMUNICATION THEORIES

Special communication theories begin with innovative practices. If novel ways of communicating catch on and a number of people become drawn to and interested in the new forms, some of the interested individuals will emerge as more expert and knowledgeable than others. These connoisseurs will become specialists in the new style of communication. They will spend time with like-minded individuals studying and talking about the ins and outs of practicing the new communication form.

The new form is novel and many who are drawn to it are novices and unaware of the nature of the form. The novices often seek help from the knowledgeable to become good communicators in the new style. The net result is that talking about the talk takes on two dimensions. The first dimension relates to criticism of the communication events. Those who participate and those who are knowledgeable often discuss specific communication events and evaluate them pro and con. The second dimension takes the criticism a step farther and adds teaching and coaching to improve future communication. As the connoisseurs discuss, criticize, and teach, their work becomes more formalized. They may give lectures, hold informal training sessions, give lessons, and write articles and books relating to the subject.

The connoisseurs often take the material they produce in their criticism, coaching, and teaching and fashion it into a coherent and consistent vision of how to communicate and the ways and means for doing it. The specialists produce a special theory of communication.

Communication is not natural in the same sense that, for example, certain rock formations or the paths of the planets around the sun of our solar system are made by nature. Communication is artificial (i.e., created by human beings), social, and conventional. Because communication is artificial, people need to be taught how to communicate. In addition, small group communication is social and all participants must agree to work cooperatively to achieve the ideals implied by good communication. Because communication is conventional, cooperating participants must know the conventions and abide by them. The conventional nature of communication ensures that when all participants succeed in their joint efforts the result is a recurring communication form. Put another way, when we find a recurring form of communication in the sensitivity training session, the encounter group, the strength group, the consciousness-raising group, the brainstorming group, the business meeting, or the group discussion, there will be a special communication theory governing the communication.

A full-blown special theory consists of three main components. The first component is a *philosophical rationale*. The philosophical rationale is a set of assumptions and value statements providing an explanation and justification for the communication form. The rationale deals with such questions as the functions and purposes of the communication, the importance and value of the efforts, and the place of the new communication form in society and the great chain of being.

The second component is an *ideal model* of the communication episode. The ideal model provides an organized description of the best, most elegant form of the communication. Scholars have developed ideal models of communication in great detail. Scholars have sometimes diagrammed the ideal model in the form of a cybernetic system (Source, Message, Channels, Receiver). Scholars have sometimes described the ideal model in terms of psychiatry, religion, and psychology (deep, significant, congruent, transactional, trusting). Scholars have sometimes described the ideal in terms of videotapes (this year's prize-winning television commercial).

Whatever form the ideal model takes, it will have tacit or explicit rules governing its operation. These rules may be *forming* or *regulating*. Forming rules describe the conventions that must be followed to achieve the ideal model. For example, turn-taking rules such as that only one person may speak at a time could be part of the forming rules of an ideal model small group communication. In many forms of communication the great majority of forming rules are followed, but some will often be broken because of ignorance, lack of skill, or self-interest. To ensure the integrity of the ideal model, participants will then employ regulatory rules to ensure that infractions are kept to a minimum. Thus people who talk out of turn may be pressured by group monitoring, by verbal admonishment, or by penalizing them in some way.

The specialists in the communication style can use the ideal model for criticism. They take a given communication episode (form) and compare it to the touchstone of the ideal model. They can then point out that a given business meeting was a time waster, or failed to accomplish its purpose, or heard all points of view, and so on. They may go further, to examine how elegant the communication was in a given sample by comparing it to the ideal model. They might then judge that a given encounter group reached a beautiful level of understanding, trust, and communion. Specialists can also use the ideal model to teach newcomers how to communicate according to the ideal model and to coach tyros in how to become better at communicating.

The final component of a special theory is concrete advice about how to improve practice. The how-to sections are collections of wisdom gathered by connoisseurs and practitioners who have wide experience practicing, criticizing, and educating others about the special communication style.

GENERAL COMMUNICATION THEORIES

The fifth meaning of the term *theory* is what I will specify as *general communication theories*. General theories are verified, consistent, and coherent generalizations that explain a class of events. General theories are often transhistorical in that they explain what took place in the past as well as what is happening in the present and anticipate or predict events in the future. General theories are also transcultural in that they explain events that take place in various cultural contexts. The generalization that accounts for the operation of the law of gravity, for example, is part of a general theory. Gravity applies to past events (Caesar crossing the Rubicon), present events (the pull of the moon on the surface of the oceans), and future events (force required by a space ship to go into orbit in the 21st century). Gravity also applies to the events in cultures as diverse as of those of ancient Romans, modern-day Black Americans, and future residents of Pakistan. By contrast, special theories apply to events of much less scope and are often time and culture bound.

Whereas special theories are conventional (governed by rules that participants can break), general theories are necessary (the law of gravity cannot be broken in the way that a member of a discussion meeting can ignore a turn-taking rule). One can try to fly but only by taking the law of gravity into account and overcoming the pull of the earth on the flying object.

General theories take a number of different forms. Some, like Newton's theory of mechanics, consist of generalizations expressing invariable relations, and these generalizations (covering laws) are often expressed in mathematical formulas. These formulas, in turn, are integrated into a consistent system by mathematical manipulations. Scholars using a general theory like Newton's need to have precise ways of applying the mathematical formulations to experience; an important way to make such application is by quantifying experience in terms of measurements that fulfill the assumptions of such mathematical systems as arithmetic. Theories of the Newtonian form can predict with precision future events such as eclipses, the flight of a rifle bullet, and the distance traveled by a uniformly accelerating automobile. Another form of general theory consists of a careful cataloging of instances of the changes in species through time. If such cataloging results in a longitudinal finding of changes through time that indicates an evolution from earlier to later forms, the theory may also include a listing of lawful forces of necessary and sufficient cause to explain the processes of evolution. General theories of evolution, such as Darwin's, may require less quantification and fewer invariable relations expressed in mathematical formulas than those of the Newtonian form. An evolutionary theory can explain the way modern humans evolved from earlier humanoid individuals. However, such theories cannot predict the future path of evolution in the same way that covering law theories can. Theories of evolution, however, do assume that their application is transhistorical and transcultural.

Symbolic Convergence as a General Theory of Communication

The symbolic convergence theory is general in the sense that it is transhistorical and transcultural. The process of symbolic convergence took place when Caesar crossed the Rubicon, is taking place in some communication events such as group meetings, and will take place in future discussions. The symbolic convergence communication theory is a general theory that accounts for the creation and use of special communication theories in the past, present, and future and in a multitude of cultures. My major thesis is that although special communication theories guide, explain, and govern practice, the general theories explain how special theories come into being, develop, and function.

Overview of the Symbolic Convergence Communication Theory

THE STRUCTURE OF THE THEORY

The structure of the symbolic convergence theory is more similar to that of evolution theories such as Darwin's than it is to Newton's or the hypothetico-deductive systems of such sciences as physics and chemistry. As a result, the symbolic convergence theory does not rely on quantitative measurement nor on mathematical application of formulas to specific cases for its operation.

The theoretical account of the evolution of the species provided by Darwin was based on explaining the dynamic tendencies within an ecological system that cause the observed variation in life forms and then encourage certain of these variations to die out and others to persist through time. The postulates of the theory explained the observable facts (the structured arrangement of life forms) but because they are tendencies and relate to possible infinite variations, the Darwinian theory could not predict which forms evolution would take in the future.

The Darwinian theory consisted of three major parts. The first part was the discovery and arrangement of life forms into structured patterns that demonstrated evolutionary development. The second part of the theory was a description of the dynamic tendencies in the ecological system that explained how the observed evolutionary changes took place. The basic dynamic was natural selection, which ensured that species evolved in terms of the survival of those life forms that were best adapted to their environment. The third part was an explanation of why and when the dynamic processes of adaptation came into play.

Symbolic convergence theory also has three parts. The first part deals with the discovery and arrangement of recurring communicative forms and patterns that indicate the evolution and presence of a shared group consciousness. The second part consists of a description of the dynamic tendencies within communication systems that explains why group consciousnesses arise, continue, decline, and disappear, and the effects such group consciousnesses have in terms of meanings, motives, and communication within the group. The basic communicative process, analogous to the principle of natural selection in evolution, is the dynamic of people sharing group fantasies. *Fantasy* is a technical term in the symbolic convergence theory and does not mean what it often does in ordinary usage, namely, something imaginary, not grounded in reality. The technical meaning for fantasy is the creative and imaginative shared interpretation of events that fulfills a group psychological or rhetorical need. Rhetorical fantasies may include fanciful and fictitious scripts of imaginary characters, but they often deal with things that have actually happened to members of the group or that are reported in authenticated works of history, in the news media, or in the oral history and folklore of other groups and communities. The third part of the theory consists of the factors that explain why people share fantasies.

The first two parts of the theory are well documented but the third part, answers to the "why" question, are more difficult to develop, and scholars are still working on formulating useful hypotheses. Currently three promising factors have been identified and others are under study.

THE FUNCTIONING OF THE THEORY

Symbolic convergence creates a symbolic climate and culture that allow people to achieve empathic communion as well as a "meeting of the minds." It is symbolic because it deals with the human tendency to interpret signs, signals, current experience, and human action and to invest these with meaning.

The power of symbolic convergence theory stems from the human tendency to try to understand events in terms of people with certain personality traits and motivations making decisions, taking action, and causing things to happen. We can understand a person making plans to achieve goals and succeeding or failing to do so, because we often interpret our own behavior in that way in our personal fantasies. We often daydream about achieving our desires and think up plans to achieve our goals. We tacitly assume that our choices and our plans are motivated, under our control, and that they can make a difference. Interpreting events in terms of human action allows us to assign responsibility, to praise or blame, to arouse and propitiate guilt, to hate and to love.

When we share a fantasy we attribute events to human action and thus make sense out of what prior to that time may have been a confusing state of affairs, and we do so in common with others who share the fantasy with us. Thus we come to symbolic convergence on the matter and we will envision that part of our world in similar ways. We have created some symbolic common ground and we can then talk with one another about that shared interpretation with code words or brief allusions along the lines of the inside-cue phenomenon. A number of studies into *attribution processes* (Berger, 1973; Insko &

Schopler, 1972; Smith, 1982) have documented the importance of our tendency to explain events in terms of attributing them to motivated human action.

Convergence refers to the way, during certain processes of communication, two or more private symbolic worlds incline toward each other, come more closely together, or even overlap. If several or many people develop portions of their private symbolic worlds that overlap as a result of symbolic convergence, they share a common group consciousness. In the instance of members of a zero-history leaderless decision-making group, if all of the members share enough fantasies so they develop a common consciousness, they have the basis for communicating with one another to raise the consciousness of new members, to sustain the consciousness of group members when challenged, to discuss their common concerns and experiences as group members, and to agree on how they are going to make decisions. Thus the members must fortuitously bring the same symbolic ground with them to the group or share fantasies together to converge their symbolic baggage into a common consciousness. Their common consciousness should ensure that they agree on what will count as legitimate forms of reasoning, good evidence, and sound decision-making procedures.

An important part of the symbolic convergence theory is the way it explains how individuals come to share enough symbolic ground to take part in logical negotiation processes, problem-solving procedures, and decision making. Equally important is the way the theory also explains how individuals come to share a common sentiment or emotional involvement and commitment to symbols. In terms of group decision making, the symbolic convergence theory accounts not only for factors in what is usually referred to as rational or logical processes, but also for factors that explain the often exciting emotional components of group work. The emotional nature of fantasy sharing and how it relates to group decision making will be spelled out in greater detail in the next section.

The Basic Communicative Dynamic of Sharing Group Fantasies

The basic communicative dynamic of the theory is the sharing of group fantasies, which brings about symbolic convergence for the participants. This is the second part of the symbolic convergence theory described above, but although it comes second in the development of the theory, it will facilitate the explanation of how one discovers and uses the evidence of fantasy sharing if I take it up first.

THE RESEARCH BACKGROUND

Investigators in small group communication laboratories (Bales, 1970; Bormann, 1990; Bormann, Pratt, & Putnam, 1978; Chesebro, Cragan, & McCullough, 1973; Dunphy, 1966; Gibbard, Hartman, & Mann, 1974) discovered the process of sharing fantasies when they investigated dramatizing messages and their effect on the group.

Bales (1950) and his associates originally developed 12 categories to use in making a content analysis of the communication in small groups. One of the categories was "shows tension release," but over the years the investigators (Bales, 1970) changed the category to "dramatizes." Continued work in which observers investigated the communication episodes associated with the dramatizes category led to the discovery of "group fantasy events."

Starting in 1959, communication investigators at the University of Minnesota (the early work is reported in Bormann, 1969) had been studying the decision-making process in group discussion using the case study method of investigation. Case studies conducted over a period of several months provided an interpretative understanding of group process that was often more complete and useful than much of the quantitative data generated by various category systems. In an attempt to develop a method of communication analysis that would capture the richness of interpretative case studies and allow for generalization, the Minnesota group had been making rhetorical analyses of the communication in group discussions by studying the transcripts of group meetings, much as a critic might analyze more public messages. The attempts to make an interpretative analysis of natural language in decision-making groups was given direction and impetus with the publication of the work of Bales and his associates on group fantasy events.

At Minnesota, we replicated the observational studies of Bales and his associates and found both the presence of group fantasy events and their influence on creating a common social reality for participants.

Because of the history of the research tradition in small group communication at Minnesota, however, we gave to the study of these communication episodes a definite rhetorical bent. That is, we asked the question, To what extent can participants in group meetings intentionally
and strategically plan and dramatize messages with the objective of
drawing others into sharing the fantasy with the consequences for
development of the group's culture that such sharing implies?

DRAMATIZING MESSAGES

A dramatizing message is one that contains one or more of the following: a pun or other wordplay, a double entendre, a figure of speech,
an analogy, or an anecdote, allegory, fable, or narrative. For the purposes of symbolic convergence relating to decision making in groups,
the narrative material in dramatizing messages is most important.

A number of scholars (Combs & Mansfield, 1976) have suggested that
it is useful to view the unfolding of a communication episode as
dramatic action, as well as to attend to the dramatic elements in messages. The symbolic convergence theory, however, distinguishes between the ongoing unfolding of experience and the messages that
discuss events in other than the here and now. If, in the middle of a
group discussion several members come into conflict, the situation
would be dramatic, but because the action is unfolding in the immediate
experience of the group it would not qualify as a basis for the sharing
of a group fantasy. If, however, the group members begin talking about
a conflict some of them had had in the past or if they envision a future
conflict, or if they dramatize a current conflict taking place somewhere
else, these comments would be dramatizing messages.

THE COMMUNICATIVE PROCESS OF SHARING A FANTASY

As they studied these messages, small group investigators found that
while observing members of either an informal social group or a task-
oriented group meeting, they could isolate moments when the discussion dropped off and members were at a stalemate. The members often
seemed tense and unsure of what to say next. Nonverbally they might
slump down in their chairs and seem bored or distracted. At this point

someone might dramatize by telling a joke, narrating a personal experience, or in another fashion portraying some persona in action at some place and time other than the here-and-now meeting of the group. Some of these dramatizing messages made little difference to the lackadaisical atmosphere: The group members did not pay much attention to them. Some dramatizing, however, caused a symbolic explosion in the form of a chain reaction. As the fantasy chain begins, a listener sits up and responds to the story. Something about it has caught the person's interest and attention. Another person responds with a laugh and adds to the story. Still another joins in and soon the entire group comes alive. They all begin talking and grow emotional. They may laugh or express fear or sadness. Then a member abruptly breaks off the episode by changing the subject, often by pulling the group back to work. The people who share in the imaginative enactment of the drama do so with appropriate responses. If the tone of the unfolding communication is humorous they laugh, if it is sad they appear dejected and melancholy. The technical term for such communicative episodes in which group members are pulled into sympathetic participation is a *fantasy chain*. They share a *group fantasy*. The content of the dramatizing message that sparks the fantasy chain is a *fantasy theme*. The fantasy theme is an observable record of the nature and content of the shared imagination. The theme is a social artifact that is public and that provides evidence of a small aspect of the common culture.

The psychological processes of being caught up in the narrative in a small task-oriented group are similar to those of being engrossed in a novel; raptly attending a play, film, or television show; enjoying a folktale or anecdote; or having a religious experience when identifying with a supernatural persona in a sacred myth.

Garland Wright (1990), artistic director of the Guthrie Theatre, portrayed the psychological process in an article titled "Celebrating a Shared Understanding." After describing a marathon production of three plays by Shakespeare, he noted that, after the first two plays as the company came onstage to begin the third play, the 1,200 people who had been together for the entire day burst into a "spontaneous and sustained ovation." This experience was, according to Wright (1990), something more than "just applause."

I began to realize that what I was seeing and participating in (I was cheering too) was the actual embodiment of that seeming abstract phrase . . . "the shared act of imagining." Here it was in the flesh—loud and alive, generating a kind of spiritual cohesion that I have rarely, if ever, experienced. . . . And suddenly all the arcane discussions about ritual and community sprang from the theoretical plane into the realm of reality. This was a dance of celebration performed by a real community with a shared sense of understanding, a shared sense of history, and a shared responsibility for the experience. (p. 7)

The psychological processes of being caught up in a drama are essentially as follows. The narrative form includes good and bad characters in a sequence of interrelated incidents. One shares the fantasy by finding one or more of the leading characters attractive. The result is the arousal of at least sympathy for or, if more strongly pulled, of empathy with the attractive characters. In the communicative moments of deepest psychological involvement the listener identifies with the protagonists. When one invests emotionally in a leading character one also becomes involved in the story line and in what happens to that character. Those who thwart the protagonists' efforts to achieve laudable goals evoke in the sympathetic participant unpleasant emotional responses and dislike. When the forces of the good characters are arrayed against those of the bad and the outcome is in doubt, sharing the fantasy results in the arousal of feelings of suspense.

When members of the small group share a fantasy, they have jointly experienced the same emotions, they have developed common heroes and villains, celebrated certain actions as laudable, and interpreted some aspect of their common experience in the same way. They have thus come to symbolic convergence about that part of their common experiences.

Not all dramatizing messages result in group apathy or in fantasy chains. Sometimes members express active disapproval when they hear the comment. They groan when they should laugh or laugh when they should be serious. This active rejection of dramatizing messages also provides data for the analysis of culture by showing the symbols, meanings, and emotions that members do not hold in common. Scholars and consultants can use differences among group members in terms of sharing, ignoring, or rejecting imaginative portrayals as evidence of symbolic divisions along rhetorical and cultural lines within the group (cliques).

GROUP FANTASIES

The result of sharing dramatizing messages is a *group fantasy.* The content of the dramatizing message that sparks the fantasy chain is called a *fantasy theme.* When someone dramatizes an event, she or he must select certain people to be the focus of the story and present them in a favorable light while selecting others to be portrayed in a more negative fashion. Shared fantasies are coherent accounts of experience in the past or envisioned in the future that simplify and form the social reality of the participants. The group's shared dreams of impending events, no matter how apocalyptic or utopian, provide artistic and comprehensible forms for thinking about and experiencing the future. Fantasy themes are always slanted, ordered, and interpreted: They provide a rhetorical means for several small task-oriented groups to account for and explain the same experiences or the same events in different ways.

Documenting the Presence of a Shared Group Consciousness

The main task in making a fantasy theme analysis is to find evidence that symbolic convergence has taken place, that participants in the decision-making group have shared a group consciousness. This is the first of the three parts of the symbolic convergence theory. Even as participant observers, members of groups often get so caught up in the fantasies that they cannot analyze them during the meeting. Certainly, nonparticipants who wish to study a group's decision making using the symbolic convergence theory must reconstruct the fantasy episodes by studying written or electronic records of the communication, using individual or focus-group interviews or employing pencil-and-paper tests to gather evidence about such fantasy episodes (Bormann, Bormann, & Harty, 1993; Cragan & Shields, 1992).

When similar dramatizing material—such as wordplay, narratives, figures, and analogies—keeps cropping up in the group's meetings in different contexts, such repetition is evidence of symbolic convergence.

CUING PREVIOUSLY SHARED FANTASIES

Other evidence of the sharing of fantasies is furnished by cryptic allusions to symbolic common ground. When participants have shared a fantasy theme, they have charged their emotional and memory banks with meanings and emotions that can be set off by a commonly agreed-upon cryptic symbolic cue.

The communication phenomenon of the inside joke is an example of such a trigger. Only those who have shared the fantasy theme that the inside joke refers to will respond in an appropriate fashion. But the symbolic cue need not be only an inside joke. The allusion to a previously shared fantasy may arouse tears or evoke anger, hatred, love, or affection as well as laughter and humor. The symbolic cue may be a code word, phrase, slogan, or nonverbal sign or gesture. It may refer to a geographical or imaginary place or the name of a persona.

FANTASY TYPES

The symbolic cue phenomenon makes possible the development of *fantasy types*. When a number of similar scenarios or outlines of the plots of fantasies, including particulars of the scenes, characters, and situations, have been shared by members of a group or larger community, they form a *fantasy type*.

A *fantasy type* is a stock scenario repeated again and again by the same characters or by similar characters. For example, our study of zero-history leaderless natural groups in the classroom has revealed several groups in which members shared personal experience fantasies about parties they had recently attended. Often these stories began to fall into a stock scenario of what the members should do at such affairs, what they celebrated as laudable, what they portrayed as enjoyable. When these stories began to have a similar form, an observer could classify them together as forming a type.

The members often seemed to make typal classifications of fantasy themes without conscious effort and began to use the more abstract and general fantasy type in their communication. Rather than dramatizing a fantasy theme with specific characters in a specific setting, they would present only the general plot line. A member might come to the meeting of a group with a fantasy type about what a good party is all about, for example, and simply allude to the type by saying, "Did I have a weekend! We took two carloads over to Wisconsin Saturday night and didn't get back until Sunday afternoon. It was a great party." Another member might respond with a laugh and say, "Let's keep the noise down for Jim's sake." A third member might use an inside cue alluding to a previously shared fantasy with something like, "Really, over under, under over? Or only over under?" and the other group members might then break out in laughter. An outsider who did not know about the shared fantasies would be confused by the cryptic remark (inside cue) concerning over and under.

Group members can also use an archetypal fantasy as a way to fit the unfolding of experience comfortably into their shared consciousness. Thus a natural group in the classroom might share a utopian archetypal fantasy portraying them as an idyllic and effective group of problem solvers who only fail when some outside persona, such as the class instructor, frustrates them. Should this group fail in trying to gain a good grade on a class assignment, they may portray the new experience as an instance of the archetypal drama. "It's our instructor's fault that we did not get an A." By using the device of a fantasy type to explain and evaluate the new events, they bring them into line with the overall values and emotions of their group consciousness. They also sustain a key element in their consciousness, namely their utopian group fantasy. Because the utopian drama is often a noncoping fantasy, it tends to make the group ineffective in dealing with changing circumstances and the environment. In this way the sharing of group fantasies can affect group decision making in such cases. In general, group decision making is affected either positively or negatively by the fantasy types that come to influence the group's culture.

When group members use fantasy types, or allusions to types, in their messages it is further evidence that fantasy themes have been shared. People cannot generalize to the more abstract type without having first shared at least several themes of a similar nature.

Why Do Group Members Share Fantasies?

The third part of the symbolic convergence theory explains why group members are predisposed to share some fantasies, to respond to others in "ho hum" fashion, and to actively reject others. Three promising factors that explain why people share fantasies are (a) the common psychodynamics and symbolic predispositions that people bring to a new small group setting, including their current symbolic baggage of personal and previously shared fantasies; (b) the current common concerns that group members have because of their experiences in the group; and (c) the rhetorical skill with which participants communicate their fantasies.

PREDISPOSITIONS BROUGHT TO THE GROUP

Bales (1970) suggested that the individual psychodynamics that each member brings to a zero-history group will influence which fantasies will be shared. Some of these personal concerns will be shared by none or only a few of the others, and these are not likely to predispose the group to share in dramatizing messages. However, unless the participants come from very different personal experiences, they will probably share some common psychodynamic concerns. Bales argued that dramatizing messages that relate to the psychodynamic concerns the members have in common are likely to be shared. He argued that a given theme might cut more closely to the personal problems of some participants than others. The members who have worked through their problem in a given area are the ones likely to dramatize material closely related to it. Those for whom the theme is enticing but not overly threatening are likely to share it, and group pressures will then tend to draw into participation those members most deeply involved in the matter. These latter members are also the most likely to break off the chain when the discussion becomes too threatening.

COMMON GROUP CONCERNS

Bales (1970) also suggested that as members of a small group meet together for a number of sessions they begin to develop current common concerns because of their experiences in the group. These concerns may relate to pressures and problems posed by the external physical or social environment or by internal problems relating to such matters as role struggles, leadership, and task conflicts. The Minnesota case studies of zero-history, leaderless, task-oriented groups indicate that shared group fantasies do, on occasion, mirror the here-and-now concerns of the group members. Bormann et al. (1978) report a case study of a group whose members had a here-and-now concern about whether to support a female contender who seemed to be the best qualified for leadership. The group members shared a number of fantasies relating to sex and power, including one about black widow spiders and their tendency to kill off their mates once fertilized, which related to that current concern.

RHETORICAL SKILL OF PARTICIPANTS

Evidence from the Minnesota case studies (Bormann, 1990, pp. 110-112) suggests a third reason why members of a small group may share a fantasy: the rhetorical skill with which a member portrays the drama. Indeed, consciousness-raising groups use dramatizing messages for persuasive purposes in just this way (Bormann, 1982; Chesebro et al., 1973). Of course, good storytellers may do a lot of dramatizing in group meetings for the enjoyment they get from being the center of attention and from releasing social tensions. The group may thus accidentally create a consciousness that is more or less conducive to good problem solving without being aware of what they are doing.

The Way Symbolic Convergence Creates Special Theories of Group Communication

To illustrate the way the general communication theory of symbolic convergence explains the creation and maintenance of special group theories, I will briefly sketch the origin and development of the recurrent form of group decision making called *public discussion.*

BACKGROUND FOR PUBLIC DISCUSSION

The early years of the 20th century were characterized by turmoil in many areas of American society. The excesses of moral indulgence and unrestrained exploitation of people and resources that characterized the years following the Civil War brought many to share fantasies of reform in large-scale movements related to Populism and Progressivism. By the 1920s, these reform efforts had moved into the field of education and, more specifically, into the area of rhetoric. In the 1920s and 1930s the newly developed field of speech grew and became established as an academic department in many colleges and universities. Faculty members in what is now called communication or speech communication were offering popular courses in public speaking and debate, but were not giving courses in small group problem solving.

At the same time, societal forces were encouraging the sharing of fantasies relating to the importance and usefulness of group meetings outside the college and university setting. Adult education programs were using discussion groups as an educational tool as early as 1920. Church groups and YMCA groups met regularly to discuss religious questions. Agricultural groups discussed farming matters and public policy. The increasing use of discussion groups by proponents of the Progressive movement's efforts to reform education resulted in more and more experimenting with various kinds of group formats. The concern with group work was accompanied by the rise of a group of connoisseurs who were dramatizing messages about the nature of such groups, their purpose, and their conduct. These dramatizations resulted in extensive fantasy chaining relating to such reform concerns as restoring democracy in government and creating democracy in the classrooms. Handbooks began to appear describing how to conduct and participate in group meetings. When the Adult Education Association published Harrison Elliott's *The Process of Group Thinking* (1928), it contained a new special theory of group problem solving.

Some teachers of speech studied the discussion formats, read what they could find on the subject, held informal talks among themselves, and began to share fantasies portraying the new form of communication as a vital breakthrough in public discourse and an important concern for all scholars of communication. These teachers were experienced in offering classes in how to speak in public and how to debate before audiences. Now one of their new salient fantasy types depicted discussion as an ethical way to make decisions in a democracy. Out of their shared fantasies came the inside cue, *public discussion*, as the emotionally charged label for their new rhetorical vision. Their fantasies contained the motives that resulted in the introduction of a unit on discussion in their established courses in public speaking and debate. In 1928, the same year that Elliott wrote his book outlining the new special theory, A. Craig Baird, a speech teacher at the University of Iowa, published *Public Discussion and Debate*. Another early textbook, by Ewbank and Auer (1952), was titled *Discussion and Debate*.

FEATURES OF THE SPECIAL THEORY OF PUBLIC DISCUSSION

The philosophical rationale that emerged from the chaining fantasies regarding public discussion was that it represented the best way to make decisions in a democracy. Indeed, an early textbook by Crowell (1963) was titled *Discussion: Method of Democracy*. As portrayed in their shared fantasies, discussion informed citizens in a democracy of basic problems and enabled them to hear all sides of a controversy. Discussion was the best way to mold public opinion and make decisions. Discussion, when contrasted with other techniques for social control such as dictatorial decree or violence and force (the thirties were the period of unrest and emerging dictatorships in Europe), was American, ethical, and noble. When compared to propaganda and persuasion, discussion was clearly superior, and even when compared to public speeches and debates, discussion was portrayed in a laudatory fashion. Indeed, so compelling and emotional were the shared fantasies of the proponents about the latter claim that many debate coaches and public speaking instructors began to argue against discussion as being less rigorous, faddish, and inappropriate for academic instruction.

The dramas of ethical and democratic social control by means of public discussions were associated with redramatizations of the importance of freedom of speech for the full advantages of discussion to come into play. These dramatizations included portrayals of the Peter Zenger case in colonial America, the amendments to the Constitution defending freedom of expression, and the holdings of the Supreme Court in regard to freedom of speech.

The values embedded in the new culture sustaining the special theory included the drama in which public discussion gives citizens a chance to hear all sides of important public questions and, although some will not act wisely, that in the long run the majority of informed citizens would make the right decision. The new special theory thus merged nicely with some revered parts of the American Saga. You can fool some of the people some of the time but you cannot fool all of the people all of the time if they have an active program of public discussion, protected by Constitutional rights of freedom of speech, in which they can discuss important questions from all angles. A second value embedded in the shared fantasies was that the individual citizen has an innate worth and dignity. The citizens are important in their own right and are not cogs in the machine of the state or a means to a more ultimate end, which is the state. Therefore, citizens have a right to participate in determining their own destinies. They should not be manipulated and treated as though their selfhood and individuality were unimportant.

For many intellectuals at the turn of the century, the ultimate tool of reason was the scientific method. Those who were becoming connoisseurs of the new special theory began to share dramas that portrayed public discussion as a way for citizens to use the main features of the scientific method to solve political and social problems. Further dramatizations portrayed the scientists in their laboratories as open-minded and objective. They weighed facts objectively. They purged themselves of all emotional prejudices, interests, and biases. They were curious. They wanted to know and would go where the facts led them. They were not prejudiced or committed to a position that they defended to the death, rather, they had a duty to the truth; they tested all evidence rigorously and when they found evidence that withstood this rigorous testing, they accepted it and accommodated their theories to it.

The second major component of a special theory is the ideal model for a good task-oriented discussion. The connoisseurs shared fantasies that motivated them to develop an ideal model for discussion that applied the scientific method to solve problems related to human affairs. The early writers suggested that the proper way to use public discussion to solve problems was to adopt the objective, empirical attitude of the scientist and the techniques of scientific inquiry. A leading proponent of progressive educational reform, John Dewey, gave a popular treatment to his analysis of reflective thinking in his book *How We Think* (1910). For the newly emerging community of connoisseurs of public discussion, Dewey's portrayal of good thinking became the basis for a series of shared fantasies that portrayed good individual thinking as also the best basis for group thinking. The result of the symbolic convergence of thought around these fantasies was the translation of Dewey's analysis of reflective thinking for individuals into the steps in the discussional process as the ideal model of public discussion.

The ideal model for good problem-solving discussion varied over the years but the basic core of Dewey's reflective thinking pattern remained in the form of (a) analyzing the problem, (b) listing the possible solutions, (c) weighing the alternative solutions, (d) selecting the best solution, and (e) taking steps to implement the solution.

The human relations dimension of the ideal model was encompassed by the concept of the *discussional attitude*. Participants were supposed to be open-minded, objective, and willing to go where the facts led. Good discussants did not have an emotional investment in their ideas and did not allow emotional responses to affect their reasoning and their ability to follow the steps of the discussional process.

In terms of role development, the special theory of group discussion dealt with only two roles, (a) the moderator and (b) the participant. The moderator handled the administrative details and led the meeting. The moderator was the procedural specialist and did not enter into the substantive discussion. The ideal participants were well informed and took an active part in the deliberations without speaking too much or too little. They integrated their comments into the overall flow of the discussion and at all times exhibited the discussional attitude.

The third major component of a special theory consists of concrete advice about how to improve practice. How-to advice on problems such as drifting from the pattern, failing to think reflectively, dealing with emotional outbursts, getting the too-talkative member to cut back, and drawing out the quiet member grew over the years into a detailed set of coaching aids. In its maturity the special theory of public discussion contained a large body of concrete advice relating to all aspects of developing a discussion that was *good* in the sense of closely approximating the ideal model.

The symbolic convergence general theory explains all of the other special theories of task-oriented group communication in the same way that it does the public discussion theory. A similar analysis of brainstorming, synectics training, and computer assisted group problem solving would reveal the same dynamic at work. The general theory also explains other forms of group communication, such as sensitivity training, encounter groups, consciousness-raising sessions, and ritualistic meetings. Furthermore, the general theory accounts for culturally diverse group meetings, such as North American business meetings and Japanese corporate meetings.

The law of gravity is an important influence on the development and launching of human artifacts such as airplanes, dirigibles, and helicopters, and the law continues to operate once an airplane is in flight. In similar fashion, the symbolic convergence theory continues to work once a group of people decide to have a task-oriented small group meeting. Thus, although the members all know that they are jointly trying to achieve a meeting that emulates the ideal model, they may continue to experience fantasy chains during the course of their deliberations. These chaining fantasies will have an effect on the group consciousness and on the group as it goes about making decisions.

The Influence of Group Consciousness on Group Decision Making

A zero-history, leaderless discussion group begins as a diffuse and unfocused symbolic and social entity. To be sure, the members should know the special theory that guides the kind of decision-making group in which they are participating, but they do not know what specific kind of group they will be within that general framework. To become an organized cohesive group, the participants must begin to communicate with one another and to create a new shared consciousness. Only after the emergence of a shared consciousness will they be able to focus their full attention on the tasks at hand and move into a phase of real work. Prior to that time, although they may appear to be working they will be expending much energy and communication on developing norms, finding roles, and creating a culture and commitment to the group.

Group consciousness, on occasion, may begin when one creative person fantasizes a powerful personal consciousness and does so with such skill that it is shared by other group members. Usually, however, the flow of communication in consciousness-creating segments of meetings is not from the speaker to the listeners. Instead, a chain is triggered by the first dramatizing message and is then picked up and elaborated by the other members. Soon a number of people are deeply involved in the discussion, excitedly adding their emotional support, and often modifying the ongoing script.

CREATING A COMMON IDENTITY

A pressing rhetorical problem for a new group is to create, in an aggregate of individuals, a sense of a common identity. People create a common identity by becoming aware that they are involved in an identifiable group and that their group differs in some important respects from other groups. They also become aware that because they are members of the group they are personally somewhat different from others who are not symbolically tied together by the experience of sharing the same fantasies. To come to such awareness the members need to identify their collective self.

A rhetorical device that members may use to identify their group is to personify it in terms of an individual, an animal, an elemental force, or by simply viewing it as a new identity.

Dealing with their identity often gets the group members to share fantasies about the boundaries of their group. Who are the outsiders? Typical personae who can symbolize the outsiders are a useful device for identifying the insiders and drawing boundaries around the group. Fantasies that clearly divide the sympathetic or good people (we) from the unsympathetic or evil people (they) aid the group's self-awareness and are crucial to the emergence of its consciousness. Indeed, an important question for a person evaluating a group relates to the way participants celebrate themselves and their group.

Once the sharing of fantasies identifies the group and distinguishes between the insiders and outsiders, the members have clear rhetorical and symbolic boundaries to serve as guidelines for terminating rituals to force members out and for initiation and acceptance rituals for recruits. Indeed, even what on the surface may appear as the trivial matter of a person missing a group meeting may be an important factor in the group's definition of membership. Often group members underestimate the importance of developing suitable norms to reintegrate a person into full group membership after that individual has missed one or more meetings.

SHARING FANTASIES ABOUT GROUP DECISION MAKING

In the beginning, members may assume that some special theory of group communication such as the special theory governing the typical business meeting is guiding their deliberations. If unchallenged this special theory may form the norms that they use in decision making. However, in the process of sharing fantasies relating to group identity the members of a task-oriented group will often include dramatizations relating to the way the group processes information, solves problems, and makes decisions. They may personify "our group" as an entity that thoroughly investigates all the facts and then, using the latest information processing techniques, "round tables" the information until "we" reach "consensus." They may characterize their discussions as completely open with "no holds barred." Ball (1992) examined the shared fantasies of the Johnson administration's small group meetings that contributed to the decisions to escalate the Vietnam conflict. In their shared fantasies, the members celebrated rational decision making that stressed factual studies, computerized information processing, fact-finding missions to the theater of operations, and thorough discussion of all options. Alternatively, the group members may share fantasies in which their mode of operation is much more intuitive, creative, and unruly.

Group members may also share fantasies about more specific details relating to problem solving, such as the nature of sound evidence, about good reasons, and about ways to make decisions. In one case study, for example, the group members were given the task of investigating a question of public policy and developing a task force report on their recommendations in terms of what should be done about the question. One member emerged in the first meeting as a central, negative person. He dramatized his personal gambling experiences in Las Vegas, his dropping out of school several times, and his commitment to the hedonistic life. The first big decision facing the group was to select a question for their task force investigation. In what seemed like an indirect but clear attempt to handle their immediate concern with the central negative person, they selected the question of legalized gambling in Minnesota. When they began to discuss the question itself, one member began quoting the results of his considerable library research to the group. He had worked very hard and if he was encouraged, such reinforcement would have obvious implications for the group's work norms. Other group members, less certain that they wanted work norms that stressed such a high level of commitment to the task, were tense and unsure as to how to respond.

The hardworking group member became a current concern for the group but one that they did not wish to confront directly this early in the history of the group. As their discussion proceeded and the well-informed member continued to quote from various authoritative sources about previous studies and task forces, the self-proclaimed gambling authority began to dramatize how misleading these written studies really were. He countered many of the findings by asserting they were in error based on his own personal authority as a gambler. All the other members save the well-informed one began to share the fantasies. Under the pressure of the group fantasizing, the well-informed member discarded his notes and ceased to do any further library research.

At that point the gambler dropped out of school, but by that time the group culture had evolved to one in which members belittled all published information and confined themselves to exchanging ignorances as though they had privileged information unavailable in print. Because they had little factual information and little authoritative opinion, their discourse was largely filled with fantasy themes composed of figurative analogies and hypothetical examples. One person adopted the role of a hypothetical evangelist he called the Reverend Ham and delivered long satirical diatribes filled with fictitious fantasy themes, which the others shared, against the sinfulness of gambling. When the group presented the results of its task force investigation, first in a panel discussion to the class and then in a written report to the instructor, they fared poorly. Their pleas that there was no sound evidence on the subject did not convince their audience and their program was unsuccessful.

SHARING FANTASIES AND GROUP MOTIVATION

The sharing of group fantasies will also provide the group with shared motivations that relate to the nature of the problem-solving activities of the group. More elaborate systems can be used, but a relatively simple and insightful way to analyze a group's shared fantasies is to classify them as implying a motive for mastery, a motive for social affiliation, or a motive for achievement.

Dramatizations that involve laudable people whose basic goals are to gain power and control are *mastery fantasies*. Dramatizations whose protagonists have basic goals related to making friends and having good times are *affiliation fantasies*. The shared fantasies about partying alluded to earlier are affiliation fantasies, as are love stories. Dramatizations that portray sympathetic people whose basic goals are to do a good job are *achievement fantasies*.

A quality circle or involvement team in a business organization whose predominant shared fantasies are mastery stories will tend to make decisions with an eye to how the decision will affect their power to control their own fate and the fate of others. How will it affect their stand vis-à-vis upper management? Their immediate supervisor? Other groups and units? Quality circles whose predominant shared fantasies are affiliation stories may make few decisions related to the job and spend most of their discussion on gossip about interpersonal relations. The team whose predominate fantasies are achievement dramas will direct its task attention to solving problems related to productivity and quality. Eyo's (1985) study of involvement teams indicates that because the organization's purposes in establishing such groups were to improve quality and productivity, achievement fantasies are better adapted to those ends than are mastery dramas.

COPING AND INEFFECTIVE FANTASIES

Shared fantasies can also influence the group members' ability to cope with changing circumstances, their external environment, and their internal conflicts. The group may share fantasies that enable members to cope more or less effectively with such matters. In evaluating a group's decision making, one would be well advised, therefore, to examine whether or not the group has shared coping fantasies or disabling fantasies.

Some fantasies may encourage members to take flight, avoid problems, and deny difficulties. If members have a strong current concern over a conflict in leadership, they may share fantasies about how they do not need a leader, or that they share leadership, or that they are all leaders. Some fantasies, indeed, may be so dysfunctional that they can be compared to psychologically disturbed thinking in individuals. Groups may share fantasies that resemble paranoia in individuals as they portray conspiratorial groups or evil individuals systematically trying to frustrate the group's task efforts. They may share fantasies that turn on the group itself and portray it as frustrating, ineffective, and evil until the group consciousness resembles that of an individual suffering from depression.

Other fantasies may encourage the group to function successfully in the task dimension. Given the range of task-facilitating and task-inhibiting fantasies that groups may share there is a kernel of good sense in the T-shirt motto that proclaims, "I have given up my search for truth and now I'm looking for a good fantasy."

SHARING FANTASIES AND GROUP CREATIVITY

Finally, we have evidence that within the problem-solving cycle of group deliberations, sharing group fantasies may function like the period of incubation in individual creativity. People caught up in a chain of fantasies may experience moments similar to the creative experience of individuals when they daydream about a creative project or an important problem and suddenly get excited about the direction of their thinking. Then the others feed back ideas and new dramatizations to add to the original comment; messages begin flowing rapidly among the participants until under the suggestive power of the group fantasy the constraints that normally hold people back are released; they feel free to experiment with ideas, to play with concepts and wild suggestions and imaginative notions.

Thus a group might emulate Wallas's (1926) description of creativity by beginning to tackle a problem (conception) and start by discussing information related to the problem in an effort to solve it (preparation). After the problem is mulled over unsuccessfully for a time, the resulting tension might encourage a member to dramatize about something that is apparently off the subject. If the drama is shared, the group may indulge in a period of fantasy sharing that contains a double meaning applicable to the problem, much as an individual might daydream without conscious purpose while working on a creative project (incubation). Suddenly the group may experience a moment of insight because something in the shared fantasies reminds them of the problem, and quickly all members realize they have found a good solution to it. With mounting enthusiasm and excitement, the members have a common "aha" experience as they realize that the solution has popped into their consciousness (illumination). Finally, the group carefully and systematically evaluates the solution to make sure that it is as good as it first seemed (verification).

Here is a sample of the case study data bearing on this finding. The quotation is from a participant's report of the meeting.

"We had picked our topic at the first meeting. By the third meeting, it was going nowhere in a hurry and not a soul was interested in pursuing it any further. However, we had 10 days before our presentation, and we all thought that the others wanted to continue with our first choice. This near-transcript is of our fourth meeting at Riverbend.

Hi, how was your weekend?

[*General comments: "Fine," "Okay."*]

Well it was pretty eventful for me." [*A stack of information literally 3 inches thick is placed before our eyes.*] "That lady I talked to at the courthouse sent me all this information. There is some good stuff in here.

[*Some brave souls pick up some sheets and skim through them.*]

It says here that there were three murders allegedly committed by juvenile offenders in the state of Minnesota last year and only one went to jail.

So we are dealing with an issue that isn't a problem.

It's still a good issue.

Come on, you can't call one thousandth of a percent a problem.

Yeah, but look at all the information she brought. We ought to be able to use it.

Look, there just aren't that many kids committing murder in the state of Minnesota.

What about [*name*]? She was murdered by kids.

That was gang-related.

[*Short yet powerful pause.*]

GANGS!!!

Yeah! We can do it on gangs!

We can call Tony Bouza and talk to him!

We can dress up like gang members during our presentation and walk in to *West Side Story* music!

We can go to North High and speak to the principal there!

This is great! It's gonna work! We're going to be great!

[*General euphoria and cohesion set in. The group was indeed great.*]"

Another case study of the fantasy themes among a group of teenagers working on a "tot lot" that was to become a playground for small children revealed a similar pattern of fantasies related to creative decision making. The teenagers were to help plan details for the playground and would work as volunteer supervisors when it was set up. Some of the fantasies of the group were analogous to the period of incubation in individual problem solving. For example, at one point group members were considering the problems of rules for the children, and they broke off their direct analysis of the problem to fantasize about how teenagers did not obey their parents. They subsequently developed an answer to their problem that resembled the content of their shared fantasies about teenage response to discipline.

Some practitioners of synectics have also discovered the importance to creative group work of such dramatizing messages as wordplay, figures of speech, analogies, and narrations that result in group fantasizing. Prince (1969), for example, suggested that when a group bogs down the members should take a fantasy vacation and think and talk about something completely removed from the problem. Thus a group might begin working on a problem by direct discussion of information relating to the difficulty. After failing to find a suitable answer, the tensions might stimulate a fantasy chain that seems unrelated to the work at hand. Suddenly the group members experience a moment of illumination and see a good solution to their problem and, with great excitement, discover that a decision has emerged. On closer examination, the shared fantasy may turn out to have been related to the decision or problem solution even though it seemed at the time to be a digression.

Scheidel (1986) discusses the use of divergent and convergent thinking in group decision making and points to the strengths and weaknesses of both. Divergent thinking often takes the form of fantasy chains and can result in contributing to solutions that are productive. Generally, the productive chains stem from problems relating to the group's task dimension. Of course, other fantasies may contribute to solutions that are not as good because they stem from internal conflicts in the social dimension. In the case study transcript above, the group has difficulty because of a bad decision about the topic they had adopted. They are torn between changing to a better topic and the fact that changing means they will have to redo much of their previous work. Their solution solves the problem. If the problem facing the group related to the irritation the other members felt because of the one member doing so much work and exercising so much power in the group, they might have rejected the topic in order to reject the member's emerging role, and been left without a good topic and with the need to study something without the help of one of their most productive researchers.

Conclusion

Symbolic convergence is a general theory of communication that provides an explanation of how the special theories governing group practice emerge and develop. It also applies to the processes of group meetings no matter what special theory governs the recurring forms. Symbolic convergence explains important elements in group consciousness, culture, and decision making. The theory provides an understanding of the context of decision making and how specific decisions come to have group support. It gives an account in terms of some of the self-conscious, rhetorical, and intentional elements of the decision-making process as well as provides an explanation of the results of the unconscious, accidental, and unplanned sharing of fantasies. The theory does not provide prediction and control of group decision making, but it does allow for understanding after the event and for anticipating possible developments.

References

Baird, A. C. (1928). *Public discussion and debate*. Boston: Ginn.

Bales, R. F. (1950). *Interaction process analysis: A method for the study of small groups*. Reading, MA: Addison Wesley.

Bales, R. F. (1970). *Personality and interpersonal behavior*. New York: Holt, Rinehart & Winston.

Ball, M. A. (1992). *Vietnam-on-the-Potomac*. New York: Praeger.

Berger, C. R. (1973). Attributional communication, situational involvement, self-esteem, and interpersonal attraction. *Journal of Communication, 23*, 284-335.

Bormann, E. G. (1969). *Discussion and group methods: Theory and practice* (1st ed.). New York: Harper & Row.

Bormann, E. G. (1982). The symbolic convergence theory of communication and the creation, raising, and sustaining of public consciousnesses. In J. Sisco (Ed.), *The Jensen lectures: Contemporary communication studies* (pp. 71-90). Tampa: University of South Florida, Department of Communication.

Bormann, E. G. (1989). *Communication theory*. Salem, WI: Sheffield.

Bormann, E. G. (1990). *Small group communication: Theory and practice* (3rd ed.). New York: HarperCollins.

Bormann, E. G., Bormann, E., & Harty, K. C. (1993). Using symbolic convergence theory and focus group interviews to develop communication designed to stop teenage use of tobacco. In L. Frey (Ed.), *Innovations in group facilitation techniques applied to research in naturalistic settings* (pp. 203-208). Cresskill, NJ: Hampton Press.

Bormann, E. G., Pratt, J., & Putnam, L. L. (1978). Power, authority, and sex: Male response to female leadership. *Communication Monographs, 45*, 119-155.

Chesebro, J. W., Cragan, J. F., & McCullough, P. W. (1973). The small group techniques of the radical revolutionary: A synthetic study of consciousness raising. *Communication Monographs, 40,* 136-146.

Combs, J. E., & Mansfield, M. W. (1976). *Drama in life: The uses of communication in society.* New York: Hastings House.

Cragan, J. F., & Shields, D. C. (1992). The use of symbolic convergence theory in corporate strategic planning: A case study. *Journal of Applied Communication Research, 20,* 199-218.

Craig, R. T. (1989). Communication as a practical discipline. In B. Dervin, L. Grossberg, B. J. O'Keefe, & E. Wartella (Eds.), *Rethinking communication* (pp. 97-122). Newbury Park, CA: Sage.

Crowell, L. (1963). *Discussion: Method of democracy.* Glenview, IL: Scott-Foresman.

Dewey, J. (1910). *How we think.* Boston: D. C. Heath.

Dunphy, D. C. (1966). Social change in self-analytic groups. In P. J. Stone, D. C. Dunphy, M. S. Smith, & D. M. Ogilivie (Eds.), *The general inquirer: A computer approach to content analysis* (pp. 287-340). Cambridge: MIT Press.

Elliott, H. (1928). *The process of group thinking.* New York: Association Press.

Ewbank, H. L., & Auer, J. J. (1952). *Discussion and debate.* New York: Appleton-Century-Crofts.

Eyo, B. (1985). *Quality circles, involvement teams, and participative management in modern business culture: Study of rhetorical visions of line unit managers, employees, and facilitators.* Unpublished doctoral dissertation, University of Minnesota.

Gibbard, G. S., Hartman, J. J., & Mann, R. D. (Eds.). (1974). *Analysis of groups.* San Francisco: Jossey-Bass.

Insko, C. A., & Schopler, J. (1972). *Experimental social psychology.* New York: Academic Press.

Prince, G. M. (1969). How to be a better meeting chairman. *Harvard Business Review, 47,* 989-1009.

Scheidel, T. M. (1986). Divergent and convergent thinking in group decision making. In R. Y. Hirokawa & M. S. Poole (Eds.), *Communication and group decision-making* (1st ed., pp. 113-130). Beverly Hills, CA: Sage.

Smith, M. J. (1982). *Persuasion and human action: A review and critique of social influence theories.* Belmont, CA: Wadsworth.

Wallas, G. (1926). *The art of thought.* New York: Harcourt, Brace.

Wright, G. (1990). Celebrating a shared understanding [In Guthrie Theatre program for *Skin of Our Teeth,* Minneapolis, MN].

The Structuration of Group Decisions

MARSHALL SCOTT POOLE
DAVID R. SEIBOLD
ROBERT D. McPHEE

Whether or not it is featured, implicit in every theory of group decision making is a theory of social interaction. Some theories give interaction a prominent place, as in Homans's (1950) theory of the group system, input-process-output models (Cragan & Wright, 1980, 1990; Gouran, 1984; Hackman & Morris, 1975; McGrath & Altman, 1966), and the other theories in this section. Others depict interaction in formal or mathematical models, as in Thibaut and Kelley's (1959) exchange theory and Davis's (1973) theory of social decision schemes. Still others give little direct attention to interaction, as in Jackson's (1987) social impact theory. Even perspectives that reduce or ignore communication express assumptions about it. For example, social decision scheme theory assumes that the function of communication is to exchange information that is combined by the social decision scheme. In social impact theory (Jackson, 1987; Latane, 1981), the function of communication is to mediate the influence (on a target person) of the strength, immediacy, and number of source persons in the group.

In our view, the value of a theory of group decision making hinges on how well it addresses the complexities of interaction. To do this effectively it must confront two overarching theoretical tensions (Poole, 1983). The first stems from the intersection of individual action and structural factors in group interaction. Interaction is conducted by knowledgeable individual members, each with particular predispositions and skills, who are influenced by structural features—norms, decision rules, communication networks—that are system-level properties. However, it is difficult to specify how the individual and system levels articulate, and as a result many group researchers bifurcate them. This creates, in effect, a polarization of micro and macro approaches in which some studies emphasize "subject" variables, such as preference for procedural order (Putnam, 1979) or motivational state, such as social comparison (Goethals & Darley, 1987), and others focus on system properties such as status hierarchies (Knotternus & Greenstein, 1981) or interaction patterns characterizing high- versus low-consensus groups (DeStephen, 1983; Sigman, 1984). Even studies that include both individual and system factors (e.g., Johnson & Miller, 1983) treat them as separate variables on different levels of analysis. This is unfortunate, because it ignores the interdependence of individuals and systems. System properties such as communication networks exist only by virtue of members' activities. In turn, actors draw on social structures to enable them to act, as when they use their connections with another member to influence a decision. An adequate theory must provide an integrative account of the interplay of member behavior and structural properties.

A corollary to this point is the neglect of social institutions by group researchers. In most studies groups have been treated as though they were isolated systems, and their embeddedness in the larger society has been ignored. However, group activities are enabled and constrained by structures drawn from institutions such as organizations, religions, legal systems, and so forth. It is important to acknowledge these influences on groups as well (Putnam & Stohl, 1990).

The second tension is between stability and change in group structures. The linkage of action and system gives rise to a tension between: (a) structure as a stable, given aspect of the group that members work with and adapt to; and (b) structure as created and negotiated, the emergent product of member activities. How do these two aspects relate and what determines the ratio of stability to change? Once again, this tension tends to result in bifurcation. Group phenomena are frequently cast either as given and stable or as created, negotiated, and transformational. For example, the symbolic interactionist perspective in *social psychology* (with its emphasis on dynamic reflexivity of gesture and symbol) contrasts sharply with the exchange perspective in social psychology (where the emphasis is on relatively static reward and alternative structures). This extends to methods as well: Naturalistic observation, discourse analytic, and rhetorical approaches characteristic of "emergent" research are radically different from the laboratory methods of most "fixed" research studies. These theoretical and methodological purifications do not reflect the real experience of groups, in which stability and change are interleaved. For example, groups that must constantly adapt to new members because of high levels of turnover do so by introducing them to traditions and norms of the ongoing group (Weick, 1979). However, the new members necessarily have a new take on these, so there is change in the stabilizing norms, too.

An adequate theory should adopt an integrative approach to study both stability and change.[1] To do this, Hernes (1976) maintains, "Structural change must be described in terms of the processes that generate change; structural stability [must be described] in terms of the processes which not only maintain the stability, but also maintain the processes which maintain the stability" (p. 514). We might add that a common basis for these processes should be specified; stability and change should be explained in the same terms.

The theory of structuration (Giddens, 1976, 1979, 1984; Poole, Seibold, & McPhee, 1985, 1986) addresses these tensions. It provides a unified theory of individual and systemic processes in groups, an account of how institutions figure in group processes, and an integrated explanation of structural stability and change. It provides a theory of group interaction commensurate with the complexities of the phenomenon.

Theory of Structuration

Groups are organized around common social practices: making decisions, sharing information, socializing, joking, teaching, doing physical labor, and more. These practices are bounded activities, meaningful to members of a social system, that occur in specific social and institutional contexts.

Structuration theory assumes that the key to understanding group practices is through analysis of the structures that underlie them. The term *structure* is used in a special sense that can best be understood in the distinction Giddens (1984) makes between system and structure. A *system* is a social entity, such as a group, pursuing various practices that give rise to observable patterns of relations, such as the pecking order often observed in groups. *Structures* are the rules and resources that actors use to generate and sustain the system. Giddens (1984) characterizes structures as "recipes" for acting. For example, it might be the rule that older members with special experience are deferred to by others in a group. This rule enables experienced members to set up and sustain a pecking order that favors them. Systems have patterns such as pecking orders because of structuring processes. The observable system is of interest and can influence structures, but the structure is what does the real work.

The nature of structures and the relations between structure and system are represented in the concept of *structuration,* which refers to *the process by which systems are produced and reproduced through members' use of rules and resources.* This definition rests on several key assumptions and distinctions. First, not only is the system produced and reproduced through structuration, but the structures themselves are, too. Structures are dualities: They are both the medium and the outcome of action. They are the medium of action because members draw on structures to interact. They are its outcome because rules and resources exist only by virtue of being used in a practice. Whenever the structure is employed, the activity reproduces it by invoking and confirming it as a meaningful basis for action. So when a group takes a vote, it is employing the rules behind voting to act, but—more than this—it is reminding itself that these rules exist, working out a way of using the rules, perhaps creating a special version of them. In short, by voting the group is producing and reproducing the rules for present and future use. So it is really somewhat misleading to focus on structures as though they are static entities. Structures have a virtual existence: They exist in a continuous process of structuration. A voting procedure does not, for all practical purposes, exist for this group if the group never employs it or makes it a regular part of its procedure. John Shotter (1983) comments on the implications of this for our understanding of the nature of social activity:

> All human action is doubly structured, for it is structured both as a product and a process, or better it is both structured and structuring. And the significance of this is that, when linked to the concept of intentionality, it explains how human action can, *in the course of its own performance*, provide itself with the conditions for its own continuation. In other words, by acting we can create the conditions for further action. (p. 19)

Action and structure both enable and constrain each other in the continuous flow of intentionality. Neither structure nor action is primary in the theory of structuration; they are a duality in that each implies the other at an ontological level. Although either structure or action may figure more prominently in a system's operation in particular times or contexts, at base neither can exist without the other.

Structuration theory shifts the focus from systems or structures to *structuration*, which emphasizes their dynamic interrelationship in interaction. Neither stability nor change is taken as the "basic state" by structuration theory. Both are explained in terms of the same model of continuous production and reproduction. On this view, neither the description of systems alone nor the enumeration of structures and their relationships is the central object of inquiry. Stability and change in system properties can be explained only by understanding their production and reproduction through structuration (Hernes, 1976). Nor can structures merely be listed or arrayed in logical or taxonomic diagrams. Extracting and describing structures may be a necessary step in any study, but it is important to remember that this is a reification of dynamic characteristics.

The study of structuration focuses directly on group interaction processes. Interaction is the locus of structuration. Through the various social processes that occur in interaction, particularly individual action and initiative, each group reproduces its own particular mix of structures. Hence factors that influence group interaction play a direct and critical role in the structuring process. Two classes of factors influence structuration. First are those concerning action in groups and its relation to social institutions. Second are the structural dynamics through which different structural features mediate and interact with each other.

ACTION AND ITS CONDITIONS

The theory assumes skilled and knowledgeable actors who reflexively monitor their activities as they navigate a continuous flow of intentionality. Reflexive monitoring means that actors project ahead according to several time frames—immediate experience, long-term life directions, and time frames imposed by social institutions such as work or the family—and that they are capable of changing course when things are not going properly. Rather than assuming that all action involves consciously formed intentions, the theory adopts Heidegger's notion of intentionality. From this flow actors sometimes formulate intentions, usually when something has gone wrong or when planning important activities. "The reflexive monitoring of behavior operates against the backdrop of the rationalization of action" (Giddens, 1979, p. 57)—our ability to give accounts of our actions to ourselves and others. As we rationalize our conduct we not only make it seem rational in socially prescribed terms, but we also give ongoing actions coherence and aid members in organizing practices (Garfinkel & Sacks, 1967).

Actors are knowledgeable about their activities in two respects. First, there is *discursive consciousness*, thoughts and knowledge that can be formulated and expressed in language, and are therefore publicly shareable. Second, there is *practical consciousness*, which is bound up with action and cannot be expressed in language; this corresponds to what Polanyi (1962) called the realm of "tacit knowledge." Of course, practical consciousness can be carried into the realm of discourse with sufficient reflection and codification.

Actors' capacity to control action is "bounded," first by factors that constrain action and second by unintended consequences of action. Three sets of factors that condition action in groups can be identified. First are the conditions imposed by the temporal order of action. Members have room to plan, sequence, and correct their activities as they unfold. A group member telling a story can expand on parts of the story, answer questions, or decide not to finish it. But being located in a temporal flow among others' acts also constrains the activity. What actors can do depends in part on the sequential behavior of others. These constraints may also serve as an important resource, because actors can use sequential expectations to control interaction as well. For example, some group members may feel empowered to bypass an "overloaded" leader to communicate with other members on an important matter, based on the expectation that the leader is too busy to pass on needed information.

Second, action is influenced by its context, including situational factors, historical precedents, structures drawn from relevant institutions, and structures reproduced earlier by the group. These structures are not just inanimate influences on action, but embodiments of previous actions. As Smith (1983) put it, "The intentionality of actors becomes objectified within social structures which have the capacity to affect the future intentionality of actors. . . . [F]uture practices are determined not only by the agency of actors, but by past practices within which past agency is objectified" (p. 13). Because preexisting structures exert intentionality in their own right, and because they are oriented to by others as well, they tend to be drawn on and reproduced in present conduct, and so they constrain that conduct. Previous structures tend to constrain later ones and perpetuate themselves.

The third set of factors are the differential distributions of knowledge and resources among members and between the group and external actors. Those members with special expertise, privileged positions, or who "know the ropes" in a group will have more control over structuration than will novices or those with few resources.

The degree to which these factors influence structuration is largely dependent on how much actors know about them. If actors are unaware of a factor or do not understand how it operates, then it is likely to be a strong influence. To the extent that members are aware of a factor, they can use it or even change it. A member who is aware of the credibility conferred by high social status can use his or her status strategically. Obviously, intermember differences in knowledge about conditions on action can also result in differential control over a group.

Action is also influenced by its unintended consequences. Because of the complexity of social systems, agents are not aware of the full consequences of their actions. These unknown outcomes may in turn constrain action or cause unintended problems. For example, a group leader who wins a point despite opposition from group members may not realize that he or she is undermining the leadership role's power by encouraging opposing members to build defensive coalitions. The consequences of action can "loop back" in a variety of ways to alter group actions (Masuch, 1985).

THE LINKAGE OF INSTITUTION AND ACTION IN MODALITIES OF STRUCTURATION

Structurational theorists have tried to link macro and micro concerns, "the global and the local." The study of group communication tends to be drawn to the micro level and to give little emphasis to larger institutions; if it includes these, there is a tendency to include them only insofar as they influence group processes (e.g., Ancona & Caldwell, 1992). A structurational approach to group decision making attempts to overcome this tendency by noting several things. First, many characteristics of groups—including their membership, assigned tasks, assigned roles, and power relations—are typically the result of larger-scale social processes, such as the design of the group by an organization or by social selection processes that incline certain types of people to take up certain career paths and thus end up in the group. Second, any group is constantly struggling to maintain its boundaries in the face of outside demands on members' time and energy, overlap in its responsibilities with other groups and roles, and its limited existence in a certain portion of time and space while members' life paths continue outside that portion (Schwartzman, 1989). What Giddens (1984) says about the time-space edges of societies as key foci of social change and breakdown applies equally well to groups. Boundary establishment and identity maintenance are critical parts of the structuration process (Poole et al., 1985).

Third, group processes themselves, no less than language and thought processes, are properties of social systems learned throughout one's life. So particular structures such as decision-making norms, leadership styles, and others, should not be regarded as natural objects but as rules and resources whose production and reproduction is contingent and variable.

Where do structures come from? In some cases they are created by the group, but more often they are appropriated by the group from enduring social institutions, such as the organization the group is embedded in; larger political, religious, or economic systems of the surrounding society; or general customs, manners, and mores of the culture or subculture. *Appropriation* involves adopting structural features from the institution and developing a situated version of them. As repositories of structural possibilities, institutions provide patterns for many group activities.

The appropriation of structural features is a skillful accomplishment, as Cicourel (1974) and Brewer (1988), among others, have shown. It results in different versions of institutional features adapted to particular contexts. For example, different groups may appropriate the political norm of majority rule in a variety of ways. One group may regard the rule as a last resort, to be used only if consensus cannot be attained, whereas another may regard it as the only way of avoiding potentially divisive conflict. For all practical purposes, these two versions are different norms: They have different meanings for members, invoke different behavior patterns, will be used differently and under different circumstances, and have different consequences for the group. Thus the mode in which groups employ institutional structures is a critical feature of structuration.

Giddens (1979, p. 129) argues that institutional features may operate in three modalities in interaction: as interpretive schemes in communication processes, as norms that guide behavior and undergird judgments about others, and as facilities in power and influence processes. The three modalities are grounded in distinctive institutional structures of signification (language, symbol structures), legitimation (religion, ethics, law, custom), and domination (resource allocation, privilege, status), respectively. This tripartite distinction is largely analytical, because the three elements tend to be compounded in every action. For instance, it is difficult to invoke a norm for purposes of legitimation without simultaneously considering its interpretation and how it is "made to count" (a matter of power). However, the degree to which particular appropriations emphasize one or the other of the three elements at a particular point in time can be distinguished. In addition, over time the modalities of structuration may change. For example, a leader calling a group to order utilizes interpretive schemes that enable members to grasp the leader's utterances and recognize them as "commencing" the meeting. The same structures can be used by members to judge whether the leader called the group to order properly. Facilities such as legitimate authority are used by leaders when they wield power, but they are also part of the meaning of leadership and imply norms about leader behavior, such as "good" ways to wield power in calling a group to order.

The process of structuration accounts for stability of structural features as well as their change. Features are stable if the group appropriates them in a consistent way, reproducing them in similar form over time. This might happen, for example, if a group very carefully followed the procedures for taking majority votes outlined in Robert's Rules of Order. In the same vein, the group may intentionally or unintentionally change a structural feature; reproduction does not necessarily imply replication. Structures may change gradually, as in a group that, through a series of small, imperceptible stages, elevates one member to "facilitator" of a procedure originally designed to promote equal participation. Structures might also be eliminated through reproduction; overuse or abuse of voting may lead groups to reject it. The rate at which these changes occur varies widely: They may come about in one fell swoop, or they may occur very gradually.

As groups appropriate institutional features, they are concomitantly contributing to the reproduction or reconstitution of the institutions. For example, effective power moves often reproduce the orders of domination that they depend on. And if a novel practice spreads through enough groups and organizations and persists for a long enough time, it may become an aspect of existing institutions, as Robert's Rules of Order did. Group structurational processes have a role in the preservation or change of institutions.

STRUCTURAL DYNAMICS AND INTERPENETRATION

Action typically draws on multiple structural features. For this reason relationships among structures are another important influence on structuration. The interpenetration of structures occurs in the joint structuration of two structures in a single system. For example, when a leader gives orders, he or she simultaneously draws on positional power resources and language, and in the process both structures are transformed to some extent. Thus the leader might use an indirect request ("We need to have this done by that date") that (a) depends for its clear meaning on the leader's position and (b) represents the leader's position as part of a "we" with the subordinate and the group. Positional resources alter what symbolic structures mean, and symbolic structures qualify positional resources.

Two fundamental forms of interpenetration can be distinguished. First, one structure *mediates* another when its production and reproduction involve the reproduction of the other. For example, the economic metaphor, in which choices are based on rationalistic cost-benefit calculations (Lakoff & Johnson, 1980), often mediates decision rules in groups (Thibaut & Kelley, 1959). Those rules consistent with the metaphor are given preferential status and reproduced, but many other possible rules, such as ethical standards, fall by the wayside.

Second, *contradiction* occurs when "the operation of one structural principle in the production of a societal system presumes that of another which tends to undermine it" (Giddens, 1979, p. 141). For example, numerous investigators have reflected on the contradiction between the social, collegial nature of group action and members' individualistic striving for control and personal position in groups. This contradiction in organizing principles, each of which conditions the other, can produce serious problems in the group. When these problems mount, the group may use time and energy to cope with them or it may change to "reprioritize" the organizing principles. Contradictions involve many complicated structural dynamics, described in more depth in Poole et al. (1985).

The dynamics of structural mediation and contradiction are explored by Smith and Berg (1987), who examine a number of inherent paradoxes in group life that set up contradictions or harmful mediations in groups. Consider, for example, the paradox of identity, in which the group that gives the individual part of his or her identity maintains its own identity by asking the individual to follow norms that submerge his or her identity. They see this paradox exhibited in processes such as artificial role division into those who do the group's work and those who nurture individuals.

STRUCTURATIONAL RESEARCH

Giddens (1984) maintains that there are two general strategies for research on structuration: the analysis of strategic conduct and institutional analysis. The *analysis of strategic conduct* takes institutions as a backdrop and focuses on how actors draw on and reproduce structures in social practices. *Institutional analysis* assumes that strategic conduct is going on, but focuses on the structural characteristics of institutions and their long-term development. Each approach "brackets" a certain part of the structurational process and uses the rest as an unanalyzed ground for its object of interest. Giddens notes that this bracketing artificially segments structuration, but argues that it is necessary for methodological purposes. Though we agree that parts of any structurational process must serve as the "ground" against which to discern the "figure," we do not believe that structurational studies have to focus on only action or only institutions. An alternative is to shift back and forth between action and institutional levels during an analysis, hoping that the "whole" will convey the nature of structuration. Studies by Smith (1983) and by Brewer (1988) do this in a single report. Research programs such as those described below tend to shift back and forth across several reports, each of which captures part of the whole.

An analysis of structuration should address a set of interlocking problems:

1. It must develop a good analysis of how the system works. This analysis defines the general field in which structuration occurs and its "surface" indicants. It forms a foundation for the analysis of constitution of the group system. By implication, this requires identification of causal links that characterize the system's operation and members' interpretive maps.

2. It must identify the array of relevant structures that are used to constitute the system. This may involve identification of both potential and active structures. All such identifications are, of course, reifications that "freeze" the modalities of structuration for purposes of analysis.

3. It must identify structuring moves or processes by which agents appropriate these structures, producing and reproducing them in activity. As Poole and DeSanctis (1992; DeSanctis & Poole, 1994) note, structuration in groups can be studied on at least three levels: the microlevel moves involved in appropriating structures into group interaction, the larger global patterns of appropriation that stretch over several meetings, and at the societal level of general discourse about the relevant structures.

4. It should also clarify the mediation of one structure by others, as well as the contradictions between structures and their role in the structurational process.

5. It ultimately should shed light on how social institutions are reproduced or shaped by the process in question.

6. Finally, the subjects or actors themselves are produced and reproduced in structuration (Poole et al., 1985). Hence we also have to account for the positioning of the subject in the social system.

These are not a set of stages for research. Working on any single problem can also produce insights on others. For example, characterizing the structuring moves and structuration in microlevel interaction may lead to identification of additional structures and also to insights as to how the system "works." Insights into how structuration shapes social institutions may shed light on structuring moves through illuminating constraints. Ideally, the finished theory should be seamless—it would incorporate all analyses into a complex whole.

Nor does structurational research have to be solely qualitative, as implied by Banks and Riley (1993). They argue for an ethnographic-ethnomethodological approach to the study of structuration (see Brewer, 1988, and Smith, 1983, for examples). Although useful, this approach is not the only path to the discovery of valid insights into structuration. Quantitative methods are useful in the study of the system level, because they permit the testing of models to determine which relationships are likely candidates for structurational analysis (Giddens, 1984). Quantitative approaches are also useful for the study of structuration itself, when many observations or cases are available for analysis and when indicators of aspects of structuration can be developed. Studies by Barley (1986) and Poole and DeSanctis (1992) illustrate the use of quantitative models in structuration research. Historical studies of structuration are also important, as Giddens's work illustrates.

Research on Structuration in Group Decision Making

This section will summarize the current state of knowledge in the research on structuration in group decision making. It focuses primarily on two long-term research projects, one by Seibold, Meyers, and colleagues on argumentation and the other by Poole, DeSanctis, and colleagues advancing adaptive structuration theory as a framework for understanding the use of computer technology in group decision making. We supplement this exposition with recent structurational investigations of teacher contract negotiations (Keough & Lake, 1993) and innovation modification during intraorganizational adoption (Lewis & Seibold, 1993).

First, we will briefly discuss the general approach of the two long-term research projects. Then we will organize the results of structurational studies around four central issues.

TWO RESEARCH PROGRAMS

Both research projects consist of a series of studies, each of which divulges parts of the structuring process. The basic approach of Seibold, Meyers, and their colleagues has been to sort out various layers of structure that underlie argument. Seibold, Canary, and Ratledge (1983) state:

> Group argument, then, can be viewed as the system of interaction produced by members engaging in advancing *arguables*, or utterances that are potentially disagreeable to other members. The advancing of these arguables is bound up in the argument *structures* (rules and resources) that the arguers draw upon, how they argue the arguable (that is, the interpretive, normative, and power-based forms of talk arguers rely upon to convey the arguable), and the ways in which the *system*, or flow of group conduct, in which they are embedded conditions what is arguable (and how arguables can be advanced). (pp. 17-18)

Initially, Seibold et al. (1981) turned to theoretical analyses of argument to identify relevant structures. They used three perspectives: Toulmin's (1969) formal model of argument as reason-giving; Perelman and Olbrechts-Tyteca's (1969) global analysis of argumentation as a sequence of dispute initiation, introduction of proof through data and technique, and convergence and amplification of the position; and Jacobs and Jackson's (1980) microlevel analysis of argumentation as discourse that interrupts the achievement of a preferred response to an adjacency pair and necessitates localized repair activity. Each of these positions is grounded in a prescriptive model and, with the possible exception of Toulmin's, assume that the goal of argumentation is ultimate convergence on a position.

In a study of a single group decision, Seibold et al. (1981) found a complex interweaving of patterns at the system level. Argumentative discourse consisted of disagreements with relatively simple repair attempts that resulted in reasoning that would be judged as flawed from Toulmin's perspective. However, there was an overall pattern of convergence as described by the Perelman model. There seemed to be a *nesting* of structures in this argumentation: The microlevel discourse rules used to manage repair were a means of implementing argument structures that contained Toulminic elements such as claim-data connections; in turn, although most argumentation only partially realized the Toulminic structures, development of the various elements served to reflect the movement from dispute initiation to convergence/amplification that the global Perelman model prescribed.

Later studies build on this study and other preliminary work (Canary, Ratledge, & Seibold, 1982; Ratledge, 1986; Seibold, Canary, & Ratledge, 1983; Seibold & Meyers, 1986). Canary, Brossman, and Seibold (1987) describe four major classes of arguments: (a) simple arguments; (b) compound arguments, which combine or embed simple ones; (c) eroded arguments, which fail to develop; and (d) convergent arguments, which combine elements of several members' arguments and are sometimes produced in "tag team" fashion by several members. The structures underlying these argument forms seem to be majority influence and the relative power or status of members. Seibold and Meyers (1986) raise the issue of how argument and decision-making structures mediate or contradict one another. For example, how does the construction of arguments acceptable to the group affect decision making so as to reproduce the requirement that decisions must be grounded in the worldview undergirding the arguments? Meyers's work (Meyers, 1989a, 1989b; Meyers & Seibold, 1987, 1990) has focused on contrasting cognitive and interactional explanations of group polarization. It explores how individual members' cognitive argument structures are mediated by collective structures developed in group interaction. Because cognitive structures are individualized, they are likely to be more fully developed, in Toulmin's terminology, than group arguments, which exhibit shifting foci and are often incomplete. Hence collective argument structures are likely to result from discourse processes similar to those described by Jacobs and Jackson.

These strands of research have yet to be woven together to show the embedding and interpenetration of structures in argumentation. However, they show how cognitive and interactional argument links to decision for polarization tasks, and they begin to trace the transformations involved in moving argument from cognitive to social venues.

Poole and DeSanctis (1990, 1992; DeSanctis & Poole, 1994) developed *adaptive structuration theory,* a version of structuration theory suited for task-oriented groups. They have applied it mainly to the study of groups using computerized group decision support systems (see McLeod, Chapter 14, this volume). They follow a two-level research process that distinguishes *functional analysis* and *constitutive analysis,* as recommended by Poole and McPhee (1994) in their discussion of dialectical explanations. Functional analysis builds models of causal relationships among variables characterizing the system level; constitutive analysis explores how the variables and relationships among them are constituted through structurational processes. Functional analysis thus establishes the relationships that are explained by constitutive analysis. But functional analysis also establishes conditions that shape structuration, and therefore also enters into the explanation of the system's constitution.

Poole and DeSanctis distinguished three levels of group systems at which a structurational analysis can be conducted. First, structuration can be studied at the micro level by tracking interaction moves that appropriate, produce, and reproduce structures (see, e.g., Poole & DeSanctis, 1992). Second, research can focus on global patterns of structuration that characterize the process across an entire decision or series of decisions (see, e.g., Heller, 1992; Poole, DeSanctis, Kirsch, & Jackson, 1995). Finally, the societal layer represents general discourse concerning appropriation of various structures that are commonly shared across a population of groups or organizations. The three layers interpenetrate, with each layer influencing the others. In their research on the bottom two layers, Poole, DeSanctis, and their colleagues have employed a mixture of qualitative and quantitative methods for both functional and constitutive analyses.

RESEARCH FINDINGS

We can organize findings from research on the structuration of group decisions into four general areas.

The Mediating Role of Interaction

A central assumption of structuration theory is that the impact of exogenous variables such as task, group size, and member resources is mediated by structuring processes. Several studies have attempted to evaluate this hypothesis. Poole, McPhee, and Seibold (1982) compared Davis's (1973) social decision scheme (SDS) model, which predicts group outcomes from the distribution of prediscussion preferences, with the valence distribution (DV) model, which predicts group outcomes from preferences expressed and developed in interaction (for later developments regarding this model see Hoffman & Kleinman, 1994, and McPhee, 1994). They found that the DV model predicted outcomes better than the SDS model, and that it mediated the impact of the SDS on outcomes. They concluded that this study yielded support for structuration theory. However, Hewes (1986; Chapter 7, this volume) argued that members' expressed valence could still reflect prediscussion preferences and that the Poole et al. study did not provide airtight evidence.

Meyers (1989a, 1989b) contrasted the non-interaction-based explanation for the polarization of group decisions offered by persuasive arguments theory (PAT) with an interaction-based explanation. PAT (Burnstein & Vinokur, 1977) accounts for the degree of polarization as a function of the arguments presented in a discussion. Typically, PAT research designs assess arguments members have prior to discussion, thus assuming that no new ideas emerge from group interaction. Meyers found that there were more distinct arguments during discussion than members generated prior to discussion and that many of these differed from prediscussion arguments. She attributed this to the emergence of arguments through interaction; qualitative analysis of the same data reported in Meyers (1987) was consistent with this interpretation. The earlier finding of Seibold et al. (1981) and Canary et al. (1987) that many group arguments were developed in "tag team" fashion buttresses this explanation as well (also see Brashers & Meyers, 1989).

Studies of computer-supported decision making illuminate the mediational hypothesis as well. A key question in technology research is whether technological support has a direct deterministic effect on group processes and outcomes or whether the appropriation of the technology in interaction mediates its impact (Poole & DeSanctis, 1990; Seibold,

Heller, & Contractor, 1994). Poole, Holmes, and DeSanctis (1991) and Poole and DeSanctis (1992) found that different groups appropriated a group decision support system (GDSS) in diverse ways and that that mode of appropriation was related to group outcomes. A test of a causal model by Poole, Lind, Watson, and DeSanctis (1992) found that communication variables mediated the impact of technology on three outcome variables: consensus change, perceived solution quality, and member satisfaction with decision procedures.

These three sets of studies cover a wide range of interaction processes—expression of preferences, argumentation, technology use in general decision making, conflict management—and a range of different types of tasks and groups. Together they suggest that interaction mediates the impact of other variables on decision-making outcomes, supporting the assumption that structuring processes make a difference. However, Poole and Roth (1989; also see Poole & Baldwin, Chapter 8, this volume) offer a caveat for this conclusion. They tested a contingency model of group decision development that posited that variables such as task and group structure would influence the sequence of decision phases groups produced. Following structuration theory, they hypothesized that a significant portion of the variance in group decision paths would remain unaccounted for due to the individualized paths generated by structuring processes in particular groups. However, their deterministic model explained up to 60% of the variance in decision paths. It seems possible that some phenomena are more tightly structured than others, leaving less room for group adaptations.

The Nature of Structuring Interaction

To study structuring interaction, it is necessary (a) to identify structures or structural features that come into play, and (b) to identify what roles they play and how they are being used. Although this abstracts structures and appropriations from interaction and runs the risk of reifying them, it is a necessary analytical move.

Identification of Structures. One approach is to distinguish general types of structures. Researchers can then use the typology as a heuristic when searching for structures in particular contexts. Poole and

DeSanctis (1992; DeSanctis & Poole, 1994) distinguished two aspects of technological structures: their *spirit,* the general goals and attitudes the technology promotes (such as democratic decision making); and the specific *structural* features built into the system (such as anonymous input of ideas, or one vote per group member). A structural feature is a specific rule or resource that operates in a group, whereas spirit is the principle of coherence that holds a set of rules and resources together. The features of a GDSS, like any technology, are designed to promote its spirit. However, features are functionally independent of spirit and may be used in ways inconsistent with it. In their analysis of 18 decision-making groups, Poole and DeSanctis (1992) further distinguished structures according to their sources, including the technology, the task, and outside norms. Meyers and Seibold (1987) distinguished argument structures according to whether they were cognitively or socially based. The different loci of these two types of structures led to differences in how they were produced and reproduced in interaction. Also, there is some evidence that social argument structures are more complex than cognitive ones (Meyers, 1989a, 1989b; Meyers & Seibold, 1987, 1990). Both of these typologies guided the identification of specific structures in discourse and actions.

In addition to delineating general distinctions, there have been efforts to enumerate specific structures. Poole (1985) described several different decision logics, structural schemes that specify basic assumptions about decision making and sequences of steps to be followed in decision making. These logics, which may be held by individual members or shared by a group, include rational logic, political logic, and assumed consensus. Keough and Lake (1993) described several value structures that came into play during a teacher negotiation session.

Because of the number and variety of possible structural features that may come into play, and because they are transformed in interaction, it is impossible to enumerate all relevant structures a priori. The specific structures enumerated will vary from case to case, depending on the nature of the phenomenon and the context. Moreover, any enumeration is inherently incomplete, because any given structure involves countless other background rules and resources (Wootten, 1976).

How Do Structures Come Into Play? One way to depict structuring interaction is as a series of *structuring moves,* microlevel actions that appropriate and may adapt structural features. A record of how structures are transformed over time by structuring moves provides a mapping of structurational processes. Poole and DeSanctis (1992) drew on Elizabethan theories of rhetorical tropes to develop a typology of appropriation moves.

Their scheme identifies 37 moves group members can use to appropriate a structure, organized into nine general categories. These categories are based on the following distinctions: (a) Does the move involve a single structure or more than one structure? (b) Does the move consist of an active use of the structure, an attempt to understand or clarify the structure, or a response to another member's appropriation move?

Two categories code moves that involve a single structure: *Direct appropriation* represents active use of the structure, whereas *constraint* represents an attempt to interpret and understand the structure. Four categories code moves involving more than one structure: *substitution* and *combination* code active uses of two or more structures, whereas *enlargement* and *contrast* code attempts to interpret and understand two or more structures in light of each other. In a substitution move, one structure replaces another, but in a combination move, two structures are melded in various ways. In enlargement moves, two structures are likened to each other, but in contrast moves, two structures are placed in opposition. *Affirmation* and *negation* represent the positive and negative modes of response to others' appropriations, whereas *ambiguity* represents uncertainty and confusion in response to some structure.

Poole and DeSanctis used this scheme to generate a timeline of appropriation moves on several types of structures used in computer-supported groups. This enabled the researchers to develop (a) profiles of the general types of appropriations made by groups as well as which members made and controlled them, and (b) maps of appropriation phases. Some results derived from this data will be discussed below. Another example of a scheme to identify structuring interaction is the previously described typology of argument structures developed by Canary et al. (1987).

Another way to characterize how structures come into play is to identify the *modalities of structuration* in which they operate. Giddens (1979, p. 129) distinguishes three general modalities: Structures can serve as interpretive schemes, as norms, or as facilities supporting the exercise of power. In an insightful analysis of teacher contract negotiations, Keough and Lake (1993) explored the transformation of modalities in interaction. Bargainers attempted to invoke different value hierarchies as interpretive schemes for a contract proposal; however, whichever interpretive scheme prevailed also defined the grounds for evaluating the merit of proposals, thus determining bargainers' power bases. The same complexity was evident in management's efforts to apply an "impact test" to issues; this served as both a normative legitimation structure and as a power structure, because it ultimately indicated which party—teachers or administration—had jurisdiction over an issue. Smith (1983) also showed how structures can operate in multiple modalities.

DeSanctis and Poole (1994; DeSanctis, Poole, DeSharnais, & Lewis, 1992) provide a related division of modalities in their discussion of instrumental uses for technologies. They classified modalities of technology use into six types of appropriations: task, process, power, social, individualistic, and playful. The six modalities were intended to complement Poole and DeSanctis's (1992) schemes of appropriation moves and structure types, which were defined previously. In a study of decision making in simulated juries, Holstein (1983) identifies similar modalities in jurors' appropriations of judges' instructions.

In addition to moves and modalities, the nature of structuring interaction can be captured in terms of overall *patterns of group use*. An important characteristic of these patterns is the attitudes the group displays toward structures, such as whether the group uses the structure reluctantly or enthusiastically. DeSanctis, Poole, and co-workers have identified several important attitudes toward GDSS structures, including: (a) the extent to which a group is confident and easy in its use of the GDSS (comfort); (b) the extent to which a group values the GDSS (respect); and (c) a group's willingness to work hard and to excel at using the GDSS (challenge) (Billingsley, 1990b; Poole & DeSanctis, 1990; Sambamurthy, 1990; Zigurs, DeSanctis, & Billingsley, 1991). These attitudes affect how groups apply the GDSS and whether they use its procedures with sufficient vigor and confidence to gain benefits from them. In common with many social attitudes, comfort and respect can be self-fulfilling prophecies: High levels of comfort, respect, and challenge breed good experiences, which increase these attitudes accordingly, and vice versa. Sambamurthy and Chin (in press) found that the higher a group's comfort (operationalized as ease of use) and respect (operationalized as perceived usefulness) for a GDSS, the higher the group's decision-making performance.

The nature of structuring interaction can also be captured in patterns of GDSS use at the global level across an entire decision process or series of decisions (Poole & DeSanctis, 1992). Heller (1992) analyzed 17 meetings of four-person GDSS groups involved in discussion of choice dilemmas using an adaptation of Billingsley's (1990a, 1990b) global-level appropriation coding system. Consistent with adaptive structuration theory expectations, results revealed that groups with 3 or 4 weeks' prior history of working together exhibited greater "GDSS salience" (observed reliance on the GDSS for completion of their tasks) than groups with little or no history together. Too, the groups with history exhibited greater use of other process structures than those offered by the GDSS, moderator, or written material resources.

Poole and DeSanctis (1991) posited five general patterns of GDSS appropriations based on qualitative observations of field and laboratory groups: (a) *autonomous* groups achieve independent mastery of the GDSS and feel free to improvise with it; (b) *dependent* groups are comfortable with the GDSS and use it properly, without excessive reliance on a facilitator or outside technician; (c) *overdependent* groups attempt to use the GDSS and value it, but require a facilitator to use the GDSS and must be helped at all stages of use; (d) *counterdependent* groups do not like the GDSS, but use it (perhaps at the insistence of a leader or facilitator)—they tend to apply it in ways inconsistent with its spirit and may use the system as a scapegoat for problems; (e) *rejector* groups refuse to use the technology. Across the five types there are marked variations in the degree to which technological structures are appropriated, the accuracy of the group's interpretation of the system's spirit, the range of modalities in which the structure will be used, and the rate of combination of structures. The researchers hypothesize that appropriation patterns will mediate outcomes for groups using GDSSs. Autonomous and dependent groups should have outcomes superior to groups that adopt the other patterns.

These typologies focus on *what* appropriations occur. Also important is *how* the appropriation process works. Poole and DeSanctis (1992) found two distinct dynamics in structuring interaction. First, there was the *continuous* production and reproduction of structures as they are employed in activities. This continuous process often has a subtle "directionality," setting up a momentum toward stabilizing or changing existing structures. Changes due to continuous structuration processes emerge very slowly and may introduce almost imperceptible changes in the structure.

Second, there were *junctures* at which groups made major choices concerning which structural features to appropriate, how they were appropriated, and whether and how they would be reproduced. Whereas members often were not aware of continuous structuring activities, they were conscious of junctures and often tried to control structuration at these points. Observation of groups using a GDSS indicated five types of regular events that could serve as junctures: the first bid to appropriate a given structure; conflict over an appropriation; a problem with the GDSS; explanations of how to use the GDSS or what its outputs or features meant; and transition points among task steps or activities. Each of these presents an occasion for introducing a new structure or a different interpretation of a structure, for combining or dissociating structural features, and for reaffirming or challenging a previous structure-in-use. The ensuing interaction sets the course for another period of continuous structuration and contributes either to maintenance or to change of the existing ensemble of structures-in-use.

Both dynamics weave together in structuration processes, with the junctures corresponding to structural "revolutions" and the continuous processes corresponding to structural "evolution." The two-way distinction is similar to what Strauss and his colleagues (Strauss, 1978) found in studies of negotiated order. Poole and DeSanctis found that how groups handled junctures related to the effectiveness with which they applied the technology to their work.

Overall, there has been a good deal of progress in understanding structuring interaction. At least two types of additional research are necessary. First, only a few studies directly investigated the process by which structures are appropriated, reproduced, and transformed. This process is the engine of structuration, however, and theories of how it works are necessary as a foundation for understanding influences on structuration. Second, more research is needed on the influence of appropriation on group and individual outcomes. Several of the studies mentioned in this section assess structuration-outcome relationships, but a much broader empirical base is needed to draw firm conclusions. As Gouran (1990) has noted, this ultimately will be the acid test of whether structuration is a significant explanatory factor in its own right or a background process that sets the stage for more important factors.

Factors That Influence Structuration

One important influence on structuration is the group's task. Poole and Roth (1989) present evidence that the nature of the decision task altered the degree of vigilance and planning that groups put into managing their processes. For tasks that were difficult and challenging, groups exhibited more organized and systematic decision processes, suggesting they were more willing to coordinate their efforts and to focus on the task at hand. For easier or more familiar tasks, groups exhibited more disorganized decision processes, suggesting less attention to the decision and less motivation to manage the process tightly. To the extent that groups are aware of the need to organize and manage their work carefully, we might expect them to be more reflective about their appropriations and structuring moves. In the short run, this should result in superior adaptation of structures to group needs and more effective applications of structures. In the long run, this might also increase members' knowledgeability concerning the grounds of action, ultimately increasing their control over the situation.

Many structures used in group decisions are formally preserved in material artifacts, such as minutes, rulebooks, or procedures incorporated into GDSSs. Characteristics of these formalized structures also influence structuration. One relevant characteristic is *restrictiveness* of a structure, the degree to which it constrains group or member behavior (DeSanctis, D'Onofrio, Sambamurthy, & Poole, 1989). Poole and De-Sanctis (1992) showed that the restrictiveness of a GDSS alters structuring behavior; specifically, members using a more restrictive GDSS were able to focus on appropriating the outputs of the GDSS, such as vote totals, whereas those with a less restrictive system had to spend more time determining how they would appropriate the system. A second characteristic influencing structuration is *degree of member control* of a structuring process. As mentioned previously, members' knowledge-ability about structuration and the conditions governing their behavior are important determinants of how well they can control it. Whether the structural feature itself favors some members over others also is important. Some GDSSs, for example, allow all members to control how the

GDSS is used, but others vest that control in a facilitator (Poole & DeSanctis, 1990).

The group's environment also influences structuration. Lewis and Seibold (1993) summarize evidence that users' coping tactics in the face of organizational innovations are influenced by the socioeconomic structure and institutional environment of the organization, the organization's structured activities for implementing the innovation, and formal and individual characteristics of the users themselves.

Task and formal properties are the only two exogenous factors that have been investigated by structurational research on groups. Clearly *much* more work is needed on this issue.

Mediation and Contradiction in Structuration

Whenever more than one distinct structure or more than one attempt to appropriate the same structure occurs, mediations and contradiction may result. For example, Poole and DeSanctis (1992) found numerous cases where two structures were combined, where one was used to clarify or interpret the meaning of another, and where one was used as a contrast with another.

In their study of teacher contract negotiations, Keough and Lake (1993) found that bargainers attempted to create or invoke value hierarchies favorable to their position. Initially the teacher and administration hierarchies seemed to mediate each other, because they divided responsibilities between teaching and administrative matters. However, this mediation was inherently unstable, because by nature *teacher* and *administrator* are oppositional terms in such negotiations; this eventuated in a breakdown of a collaboratively defined hierarchy when parties attempted to define "educational" and "administrative" spheres. A contradiction thus eroded a potential mediation. Keough and Lake also found that the mass of structural features drawn into protracted bargaining over numerous issues was extremely complex and that structuring moves on one issue might generate contradictions within the larger structural frame. One move by the teachers' negotiator to try to get the administrators to commit actually overturned an approval format favored by the union. This fundamentally altered the legal status of the contract. This structuring move had the unintended consequence of contradicting long-reproduced rules, resulting in a transformation of the system itself. The Keough and Lake study shows that contradictions that emerge in microlevel interaction may restructure the system itself.

Poole and DeSanctis (1992; DeSanctis & Poole, 1994) advance an analysis of contradiction that rests on a distinction between *faithful* and *ironic* (nonfaithful) appropriation of technological structures. This distinction is defined by the relationship between the spirit of a technology and the specific features used to implement that spirit. Features and spirit are functionally autonomous layers of structure and may come into contradiction. For example, in appropriating a GDSS intended to promote democratic decision making, a group may: (a) stick closely to both the spirit and the specific features (e.g., use a ranking feature to determine relative priorities among group ideas); (b) act in a way consistent with the spirit, but change and reinterpret the features (e.g., solicit opinions by having one person enter votes for the group, rather than having everyone vote on their own terminal); (c) violate the spirit of the structure but retain its features, thus using features in unintended ways (e.g., use a voting procedure to pressure minority members into conciliation rather than to voice opposition); or (d) alter both the spirit and the features of a structure (e.g., use a public messaging facility to make fun of others' ideas, thus inhibiting further use of the GDSS for collaborative discussion). Options (a) and (b) are faithful appropriations, whereas options (c) and (d) represent ironic appropriations. Faithful appropriations are consistent with the spirit and structural feature design, whereas ironic appropriations set up contradictions among levels of structure. Nonfaithful appropriations are not always "bad" or "improper." Sometimes they represent cases in which the system is used creatively, stretching its potential. Ironic uses are harmful, however, when the tensions they set up run counter to basic values of the spirit, or when they result in serious conflicts over the purposes of the system. Nonfaithful appropriations are important to track because they represent the formation of new structures and because they help to explain how technology structures do not always bring the outcomes that designers intended.

In a certain sense, structural mediations and contradictions give the structuration process a "life of its own." Combinations and contrapositions of structures may set into motion processes leading to unintended consequences. Such processes are not easily controlled by members, because members are often not aware of the implications of structural interpenetration, and when they are, the interactions may be quite complex.

Conclusion

This research provides a much more detailed picture of structuration in group decision making than we had when we wrote this chapter nearly 10 years ago. It suggests that structuration occurs continuously, and that this continuous process is punctuated by junctures that are occasions for changes in or reconfirmation of current practices. Influences on the structuring process in groups include members' attitudes toward structures; the modalities in which structures operate; mediations and contradictions among structures; and exogenous factors such as task, formalization, and the institutional context.

A wide range of structures has been studied, including procedural structures embodied in computerized group support systems, argument structures, decision rules, and value hierarchies in negotiation. General schemes for identifying structures or their elements include the distinction between the spirit and the features of procedural structures, between cognitive and social structures of argumentation, and between structures with various degrees of "sedimentation" or depth.

Some of these structures are embodied in material artifacts such as rulebooks and group decision support systems, but others enjoy a more evanescent existence, persisting only through repeated appropriation. Materially anchored structures are easily objectified, which enables members to develop definitive attitudes toward them and various types of dependencies on them. This also makes members more conscious of the structures and how they might be adapted and manipulated, enhancing members' discursive consciousness. It is harder to pin down structures that exist solely in the fabric of the group's activities and customs. Many such structures are not salient enough to provoke attitudes, and they are hard to bring into discursive consciousness. For example, the structure of language is appropriated unthinkingly by most.

Several schemes for identifying structuring moves, modalities of structuration, and general types of appropriations have also been developed. The different schemes represent different levels at which structuring processes may be conceptualized and studied, at the micro level, global level, or societal level. The various types of structuring moves can be seen as nested within each other, with more macro units providing context for micro moves and the micro moves constituting the macro units. The utility of identifying modalities of structuration, posited by Giddens, has been illustrated in several studies. It is particularly interesting to note that structures appropriated in one modality may be transformed to operate in other modalities.

Several lines of research provide evidence that exogenous influences on decision making, such as task, technological support, and privately produced arguments, are mediated by structuring interaction. The impacts of these exogenous influences can be discerned as structural features that the group produces and then uses to guide and to constrain its work. As a result, we would expect between-group differences in exogenous impacts, because each group will produce its own "version" of the exogenous variables and will react differently to it.

Finally, it is also evident that there are differences in the degree of freedom groups have to adapt and alter structures. Some institutions are so sedimented that groups have little freedom to alter structures, as is the case for many rituals. And exogenous variables may be so powerfully constraining that group behavior is determined, as seems to be the case in the Poole and Roth (1989) study. So it is important to gain a greater understanding of the factors that determine the degree to which groups can adapt or change structures.

This review also highlights several lacunae. Very little of this research deals with the content or substance of the decisions in question, focusing instead on the decision process. The structuration of the decisions themselves needs to be explored. Second, there is little research on the interplay among structural features at various levels—micro, global, and societal. Most analysis has focused instead on one layer of structure and its relationship with system cast at the same level. Third, little is known concerning factors that influence or constrain structuring processes. Studies that vary the context of structuration are needed. Finally, and perhaps most important, existing research has little critical edge to it. The study of structuration is inherently a critical undertaking. Current research has focused on the important task of describing how structuration occurs and the immediate effects it has on systems. However, also needed is critical penetration of how these processes subject members to domination or keep them from realizing their full potential. As Giddens (1984) has said, "Structuration theory is intrinsically incomplete if not linked to a conception of social science as critical theory" (p. 287).

Note

1. We purposely emphasize the symmetry between stability and change in this discussion. However, it is possible to favor one more than the other and still have an integrative view. In more recent writings, Giddens has emphasized ontological security based on social routines and structures as persisting features, tilting toward the stable over the changing.

References

Ancona, D. G., & Caldwell, D. F. (1992). Bridging the boundary: External process and performance in organizational teams. *Administrative Science Quarterly, 37,* 634-665.

Banks, S. P., & Riley, P. (1993). Structuration theory as an ontology for communication research. In S. A. Deetz (Ed.), *Communication yearbook 16* (pp. 167-196). Newbury Park, CA: Sage.

Barley, S. (1986). Technology as an occasion for structuring. *Administrative Science Quarterly, 31,* 78-108.

Billingsley, J. M. (1990a). *Global style level of GDSS: Resource codebook.* Unpublished manuscript, Department of Communication, Rutgers University.

Billingsley, J. M. (1990b, June). *Studying the use of technological resources: Development and test of an interaction coding instrument.* Paper presented at the annual meeting of the International Communication Association, Dublin, Ireland.

Brashers, D., & Meyers, R. A. (1989). Tag team argument and group decision-making: A preliminary investigation. In B. E. Gronbeck (Ed.), *Spheres of argument: Proceedings of the Sixth SCA/AFA Conference on Argumentation* (pp. 542-550). Annandale, VA: Speech Communication Association.

Brewer, J. D. (1988). Micro-sociology and "the duality of structure." In N. Fielding (Ed.), *Action and structure* (pp. 144-166). Newbury Park, CA: Sage.

Burnstein, E., & Vinokur, A. (1977). Persuasive argumentation and social comparison as determinants of attitude polarization. *Journal of Experimental Social Psychology, 13,* 315-322.

Canary, D. J., Brossman, B. G., & Seibold, D. R. (1987). Argument structures in decision-making groups. *Southern Speech Communication Journal, 53,* 18-37.

Canary, D. J., Ratledge, N. T., & Seibold, D. R. (1982, November). *Argument and group decision-making: Development of a coding scheme.* Paper presented at the annual meeting of the Speech Communication Association, Louisville, KY.

Cicourel, A. V. (1974). *Cognitive sociology: Language and meaning in social interaction.* New York: Free Press.

Cragan, J. F., & Wright, D. W. (1980). Small group communication research of the 1970s: A synthesis and critique. *Central States Speech Journal, 31,* 197-213.

Cragan, J. F., & Wright, D. W. (1990). Small group communication research of the 1980s: Synthesis and critique. *Communication Studies, 41,* 212-236.

Davis, J. H. (1973). *Group performance.* Reading, MA: Addison-Wesley.

DeSanctis, G., D'Onofrio, M. J., Sambamurthy, V., & Poole, M. S. (1989). Comprehensiveness and restrictiveness in group decision heuristics: Effects of computer support on consensus decision-making. In J. I. DeGross, J. C. Henderson, & B. R. Konsynski (Eds.), *Proceedings of the Tenth International Conference on Information Systems* (pp. 131-140). New York: ACM Press.

DeSanctis, G., & Poole, M. S. (1994). Capturing the complexity in advanced technology use: Adaptive structuration theory. *Organization Science, 5,* 121-147.

DeSanctis, G., Poole, M. S., DeSharnais, G., & Lewis, H. (1992). Using computing in quality team meetings: Some initial observations from the IRS-Minnesota Project. *Journal of Management Information Systems, 8,* 7-26.

DeStephen, R. J. (1983). High and low consensus groups: A content and relational interaction analysis. *Small Group Behavior, 14,* 143-162.

Garfinkel, H., & Sacks, H. (1967). On formal structures of practical actions. In J. C. McKinney & E. A. Tiryakin (Eds.), *Theoretical sociology: Perspectives and developments* (pp. 337-366). New York: Appleton-Century-Crofts.

Giddens, A. (1976). *New rules of sociological method.* New York: Basic Books.

Giddens, A. (1979). *Central problems in social theory: Action, structure, and contradiction in social analysis.* Berkeley: University of California Press.

Giddens, A. (1984). *The constitution of society: Outline of the theory of structuration.* Berkeley: University of California Press.

Goethals, G. R., & Darley, J. M. (1987). Social comparison theory: Self-evaluation and group life. In B. Mullen & G. R. Goethals (Eds.), *Theories of group behavior* (pp. 21-47). New York: Springer.

Gouran, D. (1984). The paradigm of unfulfilled promise: A critical examination of the history of research on small groups in speech communication. In T. W. Benson (Ed.), *Speech communication in the twentieth century* (pp. 90-108, 386-392). Carbondale: University of Southern Illinois Press.

Gouran, D. (1990). Exploring the predictive potential of structuration theory. In J. A. Anderson (Ed.), *Communication yearbook 13* (pp. 313-322). Newbury Park, CA: Sage.

Hackman, J. R., & Morris, C. G. (1975). Group tasks, group interaction process, and group performance effectiveness: A review and proposed integration. In L. Berkowitz (Ed.), *Advances in experimental social psychology* (Vol. 8, pp. 45-99). New York: Academic Press.

Heller, M. A. (1992). *Group decision support use: A contextual contingencies approach and the role of group history in understanding GDSS effects.* Unpublished master's thesis, University of California-Santa Barbara.

Hernes, G. (1976). Structural change in social processes. *American Journal of Sociology, 82,* 513-547.

Hewes, D. E. (1986). A socio-egocentric model of group decision-making. In R. Y. Hirokawa & M. S. Poole (Eds.), *Communication and group decision-making* (pp. 265-291). Beverly Hills, CA: Sage.

Hoffman, L. R., & Kleinman, G. B. (1994). Individual and group in group problem solving: The valence model redressed. *Human Communication Research, 21,* 36-59.

Holstein, J. A. (1983). Juror's use of judge's instructions: Conceptual and methodological issues in simulated jury studies. *Sociological Methods and Research, 11,* 501-518.

Homans, G. (1950). *The human group.* New York: Harcourt Brace.

Jackson, J. M. (1987). Social impact theory: A social forces model of influence. In B. Mullin & G. R. Goethals (Eds.), *Theories of group behavior* (pp. 111-184). New York: Springer.

Jacobs, S., & Jackson, S. (1980). Structure of conversational argument: Pragmatic bases for the enthymeme. *Quarterly Journal of Speech, 66,* 251-265.

Johnson, J. C., & Miller, M. L. (1983). Deviant social position in small groups: The relation between role and individual. *Social Networks, 5,* 51-69.

Keough, C., & Lake, R. (1993). Values as structuring properties of contract negotiations. In C. Conrad (Ed.), *The ethical nexus* (pp. 171-191). Norwood, NJ: Ablex.

Knotternus, J. D., & Greenstein, T. D. (1981). Status and performance characteristics in social interaction: A theory of status validation. *Social Psychology Quarterly, 44,* 338-348.

Lakoff, G., & Johnson, M. (1980). *Metaphors we live by.* Chicago: University of Chicago Press.

Latane, B. (1981). The psychology of social impact. *American Psychologist, 36,* 343-356.

Lewis, L. K., & Seibold, D. R. (1993). Innovation modification during intraorganizational adoption. *Academy of Management Review, 18,* 322-354.

Masuch, M. (1985). Vicious circles in organizations. *Administrative Science Quarterly, 30,* 14-33.

McGrath, J. E., & Altman, I. (1966). *Small group research: A synthesis and critique of the field.* New York: Holt, Rinehart & Winston.

McPhee, R. D. (1994). Response to Hoffman and Kleinman. *Human Communication Research, 21,* 60-63.

Meyers, R. A. (1987). *Argument and group decision-making: An interactional test of persuasive arguments theory and an alternative structurational perspective.* Unpublished doctoral dissertation, University of Illinois, Urbana-Champaign.

Meyers, R. A. (1989a). Persuasive arguments theory: A test of assumptions. *Human Communication Research, 15,* 357-381.

Meyers, R. A. (1989b). Testing persuasive arguments theory's predictor model: Alternative interactional accounts of group argument and influence. *Communication Monographs, 56,* 112-132.

Meyers, R. A., & Seibold, D. R. (1987). Interactional and noninteractional perspectives on interpersonal argument: Implications for the study of decision-making. In F. H. van Emeron, R. Grootendorst, J. A. Blair, & C. A. Willard (Eds.), *Argumentation: Perspectives and approaches* (pp. 205-214). Dordrecht, The Netherlands: Foris.

Meyers, R. A., & Seibold, D. R. (1990). Perspectives on group argument: A critical review of persuasive arguments theory and an alternative structurational view. In J. Anderson (Ed.), *Communication yearbook 13* (pp. 268-302). Newbury Park, CA: Sage.

Perelman, C. H., & Olbrechts-Tyteca, L. (1969). *The new rhetoric: A treatise on argumentation* (J. Wilkinson & P. Weaver, Trans.). Notre Dame, IN: University of Notre Dame Press.

Polanyi, M. (1962). *Personal knowledge: Toward a post-critical philosophy.* New York: Harper & Row.

Poole, M. S. (1983). Decision development in small groups III: A multiple sequence theory of decision development. *Communication Monographs, 50,* 321-341.

Poole, M. S. (1985). Tasks and interaction sequences: A theory of coherence in group decision-making. In R. Street & J. N. Cappella (Eds.), *Sequence and pattern in communicative behavior* (pp. 206-224). London: Edward Arnold.

Poole, M. S., & DeSanctis, G. (1990). Understanding the use of group decision support systems: The theory of adaptive structuration. In J. Fulk & C. Steinfield (Eds.), *Organizations and communication technology* (pp. 175-195). Newbury Park, CA: Sage.

Poole, M. S., & DeSanctis, G. (1991). *Appropriation of group decision support systems.* Unpublished manuscript, University of Minnesota, Department of Speech-Communication.

Poole, M. S., & DeSanctis, G. (1992). Microlevel structuration in computer-supported group decision-making. *Human Communication Research, 19,* 5-49.

Poole, M. S., DeSanctis, G., Kirsch, L., & Jackson, M. (1995). Group decision support systems as facilitators of quality team efforts. In L. R. Frey (Ed.), *Innovations in group facilitation techniques: Case studies of applications in naturalistic settings* (pp. 299-320). Creskill, NJ: Hampton Press.

Poole, M. S., Holmes, M., & DeSanctis, G. (1991). Conflict management in a computer-supported meeting environment. *Management Science, 37,* 926-953.

Poole, M. S., Lind, R. A., Watson, R., & DeSanctis, G. (1992). *A test of the mediating role of use processes in group support system effects.* Unpublished manuscript, University of Minnesota at Minneapolis-St. Paul, Department of Speech-Communication.

Poole, M. S., & McPhee, R. D. (1994). Methodology in interpersonal communication research. In M. Knapp & G. R. Miller (Eds.), *Handbook of interpersonal communication* (2nd ed., pp. 42-100). Newbury Park, CA: Sage.

Poole, M. S., McPhee, R. D., & Seibold, D. R. (1982). A comparison of normative and interactional explanations of group decision-making: Social decision schemes versus valence distributions. *Communication Monographs, 49,* 1-19.

Poole, M. S., & Roth, J. (1989). Decision development in small groups V: Test of a contingency model. *Human Communication Research, 15,* 549-589.

Poole, M. S., Seibold, D. R., & McPhee, R. D. (1985). Group decision-making as a structurational process. *Quarterly Journal of Speech, 71,* 74-102.

Poole, M. S., Seibold, D. R., & McPhee, R. D. (1986). A structurational approach to theory-building in group decision-making research. In R. Y. Hirokawa & M. S. Poole (Eds.), *Communication and group decision-making* (1st ed., pp. 237-264). Beverly Hills, CA: Sage.

Putnam, L. L. (1979). Preference for procedural order in task-oriented small groups. *Communication Monographs, 46,* 193-218.

Putnam, L. L., & Stohl, C. (1990). Bona fide groups: A reconceptualization of groups in context. *Communication Studies, 41,* 248-265.

Ratledge, N. T. (1986). *Theoretical and methodological integrity of a structurational scheme for coding argument in decision-making groups.* Unpublished doctoral dissertation, University of Southern California.

Sambamurthy, V. (1990). *A comparison of two levels of computer based support for communication and conflict management in equivocality reduction during stakeholder analysis.* Unpublished doctoral dissertation, University of Minnesota at Minneapolis-St. Paul.

Sambamurthy, V., & Chin, W. W. (in press). The effects of group attitudes toward using GDSS designs on the decision-making performance of computer-supported groups. *Decision Science.*

Schwartzman, H. B. (1989). *The meeting: Gatherings in organizations and communities.* New York: Plenum.

Seibold, D. R., Canary, D. J., & Ratledge, N. T. (1983, November). *Argument and group decision-making: Interim report on a structurational research program.* Paper presented at the annual meeting of the Speech Communication Association, Washington, D.C.

Seibold, D. R., Heller, M., & Contractor, N. (1994). Group decision support systems (GDSS): Review, taxonomy, and research agenda. In B. Kovacic (Ed.), *New approaches to organizational communication* (pp. 143-168). Albany: State University of New York Press.

Seibold, D. R., McPhee, R. D., Poole, M. S., Tanita, N. E., & Canary, D. J. (1981). Argument, group influence, and decision outcomes. In G. Ziegelmuller & J. Rhodes (Eds.), *Dimensions of argument: Proceedings of the second summer conference on argumentation* (pp. 663-692). Annandale, VA: Speech Communication Association.

Seibold, D. R., & Meyers, R. A. (1986). Communication and influence in group decision-making. In R. Y. Hirokawa & M. S. Poole (Eds.), *Communication and group decision-making* (1st ed., pp. 133-155). Beverly Hills, CA: Sage.

Shotter, J. (1983). "Duality of structure" and "intentionality" in an ecological psychology. *Journal for the Theory of Social Behavior, 13*, 19-43.

Sigman, S. J. (1984). Talk and interaction strategy in a task oriented group. *Small Group Behavior, 15*, 33-51.

Smith, C. W. (1983). A case study of structuration: The pure-bred beef business. *Journal for the Theory of Social Behavior, 13*, 3-18.

Smith, K. K., & Berg, D. N. (1987). *Paradoxes in group life*. San Francisco: Jossey-Bass.

Strauss, A. (1978). *Negotiations: Varieties, contexts, processes, and social order*. San Francisco: Jossey-Bass.

Thibaut, J. W., & Kelley, H. H. (1959). *The social psychology of groups*. New York: John Wiley.

Toulmin, S. E. (1969). *The uses of argument*. Cambridge, UK: Cambridge University Press.

Weick, K. E. (1979). *The social psychology of organizing* (2nd ed.). Reading, MA: Addison-Wesley.

Wootten, A. (1976). *Dilemmas of discourse*. New York: Holmes & Meier.

Zigurs, I., DeSanctis, G., & Billingsley, J. (1991). Adoption patterns and attitudinal development in computer-supported meetings: An exploratory study with SAMM. *Journal of Management Information Systems, 7*, 51-70.

Bona Fide Groups

An Alternative Perspective for Communication and Small Group Decision Making

LINDA L. PUTNAM
CYNTHIA STOHL

The role of groups in society is rapidly changing. At the organizational level, groups are playing an important role in what has been described as a management transformation (Walton, 1985). Organizations and departments consist of overlapping subgroups, ad hoc committees, and problem-solving units. Management practices promote self-regulated work teams, quality improvement programs, participation, and democratic decision making. The growth of groups in organizations reflects the role of groups in society in general. Specifically, groups form the foundation of our communities through social, political, religious, and humanitarian activities. Groups of volunteers form and execute political and religious ideals. It would be no exaggeration to say that groups are the building blocks of society.

With the increased prominence of groups in many social contexts, scholars are beginning to examine the dynamics of groups that arise independent of a researcher's intentions (Frey, 1994; Hackman, 1990). Two exciting developments, case studies of natural groups and a bona fide group perspective, are testing research and theory in social contexts and are challenging the nature of group boundaries. By focusing on naturally emerging groups, researchers capture the emotional intensity, temporal fluctuations, and historical influences of group processes (Stohl & Putnam, 1994). Specifically, case studies reveal how natural groups use communication to create and sustain a sense of identity (Adelman & Frey, 1994; Conquergood, 1994), employ status and power to influence decision outcomes (Barge & Keyton, 1994), rely on context to coordinate in-group work activities (Berteotti & Seibold, 1994), and draw from their environments to create unique decision-making processes (Ball, 1994; Scheerhorn, Geist, & Teboul, 1994). Thus studying real-life groups provides a basis for testing and altering research findings drawn from earlier laboratory groups.

A second exciting development in the study of natural groups stems from challenging the definition and nature of group boundaries. This development, represented in the *bona fide* group perspective, sets forth underpinnings of an alternative perspective for understanding what a group is and the nexus between group and context (Putnam & Stohl, 1990). The bona fide group approach is a theoretical perspective that treats a group as a social system linked to its context, shaped by fluid boundaries, and altering its environment. This chapter extends the study of bona fide groups from work on a particular type of group to a broad-range perspective that applies to different arenas of group process, especially decision making. It argues that a bona fide group serves as a prototype or an "ideal type" that functions as an alternative for studying small group communication. Departing from traditional models, the bona fide group perspective casts decision making as a process that shapes and is shaped by dynamic group boundaries and multiple contexts.

Hence this chapter examines group decision making through a bona fide group lens. It begins by developing this theoretical orientation and by distinguishing it from traditional small group research. Then it reviews studies on group decision making that demonstrate the viability and uniqueness of a bona fide group perspective. Next, the chapter sets forth distinctions between traditional models and the bona fide perspective of group decision making. Finally, it concludes with implications of the bona fide group approach for theory building and research in group decision making.

Theoretical Orientation: Bona Fide Groups

The bona fide group perspective contrasts sharply with traditional "container" models of group communication. In most studies of decision making, the group is treated as a distinct entity, located in a spatial relationship within a specific context, and surrounded by a generalized backdrop called "social context." The group is contained within a limited and structured social space with fixed and immutable boundaries. In the traditional literature, scholars rarely question the nature of these borders—group boundaries are regarded as a "given." In zero-history and laboratory studies, for example, researchers impose boundaries on groups by assembling members, assigning them to groups, and providing them with a specific task. Because a fixed structural boundary envelops the group, the social context emerges as separate from the group process. Even when "natural" groups are studied, researchers treat the environment as an external input that resides in the background.

The bona fide group perspective challenges the assumption that a group has a fixed location, an existence apart from its environment, and a boundary formed by static borders. This perspective is drawn from the study of a particular type of group. It therefore functions like a prototype that socially constitutes itself as bona fide. The bona fide group perspective incorporates the characteristics and features of this "ideal" as a means of understanding group process. Traditional theories draw from research on laboratory groups and internal group interaction. The way groups define their boundaries and negotiate relationships with their context have not been central to past research. As an alternative lens, the bona fide group perspective calls for a reinterpretation of previous findings in light of this new approach.

Two characteristics that underlie a bona fide group are *permeable and fluid boundaries* and *interdependence with context*. The idea of "groupness" itself and the social processes that form and sustain a group rest on a continual negotiation of borders, boundaries, and arenas. Boundaries, then, are not reified structures that separate groups from their environments or from other groups. Rather, boundaries are socially constructed through interactions that shape group identity, create connections with internal and external environments, and reflexively define group processes.

Boundaries simultaneously separate and link groups to multiple contexts. Group members change, redefine, and negotiate their borders through (a) multiple group membership and conflicting role identities, (b) representative roles, (c) fluctuations in membership, and (d) group identity formation. Thus members in a bona fide group interact with each other and with individuals and units outside the group as if they were interconnected and as if their boundaries were fluid. Group identity stems from a combination of internal processes of its members melded with external linkages of the group.

One feature of this alternative view is the way that groups change and redefine their boundaries. Group boundaries shift through *multiple membership and conflicting role identities.* Individuals are simultaneously members of many different groups. They may belong to departmental committees, university ad hoc groups, occupational interest groups, community service projects, and church groups. For example, a member of a church group may interact differently when he or she discovers that an elected city official is also in this group. In organizational groups, members carry residues of occupational training, hierarchical status, and departmental membership. Gender, race, political affiliations, friendships, and past relationships are considered as possible influences on the nature of group interactions and role identities. As Putnam and Stohl (1990) point out, these multiple memberships function both formally and informally in group situations.

Multiple membership also affects role identity and role conflict within a group. An individual's group role may be influenced by title, prestige, or status imported from outside the group. Hence group roles are not only linked to internal functions that a member performs but also to identities that this person enacts outside the group. Members may experience role conflicts when the demands for performance in one group contradict those of an overlapping group. For example, Ben, who serves on a college-wide promotion and tenure committee, may feel uncomfortable evaluating his friend Fred, who is an officer and valued member of his neighborhood association. Divided loyalties may also create role conflicts when individuals must choose between the demands of one group versus the needs of another one or when the values and beliefs of two groups are contradictory. Specifically, an individual who serves on a college-wide affirmative action committee may experience role conflict when her departmental search committee selects top-ranked candidates who are neither female nor minority.

Representative role implies that each member serves implicitly as a boundary spanner or as resource personnel from external units to performance within the group. The degree to which a member functions as an official or unofficial representative of another unit hinges on the group's internal dynamics and the way that representative role is enacted in group deliberations. A bona fide group perspective acknowledges that asking a female faculty member to comment on how a particular concern affects retention of women professors calls for this member to wear a representative hat that may alter decision-making dynamics in subtle yet complex ways.

From a bona fide group perspective, *fluctuations in membership* also indicate the degree of permeability of group boundaries. New members who join a group often shift role functions and patterns of group interaction (Bormann, 1975). New members import information, new ideas, resources, and perceptions that can alter a group's task deliberations, power differentiation, and role structure. Newcomers are also socialized into the norms, values, and practices of the existing group.

Group members who leave the group may also continue to influence decision making through continued interactions with and linkages to the members who remain in the group. These residual connections are important insofar as they affect group identity, access to other groups, and task performance. In effect, members influence a group as they become part of its history (Moreland & Levine, 1988). Through focusing on permeable boundaries, a bona fide group perspective incorporates the dynamic interplay among past and present members. As membership changes, boundaries may become ambiguous, unclear, alter group identity, and/or may even threaten group survival (Conquergood, 1994). If boundaries are too volatile and indistinct, the group risks being overwhelmed and losing its identity; if boundaries are too stable and exclusionary, the group may become isolated and ineffective.

A fourth characteristic, *group identity formation,* centers on the degree to which members enact a sense of belongingness, loyalty, or commitment to various groups. It focuses on the way members communicate their multiple group allegiances. Identity formation in this perspective is socially constituted through degrees of belongingness. Attention is paid to the ways that group members use pronouns, implicit and explicit group references, and comments that compare internal deliberations with external actions (Donnellon, 1994). Drawing from a symbolic rather than a linguistic view of social construction, Bormann (1975) treats group identity as stemming from shared fantasies and stories. As these fantasies chain out among members, individuals converge on values and motives that form the basis of groupness. Although identity is related to cohesion and solidarity, members do not have allegiances to only one group; rather individuals can belong to and hold strong identities with multiple groups.

Campbell's (1958) notion of "group entitativity" posits a similar view of group identity, but one rooted in perceptions rather than in social constructions. He suggests that a group varies in the degree to which it is perceived as real. Perceptions of gestalt principles such as common fate, similarity, and proximity function differently from group to group. An individual may hold multiple group identities—some shaped by perceptions of common fate and others formed on the basis of similarity. For example, individuals at a professional meeting might be regarded as a group if they wear name tags with identical employer affiliations (similarity), if they belong to the same occupational interest groups (common fate), or if they "hang around" together at the meeting (proximity). From a bona fide group perspective, individuals hold multiple group identities that vary in degrees and that change through social interactions.

Thus a bona fide group orientation treats a group as a fluid, amoeba-like entity that alters contexts as it moves and shifts. Permeable boundaries change the shape and dynamics of internal processes. In like manner, the internal dynamics of group members form and reshape the nature of boundaries and group identity. Boundaries, then, are seen as socially constructed, simultaneously integrating the group into and differentiating it from the other systems that it encompasses and in which it is embedded.

The second distinguishing characteristic of bona fide groups is *interdependence with immediate context*. In laboratory and zero-history groups, context is either assigned to the group or controlled by the investigator. Laboratory research typically focuses on only a few features of context, for example, task type, deadlines, and directives. Aspects of a group's external environment are so varied and "messy" that laboratory studies often isolate the internal dynamics of groups by controlling contextual variables. In effect, research needs to expand its conceptualization of the role of context in group life.

Although research on natural groups relies heavily on the social context for understanding external sources of influence, the bona fide group approach treats this characteristic differently. In a bona fide group perspective, *interdependence with immediate context* refers to the reciprocal relationship between the group and its environment as determined by: (a) intergroup communication, (b) coordinated actions among groups, (c) negotiation of jurisdiction or autonomy, and (d) interpretations or frames for making sense of intergroup relationships.

Intergroup communication is evident in network studies on the frequency and pattern of interaction among individuals who cross groups (Blau & Alba, 1982). Research on group linkage roles such as gatekeepers, liaisons, and linking pins show how members develop influence within and outside their groups (Rogers & Kincaid, 1981). Interorganizational network studies show how the personal nature of intergroup ties may impede an organization from acting in its own best interest (Seabright, Leventhal, & Fichman, 1992). A bona fide perspective allows researchers to extend these works by focusing on the interrelationships between group deliberations and intergroup communication.

The second component of interdependence with context, *coordinated actions among groups,* centers on interlocked behaviors among groups. Task coordination, work-flow interdependence, information specialization, and organizational structures influence the frequency, amount, and type of interactions among groups. Task characteristics such as complexity, urgency, and centrality shape the degree of coordinated action across groups (Putnam, 1989). These actions, however, are agenda items for deliberation within the group as well as for coordination with external units. More important, they are constituted socially rather than given to groups as structural characteristics.

The third component, *negotiation of jurisdiction and autonomy,* relates to interaction that shapes responsibility and accountability for a task. Internal and external communication that centers on interpreting group goals, seeking approval for actions, negotiating and legitimating authority, deciding on ownership, and accountability for decisions relates to jurisdiction and autonomy. High levels of task coordination often promote frequent within-group deliberations on decision jurisdiction (Greenwood & Jenkins, 1981).

A fourth component of this characteristic in a bona fide group perspective is consideration of *interpretative frames* that members generate to make sense of intergroup relationships. Members bring to the group a set of divergent interests, idiosyncratic languages, and disparate conceptual frames that reflect their differentiation. Through their deliberations, group members construct alternative social realities that may or may not conflict with individual interpretive frames, stereotypes of other groups, and perceptions of intergroup relationships. These social constructions form the basis of identity formation and the nature of group boundaries. Members do not have to reach convergence in their interpretations of group identity; however, group members may presume that other individuals hold similar interpretations about the group.

A bona fide group perspective recognizes that group members shape their environments as they are influenced by them. For instance, a team made up of members from different organizational departments may be influenced by priorities and biases from these departments as well as by interpretations about their teams formed from within the group. Their actions in the group may also be taken back to other groups and change how they function. Context is nested in the interactions of members because each message references and negotiates intergroup interdependence. A bona fide group perspective examines this reciprocal flow of influence between the group and its environment.

In summary, the degree to which a group's boundaries are static or fluid, permeable or impenetrable, stems from: multiple memberships and role identities, overlapping memberships and representative roles, fluctuations in membership, and group identity formation. In like manner, interdependence with immediate context indexes the degree to which a group depends on its environment to perform its task and the extent to which other units rely on the group to function effectively. Interdependence is socially constructed and assessed through: intergroup communication, coordinated actions among groups, negotiation of jurisdiction and autonomy, and interpretative frames for making sense of intergroup relationships.

A bona fide approach enters into the study of group process through focusing first on group *boundaries* and intergroup *interdependence*. That is, socially constituted boundaries form the nexus for understanding how group members interact. The notion of bona fide groups, then, serves as a lens for understanding the nature of "groupness" as constituted by individuals inside and outside that collective. All groups exhibit some degree of permeable and fluid boundaries and dependence with social context. The bona fide group approach examines how group interaction defines boundaries and interdependence with context.

A bona fide group perspective does not privilege boundary spanning and the external environment over internal group dynamics. Nor does it contend that the external context determines internal interactions. Some groups may construct their identities with limited reliance on external influences, whereas others may develop strong dependencies on units outside the group. Outside units may treat a group as dependent, isolated, or interconnected. A bona fide group perspective makes the dynamic and systemic embeddedness of group experiences central to the study of the internal workings of a group. It is a lens for describing action. Whether groups are conscious or unaware of these activities, they are continually reacting to the collective construction of boundaries and context.

As an example of how interdependence and boundaries are socially constructed, Putnam and Stohl (1990) described an interdisciplinary core curriculum committee. The college dean asked members to function as experts, not as representatives of their departmental biases. Even though committee members sought inputs from external groups, including departments, the group made decisions as if it were autonomous. The internal deliberations of committee members reflected rational decision making in that members canvassed alternatives, sought expert opinion, suspended initial judgments, and struggled with the decisions. They put their personal preferences aside, but the group failed to adapt to the political realities of its task, to develop an effective solution, and to integrate intergroup acceptability into problem analysis and evaluation of alternatives.

Related Theories

The bona fide group perspective is related to but distinct from two theories in organizational behavior—embedded intergroup relations and organizational anarchy. Alderfer's (1977, 1986, 1992) theory of embedded intergroup relations posits that groups are embedded in a suprasystem that contains interlocked subsystems. All individuals are group representatives and every interaction becomes an intergroup transaction (Alderfer & Smith, 1982). Behaviors and feelings in groups reflect a complex interplay between group memberships and the social contexts in which people find themselves. The bona fide group perspective parallels the theory of embedded intergroup relations in both characteristics—interdependence with context and permeable and fluid boundaries. Embeddedness implies that groups are interdependent with their context and engage in intergroup communication, coordinated actions among groups, and negotiations about jurisdiction and autonomy. In like manner, embedded intergroup relations theory treats an individual's emotions, cognitions, and behaviors as shaped through multiple group memberships and group representative roles. Intergroup relationships become the root of individual as well as group identity.

These two approaches, however, cast the formation and nature of groups very differently. In Alderfer's (1977, 1986) theory, intergroup relations rather than group dynamics form the basis for groupness. Representativeness is fixed through identity (e.g., sex, ethnicity, age) or organizational groups (e.g., task similarities) rather than through interactions within the group. Representativeness becomes a structural and deterministic trait, one that remains static despite the way members talk and act. Thus all individuals represent multiple groups, even when these affiliations are not socially constructed as salient. Moreover, Alderfer's theory focuses on values and perceptions of individual members rather than on group activities, such as decision making.

A bona fide group perspective, in contrast, makes interpretive frames and social interaction central to the definition of member representativeness and interconnectedness of groups. In effect, boundaries and intergroup connectedness are salient characteristics that are socially constructed inside the group and through connections among groups.

Individual and group identity form through social interactions rather than from stereotypes or sociological labels.

Unlike Alderfer's theory, *organized anarchy*, or the garbage can model of decision making, focuses directly on problem solving in organizations (Cohen, March, & Olsen, 1972; March & Olsen, 1976). It sets forth a theory of nonrational decision making aimed at the organizational level and rooted in ambiguity of situations, fluidity of processes, influence of exogenous occurrences, and timing of events. What happens in organizational decision making is not necessarily what was intended to happen.

A decision is an outcome or an interpretation of independent streams of activity rather than a systematic or rational choice (Cohen et al., 1972). The flow of individual actions, fluctuations in attention to problems, part-time participation in decisions, overload, and organizational slack impinge on how groups make decisions and how they manage consequences of their actions. In the organized anarchy model, decisions evolve over long periods of time, committee members vacillate in their attention and commitment to group tasks, and events outside of the group alter problem solving.

Even though this perspective operates at the organizational level, it posits assumptions that parallel a bona fide group perspective. In particular, both perspectives underscore the importance of part-time and fluid participation and the role of context factors on the internal processes of decision making. Both examine decision making as a contextual event that depends on the interactive flows of streams of events in choice situations. However, because the two approaches differ in foci and nexus for decision making, differences between the two approaches also exist. A bona fide group perspective is not the same as nonrational decision making. In effect, groups might adhere to a political or bargaining model and still exemplify the characteristics of permeable and fluid boundaries and interdependence with context. Variables such as attention, load, slack, and ambiguity are requisites of organized anarchy, but may not typify bona fide groups. In effect, the garbage can model centers on a form or type of decision making that incorporates features of bona fide groups; however, the bona fide group perspective is not necessarily limited to nonrational decision making.

A Review of Bona Fide Groups: Implications for Decision Making

Decision making within a bona fide group perspective, however, differs from traditional models of problem solving. A decision is a choice that group members make among alternatives available to them (Fisher & Ellis, 1990). Although decision making is only one thing a group does, it occupies a central role in group research and often overshadows other constructs. Decision making lies at the center of other group practices, including links to other groups and social relationships with other group members (Poole & Hirokawa, 1986).

Researchers have not completely ignored the influence of boundaries and context on group decision making. To uncover insights about decision making in bona fide groups, this chapter reviews studies that incorporate at least one of the characteristics or features of bona fide groups. Although a number of studies include some feature of bona fide groups, few studies examine the degree to which group boundaries are permeable, fluid, and interdependent with context. Even fewer studies explore these characteristics by examining both the internal and the external interaction of the group. These studies can be divided into two clusters: research that treats internal communication as primary while referencing external factors and research that privileges external communication while acknowledging internal group processes. None of these studies emphasize both factors equally.

INTERNAL COMMUNICATION AS PRIMARY

The studies reviewed in this section adopt a container model of group process. However, they demonstrate that incorporating as well as ignoring external inputs influences group development, information processing, proposal analysis, conflict management, and decision effectiveness.

Through incorporating external inputs, Gersick (1988, 1989) showed how vacillating between inertia and radical change led to a punctuated equilibrium model of group development. Radical changes in decision-making processes stemmed from such external interventions as requests of authority figures, the speed and timing of deadlines, and new ideas brought into the group. She found that contacts with individuals outside the group typically occurred in the first stages or at the mid-point of a group's deliberations rather than in the latter stages of development.

In a laboratory study of business decisions, Gladstein and Reilly (1985) observed that teams that experienced environmental crises (e.g., strikes, price controls, tariffs) and severe time pressures reduced group deliberations, restricted information processing, and used fewer communication channels than did groups with less pressure from the environment. In effect, crisis interventions in a group shaped decision making by accelerating group development.

Using a discourse-analytic approach, Geist and Chandler (1984) illustrated how a group negotiated interpretive frames with members of other units. By applying organizational rules and targets of identification, members of a health care team constructed images of outside groups and shaped perceptions of their own team's jurisdiction. In a follow-up study of these health care teams, Sabourin and Geist (1990) centered on the enactment of proposals in decision making. They showed how proposals expanded and developed through members' employment of organizational norms to challenge positions. By cycling and recycling proposals, group members made decisions. Premises drawn from the health care context influenced internal choices and shaped the nature of group proposals.

External inputs were also salient in Donnellon's (1994) study of cross-functional teams in a manufacturing organization. She centered on the way team talk constructed boundaries, group jurisdiction, and intergroup relations. She posited that member exaggeration of between-group differences and statements of strong identification with external groups shaped internal group processes. In Team 2000, Donnellon described how members from four different departments reached a decision on product refinement by negotiating marketing's role in evaluating the product. They sent Joan, their ambassador, as the liaison to marketing. The group decided not to drop the product, but they agreed to fine-tune it for marketing. Their forms of speech, references to their own team, and comments about outside groups reinforced team solidarity and enhanced group decision making. They managed internal conflict among members through collaboration and win-win negotiation rather than by forcing the power plays.

In contrast, "Voltometer," a cross-functional team comprised of members from five departments, experienced difficulty in deciding which peripherals to include in the final stage of product development. The decision-making process was characterized by low group identification, strong allegiance to functional departments, a win-lose style of conflict management, and power plays of members. Group members vacillated from agenda setting, to defending boundaries with functional departments, to negotiating differences through adversarial stances. Historically rooted animosities among organizational departments manifested themselves as adversarial, win-lose conflicts. Even digressions from the task reflected power plays among representatives. For instance, as the group discussed ordering lunch, members made snide comments about each other's departments, noting who should pay or could not pay. This interaction culminated when a marketing member commented, "You're on a diet when you're eating on engineering's budget" (Donnellon, 1994, p. 107).

Donnellon concluded that changing and overlapping membership also influenced decision making. Marketing members, who had high status in the organization and high stakes in the project, joined Voltometer 5 months after the group began. Although they tried to impose their agenda on the group, other members resisted. Analysis of the interaction revealed that the way group members perceived and cast overlapping membership stifled decision making and led to delays in product introduction.

Ignoring external inputs may also have a detrimental effect on decision making. Studies of groupthink showed how insularity, stable group membership, external pressures, and high levels of cohesiveness led to withdrawal from the external environment (Gouran, Hirokawa, & Martz, 1986; Hensley & Griffin, 1986; Janis, 1972, 1982). These studies demonstrated how group members ignored external information and resources, built boundaries that were static and impenetrable, and cut off communication with their social context. Moreover, the faulty decision-making processes in the groupthink model (Janis & Mann, 1977) seemed rooted in a provocative situational context.

What is unclear in this research is how forces external to these groups construct and communicate images that perpetuate group insularity. For instance, bankers and community leaders on the Board of Trustees at Kent State persisted in their decision to erect a gymnasium on the site of the deaths of the Kent State Four by casting their opponents as politically irrational (Hensley & Griffin, 1986). A bona fide group perspective would ask how communication between these constituencies contributed to these conditions for groupthink. In effect, how do groups influence their environments by developing images of external groups, and by probing and testing their constituencies as well as being shaped by them?

These studies produce evidence for an inverse relationship between sources external to the group and member deliberations within the group. Neither total dependence on nor total isolation from external groups facilitates effective decision making. On the one hand, boundaries that are too amorphous hinder decision making through weak group identity, adversarial conflict among members, and strong representative roles. On the other hand, boundaries that are too impenetrable hinder decision making through strong group identity, avoidance of conflict, and absence of accountability to external groups. Thus a balance seems necessary between overreliance on external units and too much dependence on the group itself in decision making.

Overall, these studies suggest that group members need to foster ambassador relationships with external groups (Ancona, 1990); to facilitate information processing across boundaries (Gladstein & Reilly, 1985); and to develop proposals consistent with values, norms, and changes in their environment (Sabourin & Geist, 1990). The majority of these studies, however, treat the social context as a given rather than as a social construction of the group. Donnellon's (1994) research provides a refreshing exception. However, none of these studies directly examines communication with external groups.

EXTERNAL OR BOUNDARY COMMUNICATION AS PRIMARY

A majority of the studies on embedded groups in organizations emphasize external or boundary communication among groups. Hence they focus on the frequency, pattern, and nature of communication among groups and give only passing reference to the interactions within the group. The question that these studies address is, How do groups reach out or direct their activities outward? These studies operate from the assumption that groups manage their dependence on the environment; create, enact, and adapt to their task environment; and become linked to their social context (Ancona, 1987).

This external linkage is accomplished through negotiating resources, exchanging information, scanning for problems, serving as boundary representatives, and guarding the prerogatives of the group (Ancona & Caldwell, 1988). By negotiating with other units, group members control their power-dependency relationships and their unique contributions. Gladstein and Caldwell (1985) described a product team that depended on marketing, manufacturing, and sales for its decision making. One way the team negotiated interdependence was to have its leader serve on key committees in other groups and to invite members of marketing and manufacturing to become part of the product team during peak times of coordination. Brett and Rognes (1986) demonstrated how exchanging agreements served as a form of intergroup transaction to manage turf conflicts between units.

The majority of these studies, however, do not center on decision making per se, but on overall group effectiveness. The general conclusion from this work is that isolated groups are less effective in accomplishing their tasks than are groups that reach out to their external environments (Ancona & Caldwell, 1988; Thornton, 1978). Openness and communication satisfaction within the group are critical to task effectiveness (Gladstein, 1984). Team members assess effectiveness through reliance on internal processes and they evaluate performance through probing the environment and implementing proposals (Ancona, 1990; Stohl, 1986, 1987).

In a study of interdisciplinary health care teams, Berteotti and Seibold (1994) found that overlapping role identities, departmental allegiances, group stereotypes, and turnover contributed to team ineffectiveness. Interactions of team members showed that faulty decision making, flawed information exchange, incomplete survey of alternatives, and skewed evaluation of options characterized decision making. The professionals, who aligned themselves with the hospital rather than the hospice team, treated the volunteers as overstepping their boundaries; the volunteers saw the nurses as lazy and shiftless. Volunteers emerged as isolated from problem solving and cut off from interacting with professionals. Turnover in the hospital administration, cutbacks in funding, and confusion in the organizational hierarchy exacerbated efforts to negotiate effective role relationships among the hospice team members.

Multiple and overlapping roles may also contribute to minimal participation and fluid involvement in a group. Olsen (1976) investigated a search committee's deliberations in the selection of a college dean. Working from a garbage can model of decision making, he demonstrated how the outcome of the group evolved from lengthy time delays, membership turnover, and high external load on members' time. Delays in responses to offers, game playing by the search committee chair, and objections to policies of the current dean shaped the committee's start-and-stop pattern of decision making and their eventual selection of the search committee chair to be the next dean.

These studies indicate that difficulty in negotiating multiple and overlapping roles leads to problems in decision-making and overall effectiveness. A bona fide group perspective examines how members negotiate or fail to negotiate boundaries as potential explanations for ineffective decision making.

Decision-making effectiveness, however, may be defined differently through a bona fide lens. Stohl and Holmes (1993) suggest, for example, that scholars could revitalize decision-making research by expanding the concept of decision effectiveness. Typically, research on effectiveness treats decision quality as an objective attribute that surfaces at the time of the decision. This assumption decontextualizes the task and separates it from its historical and temporal context (see, e.g., Gouran, Hirokawa, Julian, & Leatham, 1993; Hirokawa & Pace, 1983). A bona fide group perspective, however, locates decisions in the richly textured milieu of group interaction that evolves over time. Longitudinal assessments of effectiveness arise from the everyday practices faced by ongoing groups. Moreover, long-term assessments of decision quality place the task in a rich context in which identifying stakeholders, determining overlapping domains, and accommodating external constituencies are more important requisites for effectiveness than are the rational criteria previously identified.

Studies that centered directly on external communication in decision-making groups provide support for alternative patterns of problem solving. Barker, Melville, and Pacanowsky (1993) observed that changes in corporate culture and interpretations of intergroup relations influenced a self-directed work team's decisions. Initially, the team operated with a high degree of autonomy for internal deliberations. But changes in formal roles among team members, lines of external communication, and organizational culture caused the group to turn back to directives from authority figures for decision inputs. Thus, in deciding how to deal with missing parts, the group sent its coordinator to the vice president and then ultimately rejected this person's suggestion because it ran counter to the new culture. Decision premises replaced downward directives in influencing group choices. Following this incident, the group increased its productivity and its decision freedom. This study suggested that decision autonomy was negotiated among individuals and groups through testing procedures and decision premises. Changes in the external context impinged on how group members coordinated decision processes and selected criteria for evaluating alternatives.

Studies of external group communication showed how decision making focused on acceptability and implementation of the solution. In her work on embedded groups, Ancona (1987) argued for action rationality rather than for a normative model of decision making. Rather than relying on abstract criteria to judge the "best" decision, group members who embraced action rationality used "efficiency" as the top criterion. Efficiency included acceptability of the decision within and outside of the group, legitimizing group decisions in the larger context, and bolstering only a few alternatives (Brunsson, 1982).

Decision making in these groups fluctuated between formation and implementation of alternatives rather than between choosing alternatives first and then figuring out how to get them adopted (Gladstein & Quinn, 1985). Thus feasibility and commitment to a decision guided the generation and evaluation of proposals. Proposals also emanated from individuals outside the group who were likely to execute the decision. The groups balanced internal needs with external constraints and developed effective decisions that got outsiders committed to group outcomes.

A bona fide perspective recognizes that communication about the political and historical constraints in a group's environment plays a salient role in decision making. Indeed, these constraints may be more significant than are the purely rational functions that emanate from the efficacy of decisions. Ancona's (1987) study suggests that decision making in bona fide groups might follow a circular-interactive pattern rather than a linear-preformulated sequence. Group members would cycle through various phases of formation and implementation, moving back and forth from generating and evaluating alternatives to gaining commitment for courses of action to concerns for implementation. Some group members might champion particular options, form internal and external coalitions around partial decisions, and seek support for their positions (Gladstein & Quinn, 1985). The distinctions between decision making and implementation would become increasingly blurred.

This review suggests that decision making within a bona fide group lens differs from traditional studies of group problem solving. External factors influence group development, proposal analysis, and frequency and amount of group member interaction; thus groups need to negotiate a balance between dependence on and isolation from their social context. Overly strong dependence on the external context restricts internal communication, lowers group identity, and leads to ineffective decision making. Extreme isolation often produces symptoms of groupthink—namely, insularity, deference to authority, flawed information flow, and ineffective decisions. Inability to manage multiple and overlapping roles contributes to ineffective decision making through rooting group deliberations in stereotypes of external units, functional departmental allegiances, and intergroup power plays.

These findings may hinge on the type of decision or the task of the group. Some tasks, like production, are more central to external groups and require frequent coordination among units. Other tasks need very little input, approval, or coordination with outside groups. Most tasks require some type of balance and linkage between internal and external units, especially when both boundaries and interdependence are negotiated. In effect, the nature and coordination requirements of a group's task are worked out as group members negotiate jurisdiction, autonomy, and interdependence with context.

A bona fide group perspective also reframes internal processes of decision making. Proposal arguments, decision premises, and even the modus operandi for making decisions hinge on external norms, cultural changes, and directives from authority. Efficiency and acceptability surface as essential criteria for decision making. Group members vacillate between formation and implementation of decisions. Thus the decision-making process might fluctuate among analyzing the problem, generating options, gaining external commitment for options, introducing new problem analysis, working on implementation of alternatives, introducing new options, bolstering and campaigning for solutions, reassessing the problem, and reaching consensus. Decision making is as much an external process as it is internal, because the boundaries of groups are fluid and shifting.

Decision Making and Bona Fide Groups

To explore this alternative model, this section compares a bona fide group perspective with three approaches to group decision making: normative, decision emergence, and structurational (Fisher & Ellis, 1990). A case example of an ad hoc group on increasing graduate student stipends illustrates how each of these traditional approaches differs from a bona fide group view of decision making.

A NORMATIVE/FUNCTIONAL APPROACH

A normative/functional approach assumes that task-oriented groups make rational decisions. Task and decisions are isomorphic and shape group roles. Decisions are treated as intentional, conscious, rational, and nonobvious. Furthermore, the normative/functional approach assumes that relevant information is available and can be acquired. It posits that the task is within the intellectual capabilities of the group members. That is, members have access to the information that enables choice; they weigh alternatives in light of this information; and they choose the best alternative, typically through consensus (Gouran & Hirokawa, 1983). Group members have a shared commitment to make the best or the most effective decisions, and once a decision is made it becomes fixed and likely to be implemented. The normative/functional approach encompasses the work on vigilant decision making, functional views of decision making, and logical problem solving.

A bona fide group perspective differs from a normative/functional model of decision making in that it assumes decision making is not linear nor necessarily intentional. Decisions may evolve through default, omission, and even neglect. Overlapping group membership, shifting group identities, and changes in the environment suggest that groups do not fully control decisions. Decisions may be unintentional and difficult to isolate in time and space. In a bona fide view, a group may not own nor even be accountable for its decisions. Problems, alternatives, and criteria for effectiveness may arise outside the group's jurisdiction or may stem from negotiating the group's identity. Furthermore, groups often assess appropriateness of decisions based on criteria that differ from the task as it was originally conceived. How individuals outside the group talk about the problem may influence the group and provide interpretations as to what the problem means. In like manner, the group's decision-making process and the outcome it reaches may change or alter the group's context.

A DECISION EMERGENCE APPROACH

Decision emergence treats decision making in a nonlinear, nonrational way. Unlike the normative/functional approach, which assumes that interaction is meaningfully and rationally sequenced, the decision emergence approach treats choices as surfacing from a global discussion of issues that cycles back again and again in an in-depth analysis (Poole & Roth, 1989). According to Scheidel and Crowell (1964), group members engage in a reach-test pattern in which discussions reach back into prior deliberations, modify ideas, and test new proposals. Agreement on an issue surfaces by accident through role struggles, factual analyses, and the anchoring of ideas in this back-and-forth movement. Decision making is not necessarily rational or intentional, but it is bounded by time and space. Relevant communication is assumed to occur in meetings of the entire group membership, not outside the small group deliberations.

The bona fide orientation differs from decision emergence in centering on how decision making constitutes group boundaries and develops linkages with the environment. Thus issues that cycle from global to more in-depth analysis may reflect factors in a group's environment, not just the way members analyze a problem. The focus shifts from how group members attack a problem to how decision processes relate to the group environment. For example, concerns about the appropriateness of a problem might trigger a renegotiation and redefinition of the group autonomy, which alters cycles and stages of internal decision making. In like manner, changes in the group's environment (e.g., budget cuts, crises, market shifts) might alter the way members deliberate and conceive of problems, perhaps altering the reach-test pattern or the back-and-forth movement. Thus, the reflexivity between the group and its environment becomes central to the internal dynamics of group decision making.

A STRUCTURATIONAL APPROACH

A structurational view of decision making departs from the other two theories by examining the way a group produces structures and processes (Poole & Doelger, 1986; Poole, Seibold, & McPhee, 1986). Through interaction, group members appropriate rules and procedures from social systems and enact these rules within the group. For example, an individual might import a specific decision-making procedure like majority rule. Thus the group depends on and draws from individual and institutional knowledge structures in developing rules and resources for group processes. The rules and resources that members use are produced, recreated, and reinforced in group interaction. In effect, structural features of the group shape member activities and group interactions produce and reproduce these structural features.

One structure that influences a group's decision process is the group's task representation. Even though members bring impressions of the task into the group, they alter their interpretations of both the substance and the decision logic through social interactions. Cultural decision norms and objective task properties, however, surface in group deliberations as individual representations, societal conceptions of good arguments, group decision schemes, and ways of structuring coherent interaction.

The bona fide perspective is closer to a structurational view of decision making than it is to other approaches. It differs from this perspective, however, by entering the decision-making process through the intersection of internal and external processes, the negotiation of group boundaries, and the amount of interdependence between a group and its context. The bona fide group perspective does not presume that group members have control of task representation, knowledge structures, and decision schemes. Rather these structures, as structuration theory suggests, are continually infused and negotiated through the way group members interact with individuals and units outside their group. External contingencies such as changes in decisions premises

(Barker et al., 1993) and criteria for a logical argument (Sabourin & Geist, 1990) alter the surface and deep-level structures of the group. A bona fide group perspective calls into question the source and permanence of "objective" task properties and decision logic.

A bona fide group perspective also supplements structuration theory by examining the reflexivity of structure in interactions among group members as well as communication with individuals outside the group. Structures are thus produced and reproduced through the way groups form and alter their boundaries and their transactions with individuals outside the group. Group identity, then, becomes an alternative structuring modality. Structuration theory is also concerned with group identity formation and boundary issues. Communication with external groups is less prominent in this perspective (Poole et al., 1986). Another way that the bona fide group perspective supplements structuration theory is by examining how breakpoints, disruptions, and multiple phases stem from key moments of interaction outside the group or the way group members construct representations of external units (Donnellon, 1994; Gersick, 1988).

A CASE EXEMPLAR: COMPARISON OF APPROACHES

The following elaborated example shows how a bona fide group perspective differs from each of three decision-making approaches. A dean appoints a subcommittee of department chairs to study a problem with graduate student stipends. Department chairs have complained that that the stipends for graduate students are too low, have not kept up with the cost of living, and are not competitive with peer institutions. The subcommittee members are part of an Executive Council made up of all department chairs in the college. The Executive Council members represent faculty and graduate students in 11 different units in the college.

One key feature of decision making is the group's jurisdiction. This subcommittee, then, must negotiate its area of freedom, authority for collecting data, ability to represent departments, and parameters for determining what is a feasible recommendation. It must clarify its task, that is, what type of alternatives are being recommended and to whom? Rather than address these issues directly, the subcommittee proceeds with its task and negotiates the scope, breadth, and nature of the project through making and testing decisions. Members gather data through a survey of peer institutions and they ask each department to suggest items for the survey.

A normative model of decision making would examine the way the subcommittee collects data, analyzes them, develops solutions, weighs alternatives, and arrives at an effective decision. The normative model asserts that individuals assume roles to facilitate the decision-making process. Implementation of the decision is not an issue because the normative model assumes effective decisions are readily implemented.

A bona fide group perspective, in contrast, would examine the way data, analytical frameworks, solutions, and criteria for evaluation provide a means of negotiating the group's jurisdiction and decision process. Researchers might focus on the dean's desire to have the subcommittee and the dean's goal for department heads to absorb the costs of implementing any changes. The way data are collected, analyzed, and applied to the decision process also reflects how the group sees itself and its relationship to the other units on campus.

Task roles in the group carry departmental identities and overlapping memberships with other university committees. Knowledge gleaned from serving on other committees functions as a resource and a means of negotiating "groupness." Group members renegotiate their priorities when affiliations outside the group take precedence in deliberations and when members assess decisions in light of how they may influence external relationships. Finally, acceptability and likelihood of implementing a decision become critical in evaluating the proposals. A bona fide group perspective includes criteria of appropriateness and acceptability into internal and external deliberations about the decision.

The decision emergence approach examines how a group reaches a solution through cycles of development. The group members might begin with a surface view of the problem—for example, the comment, "If we could just get more money to each department, then we would have a solution"—to the point that the group cycles deeper and deeper into the problem, uncovering inequities in stipends, disparity in distribution of funds, and different bases for allocating graduate stipends. As the group wrestles with the solutions—for instance, equal versus proportional allocation of money and cost of living versus competitive salary increases—members realize that they do not understand the problem, and they cycle through analysis and testing until they get deeper into the issues. Through a reach-test model of sorting through the issues, the group engages in role struggles among members who represent different types of degree programs and who battle for authority—for example, "Why are economics graduate students paid twice the amount of philosophy graduate students? I realize that this department needs even more money to be competitive with peer institutions, but is it fair to allocate economics more stipend dollars when they already have the highest stipends in the college?" Through anchoring decision points and struggling to define the problem, a decision emerges.

Although a bona fide group perspective would also reflect a spiral pattern, this approach differs from the decision emergence view by linking cycles, testing, and role struggles to permeable boundaries and group interdependence with its context. In effect, shifts in the decision process emanate from vacillation between formation and implementation. For instance, group members might propose a tax across departments to raise money for increasing stipends and then distribute these monies in proportion to need or to the amount of tax paid. Investigating ways to implement this proposal might reveal that three departments could not afford the tax nor would they be willing to pay it, even if the funds would increase their own graduate student stipends. Information on acceptability of proposals might shift deliberations back to a reassessment of the problem, resulting in alternative solutions.

In the meantime, one committee member might advocate to external groups that any solution must enhance graduate recruitment for all departments, not just for those with the lowest stipends. During the deliberations, one member of the committee receives a major grant and asks for a replacement on the committee. The new member brings in additional values, ideas, and insights about the problem. The chair of the committee might get new information from the dean about his criteria for an efficient decision. As the group cycles among problem formation and analysis, generation of proposals, and concerns for implementation, it reshapes its boundaries and its interdependence with context. Through campaigning and advocacy of proposals, the group negotiates its jurisdiction, influences its constituents, and widens the boundaries of decision making.

A structurational approach would center on the way the subcommittee enacts individual and collective task representations from cultural norms and task properties (Poole & Doelger, 1986). In particular, it might examine the way group members develop a decision logic through task representations. Decision logics, as implicit theories for how the group should make a decision, entail stages and strategies for decisions such as problem definition, problem analysis, decision search, solution evaluation, and implementation (Poole & Doelger, 1986).

One type of decision logic is information gathering and analysis. In the subcommittee on graduate student stipends, group interaction draws from cultural and task norms for gathering and interpreting data, use of information, and procedures for evaluating it. Members begin by making presumptions as to the nature of the problem and then proceed to gather information to verify their presumptions. Specifically, their presumption is that graduate stipends throughout the college are too low. They conduct a survey across departments and universities to gather comparative data on amounts and increases in graduate students' stipends. Governed by the criterion of "gathering useful information," they draw a select sample of peer institutions, separating data for different types of degree programs, and deciphering what was included or excluded within a stipend (e.g., tuition, health benefits, fees). Hence, they enact a collective representation of the task through agreement on the problem and through collecting quantitative data to verify their presumptions.

A structuration perspective would show how these information-gathering practices produce and reproduce deep structures of what constitutes data, including rationality, modes of "unbiased" data collection, and representations of data in problem formation. Group members not only draw on these deep structures but also reproduce them through their interaction. Through reproducing and modifying them, members retain these structures for future interactions. Structures of information gathering aid in legitimating problem formation and interpreting such comments as, "Even though you think our graduate students make a lot of money, look how much lower our stipends are than those at peer institutions." "At almost every peer institution, graduate students in philosophy are paid poorly. Why should we have to raise their stipends here?" Members also use comparative data as a basis of establishing member authority and task expertise, economic cost-benefit calculations, and decision effectiveness.

A bona fide group perspective differs from structuration in locating the nexus of group interactions in representations of boundary and interdependence with context. Thus member interaction about sources outside the group, activities generated through intergroup contact, and external communication about the group would be incorporated into the surface-level analysis. At the level of deep structure, boundary and interdependence function as overarching representations that influence the production and reproduction of decisions. In structurational terms, these concepts are additional structures that the group employs.

Information gathering, in a bona fide group perspective, centers on boundaries and interdependence, not just on task representations. To return to the subcommittee example, discussions of information gathering indicate who, how, and when other individuals and groups will enter into decision making. Interactions across departments become a medium for defining jurisdiction and group boundaries. In deciding how to gather information, group members draw on their images of the Executive Council, the dean, and the disciplinary fields in the college. They design their survey to reflect their representations of which boundaries are relevant and what roles individuals outside the group play in their decision making.

Group member representations of boundaries and interdependence also interface with interactions outside the group. In particular, several department heads who are not serving on the subcommittee may decide to monitor the group's activities and send regular feedback through a group member. These surface-level interactions, then, can alter representations of boundary and shift the group's dependence on external sources. The dean's goals and criteria for a realistic decision affect how the group responds to the problem and how members generate solutions. Moreover, group members have a decision strategy to influence the actions that the dean takes on this issue. They want to shape his priorities and ways of viewing the problem. Hence, their deliberations reflect this political decision logic of "changing" the dean's and the college's attitude toward graduate education.

In effect, a bona fide group perspective expands the surface level to include interactions between the members and individuals/units outside of the group and communication among constituents about the group. It shifts the foci or locus of control from internal deliberations to representations of boundary and interdependence that permeate interactions among group members. It purports that representations of boundary and interdependence infuse and shape individual and collective task representations. At the deep structure level, representations of boundary and interdependence draw from cultural and organizational norms, particularly notions of autonomy, community, and control that are rooted in social institutions.

Summary and Conclusion

A bona fide group perspective sets forth an alternative approach for examining group decision making. Through incorporating boundaries and interdependence, features of decision making that other models omit become central to the deliberative process. Such features as negotiation of jurisdiction, representative roles, implementation of decision, criteria of acceptability and appropriateness, and communication with individuals outside the group become critical to the decision-making process. Moreover, a bona fide group perspective transforms other aspects of group decision making, such as problem definition and analysis, information gathering, generation and evaluation of solutions, argumentation and use of evidence, sequencing of activities, accountability for decisions, and role struggles.

Unlike the normative model of decision making, a bona fide group approach treats implementation as an essential element in problem analysis and generation of solutions. Rather than being the final step in a decision sequence, implementation permeates deliberations on all aspects of decision making. Group members shift back and forth from problem formation to implementation to solution analysis.

Unlike the decision emergence model, a bona fide group perspective highlights how interactions with external groups influence the way groups move between superficial and in-depth problem analysis and how they anchor decision points. Unlike a structurational approach, a bona fide perspective locates cultural norms and task properties in external as well as internal deliberations. Boundary and interdependence function as forms of representation that shape and are shaped by task deliberations.

This review and analysis of the bona fide group perspective sets forth several hypotheses for future testing. In particular, inability to negotiate the impact of multiple and fluctuating member roles may lead to ineffective decision making. Group members who develop strong dependence on other units are likely to restrict internal communications, lower group identity, have difficulty reaching consensus, and operate from diverse decision premises. Extreme isolation of groups tends to promote groupthink in problem solving. Group members who fuse the decision-making process with concerns for implementation and acceptability of decisions engage in a different form of vigilant decision making. Images or representations of external groups are socially constructed through both internal and external group deliberations.

Finally, a bona fide group perspective calls into question the fundamental notions of what constitutes a group. Definitions of a group often center on common goals among members, task-oriented activity, and identity separate from social context (Hackman, 1990). A bona fide group perspective challenges the very notion of "groupness" and boundaries as fixtures for group identity. It calls into question the systems theory model that treats groups as containers. It conceives of a group as patterns of repetitive behaviors that become interdependent and interstructured. As Weick (1979) observes, "Boundaries between [groups] and environments are never quite as clear-cut or as stable as many . . . theorists think. These boundaries shift, disappear, and are arbitrarily drawn" (p. 132). A bona fide group perspective provides an alternative theoretical model for the study of group decision making, one rooted in the social construction of boundaries and of the social context.

References

Adelman, M. B., & Frey, L. R. (1994). The pilgrim must embark: Creating and sustaining community in a residential facility for people with AIDS. In L. R. Frey (Ed.), *Group communication in context* (pp. 3-22). Hillsdale, NJ: Lawrence Erlbaum.

Alderfer, C. P. (1977). Group and intergroup relations. In J. Hackman & J. Suttle (Eds.), *Improving life at work* (pp. 227-296). Santa Monica, CA: Goodyear.

Alderfer, C. P. (1986). An intergroup perspective on group dynamics. In J. Lorsch (Ed.), *Handbook of organizational behavior* (pp. 190-222). Englewood Cliffs, NJ: Prentice Hall.

Alderfer, C. P. (1992). Contemporary issues in professional work with groups: Editor's introduction. *Journal of Applied Behavioral Sciences, 28*, 9-14.

Alderfer, C. P., & Smith, K. (1982). Studying intergroup relations embedded in organizations. *Administrative Science Quarterly, 27*, 35-65.

Ancona, D. G. (1987). Groups in organizations: Extending laboratory models. In C. Henrick (Ed.), *Annual review of personality and social psychology: Group and intergroup processes* (pp. 207-231). Newbury Park, CA: Sage.

Ancona, D. G. (1990). Outward bound: Strategies for team survival in an organization. *Academy of Management Journal, 33,* 334-365.

Ancona, D. G., & Caldwell, D. F. (1988). Beyond task and maintenance: Defining external functions in groups. *Group and Organizational Studies, 13,* 468-494.

Ball, M. A. (1994). Vacillating about Vietnam: Secrecy, duplicity, and confusion in the communication of President Kennedy and his advisors. In L. R. Frey (Ed.), *Group communication in context* (pp. 181-198). Hillsdale, NJ: Lawrence Erlbaum.

Barge, J. K., & Keyton, J. (1994). Contextualizing power and social influence in groups. In L. R. Frey (Ed.), *Group communication in context: Studies of natural groups* (pp. 85-105). Hillsdale, NJ: Lawrence Erlbaum.

Barker, J. R., Melville, C. W., & Pacanowsky, M. E. (1993). Self-directed teams at XEL: Changes in communication practices during a program of cultural transformation. *Journal of Applied Communication Research, 21,* 297-312.

Berteotti, C. R., & Seibold, D. R. (1994). Coordination and role-definition problems in health-care teams: A hospice case study. In L. R. Frey (Ed.), *Group communication in context* (pp. 107-131). Hillsdale, NJ: Lawrence Erlbaum.

Blau, J., & Alba, R. (1982). Empowering nets of participation. *Administrative Science Quarterly, 27,* 363-379.

Bormann, E. G. (1975). *Discussion and group methods: Theory and practice* (2nd ed.). New York: Harper & Row.

Brett, J. M., & Rognes, J. K. (1986). Intergroup relations in organizations: A negotiations perspective. In P. Goodman (Ed.), *Designing effective work groups* (pp. 202-236). San Francisco: Jossey-Bass.

Brunsson, N. (1982). The irrationality of action and action rationality: Decisions, ideologies, and organizational actions. *Journal of Management Studies, 19,* 29-44.

Campbell, D. T. (1958). Common fate, similarity, and other indices of the status of aggregates of persons as social entities. *Behavioral Science, 3,* 14-25.

Cohen, M. D., March, J. G., & Olsen, J. P. (1972). A garbage can model of organizational choice. *Administrative Science Quarterly, 17,* 1-25.

Conquergood, D. (1994). Homeboys and hoods: Gang communication and cultural space. In L. R. Frey (Ed.), *Group communication in context* (pp. 23-55). Hillsdale, NJ: Lawrence Erlbaum.

Donnellon, A. (1994). Team work: Linguistic models of negotiating differences. In R. J. Lewicki, B. H. Sheppard, & R. Bies (Eds.), *Research on negotiation in organizations* (Vol. 4, pp. 71-123). Greenwich, CT: JAI.

Fisher, B. A., & Ellis, D. G. (1990). *Small group decision making: Communication and the group process.* New York: McGraw-Hill.

Frey, L. R. (Ed.). (1994). *Innovations in group facilitation: Applications in natural settings.* Cresskill, NJ: Hampton Press.

Geist, P., & Chandler, T. (1984). Account analysis of influence in group decision-making. *Communication Monographs, 51,* 67-78.

Gersick, C. J. G. (1988). Time and transition in work teams: Toward a new model of group development. *Academy of Management Journal, 31,* 9-41.

Gersick, C. J. G. (1989). Marking time: Predictable transitions in work groups. *Academy of Management Journal, 32,* 274-309.

Gladstein, D. L. (1984). Groups in context: A model of task group effectiveness. *Administrative Science Quarterly, 29,* 499-517.

Gladstein, D. L., & Caldwell, D. (1985). Boundary management in new product teams. *Academy of Management Proceedings* (pp. 161-165). San Diego, CA: Academy of Management Association.

Gladstein, D. L., & Quinn, J. B. (1985). Making decisions and producing action: The two faces of strategy. In J. M. Pennings (Ed.), *Organizational strategy and change* (pp. 198-216). San Francisco: Jossey-Bass.

Gladstein, D. L., & Reilly, N. P. (1985). Group decision making under threat: The tycoon game. *Academy of Management Journal, 28*, 613-627.

Gouran, D. S., & Hirokawa, R. Y. (1983). The role of communication in decision making groups: A functional perspective. In M. S. Mander (Ed.), *Communication in transition* (pp. 168-185). New York: Praeger.

Gouran, D. S., Hirokawa, R. Y., Julian, K. M., & Leatham, G. B. (1993). The evolution and current status of the functional perspective on communication in decision-making and problem-solving groups: A critical analysis. In S. A. Deetz (Ed.), *Communication yearbook 16* (pp. 573-600). Newbury Park, CA: Sage.

Gouran, D. S., Hirokawa, R. Y., & Martz, A. E. (1986). A critical analysis of factors related to decisional processes involved in the Challenger disaster. *Central States Speech Journal, 37*, 119-135.

Greenwood, R., & Jenkins, W. I. (1981). Policy-making groups. In R. Payne & C. L. Cooper (Eds.), *Groups at work* (pp. 9-40). New York: John Wiley.

Hackman, J. R. (Ed.). (1990). *Groups that work (and those that don't): Creating conditions for effective teamwork.* San Francisco: Jossey-Bass.

Hensley, T. R., & Griffin, G. W. (1986). Victims of groupthink: The Kent State University Board of Trustees and the 1977 gymnasium controversy. *Journal of Conflict Resolution, 30*, 497-531.

Hirokawa, R. Y., & Pace, R. C. (1983). A descriptive investigation of the possible communication-based reasons for effective and ineffective group decision-making. *Communication Monographs, 50*, 363-379.

Janis, I. L. (1972). *Victims of groupthink: Psychological studies of foreign policy decisions and fiascoes.* Boston: Houghton Mifflin.

Janis, I. L. (1982). *Groupthink* (2nd ed.). Boston: Houghton Mifflin.

Janis, I. L., & Mann, L. (1977). *Decision-making: A psychological analysis of conflict, choice, and commitment.* New York: Free Press.

March, J. G., & Olsen, J. P. (1976). *Ambiguity and choice in organizations.* Bergen, Norway: Universitetsforlaget.

Moreland, R. L., & Levine, J. M. (1988). Group dynamics over time: Development and socialization in small groups. In J. E. McGrath (Ed.), *The social psychology of time* (pp. 151-181). Newbury Park, CA: Sage.

Olsen, J. P. (1976). Choice in an organized anarchy. In J. G. March & J. P. Olsen (Eds.), *Ambiguity and choice in organizations.* Bergen, Norway: Universitetsforlaget.

Poole, M. S., & Doelger, J. A. (1986). Developmental processes in group decision-making. In R. Y. Hirokawa & M. S. Poole (Eds.), *Communication and group decision-making* (1st ed., pp. 35-61). Beverly Hills, CA: Sage.

Poole, M. S., & Hirokawa, R. Y. (1986). Communication and group decision-making: A critical assessment. In R. Y. Hirokawa & M. S. Poole (Eds.), *Communication and group decision-making* (1st ed., pp. 15-31). Beverly Hills, CA: Sage.

Poole, M. S., & Roth, J. (1989). Decision development in small groups IV: A typology of group decision paths. *Human Communication Research, 15*, 323-356.

Poole, M. S., Seibold, D. R., & McPhee, R. D. (1986). A structurational approach to theory-building in group decision-making research. In R. Y. Hirokawa & M. S. Poole (Eds.), *Communication and group decision-making* (1st ed., pp. 237-264). Beverly Hills, CA: Sage.

Putnam, L. L. (1989). Perspectives for research on group embeddedness in organizations. In S. S. King (Ed.), *Human communication as a field of study* (pp. 163-181). New York: State University of New York Press.

Putnam, L. L., & Stohl, C. (1990). Bona fide groups: A reconceptualization of groups in context. *Communication Studies, 41,* 248-265.

Rogers, E., & Kincaid, D. (1981). *Communication networks.* New York: Free Press.

Sabourin, T. C., & Geist, P. (1990). Collaborative production of proposals in group decision making. *Small Group Research, 21,* 404-427.

Scheerhorn, D., Geist, P., & Teboul, J. C. B. (1994). Beyond decision making in decision-making groups: Implications for the study of group communication. In L. R. Frey (Ed.), *Group communication in context* (pp. 247-262). Hillsdale, NJ: Lawrence Erlbaum.

Scheidel, T. M., & Crowell, L. (1964). Idea development in small discussion groups. *Quarterly Journal of Speech, 50,* 140-145.

Seabright, M., Leventhal, D., & Fichman, M. (1992). Role of individual attachments in the dissolution of interorganizational relationships. *Academy of Management Journal, 35,* 122-160.

Stohl, C. (1986). Quality circles and changing patterns of communication. In M. L. McLaughlin (Ed.), *Communication yearbook 9* (pp. 511-531). Beverly Hills, CA: Sage.

Stohl, C. (1987). Bridging the parallel organization: A study of quality circle effectiveness. In M. L. McLaughlin (Ed.), *Communication yearbook 10* (pp. 416-429). Beverly Hills, CA: Sage.

Stohl, C., & Holmes, M. E. (1993). A functional perspective for bona fide groups. In S. A. Deetz (Ed.), *Communication yearbook 16* (pp. 601-614). Newbury Park, CA: Sage.

Stohl, C., & Putnam, L. L. (1994). Group communication in context: Implications for the study of bona fide groups. In L. R. Frey (Ed.), *Group communication in context* (pp. 285-292). Hillsdale, NJ: Lawrence Erlbaum.

Thornton, B. C. (1978). Health care teams and multimethodological research. In B. D. Ruben (Ed.), *Communication yearbook 2* (pp. 539-553). New Brunswick, NJ: Transaction Books.

Walton, R. E. (1985). From control to commitment in the workplace. *Harvard Business Review, 63,* 77-84.

Weick, K. E. (1979). *The social psychology of organizing* (2nd ed.). Reading, MA: Addison-Wesley.

Small Group Communication May Not Influence Decision Making

An Amplification of Socio-Egocentric Theory

DEAN E. HEWES

"Nobody likes a wiseguy," or so a colleague of mine stated after reading an earlier version of this chapter (Hewes, 1986). What moved him to comment was my claim that, as far we can prove with the evidence at hand, the content of social interaction in small groups does not affect group outcomes.[1] Or, to put it in statistical terms, we have no unambiguous evidence that group outcomes are determined either (a) by the irreducible direct causal effects of communication processes or (b) by statistical interaction effects of communication processes with variables whose values are set before the group discussion takes place (i.e., group composition, individual or shared prior knowledge, role structure, etc.). If group outcomes are not caused by irreducible communication processes, then communication itself originates no changes in group outcomes. Communication processes (**C**) are reduced to channels through which the true causes of group outcomes, mental and societal forces (M/S), act on group outcomes (O)—or, diagrammatically, M/S $\rightarrow$ C $\rightarrow$ O. If communication processes do not statistically interact with preinteraction mental and societal forces to product group outcomes, then there is no causal role left for communication processes to play.[2]

My colleague replied that this claim is unjustifiably provocative—and vaguely treasonous for a communication researcher. He argued that my claim was inconsistent with common sense, undergraduate textbooks (often the same thing), and a substantial body of evidence that suggested that communication has both positive (cf. Collins & Guetzkow, 1964; Rosenberg, Erlick, & Berkowitz, 1955; Shaw, 1932) and negative (cf. Buys, 1978; Delbecq, Van de Ven, & Gustafson, 1975; Janis & Mann, 1977; Lamm & Trommsdroff, 1973) effects on groups outcomes. My response was as follows:

a. Although we have extensive evidence that communication affects group outcomes, we do not have unambiguous evidence, in large part because our research paradigms were inadequate to the task.

b. The alternative assumption (that communication is unimportant) is also plausible, formalizable, and falsifiable.

c. Even if this alternative assumption is false, it has the additional benefit of providing a baseline description against which to test claims concerning the purported influence of communication on group decision making, a test that cannot be made with current research paradigms.

d. Even if this alternative assumption is false, falsifying it would mandate a thorough discussion of the nature of communication-as-cause, a discussion that is far from complete (Hewes, 1986, 1990).

What has become of this debate with my colleague? I did not persuade him; he did not persuade me. Why did we come to this impasse? For the same two reasons that this discussion has not resulted in more public response in scholarly journals: My claim is counterintuitive and, thus, is given less than its due consideration; the force of my earlier arguments (Hewes, 1986) was diluted by insufficient precision. I mean to correct these two deficiencies here by clarifying and updating my arguments (a) through (d) above in the order they were presented.

Evidence of the Impact of Communication on Group Decision Making

SOME KEY DEFINITIONS

Evidence relevant to the impact of communication on group decision making comes from three sources—data on inputs to group decision making, decision-making processes, and group outputs. *Inputs* are idiosyncratic or shared variables that individual group members bring to a discussion, such as cognitive abilities and limitations, knowledge of the problem or how to solve problems individually or in a group, personality characteristics, motivations both individual and shared, economic resources, and power. In other words, inputs are resources, or *structures* in the vocabulary of the structurational approach (Poole, McPhee, & Seibold, 1982; Poole, Seibold, & McPhee, 1986). *Outputs* are variables that characterize group products, such as group cohesiveness, group commitment to a decision, group productivity, decision quality, and speed of solution. Outputs are not individual characteristics (e.g., individual's satisfaction with process or outcome, etc.). *Process* consists of patterns of interaction of the group discussion displayed as trends or phases (cf. Bales & Strodtbeck, 1951; Fisher, 1970; Poole, 1981) or patterns of influence of the general form of Equation 7.1:

$$Prob\,(x_b\,(t \dotplus n)\ \mid Y_a\,(t)) \neq Prob\,(x_b\,(t \dotplus n)) \qquad (7.1)$$

That is, the odds (**Prob**) of event X (overt behavior, action, or covert mental activity) originating with person B at some time t + n given that person A originated Y (overt behavior, etc.) at some earlier time t, does not equal the odds that B would originate X despite A's earlier behavior. In other words, A's activity had an influence on B's subsequent activity. Equation 7.1 formalizes a widely accepted definition of communication (cf. Fisher, 1970; Steinfatt & Miller, 1974; Stevens, 1950) that has been applied to small group decision making in the study of the communication processes of conflict (Ellis & Fisher, 1975), socioemotional development (cf. Bales, 1950; Ellis, 1979; Poole, 1981), task-related activity (cf. Bales & Strodtbeck, 1951; Fisher, 1970; Tuckman, 1965), idea development (Scheidel & Crowell, 1964), and suasive influence of individual members on group policy choice (cf. Abelson, 1976; Poole et al., 1982).

Typically, evidence drawn from descriptions of process, inputs, and outputs has been combined in three ways to make claims concerning the relationship between communication and group outcomes—*input → output evidence, process evidence, and process → output evidence* (Hewes, 1986). The first form (input → output) is used to argue that if changing inputs affects output, then, surely, communication must have the medium that passed on this change. The second type of evidence (process evidence) is used to make the claim that because communication in group discussions shows some pattern, then, surely, this pattern must serve some purpose in determining the output. Process → output evidence is used to argue that because there is a covariation between patterns of group discussion processes and group outcomes, then, surely, processes must cause outcomes. The claims made from each of these types of evidence are flawed. Let us explore each type of evidence to find its limitations.

INPUT → OUTPUT EVIDENCE

Logically, input → output data can establish only a limited set of conclusions, assuming the manipulation of interactive factors is valid. First, if communication processes are manipulated independently of other factors (**M/S**) that could directly affect the decision output (e.g., individual problem-solving ability, prediscussion individual or shared motivation, etc.), *and* if an impact of the manipulation of communication processes is demonstrated, communication processes do have an impact on decision making. Second, if the manipulation of communication processes is confounded with noninteractive factors, and whether or not an impact of interactive factors on output is shown, communication processes may or may not have a direct impact, and they might or might not also have a nonadditive causal effect (statistical interaction) with noninteractive factors. Third, if no impact on output is shown and communication processes are not confounded with noninteractive factions, the results suggest no direct causal relationship between the communicative processes manipulated and the decision-making outcome, within the limits of statistical power. Obviously, the second alternative is not desirable if we wish to make clear causal claims. This is also the most common situation in input → output small group research.

Consider the research paradigms of decision-making agendas and computer-mediated communication research. Most common are studies of decision-making agendas—explorations of the Nominal Group Technique (Delbecq et al., 1975), versions of Dewey's model of reflective thinking applied to groups (cf. Cragan & Wright, 1980; Larson, 1969), brainstorming, and technological manipulations of interaction through the use of certain types of computer-assisted decision systems (cf. Poole & DeSanctis, 1990). These approaches were really developed to improve group performance, not to assess the causal influence of communication. For instance, decision agendas based on Dewey's (1910) model of reflective thinking, although prescribing interaction patterns, also manipulate preinteraction knowledge about the logical order in which *individual* members should think (a noninteractive factor). Thus to train groups in the use of these agendas has an affect both in communication processes and individual problem-solving skills. The same limitation exists for the more communication-oriented group decision support systems (a) that require training in the decision-agenda implicit or explicit in the support system and (b) that provide assistance for both individual and group thinking processes (cf. Poole & DeSanctis's, 1990, discussion of the precursors of adaptive structuration that could be read as a list of noninteractive factors). Do trained groups perform well with these agendas because their discussions are organized, because their members individually think about problems more rigorously, or some combination of the two? We do not know; research of this type provides equivocal results in answering questions concerning the effects of communication on decision-making outcomes.

There is another type of input → output research, often overlooked by communication researchers, that has implications for my claim. This research generates theoretical baseline models that predict outputs based solely on inputs. Because these baseline models describe what group outputs would look like if they were produced solely by noninteractive factors, any deviation between baseline model outputs and the outputs of real groups acting with the same inputs may or may not be attributed to the effects of communication processes, either as a direct or a nonadditive cause. In other words, baseline models offer evidence by negation of the variance that communication variables may be capable of explaining.

Studies employing this version of the baseline model strategy can lead to two conclusions pioneering the impact of communication on decision making: (a) If inputs are exhaustively predictive of outputs, then, at best, communication processes mediate the effects of noninteractive factors on outcomes (i.e., **M/S → C → O**), and, at worst, have no effect at all (i. e., **M/S → O**); (b) If inputs are not exhaustively predictive of decision outputs, communication processes may or may not have an independent impact on decision outputs, because we do not know if other noninteractive inputs might improve prediction. Obviously, data supporting the first conclusion should be perceived as threatening to claims that there is a relationship between communication and small group decision making—and, indeed, they are (Poole et al., 1982, 1986).

Many researchers have undertaken baseline modeling research that is capable of producing data relevant to these two possible conclusions. For example, early research on "statistized" or "concocted" groups raised important questions concerning how the quality of individual and group decisions should be compared (see, e.g., Gordon, 1923; Knight, 1921; Preston, 1938; Shaw, 1932). These questions became formalized in models of group decision making in "closed" tasks (see Davis, 1969b; Davis & Restle, 1963; Lorge & Solomon, 1955; Taylor, 1954), that is, tasks with a known correct solution. These models take some measure of input, usually individual or average individual abilities in completing some task (eureka problems, recall, sequential decisions, and the like) and use that input to predict group performance for hypothetical, noninteracting groups of some predetermined size.

Remarkably, these models of closed-task performance do a fine job of predicting interacting group decisions. As Davis (1969a) notes,

> In summary, we might conclude that the direct performance advantage displayed by groups has a simple explanation in most cases. More precisely, there exists a simple pooling hypothesis concerning member products that is at least sufficient to explain a rather wide range of group-individual results on decision-making, problem-solving, and learning tasks. However, the model developed by Taylor and by Lorge and Solomon does not explain all group performance. It has frequently overpredicted group performance, and this deviation remains to be explained in many cases. (p. 47)

Thus, particularly with Taylor's (1954) and Lorge and Solomon's (1955) models, much of group performance on closed tasks can be explained without reference to communication processes (**M/S → O**). Where communication may have an impact, it is small and negative, lowering the quality of group outputs. Still, any deviation in prediction by these models leaves open the possibility, though hardly the certainty, that communication does make a difference. When the sources of these deviations have been investigated (see Davis, 1969a; Davis & Restle, 1963), the results are open to varied interpretations. Davis has found that much of the deviation between the performance of interacting and concocted groups, with the performance of the latter based on extensions of Lorge and Solomon's (1955) model, is due to an "egalitarian process." Solution rates are not simple products of the fastest member (the hierarchical model). In the hierarchical model, when the correct solution is identified, it is automatically accepted as correct. In the egalitarian model, however, several solutions may be given consideration, thus slowing the rate of task completion. Whether this is due to an enculturated democratic (egalitarian) decision scheme largely unaffected by communication (e.g., Davis, 1969a; Davis & Restle, 1963) or due to some suasive process is not yet known. Consequently, previous work on the antecedents of closed task outputs leads to the conclusion that if communication processes do play a part in producing decision outputs, that part is only a small one and not empirically supported to date.

Of course, one could dismiss much of this closed task research by arguing that most decision-making tasks have no determinate solutions and are therefore "open," not closed. Open tasks, by virtue of the ambiguity of the solution, elicit more suasive communication and depend on it for choosing a solution. Thus the results of research on the effects of communication on group outcomes on closed tasks may not generalize to open tasks. Unfortunately for those who would dismiss the results of these modeling studies because they employ closed tasks, the results of modeling open task decision making lend no more direct support to the notion that communicative processes influence decision outputs, although some indirect support can be garnered for it. To illustrate this point, consider the best known model of group decision making in open tasks, Davis's (1973) social decision scheme theory (hereafter, the SDS). Davis argues that the choice of a decision under a specified set of alternatives is stochastically predictable given the pre-interaction dispositions of each member toward each alternative solution, a rule that combines individual dispositions to create a vector of group dispositions based on the assumption that individual members do not influence each other, and a social decision scheme that describes how group preferences map onto group decision outputs.

Although Davis and his colleagues have had remarkable success in applying SDS to jury decision making (see Davis, 1980; Penrod & Hastie, 1979), its implications have been attacked by several scholars. Driving these attacks has been the common presumption that SDS must not be complete because it excludes or hides the effects of social interaction on decision choice. Thus Penrod and Hastie (1979), for instance, in proposing their DICE simulation model, argue that by mapping preinteraction dispositions onto outputs, the SDS ignores suasive processes. Unfortunately, their own model corrects this deficiency through the addition of an input variable—the persuasibility of individual group members. Because no direct measure of this variable is taken, nor of the suasive processes themselves, the improved fit of input-output data to DICE (Penrod & Hastie, 1980) suggests only that individual difference variables (noninteractive variables) improve the fit of the data to the model by simulating differences in individual opinion trajectories through the jury's deliberation. Moreover, research on group dispositions shows that changes in them throughout the jury's deliberation do not have a marked impact on the decision output (cf. Davis, Nagao, & Stasser, 1978). As a result, like the research on baseline models of closed task performance, Penrod and Hastie's is, at best, only indirectly suggestive of an impact by communication on decision outputs.

A more direct effort to confront this issue is contained in a study conducted by Poole et al. (1982). These authors contrasted the predictions of Davis's SDS with a purportedly more communication-oriented model—the distribution valence model (DVM). This model, an extension of Hoffman's valence model (see Hoffman, 1979), contrasts with SDS in two ways that are central to this discussion. First, unlike SDS, DVM relies on the evaluative (valenced) content of remarks during a discussion to assess members' positions on a fixed set of alternative solutions, rather than on preinteraction distributions of opinions. Second, DVM allows for the possibility that individual members may vary in their impact on the outcome of a discussion. Thus DVM allows for the possibility that persuasiveness is either an emergent product of group interaction or a noninteraction factor rather like persuasibility is in DICE.

Poole et al. (1982) found that the predictions of the DVM and SDS overlapped strongly, with the DVM providing slightly more accurate predictions. They determined via structural equation modeling that the SDS seemed to determine the results of the DVM, which in turn predicted group performance, or, diagrammatically, M/S → C → O. In addition, the SDS had a small but unique effect on group performance, M/S → O. Prior research (McPhee, Poole, & Seibold, 1981) had established the importance of individual differences in affecting decision outputs, though not whether those differences arose during the interaction or before it.

How are these results to be interpreted? Originally, Poole et al. (1982) suggested that these results were supportive of the importance of communication in decision making. Later, they expressed some hesitancy in this interpretation (Poole et al., 1986; Poole, Seibold, & McPhee, Chapter 5, this volume). Although the DVM does use data coded from actual interaction to predict group outcomes, these data are not communication processes as defined by Equation 7.1. Equation 7.1 defines a communication process by stressing the importance of the dependency of one person's (B) behavior (X) on the prior behavior (Y) of another person (A). In contrast to this definition, the DVM is tested by sampling individuals' evaluative behavior across time, without reference to its temporal, contingent structure. Positive and negative evaluative remarks for each solution are summed for each person across time; the number of negative remarks is then subtracted from the number of positive remarks for each person for each solution. These figures (valence distributions) for each individual are weighted empirically to predict the final decision (McPhee et al., 1981; but cf. Hoffman & Kleinman, 1994; McPhee, 1994).

Poole et al. (1986) observe, that "as important as the previous studies are in establishing the importance of social interaction, they treat preference distribution as though it were a stable entity and the interaction structures governing valence accumulation as though they were stable rules" (p. 86). My own conclusions are less sanguine (Hewes, 1986). It is quite possible that valenced remarks during a discussion are nothing

more than imperfect reflections of individuals' preinteraction dispositions. We have no evidence that they reflect a process of changing
dispositions. If so, pooling a large sample of remarks drawn from an
underlying disposition does nothing more than reduce the standard
error of the estimate of that disposition (Hewes, 1986). Given Davis's
comparatively casual measurement of preinteraction dispositions, it
would be no wonder that the DVM's predictions are slightly more
accurate due to improved measurement alone. Further, the predictive
power that the small predictive advantage that the DVM has over the
SDS also has been gained through its use of individual difference
weighting of valence distributions and is very similar to the improved
predictions gained by Penrod and Hastie's (1980) use of the individual
difference persuasibility variable. Although both Poole et al.'s and
Penrod and Hastie's suggest communication effects, their interpretation is inherently ambiguous because we cannot determine whether or
not these effects arise from communication or noninteractive factors.
Finally, even if we take Poole et al.'s evidence at face value, it only
indicates that communication is nothing more than a proximal cause of
group outcomes, where the original, distal causes are noninteractive
factors ($M/S \rightarrow C \rightarrow O$).

What, then, can we say about the results of this and other input $\rightarrow$
output research? Given the logical limitations of such studies, their
implications are remarkably clear. The critique of decision-agenda
training studies leads to an active concern for the distinction between
communication processes and noninteractive antecedents of decision
outputs. Only by keeping this distinction in mind and exploring both
types of factors in research designs is it possible to make valid claims
about the impact of communication processes on decision outputs
(Hewes, 1986). Furthermore, when effects of communication are found,
it is essential to empirically eliminate noninteractive variables to which
communication processes could be reduced (cf. Salazar, Hirokawa,
Propp, Julian, & Leatham, 1994; and my critique of this study in the final
major section of this chapter).

The results of input $\rightarrow$ output modeling studies have been more
enlightening. That is, input $\rightarrow$ output baseline models of both closed
and open tasks have demonstrated a remarkable ability to predict small
group decision outputs without regard to communication processes.

We can thus see the utility of the baseline model strategy for investigating the impact of communication on decision making (cf. Hewes, 1986). On the other hand, the logical limitations of input → output modeling cannot be overlooked. They have all been informative but only by negation, by accounting for variation in group outcomes without reference to communication processes, leaving limited residual variance to be accounted for either by communication processes or by other noninteractive variables. To make the baseline strategy more useful, we need to develop more powerful models that not only connect inputs to outputs but also identify which apparent communication processes can themselves be reduced to input factors. I delve into this class of models in my discussion of the socio-egocentric approach to small group communication.

Evidence From Process and Process → Output Studies of Small Group Decision Making

Within the past 20 years communication researchers have answered the call for studies of the process of decision making. However, much of this research has been handicapped by underdeveloped or poorly understood process methodologies. For example, only recently has the value of the validation of coding schemes been articulated and the relevant technology developed (Folger, Hewes, & Poole, 1984). Similarly, knowledge of the assumptions of these methods has been disseminated only within the past decade and appears not to be widely understood. Nevertheless, research on communication processes reflects two positive characteristics discussed in the last section; communication processes are observed directly, and baseline models are employed. Unfortunately, a third desirable characteristic, the inclusion of noninteractive influences on decision outputs in research designs, has all but been overlooked.

Typically, process and process-output data in these studies are described using methodologies based on Equation 7.1. *Markov chains* and *lag sequential analysis* (Sackett, 1979) characterize group interaction in terms of temporally contingent probabilities of behavior. For example, Markov chains capture interaction data in *transition matrices* where the left edge indicates the category of communicative action performed at some point in time $t - n$, and the top edge indicates the category of act performed some number (n) of time periods in the future (t). Entries in these transition matrices are conditional probabilities of the form described in the first part of Equation 7.1. Under certain testable assumptions, data described in this fashion accurately capture communication processes. Similar assumptions hold for lag sequential analysis.

Studies employing these process methodologies have certain logical limitations. Consider two cases, the first in which these methodologies are used to demonstrate the existence of some communication process, and the second wherein differences in communication processes are linked to differences in decision outputs. Let us begin with the first, and by far the most common, case. Because such research is not typically concerned with process-output linkages directly, its value is restricted to the following two possible conclusions. First, if processes of communication are identified in comparison to some appropriate baseline model, they *may* or *may not* have an impact on decision outputs. (Additional evidence of the covariation between the patterns of communication that deviate from the baseline model and group outputs would make the case for communication as a cause of outputs more plausible.) Second, if communication processes are completely explained by the appropriate baseline model, then communication cannot have an unambiguous impact on decision outputs because communication patterns are reducible to input conditions. Of course, the first conclusion is premised on the assumption that the correct baseline model has been used to identify a process, and that the observed interaction patterns are not themselves explainable entirely in terms of noninteractive input variables.

With rare exceptions, studies of group communication process use the criterion for the existence of communication process contained in Equation 7.1.[3] From the earliest studies (Hawes & Foley, 1973; Scheidel & Crowell, 1964) onward, observed sequentially contingent patterns of interaction are compared to a baseline model where there is no contingent structure. This baseline model reflects the presumption that the production of behavior X by person B does not depend on previous activities Y performed by person A. In other words, it violates the criterion for a communication process defined by Equation 7.1. Statistically significant deviations between contingent patterns and the noncontingent baselines are taken as evidence that the contingent patterns (communication processes) are "real" and therefore grist for the theoretical mill.

The use of this procedure leads to two questions: Are the magnitudes of deviations from the baseline sufficiently large that they indicate the presence of substantially patterned communicative behavior? Is the baseline used adequate to rule out the effects of noninteractive forces that might be mistaken for communication processes? The answer to the first question is probably no: Many of the studies report only statistical summaries of the test implied in Equation 7.1 rather than the transition matrices themselves (see Hawes & Foley, 1973; Hewes, Planalp, & Streibel, 1980). Given the immense statistical power of the tests derived from Equation 7.1, it is quite possible to "find" a process statistically that is very weak (Hawes & Foley, 1973). As a result, only studies that report transition matrices are informative concerning the strength of the interaction processes being observed. In those studies with adequate reporting, however, the magnitude of the processes observed has been very weak (see Ellis, 1979; Hirokawa, 1980). For instance, in Ellis's (1979) study of decision-making and consciousness-raising groups, the average difference between the conditional probabilities in the transition matrices and the baseline model was .064, where the possible range of such differences is 0.00 (no pattern) to 1.00 (strong pattern)—a paltry indication of the strength of the communication processes involved and possibly imperceptible to the group members themselves (Planalp & Hewes, 1982). The results from Hirokawa's (1980) study indicate only marginally stronger, and highly limited, patterns. Observed communication behaviors, then, do not suggest the existence of substantially patterned communication processes, although some weak patterns have been observed.

Of course, one could argue that a judgment of practical significance is inherently subjective. Is 0.064 really that bad? Although I believe it is, there appears to be an even more serious problem with this research, a problem raised by the second question: Is the currently used baseline model adequate to rule out the effects of noninteractive forces that might be mistaken for communication processes? Here the answer is a more definitive no. Although the details of this argument must await the next section of this chapter, it is rather easy to demonstrate that one can observe and explain deviations from this baseline model that are produced by nonsubstantive communication processes and noninteractive factors. Thus even deviations from the current baseline cannot be accepted as direct evidence of communication processes.

Before developing this argument, however, let me close this section by discussing the logical limitations of process-output data. These data are derived from the same methodologies employed in studies looking only at process. They thus suffer from precisely the same weakness. The strength of such studies is that if a significant relationship is observed, the results are less equivocal than those derived from any other type of data. There are only two possible sources of equivocality; that the interaction patterns are completely explainable by noninteractive input variables, or that the baseline model used to identify the communication processes is inadequate. Unfortunately, the best (and practically the only) example of empirical process-output evidence (Hirokawa, 1980; but see also Hirokawa & Pace, 1983, for qualitative data) is subject to both of these limitations. Hirokawa did not examine systematically potential noninteractive input explanations for his finding that effective groups manifested conditional connections with "procedural statements providing direction" preceding "procedural agreement," whereas ineffective groups did not. However, there is preliminary evidence that a causal connection exists between antecedents as democratic leadership style. Should subsequent evidence support this, one could reduce Hirokawa's results to noninteractive factors, that is, $M/S \rightarrow C \rightarrow O$. Even without this evidence, Hirokawa's evidence for communication processes is in jeopardy because he employed the conventional baseline model to identify their existence. Thus the best of the available evidence for process and process $\rightarrow$ output evidence is in question.

My objective in critiquing input $\rightarrow$ output, process, and process $\rightarrow$ output data is to establish the logical limitations of existing approaches to the study of the relationship between communication processes and small group decision making. I hope that these logical limitations can serve as springboards for the generation of theoretical and methodological improvements, and not simply as a skeptic's contrivance. What, then, can be gleaned from this abridged review?

a. Researchers must assess both the potential interactive and noninteractive antecedents of decision outputs and control for the latter in their studies.

b. A baseline modeling strategy is a particularly rigorous approach to investigating the impact of communication on decision making.

c. Any approach to testing this relationship, including a baseline strategy, must rely on data measuring communication processes directly, and not on input → output data alone.

d. The current baseline model used to assess the existence of communicative processes is inadequate to that task.

Let me correct this last deficiency by presenting an appropriate baseline model. To do so, I must anchor it in an explanation of why communication processes might appear but are ineffectual in producing group outcomes.

A Socio-Egocentric Approach to Small Group Communication

Each of the four research guidelines above should ground any approach to small group decision making, including the approach advanced here. My approach is based on the assumption that much, if not all, small group communication is epiphenomenal—that is, identifiable noninteractive factors can explain observed patterns of group communication, and it is these noninteractive inputs that produce decision outputs. These noninteractive factors can, therefore, be used to create a new baseline model of small group communication superior to that implied by Equation 7.1. Only if observed patterns deviate substantially from this new baseline model, and only if those deviations are associated with decision output variables, are claims to the impact of communication on decision making plausible.

My approach would appear to be an advance on the input → output models discussed previously; however, it does not lead to ambiguous results as those do when inputs fail to explain output perfectly. In the new baseline model, communication is measured directly, and its impact on outcomes can be assessed directly. In addition, my approach has advantages when compared to process or process-output orientations, because it incorporates noninteractive factors into the new baseline model as well. Now to the details.

A SOCIO-EGOCENTRIC PERSPECTIVE

The term *socio-egocentric* is derived from Piaget's early developmental studies of "egocentric speech" (Piaget, 1926; see also Vygotsky, 1962, on "private speech"). Piaget (1926, p. 55) noted that children ranging in age from 3 to 8 years engage in speech characterized by "remarks that are not addressed to anyone . . . and that . . . evoke no reaction adapted to them on the part of anyone to whom they might chance to be addressed." In the most developmentally advanced type of egocentric speech, "collective monologue," children give the structural appearance of engaging in a dialogue (e.g., appropriate turn taking) but without managing to sustain the meaningful connectedness usually exemplified in adult speech (Piaget, 1926, p. 41). Piaget's explanation for the existence of egocentric speech is that children employing it are locked into "social egocentrism," wherein they find it cognitively difficult to keep in mind simultaneously both their own and another's perspective (Piaget, 1955, p. 368). Faced with this dilemma, they rely solely on their own. Other researchers, inspired by Vygotsky's work (1962) have noted that during this period, children tend to use their own speech to aid them in task performance (Zivin, 1979), using the spoken word to guide and discipline their thinking. This process is also employed in more sophisticated ways by adults under task pressure (see Sokolov, 1972). The notion of egocentric speech and the explanation that underlies it find analogy in various aspects of adult communication.

As an extreme example, consider patterns of social interaction manifested at a relaxed cocktail party. Listen closely to the "conversations," and you will hear something very akin to egocentric speech. Members of conversing dyads may follow the most basic conventions of dialogue, such as turn taking or the use of rough, often vacuous, acknowledgments of the other person's statements ("Oh, I know what you mean"), but the meaningful connectedness of a normal conversation is missing. Here, too, are collective monologues. People are talking at, rather than to, one another. Why? Because diminished capacity prevents them from integrating both halves of a conversation. So they work on their own half.

Both the developmental and cocktail party examples share common properties that can rightfully be called socio-egocentric. In both cases, the parties to these supposed dialogues apparently recognize that the situation warrants social interaction (Vygotsky, 1962). In both cases, however, the conversants are unable to manage their attention so as to meet at least two goals at the same time, formulating their own thoughts while attempting to manage the flow of conversation with full consideration of the other's contributions to it. Finally, in both cases the intereractants appear to act so as to minimize their own deficiencies by employing a structural norm of conversation (turn taking) and a cosmetic bid toward meaningful extension of the conversation (vacuous acknowledgments).

Small group decision making (especially where the task is difficult, and the group is motivated to solve it) can also be seen as a related type of multigoal task in which members' limited capacities force them to compromise on the accomplishment of some goals (Zander, 1971) or to alternate between goals to keep both active (Bales & Strodtbeck, 1951; Poole, 1981). Individual tasks, such as creating and evaluating solutions, are seen here as independent of and more important than social tasks, such as conversational management or group maintenance. Thus these two types of tasks compete for limited cognitive resources during problem solving in small group discussions, producing, as we shall see, discussions that are socio-egocentric. How might this occur? In real decision-making groups, reaching an adequate solution is usually the primary goal, although other goals (commitment, satisfaction, etc.) may also be of concern. The same is true of all the experimental groups employed in the literature reviewed here. When group members are intent on solving a problem while simultaneously pursuing social tasks, they must make compromises to make the set of tasks manageable. Two sorts of compromises are necessary. The first sort exists in terms of the individual task of solving the problem, whereas the second sort exists in the social task of conversational management. Let us consider each in turn, beginning with the individual task of problem solving. First, to ease the difficulty in solving a problem or picking a solution, each individual must have one or more methods, formal or informal, for reasoning through a problem (see, e.g., Dewey, 1910; Scandura, 1977) and/or evaluating alternative solutions. In both cases, these methods involve the operation of a set of cognitive processes that are applied in a series of temporally ordered steps. These steps aid in reasoning through a problem by reducing the cognitive load as a result of reducing memory search and increasing the efficiency of human reasoning. They further reduce the cognitive load by allowing prior experience in general problem solving to be brought to bear on new problems. Evaluation processes reduce the load in a similar fashion, though they have the added property of increasing the number (Poole & Hunter, 1979) and extremity (Tesser, 1973) of evaluations over time, even without the impact of suasive messages. Thus at least some known methods for reasoning through a problem or evaluating a solution exist at the individual level and can produce temporally ordered patterns of communication if individuals articulate their thinking.

Second, to lighten the cognitive load caused by social tasks, group members engage in a form of egocentric speech. Because members try to devote primary consideration to the pursuit of individual solutions to a problem, they add to the resources dedicated to that goal by compromising on the social goal of effective conversational management. That is, they engage in a form of socio-egocentric behavior by giving the appearance of listening and reacting to others' comments without actually doing so. Although this view of group communication may seem to fly in the face of common sense, two nonsubstantive communicative factors produce the illusion of meaningful connectedness in small group discussions: Purely structural resources may be used to manage the flow of conversation. One such structure observed in egocentric speech is turn taking. Specifically, I posit the existence of a turn-taking management device that regulates the transition between turns-at-talk from group member to group member. Whatever forces bring these devices into being—dispositions, situated factors (e.g., expertise), or habit—turn-taking management devices manifest themselves in the sequential ordering of group members' turns. In effect, these devices define windows in which each group member reports orally on the state of his or her thinking about the problem. Thus, a turn-taking management device is a nonsubstantive communication process that produces ordered discourse in its own right and facilitates public insight into the operation of temporally ordered individual, noninteractive processes. Because we might expect that people thinking about the same problem do so in similar ways, illusions of influence, idea development, and evaluation may be fostered. Do turn-taking management devices exist? Although we have no direct evidence that such devices create the opportunity for people to report on the state of their thinking, we do have evidence that sequentially ordered turn taking explains many observed patterns of communication in small group communication. A reanalysis of Hewes et al.'s (1980) interaction data derived from small group discussions reveals that a large (83.7%) and statistically significant ($p < .00001$) portion of the sequential structure of communication can be accounted for by the sequential structure of turn taking alone. That is, it is not content-related remarks that structure much of group discussion, but instead the operation of content-independent turn-taking management devices. Given the already weak sequential ordering of communication processes noted in the discussion of process and process-output data, claims as to the influence of substantive communication on decision making are further weakened.

In addition to turn-taking management devices, nonsubstantive connecting devices may also add to the illusion of influence in idea development or persuasion. In particular, vacuous acknowledgments may help create this illusion. These are statements that contain the recognition that a prior statement (or statements) has been made but that do not contain any direct reference to the content of the statement(s). Consider the following two exchanges found in decision-making groups:

A: I really believe that educating students about the dangers of bike accidents would help to reduce them.
B: Right! I've also been thinking that maybe we ought to improve bike routes as a step toward solving our problem.

Or consider this example:

C: How about building an underpass for bikes on Sierra?
D: I can see your point, but how about more money being put into traffic lights?

Both B and D make remarks that are sensible responses in the context of the problem under discussion; however, the acknowledgments are not followed by contributions that tell us, one way or the other, whether A's or C's comments have had any impact. Thus these acknowledgments are vacuous in that they are not supported by subsequent statements that demonstrate the impact of the preceding communication. They help create the illusion of meaningful connectedness, of influence and progress in decision making, but without necessarily reflecting reality. We should note two caveats concerning these claims about vacuous acknowledgments. First, the claim that an acknowledgment is vacuous concerns only its function as evidence of influence in the eyes of an objective outside observer. A vacuous acknowledgment may reflect true acknowledgment and extension in the mind of the utterer, but we cannot make that inference on the basis of the utterance alone. We are looking for hard evidence of influence by the communication processes of problem solving and evaluation, and vacuous acknowledgments do not provide such evidence. Second, although these two examples of vacuous acknowledgments are limited to one turn-exchange each, this should not imply that evidence of the status of an acknowledgment should be sought only within the turn containing it. Subsequent exchanges may indicate that an acknowledgment was, in fact, responsive to the content of an earlier statement. Remember, though, that coincidental connectedness is quite possible, because all group members are thinking about the same problem and may well be limited to the same general range of conventional categories regarding causes, solutions, and so forth.

To reprise the socio-egocentric orientation, decision making is seen as a multigoal, hierarchized process that requires of group members compromises between and among various goals. To maintain adequate cognitive capacity to achieve the primary goal of reaching an acceptable decision, group members reduce their individual task loads in this area by employing cognitive processes of problem solving and evaluation, both of which are temporally ordered. Members also reduce the overall cognitive load by simplifying the social tasks of conversational and group maintenance. They do so by engaging in an adult form of ego-centric speech that conveys a (possibly illusory) sense of involvement and extension. Turn-taking management devices regulate the flow of speech while providing the opportunity for each member to report on the state of his or her essentially individual task of problem solving or evaluation. Finally, vacuous acknowledgments, in conjunction with turn-taking management devices, help to create the impression of continuity and development in the discussion.

A SOCIO-EGOCENTRIC MODEL
AND STEPS TOWARD FALSIFICATION

Let me illustrate how this description of small group communication can be tested by providing a model of a portion of the socio-egocentric approach and some steps by which this approach might be falsified. If problem solving or solution evaluation are viewed as primarily temporally organized individual tasks, then by examining the temporal organization of each group member's activities separately, we will have a description of their thought processes. Let B be some mutually exclusive and exhaustive category system with a finite set of elements $(b_1, \ldots, b_k)$ that represent either steps in problem solving (see, e.g., Bales, 1950; Dewey, 1910; Fisher, 1970; Hewes et al., 1980) or elements of decision evaluation (McPhee et al., 1981). Let us also define M as the set of group members $(m_1, \ldots, m_q)$. In addition, let us define a vector of segments of the conversation T whose elements $(t_1, \ldots, t_w)$ segment a group discussion into an exhaustive set of units such that t_1 is the first segment and t_w is the last. The duration of these segments may be established theoretically, as in the case where there are easily identifiable phases in the discussion, or empirically (cf. Holmes & Poole, 1991). Ideally, these segments would correspond to the steps in problem solving or in evaluation mentioned earlier. Failing that, however, they may also be established empirically using techniques described elsewhere (Arundale, 1977; Poole, 1981). Combining notation from M, B, and T, the odds that a member m_j will perform some behavior b_i during segment t_n is represented as $\textbf{Prob } (m_j b_i(t_n))$. Because we know from the theoretical discussion of the cognitive processes that drive problem solving/evaluation that their steps change over time, we do not expect the values of these probabilities to remain constant over time but to change from time segment to time segment.

Let us also define a transition matrix D, a turn-taking management device whose elements (d_{ij}) indicate the odds that a member m_j will have a turn at $t + n$ within some time segment t_j, given that a member m_i had a turn immediately previously at t within the same time segment. (Note that these dependencies do not have to occur between immediately adjacent acts nor does the contingent structure necessarily involve the occurrence of only one previous behavior, though that is how I have shown it here [Hewes et al., 1980; Hewes, 1990].) If we further adopt the convention that members cannot follow themselves (Hewes et al., 1980)—that is, $d_{jj} = 0$, thus ignoring backchannel behaviors, talk-overs, and interruptions (Bales, 1950; Duncan & Fiske, 1977)— D for a dyad would have 0s in the on-diagonal elements and 1.00s for the off-diagonal elements. Obviously, D would be more complex for groups larger than two, because it could contain turn-taking hierarchies and transition probabilities less than 1.00. It is possible that the assumption that subsequent turns are determined solely by immediately previous turns, as in D currently, may be replaced by more complicated forms of dependency (see Hewes et al., 1980, for a discussion of higher-order transition matrices).

Given D and the various **Prob($m_j b_i(t_n)$)**s, it is possible to construct a socio-egocentric model of small group communication. Because the process of communication is assumed to be governed *independently* by temporally organized *individual* problem-solving/evaluation processes and turn-taking management devices, we can generate a socio-egocentric baseline model of group interaction. That is, we can describe in our baseline model the patterns of communication we would expect to see if only the temporal structure of individual problem-solving/evaluation and turn-taking management devices governed small group communication. Put another way, our baseline model describes the temporal structure of communication if communication had no influence on decision making.

By returning to Equation 7.1, we can see that the appropriate criterion for identifying communication processes converted into our current notation becomes

$$Prob\,(m_j b_i\,(t_n)\,(t + p)\mid (m_k b_l\,(t_n)\,(t)) \neq Prob\,(m_j b_i\,(t_n)\,(t + p)).\qquad(7.2)$$

This mathematical statement (Equation 7.2) defines the odds that some group member **m_j** will perform some behavior **b_i** during time segment **t_n** at **$t + p$** within that segment, given that some member **m_k** performs behavior **b_m** during the same time segment **t_n** at an earlier time **t** within that segment. In Equation 7.2 this conditional probability, or set of probabilities, for all **m**s and **b**s, would be compared to the baseline model expressed on the right side of the inequality. If the inequality holds statistically, then communication is taking place. If, however, we assume that communication processes are controlled socio-egocentrically, the appropriate baseline model against which to compare the left side of Equation 7.2 is

$$Prob\,(m_j b_i\,(t_n)\,(t \dotplus p)\ |\ m_k b_l\,(t_n)\,(t \dotplus p - a)) \times (d_{jk}).\qquad(7.3)$$

This expression (Equation 7.3) represents the assumptions of the socio-egocentric model.[4] That is, this expression assumes that the odds that some group member m_j will perform some behavior b_i during time segment t_n at $t + p$ within that segment, given that some member m_k performs behavior b_l during the same time segment t_n at an earlier time t within that segment (the left side of Equation 7.2) is determined by the product of two *independent* probabilities; the odds that person m_j performed behavior b_i during the time segment t_n at $t + p$ within that segment given that the last time the same person m_j performed any behavior (b_m) was some earlier time $t + p - q$ during time segment t_n, and the odds that person m_j's turn at talk follows some person k other than herself (d_{jk}) during that same time segment, regardless of the behavior that any person performed during the previous turn. The first part of this expression represents a sequence of thinking followed by person m_j throughout some segment of the discussion, perhaps over all of it, regardless of what others are saying or thinking. The second part of this expression represents the operation of the turn-taking management device unaffected by the content of either person's behavior or thoughts. That these two probabilities are independent of one another indicates that m_j's thought processes and speech are not influenced by the pattern of turn taking. In other words, person m_j thinks about the problem being considered by the group following a preprogramed sequence of mental behavior. When it is her opportunity to speak—that is, it is her turn—she reports on her thoughts regardless of what others have said.

This socio-egocentric baseline is a potential source of evidence for determining whether there is an influential impact of communication on problem-solving evaluations or not. If there is a difference between the left-hand side of Equation 7.2 and the socio-egocentric baseline model and that difference covaries with some group output measure, then we truly have process-output data that overcome all of the objections I have raised against it. If, on the other hand, no difference exists between the two sides of the equation, that constitutes strong evidence for the socio-egocentric approach. The baseline modeling approach reflected above thus has certain advantages for conducting studies on the impact of communication on small group decision making. First, it offers a rigorous and more realistic method for obtaining process-output evidence for the existence of influential communication processes. The traditional baseline used in Equations 7.1 and 7.2 does not take into account the fact that sequentially ordered patterns of communication can occur without communication having any influence on either problem solving or solution evaluation. The socio-egocentric baseline takes this into account and thus provides an improved method for identifying the operation of real communication influences. In addition, the socio-egocentric baseline model reflects a theoretical explanation for the absence of communication influence in decision-making groups—an explanation that already has some empirical support.

Conclusions

IS THE SOCIO-EGOCENTRIC APPROACH PLAUSIBLE?

Yes. Consider the following observations: *First,* we are faced with a truly amazing lack of adequate evidence supporting the proposition that communication processes have an impact on decision output. Why this lack of support for an intuitively satisfying claim? Perhaps it is simply the result of the use of inadequate research designs, or perhaps it is because communication has no impact on decision outputs—or that it only mediates the effects of noninteractive inputs on such outputs. Granted, these latter two claims are based on methodologically flawed, null results; the fact remains that the socio-egocentric approach offers a testable explanation of those claims. In fact, this approach has already had a salutary effect on small group communication research. *Second,* some direct support does exist for at least one aspect of the claim. For example, turn-taking management devices are hypothesized to be responsible for most of the sequential properties of small group discussion. The reanalysis of Hewes et al.'s (1980) study reported earlier supports this hypothesis. *Third,* the socio-egocentric baseline model is consistent with the results of much of the research on communication processes in small group communication. For instance, it follows naturally from the socio-egoentric model that because individuals go through sequential steps in problem solving: (a) that the *probability of occurrence* of decision-making thoughts/behaviors will change across time in small groups whose members are somewhat "in sync" cognitively, and (b) that *the probability of transitions* between those behaviors will also change across time for groups whose members are thinking along the same lines.

This first conclusion is supported by Fisher's (1970) research on the "phase hypothesis" (see also Bales & Strodtbeck, 1951; Poole & Roth, 1989; Tuckman, 1965). Fisher's results provide clear evidence that the probability of occurrence of behaviors associated with problem solving/evaluation do change over time at the level of the small group. Hewes et al.'s (1980) study shows a similar pattern at the individual level. There is also support for the second conclusion in virtually every test of the phase hypothesis that has been conducted using communication processes to identify phases (Ellis & Fisher, 1975; Hawes & Foley, 1973; Poole, 1981). In each and every case, supporting evidence for phases was obtained by identifying changes across segments of discussions in the probability of transitions between problem-solving behaviors. In three cases (Poole, 1981), evidence was garnered for the operation of different phases in different groups, again consistent with the socio-egocentric approach. These results are also consistent with Poole's theorizing and research (Poole & Roth, 1989) on his multiple sequence theory of group decision development. At present there are no data available to permit a choice between the two theories.[5] Is the socio-egocentric approach plausible? Yes, though it is lacking in direct tests of its implications.

IS THE SOCIO-EGOCENTRIC APPROACH USEFUL?

This is a question that the reader can determine better than I. Still, let me suggest three reasons to answer "yes" to this question. *First*, the socio-egocentric approach is a rigorous theoretical perspective in a subfield of Communication and Social Psychology that has had few such theories. Although the theoretical sophistication of small group research has improved markedly in the last decade, we are still at the point that rigorous thinking and theorizing is as important as, if not more important than, empirical research. The socio-egocentric approach adds to that valuable body of theory.

Second, even if the socio-egocentric approach proves to be an inadequate theory, it can still serve as a productive critical framework for examining the claims made by other theories and research. Consider, for instance, the claims made by Salazar et al. (1994) that their studies "appear to offer strong support for the importance of communication for effective group decision-making" (p. 553). On the surface, such a claim would seem to contradict the socio-egocentric approach, but if we look deeper, aided by the lens of the socio-egocentric approach, we see that this is not the case. Salazar et al. opted to test their claim concerning the causal influence of communication on group outcomes by manipulating the "opportunity to communicate" (low vs. high), as well as noninteractive factors as I have advocated earlier. Groups using free discussion (high) performed better than those using a less interactive modified Delphi procedure (low). But is "opportunity to communicate" the best way to test the causal influence of communication? It is certainly not consistent with the definition of communication contained in Equations 7.1 and 7.2, and is thus not directly relevant to the claims of the socio-egocentric approach. In addition, no contigency in behavior was measured under either experimental manipulation of "opportunity to communicate." Salazar et al. made the assumption that the Delphi procedure restricts influence, but no test of influence is available under either experimental condition to support this assumption. Further, as I noted earlier, with all training studies there is an inherent confounding of thinking and communication processes. To illustrate, compare the likely causal influence of using the relatively unfamiliar, uninvolving[6] Delphi technique in contrast to freely interactive decision making. Is it really clear that it was primarily the content of the influence processes during the group discussion that led to Salazar et al.'s results? Finally, "opportunity to communicate," even if unconfounded by noninteractive variables, is logically incapable of yielding a clear causal account of the effects of communication processes on group outcomes. Studies using "opportunity to communicate" to test the influence of communication on group outcomes cannot rule out the possibility that with this increased opportunity, communication is merely better able to more effectively mediate, rather than moderate, the influence of noninteractive factors. That is, increasing "opportunity to communicate" simply serves to open the spigot on the flow of influence of preinteraction variables. Although there may be a causal role for communication, it is hardly the one that we usually claim for it: communication as the irreducible cause of emergent social behavior or communication processes as the moderator of the causal influences of individual and/or social forces (cf. Note 2).

If we really want a direct test of the causal influence of communication on group outcomes, then the socio-egocentric approach demonstrates its heuristic value. The socio-egocentric model is the only model currently contrived that provides an adequate, falsifiable test of this claim. Moreover, the socio-egocentric approach has more heuristic value than just its model contained in Equation 7.3. The approach also contains hypotheses concerning the operation of individual cognitive processes and the use of cosmetic social resources such as vacuous acknowledgments. A full test of the approach requires that these two facets also be subject to empirical falsification. Although space does not permit a full explication of these tests, suffice it to say that protocol analysis (see Ericsson & Simon, 1993) could be used to determine individual patterns of problem solving/evaluation. These results could then be compared to observed patterns of individual problem solving/evaluation, thus providing one basis for testing the cognitive hypotheses contained in the socio-egocentric approach. Hypotheses concerning the use of vacuous acknowledgments to create the illusion of meaningful connectedness are also open to relatively straightforward empirical tests. Both sets of hypotheses, however, must be tested, along with the model, to provide adequate empirical support for the socio-egocentric approach. The socio-egocentric approach, with the heuristic value of its hypotheses, the methodological precision of its model, the critical insight it brings to other research and theory, and the plausibility of its account of communication in small group decision making, is a useful addition to small group theory.

WHAT ARE THE LIMITATIONS OF THE SOCIO-EGOCENTRIC THEORY?

Aside from the obvious lack of direct research on the socio-egocentric theory, there are at least two other limitations, limitations that might be turned into strengths. One of those is to be found in the definition of the "communication process" endemic to the socio-egocentric approach. The socio-egocentric baseline model assumes that communication processes are best represented as temporally organized contingencies of behavior (see Equations 7.1 and 7.2). Put another way, I am assuming that the influence of communication is best captured by *temporally systematic lags between the occurrence of an action and the action that triggered it.*[7] If this assumption is incorrect, we are faced with the task of producing an alternative theoretical stance on influence that is as rigorous, falsifiable, and productive as that used in the socio-egocentric baseline model. One potentially adequate, but methodologically diffi- cult, alternative to the assumption of temporally systematic lags is to assume that influence can only be demonstrated by *temporally varying but meaningful coherent contingencies in thoughts.* This would involve tracking the content of people's thoughts and using some aspect of that content to determine the conscious or nonconscious influences on them arising in others' actions. Relying on the discourse alone to track think- ing, and especially doing so using qualitative methodologies, is likely to prove to be far too imprecise to get the job done: Witness my comments on vacuous acknowledgments. Even with direct access to peoples' thoughts, it is not yet clear to me how one establishes causal necessity based solely on the content of interaction without empirically validated fixed time lags. Still, the debate over the definition of "com- munication process," and the methods each implies, could be a positive outcome of the socio-egocentric approach even if the decision goes against it.

Another related, but highly speculative, limitation of the socio- egocentric theory, and especially its current model, is its "architecture" or formal structure. This model is inherently linear. I have suggested elsewhere that this assumption of linearity may be too constraining for interpersonal communication theory (Hewes, 1990, 1995). So, too, for small group theory. Why? Because certain classes of nonlinear models (i.e., cognitive parallel processing models—cf. Rumelhart, McClelland, & the PDP Research Group, 1986) share a partial analogy to small group communication.[8] The architecture of these models is capable of explain- ing the emergence of complex system-wide activity from the simple activities of subunits by means of the operation of "laws of coopera- tion," literally principles of self-organization that operate in any system with this type of architecture (cf. Hopfield, 1982; Kelso, 1995; Rumelhart et al., 1986). In the context of small group communication, this suggests that group-level activity may emerge from the communication activity of individual members for the same reason—because communication processes are governed by these same laws of cooperation. In this view, communication is a cause of group outcomes because the architecture of communication alone invokes these laws. Sound confusing? It does to me, too. But the intellectual wave of modern systems theory is already breaching our shores and will wash us into the future (cf. Poole, in press). Perhaps the cynicism about the causal role of communication processes that I evince with socio-egocentric theory will engender the exploration of alternative architectures less prone to reductionism. This, too, could be a positive result of a potential weakness in socio-egocentric theory.

SUMMING UP

Too little care has been taken in testing claims concerning the ability of communication to constitute, guide, create, enhance, or inhibit small group decision making. The evidence for these claim is weak; yet the claims continue to be accepted as if they were firmly established. Current work on small group communication reflects the belief that we must study the *how* of communication influence rather than the *if*. We students of small group decision making have let our intuitive beliefs about the importance of communication overwhelm our critical faculties. With few exceptions (e.g., Poole et al., 1982), researchers have failed to meet the challenge to their beliefs issued by input → output models of group performance. Unless we meet this challenge, we face the very real possibility of erecting our theoretical foundations on sand.

Notes

1. My claim here is limited to the causal influence of the *content* of communication that takes place in the decision-making discussion on changes in outcomes at the group level, not the individual level. For example, excluded from my analysis are the effects of having the *opportunity* to discuss an issue on perceptions of the legitimacy of the decision-making process or on individual member satisfaction.

2. This may be a controversial claim. I am suggesting that to see communication as merely a delivery system for mental and societal forces means that communication has no unique predictive value. Moreover, it has no explanatory value under this condition in the way we want to think of explaining the effects of communication. For example, if we assume that communication is purely the product of preinteraction mental and

societal forces, then communication does not constitute mental and societal forces; it does not form social identity, change beliefs, alter social structure, and so on. If communication is reduced to a mediating role, this kind of explanation is not possible because communication must be reducible to preinteraction mental and societal forces.

3. An alternative, and even more flawed, approach is to avoid measuring communication processes directly and simply group performance under varying levels of opportunities to communicate (cf. Salazar, Hirokawa, Propp, Julian, & Leatham, 1994). In the last major section of this chapter, I return to the problems faced by this approach.

4. I have assumed that the processes being modeled are "first order," that is, that the sequential structure that they represent depends on only one previous act. As with the baseline model in Equations 7.1 and 7.2, the socio-egocentric model can be extended to more complicated cases without violating anything fundamental theoretically.

5. The details of the comparison and contrasts between Poole's multiple sequence model and the socio-egocentric approach require more space than I have here. They will be discussed in a manuscript soon to be completed.

6. Salazar et al. (1994) attempt to make task performance as involving as possible by making extra credit for the subjects dependent on successful performance for both high and low communication opportunity conditions. That does not mitigate the obvious point that face-to-face communication is simply more involving than reading material in the Delphi technique. That involvement provides motivation for both individual and interactive group problem-solving effectiveness.

7. Actually, we could assume that what is fixed is not simply the time interval between two actions, but rather the action and the temporal probability distribution of action that follows it. The time interval is not simply of a fixed length but of random length governed by a probability distribution whose form is contingent only in the previous action that triggered it.

8. Parallel processing systems share the following positive and negative analogies with small group communication. Both are made up of numerous nodes with the ability to process information, though the processing capacities of human nodes are much greater than those usually employed in parallel processing systems. The links between both kinds of nodes describe the state of the system, including its knowledge. The systems in both cases are assumed to be irreducible to the activity of individual nodes. On the other hand, parallel processing systems are purely parallel; that is, the nodes process information simultaneously. In groups, processing would appear to be both serial and parallel; that is, some of the information is being processed sequentially as it is presented in communication, but other aspects of it are being processed simultaneously in parallel. In addition, the nodes in groups, unlike those in parallel processing systems, do not attend to the activity of all other nodes all the time. They do adapt their communication rhetorically to other nodes—which does not happen in parallel processing systems. I am beginning to explore whether or not the insights obtained for parallel processing systems are relevant to small group communication given these negative analogies. I think they are.

References

Abelson, P. (1976). Script processing in attitude formation and decision-making. In J. S. Carroll & J. W. Payne (Eds.), *Cognition and social behavior* (pp. 33-45). Hillsdale, NJ: Lawrence Erlbaum.

Arundale, R. B. (1977). Sampling across time for communication research: A simulation. In P. M. Hirsch et al. (Eds.), *Strategies for communication research* (pp. 123-131). Beverly Hills, CA: Sage.

Bales, R. F. (1950). *Interaction process analysis: A method for studying small groups.* Reading, MA: Addison-Wesley.

Bales, R. F., & Strodtbeck, F. L. (1951). Phases in group problem-solving. *Journal of Abnormal and Social Psychology, 46,* 485-495.

Buys, C. J. (1978). Humans would do better without groups. *Personality and Social Psychology Bulletin, 4,* 123-125.

Collins, B. F., & Guetzkow, H. (1964). *A social psychology of group processes of decision-making.* New York: John Wiley.

Cragan, J. F., & Wright, D. W. (1980). Small group communication research of the 1970s: A synthesis and critique. *Central States Speech Journal, 31,* 197-213.

Davis, J. H. (1969a). *Group performance.* Reading, MA: Addison-Wesley.

Davis, J. H. (1969b). Individual, group problem-solving, subject preferences and problem type. *Journal of Personality and Social Psychology, 3,* 362-374.

Davis, J. H. (1973). Group decision and social interaction: A theory of social decision schemes. *Psychological Review, 80,* 97-125.

Davis, J. H. (1980). Group decision and procedural justice. In M. Fishbein (Ed.), *Progress in social psychology* (Vol. 1, pp. 157-229). Hillsdale, NJ: Lawrence Erlbaum.

Davis, J. H., & Restle, F. (1963). The analysis of problems and predictions of group problem solving. *Journal of Abnormal and Social Psychology, 66,* 103-116.

Davis, J. H., Spitzer, C. E., Nagao, C., & Stasser, G. (1978). The nature of bias in social decisions by individuals and groups: An example from mock juries. In H. Brandstatter, J. Davis, & H. Schuler (Eds.), *Dynamics of group decisions* (pp. 33-52). Beverly Hills, CA: Sage.

Delbecq, A. L., Van de Ven, A. H., & Gustafson, D. H. (1975). *Group techniques for program planning: A guide to nominal group and Delphi processes.* Glenview, IL: Scott, Foresman.

Dewey, J. (1910). *How we think.* Boston: D. C. Heath.

Duncan, S., & Fiske, D. (1977). *Face-to-face interaction: Research, methods, and theory.* Hillsdale, NJ: Lawrence Erlbaum.

Ellis, D. G. (1979). Relational control in two group systems. *Communication Monographs, 46,* 153-166.

Ellis, D. G., & Fisher, B. A. (1975). Phases of conflict in small group development: A Markov analysis. *Human Communication Research, 1,* 195-212.

Ericsson, K., & Simon, H. A. (1993). *Protocol analysis: Verbal reports as data* (2nd ed.). Cambridge: MIT Press.

Fisher, B. A. (1970). Decision emergence: Phases in group decision-making. *Speech Monographs, 37,* 53-66.

Folger, J. P., Hewes, D. E., & Poole, M. S. (1984). Coding social interaction. In B. Dervin & M. Voight (Eds.), *Progress in communication science* (Vol. 4, pp. 115-161). Norwood, NJ: Ablex.

Gordon, K. (1923). A study of aesthetic judgments. *Journal of Experimental Psychology, 6,* 36-43.

Hawes, L., & Foley, J. (1973). A Markov analysis of interview communication. *Speech Monographs, 40,* 208-219.

Hewes, D. E. (1986). A socio-egocentric model of group decision-making. In R. Y. Hirokawa & M. S. Poole (Eds.), *Communication and group decision-making* (1st ed., pp. 265-291). Beverly Hills, CA: Sage.

Hewes, D. E. (1990). *Challenging interaction influence on group decision-making: Extending the socioegocentric model.* Paper presented to the Speech Communication Association, Chicago.

Hewes, D. E. (1995). Cognitive interpersonal communication research: Some thoughts on criteria. In B. R. Burleson (Ed.), *Communication yearbook 18* (pp. 162-179). Thousand Oaks, CA: Sage.

Hewes, D. E., Planalp, S., & Streibel, M. (1980). Analyzing social interaction: Some excruciating models and exhilarating results. In D. Nimmo (Ed.), *Communication yearbook 4* (pp. 123-144). New Brunswick, NJ: ICA-Transaction Books.

Hirokawa, R. Y. (1980). A comparative analysis of communication patterns within effective and ineffective decision-making groups. *Communication Monographs, 47,* 312-321.

Hirokawa, R. Y., & Pace, R. C. (1983). A descriptive investigation of the possible communication-based reasons for effective and ineffective group decision-making. *Communication Monographs, 50,* 363-379.

Hoffman, L. R. (1979). *The group problem-solving process: Studies of a valence model.* New York: Praeger.

Hoffman, L. R., & Kleinman, G. B. (1994). Individual and group in group problem solving: The valence model redressed. *Human Communication Research, 21,* 36-59.

Holmes, M., & Poole, M. S. (1991). The longitudinal analysis of interaction. In B. Montgomery & S. Duck (Eds.), *Studying interpersonal interaction* (pp. 286-302). New York: Guilford.

Hopfield, J. J. (1982). Neural networks and physical systems with emergent collective computational abilities. *Proceedings of the National Academy of Sciences, 79,* 2554-2558.

Janis, I. L., & Mann, L. (1977). *Decision making: A psychological analysis of conflict, choice, and commitment.* New York: Free Press.

Kelso, J. A. S. (1995). *Dynamic patterns.* Cambridge: MIT Press.

Knight, H. C. (1921). *A comparison of the reliability of group and individual judgments.* Unpublished master's thesis, Columbia University.

Lamm, H., & Trommsdorff, J. (1973). Group versus individual performance on tasks requiring ideational proficiency (brainstorming): A review. *European Journal of Social Psychology, 3,* 361-388.

Larson, C. E. (1969). Forms of analysis and small group problem-solving. *Speech Monographs, 36,* 452-455.

Lorge, I., & Solomon, H. (1955). Two models of group behavior in the solution of eureka-type problems. *Psychometrika, 20,* 139-148.

McPhee, R. D. (1994). Response to Hoffman and Kleinman. *Human Communication Research, 21,* 60-63.

McPhee, R. D., Poole, M. S., & Seibold, D. R. (1981). The valence model unveiled: A critique and alternative formulation. In M. Burgoon (Ed.), *Communication yearbook 5* (pp. 259-278). New Brunswick, NJ: Transaction Books.

Penrod, S., & Hastie, R. (1979). Models of jury decision-making: A critical review. *Psychological Bulletin, 86,* 462-492.

Penrod, S., & Hastie, R. (1980). A computer simulation of jury decision-making. *Psychological Bulletin, 87,* 133-159.

Piaget, J. (1926). *The language and thought of the child.* New York: Harcourt & Brace.

Piaget, J. (1955). *The construction of reality in the child.* London: Routledge & Kegan Paul.

Planalp, S., & Hewes, D. E. (1982). A cognitive approach to communication theory: Cogito ergo dico? In M. Burgoon (Ed.), *Communication yearbook 5* (pp. 49-78). New Brunswick, NJ: Transaction Books.

Poole, M. S. (1981). Decision development in small groups I: A comparison of two models. *Communication Monographs, 48*, 1-24.

Poole, M. S. (in press). A turn of the wheel: The case for a renewal of systems inquiry in organizational communication research. In G. Barnett & L. Thayer (Eds.), *Organizations-communication V*. Norwood, NJ: Ablex.

Poole, M. S., & DeSanctis, G. (1990). Understanding the use of group decision support systems: The theory of adaptive structuration. In J. Fulk & C. Steinfield (Eds.), *Organizations and communication technology* (pp. 175-195). Newbury Park, CA: Sage.

Poole, M. S., & Hunter, J. E. (1979). Change in hierarchically-organized attitudes. In D. Nimmo (Ed.), *Communication yearbook 3* (pp.157-176). New Brunswick, NJ: Transaction Books.

Poole, M. S., McPhee, R. D., & Seibold, D. R. (1982). A comparison of normative and interactional explanations of group decision-making: Social decision schemes versus valence distributions. *Communication Monographs, 49*, 1-19.

Poole, M. S., & Roth, J. (1989). Decision development in small groups IV: A typology of decision paths. *Human Communication Research, 15*, 323-356.

Poole, M. S., Seibold, D. R., & McPhee, R. D. (1986). A structurational approach to theory-building in group decision-making research. In R. Y. Hirokawa & M. S. Poole (Eds.), *Communication and group decision-making* (1st ed., pp. 237-264). Beverly Hills, CA: Sage.

Preston, M. (1938). A note on the reliability and validity of group judgment. *Journal of Experimental Psychology, 22*, 462-471.

Rosenberg, S., Erlick, D. S., & Berkowitz, L. (1955). Some effects of varying combinations of group members on group performance measures and leadership behaviors. *Journal of Abnormal and Social Psychology, 51*, 195-203.

Rumelhart, D. E., McClelland, J. L., & the PDP Research Group. (1986). *Parallel distributed processing*. Cambridge: MIT Press.

Sackett, G. P. (1979). The lag sequential analysis of contingency and cyclicity in behavioral interaction research. In J. D. Osofsky (Ed.), *Handbook of infant development* (pp. 210-223). New York: John Wiley.

Salazar, A. J., Hirokawa, R. Y., Propp, K., Julian, K. M., & Leatham, G. B. (1994). In search of true causes: Examining the effects of group potential and group interaction on decision performance. *Human Communication Research, 20*, 529-559.

Scheidel, T. M., & Crowell, L. (1964). Idea development in small discussion groups. *Quarterly Journal of Speech, 59*, 140-145.

Shaw, M. E. (1932). A comparison of individuals and small groups in the rational solution of complex problems. *American Journal of Psychology, 44*, 491-504.

Sokolov, A. N. (1972). *Inner speech and thought*. New York: Plenum.

Steinfatt, T., & Miller, G. R. (1974). Communication in game theoretic models of conflict. In G. R. Miller & H. Simmons (Eds.), *Perspectives on communication in social conflicts* (pp. 14-75). Englewood Cliffs, NJ: Prentice Hall.

Stevens, S. (1950). A definition of communication. *Journal of the Acoustical Society of America, 22*, 689-690.

Taylor, D. W. (1954). *Problem solving in groups*. Proceedings of the 14th International Congress on Psychology, Montreal.

Tesser, A. (1978). Self-generated attitude change. In L. Berkowitz (Ed.), *Advances in experimental social psychology* (pp. 289-338). New York: Academic Press.

Tuckman, B. W. (1965). Developmental sequence in small groups. *Psychological Bulletin, 64*, 384-399.

Vygotsky, L. (1962). *Thought and language*. Cambridge: MIT Press.

Zander, A. (1971). *Motives and goals in groups*. New York: Academic Press.

Zivin, G. (1979). *The development of self-regulation through private speech*. New York: John Wiley.

PROCESSES

Developmental Processes in Group Decision Making

MARSHALL SCOTT POOLE
CAROLYN L. BALDWIN

Interaction is the essence of group decision making. In its complex interplay, ideas and options are advanced and discredited; goals are set, elaborated, challenged, shown to be ambiguous; commitments are offered and assessed; actors enter and withdraw from discussions; decision proposals are tested, refined, modified, and confirmed. Even when outside political maneuvering has already decided the issues, groups meet to clarify, justify, and "talk through" the decision, or to cloak machinations in ceremonial debate. These elaborations are just as important to the ultimate effectiveness of a decision and just as much a part of "decision making" as idea development or deliberations.

The study of decision development is concerned with how group interaction creates and elaborates decisions over time. The developmental research strategy has several advantages. It focuses attention on temporal patterns in decision making, uncovering distinctive features and differences not detectable with other strategies. It also centers squarely on the group interaction processes through which decisions are constituted. As McGrath and Altman (1966) argued, research that simply relates inputs to outputs and ignores the process by which a group arrives at a decision is seriously flawed. Because it establishes the temporal order of events, the developmental strategy also facilitates causal analysis.

When the chapter on decision development was written for the first edition of this book (Poole & Doelger, 1986), there was relatively little research on decision development per se. However, in the succeeding years a number of gaps have been filled, and theoretical development has proceeded apace. The current chapter will review various models of decision development and weigh the evidence for each. It will also take a broader look at what the accumulated evidence tells us about decision development.

Before proceeding it is necessary to distinguish two developmental processes that may influence decision making: development of the decision itself and the longer-term development of the group as an entity. This chapter is primarily concerned with development of single decisions. Such decisions may be very brief or extend over numerous meetings; they may involve as few as three members or a very large group. This means that we are not directly concerned with the extended life cycle of groups, as exemplified by Lacoursiere's (1980) work, although this is relevant insofar as it influences individual decisions.

Theoretical Perspectives on Decision Development

At least four distinct models of decision development have been offered during the past 10 years: phase models, critical event models, continuous models, and social construction models. Each model advances a unique description of decision development and a different generative mechanism. This section briefly reviews the basic assumptions and leading exemplars of each type.

PHASE MODELS

Most studies of decision development picture it as a series of phases groups pass through on their way to a choice. A *phase* is defined as a period of coherent activity that serves some decision-related function, such as problem definition, orientation, solution development, or socioemotional expression (which is assumed to contribute to decision making by enabling groups to vent frustrations or to integrate themselves).

The best established models of decision development posit a single, set sequence of phases leading to a decision. Bales and Strodtbeck (1951) posited the classic model of decision development as a *unitary sequence* of three phases—a period of orientation followed by an evaluation phase followed by a control phase. Upon testing this model on a sample of 22 groups, they found it supported for 7 out of 8 groups that had fulfilled a set of conditions for a "full-fledged" problem-solving session. Later research by Landsberger (1955), Heinecke and Bales (1956), and Morris (1970) also supported this model. Fisher (1970) coded 10 groups with his Decision Proposal Coding System, divided the coded data into four equal segments, and tested for differences in segment interaction profiles to derive a four-phase unitary sequence model: orientation, conflict, emergence, and reinforcement. Mabry (1975) developed and tested another unitary sequence model based on Parsons's pattern variable model (Parsons, Shils, & Olds, 1951).

Unitary sequence models explain decision behavior in terms of the group's response to an ordered sequence of problems or requirements for building a decision, such as Bales and Strodtbeck's (1951) logically based sequence of decision problems or Fisher's (1970) four-step conflict resolution pattern. Implicitly, they assume that all groups—or at least the average group—will follow an identical sequence of phases. Unitary sequence models are widely used in textbooks on group communication, in part because their clarity and logic make them good teaching tools.

Another class of phase models argues that groups may follow different developmental sequences, depending on various contingencies. These *multiple sequence models* do not deny the occurrence of the set sequence posited by unitary sequence models, but argue that this is only one of many paths decisions may follow. Groups may also follow more complicated paths in which phases repeat themselves and groups cycle back to previously completed activities as they discover problems or encounter difficulties. Also possible are shorter, degenerate sequences containing only part of the complement of unitary sequence phases.

Poole (1981) argued that unitary sequence studies had problems of design and analysis that biased them in favor of finding a single sequence of phases. These problems included (a) dividing discussions into the same number of segments as expected phases, thereby hiding developmental complexities that might refute the hypothesis of a single sequence; and (b) summarizing data across groups, thereby preventing the discovery of between-group differences in development. Poole conducted a comparative test of the unitary and multiple sequence models on data segmented into 10 divisions (many more phases than any unitary model posited) and used a design that permitted between-group comparisons. For two different operationalizations of phases, Poole found significant between-group differences in development, suggesting rejection of the unitary sequence model. The multiple sequence models accounted for 2.5 times more variance in developmental trends than did the unitary model. The existence of multiple decision sequences has also been documented in a number of studies of group and organizational decision making (Chandler, 1981; Hirokawa, 1983; Mintzberg, Raisinghani, & Theoret, 1976; Nutt, 1984b; Poole, 1983a; Poole & Roth, 1989a).

Multiple sequence studies suggest that differences in development can be explained by contingency variables that cause groups to take different decision paths. Possible contingency variables include task characteristics (Poole, 1983b; Poole & Roth, 1989b), degree of conflict in the decision (Mintzberg et al., 1976; Poole & Roth, 1989b), group composition (Sorenson, 1971), group size (Poole & Roth, 1989b), and group cohesiveness (Poole & Roth, 1989b). Depending on these contingency variables, group decision paths may vary in terms of the types of group activities and the order in which they occur, the number of cycles of repetitive phases a group passes through, and the degree to which the decision path follows the normative sequence of phases posited in unitary sequence models (Mintzberg et al., 1976; Nutt, 1984b; Poole & Roth, 1989b).

Multiple sequence models are advantageous because they take into account the observable complexity in group decision paths; they do not confine the researcher to an ideal type sequence or to labeling cases that fail to fit the ideal "non-full-fledged" decisions, as did Bales and Strodtbeck (1951). These models also take into account the responsiveness of groups to their context and the constraints imposed by outside factors. They promise to provide normative models to help practitioners adapt to changing demands.

However, there is also evidence that phase models provide only a limited picture of decision behavior. Studies examining the detailed local structure of group activities yield a more complicated view of decisions. Poole (1981) isolated clusters of associated behaviors from 10-act segments of decision-making discussions by student and physician groups. He found 19 distinct activity clusters for student groups and 17 for physician groups, only some of which were redundant across both samples. In a factor analytic study of member-leader behavior in classroom groups, Mann (1966) found six dimensions of behavior that combined in complex ways to produce different activity patterns. Cyclic studies discussed in more detail below also found more complex behavior patterns than can be captured by phase descriptions (Scheidel & Crowell, 1964; Segal, 1982). Research on the distribution and duration of content themes in task-oriented groups also suggests a complex pattern of attention and activity shifts. Though the phase concept is generally accepted, it may also limit our thinking about decision development.

CRITICAL EVENT MODELS

Another class of models argues that decision development can best be understood by identifying key milestones or turning points in the decision process. The focus is on the general strategies behind group decision behavior and on shifts in strategy and direction, rather than on detailed maps of decision behavior. So decision development is described in terms of a succession of strategies or approaches a group adopts; it is explained by accounting for causes of shifts in strategy or direction.

MacKenzie (1976) describes decision development in terms of a series of milestones groups must attain to complete a task. For each task a group undertakes, a set of milestones can be defined that represents the subtasks or steps that must be accomplished to complete the task; MacKenzie refers to this as the task structure. For example, with a ranking task like "Lost on the Moon," the milestones might be:

1. Members finish their individual rankings;
2. Information on other members' rankings held by all members;
3. Group agrees on top-ranked item;

4. Group agrees on second-ranked item;

   [Group agrees on third-, fourth-, and so forth, ranked item through item 15];

16. Group agrees on entire ranking of list;

17. Group reports answer to experimenter.

For most tasks there is a normative ordering of milestones so that groups can be said to attain them in a timely (in order) or untimely (out of order) fashion. Associated with each milestone are related behaviors and messages that can be used to determine which milestone a group is working on as well as group progress toward a decision. Milestone structures are part of a formal stochastic model of decision making that also includes role structures and communication structures. The model tries to account for decision making and group evolution in terms of dynamic changes in these structures. Of course, the definition of milestones limits the scope of the model to well-defined tasks.

Gersick (1988), drawing on the paradigm of punctuated equilibrium, articulates a model of group development that frames the history of a group as phases of inertia punctuated by transitory periods of upheaval and quantum change. Gersick highlights two elements of organizational groups that have not traditionally been central to small group research: timing as a trigger of critical events, and groups' dynamic relationships with their environments (Gersick, 1988).

There are three key components in Gersick's model: deep structure, equilibrium periods, and revolutionary periods. The first construct, deep structure, describes the fundamental and highly stable elements of a system that define the system's basic units of organization and the activity patterns required to maintain the system's existence (Gersick, 1991). For an organizational group, this deep structure includes, for example, interpretive frameworks that describe patterns of interaction, performance strategies, or assumptions about the group's task or external environment. Gersick (1991) describes deep structure as "the rules of the game" and equilibrium periods as "the game in play" (p. 16). Though groups in equilibrium may exhibit enough variability and incremental change to mask underlying deep structures, basic patterns of activity and organization remain constant. The final element of the punctuated equilibrium model is the revolutionary period. Continuing Gersick's (1991) analogy, the revolutionary period is a critical event that changes the rules of the game: "The definitive assertion in this paradigm is that systems do not shift from one kind of game to another through incremental steps: such transformations occur through wholesale upheaval" (p. 19).

In her research, described below, Gersick found that this revolutionary period coincided with the halfway point in a group's work, as members evaluated what they had done and tried to get organized to finish their tasks. This period triggered an attempt to change the strategy that was set throughout the first equilibrium period. If this change is successful, then the group settles into a new equilibrium period and completes its work. If it is not, the group continues enacting problems that prevented progress in the first equilibrium. Hence Gersick presents a macro-level view of decision development as a series of (usually two) uniform periods of work punctuated by a critical transition period.

One strength of critical event models is that they seem to describe decision development in terms similar to how it would be recalled by participants: as a series of global events and turning points. In addition, critical event models give a more general, summative account of decision activities at the strategy level. This has theoretical utility because it isolates a relatively small number of strategies, each of which might be executed in a wide variety of different behavioral sequences, thus yielding wider generality across groups. It is also useful to practitioners because it focuses on strategies rather than on hard-to-grasp, multiplicitous behavior.

These strengths also bring with them limitations. By abstracting from the stream of decision behavior, critical event models run the risk of oversimplifying, of missing important distinctions in different implementations of the same strategy. Also, critical event models key on changes or shifts in direction to describe decision paths, rather than focusing attention on how strategies are implemented. They thereby downplay the role of small, incremental changes and of repetitive, cyclical activity in decision making.

CONTINUOUS MODELS

A third group of models depicts decision development as a continuous process of change rather than as a series of phasic "blocks" dropped in a row. As such, development is better captured by models that track changes in continuous variables rather than by those that identify categorical constructs such as phases. Continuous models focus on cyclical patterns of development and on the ebb and flow of state variables (Segal, 1982). For instance, one feature of decision development is the regular cycling of socioemotional activity, which reflects alternations in attention to the task and to group maintenance (Bales, 1953; Poole, 1981). Continuous descriptions can also be translated into phasic descriptions; characteristic patterns among continuous variables can be used as phase indicators, permitting segmentation of continuous processes into phase sequences (e.g., Poole, 1981). However, this partitioning is artificial, because the processes that drive development are assumed to operate continuously.

One of the most influential continuous models was developed by Scheidel and Crowell (1964). They posit that groups develop ideas through a " 'reach-test' type of motion" in which one member advances an idea and then the group elaborates on it at length and expresses approval before going on to the next idea. They propose that this cyclical process of introduction, discussion, and anchoring of group positions is important to building commitment to the group's solution.

Building on Scheidel and Crowell, Poole (1983b) proposed a contingency model that attempted to reconcile phasic models with the evidence that development was more complex than phase theories allowed. Poole's model portrays development as a series of intertwining threads of activity that evolve simultaneously and interweave in different patterns over time. Poole proposed three threads initially: (a) task process activities (e.g., problem analysis, solution evaluation); (b) relational character (activity patterns that reflect the working relationship among members at a given point in time—e.g., integration, focused work, conflict); and (c) topical focus (the substantive issues being dealt with in group activities). When these three threads develop in a coordinated fashion (which probably happens most of the time), the coherent phases assumed by unitary or multiple sequence models result. These phases can be characterized by an ordered triple of activities along these dimensions, such as

{problem analysis::focused work::topic a},

a combination that could be labeled a *problem definition phase*. However, when the threads are not coordinated and the group shifts behavioral patterns very rapidly, there will be no coherent pattern and no phases can be discerned. In such cases it is more sensible to consider each thread in its own right.

Completing the descriptive model are three types of *breakpoints*, events that represent discontinuities in interaction and that may signal developmental transitions. These breakpoints show the operation of intermittent causal processes that locally redirect group interaction. *Normal breakpoints* (topic shifts and adjournments) institute breaks without disrupting group activities. Second, there are *delays* during which the group cycles back to rework previously completed points; generally these are spurred by the need to comprehend or to adapt to new contingencies. Third, there are *disruptions,* either when a major conflict halts the group's progress or when failures cause the group to reconsider its work. The developmental pattern of the three threads and the breakpoints reveals phases as well as periods of noncoherent activity in group work.

Developmental paths are determined by the interplay of two forces: an "underlying" requisite structural model and a set of contingency factors. The structural model represents the basic requirements for task completion, which may vary from task to task. For a problem-solving group these include problem recognition, problem definition, the search for and generation of solutions, the adaptation of solutions to the problem, evaluation of solutions in light of criteria for solving the problem, and implementation planning. This structure of requirements defines logical prerequisites for task completion and entails a definite order of activities. As such, it sets basic parameters for decision development. However, this basic sequence is complicated by contingency factors—task and group structural characteristics—that determine the adaptations groups must make in the basic sequence. These influence four aspects of decision development: (a) types of group activities and the order in which they occur; (b) the number of cycles of repetitive activities; (c) the types and frequencies of breakpoints; and (d) the degree of coordination among the three activity threads.

Poole and Roth (1989a, 1989b) conducted a partial test of this model with a sample of 47 group decisions drawn from a variety of contexts.

They coded task and relational activities in these discussions and developed a flexible phase mapping procedure to identify the sequence of decision-making phases in each. The flexible phase mapping procedure, formalized by Holmes and Poole (1991), makes no assumptions about the number or nature of the phase sequences that will be found: Sequences may differ in number and order of phases, and phases may repeat. The procedure is capable of identifying a wide range of decision paths, from simple unitary sequences to complicated paths with many recycles.

Poole and Roth measured three sets of contingency variables for each group: objective task characteristics (those that did not depend on the group's experience with the task: e.g., goal clarity, solution multiplicity); group task characteristics (those that depended on the group's experience with the task: e.g., novelty); and internal structural variables (cohesiveness, degree of concentration of power, history of conflict, and group size). As we will detail below, variables from all three sets predicted the degree to which the path departed from the unitary sequence, complexity of developmental path, and the particular decision activities that occurred. The variables did not predict degree of coordination among threads.

Poole's contingency model integrates several aspects of other models. It accounts for the relationship among unitary and other possible developmental paths, and explains the role of the requisite structures that generate unitary sequences in decision development. The conception of intertwining threads interspersed with breakpoints offers a more complex picture of decision processes than do phase models. Breakpoints capture some of the properties of critical events. If the variety of decision paths can be determined and effective contingency variables identified, the model will also have practical utility.

However, there are also problems. Poole and Roth did not assess continuous properties of decision paths, but rather translated continuous variables into phase sequences. Hence the contingency model has yet to be tested in the terms in which it was originally cast. In addition, the generative mechanism for coordinating activity threads is not very well specified by Poole (1983b). Threads "intertwine," but it is unclear what drives or influences this process. Attempts to solve these and other problems have led some to posit social construction models of decision development.

SOCIAL CONSTRUCTION MODELS

Poole (1985) states the reasoning behind social construction approaches:

Without reference to microlevel processes, a complete explanation of decision development is impossible. Contingency theories promise extremely effective prediction and explanations of group developmental sequences. However, knowing the order of a group's phases does not tell us *how* the sequence developed as it did. Existing accounts of logical requirements and the effects of contingency variables on group activities give us some penetration of this question, but they still leave open the mechanism through which these factors operate. An adequate explanation must lay out the generative mechanism whereby causes have their effects. And any generative mechanism for the explanation of group activity must be tied to an account of members' activity and interaction, because this is the only means by which any group activity can be carried out. It is not satisfactory simply to assert that the decision structure, the contingency factors, and the phases relate to each other. An adequate theory must account for how a decision is constituted in and through interaction, how the contingency factors are mediated by member reactions, and how interaction advances the group toward a decision. (p. 212)

Several researchers have studied aspects of the social construction of decisions. In her excellent study, *The Meeting*, Schwartzman (1989) discusses how decisions are framed by discursive moves both during and after meetings. Schwartzman observes that decision making per se comprises a relatively small proportion of meeting time; functions such as sensemaking, solidification of the group, meeting members' individual needs for status and power, and socializing often receive more attention (see also Weick, 1979). Moves that frame decisions include labeling a segment of discussion "decision making," treating statements as assertions or arguments rather than some other type of speech act, and confirming agreement on a conclusion to bring the segment of discussion to an end. In addition, decisions may be made post hoc, during postmeeting discussions in which members make sense of their meeting by formulating what was done as a decision. Schwartzman's study highlights the varied ways in which groups actively construct decisions.

Fisher and Stutman (1987) analyze breakpoints as tools for social construction. They argue that Poole's contingency model does not adequately recognize the role of breakpoints in framing decisions. For them, breakpoints are key points at which the group has a chance either to change direction or to reaffirm its current direction. At breakpoints members seek to influence discussion through prospective and retrospective routing statements. Prospective routing statements try to move the discussion in a certain direction, whereas retrospective routing statements try to set direction by summarizing and reformulating what the group has done. Both of these statement types serve to frame the beginnings and endings of discussion phases. If routing statements are accepted, they serve to redirect discussion; if they are rejected, the group is reaffirming its current direction.

Another social construction approach was offered by Poole and Doelger (1986; Poole, 1985) in their model of the structuration of decision paths. This model addresses two questions: (a) How are coherent phases constituted in group interaction; and (b) how does the group manage transitions between phases? Building on Poole's contingency model, it attempts to show how micro-level structuring processes in group interaction generate molar-level phase sequences. Group members draw on structures of rules and resources to conduct their activities; this constitutes the path to a decision and the decision itself. In turn, these structures are themselves produced and reproduced as they are used to generate a decision. There is thus a double constitution of the decision system and its underlying structures in a continuous process of structuration (see Poole, Seibold, & McPhee, Chapter 5, this volume, for a more complete discussion).

Poole and Doelger (1986) discuss two types of structures important in the social construction of group decisions: task representations and rules for maintaining discursive coherence. Task representations are mental models of how the task should be done; they are made up of a substantive representation of the nature of the task and a decision logic specifying how the group should make decisions. Several decision logics are available to groups, including rational logic, political logic, and assumed consensus (Poole, 1985). These logics represent different social norms that have evolved to govern decision making and specify different idealized sequences of steps for the decision process; for example, rational logic embodies the classical unitary model. Task representations may be individual or shared, and one purpose of interaction is the development of shared representations. Coherence structures are the discourse rules that members can draw on to make their discourse coherent and cohesive, such as the rules underlying the use of lexical ties, motive talk, or side sequences. These are not the only structures involved in decision making; Poole and DeSanctis (1992) show how technological and procedural structures influence decision making, and other structures such as custom, special knowledge, and members' power may be used to influence decision-making discussions.

Here is how the structuring process works: Members advance various task representations, and the group constructs one or more representations through interaction. Coherence structures are applied to give continuity and cohesiveness to discussion. If the group converges on a single representation that adequately addresses the objective requirements of the task, then a relatively simple decision path will result, one likely to conform to a unitary sequence model. More complex paths result when more than one representation is utilized at different points in a discussion, when two or more representations compete with each other, or when a representation is not adequate to deal with objective task demands and the group experiences failure or must cycle back to rework its representation. Each of these cases corresponds to various types of breakpoints from Poole's contingency model. Nonorganized periods of interaction result when the group's appropriation of coherence structures is not sufficient to overcome problems introduced by difficulties with the task or conflicts among task representations.

The structurational model is concerned with how the developmental paths described in phase models and Poole's contingency model are constituted in group interaction. It portrays the generative process underlying decision development. According to the theory, the contingency variables that influence decision paths operate through their influence on group interaction. Because interaction processes mediate contingency relationships, members' interpretations of and reactions to contingencies play an important role in decision development. As a result, there can be no strong deterministic explanations for decision development; rather than being regarded as error variance, individual differences among groups with the same combination of contingency variables are predicted by the theory. The theory explains these differences as emergents, constructed according to the particular pattern of structural appropriations each group develops. These emergents are influenced by, among other things, the nature of the structures that are appropriated (a group using Robert's Rules of Order to organize its process will have a different path than one using consensus decision-making techniques), the degree of consensus on which structures should be used and how they are used, and members' degree of insight into structures (greater insight into structures allows better control and ability to adapt a structure to contextual demands).

The structurational model of decision development has several strong points. It concentrates on how decisions are constituted by micro-level group interaction, providing a more specific explanation for social construction than many other theories. Although many theories acknowledge the importance of social construction, most simply assert it and concentrate on traditional variable-based models. Many social construction theories, on the other hand, underplay the importance of exogenous variables and focus primarily on interaction dynamics. Structuration theory is concerned with the nexus of action and context and attempts to give each its measure.

One disadvantage is the relative lack of parsimony of social construction models compared to phase theories or contingency models. These models offer a complex view that defies simple propositional theory building and complete specification of influences. For example, Poole and Doelger (1986) did not specify the different ways in which groups may appropriate structures; this was left for a later study by Poole and DeSanctis (1992) and will be a useful addition to the theory just described. Another problem specific to the structurational models is that they cannot be tested in the same terms in which they are written. These theories posit a duality of structure whereby system and structure are both simultaneously and continuously produced and reproduced. However, it is impossible to study both sides of the duality simultaneously. Either social structures must serve as ground as action becomes the figure, or action must be pushed into the background in the study of structures and social institutions. This methodological convenience is somewhat uncomfortable.

At this point, the social construction perspective on decision development is still in its infancy. Accounts of the constitution of decisions are for the most part fragmentary, and relatively little evidence is available on the utility or nature of the social construction process.

RELATIONSHIPS AMONG THE MODELS

The models in this section do not seem to offer competing explanations, but rather different views of a complicated phenomenon. The phase, critical event, and cyclical models focus on overt, observable decision-making activities, whereas the social construction models, and Gersick's critical event model, are concerned with more subtle processes whereby the observable level is constituted. Moving from phase to cyclical to social construction models introduces increasing complexity to our descriptions and explanations. Because more complex descriptions can always be transformed into simpler ones, aspects of social construction models can be studied with cyclical and phase representations (see, e.g., Poole & DeSanctis, 1992), and aspects of cyclical models can be studied from a phasic perspective (see, e.g., Poole & Roth, 1989a). Critical events are useful supplements to the other descriptions, offering explanations for phase transitions or directional shifts. As Fisher and Stutman (1987) showed, the social construction of critical events and the group's response to them can be used to show how decision paths are constituted by the group. In short, the pictures offered by the various models are susceptible to integration in a common frame. The structuration model has already offered a partial integration, and a more thoroughgoing one seems likely to emerge in the future.

Evidence About the Nature of Decision Development

Certainly no observation is totally independent of the theory or model that spawns it, but results of studies conducted under one model can inform another. This section gathers empirical results on four key issues from a broad range of studies. These results may provide parameters for future models and stimulate additional questions.

TYPES OF DECISION PATHS

As noted in the discussion of phase models, numerous studies suggest that the classical unitary sequence is only one of a number of decision paths that may occur. These studies vary widely in type of groups sampled, group size, task, and context, so support for the existence of multiple sequences seems robust and general. Several studies have classified developmental sequences into distinct types, and they indicate that the rational unitary sequence does occur fairly often but that it is not the predominant type. Poole (1983a) found that 3 out of 10 groups in his study had clear unitary sequences, whereas 2 others were "borderline" cases. Poole and Roth (1989a) sampled a very diverse set of groups and found 11 out of 47 decisions to follow a unitary sequence. Segal's (1982) study of cycles in decision making found that about 25% of the cycles followed a unitary sequence. In Nutt's (1984b) study of organizational decision processes (most of which were made by strategic groups), 25% of the identified decision paths resemble the unitary sequence. Based on this evidence, a good guess would be that about a quarter of the decisions in a given sample will approximate the rational decision sequence.

What other sequences occur? Poole and Roth (1989a) found that 22 of 47 decisions in their sample had complex cyclic paths in which the same phases recurred repeatedly; about half these cycles were full or partial unitary sequences. Chandler (1981) and Segal (1982) also found cyclic patterns in group decisions. Segal found that the phases in her groups' cycles occurred in the expected unitary order less than 25% of the time. Nutt (1984b) and Mintzberg et al. (1976), too, found cycling in almost all their organizational decisions.

Also common are decision paths that start with discussion of solutions, counter to the rational norms underlying most unitary models. Poole and Roth (1989a) found that 14 out of 47 decisions in their sample followed paths in which the discussion of solutions was the primary focus; moreover, several of the groups that followed the unitary sequence started out with a short period of solution development and then shifted to the rational sequence. In Nutt's (1984b) study, 37% of the decision paths were primarily solution-centered.

What accounts for the existence of these other types of paths? One possibility is that other normative models of decision making inspire members to take paths different from the rational unitary sequence. In his discussion of decision logics, Poole (1985) identified rational, assumed consensus, and political models that could guide members' decision strategies. Each of these implies a different sequence of activities for decision making; for example, the political model implies that members start with solutions and try to work out acceptable compromises. Honeycutt and Poole (1994) found that individuals' procedural schemata for decision making could be classed into three general types: rational, political, and information sharing. There were also a number of schemata in their study that did not fall into these three categories. In a later section we discuss the possible influence of contingency variables in the multiplication of decision paths.

We have noted that a large proportion of decision-making groups appear to follow cyclic paths that loop back as the group goes through various iterations in its decision process. In addition to these task-related cycles, cycles of socioemotional expression have also been found. Poole (1983a; Poole & Roth, 1989a) found two types of such cycles: (a) cycles with short periods in which joking and other positive socioemotional expression occur briefly and often break up task discussions, and (b) longer period cycles in which work on the task is broken by periods of integration characterized by joking and tangential comments. Poole (1983a) also found cycles of conflict in some decisions. These cyclic patterns are consistent with Bales's equilibrium hypothesis, which asserted that working groups build up tension that must be vented through socioemotional activity.

CRITICAL EVENTS AND DECISION DEVELOPMENT

Several studies shed light on various types of critical events. Poole discussed breakpoints in decision paths as one type of critical event. Poole and Roth (1989a) found that 34 out of 47 decision paths had delays, signaled by recycling to previous phases, and that 20 out of 47 decision paths had disruptions, indicated by conflicts.

Fisher and Stutman (1987), mentioned earlier, interpreted breakpoints as potential junctures at which members decide whether to change the group's direction. At breakpoints, members attempt to influence the course of the discussion through routing statements, prospective and retrospective. Based on an analysis of several decisions, Fisher and Stutman venture that prospective routing statements are most likely to be effective if they are timed properly, are tied to a substantive issue, are not overly controlling or authoritarian, and do not try to project too far ahead. Retrospective routing statements are most likely to be effective if they exhibit a positive tone about previous group interaction. Fisher and Stutman emphasize that routing statements are only bids to redirect the discussion. The group may reject them and, in effect, confirm its present direction at the breakpoint. Fisher and Stutman posit two additional functions of breakpoints, beyond serving as discussion watersheds. They serve a maintenance function in that they help to anchor developing group consensus, and they help to "recycle" ideas. In this sense, breakpoints are tied to the "reach-test" process described by Scheidel and Crowell (1964).

Gersick's (1983, 1988, 1989) studies of field and laboratory task groups elucidate the operation of critical events as transition periods—time-limited and time-sensitive opportunities for radical group progress—that consistently occur precisely at the halfway point in groups' official calendars. This has been a stable finding despite considerable variation in the amount of time allotted for task completion and the type of task involved (Gersick, 1988). The critical event, then, marks off two distinct phases of activity.

Within the Phase I-Transition-Phase II pattern, three points are of particular interest: a group's first meeting, in which members implicitly and explicitly set forth the patterns of Phase I; the transition point itself; and the last group meeting, or more broadly, the completion phase, in which groups accelerate and finish work generated in Phase II. Gersick found that as early as one minute into a group's first meeting, a framework of behaviors and themes could emerge to dominate the first half of a group's life. This framework was implicitly established through topics and premises of discussion, problem definition, performance strategies, and behavior toward external contexts.

The midpoint transition for each group was marked by five general characteristics. *First,* transition began with the completion or abandonment of Phase I agendas. *Second,* team members expressed urgency about finishing on time. *Third,* transition occurred precisely at the midpoint of groups' official calendar regardless of the number or length of meetings teams had prior to or after that point. *Fourth,* new contact between teams and their organizational contexts played an important role in the transition. *Fifth,* new agreements on the ultimate direction of teams' work were made at the transition point. Transitions were accomplished through the completion, revision, or abandonment of Phase I agendas combined with new ideas or insights, often in conjunction with an explicit interest in the match between their product and external requirements and resources. After successful transitions, groups settled into a new Phase II period of inertia during which transitional plans were executed. Not all teams used transitional opportunities equally well: Internal problems that went unaddressed during Phase I, if not addressed at the transition, often worsened in Phase II, and teams that failed to match their work to outside requirements suffered lasting effects (Gersick, 1988).

Phase II of Gersick's model culminates at a groups' final meeting, the completion period. It is at this point that all teams are most similar to one another and illustrate three general patterns: a move from generating new materials to editing a final product for external use, explicit attention to outside requirements and resources, and the expression of more positive or negative feelings toward group work and group members than at any prior time. These activities did not alter basic product revisions established during the transition period.

The third line of work that can shed light on critical events in group decision making is connected with Bormann's symbolic convergence theory. Periods of fantasy chaining, during which the group focuses its attention away from its immediate task, serve as critical events that give a group its identity and unify members around common courses of action. Fantasy chains thus have the potential to fundamentally shape group decision paths. In Chapter 4 of this volume Bormann discusses these in some detail.

FACTORS INFLUENCING DECISION DEVELOPMENT

The most widely studied explanatory variable in decision development research is the group's task. Comparison of studies using different tasks provides some evidence on this point. For example, phase sequences for bargaining tasks are different from those found by other researchers for problem-solving tasks (Holmes, 1992; Morley & Stephenson, 1977).

More useful are studies that have manipulated or varied tasks. Segal (1982) varied task complexity and found that number of cycles varied directly with task complexity. Mintzberg et al. (1976) reported that degree of uncertainty about the situation led to more complex decision paths. Poole and Roth (1989b) measured a number of dimensions of tasks for a varied sample of 47 decisions, grouping them into two panels—*objective task characteristics,* which are those aspects of the task that are independent of the group's experience with the task and the immediate situation in which it is executed (the dimensions were goal clarity, whether solutions were predefined or not [openness], required expertise, fact vs. value orientation, policy vs. action orientation, and degree of direct impact on the group), and *group task characteristics,* those aspects of the task that depend on the group's prior experience with the task and the immediate situation (the dimensions were novelty, degree of innovativeness, and urgency). They found that the decision path's conformity to the unitary sequence and degree of solution orientation was predicted by several objective task characteristics (value orientation, goal clarity, openness), but not by group task characteristics. Complexity of the decision path was predicted by dimensions of both types of task characteristics (it was *inversely* related to novelty, goal clarity, and value orientation), whereas degree of conflict was weakly predicted by group task characteristics only (novelty and innovativeness). Proportions of various types of decision behaviors, including problem analysis, solution activity, and integrative activity, were predicted by both types of task characteristics.

Building on these findings, Mennecke, Hoffer, and Wynne (1992) postulate a "meta-variable," *task perplexity,* which is a composite of familiarity, perceived complexity, and time pressure. They argue that increased perplexity results in a more complex path up to a point at which even groups' best efforts at organizing fail and the path becomes more simple again, that is, an inverted-U relationship between perplexity and path complexity.

Procedures for carrying out the decision task also seem likely to influence decision paths. Gersick (1988, 1989) found that one type of procedure, having a time limit, served as a trigger for the critical events that changed the course of decision activity. Several studies on the use of group decision support systems (GDSSs) to manage implementation of procedures have generated findings on decision development. Three studies (Chidambaram, Bostrom, & Wynne, 1990; Easton, Vogel, & Nunamaker, 1989; Poole, Holmes, Watson, & DeSanctis, 1993) found that groups using a GDSS had less complex decision paths than those managing the same procedures manually and those with no procedures at all. These studies suggest that procedures in themselves are not sufficient to lower complexity, but that procedures that are enforced (as they are more likely to be when computerized than manually executed) result in simpler paths. None of these studies, however, suggest that the simpler paths resemble unitary sequences. Poole and Holmes (in press) identified decision path types for the groups studied in Poole et al. (1993). Their results indicated that only a relatively small number of paths are unitary sequences and that different types of procedural support lead to distinctly different decision path types.

Poole and Roth (1989b) identified a third panel of variables that influenced decision development, *group structural variables.* The panel included group cohesiveness, degree of power concentration, conflict management style, and group size. Poole and Roth found that variables from this panel predicted the decision path's degree of conformity to the unitary sequence and solution orientation, degree of conflict in the path, and the amount of problem analysis activity. Group structural variables did not predict complexity or amount of solution-related activity. In a head-on comparison of the panels, group structural variables proved to be much more effective than the task panels as predictors of conformity to the unitary sequence, solution orientation, degree of conflict, and problem analysis activity. The group task panel was the most effective predictor of complexity. These results are consistent with those of Mintzberg et al. (1976), who found that degree of consensus on values and interests influenced type of decision path. Sorenson (1971) reported that a different type of structural characteristic, group composition, affected decision paths.

RELATIONSHIP OF DECISION DEVELOPMENT TO OUTCOMES

The relationship of decision development variables to group outcomes has been a neglected subject. In part, this may be due to the extreme effort required simply to map multiple sequences. It may also be because it is difficult to think through how the many possible sequences might affect outcomes.

Randy Hirokawa's research provides most of the available evidence. Hirokawa (1983) had groups work on a task that required them to analyze a traffic flow problem and suggest solutions; effectiveness of solutions was evaluated based on judgments of experts. Hirokawa selected five clearly successful and four unsuccessful groups from this sample and coded their decision-making interaction. His analysis found that no distinctive sequence of phases was associated with either success or failure. However, there were clear differences in decision paths between successful and unsuccessful groups: Successful groups engaged in problem analysis at the beginning of their sessions, but unsuccessful groups did not; solution discussion peaked in the middle of most of the successful groups, but it was scattered uniformly throughout unsuccessful groups; evaluation peaked near the end of successful groups, but there was no uniformity in evaluation in unsuccessful groups; there was more concern with establishing procedures in successful than in unsuccessful groups. At least some of the successful groups appear to have followed a unitary sequence. In a later study, Hirokawa (1985) compared quality of decisions of groups using four different discussion formats, each of which specified a different sequence of decision steps: reflective thinking, ideal solution, single question, and free-form discussion (i.e., no procedure). He found no difference in quality among the formats.

Poole and Holmes (1995) correlated their typology of developmental paths to three outcome variables, pre- to postdiscussion change in member consensus, members' perceptions of decision quality, and member satisfaction with the group's decision process. They found that the three decision path types that most closely resembled the rational unitary sequence had greater consensus change than the types that differed from the unitary sequence. For both perceived quality and decision scheme satisfaction, two of the three types that resembled the unitary sequence had significantly higher ratings than the four types that differed from the unitary sequence.

Sambamurthy and Poole (1992) studied the relationship of conflict management paths to consensus change, perceived decision quality, and decision scheme satisfaction in decision-making discussions by computer-supported groups. They found that groups with most consensus change and highest perceived quality and decision scheme satisfaction followed paths that first engaged in focused discussion, then had a period of open opposition and clash, then engaged in open problem-solving or negotiation to resolve the conflict; this resembles the normative phase sequence suggested as optimal for negotiation

(Holmes, 1992). Groups that never openly surfaced conflict or that resolved open oppositions by tabling the issue or with a win-lose resolution had significantly lower results.

Nutt (1984a) gathered organizational data from records and decision-maker ratings to evaluate the effectiveness of his decision paths. He found that those paths that started with debate over a specific solution proposal resulted in decisions that were rated highest in quality and success of adoption; decisions following the complete sequence from problem definition through testing through decision did not perform as well. Of interest, decisions focused on solutions developed in-house had results superior to cases in which solutions were borrowed from other contexts or firms. The general superiority of solution-oriented groups may, in part, have been due to the fact that having a specific proposal eased the political tasks of building a constituency and preventing the proposal from being prematurely scuttled.

Though the results of these studies are suggestive, it would be premature to draw any general conclusions about decision path-outcome relationships. This is a very important area for future research, because a true contingency model will only be possible when research has identified the outcomes produced by various decision paths and their dependence on input and contextual variables.

Conclusion

The theoretical models laid out in this chapter provide a range of explanations for decision development, though the empirical results delimit the realm of possible explanations and pose some puzzles that theory must solve. The various models differ in several respects. They differ in granularity of description, whether they attempt to describe a continuous stream of behavior or more general phases of activity or general strategies broken by a few critical events. They also differ in whether they describe decision-making behavior in terms of the functions various acts serve or in terms of the content of the decision. They also differ in the degree to which they explain development as a result only of deterministic variables or add the role of active human agency to the mix. Yet despite these differences, consideration of the models shows that for the most part they are not incompatible. The less complex and more deterministic can be nested within the more complex formulations. The unitary sequence model is encompassed within the contingency model. Both the contingency model and the punctuated equilibrium model can be encompassed within the structurational model.

The punctuated equilibrium and structurational models, undoubtedly the two most complex formulations, have several features in common. Both attempt to characterize deeper-level determinants of recognizable behavioral complexity. Both models posit that the generation of decision paths is mediated by members' mental models of tasks and decision procedures. For the punctuated equilibrium model these take the form of "deep structure," members' interpretive rules and task representations that maintain the group's general direction. For the structurational model they are task representations—made up of decision logics combined with interpretations of substantive task demands—held by members and enacted in one or more group task representation(s). Both punctuated equilibrium and structurational models recognize the complex dynamics involved in enacting these deeper structures in the group's decision. Both also recognize the influence of external forces on the group, but posit that their impact is mediated through the interaction system. Although there is certainly much more diversity in current theories of decision development than when Poole and Doelger (1986) wrote their chapter, it is hard to ignore the possibilities for synthesis and convergence among existing views.

At this point there has been little research on any of the representations of the "logic" underlying decision development. Abric (1971) found different levels of performance in groups with two different task representations of the same objective task. Meyer (1984) studied several cases in which organizational decisions shifted among different decision logics. Poole and DeSanctis (1992) developed a method for identifying and charting development of task representations, and applied it in a study of structures appropriated from group decision support technology and its impact on decision-making interaction. More extensive and definitive research is needed before we can draw any conclusions concerning the validity of the punctuated equilibrium or structurational models. Certainly the relative simplicity of contingency or multiple sequence theories is appealing, if research suggests rejection of these two models.

Also needed is continuing improvement of methods of data collection and analysis. Holmes and Poole (1991) describe a computer program for flexible phase mapping, which is available from Holmes.[1] Poole and Holmes (1995) describe how large numbers of complex sequences can be classified into typological categories with the aid of optimal matching and clustering techniques. Poole and DeSanctis (1992) report on an analytical scheme designed to identify structuring moves in group interaction. Gersick (1983) describes a multilayered qualitative and quantitative analysis methodology that was used in her initial studies. Van Lear (1991) describes methods for spectral analysis of continuous longitudinal data. Though useful, these advances certainly do not conquer the complexity of decision-making interaction. It is a hard nut to crack, and progress will hinge to some extent on methodological advances.

Aeschylus wrote, "Time brings all things to pass." Research on decision development explicitly brings the temporal nature of decision making into the foreground. It puts flesh on the skeleton of input-output models of decision making. Recent research has greatly enhanced our understanding of decision development, and the pursuit of the models discussed in this chapter promises to add a great deal more.

Note

1. The computer program for flexible phase mapping is available from Michael Holmes, Department of Communication, LNCO 2400, University of Utah, Salt Lake City, UT 84112.

References

Abric, J. C. (1971). An experimental study of group creativity: Task representation, group structure, and performance. *European Journal of Social Psychology, 1*, 311-326.

Bales, R. F. (1953). The equilibrium problem in small groups. In T. Parsons, E. A. Shils, & R. F. Bales (Eds.), *Working papers in the theory of action* (pp. 111-161). New York: Free Press.

Bales, R. F., & Strodtbeck, F. L. (1951). Phases in group problem-solving. *Journal of Abnormal and Social Psychology, 46*, 485-495.

Chandler, T. A. (1981). *Decision-making in small groups: A comparison of two models.* Unpublished master's thesis, Cleveland State University.

Chidambaram, L., Bostrom, R. P., & Wynne, B. E. (1990). A longitudinal study of the impact of group decision support systems on group development. *Journal of Management Information Systems, 7*, 7-25.

Easton, A. C., Vogel, D. R., & Nunamaker, J. F. (1989). Stakeholder identification and assumption surfacing in small groups: An experimental study. In R. Blanning & D. King (Eds.), *Proceedings of the Twenty-Second Annual Hawaii International Conference on System Sciences* (Vol. 3, pp. 344-352). Los Alamitos, CA: IEEE Computer Society Press.

Fisher, B. A. (1970). Decision emergence: Phases in group decision-making. *Communication Monographs, 7,* 53-66.

Fisher, B. A., & Stutman, R. K. (1987). An assessment of group trajectories: Analyzing developmental breakpoints. *Communication Quarterly, 35,* 105-124.

Gersick, C. J. G. (1983). *Life cycles of ad hoc task groups* (Tech. Rep. No. 4). New Haven, CT: Yale School of Organization and Management, Research Program on Group Effectiveness.

Gersick, C. J. G. (1988). Time and transitions in work teams: Toward a new model of group development. *Academy of Management Journal, 31,* 9-41.

Gersick, C. J. G. (1989). Marking time: Predictable transitions in work groups. *Academy of Management Journal, 32,* 274-309.

Gersick, C. J. G. (1991). Revolutionary change theories: A multilevel exploration of the punctuated equilibrium paradigm. *Academy of Management Review, 16,* 10-36.

Heinecke, C., & Bales, R. F. (1956). Developmental trends in the structure of small groups. *Sociometry, 16,* 7-25.

Hirokawa, R. Y. (1983). Group communication and problem-solving effectiveness: An investigation of group phases. *Human Communication Research, 4,* 312-321.

Hirokawa, R. Y. (1985). Discussion procedures and decision-making performance: A test of a functional perspective. *Human Communication Research, 12,* 203-224.

Holmes, M. E. (1992). Phase structures in negotiation. In L. L. Putnam & M. E. Roloff (Eds.), *Communication and negotiation* (pp. 83-107). Newbury Park, CA: Sage.

Holmes, M., & Poole, M. S. (1991). The longitudinal analysis of interaction. In B. Montgomery & S. Duck (Eds.), *Studying interpersonal interaction* (pp. 286-302). New York: Guilford.

Honeycutt, J., & Poole, M. S. (1994, November). *Procedural schemata for group decision-making.* Paper presented at the 1994 Speech Communication Association Convention, New Orleans.

Lacoursiere, R. (1980). *The life cycle of groups.* New York: Human Sciences Press.

Landsberger, H. A. (1955). Interaction process analysis of the mediation of labor management disputes. *Journal of Abnormal and Social Psychology, 51,* 552-558.

Mabry, E. A. (1975). An exploratory analysis of a developmental model for task-oriented small groups. *Human Communication Research, 2,* 66-74.

MacKenzie, K. D. (1976). *A theory of group structures* (2 vols.). New York: Gordon & Breach.

Mann, R. D. (1966). The development of member-trainer relationships in self-analytic groups. *Human Relations, 19,* 85-115.

McGrath, J. E., & Altman, I. (1966). *Small group research: A synthesis and critique of the field.* New York: Holt, Rinehart & Winston.

Mennecke, B. E., Hoffer, J. A., & Wynne, B. E. (1992). The implications of group development and history for group support system theory and practice. *Small Group Research, 23,* 524-572.

Meyer, A. D. (1984). Mingling decision-making metaphors. *Academy of Management Review, 9,* 6-17.

Mintzberg, H., Raisinghani, D., & Theoret, A. (1976). The structure of "unstructured" decision processes. *Administrative Science Quarterly, 31,* 246-275.

Morley, I. E., & Stephenson, G. M. (1977). *The social psychology of bargaining*. London: Allen & Unwin.

Morris, C. (1970). Changes in group interaction during problem solving. *Journal of Social Psychology, 81*, 157-165.

Nutt, P. C. (1984a). Planning process archetypes and their effectiveness. *Decision Sciences, 15*, 221-238.

Nutt, P. C. (1984b). Types of organizational decision processes. *Administrative Science Quarterly, 29*, 414-450.

Parsons, T., Shils, E. A., & Olds, J. (1951). Values, motives, and systems of action. In T. Parsons & E. A. Shils (Eds.), *Toward a general theory of action* (pp. 47-275). New York: Harper & Row.

Poole, M. S. (1981). Decision development in small groups I: A comparison of two models. *Communication Monographs, 48*, 1-24.

Poole, M. S. (1983a). Decision development in small groups II: A study of multiple sequences in decision-making. *Communication Monographs, 50*, 206-232.

Poole, M. S. (1983b). Decision development in small groups III: A multiple sequence theory of decision development. *Communication Monographs, 50*, 321-341.

Poole, M. S. (1985). Tasks and interaction sequences: A theory of coherence in group decision-making. In R. Street & J. N. Cappella (Eds.), *Sequence and pattern in communicative behavior* (pp. 206-224). London: Edward Arnold.

Poole, M. S., & DeSanctis, G. (1992). Microlevel structuration in computer-supported group decision-making. *Human Communication Research, 19*, 5-49.

Poole, M. S., & Doelger, J. A. (1986). Developmental processes in group decision-making. In R. Y. Hirokawa & M. S. Poole (Eds.), *Communication and group decision-making* (1st ed., pp. 35-62). Beverly Hills, CA: Sage.

Poole, M. S., & Holmes, M. E. (1995). Decision development in computer-assisted group decision-making. *Human Communication Research, 22*, 90-127.

Poole, M. S., Holmes, M., Watson, R., & DeSanctis, G. (1993). Group decision support systems and group communication: A comparison of decision-making processes in computer-supported and nonsupported groups. *Communication Research, 20*, 176-213.

Poole, M. S., & Roth, J. (1989a). Decision development in small groups IV: A typology of decision paths. *Human Communication Research, 15*, 323-356.

Poole, M. S., & Roth, J. (1989b). Decision development in small groups V: Test of a contingency model. *Human Communication Research, 15*, 549-589.

Sambamurthy, V., & Poole, M. S. (1992). The effects of variations in capabilities of GDSS designs on management of cognitive conflict in groups. *Information Systems Research, 3*, 224-251.

Scheidel, T. M., & Crowell, L. (1964). Idea development in small discussion groups. *Quarterly Journal of Speech, 50*, 140-145.

Schwartzman, H. B. (1989). *The meeting: Gatherings in organizations and communities*. New York: Plenum.

Segal, U. A. (1982). The cyclical nature of decision making: An exploratory empirical investigation. *Small Group Behavior, 13*, 333-348.

Sorenson, J. R. (1971). Task demands, group interaction, and group performance. *Sociometry, 34*, 483-495.

Van Lear, C. A. (1991). Testing a cyclical model of communication openness in relationship development: Two longitudinal studies. *Communication Monographs, 58*, 337-361.

Weick, K. E. (1979). *The social psychology of organizing* (2nd ed.). Reading, MA: Addison-Wesley.

Communication and Influence in Group Decision Making

DAVID R. SEIBOLD
RENÉE A. MEYERS
SUNWOLF

Social scientists have long been interested in influence that occurs during and as a result of group interaction. Interaction and influence in *group* contexts have been central to such disparate research areas as analyses of government committees (Barber, 1966), examinations of group psychotherapy (Page, Davis, Berkow, & O'Leary, 1989), treatments of collective action (Bonacich, 1987), intergroup relations (Messick & Mackie, 1989), social movements (Brown & Hosking, 1986), investigations of work groups in organizations (Bramel & Friend, 1987; Hackman, 1990; Sundstrom, deMeuse, & Futrell, 1990), and reviews of the dynamics of healing (Glik, 1988) as well as burnout among social services providers (Leiter, 1988) and studies of technologically linked groups (Siegel, Dubrovsky, Kiesler, & McGuire, 1986). Too, interpersonal influence has been at the core of classic studies of group conformity (Asch, 1951, 1956), cohesiveness (Back, 1951), and comparison (Festinger, 1950, 1954). More recently, group influence processes also have received prominent treatment in major reviews in management (Bettenhausen, 1991), psychology (Levine & Moreland, 1990), and communication (Cragan & Wright, 1990).

The subdomain of group decision-making research appears to parallel these larger trends. For example, the research literature is replete with studies of decision making by top-level government groups (Burnstein & Berbaum, 1983), decision making in computer-mediated conferences (Hiltz, Johnson, & Turoff, 1986), decision making among groups of visually handicapped members (Dixit, 1986), and decision making and work group effectiveness in organizations (Guzzo, 1982, 1986). Too, the group decision-making literature abounds with studies emphasizing such determinants of decision making as task type (see studies in Brandstatter, Davis, & Stocker-Kreichgauer, 1982; also see McGrath, 1984), individual differences (Kirchler & Davis, 1986), decision rules (Stasser, Kerr, & Davis, 1989), and group composition (Kerr, 1989; Wood, 1985).

However, problems exist concerning our understanding of communication and influence in group decision making. First, few studies of influence in group contexts—including influence in decision-making groups—actually study members' communication. For example, even reviews demonstrating precise and strong links between members' participation in group decision making and their subsequent opinions about the discussion topic (e.g., Sande & Zanna, 1987) are notably imprecise about the role of interpersonal messages and influence in those process-outcome relationships. This is not surprising, considering that many of these researchers equate information with communication, and/or pay little attention to the form, function, and responses to message exchanges in group decision making.

A second problem for our understanding of communicative influence in groups is its taken-for-granted character. Depending on the presuppositions of researchers, many studies have ignored the communication dynamics of influence because communication has been assumed to attenuate or add little to input-output relationships of interest (e.g., Davis, 1973; Steiner, 1972). Though this has been particularly true of researchers outside communication, the opposite problem has prevailed within the field of communication. The mediating and enhancing effects of communication on input-outcome relationships have so often been assumed that the field is replete with communication "process" studies that offer scant insight into inputs affecting the process, whether and how they are mediated in communication, and the relative effects (on outcomes) of each. For these reasons, Hewes (1986) urged a "baseline modeling strategy" (input-output) to determine *whether* communication affects group outcomes and—when used in conjunction with process-output models—to determine *how* communication affects the process. Somewhat consonant with Hewes's injunction, Poole, McPhee, and Seibold (1982) tested an interaction-based analogue of Davis's proportionality decision scheme against the noninteractional social decision scheme theory counterpart. They found that (a) communication was a necessary and independent causal factor in the decision making of the groups studied; (b) the effects of decision rules on group outcomes were not independent of, but were mediated by, the interactional model; and (c) members' interaction served not merely as medium but as the locus for these normative structures. More recently, and more consonant with Hewes's recommendations, Jarboe (1988) found that an independent conditions model (input-output) accounted for more variance in group problem-solving productivity measures than did a communication model (process-output). However, the communication model accounted for significantly more variance in group satisfaction measures than did the independent conditions model. Most telling, a total model (input-process-output) consisting of significant independent conditions, communication behaviors, and interaction effects between communication and procedure, accounted for the most variance in two of three satisfaction measures and all three measures of productivity.

A third problem for our understanding of communication and group influence, related to but separable from the taken-for-granted problem above, is the potential for both lay persons' and researchers' beliefs about group decision-making behavior to persist despite contrary empirical evidence. For example, Davis (1992) offered an intriguing argument that intuitive explanations of consensus decision making by group members often run counter to analysis rooted in empirical data and statistical reasoning. He described group decision-making research examples from the past four decades, including problems surrounding assumptions concerning group superiority relative to individual performance (1950s), exaggerated group risk-taking relative to individual risk-taking (1960s), group size relative to performance level (1970s), and "free discussion" in decision making relative to procedural constraints

(1980s). Davis's analysis in the last area is especially germane to this chapter and to the caveats we have offered thus far concerning not only the paucity of studies of members' *actual* messages (problem 1) but the dearth of studies that examine inputs and communication processes separately and in combination to ascertain their effect on outcomes (problem 2). In this case, as we shall try to illuminate subsequently, unwarranted *assumptions* concerning each of these and their relationship can exacerbate the difficulty of understanding communicative influence in group decision making (problem 3).

As Davis (1992) accurately noted, most group decision-making researchers instruct members to "discuss freely" the intellective task in the study. Such free discussion is assumed to promote optimal interpersonal interaction and information sharing that, unfettered by the imposition of social constraints, power imbalances, or obvious member status differences, is assumed to lead to optimal outcomes. Of course, *how* the group engages in this discussion (i.e., its "structuring" of the task—see Poole, Seibold, & McPhee, Chapter 5, this volume) can produce widely different outcomes in ostensibly similar groups. As Davis (1992) observed,

> One may surmise that procedural routines influence such group functions as task definition (e.g., composing, structuring, and adopting an agenda), discussion scheduling (e.g., speaker recognition and turn-taking), publicizing of decision preferences (e.g., various voting mechanisms), and selection and use of consensus rules or criteria for arriving at a decision (e.g., majority rule, averaging). (p. 23)

Drawing on extensive studies of two such procedural constraints—agenda factors and polling practices—Davis demonstrated that, instructions to discuss freely notwithstanding, (a) the mere order in which group members take up issues can have important effects on outcome, and (b) even a routine procedure such as straw polling can empirically influence aggregate outcomes. Davis's conclusions do not vitiate the effects of communication on decision outcomes. Indeed, from a structuration theory perspective, they encourage theorizing and empirical study of how these structures are mediated in discourse to produce decisions and reproduce the agenda and polling structures that enable them (see Poole et al., Chapter 5, this volume). From the standpoint of this chapter, however, Davis's conclusions underscore the difficulty of making reliable claims about communicative influence in decision-making groups when so few studies have examined both communication processes and constraints on them that may, correlatively, affect decision outcomes.

Bearing in mind both the prevalence of research that *ostensibly* addresses communication and influence in decision-making groups, and the paucity of research that *actually* assesses this relationship given the three problems noted above, this chapter examines the most relevant literature for understanding group influence and decision making. It is divided into two sections: (a) prominent theoretical perspectives on group influence, and (b) communication issues and group influence. In the first section, we review three prominent theoretical positions outside the domain of communication that offer explanations of influence processes in group decision making, especially the phenomenon of group discussion-induced opinion shift. These theories typically relegate communication to a secondary (or nonexistent) role in the influence process, concentrating instead on various individual or situational input factors as explanatory mechanisms. Still, they are important because of the research domain to which they have been applied: choice shift and group polarization. Unlike much of the majority influence and minority influence group research, the group polarization literature is rooted in members' *interactions* (even if the theories of that "process" have not been as specific as communication scholars might wish). In contrast to discussion-induced polarization studies, in which the interactional determinants of how group members are *influenced* are of central research concern (even if how individuals *influence* the group are not), majority- and minority-influence investigators often focus on noninteractional determinants of influence such as real and perceived group majority size effects on conformity, the self-generated persuasion that stems from recognition of one's own deviate position relative to other members, and the conforming force of a group member's own needs for being correct (informational influence) or for social approval (normative influence). Kitayama and Burnstein (1994) provide a useful and fuller treatment of this discussion-based versus noninteractional basis of influence in group decision making.

In the second section of the chapter, we review research that focuses more specifically on the relationship between communication and group influence, including some minority-influence research that does address the communication dynamics of minority members' influence on the group majority. Although this latter set of studies is not as theoretically developed or integrated as the research treated in the first part of the chapter, it does provide insight into some of the input, process, and output factors that impact the communication-influence relationship.

Prominent Theoretical Perspectives on Group Influence

The interaction-influence-outcome link is rarely the central focus of group influence investigations outside communication research. The principal theoretical positions associated with research on group decision making, for example, typically ignore or relegate interaction to an "information carrier" role, focusing instead on various individual or situational input variables affecting group outcomes. The most prominent theoretical positions on psychological input-influence-group outcome linkages are those associated with research on decision "choice shift."

"Choice shift" has been an important research area since Stoner (1961) reported that average individual postdiscussion decision choices were more polar (in a risky direction) than average individual prediscussion choices. Researchers initially investigated choice shift for practical reasons. The discovery that groups often polarize in a risky direction challenged the conventional assumption that groups were more conservative than individuals (Clark, 1971), and appeared to have important implications for groups responsible for making decisions involving risk (e.g., juries, military groups, political action groups). It was thought that understanding "risky shift" would provide information about when to employ groups and when to employ individuals in decision-making situations.

As researchers discovered that choice shifts were not unique to "risky" decision issues but were a general outcome of group decision-making discussion (Moscovici & Zavalloni, 1969; Myers & Bishop, 1971), choice shift invited various theoretical explanations. Investigations have been conducted in several nations and have examined effects on choice shifts of consensus achievement (Teger & Pruitt, 1967), relevance of the decision task to the subjects (Madsen, 1978), group size (Myers & Arenson, 1972), ambiguity of the task (Boster & Hale, 1989;

Hale & Boster, 1988), and task type (Moscovici & Zavalloni, 1969; Myers, 1975), among others.

The three theoretical perspectives we examine below attempt to provide a unified account of why choice shifts occur and how they function in group decision making. In order, we review social comparison theory (SCT), persuasive arguments theory (PAT), and social identity theory (SIT). The first two models, SCT and PAT, have enjoyed a long and healthy rivalry. Since the 1970s, researchers have continued to test the merits of these two alternative explanations, with investigators in both camps often claiming victory. The third theory, social identity theory, is a relatively new theory and has helped to spark a reexamination of the polarization phenomenon from a new theoretical foundation. Each of these models provides important information about individual and situational factors affecting group choices.

SOCIAL COMPARISON THEORY

Social comparison theory (SCT) proposes that group influence is embedded in (a) members' drives to reevaluate their own preferences in light of thinking about others' choices, and (b) members' feelings of either external pressures (reward/punishment) or internal pressures to conform. Although Brown (1965) was among the first explicitly to propose social comparison as a theoretical mechanism for individual choice shifts in groups, early research on conformity suggested its relevance (Asch, 1951, 1956; Festinger, 1954). The social comparison perspective emphasizes that values underlie attraction toward the dominant alternative in decision-making groups. In many "choice-dilemma" cases, for example, riskiness is thought to be a culturally coveted value that causes the typical American to want to be at least as risky as other individuals in the group. A group member will attempt to discern where other members stand on an issue and then choose as his or her initial decision a level of risk that is at or above the perceived group average. The main function of group discussion is simply to allow group members to compare their positions to those of others. As a result of members' privately enacted social comparisons, groups or individual members may shift toward greater risk or caution following group discussion.

Evidence exists that mere exchange of information among members about initial choices causes shifts toward greater risk by initially cautious individuals (Jellison & Arkin, 1977; Jellison & Riskind, 1970; Teger & Pruitt, 1967; Willems & Clark, 1971). Still, the consistent finding that mere exchange of information is not as effective in promoting shifts as is actual group discussion suggests that social comparison by itself is not sufficient to account for the "shift" phenomenon (Kogan & Wallach, 1967; Sanders & Baron, 1977; Vinokur, 1971). As Vinokur (1971) stated,

> In spite of some indirect supportive evidence, Brown's hypothesis that information about others' choices is sufficient to produce shifts must be rejected. The evidence suggests that the crucial factor responsible for both risky and conservative shifts is something in the *flow of information* relevant to the issues being decided upon, and not the mere knowledge of others' choices. (p. 236; emphasis added)

In a later article, Goethals and Darley (1987) attempted to update and revise the theoretical tenets of SCT. They drew comparisons to social identity theory (to be described subsequently), stating that social comparison may involve across-group comparisons (rather than just individual comparisons); may be an automatic rather than a sought-out activity; and may be undertaken for both self-validation and self-knowledge reasons. Given these revisions, it seems likely that SCT could be subsumed within the broader theoretical framework of SIT.

PERSUASIVE ARGUMENTS THEORY

The inability of SCT to account fully for the choice shift phenomenon was an impetus for development of persuasive arguments theory (PAT), which focuses on informational rather than normative influence and on the cognitive processing of arguments by individuals. On this view, influence accrues because of the manner in which group members process arguments and the effects of those positions on individual and group decision choices (Burnstein & Vinokur, 1973, 1977; Vinokur & Burnstein, 1974, 1978). Burnstein (1982) explained that when individuals evaluate or reevaluate alternative decision choices prior to group discussion, they construct "arguments" (reasons, considerations) describing the attributes of each choice. Each person possesses a culturally given pool (a standard set) of arguments relevant to each alternative, although each member may possess a pool of unique arguments in addition to those common to other group members. Consequently, neither all arguments nor the same arguments are equally available to all individuals in a particular group. To judge the relative merit of any alternative, each individual samples from his or her own pool (i.e., retrieves arguments from memory). An individual weighs the relative importance of the arguments she or he possesses for each alternative and, based on this knowledge, chooses the alternative that elicits the best and most persuasive arguments.

The average group prediscussion decision choice is the alternative for which most members hold the greatest number of arguments. Further thought by the individual or group discussion will lead to polarization toward the alternative that elicits more arguments. On this view, the main function of group interaction is to allow group members to state and share previously considered arguments, and to provide a forum for increasing individual information processing about various alternatives. As Myers and Lamm (1976) argued, it is not interaction per se that influences individual opinion change, but interaction as a context for further individual private and public rehearsal and personal learning that causes subjects to reconsider their prediscussion choices.

Burnstein (1982) stated that research concerning PAT demonstrated that (a) when an individual could argue but not compare, shifts still occurred; (b) when she or he could compare but not openly argue, shifts vanished or were greatly attenuated; and (c) even in attenuated form, choice shifts seem to depend directly on tacit argumentation. He contended that PAT better predicts, and more adequately explains, group choice shifts than does SCT. Indeed, there is evidence that the greater the total number of arguments held by group members for a given alternative, the greater the likelihood of group shift toward that alternative (Myers & Bishop, 1971; Silverthorne, 1971). Moreover, research utilizing a more complex PAT model that incorporates argument "persuasiveness" and "novelty" has been shown to be a good predictor of the direction of choice shifts and of shifts calculated across groups for a particular choice or across choices for a particular group (Madsen, 1978). It is less accurate in predicting magnitude of shifts and shifts that obtain for specific choices or groups (Bishop & Myers, 1974).

Recent research within the communication discipline echoes these doubts about the predictive power of PAT. In two investigations designed to test the assumptions and models of PAT, Meyers (1989a, 1989b) found that more interactional assumptions and models of argument provided a truer picture of what actually occurred in group choice shift discussions than did the cognitive-based models and assumptions of PAT. As Meyers (1989a) concluded, "This investigation does not purport to sound the deathknell for PAT research, but it does point up ways in which interaction mediates and moderates cognitive arguments" (p. 376).

Although both SCT and PAT offer plausible explanations of the group choice shift process, researchers in recent years have concluded that these two theories are complementary, rather than competing, explanations of polarization. Following a meta-analysis of 21 polarization studies published between 1974 and 1982, Isenberg (1986) concluded that "given the support for both PAT and SCT as mediating processes, it behooves investigators to develop theories that account for the interaction between SCT and PAT and that address the factors that moderate the emergence of one or the other form of influence" (p. 1149). As a result, some researchers have begun to search for mediating or moderating factors that might help explain when normative or informational influence will be more prominent. For example, recent investigations suggest that a group's goal may play a significant role in determining the type of influence that will be most prevalent. In a program of research aimed at distinguishing the effects of "task" and "social" group goals, Kaplan and colleagues (Kaplan 1987, 1989; Kaplan & Miller, 1987; Rugs & Kaplan, 1993) have found that "variations in the group's interactive goal affect the impact of normative and informational influence on member attitudes" (Rugs & Kaplan, 1993, p. 155). These researchers found that when instructions provided task goals, informational communication was more influential. But when instructions provided group goals, normative communication became more important. In a similar investigation of the moderating impact of goals, Earle (1986) found that subjects who worked under a group goal were far more rejecting of a deviant than were those who worked under an individual goal condition. Earle (1986) concluded that different types of goals can affect whether subjects attend to normative or informational influence.

Perhaps more germane to this chapter than these isolated studies is the advancement of a theory that purports to be able to account for *both*

PAT and SCT explanations of influence within a single framework. Typically referred to as social identity theory (although it is sometimes called *referent informational influence* or *self-categorization theory*), this perspective offers an "alternative path which avoids the two-process dependency model and seeks an explanation of group polarization in terms of a unitary process of conformity to salient self-defining in-group norms" (Turner, Wetherell, & Hogg, 1989, p. 136).

SOCIAL IDENTITY THEORY

According to social identity theory (SIT), group membership plays an important and causal role in the polarization phemonenon (Mackie & Cooper, 1984; Tajfel & Turner, 1979; Turner, 1982, 1985). SIT is a theory of self-evaluation that emphasizes across-group comparisons. Social identification occurs in a three-step process (Mackie, 1986). The first step is called *social categorization* and occurs when group members perceive, define, and recognize both themselves and others as members of distinct social groups. Once this categorization into in-groups and out-groups occurs, the second step involves assigning and distinguishing the representative attributes, behaviors, and norms of both the in-group and the out-group. As a consequence of this process, "groups are likely to be perceived as being stereotypically extreme" (Mackie, 1986, p. 720). The final step in the social identification process is self-stereotyping, during which the perceived characteristics of the in-group are adopted by the self.

Social identity researchers and theorists (McLachlan, 1986; Turner & Oakes, 1986) suggest that this model can account for the attitude change that occurs in group polarization. They assert that many typical group polarization experiments are in fact manipulations of social categorizations. Exposure to the opinions of others, or participation in a discussion, allows group members to perceive how similar (or different) they are from others in the group. This promotes the creation of in-group and out-group categorizations, which results in a perception of an in-group being more stereotypically extreme than is truly the case. The in-group's position on the polarization item also will be perceived to be more stereotypically extreme, and conformity to this extreme group norm causes group polarization.

Recent investigations tested the SIT explanation of group polarization. Wetherell (1987) reported a study in which subjects listened to a tape recording of a group of people who discussed a series of choice dilemmas to a polarized consensus. Subjects were informed that this discussion group was to be either their in-group or their out-group for a later group activity. They also were told that the group contained subjects with similar or dissimilar attitudes to their own. In all four cases, the taped discussion was identical. When subjects' own opinions from before and after listening to the taped discussion were compared, it was discovered that subjects were more persuaded by the same arguments if they emanated from their in-group than an out-group, and from similar than dissimilar others. In another experiment, Mackie and Cooper (1984) asked subjects to listen to a taped discussion attributed to either the subject's group or to a group competing with the subject's in-group. Only when the discussion was attributed to the subject's in-group did the subject's attitudes polarize in the direction advocated on the tape. In addition, subjects in this study did judge their own group's position to be significantly more extreme than did other participants unrelated to that group. In a later experiment, Mackie (1986) manipulated subjects' perceptions of whether they were acting as a group or as an individual in making group decisions. She found that "the characteristics of groups were perceived to be more extreme than the characteristics of individuals inferred from identical information" (p. 727). In addition, results indicated that this increasingly extreme perception of group characteristics was dependent on an acceptance, and focus on, group membership. If a subject perceived him- or herself to be acting individually, the perception was attenuated. Finally, Turner et al. (1989) corroborated Mackie's (1986) conclusion when they found that stereotypically risky groups polarized toward risk and stereotypically cautious groups toward caution. But risky and cautious individuals tended to shift away from the direction of their label or not to shift significantly. Turner et al. (1989) concluded,

> It seems that the social normative/group context needs to be taken into account in determining which arguments will be perceived as persuasive and the conditions under which extremity will be valued. The experiment supported the hypothesis that the persuasiveness of material (arguments, positions, etc.) generated spontaneously in group discussion (as inferred

from the subsequent direction of shift) is mediated by the degree to which it is perceived as prototypical of an in-group consensus. (p. 144)

A social identity explanation, then, assumes that a participant's perception of group membership directs and controls other processes. Mackie (1986) explained that, "According to the social identity model, group membership informs the subject of what information is important, why it is valued by the group, and how it should be interpreted" (p. 727). By extension, social identity theorists claim that this theory can account for both SCT and PAT within a single framework. Turner et al. (1989) stated that, "In many respects the important contribution of the present theory is to bring together the concepts of social value and informational influence in that it explains persuasion in terms of the processes whereby explicit or implicit informational content becomes socially valued or validated" (p. 145).

In sum, all three theoretical perspectives (SCT, PAT, and SIT) offer explanations of group influence. Yet from a communication standpoint, these models ignore crucial features of group decision making because they minimize the facilitative and transforming character of *interaction* about decision choices. As Moscovici and Lecuyer (1972) stated more than two decades ago, "A real theory of decision-making processes in groups has to be a theory of interaction between the members of those groups" (p. 243). In the next section we explore research that is more responsive to Moscovici and Lecuyer's call for group decison-making research that is inherently communication based.

Communication Issues and Group Influence

Recent research has begun to examine more closely the role communication plays in the group influence process. Although many of these investigations have been conducted within the communication discipline, some equally exciting research in this domain has been conducted outside the field. At this time, no one theoretical perspective guides this body of research, yet the findings provide important information about how communication-as-influence is shaped by various input factors, and in turn shapes the group's outcomes. In this final section, we focus on research that establishes a relationship between group communicative influence and input factors (e.g., various individual characteristics, task information, and participation factors—including minority influence) or output factors (choice shift, consensus).

GROUP INFLUENCE AND INPUT FACTORS

A number of studies have focused on individual characteristics of group members and the influence such attributes have on small decision-making group processes. Using an expectation states approach, Bradley (1980) examined the problem of women attempting to enter mutually influencing relationships in organizations typically populated by male members with a history of working together as a team. The expectation states perspective argues that social influence in small task groups is determined by the group member's status in the "outside" world, which is then used by the members to infer this group member's ability to contribute to, and influence, the group. Bradley argued that gender could be assumed to function in a small decision-making group as a status characteristic.

The study examined the relationship between male and female opinion deviation, under conditions of either high competence (prior announced relevant experience) or low competence (operationalized as no demonstrated task-related ability, typically experienced by women who enter organizations without prior opportunities to demonstrate skills). In general, the results substantiated the hypothesis that highly competent male and female opinion deviates would be treated more positively than their low-competence counterparts, although the impact of the competence variable was more pronounced for female deviates. Surprisingly, majority attitude shifts were quantitatively greatest in the high-competence/female condition (influence due to the male "surprise" element at confronting female expertise was suggested). At the same time, the highly competent females, though succeeding in their influence attempts, were not particularly well liked.

Complementing Bradley's research on influence deriving from perceived memberships in other status groups, McGarty, Haslam, Hutchinson, and Turner (1994) studied the influence of a group member's own perceived group membership on choice. Would differences in the persuasive power of in-groups and out-groups be mediated by peripheral cues rather than the persuasive nature of the message? Findings indicated that the pattern observed was consistent with a reduction in the influence of the out-group member (when group membership was made salient), rather than an increase in the persuasiveness of the in-group speaker; increased salience led to rejection of the out-group speaker rather than increased acceptance of the in-group speaker. Findings were consistent with self-categorization theory, holding that for group memberships to have influence, it is not sufficient for people merely to be aware of the category; they must see the category as relevant to self. It is important that future testing of salient group memberships' effect must identify variables mediating the relationship between group membership salience and influence.

Contrasting with work on the influence of accessible *external* characteristics of group members, Stasser (1992) studied the effect of *hidden* information (highly salient unshared information) and the presence or absence of advocacy during discussion on the ability of groups to reach more informed decisions. Stasser created a *hidden profile* by distributing among group members pieces of information that would support a (superior) decision alternative; in fact, the group as a whole had the entire set of information. Expanding on prior findings (Stasser & Titus, 1985) that groups often failed to pool unshared information, the simulations demonstrated similar failures, with four-member groups faring somewhat better than eight-member groups if information was rendered salient prior to discussion, if salience was maintained during discussion, and if a nonadvocacy approach was employed by members. Confounding the popular principle that a group can reach a more informed decision than any of its members acting alone, Stasser suggested that the failure of groups to discover hidden profiles reflects the inadequacies of group discussions that are unstructured. The results suggest conditions under which information held by individual group members may not be shared during discussion, indicating that for tasks that encourage advocacy (e.g., juries) or groups that choose advocacy as group process, even salient unshared information may remain undetected and may potentially affect decision making adversely.

Wright, Luus, and Christie (1990), on the other hand, argue that discussion will enhance the use of some typically underused piece of information if the information appears relevant to task and if arguments regarding the causal significance of the information are shared. These researchers found that group discussion moderates the tendency of attributors to underuse consensus information (consensus underutilization effect). Such a finding could have practical significance, for example, for trial attorneys who have the opportunity to discuss with jurors prior to their selection the consensus information the jurors hold about behavior relevant to the case (e.g., under what circumstances would jurors who declare contrary positions about attributions and consensus information about case-relevant behavior be influenced during deliberations to surrender their dispositional biases?).

Although information that group members assume they know about other members (external characteristics) and information that group members hold independently (hidden information) can affect the influence processes in group decision making, other studies demonstrate ways in which the *communication behavior characteristics* of group members impact intragroup influence. Koomen (1988) studied the relationship between participation rate in five-person male groups and liking ratings. Results showed that the greater the attraction the group had for a member-rater, the more positive the relationship between participation rate and liking rating. Koomen concluded that the incorporation of "cohesiveness" as a moderating factor in the relationship between participation rate and likableness is essential. Noting the lack of direction for causation in the relationship, Koomen encouraged the study of other factors that may affect the participation rate/liking relationship (e.g., the standard of participation that members hold as appropriate, time pressures, group size, need for leadership).

Communicative behavior characteristics of group members not only involve *how much* they participate, but also *when* their participation takes place. Turn-taking by interruption or noninterruption was the central focus of research in recent work by Ng, Bell, and Brooke (1993). It follows that group members who obtain more turns will participate more and may earn higher influence rankings than members who have fewer turns. Interruptions were operationalized as acts that enabled the interrupter successfully to gain a speaking turn. Results of this investigation indicated that high-ranking members had a greater proportion of turns, and divided turns into interruption-turns and noninterruption-turns. Ng et al. interpreted the results as supporting a resource perspective of influence, concluding that members who gained the largest share of turns had the most opportunity to influence the discussion (in fact, interruption-turns were a better predictor of influence). The small number of students involved ($N = 19$), however, suggests that this study be viewed as a foundation for further work rather than as a basis for generalization about interruptions and social influence in other small group contexts.

In addition to how much and when members' communication behaviors affect influence in the group, the corpus of studies on minority influence (Nemeth & Staw, 1989) has offered insight into group influence associated with different *types* of communication behaviors.

First, however, it appears that minority influence on the group majority is the exception rather than the rule (movies such as *Twelve Angry Men* notwithstanding). For example, as reviewed in Nemeth (1986), analyses of 225 jury decisions revealed that the majority position on the first ballot became the final verdict in more than 85% of the cases. Second, there is nonetheless a great deal of evidence dating from Moscovici, Lage, and Naffrechoux (1969) that minority members can influence the group majority by inducing issue-relevant thought that is consonant with the minority's stance. Third, such influence is most likely when the minority member(s)' views are correct, the majority is wrong, and the minority is willing to communicate this (Staw & Boettger, 1988, cited in Nemeth & Staw, 1989); when the position is communicated "consistently" (Maass & Clark, 1984) but not "rigidly" (Mugny, 1982); and when the minority members are perceived to be "confident"—either because of their communicative style or their few numbers (see review by Nemeth & Staw, 1989). Finally, there is evidence that the mere presence of a (vocal) minority improves decision outcomes of the majority simply by requiring more attention, thought process, information recall, and detection of correct solutions inherent in the "divergent thinking" stimulated by the minority as opposed to the "convergent thinking" stimulated by majority arguments (e.g., Nemeth & Kwan, 1987; Nemeth & Staw, 1989).

GROUP INFLUENCE AND OUTPUT FACTORS

Choice Shifts. Research on the relationship between group interaction and risky or cautious choice shifts is fragmented and not well tied to the social psychological research on choice shift we reviewed at the outset, but findings indicate that communication patterns differ in risky- and cautious-shift groups (Cline & Cline, 1979; Cline & Cline,

1980). Risky groups disagreed more, produced more than twice as many statements, focused on task considerations, and utilized more "non-self"-oriented statements than did cautious groups. In other research, Alderton (1981) found that the direction of arguments in a group during the initial and final stages of group decision making predicted the direction of group shifts. Alderton and Frey (1983) also reported that positive communicative responses to minority arguments in a group discussion caused groups to shift less strongly in the majority direction.

In a related investigation, Mayer (1985) compared three theories of why groups make more extreme decisions than their members have made: diffusion of responsibility theory, social comparison theory, and persuasive arguments theory. He found strong support for persuasive arguments theory, further suggesting the importance of communication to group influence processes. Finally, Boster and colleagues have articulated and modeled the persuasive process by which choice shifts occur (Boster & Mayer, 1984; Boster, Mayer, Hunter, & Hale, 1980). Similar to the social identity theorists, Boster and colleagues contend group membership mediates how arguments are viewed and interpreted. They found that majority opinion in a group affects how members perceive the quality of the arguments presented and that this perception then influences the direction and magnitude of group shifts. Boster and Mayer (1984) posited a causal model in which majority opinion affects members' perceptions of the quality of their arguments, which then has a direct effect on opinion change. Given recent findings associated with social identity theory research, this model of group argument appears promising.

Yet one investigation contends that the position of the majority was confounded with order of presentation in Boster and Mayer (1984). When Mongeau and Garlick (1988) varied the order of presentation of majority and minority arguments, they found support for the persuasive arguments explanation of polarization only. That is, participants in this investigation concentrated primarily on the manipulated quality of the arguments and generally ignored social comparison information (majority or minority) when evaluating message arguments or developing attitudes. The authors admit, however, that "the primary limitation of this study lies in the fact that it did not observe respondents actively participating in group discussions" (Mongeau & Garlick, 1988, p. 124).

Like researchers in other disciplines, communication scholars also have begun to search for the mediating factors that explain when normative or informational influence will be most prominent. Hale and Boster (1988) found that ambiguity was an effective moderator of choice shift explanations. As ambiguity related to the task increased, social comparisons exerted greater influence over decisions, and as ambiguity decreased, the influence of persuasive arguments increased. Boster and Hale (1989) created an *ambiguity moderated model* (AMM), which is a "dual-process model that predicts that the process detailed by PA theory will be activated to a greater extent under conditions of low ambiguity, whereas the process detailed by SC theory will be activated to a greater extent under conditions of high ambiguity" (p. 546). Tests of the model (Boster & Hale, 1989) showed AMM to be a better predictor of group decision results than either the PAT or SCT models.

Group Consensus. Other research on the relationship between group influence and outputs has investigated communication patterns indicative of and contributing to consensus decision making. Results indicate that groups achieving consensus not only exhibit more agreement (Giffin & Ehrlich, 1963; Lumsden, 1974), but also are characterized by less opinionatedness and more objectivity (Gouran, 1969; Hill, 1976) and fewer redundant statements (Kline & Hullinger, 1973). Moreover, orientation behaviors (statements that facilitate goal achievement by using facts, making helpful suggestions, resolving conflict, or lessening tension) consistently have been found to be related to consensus achievement (Gouran, 1969; Kline, 1972; Knutson, 1972; Knutson & Holdridge, 1975; Knutson & Kowitz, 1977). DeStephen (1983) discovered that, in addition to these types of communication, clarification and substantiation statements (designed to clarify undeveloped interpretations) contributed to a group's ability to achieve consensus. Finally, members' communication has been found to be more random and less responsive in non-consensus groups than in consensus groups (Gouran & Geonetta, 1977; Saine & Bock, 1973).

In related research, Kerr, MacCoun, Hansen, and Hymes (1987) sought to address the question of whether, as group members change sides, a momentum-like effect occurs in decision-making groups. Kerr et al. (1987) investigated (a) whether a person was more or less likely to yield to an opposing faction after losing or gaining a supporter, and

(b) why the social support would increase susceptibility to social influence in decision-making groups. Results showed no evidence for a momentum effect. In fact, an *antimomentum* effect occurred, with verdict change in the direction of the prior change less likely to occur than if there had been no prior switch. Results indicated that supporters with low levels of support were most likely to switch verdicts, disconfirming the informational influence model, which predicted that switches would occur simply because a larger number of arguments was generated. This study introduced for the first time data suggesting that the *level of support* received from the group could affect the way a group member defends a position; this was particularly true for male subjects.

Of course, there is a long line of research indicating that the total of *all* group members' expressed positions greatly influences the decision outcome. For example, the valence model associated with the work of Norman Maier, Richard Hoffman, and others (see Hoffman, 1979) generalizes the models developed in "persuasive argument" explanations of group choice shifts by focusing on the evaluative dimensions of members' verbal contributions during discussion. *Valence* represents the (cumulative) degree to which any particular suggestion is acceptable to all group members. Valence strongly predicts group choice: In about 85% of cases the final choice of a group is the option that has received the highest valence based on members' expressions of positivity. There also appear to be "threshold adoption levels," such that once an option's cumulative valence passes the adoption threshold it is chosen by the group. Finally, it is not merely the total valence but the *distribution* of that valence across participating group members that best predicts final group decision. McPhee, Poole, and Seibold (1981) provide a more complete review of Hoffman's research, and they report a study with findings that support all three of the claims above concerning valence, distributed valence, and the adoption threshold.

Even this brief review of recent communication investigations of group decision making reveals the important role interaction plays in the group influence process. Communication is shaped by various input factors and, in turn, shapes group outcomes. Certainly additional research is needed before an integrated theory of group influence is realized. Nevertheless, this set of studies offers valuable information about how influence in groups develops, is interpreted, and affects final group decisions.

Conclusion

We began this chapter by noting the paucity of empirical studies of interpersonal influence processes in decision-making groups and the dearth of powerful theories available for accounting for these processes. We identified three problems that characterize our current understanding of communication and influence in group decision making: (a) few studies of group influence actually study members' communication, (b) too often communication in group decision making assumes a taken-for-granted character, and (c) there is a potential for researchers' beliefs about group decision making to persist despite contrary empirical evidence. Each of these problems is evident in the research reviewed in this chapter. Ironically, some of the strongest theories of group influence underemphasize the role of interaction, whereas most studies of decision-making group interaction resist theoretical integration. Certainly we cannot presume to conclude here that our understanding of the communication-influence relationship is complete. Still, much progress has been made in the past few decades. As researchers continue to avoid the three problems noted above, and strive to make the investigation of communication central in their research endeavors, our understanding of the interaction-influence relationship in group practices will steadily increase. Our hope is that future researchers in this domain will continue to work toward the goal Moscovici and Lecuyer (1972) set more than two decades ago: "A real theory of decision-making processes in groups has to be a theory of interaction between the members of those groups" (p. 243).

References

Alderton, S. M. (1981). A processual analysis of argumentation in polarizing groups. In G. Ziegelmuller & J. Rhodes (Eds.), *Proceedings of the Second Summer Conference on Argumentation* (pp. 693-703). Annandale, VA: Speech Communication Association.

Alderton, S. M., & Frey, L. R. (1983). Effects of reactions to arguments on group outcome: The case of group polarization. *Central States Speech Journal, 34*, 88-95.

Asch, S. E. (1951). Effects of group pressure upon the modification and distortion of judgments. In H. Guetzkow (Ed.), *Groups, leadership, and men* (pp. 177-190). Pittsburgh, PA: Carnegie Press.

Asch, S. E. (1956). Studies of independence and submission to group pressure I: On minority of one against unanimous majority. *Psychological Monographs, 70*(10, Whole No. 417).

Back, K. W. (1951). Influence through social communication. *Journal of Abnormal and Social Psychology, 46*, 9-23.

Barber, J. D. (1966). *Power in committees: An experiment in governmental process.* Chicago: Rand McNally.

Bettenhausen, K. L. (1991). Five years of groups research: What we have learned and what needs to be addressed. *Journal of Management, 17*, 345-381.

Bishop, G. D., & Myers, D. G. (1974). Information influence in group discussion. *Organizational Behavior and Human Performance, 12*, 92-104.

Bonacich, P. (1987). Communication networks and collective action. *Social Networks, 9*, 389-396.

Boster, F. J., & Hale, J. L. (1989). Response scale ambiguity as a moderator of the choice shift. *Communication Research, 16*, 532-551.

Boster, F. J., & Mayer, M. E. (1984). Choice shifts: Argument qualities or social comparisons. In R. Bostrom (Ed.), *Communication yearbook 8* (pp. 393-410). Beverly Hills, CA: Sage.

Boster, F. J., Mayer, M. E., Hunter, J. E., & Hale, J. L. (1980). Expanding the persuasive arguments explanation of the polarity shift: A linear discrepancy model. In D. Nimmo (Ed.), *Communication yearbook 4* (pp. 165-176). Beverly Hills, CA: Sage.

Bradley, P. H. (1980). Sex, competence, and opinion deviation: An expectation states approach. *Communication Monographs, 47*, 101-110.

Bramel, D., & Friend, R. (1987). The work group and its vicissitudes in social and industrial psychology. *Journal of Applied Behavioral Science, 23*, 233-253.

Brandstatter, H., Davis, J. H., & Stocker-Kreichgauer, G. (Eds.). (1982). *Group decision making.* London: Academic Press.

Brown, M. H., & Hosking, D. M. (1986). Distributed leadership and skilled performance as successful organization in social movements. *Human Relations, 39*, 65-79.

Brown, R. (1965). *Social psychology.* New York: Free Press.

Burnstein, E. (1982). Persuasion as argument processing. In H. Brandstatter, J. H. Davis, & G. Stocker-Kreichgauer (Eds.), *Group decision making* (pp. 103-124). New York: Academic Press.

Burnstein, E., & Berbaum, M. L. (1983). Stages in group decision making: The decomposition of historical narratives. *Political Psychology, 4*, 531-561.

Burnstein, E., & Vinokur, A. (1973). Testing two classes of theories about group induced shift in individual choice. *Journal of Experimental Social Psychology, 9*, 123-137.

Burnstein, E., & Vinokur, A. (1977). Persuasive argumentation and social comparison as determinants of attitude polarization. *Journal of Experimental Social Psychology, 13*, 315-332.

Clark, R. D., III. (1971). Group-induced shift toward risk: A critical appraisal. *Psychological Bulletin, 76*, 251-270.

Cline, R. J., & Cline, T. R. (1980). A structural analysis of risky-shift and cautious-shift discussions: The diffusion of responsibility theory. *Communication Quarterly, 28*, 26-36.

Cline, T. R., & Cline, R. J. (1979). Risky and cautious decision shifts in small groups. *Southern Speech Communication Journal, 44*, 252-263.

Cragan, J. F., & Wright, D. W. (1990). Small group communication research of the 1980s: A synthesis and critique. *Communication Studies, 41*, 212-236.

Davis, J. H. (1973). Group decision and social interaction: A theory of social decision schemes. *Psychological Review, 80*, 97-125.

Davis, J. H. (1992). Some compelling intuitions about group consensus decisions, theoretical and empirical research, and interpersonal aggregation phenomena: Selected examples, 1950-1990. *Organizational Behavior and Human Decision Processes, 52,* 3-38.

DeStephen, R. S. (1983). High and low consensus groups: A content and relational interaction analysis. *Small Group Behavior, 14,* 143-162.

Dixit, A. K. (1986). Individual and group decisions of visually handicapped on risk taking. *International Journal of Rehabilitation Research, 9,* 66-68.

Earle, W. B. (1986). The social context of social comparison: Reality or reassurance? *Personality and Social Psychology Bulletin, 12,* 159-168.

Festinger, L. (1950). A theory of social comparison processes. *Human Relations, 7,* 117-140.

Festinger, L. (1954). Informal social communication. *Psychological Review, 57,* 271-282.

Giffin, K., & Ehrlich, L. (1963). The attitudinal effects of a group discussion on a proposed change in company policy. *Communication Monographs, 30,* 377-379.

Glik, D. C. (1988). Symbolic, ritual, and social dynamics of spiritual healing. *Social and Science Medicine, 27,* 1197-1206.

Goethals, G. R., & Darley, J. M. (1987). Social comparison theory: Self-evaluation and group life. In B. Mullen & G. R. Goethals (Eds.), *Theories of group behavior* (pp. 21-47). New York: Springer.

Gouran, D. S. (1969). Variables related to consensus in group discussions of questions of policy. *Speech Monographs, 36,* 387-391.

Gouran, D. S., & Geonetta, S. C. (1977). Patterns of interaction in decision-making groups at varying distances from consensus. *Small Group Behavior, 8,* 511-524.

Guzzo, R. A. (Ed.). (1982). *Improving group decision making in organizations.* New York: Academic Press.

Guzzo, R. A. (1986). Group decision making and group effectiveness in organizations. In P. S. Goodman & Associates (Eds.), *Designing effective work groups* (pp. 34-71). San Francisco: Jossey-Bass.

Hackman, J. R. (Ed.). (1990). *Groups that work (and those that don't): Creating conditions for effective teamwork.* San Franciso: Jossey-Bass.

Hale, J. L., & Boster, F. J. (1988). Comparing effects coded models of choice shifts. *Communication Research Reports, 5,* 180-186.

Hewes, D. E. (1986). A socio-egocentric model of group decision-making. In R. Y. Hirokawa & M. S. Poole (Eds.), *Communication and group decision-making* (1st ed., pp. 265-291). Beverly Hills, CA: Sage.

Hill, T. A. (1976). An experimental study of the relationship between opinionated leaders and small group consensus. *Communication Monographs, 43,* 246-257.

Hiltz, S. R., Johnson, K., & Turoff, M. (1986). Experiments in group decison making: Communication process and outcome in face-to-face versus computerized conferences. *Human Communication Research, 13,* 225-252.

Hoffman, C. R. (1979). *The group problem solving process.* New York: Praeger.

Isenberg, D. J. (1986). Group polarization: A critical review and meta-analysis. *Journal of Personality and Social Psychology, 50,* 1141-1151.

Jarboe, S. (1988). A comparison of input-output, process-output, and input-process-output models of small group problem-solving effectiveness. *Communication Monographs, 55,* 121-142.

Jellison, J. M., & Arkin, R. M. (1977). Social comparison of abilities: A self-presentational approach to decision-making in groups. In J. M. Suls & R. L. Miller (Eds.), *Social comparison processes* (pp. 235-257). New York: Halsted Press.

Jellison, J. M., & Riskind, J. A. (1970). A social comparison of abilities in interpretation of risk-taking behavior. *Journal of Personality and Social Psychology, 15,* 375-390.

Kaplan, M. F. (1987). The influencing process in group decision-making. In C. Hendrick (Ed.), *Review of personality and social psychology: Group processes* (Vol. 8, pp. 189-212). Newbury Park, CA: Sage.

Kaplan, M. F. (1989). Task, situational, and personal determinants of influence processes in group decision-making. In E. J. Lawler & B. Markovsky (Eds.), *Advances in group processes* (Vol. 6, pp. 87-105). Greenwich, CT: JAI.

Kaplan, M. F., & Miller, C. E. (1987). Group decision making and normative vs. informational influence: Effects of type of issue and decision rule. *Journal of Personality and Social Psychology, 53,* 306-313.

Kerr, N. L. (1989). Illusions of efficacy: The effects of group size on perceived efficacy in social dilemmas. *Journal of Experimental Social Psychology, 25,* 287-313.

Kerr, N. L., MacCoun, R. J., Hansen, C. H., & Hymes, J. A. (1987). Gaining and losing social support: Momentum in decision-making groups. *Journal of Experimental Social Psychology, 23,* 119-145.

Kirchler, E., & Davis, J. H. (1986). The influence of member status differences and task type on group consensus and member position change. *Journal of Personality and Social Psychology, 51,* 83-91.

Kitayama, S., & Burnstein, E. (1994). Social influence, persuasion, and group decision-making. In S. Shavitt & T. C. Brock (Eds.), *Persuasion: Psychological insights and perspectives* (pp. 175-193). Needham Heights, MA: Allyn & Bacon.

Kline, J. A. (1972). Orientation and group consensus. *Central States Speech Journal, 23,* 44-47.

Kline, J. A., & Hullinger, J. L. (1973). Redundancy, self-orientation, and group consensus. *Speech Monographs, 40,* 72-74.

Knutson, T. J. (1972). An experimental study of the effects of orientation behavior on small group consensus. *Speech Monographs, 39,* 159-165.

Knutson, T. J., & Holdridge, W. E. (1975). Orientation behavior, leadership, and consensus: A possible functional relationship. *Speech Monographs, 42,* 107-114.

Knutson, T. J., & Kowitz, A. C. (1977). Effects of information type and levels of orientation on consensus achievement in substantive and effective small group conflict. *Central States Speech Journal, 28,* 54-63.

Kogan, N., & Wallach, M. A. (1967). Effects of physical separation of group members upon group risk taking. *Human Relations, 20,* 41-48.

Koomen, W. (1988). The relationship between participation rate and liking ratings in groups. *British Journal of Social Psychology, 27,* 127-132.

Leiter, M. P. (1988). Burnout as a function of communication patterns: A study of a multidisciplinary mental health team. *Group and Organization Studies, 13,* 111-128.

Levine, J. M., & Moreland, R. L. (1990). Progress in small group research. *Annual Review of Psychology, 41,* 585-634.

Lumsden, G. (1974). An experimental study of the effect of verbal agreement on leadership maintenance in problem-solving discussion. *Central States Speech Journal, 25,* 270-276.

Maass, A., & Clark, R. D., III. (1984). The hidden impact of minorities: Fifteen years of minority influence research. *Psychological Bulletin, 95,* 428-450.

Mackie, D. M. (1986). Social identification effects in group polarization. *Journal of Personality and Social Psychology, 50,* 720-728.

Mackie, D. M., & Cooper, J. (1984). Group polarization: The effects of group membership. *Journal of Personality and Social Psychology, 46,* 575-585.

Madsen, D. B. (1978). Issue importance and group choice shifts: A persuasive arguments approach. *Journal of Personality and Social Psychology, 36,* 1118-1127.

Mayer, M. E. (1985). Explaining choice shift: An effects coded model. *Communication Monographs, 52,* 92-101.

McGarty, C., Haslam, S. A., Hutchinson, K. J., & Turner, J. C. (1994). The effects of salient group memberships on persuasion. *Small Group Research, 25,* 267-293.

McGrath, J. E. (1984). *Groups: Interaction and performance.* Englewood Cliffs, NJ: Prentice Hall.

McLachlan, A. (1986). The effects of two forms of decision reappraisal on the perception of pertinent arguments. *British Journal of Social Psychology, 25,* 129-138.

McPhee, R. D., Poole, M. S., & Seibold, D. R. (1981). The valence model unveiled: A critique and alternative formulation. In M. Burgoon (Ed.), *Communication yearbook 5* (pp. 259-278). New Brunswick, NJ: Transaction Books.

Messick, D. M., & Mackie, D. M. (1989). Intergroup relations. *Annual Review of Psychology, 40,* 45-81.

Meyers, R. A. (1989a). Persuasive arguments theory: A test of assumptions. *Human Communication Research, 15,* 357-381.

Meyers, R. A. (1989b). Testing persuasive argument theory's predictor model: Alternative interactional accounts of group argument and influence. *Communication Monographs, 56,* 112-132.

Mongeau, P. A., & Garlick, R. (1988). Social comparison and persuasive arguments as determinants of group polarization. *Communication Research Reports, 5,* 120-125.

Moscovici, S., Lage, E., & Naffrechoux, M. (1969). Influence of a consistent minority on the responses of a majority in a color perception task. *Sociometry, 32,* 365-380.

Moscovici, S., & Lecuyer, R. (1972). Studies in group decision I: Social space, patterns of communication, and group consensus. *European Journal of Social Psychology, 2,* 221-244.

Moscovici, S., & Zavalloni, M. (1969). The group as polarizer of attitudes. *Journal of Personality and Social Psychology, 12,* 125-135.

Mugny, G. (1982). *The power of minorities.* London: Academic Press.

Myers, D. G. (1975). Discussion-induced attitude polarization. *Human Relations, 28,* 699-714.

Myers, D. G., & Arenson, S. J. (1972). Enhancement of dominant risk tendencies in group discussion. *Psychological Reports, 30,* 615-623.

Myers, D. G., & Bishop, G. D. (1971). Enhancement of dominant attitudes in group discussion. *Journal of Personality and Social Psychology, 20,* 386-291.

Myers, D. G., & Lamm, H. (1976). The group polarization phenomenon. *Psychological Bulletin, 83,* 602-627.

Nemeth, C. J. (1986). Differential contributions of majority vs. minority influence. *Psychological Review, 93*(1), 23-32.

Nemeth, C. J., & Kwan, J. L. (1987). Minority influence, divergent thinking, and the detection of correct solutions. *Journal of Applied Social Psychology, 9,* 788-799.

Nemeth, C. J., & Staw, B. M. (1989). The tradeoffs of social control and innovation in groups and organizations. In L. Berkowitz (Ed.), *Advances in experimental social psychology* (Vol. 2, pp. 175-210). San Diego, CA: Academic Press.

Ng, S. H., Bell, D., & Brooke, M. (1993). Gaining turns and achieving high influence ranking in small conversational groups. *British Journal of Social Psychology, 32,* 265-275.

Page, R. C., Davis, K. C., Berkow, D. N., & O'Leary, E. (1989). Analysis of group process in marathon group therapy with users of illicit drugs. *Small Group Behavior, 20,* 220-227.

Poole, M. S., McPhee, R. D., & Seibold, D. R. (1982). A comparison of normative and interactional explanations of group decision-making: Social decision schemes versus valence distributions. *Communication Monographs, 49,* 1-19.

Rugs, D., & Kaplan, M. F. (1993). Effectiveness of informational and normative influences in group decision making depends on the group interactive goal. *British Journal of Social Psychology, 32,* 147-158.

Saine, T. J., & Bock, D. G. (1973). A comparison of the distributional and sequential structures in high and low consensus groups. *Central States Speech Journal, 24,* 125-130.

Sande, G. N., & Zanna, M. P. (1987). Cognitive dissonance theory: Collective actions and individual reactions. In B. Mullen & G. R. Goethals (Eds.), *Theories of group behavior* (pp. 49-69). New York: Springer.

Sanders, G. S., & Baron, R. S. (1977). Is social comparison irrelevant for producing choice shifts? *Journal of Experimental Social Psychology, 13,* 303-314.

Siegel, J., Dubrovsky, V. J., Kiesler, S., & McGuire, T. W. (1986). Group processes in computer-mediated communication. *Organizational Behavior and Human Decision Processes, 37,* 157-187.

Silverthorne, C. P. (1971). Information input and the group shift phenomenon in risk taking. *Journal of Personality and Social Psychology, 20,* 456-461.

Stasser, G. (1992). Information salience and the discovery of hidden profiles by decision making groups: A "thought experiment." *Organizational Behavior and Human Decision Processes, 52,* 156-181.

Stasser, G., Kerr, N. L., & Davis, J. H. (1989). Influence processes and consensus models in decision-making groups. In P. B. Paulus (Ed.), *Psychology of group influence* (2nd ed., pp. 279-326). Hillsdale, NJ: Lawrence Erlbaum.

Stasser, G., & Titus, W. (1985). Pooling of unshared information in group decision making: Biased information sampling during group discussion. *Journal of Personality and Social Psychology, 48,* 1476-1478.

Steiner, I. D. (1972). *Group process and productivity.* New York: Academic Press.

Stoner, J. A. F. (1961). *A comparison of individual and group decisions involving risk.* Unpublished master's thesis, Massachusetts Institute of Technology.

Sundstrom, E., deMeuse, K. P., & Futrell, D. (1990). Work teams: Applications and effectiveness. *American Psychologist, 5,* 120-133.

Tajfel, H., & Turner, J. C. (1979). An integrative theory of intergroup conflict. In W. G. Austin & S. Worchel (Eds.), *The social psychology of intergroup conflict* (pp. 33-47). Monterey, CA: Brooks/Cole.

Teger, A. I., & Pruitt, D. (1967). Components of group risk taking. *Journal of Experimental Social Psychology, 3,* 189-205.

Turner, J. C. (1982). Toward a cognitive redefinition of the social group. In H. Tajfel (Ed.), *Social identity and intergroup relations* (pp. 15-40). Cambridge, UK: Cambridge University Press.

Turner, J. C. (1985). Social categorization and the self-concept: A social cognitive theory of group behavior. In E. J. Lawler (Ed.), *Advances in group processes: Theory and research* (Vol. 2, pp. 77-122). Greenwich, CT: JAI.

Turner, J. C., & Oakes, P. J. (1986). The significance of the social identity concept for social psychology with reference to individualism, interactionism, and social influence. *British Journal of Social Psychology, 25,* 237-252.

Turner, J. C., Wetherell, M. S., & Hogg, M. A. (1989). Referent informational influence and group polarization. *British Journal of Social Psychology, 28,* 135-147.

Vinokur, A. (1971). Review and theoretical analysis of the effects of group processes upon individual and group decisions involving risk. *Psychological Bulletin, 76,* 231-250.

Vinokur, A., & Burnstein, E. (1974). Effects of partially shared persuasive arguments on group induced shifts: A group problem-solving approach. *Journal of Personality and Social Psychology, 19,* 305-315.

Vinokur, A., & Burnstein, E. (1978). Novel argumentation and attitude change: The case of polarization following discussion. *European Journal of Social Psychology, 8,* 335-348.

Wetherell, M. S. (1987). Social identity and group polarization. In J. C. Turner, M. A. Hogg, P. J. Oakes, S. D. Reicher, & M. S. Wetherell (Eds.), *Rediscovering the social group: A self-categorization theory* (pp. 142-170). New York: Blackwell.

Willems, E. P., & Clark, R. D., III. (1971). Shift toward risk and heterogeneity of groups. *Journal of Experimental Social Psychology, 7,* 304-312.

Wood, W. (1985). Meta-analytic review of sex difference in group performance. *Psychological Bulletin, 102,* 53-71.

Wright, E. F., Lüüs, C. A. E., & Christie, S. D. (1990). Does group discussion facilitate the use of consensus information in making causal attributions? *Journal of Personality and Social Psychology, 59,* 261-269.

Communication and Group Decision-Making Effectiveness

RANDY Y. HIROKAWA
LARRY ERBERT
ANTHONY HURST

Groups, and the decisions that emerge from them, clearly play an important role in our society. Our government would come to a grinding halt without the aid of decision-making groups of various kinds; our legal system would certainly be hampered without juries; our educational system depends (almost too much) on faculty committees; and we cannot overstate the importance of decision-making groups for our many private and public organizations (Hackman, 1990; Putnam, 1992).

Our current dependence on groups to make important decisions is, unfortunately, not a cause for optimism. Humorous sayings like, "A camel is a horse designed by a committee," or "A committee is a group that keeps minutes and wastes hours," attest to the fact that groups often do not perform as they should. Indeed, some of our government's most foolhardy and embarrassing foreign policy decisions were made by presumably well-informed and well-intentioned groups (Janis, 1982).

To be sure, asking groups to make important decisions involves risk. Groups are just as likely to make "bad" decisions as they are to make "good" ones.[1] It is not surprising, then, that the question of why some groups arrive at high-quality decisions while others do not has long been of interest to small group scholars from a variety of academic disciplines (see, e.g., Collins & Guetzkow, 1964; Hackman, 1990; McGrath, 1984; Steiner, 1972). Fortunately, the results of these studies indicate that the performance of decision-making groups is, in most cases, attributable to factors group members can control.

General Influences on Decision Performance

One important factor is the *informational resources* available to group members. In general, researchers have found that the better informed members are about the problem they are required to solve, as well as the positive and negative qualities of available choices, the better able they are to reach a high-quality decision. In fact, several authors have indicated that the quality of information available to a group is one of the most important determinants of successful group decision making (Kelley & Thibaut, 1969).

A second factor known to influence the performance of decision-making groups is the *quality of effort* group members put forth in trying to reach a decision. According to Janis and Mann (1977), groups are more likely to reach high-quality decisions when their decision-making processes are characterized by careful and painstaking examination and reexamination of the information on which the choice is to be based. They suggest that this perseverant effort, which they label "vigilance," enables group members to catch and remedy errors of thinking that, if left unchecked, can lead the group to a remarkably bad decision.

A third factor known to affect the performance of decision-making groups is the *quality of thinking* displayed by group members as they attempt to reach a collective decision. In particular, studies have shown that the ability of a group to reach a high-quality decision is dependent on its members' ability to arrive at warranted or appropriate inferences (or conclusions) from decision-relevant information available to them. NASA's regrettable decision to launch the ill-fated space shuttle *Challenger* in the face of information suggesting a postponement of that launch provides a good example of this point. During the pre-launch deliberation, engineers from Morton Thiokol, manufacturers of the solid-fuel rocket boosters that propelled the shuttle, provided NASA officials with data indicating that a crucial component of the rocket motor had malfunctioned on previous shuttle flights when launch temperatures fell below 52 ° Fahrenheit. Because the temperature at the time of the *Challenger* launch was expected to be 32 ° F, the conclusion that NASA should have drawn from those data was that the component was likely to malfunction on this flight as well. Such a conclusion would obviously justify a decision to postpone the launch until the temperature reached or exceeded 52 degrees. Yet the conclusion that NASA officials actually drew from the data was that, because malfunctions of the rocket component had *not* resulted in any serious problems with previous shuttle flights, there was no reason to believe that any problems would result in the present instance. This conclusion supported the decision to proceed with the launch of the *Challenger*—a decision that ultimately cost the lives of the eight crew members (Hirokawa, Gouran, & Martz, 1988).

A fourth factor known to affect the performance of a decision-making group is the *decision logic* its members employ in reaching a decision. A group's decision logic refers to the "system of reasoning" it employs in selecting and justifying a choice from among a set of alternatives (Hirokawa & Keyton, 1991). Peter Senge, in his influential book, *The Fifth Discipline* (1990), observes that groups usually employ either a "rational" or a "political" logic in arriving at a decision. A rational decision logic is one in which the group arrives at a final decision by carefully considering the positive and negative qualities of all available choices, and then selecting the alternative that offers the most positive, and least negative, attributes. A political decision logic, on the other hand, is one in which "factors other than the intrinsic merits of alternative courses of action weigh in making decisions—factors such as building one's own power base, or 'looking good,' or 'pleasing the boss' " (Senge, 1990, p. 60). In short, a group using a political logic is guided by its self-interests and selects either the most expedient alternative or the alternative that offers the path of least resistance. According to Senge, groups are more likely to arrive at high-quality decisions when they employ a rational, as a opposed to a political, logic in arriving at a final decision (p. 60).

Importance of Group Communication

Although it is clear that group decision-making performance is affected by a variety of factors, there are many who suggest that the quality of communication that occurs as a group attempts to reach a collective decision may well be the single most important influence on the decision-making success or failure of a group (see, e.g., Collins & Guetzkow, 1964; Gouran & Hirokawa, 1983; Hackman & Morris, 1975; Janis & Mann, 1977; McGrath, 1984; Taylor & Faust, 1952). Such a conclusion, for instance, is implied in Steiner's (1972, p. 9) oft-cited equation:

$$\text{Actual (group) productivity} = \text{potential (group) productivity} - \text{losses due to faulty processes.}$$

Although many believe that the quality of a group's communication is directly related to the quality of its decision-making performance, other authors have questioned the inherent existence of such a relationship. For example, a major research tradition in social psychology growing out of the pioneering work of Lorge and Solomon (1955), and extending to theories by Steiner (1972) and Davis (1973), explains group decision outcomes primarily in terms of noncommunication input variables like member intelligence, ability, knowledge, or skills. Getting back to Steiner's (1972) oft-cited equation, "actual group productivity = potential productivity – losses due to faulty processes," group communication is actually unceremoniously included among "losses due to faulty processes" and is assumed, at best, to hinder group decision performance. Moreover, what negative impact communication has in Steiner's model is dependent on what he regards as the primary determinants of productivity—namely, member characteristics and task type.

Davis's (1973) theory of social decision schemes likewise accounts for group decision performance on the basis of noncommunication variables. His model explains decisions as a function of overarching decision norms (e.g., consensus or majority rule) that combine members' prediscussion preferences into a final group choice. For Davis, the quality of a group's final decision is largely dependent on the quality of members' prediscussion preferences as combined through a social decision scheme. Group discussion, at best, serves as a less-than-perfect medium through which individual preferences are made known to others in the group.

To be sure, the existing literature reveals a very confusing state of affairs regarding the relationship between group communication and group decision-making performance. In short, the belief that group communication is essential for the achievement of high-quality decisions appears to be counterbalanced by claims that communication, at best, merely inhibits group decision-making performance. The remainder of this chapter focuses on what we have learned (and still need to learn) about the relationship between group communication and group decision-making performance. It is organized into three general sections. First, I provide a brief review of existing research on the relationship between group communication and group decision-making performance. Next, I critique this research, noting several persistent problems that need to be overcome to advance our understanding of this relationship. Finally, I identify several key research questions for small group scholars interested in investigating the relationship between group communication and group decision-making performance.

Communication and Group Decision-Making Performance

Efforts to investigate the relationship between group communication and group decision-making performance can be organized around four general concerns: (a) What communication *structures* are related to group decision-making performance? (b) What communication *modalities* are related to group decision-making performance? (c) What communication *procedures* are related to group decision-making performance? and (d) What communication *behaviors* are related to group decision-making performance?

COMMUNICATION STRUCTURES AND PERFORMANCE

Early research examining the relationship between group communication and group decision-making performance sought to determine whether group performance can be facilitated through the manipulation of a group's communication *network* structure (see, e.g., Bavelas, 1948, 1950; Leavitt, 1951; Shaw, 1964, 1981). Researchers pursuing this line of investigation were interested in discovering the effects of various network structures (or configurations of communication channels among group members) on group problem-solving and decision-making effectiveness. Laboratory experiments addressing this question placed group members in various arrangements of communication channels, including: (a) the *circle*—where each member can communicate with only two adjacent members, the complete set of linkages forming a circle; (b) the *chain*, a circle with one link removed; (c) the *wheel*, where one member is linked to all others, but none of those others are linked to each other; and (d) the *all-channel*, where every member can communicate with every other member.

The findings from these studies collectively indicate that no network structure is universally superior in facilitating group decision-making or problem-solving performance. However, some network structures appear to be more facilitative for certain types of tasks. Leavitt (1951), for example, used a simple symbol identification task and found that centralized structures (like the wheel) produced higher-quality group performance than did decentralized structures (like the circle). Shaw (1964), on the other hand, used a more complex mathematical problem and found that decentralized structures produced more accurate decisions than did centralized structures. Similar findings have been obtained by Guetzkow and Simon (1955), Hirota (1953), Kano (1971), and Lawson (1964).

In short, research examining the relationship between communication network structures and group decision-making performance have found that such a relationship appears to be mediated by the type of task a group is required to perform. As Shaw (1981) notes, the influence of network structures on group performance "is limited by the size of the group, the subject population, and the kind of task. Of these, task seems to be the most critical variable" (p. 155). Thus when the task is relatively simple and requires only the collation of information, centralized structures are likely to be more facilitative than decentralized ones. However, when the decision task is more complex and requires a variety of subdecisions, decentralized structures appear to be more facilitative of performance than centralized ones.

COMMUNICATION MODALITIES AND PERFORMANCE

A second line of research examining the relationship between group communication and group decision-making performance has focused on the effects of communication modalities available to group members. Researchers pursuing this line of study have typically compared the decision-making performance of face-to-face communication groups with comparable groups operating under one or more modality restrictions—for instance, written communication only, audio communication only, electronically mediated audio/visual communication, and the like (see, e.g., Argyle & Cook, 1976; Cook & Lallijee, 1972; Williams, 1977).

The results of these investigations have been mixed and again appear to be influenced by the type of task employed. In general, researchers have found virtually no differences among various communication modalities for brainstorming or simple problem-solving tasks, but have discovered that less restrictive modalities tend to be associated with higher-quality decisions than more restrictive modalities when more complex and difficult decision-making tasks have been employed (Hiltz, Johnson, & Turoff, 1986).

In summary, the data from this line of investigation indicate that the relationship among communication modalities and group decision-making performance is mediated by the complexity of the task facing the group. When the task is simple and can be accomplished with little or no group discussion, restrictive modalities (like audio-only) appear to be as facilitative of group performance as less restrictive modalities (like face-to-face). For more complex (and presumably difficult) tasks, however, less restrictive modalities appear to be more facilitative of performance than more restrictive ones. This is likely to be the case because, ostensibly, less restrictive modalities provide group members with increased opportunity to exchange and utilize information in arriving at a solution to the problem (McGrath, 1984).

COMMUNICATION PROCEDURES AND PERFORMANCE

A third line of research examining the relationship between group communication and group decision-making performance has focused on the effects of discussion procedures and agenda formats on group performance (see, e.g., Bayless, 1967; Brilhart & Jochem, 1964; Burleson, Levine, & Samter, 1984; Gustafson, Shukla, Delbecq, & Walster, 1973; Hirokawa, 1985; Jarboe, 1988; Larson, 1969; Maier & Maier, 1957; Maier & Thurber, 1969; Stephenson, Michalson, & Franklin, 1982). These studies are based on the assumption that the manner in which a group attempts to solve its problem or to reach a decision is an important determinant of its eventual performance effectiveness. Among the types of formats compared by researchers are reflective-thinking, nominal group technique, Delphi method, PERT, ideal solution, and single-question formats.

Results from these investigations have been mixed. Some studies have shown that simplified versions of Dewey's (1910) reflective-thinking agenda increase the problem-solving and decision-making ability of groups over other types of procedures (Brilhart & Jochem, 1964; Maier & Thurber, 1969). Other studies have found no differences among discussion formats (Bayless, 1967; Hirokawa, 1985; Larson, 1969). Still other investigations have shown that certain limited interaction formats (like the nominal group technique), when compared to free-discussion and no-discussion formats, tend to produce more and better quality solutions and decisions. In contrast, however, other studies have found that free-discussion formats are associated with higher quality decisions than no- or limited-interaction formats (Burleson et al., 1984; Jarboe, 1988).

The findings from this line of investigation indicate that the relationship between discussion formats and group decision-making performance appears to be dependent on two factors. First is the *nature of the task*. When a group is faced with an easy decision task (e.g., one that can be completed by competent group members without extensive consultation with others), the discussion agenda or format followed by the group is of little consequence. In this instance, the decision-making skills, as well as the amount of relevant information possessed by group members, are the key facilitators of group performance. As the difficulty of the decision task increases, however, formats that encourage vigilant and systematic face-to-face interaction tend to result in higher-quality outcomes (Hirokawa, 1988; Jarboe, 1988).

A second factor mediating the relationship between discussion formats and group decision-making performance is the *functional potential* of the respective formats. Studies indicate that any discussion format that encourages a group to analyze a problem thoroughly, to establish criteria for a good solution, and to evaluate the positive and negative qualities of alternative choices in light of those criteria leads more often to higher-quality decisions than do formats that do not permit the group to perform those functions in reaching a decision (Hirokawa, 1985). Little research, however, has focused on the relationship between a group's discussion agenda and its ability to satisfy critical task requirements during the decision-making process.

COMMUNICATION BEHAVIORS AND PERFORMANCE

Studies examining the relationship between various types of communicative behaviors and group decision-making performance constitute the fourth, and perhaps most extensive, line of research. These investigations have followed two general paths. First, a number of studies have sought to identify correlations between the frequency of various types of communicative behaviors and the quality of group decisions (see, e.g., Gouran, Brown, & Henry, 1978; Hackman & Morris, 1975; Harper & Askling, 1980; Hirokawa, 1980, 1983a, 1983b, 1985, 1987, 1988; Hirokawa & Pace, 1983; Hirokawa & Rost, 1992; Katzell, Miller, Rotter, & Venet, 1970; Landsberger, 1955; Lanzetta & Roby, 1960; Leathers, 1972; Sorenson, 1971). These investigations generally indicate that group decision-making performance is *not* affected by the production of specific types of communicative behaviors, per se, but by the extent to which those behaviors allow group members to perform important decision-making subtasks or functions (Gouran & Hirokawa, 1983, p. 170).

Leathers (1972), for example, manipulated the quality of communication within decision-making groups and found that groups experiencing low-quality communication (i.e., numerous highly abstract statements, internally inconsistent statements, irrelevant statements, negatively reinforcing statements, facetious statements, and statements reflecting a desire to withdraw from the group) led to decisions of significantly lower quality than was the case with groups characterized by high-quality communication (i.e., precise statements, internally consistent statements, relevant statements, positive reinforcement statements, and statements emphasizing cooperation and teamwork).

Gouran et al. (1978) compared the interactions of a number of decision-making groups and observed strong positive correlations among a measure of perceived quality and several behavioral attributes that included addressing relevant issues, analysis of issues, amplification of contributions, making goal-directed statements, using and testing evidence, performing necessary leadership functions, promoting interpersonal relations, and maintaining an even distribution of participation. Another investigation, by Harper and Askling (1980), produced similar findings. Their study found that groups making high-quality decisions displayed higher-quality leadership, more open communication, and a higher proportion of active participants than did groups whose decisions were judged to be of low quality.

Investigations by Hirokawa and his associates (see, e.g., Hirokawa, 1980, 1983a, 1983b, 1985, 1987, 1988; Hirokawa & Pace, 1983; Hirokawa & Rost, 1990) further indicate that the facilitative influence of communication behaviors lies in its ability to assist the group in satisfying important decision-making subtasks. In one study, Hirokawa (1980) pursued the question of what distinguishes effective from ineffective group decision making by focusing on instrumental functions of communication. His analysis revealed that in effective groups procedural statements providing direction were produced with greater than chance frequency, but this pattern was not evident in the ineffective groups. In another study, Hirokawa (1983a) correlated ratings of the quality of group decisions with the frequency of communicative behaviors that performed five decision-related functions. Decision quality correlated positively with behaviors "analyzing the problem" and negatively with behaviors "establishing operating procedures," suggesting that the more attention a group must invest in discussing the procedures it will follow, the less attention it will focus on other functions necessary for reaching effective solutions. In more recent investigations, Hirokawa (1985, 1988; Hirokawa & Rost, 1990) has provided still more evidence that group communication behaviors are related to group decision-making performance to the extent that they contribute to the accomplishment of such decision-related subtasks as problem analysis and the evaluation of the positive and negative aspects of available choices.

Limitations of Existing Research

Though scholarship to date supports the existence of a relationship between group communication and group decision-making performance, it is also clear that this research is inconclusive in establishing definite connections among specific communication attributes and differences in group decision-making performance. As Hewes (1986) concludes,

> Too little care has been taken in testing claims concerning the ability of communication to constitute, guide, enhance, or inhibit small group decision-making. When the evidentiary base of this claim was closely examined, it was found to be weak, yet the claim continues to be accepted as if it were firmly established. (pp. 288-289)

There are at least four reasons why current scholarship has failed to provide a greater understanding of the relationship between group communication and group decision-making performance. They include (a) imprecise measures of group decision-making performance, (b) absence of integrative theories, (c) conceptual confusion over the relationship between communication and group decision-making performance, and (d) failure to account for the influence of contextual variables on the relationship between communication and group decision-making performance.

IMPRECISE MEASURES OF DECISION PERFORMANCE

Several critics (e.g., Gouran, 1988; Janis & Mann, 1977; Poole, 1990) have argued that the study of group decision-making performance in general, and the relationship between group communication and group performance in particular, have been hampered by the absence of a problem-free way to assess group decision-making *performance*. According to Gouran (1988), researchers have employed at least three different approaches—correctness, quality, and utility—none of which is totally satisfactory as an operational definition of group decision-making performance.

Correctness of Decision. A number of investigations have operationalized group decision-making performance in terms of the *correctness* of the group's choice. The notion of correctness implies that the choice can be proven to be logically and objectively free from error or flaw. Gouran (1988) notes that such an operationalization of group performance has the obvious advantage of permitting a researcher "to say with both accuracy and confidence how closely the members of a group have approached their objective, what they have achieved, and how they compare with other groups" (p. 249). At the same time, he points out that evaluating a group's decision-making performance on the basis of the correctness of its decision is problematic because it is not reflective of the types of decisions groups usually address. According to Gouran, even when groups are asked to resolve issues for which the accuracy or correctness of their decision is a concern (e.g., determining the guilt or innocence of someone who has been accused of a crime), the correctness of their decision is usually, if not always, unverifiable. Gouran therefore maintains that the concept of correctness is unacceptable as an operationalization of decision-making performance because it cannot be easily applied to most of the kinds of decision-making tasks groups usually face.

Quality of Decision. A second way that researchers have evaluated the performance of a decision-making group is in terms of the quality of its decision. Typically, the quality of a group's decision is assessed by asking knowledgeable individuals, or those presumably affected by the decision, to indicate whether a given decision possesses certain attributes (e.g., economic feasibility or equity) that are assumed to be desirable under the circumstances specified. As such, the more desirable attributes a decision is judged to possess, the higher its overall quality is assumed to be. Gouran (1988) maintains that, "A focus on the quality of decisions has permitted scholars to investigate the behavior of groups pursuing tasks that more nearly resemble realistic situations" (p. 251). He also notes, however, that "A number of problems are associated with its use" (p. 251). The most serious problem concerns the inherent subjectivity of the notion of "quality." According to Gouran, the assessment of a decision's quality is so heavily reliant on perceptions that "the criteria do not have any specific referents in decisions themselves" (p. 252). In other words, just because a panel of judges determines that a choice possesses certain desirable attributes does not mean that it necessarily possesses them; indeed, a different panel of judges could arrive at an opposite conclusion, depending on their perspective. In short, Gouran (1988) contends that the concept of quality is "too abstract and nebulous" to be useful in evaluating the performance of decision-making groups (p. 252).

Utility of Decision. A number of researchers have assessed the performance of decision-making groups in terms of the utility of their decisions. As used in this context, the utility of a decision refers to the ratio of costs and benefits associated with it relative to other available choices (Gouran, 1988, p. 252). Those who have used this concept to evaluate group performance have usually done so in a post hoc manner. That is, they have examined actual cases of group decision making for which the positive and negative consequences are known and then tried to reconstruct the process that led to those decisions (see, e.g., Gouran, 1984; Head, Short, & McFarlane, 1978; Hirokawa et al., 1988; Janis, 1972, 1982; Stein & Tanter, 1980). Included among the many decisions examined in this manner are the Watergate coverup (Gouran, 1984; Janis, 1982) and the *Challenger* disaster (Hirokawa et al., 1988). The concept of utility is a straightforward and objective basis for evaluating the performance of decision-making groups. That is to say, once a decision has been made, and its consequences are known, it is relatively easy to classify it as beneficial or costly. Yet as Gouran (1988) and others (Janis & Mann, 1977; March & Simon, 1958; Poole, 1990) have noted, the fact that the consequences of any decision are not always immediate and, in fact, are often separated from the decision by considerable time intervals, it is problematic to evaluate a group's performance on the basis of the utility of its decision. Simply put, any number of unforeseen factors can intervene between the time of a decision and its known consequences. Hence a group that makes a "good" decision on the basis of the information available to it may later be viewed as having made a "bad" decision because of unforeseen changes in the environment, just as a group that makes a "bad" choice can later be credited with making a "good" one. In short, the concept of utility makes it difficult to link group communication processes directly to group decision-making performance.

The Need for a Better Measure. Clearly, existing approaches to the assessment of group decision-making performance are deficient in various ways—*correctness* can only be applied to a very limited range of decision-making tasks; *quality* is too subjective and idiosyncratic for precise social scientific measurement; and *utility* can only be applied post hoc, when there is an inherent difficulty in linking communication processes to decision outcomes (Gouran, 1988, p. 255). To be sure, research on the relationship between group communication and group decision-making performance will continue to be hindered unless we can develop a way of assessing group decision-making performance that meets at least two criteria. First, it must apply to the full range of decision-making tasks and activities in which groups engage. Gouran (1988) identifies at least four types of decision-making tasks that a group could encounter. They include questions of *fact* ("What caused the crash of the space shuttle *Challenger?*"), *conjecture* ("Will passage of NAFTA help or hurt the U.S. economy?"), *value* ("Should capital punishment be permitted?"), and *policy* ("What should be done to prevent the proliferation of nuclear weapons among Third World nations?"). Current approaches to assessing group performance are limited to only a few of these questions, but not to all of them. What is needed is a way of assessing performance that applies to all four basic types of group decision-making activities. The development of such a common measure of performance will enable scholars to better generalize and integrate their findings across a variety of group decision-making settings.

The generalizability of the measure notwithstanding, it is perhaps more important that we develop a more sensitive way of assessing group decision-making performance. This is not merely a call for more valid scientific measures of performance. Indeed, the quest for such measures has led to the use of "play problems that have no real relevance to [group] members and generally have fairly pat, simple answers that can be scored as right or wrong" (Poole, 1990, p. 245). Rather, what is needed is a way of evaluating group decision-making outcomes that better accounts for the complex and often shifting notion of what constitutes "good" and "bad" group decisions. As Poole (1990, p. 245) puts it,

> [Existing] measures are chosen, in part, because we have an academic view of outcomes. We want outcomes that can be clearly defined and cleanly measured. Getting the "right" answer [seems] valid and clean.

However . . . in the real world, there are rarely right answers, just better or worse ones. Moreover, what is good in the short run sometimes looks bad over the long run and vice versa. And are correct answers what we want, or do we want practical solutions, or politically smart ones, or fair ones? Unfortunately, as decades of evaluation research have shown, most real world outcomes are soft and elusive and difficult to measure. We do a disservice to ourselves and to those who want to use our research if we reduce complex, changeable, and politically determined outcomes to correct or best answers or to sometimes flippant [ratings of performance]. (p. 245)

Poole's point is that we need to formulate a way of assessing group decision-making performance that has more direct relevance to what really counts as good or bad decisions in the real world. To this end, perhaps Gouran's (1988, p. 257) notion of *appropriateness* ("the choice that a group is obliged to make in light of its purpose, the requirements of the task, and what the analysis of information bearing on the available alternatives establishes as reasons for endorsing and rejecting each") offers promise as a basis for evaluating group decision-making performance.

ABSENCE OF INTEGRATIVE THEORIES

A number of authors have suggested that a second reason why research to date has not been more successful in enhancing our understanding of the relationship between group communication and group decision-making performance is because it has, in most cases, not been guided by integrative theories of group decision making. Nearly two decades ago, Hackman and Morris (1975) criticized group process-performance scholarship on the grounds that it was not guided by a cogent theoretical framework that identified the specific process variables that, at least in principle, should be related to group performance. As a result, they suggested that researchers' selection of communication attributes and variables were often based on speculation and intuition, rather than on sound theoretical insights. Since then, other authors have advanced similar criticisms of group decision-making research (see, e.g., Bormann, 1980; Cragan & Wright, 1990; Gouran, 1984; Gouran & Hirokawa, 1983; Shaw, 1981).

As the chapters in this volume indicate, research on group decision-making communication has increasingly been theory-driven. Yet we still lack comprehensive and integrative theories that can serve as general frameworks for guiding and incorporating research efforts to understand the link between communication and group decision-making performance. In short, what we need are theoretical frameworks that enable researchers to understand how communication structures, modalities, procedures, and behaviors independently—and interdependently—affect group decision-making performance. At best, we currently possess a rudimentary understanding of how certain types of communication behaviors affect group performance (see Gouran & Hirokawa, Chapter 3, this volume). However, we possess little or no theoretical understanding of the separate and collective roles that structures, modalities, procedures, and behaviors play in group decision-making outcomes. The development of such integrative theories is a necessary step in the advancement of group communication-performance research.

CONFUSION OVER THE NATURE OF THE COMMUNICATION-PERFORMANCE RELATIONSHIP

A third reason why scholars have failed to provide a better understanding of the relationship between group communication and group decision-making performance is attributable to conceptual confusion regarding the nature of that relationship. The literature indicates that the relationship between group communication and group decision-making performance has been conceptualized in two ways. The first is to view group communication as *a medium* for the effects of various exogenous factors on group decision-making outcomes; and the second is to view group communication as *constitutive* of group decisions—that is, as the means for creating the social context or reality within which a decision is shaped and enacted. Although these two conceptions are by no means incompatible, group scholars have tended to favor one or the other in studying the relationship between communication and group decision-making performance, and this bias has limited the development of theory and research in this area.

Mediational Role of Communication. The prevailing view held by many small group scholars is that group communication serves as a medium through which the true determinants of group decision performance are able to exert their influence. This perspective assumes that factors or processes other than communication itself account for the performance of decision-making groups. The mediational role of communication has been discussed in the research literature in several different ways. Barnlund (1959) and others (Leavitt, 1951; Shaw, 1981) claim that communication enhances group decision-making performance by allowing members to distribute and pool available informational resources necessary for effective decision making. These authors suggest that the true determinant of decision-making performance is the presence of relevant information in the group; communication provides the medium through which this information is distributed among group members and subsequently brought to bear on the decision task. Similarly, other authors (Janis, 1972, 1982; Taylor & Faust, 1952) have indicated that communication facilitates group decision-making performance by allowing group members to catch and remedy errors of individual judgment. Here again, the major determinant of group decision-making effectiveness is a group's ability, through discussion, to detect and correct errors by group members before these can adversely affect the group's decision. This determinant of performance is external to the group's communication, but it is through communication that this variable is able to influence the group's decision-making performance.

Constitutive Role of Communication. In contrast to group scholars who view communication as a medium that allows exogenous factors to affect group decision performance, several recent authors suggest that communication plays a more fundamental role in effective group decision making. These scholars maintain that group communication is more than a convenient channel or conduit that transmits the effects of exogenous factors like knowledge, effort, or thinking on decision performance. Rather, it is a social tool that group members use to create the social context within which decisions are made. As a social tool for the constitution of decisions, then, communication exerts its own effects on the quality of group decisions (Poole & Hirokawa, 1986, p. 21).

For example, the work of Hirokawa and his associates (see Gouran & Hirokawa, Chapter 3 in this volume; Gouran, Hirokawa, Julian, & Leatham, 1993) adopts such a constitutive perspective. Briefly, their research is based on the notion that a group's ultimate decision is the end result of a series of prior subdecisions reached by members in regard to various issues—such as what choices are available to members, and what are the desirable and undesirable aspects of each choice? The conclusions that members collectively reach form the social context within which the group's final decision is made. Furthermore, this social context is largely shaped by group communication. That is, it is through communication that members address and subsequently reach conclusions regarding decision-relevant issues and questions. In short, the work of Hirokawa and his associates links communication to group decision-making performance by asserting that group communication directly shapes the quality of a group's decision by constituting the social context from which that decision ultimately emerges.

The Need for Integration. Although some have attempted to defend one or the other perspective as a more accurate representation of the role of group communication, I believe that both perspectives have validity and, therefore, importance for our understanding of group decision-making performance. The *mediational* view is important because it emphasizes the fact that the effects of knowledge, effort, thinking, decision logic, task characteristics, and scores of other influences on decision-making performance exist only through the mediation of the group discussion process. Likewise, the *constitutive* view is important because it emphasizes the active role of group communication in creating and sustaining social practices like decision making. Moreover, unlike the mediational view, which relies on factors other than discussion to account for decision outcomes, the constitutive perspective regards the group communication process as the primary force in decision-making performance. Because both the mediational and constitutive views of group communication appear to have merit, it seems clear that future scholars need to discover ways to integrate both perspectives in their theorizing and investigation of the relationship between communication and group decision-making performance. To do otherwise will cause us to discover only portions of that relationship without understanding its full complexity.

INFLUENCE OF CONTEXTUAL VARIABLES

Yet another reason why previous research has failed to provide us with a better understanding of the relationship between group communication and group decision-making performance is because those investigations have not been particularly sensitive to contextual influences. Previous research generally supports the argument that the nature of the decision-making task influences the decision-making process a group follows in reaching a decision (see, e.g., Hackman, 1968; Kabanoff & O'Brien, 1979). For example, studies have found that task-related variables like task complexity (Payne, 1976), significance of the task, and task uncertainty (Waller & Mitchell, 1984) affect various aspects of a group's decision-making process, including analytical strategies and information search behaviors.

Given the task-contingent nature of the group decision-making process, most students of group decision making would agree that a thorough understanding of the relationship between group communication and group decision-making performance must somehow take into account the influence of various task characteristics. And yet, surprisingly little systematic research has focused on how task characteristics affect the relationship between group communication and group decision-making performance. Nevertheless, data from the various lines of research, most of which were reviewed early in this chapter, collectively suggest that the relationship between group communication and group decision-making performance is mediated by at least three task-related contextual factors: (a) information distribution, (b) information-processing requirements, and (c) analytical and evaluation demands.

Information Distribution. The literature suggests that the relationship between communication and group decision-making performance is affected by the distribution of decision-relevant information among group members (Hirokawa, 1990). When information is equally distributed among group members, communication appears to be unrelated to group decision-making performance. However, when the distribution of information is skewed so that only a few members possess the information needed to reach a high-quality decision, a positive relationship between group communication and group decision-making performance emerges. For example, early group network studies found that when all group members were provided with the information needed to reach a high-quality decision, no differences were found in the facilitative effects of centralized or decentralized structures (Leavitt, 1951). In contrast, when none of the group members were provided with complete information, decentralized structures tended to be associated with more effective group performance than did centralized structures (Shaw, 1964). According to Hirokawa (1990), the reason group communication is unrelated to decision-making performance when informational homogeneity is high is because the presence of group communication, or the structures and modalities providing such communication, is unnecessary for effective group decision-making performance. Simply put, because group members already possess the information needed to complete the task, intragroup communication is not needed to distribute and pool the information required to reached a high-quality group decision. When informational homogeneity is low, however, effective group decision making requires group members to engage in open communication to distribute needed information properly among group members. In such cases the presence of such communication, as well as the structures and modalities that facilitate it, are likely to be associated with effective group decision-making performance.

Information-Processing Requirements. A second task-related variable that appears to influence the relationship between group communication and group decision-making performance is the information-processing requirements presented to the group by the decision-making situation. As used here, *information-processing requirements* refers to the extent to which (a) the validity or accuracy of information bearing on a group's decision can be objectively verified,[2] and (b) the implications of available information for the group's decision are clearly evident to its members. The literature indicates that group communication is unrelated to group performance when information-processing requirements are low—that is, the accuracy of available information can be objectively verified, and the implications of the information for the group's decision are clear. When information-processing requirements are high, however, a positive relationship between group communication and group decision-making performance emerges. For example, studies examining the effects of communication modalities on group decision-making performance (see, e.g., Argyle & Cook, 1976; Cook & Lallijee, 1972; Williams, 1977) have discovered no differences in decision-making performance among groups employing various modalities when the information-processing requirements of the task were low. However, when successful completion of the task required group members to deal with ambiguous and equivocal information, face-to-face discussion tended to be associated with significantly higher levels of performance than did more restricted modalities (Hiltz et al., 1986). Hirokawa (1990) suggests that unrestricted discussion is essential for effective group decision making when information-processing requirements are high, because group members have no way of establishing the accuracy or implication of information bearing on their decision other than to discuss and reach a consensus on whether the data should be taken into account in reaching a decision. The extent to which such discussion enables the group to make appropriate decisions regarding the information that should and should not be used in reaching its final decision obviously has important implications for the quality of that decision. In contrast, when information-processing requirements are low, unrestricted discussion is less crucial for effective group decision making because group members can verify the accuracy of information, and see its decisional implications, without interacting with others in the group.

Analytical and Evaluation Demands. A third task-related factor that appears to mediate the relationship between communication and group decision-making performance is the analytical and evaluation demands facing the group. Simply stated, these demands pertain to (a) the degree to which the group understands the problem it needs to solve or the goal(s) it needs to reach; and (b) the extent to which the criteria for a good decision are clearly presented to the group. Prior research suggests that no relationship between group communication and group decision-making performance is likely to be found when the analytical and evaluative demands facing a group are low—that is, when the group clearly understands the problem it needs to solve or the goals it needs to achieve, and the criteria for a good decision are evident to all group members. In contrast, when the analytical and evaluation demands are high, a positive relationship between communication and group decision-making performance is likely to be observed.

Studies comparing the decision-making performance of groups employing various procedural formats have found no significant differences in the decision-making performance of free-interaction and limited-interaction groups when the tasks presented to the groups had low analytical and evaluation demands (see, e.g., Campbell, 1968; Emmons & Kaplan, 1971; Kanekar & Rosenbaum, 1972; Lamm & Tromsdorff, 1973). However, studies employing tasks that had more ambiguous problems and/or goals, and unspecified criteria for evaluating available choices, have found that the opportunity for open discussion is positively related to decision performance (Burleson et al., 1984). According to Hirokawa (1990), group communication is more likely to be related to group performance when the decision task is characterized by high analytical and evaluation demands, because communication helps group members become more aware of the problem they need to resolve, the criteria they need to employ in reaching a decision, and the comparative advantages and disadvantages of available choices in light of those criteria. When those demands are absent, group performance is largely dependent on the ability of individual members to recognize the problem or goal(s) to be achieved, and to apply the appropriate criteria systematically in selecting an available choice. Little or no communication among groups members is needed to perform these functions.

The Need for Contingency Models. In summary, the preceding discussion suggests that the overall importance of group communication for effective group decision making is dependent on particular characteristics of the task situation facing the group. It appears that a relationship between group communication and group decision-making performance is more likely to emerge as the "unfavorableness" of the task situation increases. That is, we can expect communication to have the greatest impact on effective group performance when the task situation is characterized by unequal distribution of information, high information-processing requirements, and high analytical and evaluation demands. Stated another way, the literature suggests that a relationship between group communication attributes and group decision performance outcomes is likely to emerge only under certain task conditions and situations. Thus there is little doubt that future research needs to be guided by theoretical frameworks that adopt a contingency perspective on the relationship between communication and group decision-making performance (Hirokawa & McLeod, 1993; Poole & Roth, 1989).

Implications for Future Research

Research on the relationship between group communication and group decision-making performance is well past its incipient stage. Indeed, we have learned a good deal about the nature of this complex relationship. At the same time, it is obvious that there is still more that needs to be learned. In concluding this chapter, then, I would like to identify some of the questions that remain to be answered regarding the relationship between communication and group decision-making performance.

WHEN DOES COMMUNICATION MAKE A DIFFERENCE?

At the outset of this chapter, I noted that although many group scholars believe that the performance of decision-making groups is directly related to their communication attributes, not all group decision-making theorists agree with this notion. Indeed there are some who assert that group communication exerts little or no influence on group decision-making outcomes. Moreover, even those who accept the relationship between group communication and group decision-making performance do not necessarily agree on the direction of that relationship. In light of these mixed views, the natural inclination of researchers has been to search for a definitive answer to the question: *Is group communication related to group decision-making performance?*

I maintain that the search for a definitive answer to such a question is somewhat misguided. Instead of asking whether communication is related to performance, future researchers should ask: *Under what particular circumstances and conditions is group communication related to group decision-making performance?* The extant literature makes it clear that we can no longer assume that group communication always influences group decision-making performance. Indeed Hewes (1986) is correct in admonishing group communication scholars that "We . . . have let our intuitive beliefs about the importance of communication overwhelm our critical faculties" (p. 289). Simply stated, then, future researchers must identify the *parameters* within which group communication is related to group performance outcomes. To that end, recent theoretical work by Hirokawa and McLeod (1993) and Poole and Roth (1989), as well as empirical research by Hirokawa et al. (1992), Salazar (1991), and Salazar, Hirokawa, Julian, Leatham, and Propp (1994), provide examples of the kind of contingency-based scholarship that is required to enhance our understanding of the relationship between communication and group decision-making performance.

In the Salazar et al. (1994) study, for instance, the researchers demonstrate that communication opportunity is largely unrelated to group decision-making performance when group potential (as measured by the individual knowledge and skills of group members) is either high *or* low. A relationship between communication and performance emerged only under conditions of moderate group potential. The authors account for this finding by noting that when group potential is high, a natural "ceiling effect" results whereby group communication has very little to contribute to group performance above and beyond the individual knowledge and skills of group members. At the same time, when group potential is low, the needs of the group usually exceed that which communication alone can provide. Under conditions of moderate potential, however, group communication can facilitate the exchange of information and the development of choices such that group members appear to take better advantage of their potential.

HOW DOES COMMUNICATION INFLUENCE PERFORMANCE?

Once researchers are successful in identifying the parameters within which a relationship between group communication and group decision-making performance exists, attention needs to focus on the question: *How does group communication influence group decision-making performance?* As noted earlier, there appears to be some confusion in the literature regarding the precise role that communication plays in determining group decision-making outcomes. Some have argued that communication mediates group decision-making performance by serving as a conduit through which various exogenous factors exert their influence on group performance. Others contend that communication actually produces group decisions by creating and shaping the contexts within which those decisions are made and enacted.

The concern here is not to determine which perspective—the mediational or constitutive—has more merit. Rather, it is to understand better *how* group communication both mediates *and* constitutes group decision-making performance. Within a mediational framework, for example, future researchers need to discover precisely how communication mediates the relationship between exogenous variables and group decision-making outcomes. For instance, Hackman (1990) contends that group decision-making performance is determined by three "enabling conditions": sufficient group *effort*, adequate *knowledge and skills* possessed by group members, and appropriate performance *strategies and procedures* employed in reaching a decision. Moreover, he suggests that these enabling conditions exert their influence on group performance through the mediation of group communication and interaction. However, the precise nature of that role is left largely unstated by Hackman. Thus future researchers need to be concerned with understanding how group communication mediates the effects of exogenous factors like knowledge and skills, or strategies and procedures, on group decision-making performance.

In the same way, those adopting a constitutive view of the relationship between communication and group decision-making performance need to understand better how group communication functions to create the social contexts within which group decisions are made and enacted. That is, scholars need to focus attention on how group discourse functions to give rhetorical weight and force to the information, assumptions, and values that ultimately figure in the making of group decisions. Bormann's (1986, Chapter 4 in this volume) research on the formation of shared group reality through the production of fantasy chains represents such a focus. Moreover, future research efforts should also be directed toward the identification of the critical skills or competencies required by group members communicatively to construct appropriate decisions. As alluded to earlier in my cursory review of functional communication theory, the appropriateness of a group's decision can be seen as inextricably tied to the appropriateness of the social context within which that decision is made. The question that a constitutive perspective suggests, then, is why some groups construct appropriate social realities while others do not. Because these social realities are assumed to be communicative accomplishments of members, an understanding of the kinds of communicative skills members need to facilitate the construction of appropriate social contexts for group decision making seems crucial. Gouran's (1986) work on how group members communicatively counteract errors in reasoning during the group decision-making process represents an example of this concern.

CAN COMMUNICATION BE ALTERED TO ENHANCE GROUP PERFORMANCE?

The identification of the parameters within which communication is related to group performance, and the stipulation of the precise nature of that relationship, leads to perhaps the most crucial challenge facing future researchers. That is, we must ultimately be able to answer the question: *Can group communication be altered to enhance group decision-making performance?* Clearly, answering this question requires us first to understand *what* communication attributes need to be altered to enhance group performance. This is why a comprehensive understanding of the relationship between various communication attributes and group decision-making performance represents a logical prerequisite to determining whether the process can be altered. Beyond that, however, researchers need to determine whether the communication process *can* be systematically altered to enhance group decision-making performance. Moreover, future researchers need to discover *how* best to alter the communication process to achieve those desired ends. That is, what specific methods, procedures, and strategies need to be employed to alter successfully the group communication process in planned ways that facilitate effective decision making. Toward this end, recent research exploring the use of social technologies like group decision support systems (GDSSs) to improve the group decision-making process (McLeod, Chapter 14, this volume) represent the kind of direction that future researchers need to take in their efforts to determine whether the group communication process can be altered to enhance group performance.

Concluding Comments

Nearly two decades ago, Hackman and Morris (1975) observed,

[Although] there is substantial agreement among researchers and observers of task-oriented groups that something important happens in group interaction that can affect performance outcomes . . . there is little agreement about just what that "something" is, when it will enhance (or when it will impair) group effectiveness, and how it can be monitored, analyzed, and altered. (p. 49)

Despite recent advances, the authors' indictment of the research literature pertaining to the relationship between group communication and group decision-making performance remains valid. Clearly there is much that we still need to understand about this deceptively complex relationship. However, armed with a keen awareness of the problems and limitations of prior research, as well as a clear understanding of the important questions in need of address, future researchers should prove more successful in enhancing our understanding of the link between group communication and group decision-making performance.

Notes

1. The lay person typically equates a "good" decision with one that is "correct" (i.e., one that can be objectively proven to be free from error or flaw). In principle, at least, there are some group decisions that can be evaluated on the basis of their correctness. However, "correctness," as an evaluative term, refers to matters of accuracy or truth, and therefore can only serve as an acceptable operationalization of "goodness" when the decision to be reached concerns matters of fact alone. Most group decisions do not meet this criterion. They involve an amalgam of factual and value issues and, therefore, cannot be evaluated solely on the basis of their "correctness." In such cases, we must employ a more subjective perspective in determining whether a group decision is a good or bad one. For the purposes of this chapter, then, I will define a "good" decision as one that is judged, at the time of the evaluation, to serve the needs and interests of those affected by that decision. Simply put, a decision is a good one if it yields (or has the potential to yield) more benefit than harm to those affected by the choice. The more a decision serves the best interests and needs of those affected by it, the "better" the decision is; the less it serves those interests and needs, the "worse" the decision is.

2. A jury is an example of a group that is provided with information that possesses either low or high informational veracity. For instance, the jury may be presented with information regarding the type of gun used to shoot and kill a victim, or the approximate

time that the victim was killed. These data possess high informational veracity because they can be objectively verified to be correct or incorrect. At the same time, the jury may also be presented with information concerning the possible reasons why the defendant may have shot and killed the victim. This information possesses low informational veracity because there is no way to verify objectively the accuracy of those speculations regarding the defendant's motives.

References

Argyle, M., & Cook, M. (1976). *Gaze and mutual gaze.* London: C.U.P.

Barnlund, D. C. (1959). A comparative study of individual, majority, and group judgment. *Journal of Abnormal and Social Psychology, 58,* 55-60.

Bavelas, A. (1948). A mathematic model of group structure. *Applied Anthropology, 7,* 16-30.

Bavelas, A. (1950). Communication patterns in task-oriented groups. *Journal of the Acoustical Society of America, 22,* 725-730.

Bayless, O. L. (1967). An alternative pattern for problem solving discussion. *Journal of Communication, 17,* 188-197.

Bormann, E. G. (1980). The paradox and promise of small group communication revisited. *Central States Speech Journal, 31,* 214-220.

Bormann, E. G. (1986). Symbolic convergence theory and communication in group decision-making. In R. Y. Hirokawa & M. S. Poole (Eds.), *Communication and group decision-making* (1st ed., pp. 219-236). Beverly Hills, CA: Sage.

Brilhart, J. K., & Jochem, L. M. (1964). Effects of different patterns on outcomes of problem-solving discussion. *Journal of Applied Psychology, 48,* 175-179.

Burleson, B. R., Levine, B. J., & Samter, W. (1984). Decision-making procedure and decision quality. *Human Communication Research, 10,* 557-574.

Campbell, J. P. (1968). Individual versus group problem solving in an industrial sample. *Journal of Applied Psychology, 52,* 205-210.

Collins, B. E., & Guetzkow, H. (1964). *A social psychology of group processes for decision-making.* New York: John Wiley.

Cook, M., & Lallijee, M. (1972). Verbal substitutes for visual signals in interaction. *Semiotica, 3,* 212-221.

Cragan, J. F., & Wright, D. W. (1990). Small group communication research of the 1980s: A synthesis and critique. *Communication Studies, 41,* 212-236.

Davis, J. H. (1973). Group decision and social interaction: A theory of social decision schemes. *Psychological Review, 80,* 97-125.

Dewey, J. (1910). *How we think.* Boston: D. C. Heath.

Emmons, J. F., & Kaplan, L. M. (1971). *The delphi method of decision-making: A futuristic technique.* Paper presented at the annual meeting of the International Communication Association.

Gouran, D. S. (1984). Communicative influences related to the Watergate coverup: The failure of collective judgment. *Central States Speech Journal, 35,* 260-268.

Gouran, D. S. (1986). Inferential errors, interaction, and group decision-making. In R. Y. Hirokawa & M. S. Poole (Eds.), *Communication and group decision-making* (1st ed., pp. 93-112). Beverly Hills, CA: Sage.

Gouran, D. S. (1988). Group decision making: An approach to integrative research. In C. H. Tardy (Ed.), *A handbook for the study of human communication* (pp. 247-267). Norwood, NJ: Ablex.

Gouran, D. S., Brown, C. R., & Henry, D. R. (1978). Behavioral correlates of perceptions of quality in decision-making discussions. *Communication Monographs, 45,* 51-63.

Gouran, D. S., & Hirokawa, R. Y. (1983). The role of communication in decision-making groups: A functional perspective. In M. S. Mander (Ed.), *Communications in transition* (pp. 168-185). New York: Praeger.

Gouran, D. S., Hirokawa, R. Y., Julian, K. M., & Leatham, G. B. (1993). The evolution and current status of the functional perspective on communication in decision-making and problem-solving groups: A critical analysis. In S. A. Deetz (Ed.), *Communication yearbook 16* (pp. 573-600). Newbury Park, CA: Sage.

Guetzkow, H., & Simon, H. A. (1955). The impact of certain communication nets upon organization and performance in task-oriented groups. *Management Science, 1,* 233-250.

Gustafson, D. H., Shukla, R. K., Delbecq, A., & Walster, G. W. (1973). A comparative study of differences in subjective likelihood estimates made by individuals, interacting groups, delphi groups, and nominal groups. *Organizational Behavior and Human Performance, 9,* 280-291.

Hackman, J. R. (1968). Effects of task characteristics on group products. *Journal of Experimental Social Psychology, 4,* 162-187.

Hackman, J. R. (Ed.). (1990). *Groups that work (and those that don't): Creating conditions for effective teamwork.* San Francisco: Jossey-Bass.

Hackman, J. R., & Morris, C. G. (1975). Group tasks, group interaction process, and group performance effectiveness: A review and proposed integration. In L. Berkowitz (Ed.), *Advances in experimental social psychology* (Vol. 8, pp. 45-99). New York: Academic Press.

Harper, N. L., & Askling, L. R. (1980). Group communication and quality of task solution in a media production organization. *Communication Monographs, 47,* 77-100.

Head, R. G., Short, F. W., & McFarlane, R. C. (1978). *Crisis resolution: Presidential decision making in the Mayaquez and Korean confrontations.* Boulder, CO: Westview.

Hewes, D. E. (1986). A socioegocentric model of group decision-making. In R. Y. Hirokawa & M. S. Poole (Eds.), *Communication and group decision-making* (1st ed., pp. 265-291). Beverly Hills, CA: Sage.

Hiltz, S. R., Johnson, K., & Turoff, M. (1986). Experiments in group decision-making: Communication process and outcome in face-to-face versus computerized conferences. *Human Communication Research, 13,* 225-252.

Hirokawa, R. Y. (1980). A comparative analysis of communication patterns within effective and ineffective decision-making groups. *Communication Monographs, 47,* 312-321.

Hirokawa, R. Y. (1983a). Group communication and problem-solving effectiveness II: An exploratory investigation of procedural functions. *Western Journal of Speech Communication, 47,* 59-74.

Hirokawa, R. Y. (1983b). Group communication and problem-solving effectiveness: An investigation of group phases. *Human Communication Research, 9,* 291-305.

Hirokawa, R. Y. (1985). Discussion procedures and decision-making performance: A test of a functional perspective. *Human Communication Research, 12,* 203-224.

Hirokawa, R. Y. (1987). Why informed groups make faulty decisions: An investigation of possible interaction-based explanations. *Small Group Behavior, 18,* 3-29.

Hirokawa, R. Y. (1988). Group communication and decision-making performance: A continued test of the functional perspective. *Human Communication Research, 14,* 487-515.

Hirokawa, R. Y. (1990). The role of communication in group decision-making efficacy: A task-contingency perspective. *Small Group Research, 21,* 190-204.

Hirokawa, R. Y., Gouran, D. S., & Martz, A. E. (1988). Understanding the sources of faulty group decision making: A lesson from the *Challenger* disaster. *Small Group Behavior, 19,* 411-433.

Hirokawa, R. Y., & Keyton, J. K. (1990, November). *Toward a theory of decision logics in group decision-making.* Paper presented at the annual meeting of the Speech Communication Association, Chicago.

Hirokawa, R. Y., & McLeod, P. L. (1993, November). *Communication, decision development, and decision quality in small groups: An integration of two approaches.* Paper presented at the annual meeting of the Speech Communication Association, Miami Beach.

Hirokawa, R. Y., & Pace, R. C. (1983). A descriptive investigation of the possible communication-based reasons for effective and ineffective group decision-making. *Communication Monographs, 50,* 363-379.

Hirokawa, R. Y., & Rost, K. M. (1992). Effective group decision-making in organizations: A field test of the vigilant interaction theory. *Management Communication Quarterly, 5,* 267-288.

Hirota, K. (1953). Group problem solving and communication. *Japanese Journal of Psychology, 24,* 176-177.

Janis, I. L. (1972). *Victims of groupthink: Psychological studies of foreign policy decisions and fiascoes.* Boston: Houghton Mifflin.

Janis, I. L. (1982). *Groupthink* (2nd ed.). Boston: Houghton Mifflin.

Janis, I. L., & Mann, L. (1977). *Decision making: A psychological analysis of conflict, choice, and commitment.* New York: Free Press.

Jarboe, S. (1988). A comparison of input-output, process-output, and input-process-output models of small group problem-solving effectiveness. *Communication Monographs, 55,* 121-142.

Kabanoff, B., & O'Brien, G. E. (1979). The effects of task type and cooperation upon group products and performance. *Organizational Behavior and Human Performance, 23,* 163-181.

Kanekar, S., & Rosenbaum, M. E. (1972). Group performance as a function of available time. *Psychonomic Science, 27,* 279-296.

Kano, S. (1971). Task characteristics and network. *Japanese Journal of Educational Social Psychology, 10,* 55-66.

Katzell, R. A., Miller, C. E., Rotter, N. G., & Venet, T. G. (1970). Effects of leadership and other inputs on group processes and outputs. *Journal of Social Psychology, 80,* 157-169.

Kelley, H. H., & Thibaut, J. W. (1969). Group problem-solving. In G. Lindzey & E. Aronson (Eds.), *Handbook of social psychology* (pp. 1-101). Cambridge, MA: Addison-Wesley.

Lamm, H. S., & Tromsdorff, G. (1973). Group versus individual performance on tasks requiring ideational proficiency (brainstorming): A review. *European Journal of Social Psychology, 3,* 361-388.

Landsberger, H. A. (1955). Interaction process analysis of the mediation of labor-management disputes. *Journal of Abnormal and Social Psychology, 51,* 552-558.

Lanzetta, J. T., & Roby, T. B. (1960). The relationship between certain group process variables and group problem solving efficiency. *Journal of Social Psychology, 52,* 135-148.

Larson, C. E. (1969). Forms of analysis and small group problem-solving. *Speech Monographs, 36,* 452-455.

Lawson, E. D. (1964). Reinforced and non-reinforced four-man communication nets. *Psychological Reports, 14,* 287-296.

Leathers, D. G. (1972). Quality of group communication as a determinant of group product. *Speech Monographs, 39,* 166-173.

Leavitt, H. J. (1951). Some effects of certain communication patterns on group performance. *Journal of Abnormal and Social Psychology, 46,* 38-50.

Lorge, I., & Solomon, H. (1955). Two models of group behavior in the solution of eureka-type problems. *Psychometrika, 20,* 139-148.

Maier, N. R. F., & Maier, R. A. (1957). An experimental test of the effects of "developmental" vs. "free" discussion on the quality of group decisions. *Journal of Applied Psychology, 41,* 320-323.

Maier, N. R. F., & Thurber, J. A. (1969). Limitations of procedures for improving group problem solving. *Psychological Reports, 25,* 639-656.

March, J. G., & Simon, H. A. (1958). *Organizations.* New York: John Wiley.

McGrath, J. E. (1984). *Groups: Interaction and performance.* Englewood Cliffs, NJ: Prentice Hall.

Payne, J. W. (1976). Task complexity and contingent processing in decision making: An information search and protocol analysis. *Organizational Behavior and Human Performance, 16,* 366-387.

Poole, M. S. (1990). Do we have any theories of group communication? *Communication Studies, 41,* 237-247.

Poole, M. S., & Hirokawa, R. Y. (1986). Communication and group decision-making: A critical assessment. In R. Y. Hirokawa & M. S. Poole (Eds.), *Communication and group decision-making* (1st ed., pp. 15-31). Beverly Hills, CA: Sage.

Poole, M. S., & Roth, J. (1989). Decision development in small groups V: Test of a contingency model. *Human Communication Research, 15,* 549-589.

Putnam, L. L. (1992). Rethinking the nature of groups in organizations. In R. S. Cathcart & L. A. Samovar (Eds.), *Small group communication: A reader* (6th ed., pp. 57-66). Dubuque, IA: William C. Brown.

Salazar, A. J. (1991). *Assessing the impact of interaction on group decision-making performance: Some conditions and patterns of interaction.* Unpublished doctoral dissertation, Department of Communication Studies, University of Iowa.

Salazar, A. J., Hirokawa, R. Y., Julian, K. M., Leatham, G. B., & Propp, K. M. (1994). In search of true causes: Examination of the effects of group potential and group interaction on decision performance. *Human Communication Research, 20,* 529-559.

Senge, P. M. (1990). *The fifth discipline.* Garden City, NY: Doubleday.

Shaw, M. E. (1964). Communication networks. In L. Berkowitz (Ed.), *Advances in experimental social psychology* (Vol. 1). Orlando, FL: Academic Press.

Shaw, M. E. (1981). *Group dynamics: The psychology of small group behavior* (3rd ed.). New York: McGraw-Hill.

Sorenson, J. R. (1971). Task demands, group interaction, and group performance. *Sociometry, 34,* 483-495.

Stein, J. G., & Tanter, R. (1980). *Rational decision making: Israel's security choices, 1967.* Columbus: Ohio State University Press.

Steiner, I. D. (1972). *Group process and productivity.* New York: Academic Press.

Stephenson, B. Y., Michalson, L. K., & Franklin, S. G. (1982). An empirical test of the nominal group technique in state solar energy planning. *Group and Organizational Studies, 7,* 320-334.

Taylor, D. W., & Faust, W. L. (1952). Twenty questions: Efficiency in problem-solving as a function of size of group. *Journal of Experimental Psychology, 44,* 360-368.

Waller, W. S., & Mitchell, T. R. (1984). The effects of context on the selection of decision strategies for the cost variance investigation problem. *Organizational Behavior and Human Performance, 33,* 397-413.

Williams, E. (1977). Experimental comparisons of face-to-face and mediated communication: A review. *Psychological Bulletin, 84,* 963-976.

Leadership Skills and the Dialectics of Leadership in Group Decision Making

J. KEVIN BARGE

The common textbook image of decision-making groups portrays groups as being given an unambiguous task to perform, having sufficient time to select rationally among competing alternatives, and in light of valid information, selecting the best solution apart from any outside pressure. Yet when fact is separated from fiction, the reality is that many decision-making groups do not exist in calm and stable environments; rather, decision-making groups are finding themselves in more complex, fast-paced, and turbulent environments than ever before. The increased use of information and communication technologies, which have flooded government, business, and social service groups with information, necessitates managing numerous problems and tasks simultaneously and makes it difficult to identify critical problems from the mass of information (Naisbett, 1994). Decision-making groups may also face intense time pressure (Janis, 1989) and are under growing pressure to respond quickly to environmental changes (Cushman & King, 1993). External pressure by key constituencies and stakeholders has increased as consumers of a decision-making group's products have become more sophisticated; are demanding higher quality goods and services; and are requiring that governmental, social service, and business groups be held accountable for their decisions (Hammer & Champy, 1993). The diversity of individuals participating in corporate, governmental, and social service organizations is increasing as women and minorities enter the workforce in increasing numbers (Johnston & Packer, 1987). Simply, decision-making groups now find themselves in a constant state of flux as they must be sensitive to changes within their environment and their group's membership.

What is the implication of these trends for the leaders of decision-making groups? The impact of these changing environmental conditions necessitates flexible and adaptable leadership. Traditional conceptions of group leadership where one or two individuals perform a small set of leadership functions will not be able to cope with the changing internal and external environments of decision-making groups. Decision-making groups, like the environment they belong to, will also be in a state of flux as new members join the group and old members leave, new configurations among individual group members and other groups will replace old ways of performing their task, and demands by internal and external constituents will continually change. Relying on tried and true methods that have worked well in the past when leading groups may turn out to be a formula for future disaster. Contemporary group leaders must not only be adaptable and flexible in the strategies, techniques, and methods they employ, they must also be open to learning and changing their behavior (Conger, 1992). Learning from the mistakes of the past and accurately forecasting the needs of the future are critical for effective group leadership.

Being an effective group leader turns on managing the tensions associated with two key dialectics. Effective group leaders need to be able to manage the tensions associated with the *universal-situational dialectic*. This dialectic is concerned with whether leaders need to perform in a uniform way across all people and all types of situations or to adapt their behavior according to the nuances of the situation. Effective group leaders must also manage the tensions associated with the *internal-external dialectic*. They are members of a specific group that possesses its own unique values, attitudes, rituals, and beliefs and are simultaneously members of groups located in the larger environment. Leaders as well as group members not only belong to a particular group, they are also members of multiple groups that may compete for their loyalty. Group leaders must help manage the boundary separating the group and the environment. Issues such as how much information the group should give to key players or constituents in the environment regarding its activities and how much information the group needs to know about key players' or constituents' beliefs and attitudes are of chief concern to the group leader.

Contemporary decision-making groups require a new view of leadership. They require a view of leadership that at its heart emphasizes the coordinated activities of the group members as they manage their work and relationships with one another as well as with the external environment. As Leonard Sayles (1993) puts it, traditional work on leadership has "ignored the application of leadership to the accomplishment of work, of coordination and integration" (p. 229). Effective group leaders must address these issues of balancing the internal demands of the group with the external demands created by the environment, and in so doing, grapple with the need to be consistent in their behavior as well as to change according to the situation. In this chapter, I take the position that leadership is more profitably viewed as a form of mediation and coordination. By viewing leadership as a mediation, the dualism between internal and external audiences and treating work and relational problems as separate dissolves. Moreover, I will argue that effective leaders are best able to change and adapt their behaviors when they are competent communicators. This means that effective leaders need to possess particular communication skills that facilitate their adaptation to changing circumstances.

The Dialectics of Leadership

Numerous definitions of leadership have been offered, with a recent accounting of more than 300 definitions (Bennis & Nanus, 1985). Definitional debates have occurred over whether leadership is best equated with a structured role in an authority hierarchy or if it is the process of negotiating the social order (Hosking, 1988), whether leadership should be equated with management or is a type of personal relationship formed among people (Graen & Scandura, 1987), or whether leadership is premised on the ability of individuals to use methods that intrinsically or extrinsically motivate followers (Bass, 1985). Despite the variety of definitions offered, most theorists agree that leadership is a type of social influence process. Shaw (1981) explains, "Leadership is an influence process which is directed toward goal achievement" (p. 317).

Communication researchers, for the most part, have adopted this definition of leadership and have focused on the relationship between the communicative activities of a leader and a group's success in achieving goals. Communication researchers, however, can be differentiated according to the choices they make regarding the pole they emphasize on the universal-situational dialectic and the internal-external dialectic. Leadership researchers have distinguished themselves on the universal-situational dialectic by viewing the needed leadership traits and behaviors to manage group interaction as either remaining stable across situations or as changing according to the characteristics of the situation. The internal-external dialectic is reflected in the choice leadership researchers make whether to focus on how leadership facilitates the internal group dynamics or how leadership allows groups to manage their external environment. Traditionally, most group communication research focuses on the stable set of traits and behaviors leaders use to manage the internal workings of the group. Yet contemporary research and analysis is signaling the need to adopt a more situationally based approach that manages the boundary separating the group from the environment.

THE UNIVERSAL-SITUATIONAL DIALECTIC

A central choice researchers make regarding small group leadership is whether to view leadership as a universal or a situational phenomenon. Universal theories contend that a single set of leadership traits or behaviors can be identified that remain consistent across all situations. Knutson and Holdridge (1975) utilized a universal approach when they discovered that individuals who perform orientation functions during group discussion emerge as leaders. The underlying assumption was that orientation behaviors would always predict leadership emergence regardless of situation. On the other hand, situational approaches to leadership maintain the needed traits or behaviors vary according to the situation. Fiedler's (1967, 1993) contingency theory, House's path-goal theory (1974), and Vroom and Jago's (1988) decision-making model contend that the needed combination of leadership traits or behaviors is dictated by the nature of the situation. For example, when the nature of the task is ambiguous, leaders may need to provide more structure during the discussion (House, 1974). A situational approach is much like the "it all depends" hypothesis whereby what leadership trait or style is required depends on the variables that are associated with the situation, followers, and leaders (Fisher, 1986, p. 203). Whether leadership researchers explain leadership using traits or interaction behavior, both approaches point to the need to view leadership as a more complex phenomenon that is situationally based. This tension is best reflected by two streams of research characterizing group leadership: (a) communication traits, and (b) interaction behaviors.

Communication Traits

Trait theories remained popular until the mid-1940s when Ralph Stogdill (1948) published a seminal article that argued that although hundreds of leadership traits had been discovered, few consistent patterns of traits appeared to distinguish leaders from nonleaders. Recently, trait theories of leadership have regained their popularity. Kirkpatrick and Locke (1991) contend that certain core traits such as honesty, integrity, self-confidence, cognitive ability, and knowledge of the business have been consistently demonstrated through research to distinguish leaders from nonleaders. In a recent meta-analytic study of trait theory, Lord, DeVader, and Alliger (1986) suggest that abandoning trait explanations of leadership may be premature. They discovered that leader emergence can be predicted by dominance, intelligence, and masculinity-femininity of the leader. Kenny and Zaccaro (1983) reinforce the importance of traits as they relate to leadership by arguing,

> Persons who are consistently cast in the leadership role possess the ability to perceive and predict variations in group situations and pattern their own approaches accordingly. Such leaders may be highly competent in reading the needs of their constituencies and altering their behaviors to more effectively respond to these needs. (p. 683)

It is this ability to read and to react to social situations that is of interest to those who study communication. It is important to articulate those traits that allow persons to decipher communicative cues within a variety of situations and to construct actions that are consistent with situational demands. In the recent leadership emergence literature, two traits related to the communicative abilities of individuals have been emphasized: (a) self-monitoring and (b) gender.

Self-monitoring refers to the ability of individuals to monitor their self-presentations during social interaction (Snyder, 1974). High self-monitors are individuals who are socially sensitive to situations and utilize situational cues that dictate appropriate social behavior to adapt their own actions. Low self-monitors utilize their own personal attitudes to construct their actions and do not adapt their behavior according to situational constraints. Several studies have indicated that high self-monitors tend to emerge as leaders (Cronshaw & Ellis, 1991; Dobbins, Long, Dedrick, & Clemons, 1990; Ellis, 1988; Ellis, Adamson, Deszca, & Cawsey, 1988; Ellis & Cronshaw, 1992; Kent & Moss, 1990; Zaccaro, Foti, & Kenny, 1991).

The relationship between self-monitoring and leadership emergence appears to be moderated by two factors. First, *gender* moderates the relationship between self-monitoring and leadership emergence. In research using mixed-sex groups, Ellis (1988) and Ellis and Cronshaw (1992) discovered a strong relationship between self-monitoring and leadership emergence for males but not for females. On the other hand, Dobbins et al. (1990) did not find a significant interaction between gender and self-monitoring on the outcome of leadership emergence. They did, however, find that men tended to emerge more frequently as leaders than did women. Garland and Beard (1979) found in their study using same-sex groups that self-monitoring was positively associated with leadership emergence for female groups. No correlation was found between leadership emergence and self-monitoring for male groups. Second, the *nature of the task* moderates self-monitoring and leadership emergence. High self-monitors tend to emerge as leaders when the task requires discussion, information relating to the competence of the group members is not available (Garland & Beard, 1979), and they are cued to the demands of the task (Cronshaw & Ellis, 1991). Additional support is provided by Ellis and Cronshaw (1992), who found that self-monitoring was strongly tied to leadership emergence in low- versus high-feedback tasks. However, the difference between the correlations was not statistically significant.

A second trait that has garnered much attention by group leadership researchers has been *gender*. Gender research in group leadership has been divided along two lines. One line has examined how gender is associated with particular communication patterns and how this, in turn, influences men and women emerging into and maintaining leader roles. A second line of research has examined how gender may influence perceptions of leadership effectiveness.

Researchers have argued that gender exercises a strong influence on the communication patterns men and women produce. According to gender role theory, men are socialized to be agentic and highly instrumental in their behavior as marked by being assertive, task-oriented, or competent. Women are socialized into communal or expressive patterns of communication as referenced by cooperation, friendliness, and concern for others' feelings (Eagly, 1987). Because decision-making and problem-solving groups are primarily task-oriented, the instrumental behavior exhibited by males is needed to facilitate the group's accomplishment of its task. Therefore, males versus females should emerge in and maintain leadership positions because their forms of communication are better suited to the demands of the group task.

Several studies have confirmed this line of reasoning (see Andrews [1992, pp. 75-78] for a review; Eagly & Karau, 1991). At the base of this argument is the expectation that men and women communicate differently. Several studies have associated male leaders with exhibiting high levels of initiation whereas female leaders tend to exhibit more consideration behavior (e.g., Instone, Major, & Bunker, 1983). The rhetorical styles that characterize leadership emergence among women also emphasize consideration behavior. Owen (1986) discovered that females who emerged as leaders tended to use one of two rhetorical themes. On one hand, women became leaders through hard work and by default. On the other hand, women tended to frame their contributions to the group in terms of being an organizer or coordinator but not a leader. Both themes point to the fact that women emphasize expressive and cooperative behavior during group discussion. More contemporary research disputes the blanket endorsement that men and women communicate in different ways. Hawkins (1992) found that men and women communicate in similar ways regarding the task. Eagly and Johnson (1990) discovered that studies conducted in a laboratory setting do generate the stereotypic patterns of communication. In studies conducted in ongoing organizations, however, these communication differences did not emerge. This suggests that some of the differences attributed to gender may be artifacts of the research setting.

Whether women or men emerge as leaders within small groups may be better explained by relating gender to other personal and situational factors. For example, Bunyi and Andrews (1985) discovered that although individuals who are skilled in organizing group discussions and facilitating evaluation of ideas tend to emerge as leaders more often than individuals who are unskilled, males who were in mixed-gender groups tended to emerge as leaders more often than females. Group composition may serve as a critical variable in moderating the gender-leadership emergence relationship. The nature of the task also appears to influence whether women will emerge as leaders. Wentworth and Anderson (1984) discovered that women emerged as leaders in "feminine" task conditions. Eagly and Karau (1991) discovered that tasks requiring more complex interpersonal interaction were more likely to be associated with women emerging as leaders.

A second group of studies has examined how gender relates to the stereotypical perceptions of females in leadership roles. Kushell and Newton (1986) found subjects were more satisfied in democratically versus autocratically led groups and leader gender made no difference to their level of satisfaction. However, female subjects were highly dissatisfied when their group was led by a male exhibiting an autocratic style. Jurma and Wright (1990) found subjects were satisfied with a leader's performance when the leader had lost reward power. The gender of the leader did not influence the satisfaction ratings with the leader's performance and intrinsic satisfaction with the task. Similarly, Alderton and Jurma (1980) found group members were equally satisfied with male and female leaders as long as they exhibited similar levels of task behavior. Bradley (1980) found that women who were perceived as competent were treated with reason and friendliness by all-male majorities. In a recent meta-analysis, Eagly, Makhijani, and Klonsky (1992) found that female leaders tended to be rated less favorably than male leaders when they acted autocratically and were directive. Moreover, women were viewed less favorably when they occupied roles that were associated with men.

Trait explanations have difficulty accounting for an individual's ability to sustain and maintain leadership roles over time. Though traits may successfully predict leadership emergence within single-meeting leaderless group discussions, traits do not successfully predict who will maintain leadership across the life of a group. For example, Spillman, Spillman, and Reinking (1981) tested biological gender and sex role orientation influence on leadership emergence and perceptions. Sex role orientation was measured using Bem's Sex Role Inventory with group members being classified into one of the following sex roles: (a) masculine, (b) feminine, or (c) androgynous. Individuals participating in a small group communication class were randomly assigned to groups at the beginning of the semester. At four different points throughout the semester, group members rated one another regarding their leadership perceptions. Spillman et al. (1981) found that initial group characteristics of gender did influence leadership perceptions. Women were perceived as being higher in leadership during the early part of the semester. Similarly, individuals who adopted masculine and androgynous sex roles were perceived as higher in task leadership in the beginning of the semester than were individuals who adopted a feminine sex role. However, over time the personality variables of biological and psychological gender could not account for leadership perceptions. Spillman et al. (1981) observed, "Group history and communication sequences became more important as group problem-solving continued, diminishing the effect of initial group member characteristics" (p. 149).

The diminishing association between leadership and gender as a function of time is also indicated in Eagly and Karau's (1991) meta-analytic study examining the relationship between gender and leadership emergence. They argued that gender has less effect on leadership emergence as groups meet for longer periods of time. They explain,

> The gender role perspective suggests that the tendency for men to lead should diminish to some extent over time because as interaction progresses group members obtain detailed information about attributes other than gender. Specifically members become more knowledgeable about each other's task-relevant competence—for example, about training or skills specifically relevant to the group's task. This knowledge should establish expectations about members' task contribution, and the importance of expectations based on gender should diminish. (p. 687)

Eagly and Karau (1991) discovered that meeting length weakened the tendency for males to emerge as leaders. Both the Spillman et al. (1981) and the Eagly and Karau (1991) studies point to the fact that gender becomes less important in maintaining leadership roles over time.

Interaction Behaviors

An alternate stream of leadership research has centered on the quantity and quality of communicative behaviors exhibited by leaders. Historically, several studies have documented that leadership emergence is tied to an individual's verbal (Lumsden, 1974; Riecken, 1975) and nonverbal (Baird, 1977) *rate of participation* in group discussion. A comprehensive study by Mullen, Salas, and Driskell (1989) examined the linkage between participation rate and leadership emergence. Using meta-analysis, they tested for the possibility of six alternative explanations for this relationship:

1. *Artifact influence:* The relationship between participation and emergence will be stronger in studies that utilize judgments from outside observers versus group members.
2. *Reward account:* Because groups reward individuals who facilitate goal achievement by nominating them as leaders, the relationship between participation and emergence will be strongest when the participator is high versus low in expertise.
3. *Leadership sign account:* If participation is taken as a sign of high expertise and the ability to perform task functions successfully, the relationship between participation and emergence will be strongest when the person's participation unambiguously denotes competence.
4. *Self-presentation account:* The participation rate and leadership emergence relationship is stronger when outside observers are present, because leaders try to "look good" in front of the observers.
5. *Motivation account:* The participation and leadership emergence is stronger in real ongoing versus zero-history groups, because the participants are more motivated and invested in the group's success.
6. *Salience account:* Because individuals who participate at high levels will become more salient in the group, the participation rate and leadership emergence relationship will be stronger as the size of the group decreases.

The results of Mullen et al.'s (1989) meta-analysis found overall that participation rate and leadership emergence were strongly related.

Moreover, the relationship between participation rate and leadership emergence (a) decreases as a function of participator expertise, (b) increases as the groups are likely to have more contact with constituencies outside the laboratory, and (c) increases as the salience increases. The results tend to diminish the importance of the reward, leadership sign, or self-presentation accounts.

Several studies have also examined how the *quality of leadership discourse* is related to leadership emergence and perceptions of leadership. Schultz (1974, 1978, 1980, 1986) was concerned with isolating the types of communicative functions that could predict leadership emergence. Using laboratory problem-solving groups, Schultz (1974, 1978) found that positive communication functions such as setting goals, giving directions, summarizing, and being self-assured were particularly important factors in predicting leadership emergence. To a lesser degree, the negative communication functions of quarrelsomeness and diminished sensibility embodied emergent leaders. These same variables were also found to predict leadership emergence in group meetings that occurred over time (Schultz, 1980, 1986).

Studies have also examined how other group members react to leaders. For example, Schultz (1982) argued that one of the key aspects of effective decision making is the ability to express opinions and disagreement to extend the discussion and explore a range of solutions. Yet individuals performing these behaviors may be perceived as quarrellsome, which would prompt other group members to perceive them negatively and would subsequently inhibit those individuals from emerging as leaders. Using the communicative functions she had identified in earlier studies, Schultz selected out potential leaders in a number of small groups and trained them in argumentation skills. In subsequent discussions, she discovered in groups that had only one potential leader that the leader was selected regardless of how argumentative they were perceived to be. In groups that had two or more potential leaders, the trained leaders received few leadership nominations. Argumentativeness was also curvilinearly related to perceptions of leadership, as low and extremely argumentative leaders were rated lower than leaders who were moderately argumentative. The same type of relationship also emerged for leader's influence on the group's decision-making process.

Ketrow (1991) contended that most group leadership theories classify leadership behaviors into two categories: (a) task oriented, and (b) socioemotional. She argued that a third class of leadership behavior, procedural behavior, must also be considered. This is consistent with previous research that has examined issues of procedural functions in group decision making at both the group (e.g., Gouran, 1986; Hirokawa, Ice, & Cook, 1988) and individual levels (e.g., Knutson & Holdridge, 1975). In her study, Schultz found that individuals who primarily performed procedural functions during discussion were overwhelmingly selected as leaders whereas individuals who performed task functions were typically perceived as the most influential member of the discussion. Individual group members' preferences for task, socioemotional, and procedural behaviors did not influence the findings. Ketrow (1991) concluded the results indicated that "(a) subjects distinguish sharply between leader[s] and [the] most influential [person]; (b) procedurally oriented behavior is equated with leadership behavior; and (c) task-oriented behavior generally is seen as most influential to the outcome of a decision for a small group discussion" (p. 508). Bacon and Severson (1986) discovered that the variables of assertiveness, responsiveness, and versatility successfully predicted procedural leaders and nonleaders. Procedural leaders tend to be more assertive, responsive, and versatile than nonleaders. The importance of being responsive and versatile was reflected in Witteman's (1991) study when he found that group members were more satisfied with leaders who employed more solution-oriented conflict management behavior. Conversely, leaders who employed nonconfrontation as a means of managing conflict were less satisfying to group members.

Some researchers have argued that leadership cannot be reduced to a small set of leadership functions that are frequently performed. Rather, leadership behavior is better characterized by its variety as leaders adapt their behavior when interacting with different people, at different times, in different situations. In a study examining the relational control of small groups, Ellis (1979) found that nonleaders tended to interact in similar ways with other group members. However, leaders tended to be highly idiosyncratic in the manner in which they interacted with other group members. Drecksel (1985) later confirmed this observation. She coded 18 group discussions over time using two coding schemes: (a) SIPA, and (b) RELCOM. In her analysis, she found that the interaction patterns of emergent leaders were distinctive whereas the interaction patterns of nonleaders were similar to the overall group interaction. Although leader-follower dyads tended to be characterized by a higher rate of participation than nonleader-nonleader dyads, the communicative functions performed by the dyads differed from the group interaction in unique ways and also differed from group to group.

Leadership Is a Situational Phenomenon

Current leadership literature as it relates to universal and situational positions is divided in focus. On one hand, much of the leadership emergence literature that stems from leaderless discussion groups uniformly documents that traits such as self-monitoring (Cronshaw & Ellis, 1991; Ellis & Cronshaw, 1992) and high rates of participation (Mullen et al., 1989) are associated with an individual emerging as a leader. Yet research in ongoing groups diminishes the importance of certain traits and behaviors in predicting who will emerge in and maintain leadership roles. Geier (1967) found that the traits that predicted leadership emergence at one stage of group development did not allow individuals to sustain their leadership position. Spillman et al. (1981) discovered that the importance of gender decreased during ongoing groups in predicting who would emerge as leaders. Similarly, Eagly and Karau (1991) found that increased meeting time decreased the importance of gender in predicting emergent leaders. Leadership behavior also changes across time and groups. Wood (1977) found that leaders adapted their discussion behavior at later meetings, provided they did not achieve their goals during earlier meetings. Drecksel (1985) found that the leaders of ongoing discussion groups adapted their behavior across meeting and individuals. Although the leadership emergence literature appears to be tied to articulating those sets of traits and behaviors that allow individuals to emerge as leaders regardless of situation, the literature examining ongoing groups appears to adopt a situational approach that recognizes the adaptable nature of leadership.

THE INTERNAL-EXTERNAL DIALECTIC

A common complaint leveled against most group communication research has been its heavy use of zero-history college groups (Bormann,

1970). Because many real-world groups meet over a period of time and consist of people other than college students, generalizing research findings from zero-history groups to other populations has been challenged. Certainly, when researchers desire to focus on one set of relationships without the interference of confounding variables, such a methodology is appropriate. Sorenson and Savage (1989) used zero-history groups because they wanted to strip away the historical context of the group. They argued that their chief concern was with the immediate influence of relational messages within a group, which necessitated that "we examine groups that have no prior leader-member relationships" (p. 327). The focus of the research is on the interaction within the group apart from its historical and hierarchical context.

Those researchers who acknowledge the importance of situational variables attempt to model them into the research design. The typical research protocol is as follows:

1. Identify the situational variable of interest.
2. Articulate a theoretical relationship between a communication trait or behavior and some outcome such as leadership emergence. Explain how the situational variable moderates the relationship between communication and the specified outcome.
3. Place individuals in a leaderless group discussion (LGD) that will meet only one time.
4. Prior to the discussion, manipulate the variable of interest.
5. Provide the LGD a task to solve.
6. Collect observations regarding the variable of interest through either administering a survey to group members or coding the group's dialogue.

Research by Garland and Beard (1979) and others utilizes such a research method. This approach emphasizes leadership's role in helping the group coordinate itself according to the demands of the situation. The emphasis is on how the situation causes group behavior and influences how group members manage their relationships with one another. Communicative behavior is treated as a response to manage the situation, and the emphasis is on how group members organize themselves to solve successfully the task or problem they have been given.

This research paradigm has focused on the kinds of behaviors leaders need to perform to manage the group. Not surprisingly, two general types of behavior have emerged that characterize leadership: (a) task behavior—messages aimed at coordinating the activities of the group; and (b) socioemotional behavior—messages aimed at maintaining the interpersonal and relational climate of the group. Behavioral functions that manage the relationship with the group's environment have not been examined. This is sensible if the purpose of the research is to examine a theoretical relationship between communication and a group outcome. The focus of the research must be on the internal workings of the group apart from the larger environment. Similarly, if the situation is viewed as an independent variable that causes group behavior, the focus is once again on the internal workings and activities of the group. This emphasis on the internal activities of the group apart from the larger environment is the chief reason for the prevalence of "two-factor" theories of leadership that characterize leadership according to task or relational behavior.

The assumption that leadership is primarily concerned with managing the internal workings of a group apart from its external environment and that the situation causes group behavior has been challenged on two fronts. First, real-world groups do not exist in a vacuum. Work groups are embedded within an organizational hierarchy and this hierarchical arrangement exists over time. Ancona (1987) contends that a chief problem confronting group leadership research is that much of it has been produced in laboratory settings. Such research precludes the possibility that a group's effectiveness "may be as much a function of how they deal with problems in their environment as of how well the group members deal with each other" (Ancona & Caldwell, 1988, p. 468). Leadership is more than simply managing the task and relational activities of group members; it also entails helping the group manage its relationship with the larger organizational environment. It serves an important boundary-spanning function in which it manages how much information from the external environment should be imported into the group discussion and how much information regarding the group's activities should be made available to external constituencies. As a result, leaders must monitor and take action both within and outside the group (Hackman & Walton, 1986).

Leaders may need to undertake action that creates a supportive organizational context for the group. Ancona and Caldwell (1988) identified five external functions leaders perform in groups that may help create an environment that groups can use to be productive.

1. *Scout Activities:* Activities aimed at collecting and bringing information into the group.
2. *Ambassador Activities:* Activities aimed at exporting information to the environment that helps keep outsiders informed of the group's activities and may be used to help build a positive image of the group to outside groups.
3. *Sentry Activities:* Activities that serve a gatekeeping function, that monitor the type and amount of information that external groups are able to send to the group. The aim is to avoid sending information to the group that disrupts or distracts the group from working on its task.
4. *Guard Activities:* Activities that monitor and censor information that the group gives in response to requests for information by outside individuals and groups.
5. *Immigrants, Captives, and Emigrants:* These represent differing types of boundary spanning roles performed by individuals, such as transferring information. Immigrants are individuals who join a group voluntarily, whereas captives are typically assigned to a group. Emigrants serve as representatives for the group to external audiences.

In a follow-up study, Ancona (1990) discovered that group leaders tended to use three basic strategies when managing their environment. *Informing* concentrated on the internal group process and the holding back of information to external audiences until the intentions of the group were clear. *Parading* balanced the focus on team building with an attention to letting outside groups know of the group's concern and commitment. *Probing* was mainly externally focused with a premium placed on collecting information from outsiders. Ancona (1990) argues that groups that depend on their external environment will be more effective when they use probing. Highly isolated groups that overemphasize the informing strategy will have a higher likelihood of failing. Her set of studies provide one set of data that highlights the necessity of dealing with the group's external environment.

A second line of attack on the position that the situation dictates group behavior has been that environments may not be imposed on groups; rather, groups may create their own environments. Recent literature in the strategic management literature has suggested that viewing the group's environment as objective may be inaccurate (Smircich & Stubbart, 1985). Stemming from Weick's (1979) theory of organizing, group members may enact or create their environment. Groups may use decision premises, analogies and metaphors, prototypes, and scripts to help them frame their environment (e.g., Duhaime & Schwenk, 1985; Gioia & Poole, 1984; Schwenk, 1988). The old adage, "Seeing is believing," is turned around to "Believing is seeing." This shift from viewing a group environment as an objective phenomenon to a phenomenon that is socially created by group members broadens leadership's function from managing task and relational problems within the group. Leadership plays an important role in helping the group create and sustain its environment.

An excellent example of how leadership helps group members renegotiate their view of their environment is provided by Howell and Frost's (1989) study on charismatic leadership. They examined the influence of charismatic leadership, a form of leadership that attempts to inspire followers to transcend their own political self-interest for higher-level goals on group conformity to norms. Charismatic leaders are able to articulate overarching goals and communicate high expectations through providing individual members with individualized consideration. In their study, Howell and Frost discovered that charismatic leaders were able to transcend situational constraints such as norms for low productivity. Through their charisma, they were able to lead individuals to higher levels of productivity and to facilitate their adjustment to the task. This study indicates that leaders may be able to articulate visions of what the group can do and achieve. Such visions create a context or definition of a situation that groups may adopt.

Managing the Dialectics: Leadership as Mediation

The preceding review of literature highlights the recognition by researchers that leadership is a more complex phenomenon than originally thought. Reducing leadership to a set of traits or behaviors that are consistently effective across situations provides a neat package to describe leadership but is impractical due to numerous differences in tasks, personalities, and organizational cultures. Although acknowledging that leadership is inherently situational is more intuitively sensible, it also is problematic because determining which situational factors should be included in a model of leadership is difficult. Similarly, leadership must be internally constrained and manage the interactions among group members but must also recognize that the internal workings of a group are in part dependent on people and forces external to the group. Leaders must engage in a delicate balancing act as they take into account the needs of the group members as well as the needs of constituencies external to the group. Currently, researchers have tended to opt for either one of the extremes of the two dialectics. What is needed is a metaphor for leadership that transcends these dichotomies and allows for an integrative approach that (a) facilitates our explaining the stable and universal aspects of group leadership as well as its situational characteristics, and (b) acknowledges the balancing act between internal and external constituencies. Viewing leadership as "medium" is one metaphor that provides a means for transcending these dialectics and was initially proposed by Karl Weick (1978) and later developed by Aubrey Fisher (1985, 1986).

Viewing leadership as a form of mediation provides a more parsimonious means of managing its attendant complexities. In one sense, Weick's (1978) use of the term *medium* is meant figuratively, as it conjures up images of mystics who attempt to help people communicate with loved ones who have died. Mediums and mystics use a variety of devices such as tea leaves and crystal balls to cross the boundary of the living and make contact with the souls of the dear departed. Upon contacting those dear departed ones, the medium must interpret for the client the messages that she or he has obtained from the person who has died. Mediums must interpret the meaning of the mysterious knock occurring during the seance or the chilly gust of wind that breezes through the room. Many times, in the process of interpreting the meaning of the message, mediums help the client plan what actions to take next. This may include determining what clients need to do with their lives, whether to contribute their money to charity, to get married, to get divorced, or to give their life savings to the mystic.

In a literal sense, leadership as medium means that the primary function of leadership is to help overcome the variety of task and relational problems encountered by the group. What is it that leadership mediates? Leadership mediates the information inputs collected by the group and the group outcomes. Leadership must help the group understand what these information inputs mean and facilitate the group toward taking action that helps the group achieve its goals. For groups to meet their goals, they must develop an organizing system or set of procedures that helps them interpret information inputs and plan and execute action based on those interpretations. Leadership is the process of helping groups create this organizing system and helping the group overcome barriers to achieving goals. Leadership entails devising a system of helping the group get its work done that is simultaneously stable and flexible and assists in managing the information shared among group members and between the group and its external audiences.

Leadership is a good medium when it is as complex as its information environment. According to Ashby's (1968) law of requisite variety, only variety can regulate variety. As the information environment becomes more complex, the number and variety of behaviors, processes, strategies, and tactics that can be used to make sense of the environment and to take action must also increase. According to Weick (1978), there are two processes associated with leadership: (a) object mediation, and (b) action mediation. The concept of *object mediation* is best embodied in the notion of a contour gauge. A contour gauge is similar to the wax or clay that allows a locksmith to take an impression of a key. The wax or clay is the medium through which impressions may be recorded. Just like a contour gauge allows you to take imprints of the environment, so does object mediation. Effective leadership must initially be externally constrained with an emphasis toward collecting imprints of the environment. Whether leadership is a good object mediator or gauge depends on two factors: (a) the number of elements that comprise the gauge, and (b) the independence of the elements. Object mediation is improved when a large number of independent elements versus small numbers of highly dependent elements make up the gauge. Using the previous example, wax is a better medium than a block of wood for taking impressions of a key because wax is malleable and can be molded in different ways because each section of the wax is independent. Wood, on the other hand, is solid and rigid and cannot easily record impressions. *Action mediation* references the behavioral actions and sequences leadership must perform to move the group toward goal achievement. Action mediation encompasses those processes that are aimed at helping the group make decisions and take actions that alleviate the demands placed on the group.

MEDIATION AND COMMUNICATION SKILLS

Barge and Hirokawa (1989) contend that the mediation process occurs through communication. It is through interaction that group members come to recognize problems facing the group and to take collective action that allows the group to meet the challenges posed by its environment. Group members who serve as mediums must not only "know" what problems the group is facing and "know" what kinds of processes must be undertaken to meet them; they must be able to express themselves in ways that other group members can understand and agree with. The key is to communicate in a way that other group members can understand. How, then, does one manage the tension between learning a set of communication strategies that are equally effective in all situations as opposed to adapting and tailoring one's communication to the situational demands? The answer lies in the concept of communication skill.

Communication skills have been defined in a number of ways ranging from the specific performance of a behavior (e.g., a person is skilled at seeking information if she or he can produce a question) to including those cognitive and behavioral processes associated with a person having the skill (Spitzberg & Cupach, 1989). For purposes of this chapter, *communication skill* refers to the general ability an individual has to perform a behavior successfully. This view of skill helps dissolve the dichotomy between the universal and situational approaches to leadership. Using skill as the primary mechanism for explaining leadership allows the researcher to identify a small set of core skills that allow leaders to be effective in a majority of situations. Although the necessary skills have been identified at a general abstract level, the specific communication choices associated with leadership have not been predetermined. To act in a skilled manner means leaders need to adapt their communication to the dictates of the situation. How the skill manifests itself in overt communication messages will vary according to the situation.

At this point, an example may be warranted. A common skill associated with leadership of decision-making groups is the thorough and thoughtful assessment of alternatives (Janis, 1989). Assume that a task force at a university has been given the challenge of redesigning the undergraduate core curriculum. Although the task force has been meeting for a long time and members know one another quite well, they may still be facing problems in evaluating alternative proposals to the existing core curriculum. If a leader is skillfully to lead a group in evaluating various proposals, the leader may perform a number of behaviors:

1. Proposing specific criteria to be applied to all proposals
2. Offering an opinion on a specific proposal
3. Combining two or more proposals into a new proposal
4. Offering a one-sided (pro or con) assessment of a proposal to generate discussion
5. Requesting feedback on a specific proposal

We have probably all seen individuals occupying leadership roles perform these differing kinds of behavior aimed at helping the group to evaluate thoroughly a set of alternatives. If we examine skill at the ability level, this allows researchers initially to examine the complexity of the various ways in which leadership manifests the skill known as evaluating solutions. Leaders use a variety of messages to achieve this goal, and they may change their messages as the discussion unfolds. However, the goal remains the same—fully evaluating the alternatives. The types of messages and their sequence may vary according to the nature of the situation. The skill level of the individual cannot be reduced to the specific type of message uttered or whether the specific pattern of messages followed a prescribed pattern. Rather, the skill level of the individual can be assessed according to the ability of leaders to adapt their messages and act in concert with other group members to achieve a particular goal.

COMMUNICATION SKILLS AND LEADERSHIP

Constructing a model of leadership based on the notion of communication skills involves two distinct activities. First, the specific types of communication skills associated with object and action mediation need to be identified. Second, the relationship between a group's decision-making environment and the needed communication skills to manage it must be articulated. The present model is based on an earlier model created by Barge and Hirokawa (1989) and is expanded to account for the embedded nature of groups.

Communication Skills

Viewing leadership as a form of mediation shifts from conceptualizing leadership skills solely in reference to task and people problems to couching skills in the language of information processing and the strategies associated with acquiring, retrieving, managing, and using information. Leaders attempt to establish a dialogue among group members and external stakeholders and constituencies that allow groups to acquire needed information regarding their environment and subsequently to act on that information by structuring a system of organizing to achieve their goals. From this perspective, two key questions emerge. What kinds of communication skills allow leaders and groups to connect with their environment and make sense of it? On arriving at an understanding of their environment, what kinds of communication skills facilitate leaders and groups being able to transform their interpretations into taking action to achieve their goals? These two questions parallel the concepts of object and action mediation.

Object Mediation. Object mediation regards collecting information about a group's environment and drawing accurate inferences from the collected information. Leaders initially need to engage with the group's environment to familiarize themselves with the constraints and opportunities afforded them by the environment. This means they must devote time to collecting information regarding the environment from other group members as well as seeking information and cultivating contacts from outside the group. What effective leadership attempts to do is to build a rich description of the various images of the group's environment created by multiple parties, internal and external to the group, and to connect the various facts and perceptions together to provide a coherent image and understanding of the environment.

Becoming successful at object mediation necessitates leaders becoming skilled at cultivating and accessing information sources within and outside the group, being able to tease out the nuances and uniqueness of the group's situation, and being able to construct a coherent story regarding the environment. The former set of abilities references the skill of networking whereas the latter references the skill of data-splitting. *Networking* enables effective leaders to collect needed information to make quality decisions and enhances their ability to distinguish between genuine and "pseudo" problems. Networking allows leaders to scout out pockets of resistance by identifying potential external opponents and adversaries to the group's decisions (Ancona & Caldwell, 1988) as well as collecting information regarding individual members' viewpoints and potential coalitions emerging within the group. How leaders go about networking varies as some may resort to simple information-seeking strategies such as direct requests or surveying the scene (Miller & Jablin, 1991), whereas others may establish mentoring relationships with key external constituencies or may try to enhance their power so others will come to them for information (Pfeffer, 1990). Regardless of the specific manifestation of the skill of networking, the ability to collect and gather information regarding the environment is crucial to successful leadership.

Leaders must be careful to avoid confusing the information collected regarding the environment with the medium used to collect the information. Leaders do not enter a situation tabula rasa but typically carry with them predispositions and preexisting hypotheses that influence who they decide to network with and the kind of information they may collect. If leaders are not careful, they can create a self-fulfilling prophecy in which they discover a group's environment is exactly as they initially imagined it. For example, leaders may have a preexisting theory that the group's environment is highly political and turbulent. Such a hypothesis may predispose both a leader and a group to seek out information that already confirms this preexisting hypothesis and to ignore information that counters this hypothesis and suggests that a different kind of environment exists. As a result, when leaders collect information, they must be careful that they do not hastily impose their own preexisting ideas regarding the situation and gloss over the unique qualities of the present situation.

Weick (1978) contends that the skill of *data-splitting* allows leaders and groups to avoid such a glossing process and more closely attend to the uniqueness of the present situation. Leaders should pay close attention to the kinds of assumptions they make regarding situations and continually challenge their existing hypotheses and create new ones that counter old hypotheses. Injecting self-doubt, cynicism, and second-guessing may allow leaders to help themselves and their groups formulate an image of the environment that takes into account its unique qualities (Hogarth & Makridakis, 1981). A key to effective data-splitting is the challenging and testing of the assumptions regarding how the information collected fits together. Believing what you know to be false and rejecting what you know to be true is a philosophy that leaders can use to avoid creating a poor description of the environment. Although a number of strategies reflect the skill of data-splitting, such as counter-attitudinal role playing, assigning someone a Devil's Advocate role during discussion, and actively debating the underlying assumptions of the information (Makridakis, 1990), leaders need to develop a broad repertoire of data-splitting strategies that allows them to unpack and make sense of information to create a rich and coherent picture of the group's environment.

Action Mediation. Action mediation is at the heart of leadership because it involves selecting from among competing courses of action and helping the group create a system of organizing that allows it to make quality decisions (Weick, 1978). The ability of leaders to be effective action mediators turns on two key skills. First, leaders must be able to facilitate group members in decision making, or in selecting from among competing alternatives, that will move them in the direction of meeting the group's goals and tasks. This necessitates leaders being skilled in various communication activities that allow the group to arrive at quality decisions. Second, leaders need to be skilled at managing personal relationships among group members. As leaders and group members analyze information and select from among alternative solutions, disputes will arise over issues such as the relevance of certain pieces of information, the validity of particular viewpoints, the viability of solutions, and the personality characteristics of members. Disputes over substantive issues as well as the personalities of group members may emerge that necessitate group leaders to be able to manage the relationships among group members. This is the domain of relational management.

The base work of decision-making groups is to select from among alternatives the one that meets the requirements of the group's task. This means that leaders need to be skilled at facilitating *decision making*.

Although a number of typologies of decision-making functions have been derived (e.g., Hirokawa, 1988; Poole & Roth, 1989), several common functions associated with decision making can be identified. This set of common decision-making functions suggests that leaders need to possess the following skills:

Problem Analysis: Delineation of the nature of the problem, the causes of the problem, and its consequences.

Solution Generation: Producing possible alternatives to solve a problem. May utilize such idea generation tools as brainstorming, nominal group technique, or synectics to produce a variety of alternatives from which the group may select (Poole, 1991).

Solution Evaluation: Analyzes the positive and negative consequences of adopting a particular solution. Good solution evaluation also includes second-guessing previous decisions to reexamine old information.

Solution Implementation: Plans and procedures must be established to implement the selected solution. Contingencies that may influence the success of an implemented plan must be considered and planned.

Procedural Competencies: Groups that establish and follow procedures tend to make better decisions. Part of the skill of decision making is establishing a set of procedures that can be followed by group members.

The primary work of decision-making groups is making decisions. This means that group leaders need to be able to produce messages that facilitate the decision-making process. Whether these skills are directed at the members of the group or are directed toward external constituencies, the importance of making decisions to facilitate accomplishing goals cannot be denied.

The skill of *relational management* refers to the ability of leaders to coordinate and construct interpersonal relationships that allow an appropriate balance of cohesion, unity, and task motivation within a group. Groups need to construct a sense of cohesion within the group that brings group members together and allows them to perform their task. Groups that are more cohesive tend to be higher-level performers and to increase group member motivation to complete the task. It is important not to confuse highly cohesive groups with groups that do not permit voicing differing viewpoints and ideas, as in the case of groupthink (Janis & Mann, 1977). Group leaders must provide a space for dissenting views to be voiced within a group and create an understanding that dissenting views should be appreciated and valued. Conflicts within groups are inevitable, and the central task for leaders is to construct jointly with group members a climate that allows conflicts to surface and be dealt with in a constructive fashion. This requires leaders not only to be able to resolve conflicts among group members, but also to provide criticism and feedback to group members that encourages them to continue participating in the group. Though feedback plays a valuable role in correcting errant ideas and helping individuals adjust to one another, it must be done in a manner that confirms the group members' sense of competence and invites future participation. Otherwise, group members may become discouraged if they feel that their contributions are not valued, and subsequently lose motivation to perform the task. The importance of leaders being able to create a space whereby other group members can feel ownership of their ideas and feel they are making a valued contribution to the group is acknowledged in several contemporary leadership approaches that recognize the primary defining characteristic of leaders, as opposed to nonleaders, is their ability to inspire and motivate followers (Bass, 1985; Conger, 1989; Nanus, 1992).

Although several skills may assist leaders in managing interpersonal relationships within groups, two skills are of particular importance in managing cohesion and motivation within groups. First, leaders need to be skilled at *conflict resolution* if they are to resolve potential obstacles arising from disagreements over substantive issues and personal conflicts emerging among group members. A number of potential communicative strategies exist that may assist in reducing conflict. For example, leaders may use conflict management styles to resolve conflict. Conflict management styles are stylized patterns of behavior that allow leaders to manage conflict by promoting win-lose conflict situations through dominating other people or obliging others' wishes at the expense of their own; or through creating lose-lose situations by avoiding the conflict altogether or compromising—both parties give up something of value; or by creating win-win situations where the wishes of both parties are integrated (Nicotera, 1994). The selection and use of the particular style would depend on the kind of situation the leader is facing. An alternative way of managing conflict is through negotiation (Sayles, 1993). Particularly when leaders are engaged with individuals and groups external to their group, they may need to broker a deal that allows for the continued existence of the group. Leaders may need to learn both win-win approaches such as integrative bargaining and win-lose approaches such as distributive bargaining if they are to be successful negotiators. Maintaining variety in one's personal repertoire is critical, because the kinds of negotiating strategies selected depend on the situation and the goals the leader is trying to achieve (Wilson & Putnam, 1990).

Second, the ability to *motivate* group members to perform a task is key to managing relational issues effectively. As part of the organizing process, groups will at times need to adopt role structures that they are uncomfortable with and that they perceive as not meeting their personal needs. This role strain may cause them to be less motivated to participate in the group and to engage with the task. Motivation problems are not tied solely to issues of being forced to perform a role with which one is not comfortable. Motivation to perform the task may also decline when the task of the group is unclear, group members fail to see the importance of the task, or the group is not making timely progress to complete the task. Contemporary theorists contend that there are a number of communication strategies that can be used to motivate group members. For example, feedback has been linked to motivation to perform a task (Haslett & Ogilvie, 1992) and learning (Cusella, 1987). A key portion of managing conflict and making decisions is being able to give criticism and feedback to individuals regarding their ideas, actions, and the possible consequences of their actions. Feedback serves as a corrective mechanism that can allow individuals to know when their ideas or assumptions are incorrect and that highlights when their behavior is counterproductive. Visioning has been another strategy suggested for improving group member motivation and loyalty (Nanus, 1992). Visioning involves communicating images of the task that stimulate individuals to diminish their personal goals in lieu of pursing group-level objectives. Leaders may use a variety of communicative strategies, such as metaphors, stories, and personification, to demonstrate the worth of the goal and task the group has set before it (Conger, 1989). Although a number of strategies may be used to motivate group members, the underlying assumption of motivation is that group members need to recognize the importance and value of their task and be willing to put forth the effort to ensure that it is completed at a high level of quality.

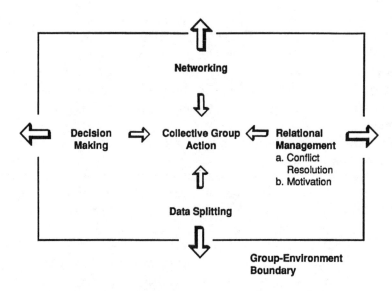

Figure 11.1. Communication skills and group leadership.

In Figure 11.1, a model of leadership communication skills is presented. The vertical axis highlights the importance of object mediation to leadership. Networking and data-splitting are central to groups making sense of their environment as well as helping key stakeholders and constituencies in the environment make sense of the group's actions. The horizontal axis references the skills of decision making and relational management that are associated with action mediation. Although the specific skills associated with each axis reflect their primary function, it is important to note that skills associated with object and action mediation skills are interconnected. For example, networking may be instrumental to decision making, and managing conflict may be key to networking successfully. Effective mediation is contingent on object and action mediation complementing and augmenting one another. The arrows linking the group to the larger environment illustrate that leadership must help manage the boundary between the group and its larger environment. The intersection of these skills with collective group action recognizes that leadership also manages the internal workings of the group and that the collective group interaction influences how leadership may manage the group's boundary.

COMMUNICATION SKILLS AND THE GROUP ENVIRONMENT

A group's environment provides both constraints against and opportunities for decision making. According to Janis (1989), groups must fulfill certain decision-making prerequisites, such as analyzing the problem and carefully evaluating the advantages and disadvantages of potential solutions, if they are to arrive at quality decisions. A variety of obstacles such as time constraints or the need for group members to maintain cohesiveness at all costs may negatively influence the group's ability to satisfy these decision-making prerequisites. Though a number of situational factors may influence the group's decision-making process, Barge and Hirokawa (1989) identify three general situational factors that influence the kinds of communication skills and messages that must be emphasized if groups are to reach high-quality decisions. If the nature of the group's relationship with the environment is believed to influence leadership and decision making, then a fourth factor, the group's level of coupling with the environment, must also be taken into account.

Task Complexity. Task complexity may influence the kinds of leadership skills required to manage the group's situation. Simple tasks are typically viewed as requiring little effort; not requiring the cooperation of group members; and having a small, finite set of possible alternative solutions from which to select. On the other hand, complex tasks typically require greater amounts of effort, require the joint collaboration of all group members, and possess multiple solutions. Many group researchers have contended that the nature of the task influences the kinds of communication choices and patterns that must be made during discussion (Hirokawa, 1988, 1990). For example, as decision-making tasks become more complex, communication activity must also become more complex as large amounts of information need to be consolidated, in-depth problem analysis needs to be conducted, and a solution must be decided on from a wide variety of alternatives. Similarly, Barge, Schlueter, and Duncan (1990) found that when the task was extremely structured (e.g., simple), the encoding and decoding skills of the leader made little difference on performance-based outcomes. This finding was consistent with a *substitutes for leadership perspective* that argues that leadership behavior's influence on performance outcomes may be neutralized by a number of task, subordinate, and organizational characteristics (Howell, Bowen, Dorfman, Kerr, & Podsakoff, 1990; Howell & Dorfman, 1986; Kerr, 1977). Moreover, when the task is more complex (e.g., policy driven), some evidence shows that the contributions of the entire group as opposed to a single leader make a difference on decision quality (Barge, 1989). When decision-making tasks become more complex, therefore, leadership skills must also become more complex as it becomes critical for leadership to manage and coordinate successfully the collective activity of the group. This line of reasoning leads to the following proposition linking task complexity to communication skills.

> Proposition 1: Complex group tasks require a greater depth and breadth of networking, data-splitting, decision-making, conflict resolution, and motivation skills.

Role Relationships. The nature of role relationships within the group may affect the necessary leadership communication skills. Groups may range from having highly defined and structured group roles to loosely defined and unstructured roles. Group roles are typically negotiated during the beginnings of a group but may also be renegotiated due to significant changes in group composition, the nature of the task, or development shifts (Worchel, Coutant-Sassic, & Grossman, 1992). When groups have a looser and more ambiguously defined role structure, the breadth and range of communication skills needed to manage the situation are increased. For example, Bottger and Yetton (1988) found that when a group has less consensus on selecting solutions, the need for conflict management skills is increased. Similarly, as group members lack consensus on the group structure, leadership will have to be aimed at establishing a space where group members can create roles that aid the group's development. Given that a role system must be established, leadership must aid in consolidating the various views on group member's positions within the group and in reconciling disparate views of the group's organization, and facilitate the group toward establishing a role structure that allows it to perform its task.

Furthermore, leadership must also be sensitive to the pressures contained in the environment to forge a role structure. As Ancona (1990) observes, individuals performing leadership roles may need to shield the group from external pressures and at the same time need to keep constituents in the environment informed of the group's activities. This means that leadership must monitor the environment to find out what expectations are held in reference to group structure.

> Proposition 2: Groups with ambiguously defined roles will require more networking, data-splitting, decision-making, conflict resolution, and motivation skills.

Group Climate. Group climate can affect the kinds of leadership skills required to manage the situation. Group climate reflects the affective reaction of group members toward one another and may range from positive to negative. Janis (1989) observes that a group's climate influences decision making. When groups are dominated by individuals set on pursuing their own individual goals (e.g., a competitive climate) or intent on maintaining the positive group feelings so as to diminish critical evaluation of the decision, then group climate negatively influences decision making. The task of effective leadership is to create a climate in which individuals have positive affect for one another, yet are not wed to maintaining the positive affect at the expense of rigorously debating and challenging ideas. To transform a negative climate to one in which positive affect and substantive debate over ideas can occur is a difficult task. It requires leaders to be skilled at acquiring the various group member's perceptions and feelings regarding the situation and to find a way to mesh the competing views together.

> Proposition 3: Negative group climates will be marked by the increased use of networking, data-splitting, decision-making, conflict resolution, and motivation skills.

Environmental Coupling. A fourth situational factor is the type of relationship between the group and its environment, or *coupling*. Groups do not exist apart from their environment. Group leadership needs to interpret the actions of the group to the larger environment and also interpret the desires and expectations of stakeholders and constituencies within the environment to the group (Ancona, 1990; Ancona & Caldwell, 1988). Organizations may pressure decision-making groups to arrive quickly at decisions that meet particular criteria. Therefore, it is necessary to consider how the additional factor of coupling—the type of relationship the group has with its larger environment—influences the kinds of leadership skills needed to manage the situation. Groups may be loosely coupled with the larger environment, meaning they are less dependent on the environment and are more autonomous (Weick, 1979). On the other hand, groups may be tightly coupled to the environment. This heightened state of inter-dependency causes changes in group behavior to be paralleled by changes in the environment. Action-reaction becomes common when groups and environments are tightly coupled.

Leadership faces a delicate balancing act of having to manage the boundary between a group and the larger environment. Leadership is more than simply coordinating the activities of the group members with each other; it also involves coordinating the group's activity in the larger scheme of the environment. This entails leadership managing the image of the group in the larger environment by appropriately transmitting information regarding group activities as well as by relaying the expec-tations of constituencies in the environment to the group and shielding the group from external pressure (Ancona, 1987). The degree to which leadership performs a boundary-spanning function and requires high levels of skill at object mediation depends on the level of coupling the group has with the environment. Moreover, when the needs of the group come into conflict with the demands created by the environment, group leadership will need to be highly skilled at managing disputes between the stakeholders in the environment and the group.

> Proposition 4: When groups are tightly coupled with the organiza-tion, leaders will need to be more highly skilled at networking, data-splitting, and conflict resolution skills with external stakeholders and constituencies.

The degree of coupling may also influence the relationship among leadership skills, individual outcomes, and group outcomes. At an individual level, persons performing leadership roles are constantly evaluated, whether by fellow group members or by individuals exter-nal to the group. Because the standards evaluators use to judge the effectiveness of a leader vary according to their position with the leader, the degree to which the group is coupled to the environment will influence which factors become more salient in assessing effectiveness. Group members who perceive individuals as performing behaviors that are viewed as prototypical of leadership will tend to classify those individuals as leaders (Phillips & Lord, 1986). Followers may also judge a leader positively if a leader's behavior fits their image of effectiveness and may even be willing to forgive, ignore, or excuse unusual leader behavior if the leader has been successful in the past (Conger, 1989; Hollander, 1960, 1978). It therefore makes sense to argue that leaders will be perceived as effective by group members when they are skilled at managing disputes, motivating group members, and making decisions during discussion. The overt behavior that leaders exhibit during group discussion becomes the primary basis for formulating judgments of effectiveness.

> Proposition 5: Group members will base their perceptions of leadership effectiveness on their leader's data-splitting, decision-making, conflict resolution, and motivation skills performed during discussion.

During discussion, the goals and objectives of group members may become the dominant criteria by which they assess the effectiveness of a leader. As Barge and Hirokawa (1989) point out, group goals may influence perceptions of leadership effectiveness. Typically, group goals have been distinguished according to task and relational foci. Task goals emphasize a need to get the job done or to make a decision. The ability to collect information, appropriately analyze information, and draw valid inferences from it, as well as to select among competing alternatives, is at the heart of making decisions. Relational goals emphasize maintaining the group climate and may vary in their intensity according to the particular group. For example, Janis (1989) observes that some groups suffer from a preoccupation with maintaining cohesion within the group, which causes group members to refrain from voicing negative criticism or second-guessing others' ideas in an effort to maintain the high level of cohesion among group members. This preoccupation with maintaining cohesion also sets a standard by which to judge effective and ineffective leader behavior. In this instance, effective communication is marked by messages that reinforce, as opposed to challenge, the feeling of cohesion. When relational goals are dominant within a group, a premium is placed on maintaining a harmonious climate and maintaining a positive feeling toward the task. Group goals influence perception of leadership effectiveness in two ways.

Proposition 6: When task goals are more salient, leadership effectiveness will be more strongly predicted by networking, data-splitting, and decision-making skills.

Proposition 7: When relational goals are more salient, leadership effectiveness will be more strongly predicted by conflict resolution and motivation skills.

It is possible for leaders to perform skillfully during discussion in the eyes of other group members, and yet those actions may not lead to wider acceptance of the group's decisions and activities by the larger environment. Certainly, leaders can resolve conflict and facilitate making decisions within groups apart from any affordances and constraints present in the environment. Yet for leaders to have success in tightly coupled environments means they must have successfully engaged with the environment to form and construct an interpretation of the environment that allows the group to take actions that fit within the environment. Sayles (1993) argues that leaders need to be skilled at managing interdependencies. Particularly as groups become more tightly coupled with their environments, the need to manage the interdependency between the group and the environment becomes more critical. Therefore, skills such as networking, data-splitting, and conflict resolution become critical in managing the group's boundary so the leader can help the group collect needed information to make decisions and also to promote the group's interest. This means that leaders' ability to construct such interpretations through networking, data-splitting, and dispute resolution skills will indirectly affect their ability to perform effectively during discussion. Leaders who are more "in touch" with their environment will be more likely to facilitate the group in directions that will allow the group to align its actions with the larger environment. This means that a leader's skill at managing external audiences and constituencies will directly influence how external audiences assess leadership effectiveness and have an indirect effect on how internal group members perceive leadership effectiveness.

Proposition 8A: When the group is tightly coupled with the environment, a leader's skill at networking, data-splitting, and conflict resolution with external audiences will be strong predictors of leadership effectiveness by external audiences.

Proposition 8B: When the group is tightly coupled with the environment, a leader's skill at networking, data-splitting, and conflict resolution with external audiences will moderate perceptions of leadership effectiveness by internal group members.

The degree of coupling between a group and its environment not only affects the outcome of leadership effectiveness, it also influences group-level outcomes such as decision acceptance and quality, as well as relational outcomes. Groups make decisions and they will ultimately be evaluated on the outcomes of their decisions by both group members and external constituencies. Although criteria for evaluating decisions have ranged from assessing the decision outcome, to the processes and procedures associated with reaching the decision, it may be more profitable to link group process to outcomes and to argue that, in most instances, a careful assessment of consequences associated with decisions and proper evaluation of the problem and potential solutions will be associated with high-quality decisions (Gouran, 1990; Janis, 1989). From this viewpoint, it becomes critical that groups engage in processes that facilitate effective decision making. When groups are highly interdependent with the environment, this necessitates leadership aiding the collection of environmental information to form the basis for a good decision. As part of this process, leadership may become aware of potential obstacles that the group needs to be aware of when making its decision. By becoming aware of the obstacles to decision making, not only does acceptance of the decision by the larger environment become more likely, a higher quality decision is more likely to occur because the constraints are recognized and can be managed.

Relational outcomes such as cohesion are also likely to be influenced by how tightly coupled the group is with the environment. Groups are more likely to become cohesive and satisfied when they are productive and successful (Greene, 1989). When a group is tightly coupled with the environment, its success depends heavily on the group being able to acquire needed information from the environment and subsequently to take actions that fit with the environment. On the other hand, when groups are loosely coupled with the environment and are less dependent on environmental stakeholders for acceptance or resources, how a leader manages the internal workings of the group becomes important. Success becomes predicated on the leadership's management of the group's internal dynamics. This line of reasoning linking coupling to group-level outcomes leads to the following two propositions.

Proposition 9: When groups are tightly coupled with the environment, acceptance of the decision, the decision quality, and group cohesion are predicted by the skills of networking, data-splitting, and conflict resolution with external stakeholders and constituencies.

Proposition 10: When groups are loosely coupled with the environment, the skills of data-splitting, decision making, conflict resolution, and motivation with group members will strongly predict acceptance of the decision, decision quality, and group cohesion.

Conclusion

Viewing leadership as a form of mediation moves leadership researchers away from conceiving of leadership in hierarchical terms toward viewing leadership in more systemic and horizontal terms. When we view leadership in systemic terms, two important changes occur in our worldview. First, we begin to recognize that leadership involves dealing with complexity. Rather than viewing complexity as a problem to be managed or another situational variable to be incorporated into our leadership models, viewing leadership as mediation places complexity at the heart of leadership. When leadership is placed in hierarchical terms where leaders are viewed primarily in terms of controlling and directing followers, complexity is typically viewed as a problem that must be resolved. On the other hand, the mediation view of leadership recognizes that leaders must be complex information processors if leadership is to aid a group in managing challenges within its environment. Viewing leadership as a form of mediation not only recognizes the inherent complexity of the group and its environmental system, it also embraces the idea that leadership communication must also be as complex as the environment if it is to be effective.

Second, viewing leadership as medium recognizes that groups do not exist in a vacuum and that they must be successful at managing the boundary between the group and its environment. Group leadership cannot simply be reduced to helping group members make good decisions and managing conflicts. The ability to make good decisions, in many instances, is directly dependent on the ability of the group to acquire information from constituencies external to the group. Viewing leadership as mediation necessitates working through problems arising from the group's boundary with the environment. Leadership must help groups manage challenges and difficulties arising from the interconnections of the group with other groups and the overlapping formal and informal memberships of individuals with other groups (Putnam & Stohl, 1990).

Leadership is an inherently complex process and one that remains ambiguous and misunderstood (Bennis & Nanus, 1985). By developing concepts that allow us to examine the complexity of leadership, we can perhaps gain a better understanding of how leaders assist groups in making good decisions.

References

Alderton, S. M., & Jurma, W. E. (1980). Genderless, gender related task leader communication and group satisfaction: A test of two hypotheses. *Southern Speech Communication Journal, 46,* 48-60.

Ancona, D. G. (1987). Groups in organizations: Extending laboratory models. In C. Hendrick (Ed.), *Annual review of personality and social psychology: Group and intergroup processes* (pp. 207-231). Newbury Park, CA: Sage.

Ancona, D. G. (1990). Outward bound: Strategies for team survival in an organization. *Academy of Management Journal, 33,* 334-365.

Ancona, D. G., & Caldwell, D. F. (1988). Beyond task and maintenance: Defining external functions in groups. *Group and Organizational Studies, 13,* 468-494.

Andrews, P. H. (1992). Sex and gender differences in group communication: Impact on the facilitation process. *Small Group Research, 23*(1), 74-94.

Ashby, W. R. (1968). Variety, constraint, and the law of requisite variety. In W. Buckley (Ed.), *Modern systems research for the behavioral scientist* (pp. 129-136). Durham, NC: Duke University Press.

Bacon, C. C., & Severson, M. L. (1986). Assertiveness, responsiveness, and versatility as predictors of leadership emergence. *Communication Research Reports, 3,* 53-59.

Baird, J. E. (1977). Some nonverbal elements of leadership emergence. *Southern Speech Communication Journal, 42,* 352-361.

Barge, J. K. (1989). Leadership as medium: A leaderless group discussion model. *Communication Quarterly, 37*(4), 237-247.

Barge, J. K., & Hirokawa, R. Y. (1989). Toward a communication competency model of group leadership. *Small Group Behavior, 20*(2), 167-189.

Barge, J. K., Schlueter, D. W., & Duncan, G. (1990). Task structure as a moderator of task and relational skills. *Communication Studies, 41*(1), 1-18.

Bass, B. M. (1985). *Leadership and performance beyond expectations.* New York: Free Press.

Bennis, W. G., & Nanus, B. (1985). *Leaders: The strategies of taking charge.* San Francisco: HarperCollins.

Bormann, E. G. (1970). The paradox and promise of small group research. *Communication Monographs, 37,* 211-217.

Bottger, P. C., & Yetton, P. W. (1988). An integration of process and decision scheme explanations of a group problem-solving performance. *Organizational Behavior and Human Decision Processes, 42*(2), 233-249.

Bradley, P. H. (1980). Sex, competence, and opinion deviation: An expectation states approach. *Communication Monographs, 47,* 101-110.

Bunyi, J. M., & Andrews, P. H. (1985). Gender and leadership emergence: An experimental study. *Southern Speech Communication Journal, 50,* 246-260.

Conger, J. A. (1989). *The charismatic leader: Behind the mystique of exceptional leadership.* San Francisco: Jossey-Bass.

Conger, J. A. (1992). *Learning to lead.* San Francisco: Jossey-Bass.

Cronshaw, S. F., & Ellis, R. J. (1991). A process investigation of self-monitoring and leader emergence. *Small Group Research, 22,* 403-420.

Cusella, L. P. (1987). Feedback, motivation, and performance. In F. M. Jablin, L. L. Putnam, K. H. Roberts, & L. W. Porter (Eds.), *Handbook of organizational communication* (pp. 624-678). Newbury Park, CA: Sage.

Cushman, D. P., & King, S. S. (1993). High-speed management: A revolution in organizational communication in the 1990s. In S. A. Deetz (Ed.), *Communication yearbook 16* (pp. 209-236). Newbury Park, CA: Sage.

Dobbins, G. H., Long, W. S., Dedrick, E. J., & Clemons, T. C. (1990). The role of self-monitoring and gender on leader emergence: A laboratory and field study. *Journal of Management, 16*(3), 609-618.

Drecksel, G. L. (1985, May). *Interaction characteristics of emergent leaders.* Paper presented at the annual meeting of the International Communication Association, Honolulu.

Duhaime, I. M., & Schwenk, C. R. (1985). Conjectures on cognitive simplification in acquisition and divestment decision making. *Academy of Management Review, 10*(2), 287-295.

Eagly, A. H. (1987). *Sex differences in social behavior: A social-role interpretation.* Hillsdale, NJ: Lawrence Erlbaum.

Eagly, A. H., & Johnson, B. T. (1990). Gender and leadership style: A meta-analysis. *Psychological Bulletin, 108*(2), 233-256.

Eagly, A. H., & Karau, S. J. (1991). Gender and the emergence of leaders: A meta-analysis. *Journal of Personality and Social Psychology, 60*(5), 685-710.

Eagly, A. H., Makhijani, M. G., & Klonsky, B. G. (1992). Gender and the evaluation of leaders: A meta-analysis. *Psychological Bulletin, 111*(1), 3-22.

Ellis, D. G. (1979). Relational control in two group systems. *Communication Monographs, 46,* 153-166.

Ellis, R. J. (1988). Self-monitoring and leadership emergence in groups. *Personality and Social Psychology Bulletin, 14*(4), 681-693.

Ellis, R. J., Adamson, R. S., Deszca, G., & Cawsey, T. F. (1988). Self-monitoring and leadership emergence. *Small Group Behavior, 19*(3), 312-324.

Ellis, R. J., & Cronshaw, S. F. (1992). Self-monitoring and leader emergence: A test of moderator effects. *Small Group Research, 23,* 113-129.

Fiedler, F. E. (1967). *A theory of leadership effectiveness.* New York: McGraw-Hill.

Fiedler, F. E. (1993). The leadership situation and the black box in contingency theories. In M. M. Chemers & R. Ayman (Eds.), *Leadership theory and research: Perspectives and directions* (pp. 1-28). San Diego, CA: Academic Press.

Fisher, B. A. (1985). Leadership as medium: Treating complexity in group communication research. *Small Group Behavior, 16,* 167-196.

Fisher, B. A. (1986). Leadership: When does the difference make a difference? In R. Y. Hirokawa & M. S. Poole (Eds.), *Communication and group decision-making* (1st ed., pp. 197-218). Beverly Hills, CA: Sage.

Garland, H., & Beard, J. F. (1979). Relationship between self-monitoring and leader emergence across two task situations. *Journal of Applied Psychology, 64,* 72-76.

Geier, J. G. (1967). A trait approach to the study of leadership in small groups. *Journal of Communication, 17,* 316-323.

Gioia, D. A., & Poole, P. P. (1984). Scripts in organizational behavior. *Academy of Management Review, 9*(3), 449-459.

Gouran, D. S. (1986). Inferential errors, interaction, and group decision-making. In R. Y. Hirokawa & M. S. Poole (Eds.), *Communication and group decision-making* (1st ed., pp. 93-112). Beverly Hills, CA: Sage.

Gouran, D. S. (1990). Evaluating group outcomes. In G. R. Phillips & B. Dervin (Eds.), *Teaching how to work in groups* (pp. 125-196). Norwood, NJ: Ablex.

Graen, G. B., & Scandura, T. A. (1987). Toward a psychology of dyadic organizing. In L. L. Cummings & B. M. Staw (Eds.), *Research in organizational behavior* (Vol. 9, pp. 175-208). Greenwich, CT: JAI.

Greene, C. M. (1989). Cohesion and productivity in work groups. *Small Group Behavior, 20,* 70-86.

Hackman, J. R., & Walton, R. E. (1986). Leading groups in organizations. In P. Goodman (Ed.), *Designing effective work groups* (pp. 72-119). San Francisco: Jossey-Bass.

Hammer, M., & Champy, J. (1993). *Reengineering the corporation.* New York: Harper-Business.

Haslett, B., & Ogilvie, J. R. (1992). Feedback processes in task groups. In R. S. Cathcart & L. A. Samovar (Eds.), *Small group communication: A reader* (pp. 342-356). Dubuque, IA: William C. Brown.

Hawkins, K. W. (1992, November). *Effects of gender and communication content on leadership emergence in small task-oriented groups.* Paper presented at the annual meeting of the Speech Communication Association, Chicago.

Hirokawa, R. Y. (1988, April). *The role of communication in group decision-making efficacy: A task-contingency perspective.* Paper presented at the annual meeting of the Central States Speech Association, Schaumburg, IL.

Hirokawa, R. Y. (1990). The role of communication in group decision-making efficacy: A task-contingency perspective. *Small Group Research, 21,* 190-204.

Hirokawa, R. Y., Ice, R., & Cook, J. (1988). Preference for procedural order, discussion structure, and group decision performance. *Communication Quarterly, 3,* 217-226.

Hogarth, R. M., & Makridakis, S. (1981). Forecasting and planning: An evaluation. *Management Science, 27*(2), 115-138.

Hollander, E. (1978). *Leadership dynamics: A practical guide to effective relationships.* New York: Free Press.

Hollander, E. P. (1960). Competence and conformity in the acceptance of influence. *Journal of Abnormal and Social Psychology, 61,* 365-369.

Hosking, D. M. (1988). Organizing, leadership, and skilful process. *Journal of Management Studies, 25*(2), 147-166.

House, R. J. (1974). Path-goal theory of leader effectiveness. *Journal of Contemporary Business, 3,* 81-97.

Howell, J. M., & Frost, P. J. (1989). A laboratory study of charismatic leadership. *Organizational Behavior and Human Decision Processes, 43*(2), 243-269.

Howell, J. P., Bowen, D. E., Dorfman, P. W., Kerr, S., & Podsakoff, P. M. (1990). Substitutes for leadership: Effective alternatives to ineffective leadership. *Organizational Dynamics, 19*(1), 20-38.

Howell, J. P., & Dorfman, P. W. (1986). Leadership and substitutes for leadership among professional and nonprofessional workers. *Journal of Applied Behavioral Science, 22,* 29-46.

Instone, D., Major, B., & Bunker, B. (1983). Gender, self confidence, and social strategies: An organizational simulation. *Journal of Personality and Social Psychology, 44,* 322-333.

Janis, I. L. (1989). *Crucial decisions: Leadership in policymaking and crisis management.* New York: Free Press.

Janis, I. L., & Mann, L. (1977). *Decision making: A psychological analysis of conflict, choice, and commitment.* New York: Free Press.

Johnston, W. B., & Packer, A. E. (1987). *Workforce 2000: Work and workers for the 21st century.* Indianapolis, IN: Hudson Institute.

Jurma, W. E., & Wright, B. C. (1990). Follower reactions to male and female leaders who maintain or lose reward power. *Small Group Research, 21*(1), 97-112.

Kenny, D. A., & Zaccarro, S. J. (1983). An estimate of variance due to traits in leadership. *Journal of Applied Psychology, 69,* 678-685.

Kent, R. L., & Moss, S. E. (1990). Self-monitoring as a predictor of leader emergence. *Psychological Reports, 66*(3, Pt. 1), 875-881.

Kerr, S. (1977). Substitutes for leadership: Some implications for organizational design. *Organization and Administrative Sciences, 8,* 135-146.

Ketrow, S. M. (1991). Communication role specializations and perceptions of leadership. *Small Group Research, 22*(4), 492-514.

Kirkpatrick, S. A., & Locke, E. A. (1991). Leadership: Do traits matter? *The Executive, 5,* 48-60.

Knutson, T. J., & Holdridge, W. E. (1975). Orientation behavior, leadership, and consensus: A possible functional relationship. *Speech Monographs, 42,* 107-114.

Kushell, E., & Newton, R. (1986). Gender, leadership style, and subordinate satisfaction: An experiment. *Sex Roles, 14*(3-4), 203-209.

Lord, R. G., DeVader, C. L., & Alliger, G. M. (1986). A meta-analysis of the relation between personality traits and leadership perceptions: An application of validity generalization procedures. *Journal of Applied Psychology, 71,* 402-410.

Lumsden, G. B. (1974). An experimental study of the effect of verbal agreement on leadership maintenance in problem-solving discussion. *Central States Speech Journal, 25,* 270-276.

Makridakis, S. (1990). *Forecasting, planning, and strategy for the 21st century.* New York: Free Press.

Miller, V. D., & Jablin, F. M. (1991). Information seeking during organizational entry: Influences, tactics, and a model of the process. *Academy of Management Review, 16*(1), 92-120.

Mullen, B., Salas, E., & Driskell, J. E. (1989). Salience, motivation, and artifact as contribution to the relation between participation rate and leadership. *Journal of Experimental Social Psychology, 25*(6), 545-559.

Naisbett, J. (1994). *Global paradox.* New York: William Morrow.

Nanus, B. (1992). *Visionary leadership.* San Francisco: Jossey-Bass.

Nicotera, A. M. (1994). The use of multiple approaches to conflict: A study of sequences. *Human Communication Research, 20,* 592-621.

Owen, W. F. (1986). Rhetorical themes of emergent female leaders. *Small Group Behavior, 17,* 475-486.

Pfeffer, J. (1990). *Managing with power.* Boston: Harvard Business School Press.

Phillips, J. S., & Lord, R. G. (1986). Notes on the practical and theoretical consequences of implicit leadership theories for the future of leadership measurement. *Journal of Management, 12*(1), 31-41.

Poole, M. S. (1991). Procedures for managing meetings: Social and technological innovation. In R. A. Swanson & B. O. Knapp (Eds.), *Innovative meeting management* (pp. 53-110). Austin, TX: 3M Meeting Management Institute.

Poole, M. S., & Roth, J. (1989). Decision development in small groups V: Test of a contingency model. *Human Communication Research, 15,* 549-589.

Putnam, L. L., & Stohl, C. (1990). Bona fide groups: A reconceptualization of groups in context. *Communication Studies, 41*(3), 248-265.

Riecken, H. (1975). The effects of talkativeness on ability to influence group solutions of problems. In P. Crosbie (Ed.), *Interaction in small groups* (pp. 238-249). New York: Macmillan.

Sayles, L. R. (1993). *Working leadership.* New York: Free Press.

Schultz, B. (1974). Characteristics of emergent leaders of continuing problem-solving groups. *Journal of Psychology, 88,* 167-173.

Schultz, B. (1978). Predicting emergent leaders: An exploratory study of the salience of communicative functions. *Small Group Behavior, 9,* 9-14.

Schultz, B. (1980). Communication correlates of perceived leaders. *Small Group Behavior, 11,* 176-201.

Schultz, B. (1982). Argumentativeness: Its effect in group decision-making and its role in leadership perceptions. *Communication Quarterly, 30,* 368-375.

Schultz, B. (1986). Communication correlates of perceived leaders in the small group. *Small Group Behavior, 17,* 51-65.

Schwenk, C. R. (1988). The cognitive perspective on strategic decision-making. *Journal of Management Studies, 25*(1), 41-55.

Shaw, M. E. (1981). *Group dynamics: The psychology of small group behavior.* New York: McGraw-Hill.

Smircich, L., & Stubbart, C. (1985). Strategic management in an enacted world. *Academy of Management Review, 10*(4), 724-736.

Snyder, M. (1974). The self-monitoring of expressive behavior. *Journal of Personality and Social Psychology, 30,* 526-537.

Sorenson, R. L., & Savage, G. T. (1989). Signalling participation through relational communication: A test of the leader interpersonal influence model. *Group and Organization Studies, 14*(3), 325-354.

Spillman, B., Spillman, R., & Reinking, K. (1981). Leadership emergence: Dynamic analysis of the effects of sex and androgyny. *Small Group Behavior, 12,* 139-157.

Spitzberg, B. H., & Cupach, W. R. (1989). *Handbook of interpersonal competence research.* New York: Springer.

Stogdill, R. M. (1948). Personal factors associated with leadership: A survey of the literature. *Journal of Psychology, 25,* 35-71.

Vroom, V. H., & Jago, A. G. (1988). *The new leadership: Managing participation in organizations.* Englewood Cliffs, NJ: Prentice Hall.

Weick, K. E. (1978). The spines of leaders. In M. McCall & M. Lombardo (Eds.), *Leadership: Where else can we go?* (pp. 37-61). Durham, NC: Duke University Press.

Weick, K. E. (1979). *The social psychology of organizing* (2nd ed.). Reading, MA: Addison-Wesley.

Wentworth, D. K., & Anderson, L. R. (1984). Emergent leadership as a function of sex and task type. *Sex Roles, 11,* 513-524.

Wilson, S. R., & Putnam, L. L. (1990). Interaction goals in negotiation. In J. A. Anderson (Ed.), *Communication yearbook 13* (pp. 374-406). Newbury Park, CA: Sage.

Witteman, H. (1991). Group member satisfaction: A conflict-related account. *Small Group Research, 22*(1), 24-58.

Wood, J. (1977). Leading in purposive discussions: A study of adaptive behavior. *Communication Monographs, 44,* 152-166.

Worchel, S., Coutant-Sassic, D., & Grossman, M. (1992). A developmental approach to group dynamics: A model and illustrative research. In S. Worchel, W. Wood, & J. A. Simpson (Eds.), *Group process and productivity* (pp. 181-202). Newbury Park, CA: Sage.

Zaccaro, S. J., Foti, R. J., & Kenny, D. A. (1991). Self-monitoring and trait-based variance in leadership: An investigation of leader flexibility across multiple group situations. *Journal of Applied Psychology, 76*(2), 308-315.

PROCEDURES

Procedures for Enhancing Group Decision Making

SUSAN JARBOE

Pick up any basic text on group communication and one will find a section on "procedures." With the goal of making groups more effective, communication scholars convey to students various ways to tackle the issues that face any problem-solving or decision-making group. The range of procedures addressed in our texts reflects many of the difficulties inherent in group work; there are procedures to manage problems, procedures to manage meetings, procedures to make decisions, procedures to manage conflict, and even procedures for group self-reflection. Some procedures are rather descriptive, derived from what groups tend to do; but most are prescriptive, mandating what a group should or should not do.

We generally give our students an adequate sample of the range of options available, a compendium of approaches. But the collation of these approaches can overwhelm the students, who ask, "What procedure should be used in what group under what circumstances?" Unfortunately, the answer to such a question is not altogether straightforward. The advice can rest on common sense, perhaps derived from experience; in some cases, limited laboratory or case study research is informative, but most often, as Pavitt (1993) recently observed, "Those of us who continue to teach and recommend the use of formal procedures must do so on faith rather than on solid ground" (p. 231).

A useful answer to the question would emerge from systematic research and scholarship on group procedures, but before that can occur, scholars first need to identify the critical questions we should be asking about procedures. The purposes of this chapter are to describe the activities that are subsumed under the notion of group procedures; to review some of the most common procedures within and outside the speech communication discipline; to explore the role of communication in the manifestation of procedures; and to introduce, not a course of research, but a set of issues that should be addressed before we can hope to illuminate the interplay among procedures, communication, and group effectiveness.

What Is a Procedure?

Scholarship in group communication has always been plagued by problems with terminology. More than 20 years ago, Mortensen (1970) wrote,

> It is bad enough for the consumer of the literature to confront subject matter that is represented alternately as "group process," "group interaction," "group dynamics," "group relations," "group discussion," "group behavior," "group skills," "group performance," and "group communication." But what is even worse is to find such an unwieldy assortment of terms treated as interchangeable and synonymous. The obvious consequent of such a mixture of terminology is conceptual confusion. (p. 305)

Not only have we neglected Mortensen's concern, we have created a similar one by representing *procedures* variously as procedure, discussion, method, agenda, format, system, pattern, process, scheme, approach, strategy, technique, and model, among other labels. For example, *agenda* can refer to a general approach to problem solving, as in the "Standard Agenda" (Wood, Phillips, & Pedersen, 1986), but in more common parlance it refers to the list of items to be discussed at a particular meeting of the group. Ross (1989) referred to problem-solving procedures as *patterns* or *procedural formats* to "distinguish them from specific business agendas" (p. 75), but the words *pattern* and *format* are also problematic; for example, Seibold (1992) used *format* for organizing meetings and conferences.

Procedure and its synonyms are used as umbrella terms for myriad approaches to discussion that are directly or indirectly related to problem solving. Seibold (1992) included under the rubric of problem-solving procedures the following: problem census, rational reflection, brainstorming, buzz groups, nominal group technique, Delphi, listening teams, role playing, two-column method, risk, and PERT. Similarly, Tubbs (1992), using the alternative term *decision-making processes*, listed the reflective thinking process, the Kepner-Tregoe approach, the single-question form, brainstorming, incrementalism, mixed scanning, and tacit bargaining. Poole (1991), with the header "Procedures for Managing Meetings," included Robert's Rules of Order, brainstorming, nominal group technique, multiattribute decision analysis, Hall's consensus rules, devil's advocate, synectics, and Delphi technique.

A recent definition by Pavitt (1993) illustrates the difficulty in defining *procedure* and its related concepts. He described a formal discussion procedure as "an ordered sequence of steps for decision-making groups to follow in their discussions" (p. 217). Embedded in this definition are several complex issues. First, there is the implication that formal discussion procedures are of no use to groups that do not make decisions. This is a questionable assumption. Second, the word *formal* is misleading—its conventional association is with public discussion formats such as the panel or symposium. Finally, as we shall see, the terms *ordered, sequence,* and *steps* are not applicable to all procedures designed for problem-solving groups.

One source of the difficulty in defining *procedure* for groups lies in our orientation to the purposes of groups. Several scholars have commented on the bewilderment that arises when people use the terms *problem solving* and *decision making* interchangeably. Problem solving is often seen as a comprehensive, multistage process that begins with problem identification and ends with selection and/or implementation of a preferred alternative, whereas decision making is the process of evaluating and choosing among alternatives (Barker, Wahlers, Watson, & Kibler, 1987; Brilhart & Galanes, 1992; Ross, 1989; Simon & Associates, 1992; Zander, 1982). Other authors apparently see the terms in reverse (Poole, 1991), whereas Gulley and Leathers (1977) perceive the scope of decision-making behavior to include the procedures and rules the group uses.

These varying perceptions may be due to the level of abstraction at which the terms *problem* and *decision* are used. Zander (1982) defined a problem as "a specific situation to which members must respond if the group is to function effectively" (p. 13). Barker et al. (1987) defined a problem as "a question proposed for solution or consideration implying certain obstacles that must be overcome" (p. 103). Brilhart and Galanes (1992) identified three major components of problems: an undesirable present situation, a goal, and obstacles. Similarly, Klopf (1985) described these problem elements as a goal, obstacles to achieving it, and a point of awareness of the obstacles.

A group whose charge is to solve a problem clearly has to decide on a course of action to be implemented to manage the problem or achieve its goal. But within that overall process, other problems must be tackled and decisions made about them. For example, a group might ask, "What are the best sources of information about the situation?", or "How can we resolve our conflict about this?", or even "What is the best time for us to meet next?" These are "micro problems," and decisions must be made about them, too. In short, any dilemma facing the group can be conceived of as a problem. It may be task or social. It may call for extensive analysis and/or lengthy discussion of alternatives, or it may have a readily apparent and acceptable solution. As Zander (1982) asserted, "If there is no problem, no decision is needed, and things continue as they are" (p. 13). Because problems drive decisions rather than the reverse, this chapter treats problem solving as the larger process in which decision making and other activities occur.

Given that orientation, this chapter employs the following categories of procedures. *Problem-solving models* are procedures designed to tackle the overall problem facing the group, the major goal. These emphasize problem analysis and solution evaluation. Essentially, they operate at a macro level by providing a cognitive framework to take the group from start to finish to get the problem solved. They may, but do not necessarily, prescribe communicative behavior. When adopted or adapted by a group, their practical manifestation is a *problem-solving strategy*. Procedures that operate at the micro level, designed for subgoals of the problem-solving process such as idea generation or decision making, are *problem-solving devices*. One set of micro-level procedures of particular interest to communication scholars is focused on the range or nature of participation in the group endeavor. They deal primarily, if not solely, with social interaction in the group. They offer no advice on how a group should approach solving a problem, but rather on how to manage *talk*, which could be about a problem or something else entirely. These are called, simply, *interaction rules*. One other term should be clarified; a *tactic* is a specific communicative behavior, displayed by a group member, that supports a particular device.

Macro-Level Procedures: Problem-Solving Models

The recurrent issue on procedures is whether they enhance group effectiveness over groups that are simply free to interact however they wish. Free or naturally interacting groups can suffer from any number of ills, such as the focus effect, in which the group falls into a rut (Dunnette, Campbell, & Jaastad, 1963; Taylor, Berry, & Block, 1958); premature evaluation of ideas (Collaros & Anderson, 1969); conformity pressures due to status differences (Torrance, 1957); influence of dominant personalities (Chung & Ferris, 1971); and unexpressed judgments made by group members (Collaros & Anderson, 1969). In addition to minimizing these problems, procedures also specify a goal path for the group; early work in this area showed that the use of formats specific to the task have yielded better solutions than free groups (Maier & Hoffman, 1960; Maier & Maier, 1957; Maier & Solem, 1962; Maier & Thurber, 1969). Pavitt (1993), summarizing research on a limited number of procedures, reported that procedures improve effectiveness with tasks that have objective measures of outcome, but the results are mixed with other kinds of tasks. He still concluded, however, that "the majority of evidence finds in their favor" (p. 221).

One way in which procedures are believed to work is by enhancing quality of thought of group members. By specifying "Discuss this" or "Think about that," some procedures promote critical and/or creative thinking of group members. Isaksen (1988a) described critical thinking as the process "in which one analyzes and develops mechanisms to compare and contrast ideas; improve and refine concepts; screen, select, and support alternatives; and make judgments and effect decisions" and creative thinking as the process "in which one makes and communicates meaningful new connections by devising unusual new possibilities" (p. 140). Creative thinking is often labeled *divergent* and analytical thinking, *convergent* (Albrecht, 1987; Rawlinson, 1981; Scheidel & Crowell, 1979; Whitfield, 1975). Both divergent and convergent thinking are necessary for effective group problem solving (Scheidel, 1986), and their relevance is seen in specific devices.

In addition to their minimizing group problems, providing clearer goal paths, and improving thought, Poole (1991) summarized other potential benefits to using procedures: They help coordinate members' thinking; they provide a set of objective ground rules; they prevent counterproductive behavior; they capitalize on the strengths of groups; they balance member participation; they can reveal and manage conflicts; they give groups a sense of closure; they make groups reflect on their process; and they empower groups. This is not to say that every procedure can yield every benefit; or that individual procedures promote each benefit to the same degree; or that every group responds in the same way to procedures. Macro-level procedures have, as their primary goal, a high-quality final solution achieved by means of a systematic approach to thinking and discussing the problem.

RATIONAL MODELS

A host of problem-solving and decision-making models for groups have been derived from Dewey's (1910) five-step model of individual reflective thinking: awareness of the problem, assessment of the problem, suggesting solutions, assessing solutions, and testing solutions. McBurney and Hance (1939) adapted these five elements for group agendas. Ross (1974) added the concept of explicit criteria steps and the final step of implementation (Cragan & Wright, 1986; Ross, 1989). Wright's (1975) model included these elements, too, and he added an initial period of ventilation in which the group copes with tension as members come to grips with their task (Cragan & Wright, 1986; Ross, 1989).

Some authors incorporate elements of reflective thinking and its subsequent variations into their own prescriptive agendas, such as the *general procedural model for problem solving* (Brilhart & Galanes, 1992) and the *problem management sequence* (Scheidel & Crowell, 1979). Wood et al.'s (1986) *standard agenda* emphasized the group's relationship with the environment by taking groups from understanding their charge to preparing a final report, with the problem-solving phases sandwiched in between (Klopf, 1985; Ross, 1989; Rothwell, 1992). Although rational approaches have varying numbers of steps, various combination of steps, and various sequences of those steps, they are strongly influenced, if not actually derived, from the reflective thinking model (see Barker et al., 1987; Bormann & Bormann, 1988; Ellis & Fisher, 1994; Jensen & Chilberg, 1991; Ross, 1989; Rothwell, 1992; Wilson & Hanna, 1990).

On the whole, there is a paucity of research on reflective thinking and its variations; rational models "have not been subjected to substantial critical scrutiny or empirical inquiry" (Gouran, 1991, p. 345). Simplified versions of the reflective thinking model have been shown to increase the problem-solving ability of groups over other types of procedures (Brilhart & Jochem, 1964; Maier & Thurber, 1969), although Jarboe (1988) found no difference in solution quality when compared to the nominal group technique. Furthermore, as Gouran (1991) wrote,

> Existing research evidence leaves a mixed view of the value of rational approaches to decision-making and problem-solving discussion. Results of studies have been inconsistent, and even when they have been supportive, conceptual and methodological deficiencies raise other questions about the strength of the reported relationships. (p. 346)

Rational models of problem solving may be ideal, but they are not always practical. Braybrooke and Lindblom (1970) pointed out that rational procedures are too complex and are costly in time. Furthermore, it is difficult to agree on values, and necessary information may not be available. And aside from whether or not rational models are necessarily effective, their emphasis could mislead students about the myriad ways in which problems can be approached. Etzioni (1992) argued that normative and affective factors are a part of many decision processes and can have a positive effect. As Zey (1992) explained,

> We do our students a disservice by teaching them that the rational choice models of decision making are the only acceptable models. Students may perceive rational choice models not only as explanation, but also as justification for making decisions on rational bases only. (p. 27)

CREATIVE MODELS

Although not strongly reflected in the communication literature, trade magazines, management journals, and other literature focused on the business world have addressed individual and group performance in the context of "creative problem solving." Although there is no consensus on the number of steps that do or should occur, Rawlinson (1981) outlined the basic stages of the creative thinking process in a group: Preparation, which is gathering facts and restating the problem; effort, which is necessary to overcome mental blocks; incubation, which is letting the problem rest while attention is given to other things; insight, which is the "Aha!" stage when ideas are discovered; and evaluation, which is entirely convergent. Effort, incubation, and insight are the creative phases, and Rawlinson noted that "laughter plays a large part in these three stages" (p. 28). Kuhn (1988) differentiated two kinds of incubation: naive gestation, which occurs after problem recognition but before the information search; and knowledgeable gestation, which occurs after detailed preparation. Other characteristics of the process include arousing interest in and motivation for the task at hand (Hurst, Rush, & White, 1989; Kao, 1991) and discovering challenges and defining opportunities (Greene, 1986).

The model in the communication discipline that is most attentive to creative activity is that of Scheidel and Crowell (1979). Although their *problem management sequence* is clearly derived from the rational tradition with its four steps of describing the problem, analyzing the problem, proposing plans, and selecting the best plan, they argued—as did Isaksen (1988b)—that the overall phasic sequence of the discussion first reflects divergence, then convergence. Furthermore, within each phase there are divergent and convergent components.

Research on creative problem-solving models is well under way. In a controlled field experiment, Basadur, Graen, and Green (1982) found effects immediately after training participants in creative problem solving; in addition, 2 weeks later trained participants showed greater preference for ideation, more practice of ideation in problem finding and problem solving, and higher performance in problem finding. Firestien (1990) found that groups trained in creative problem solving participated more, criticized ideas less, supported ideas more, exhibited humor, and produced more ideas, but participation was more uneven.

Creative models contain components of classic, rational problem solving, such as data gathering, problem definition, solution generation, and solution evaluation. But they have unique elements unspecified in rational models of problem solving. For example, attention is granted to arousing interest, motivation, and effort for the task, reflecting the belief that individual reactions to the problem situation are relevant to effectiveness. A second difference is the incubation phase, where nothing to do with the task is scheduled. Although this may happen naturally in groups that meet over a period of time, creative models aver that this is an important step that must be programmed into the process for a "creative shift" (Hare, 1992) to occur. Another difference is in imagination. Rational strategies may incorporate an idea generation technique such as brainstorming, which, if done properly, requires imagination; but the model does not label it an "imagination" phase. Similarly, phases such as illumination and insight are not a part of the rational tradition. Finally, creative models attend to the social dimension. The concept of having fun is an important part of being creative, as many case studies reveal.

PLANNING MODELS

Broader conceptually than the models above, planning models are focused less on specific problems and more on general group goals. Nutt (1984) explained that different models of planning—such as research and development, social change, problem solving, and design— have different stages, but the generic process can be portrayed as formulation, conceptualization, detailing, evaluation, and implementation. Each stage has research, synthesis, and analysis steps. Delbecq and Van de Ven (1971) developed a *program planning* model of problem exploration, knowledge exploration, priority development, program development, and program evaluation. Each phase is targeted at different interest groups, such as consumers, external personnel, resource controllers, and administrators. *Strategic planning* models are designed to help organizations cope with rapid change to enhance an organization's long-term prospects. Although long-range planning predicts the future from the past, strategic planning anticipates new trends to which the organization must adapt. Although the focus could be a problem such as a performance gap, usually these models address a "strategic issue," that is, "a forthcoming development . . . which is likely to have an important impact on the ability of the enterprise to meet its objectives" (Ansoff, 1980). Such situations are characterized by complexity, ambiguity, interconnectedness with other problems, and trade-offs with alternative solutions (Rajagopalan, Rasheed, & Datta, 1993).

One frequently cited strategic decision process, based on a field study, is that of Mintzberg, Raisinghani, and Theoret (1976). The identification phase consists of decision recognition and diagnosis routines; the development phase consists of search and design routines; and the selection phase consists of screen, evaluation choice, and authorization routines. The entire process is supported by decision control routines such as resource allocation; communication routines such as explanation, investigation, and dissemination; and political routines such as bargaining. Chakravarthy and Lorange (1991) suggested five distinct steps to the strategy process: objectives setting; strategic programming; budgeting; monitoring, control, and learning; and incentives and staffing.

Strategic planning models incorporate many of the elements of rational and creative models: They require diagnosis, analysis, and synthesis. Yet because they are driven by change, strategic planning models place more emphasis on assessment of the external environment and the internal environment, increasing organizational learning, communication between groups, and processes tailored to the organization as well as to the situation at hand. Given the need for organizations to have systems in place for strategic planning, "strategic management" has come to the fore; that is, creating a system within the organization by which assessment and management of change becomes a constant. Because such models of change require organizations to take a long, hard look at themselves, outside help is often required. Lorange (1982) described an intervention model for increasing an organization's capability to manage change: scouting, entry, diagnosis, planning, action, evaluation, and termination.

Micro-Level Procedures: Problem-Solving Devices

One of the questions that frequently arises about problem-solving procedures is whether it is the procedure as a whole that is having the effect, or whether it is some subset of activities related to the model that is responsible for outcomes. This question has led to a line of research on "critical functions" for decision making (see Gouran, Hirokawa, Julian, & Leatham, 1993; see also Chapter 7 in this volume). Some of these functions, influenced by Janis and Mann's (1977) notion of vigilant decision making, are clearly within the rational framework: understanding the problem, establishing goals for an acceptable solution, generating alternatives, evaluating positive and negative consequences, and deciding on the most appropriate solution. Whether or not these are critical functions or, even if they are, whether this is a comprehensive list of such functions, is yet to be determined. Furthermore, the way in which each function is achieved can vary. For example, Van-Gundy's (1988) reference book described 10 methods for defining and analyzing problems, 61 methods for idea generation, 16 methods for evaluating ideas, 4 methods for implementing ideas, and 14 other miscellaneous techniques. Scheidel and Crowell (1979) sorted procedures into those designed for making lists, pruning lists, creating new products or procedures, developing and handling ideas, building involvement and/or understanding, handling conflicts, or planning implementation. Although many devices can be used for multiple purposes, they are loosely grouped according to their support of important problem-solving activities.

IDENTIFYING GOALS AND PRIORITIZING PROBLEMS

Obviously, the group must be aware of its purposes, functions, and goals before problem solving can begin. Occasionally a crisis arises where a group's priorities are immediately apparent (Smart & Vertinsky, 1977). Some groups have ongoing responsibility to identify problems and then manage them on a continuous basis; *Quality circles*, for example, are charged with assessing their working circumstances to improve production. If an organization has a strategic management system in place, the organization's capability for early detection of problems and trends increases the available time to deal with the situation, increasing the likelihood of a successful decision.

Other groups are more ad hoc; the members come together for a specific purpose and then disband. Sometimes the problem is presented to the group from an outside source in its environment, as when management appoints a task force in an organization. But often groups have to decide what their problem is. *Problem census* (Maier, 1963) is a method used at the beginning of a meeting, in which group members introduce, list, and rank problems to be considered at that or future meetings; if desired, anonymity of contributors can be maintained (Brilhart & Galanes, 1992; Klopf, 1985; Seibold, 1992). The *single-question form* (Larson, 1969) focuses on the one thing the group aims to accomplish, subquestions and their answers are generated, and then a solution is identified (Cragan & Wright, 1986; Tubbs, 1992; Wilson & Hanna, 1990). Idea generation devices (see below) are also ways to produce lists of problems or concerns.

Given the complexity of contemporary decision environments, sheer ranking of problems to set priorities is simplistic because of connected and overlapping concepts. It may be necessary to analyze the problem before goals or priorities can be set. In strategic planning, trends emerge from the internal strengths and weaknesses of the organization, and the opportunities and threats from the external environment (SWOT). Each trend is evaluated in terms of impact and urgency, which determines whether the problem should be dropped, monitored, or handled immediately (Ansoff, 1980). Personal constructs of team members can be used to build models of problems, or *cognitive maps* (Eden, Jones, & Sims, 1983). These idea structures demonstrate the interrelatedness of problem components. Consensus mapping (Hart, Boroush, Enk, & Hornick, 1985) utilizes individual idea cards that are sorted into classifications to build the model.

Although methods to set priorities are increasing in sophistication (see "Designing and Evaluating Solutions" below), of the several phases of problem solving, Simon and colleagues (1992) wrote, "The very first steps in the problem-solving process are the least understood. What brings (and should bring) problems to the head of the agenda?" (p. 46). He continued, "relatively little has been accomplished toward analyzing or designing effective agenda-setting systems" (p. 46).

ANALYZING PROBLEMS

One of the common dangers to group effectiveness is becoming "solution minded" too soon; that is, generating solutions before a full understanding of the problem is available. Models of problem solving suggest a systematic assessment of the problem: its symptoms, its causes, the limitations of present efforts, and so on. To accomplish this phase well, group discussion texts emphasize gathering, evaluating, and using various types of information. Gulley and Leathers (1977) mention observation, interviews, and reading. From the applied realm, Gamache and Gagliano (1988) describe the use of internal and external experts and the expert survey. The nature of information includes examples, statistics, facts, opinions, and ways to evaluate them (Baird & Weinberg, 1981; Barker et al., 1987; Cragan & Wright, 1986; Scheidel & Crowell, 1979; Wood et al., 1986), although the management literature warns readers about information overload, difficulties with information storage and retrieval, and appropriate transmission and dissemination of information (MacCrimmon, 1974).

Critical thinking, including inductive and deductive reasoning and common fallacies, is important for problem analysis (Baird & Weinberg, 1981; Barker et al., 1987; Brilhart & Galanes, 1992; Cragan & Wright, 1986; Gulley & Leathers, 1977; Klopf, 1985; Rothwell, 1992; Scheidel & Crowell, 1979; Wood et al., 1986). Awareness of nonlogical forms of reasoning, such as shifting ground, forced dichotomy, and the bandwagon effect, is useful as well (Baird & Weinberg, 1981; Klopf, 1985). This legacy of the rhetorical tradition serves critical thinking functions well.

Creative approaches to problem analysis are also available. *Role playing* (Maier, Solem, & Maier, 1957) can be useful for human relations or social problems in the group (Klopf, 1985; Scheidel & Crowell, 1979; Seibold, 1992). *Synectics* (Gordon, 1961) uses analogies, metaphors, and fantasizing to see the problem in a new way. *Lateral thinking* (de Bono, 1967) encourages group members to break out of the frame of reference in which the problem is usually viewed.

SETTING CRITERIA

When a group has an overall problem to solve, members should have ideas about what that solution should accomplish. In some models, this phase, often known as criteria, occurs after problem analysis but before solution generation and evaluation, but Brilhart (1974) suggested that criteria follow rather than precede solutions (Cragan & Wright, 1986; Ross, 1989). In practice, however, criteria often emerge as solutions are evaluated. As general guidelines for criteria, Scheidel and Crowell (1979) argued for utility, whether the solution will work and how fully; feasibility, whether the solution is practical in terms of resources such as money, equipment, or personnel; promptness, the amount of time to get the solution under way; and congruency with boundaries, whether the solution protects, or at least does not damage too much, values operant in the system. Kepner and Tregoe (1965) sorted criteria into "musts," which are absolute requirements, and prioritized "wants," which are desirable.

GENERATING IDEAS

In every phase of the problem-solving process, there is always a need for ideas. Often associated with the solutions phase, one of the most frequently mentioned methods is Osborn's (1957) *brainstorming* (Barker et al., 1987; Brilhart & Galanes, 1992; Cragan & Wright, 1986; Jensen & Chilberg, 1991; Klopf, 1985; Rothwell, 1992; Scheidel & Crowell, 1979; Tubbs, 1992; Wilson & Hanna, 1990). Its goals are to generate as many ideas as possible by being creative, suspending judgment, and combining or adapting ideas. *Excursion* (Gryskiewicz, 1987) uses scenarios to stimulate ideas. The *nominal group technique* (NGT) (Delbecq, Van de Ven, & Gustafson, 1975) is also frequently suggested (Brilhart & Galanes, 1992; Cragan & Wright, 1986; Klopf, 1985; Rothwell, 1992; Scheidel & Crowell, 1979; Wilson & Hanna, 1990). The idea generation phase is silent at the individual level, similar to *brainwriting* (Geschka, Schaude, & Schlicksupp, 1975). A round-robin listing presents the ideas to the group, and discussion occurs after listing with the goal of clarification rather than decision. Voting, with a discussion of the vote when necessary, prioritizes the ideas.

Contemporary research on brainstorming is centered on barriers to its effectiveness and ways to remove them. From the speech communication discipline, low apprehensive participants produced more on a brainstorming task than high apprehensives (Jablin, Seibold, & Sorenson, 1977). Harkins and Jackson (1985) found that social loafing decreased when participants believed their outputs were individually identifiable and could be compared with the products of their peers. Basadur and Thompson (1986) tested the brainstorming principle of "extended effort" (i.e., getting as many ideas as possible and not stopping after the first few). They found that the most preferred ideas came in the latter two thirds of the idea list, indicating the desirability of extended effort. Diehl and Stroebe (1987) explored the free-riding tendency, evaluation apprehension, and production blocking. Kelly and Karau (1993) studied the effects of varying levels of time pressure on a brainstorming task.

The NGT has been tested in both laboratory and applied settings. When compared to consensus and conventional interacting groups on a ranking task, both the NGT and consensus produced better quality decisions than conventional groups (Nemiroff, Pasmore, & Ford, 1976). The NGT and the Delphi produced more ideas when compared to interacting groups, and the NGT produced more unique ideas (Van de Ven & Delbecq, 1974). However, Green (1975) found no difference between the NGT and interacting groups on the number of ideas generated, the number of unique ideas, or the quality of responses. In a comparison of interacting, consensus, NGT, and Delphi groups, the Delphi had the highest quality decisions and the NGT the lowest (Erffmeyer & Lane, 1984). NGT was superior in decision quality on a structured problem compared to consensus (Herbert & Yost, 1979). In an applied study of implementation attempts, the NGT and "structured discussion" (essentially, the reflective thinking model) produced higher rates of implementation than interacting groups, with the NGT more effective on simple tasks, structured discussion best on moderate tasks, and no difference on complex tasks (White, Dittrich, & Lang, 1980). *Problem centered leadership,* which relies on a leader's ability to facilitate the entire problem-solving process (Maier, 1952), yielded greater decision effectiveness on an index of quality and acceptance with a personnel task than did NGT or Delphi (Miner, 1979). In terms of satisfaction, NGT groups were more satisfied than Delphi and interacting groups (Van de Ven & Delbecq, 1974), but consensus groups were more satisfied with their decisions and with their own performance than NGT or interacting groups (Nemiroff et al., 1976).

New modifications and applications of the NGT continue to develop. For example, Fox (1989) substituted written cards for the verbal input phase and discovered that this anonymity increased participant satisfaction. Hegedus and Rasmussen (1986) eliminated the round-robin recording and polling phases and, instead, relied solely on individual work, unstructured discussion, and social facilitation for evaluation problems. They found that there was more task-related discussion in the nominal group condition than in unstructured groups and that the nominal group technique condition produced more participant satisfaction. Bartunek and Murninghan [sic] (1984) introduced structured pauses and expanded the discussion phase beyond clarification, changes that they believed increased decision acceptance and the ability to tackle unstructured problems.

DESIGNING AND EVALUATING SOLUTIONS

Although idea generation strategies can provide ideas for solutions, there are specific procedures for an overall approach. With the *ideals* method (Nadler, 1970), the group looks at the function of the solution and then gathers the necessary information, designs the system, and evaluates its effectiveness (Cragan & Wright, 1986; Scheidel & Crowell, 1979; Wilson & Hanna, 1990). Braybrooke and Lindblom (1970) bypassed the complexities of problem analysis by exploring solutions that are small changes from the status quo. *Incrementalism* is less risky than sweeping solutions, and short steps can eventually accumulate into meaningful change (Scheidel & Crowell, 1979; Tubbs, 1992).

Before a particular solution is selected, its attributes and potential effectiveness must be evaluated; as with problem analysis, reasoning and inference are important skills in this phase. The vigilant decision-making perspective suggests a step of exploring positive and negative consequences, which may or may not have emerged in the criteria phase. Another method of evaluation is to compare each solution against preset criteria, sometimes with numerical ratings (Kepner & Tregoe, 1965). *Multidimensional scaling* (Frankel, 1987) rates top-ranked items numerically on criteria such as desirability and importance, and items are sorted into similar groupings; however, this method requires technological sophistication. *Multi-attribute utility models* (Eils & John, 1980; Thomas, McDaniel, & Dooris, 1989) are similar: Alternatives are rated on criteria, the importance of the criteria are weighed, and the final rankings emerge from applying a utility algorithm; for example, the sum of weights times rates. The advantage to these systematic approaches is that each solution is measured against the same set of standards.

To ensure that each solution is thoroughly assessed, criticism can be structurally induced. For example, in the *devil's advocate* (DA) method (Cosier, 1978), one group develops solutions, another critiques the facts and assumptions on which the solutions are based, and the solutions thus evolve as they are changed by criticism. Mason (1969) commented that if devil's advocacy does not provide alternative assumptions or plans, the criticism can be destructive, possibly making future plans "safe" ones. *RISK* (Maier, 1963) is similar to the devil's advocate. It seeks input from affected parties about their doubts and fears about the solution. Members (and others) are asked to brainstorm any risks or problems they see with the solution. These can be discussed, weighed, and if necessary, the solution can be readjusted (Brilhart & Galanes, 1992; Rothwell, 1992; Seibold, 1992). In *dialectical inquiry* (DI) (Cosier, Ruble, & Aplin, 1978), the group considers potential solutions and their bases or assumptions and then considers the negative form of each solution and generates countersolutions based on the negative forms of the assumptions; this leads to a pool of more potential solutions when the solutions from each end of the dialectical continuum are synthesized.

DA and DI have often been compared as to their effectiveness. In a laboratory study of strategic decision making, they were superior to *consensus* in producing higher-quality recommendations, but the consensus groups were more satisfied, more accepting of the decisions, and more desirous of continuing to work in their groups (Schweiger, Sandberg, & Ragan, 1986). A similar finding occurred in a study of middle and upper-middle managers (Schweiger, Sandberg, & Rechner, 1989). Such effects on quality may be due to maximizing the capabilities of individuals with the DA and DI methods (Schweiger & Sandberg, 1989). In a field study comparing DA, DI, and expert systems on strategic plans, the DI groups received the lowest ratings, and on one criterion DA groups were judged better (Cosier & Aplin, 1980). In a meta-analysis of these methods with the *expert-based* approach, Schwenk (1990) concluded that DA and DI were superior when the world-state is inconsistent with the experts' views; there was also some evidence that DI is better than DA when groups are used. However, Schweiger and Finger (1984) noted that many of the research operationalizations of these methods in research did not conform to the original intent of the device.

DECISION-MAKING SCHEMES

One set of procedures is concerned with who makes the decision and/or how it is made. These are sometimes referred to as *decision-making methods* as well as *decision-making procedures;* Rothwell (1992) calls them "rules." Most communication texts presume a "leaderless group discussion" setting, in which all (or most) members have an equal share in the power to make decisions, but for many problem-solving groups, the environment in which the group exists determines the method by which decisions will be made. The power of a group may only be advisory, or the group may have actual authority. Common methods are *consensus, majority vote,* and *decision by authority.* Other methods include *minority decision,* where a subgroup decides, with or without the goodwill of the other group members; the average of members' opinions; and occasionally the decision is made by an expert, with or without previous discussion. Bargaining, arbitration, and compromise are also possibilities (for descriptions of these schemes, see Brilhart & Galanes, 1992; Gulley & Leathers, 1977; Jensen & Chilberg, 1991; Johnson & Johnson, 1987; Klopf, 1985; Ross, 1989; Rothwell, 1992; Wilson & Hanna, 1990).

It is difficult to measure which scheme achieves the most effective decision for problem solving because schemes are seldom compared directly in research. Furthermore, in practice, they are not necessarily discrete; bargaining can be a prelude to a vote, and a vote can be a prelude to decision by authority. When compared to uninstructed groups, consensus (Hall & Watson, 1970) produced better quality decisions but took more time (Nemiroff & King, 1975; Nemiroff et al., 1976). A modified consensus technique produced more accurate judgments on a forecasting task while the NGT showed no effect on pre- and postdiscussion measures (Ang & O'Connor, 1991). Comparing unanimous decision rules and majority decision rules on a bargaining/negotiation task, members of unanimous groups were more likely to coordinate their interests to achieve higher rewards (Thompson, Mannix, & Bazerman, 1988). Exposure to minority concerns increased solution quality over exposure to only majority views (Nemeth & Kwan, 1987).

In terms of social outcomes, consensus enhanced member commitment to the decision over Delphi, NGT, and interacting groups (Erffmeyer & Lane, 1984). In a comparison of nominal voting, majority voting, and consensus groups, satisfaction with personal participation was lowest in the nominal vote and highest in the consensus; negative socioemotional behavior was lowest in the nominal vote; but there were no differences in satisfaction with the final decision or conformity to the group decision (Green & Taber, 1980). In a study of jury deliberations under two-thirds majority and unanimity rules, no effects were found on the nature of the verdict, although unanimity groups became hung juries more often. The requirement for unanimity increased the likelihood of full consensus as well as agreement with the verdict (Nemeth, 1977).

When deciding which scheme is most suitable, there are several factors to be weighed. Vroom and Yetton (1973) designed a system for leaders to determine the decision scheme: should the leader make the decision; or, should the group be involved; and, if so, to what extent? It offers a decision tree that assesses problem attributes (quality requirements, information needed, and structure) and member commitment (necessity of acceptance, likelihood of acceptance, shared organizational goals, and likelihood of conflict). The interplay of these factors determines who should decide. Wood (1984) offered a selection model for voting, negotiation and consensus that outlined the constraints related to the characteristics of the members, the task, and the outcomes.

IMPLEMENTATION AND EVALUATION OF SOLUTIONS

However the solution is chosen, the way to put it into effect can be the source of an entirely new problem-solving process. This phase is centered on feasibility requirements. Less attention has been given to this area of problem solving than to the ways to arrive at a decision. The *program evaluation and review technique* (PERT) (Phillips, 1966) focuses on the final event that would signify that the problem has been solved. Preceding necessary events are determined, with estimates of time required to arrive at the goal (Barker et al., 1987; Brilhart & Galanes, 1992; Cragan & Wright, 1986; Klopf, 1985; Ross, 1989; Rothwell, 1992; Scheidel & Crowell, 1979). The *standard agenda performance system* incorporates a PERT-like implementation plan into the standard agenda; events are evaluated as they are implemented (Klopf, 1985). As noted above, the *ideals* method combines solution generation with solution implementation. *Mixed scanning* (Etzioni, 1968) takes an incremental approach to implementing the solution; the solution should be broken down into small steps and implemented sequentially, with the least costly and most reversible changes at the beginning (Scheidel & Crowell, 1979; Tubbs, 1992). It includes a review procedure to identify potential problems as the solution matures, clearly along the lines of contemporary strategic management.

Regulating Involvement Through Interaction Rules

The preceding array of procedures illustrates the range of methods available to groups to use when coping with problems. There are other procedures that focus on ways to involve people in the problem-solving process. Procedures for building involvement can operate at the macro level of problem solving, in various phases of the problem-solving process, or even outside the context of the group task. Furthermore, they can be targeted at both group and nongroup members.

INTERFACING WITH OUTSIDERS

There may be occasions when a problem-solving group needs to interact with nongroup members to gather information, perceptions, or ideas. *Focus groups* (Stewart & Shamdasani, 1990), for example, are not problem-solving groups, but operate on one component of the problem-solving process. A focus group is intended to gather public reactions to an issue; A general topic is announced, and participants can free-associate (Brilhart & Galanes, 1992). At other points, a group might wish to seek feedback or to present its findings to its "public." Some discussion formats are geared to public discussion, where the group interacts in front of, or with, other people; Ross (1989) called these *standard forms of discussion*. The *symposium* is a series of set speeches, whereas the *panel* is a more interactive discussion by experts. The *colloquy* allows questions of experts from a few selected members of the audience and the *forum* allows for interaction with any audience member; these may follow a symposium or a panel (Baird & Weinberg, 1981; Barker et al., 1987; Bormann & Bormann, 1988; Cragan & Wright, 1986; Jensen & Chilberg, 1991; Klopf, 1985; Ross, 1989; Wilson & Hanna, 1990). Conference planning is essentially managing a series of discussions; it involves creating groups at the beginning and synthesizing findings at the end. Various problem-solving models at the macro or micro levels can be incorporated into conferences, and formats from the *roundtable* to the *panel* can be used (Barker et al., 1987; Scheidel & Crowell, 1979). The *charette* (Napier & Gershenfeld, 1973) is a conference consisting of an intense series of meetings of those who will be most affected by the decision; information and experts are made available to the discussants (Scheidel & Crowell, 1979).

BUILDING INTERNAL INVOLVEMENT

Involvement can begin with the careful selection of group members. A task force, for example, may be designed to ensure representation from various departments in the organization. One of the currently popular approaches is *quality circles* (Thompson, 1982). A circle is a small group of people, often from the same work area, that identifies, analyzes, and resolves problems (Barker et al., 1987; Brilhart & Galanes, 1992; Rothwell, 1992; Wilson & Hanna, 1990). The members are trained in problem analysis and meeting skills and have access to outside facilitation. As experience and sophistication increases, circles can be formed across different work areas to explore organizational problems. The assumption behind circles is that those closest to the work understand the problems best, thus the problem identification phase is a major part of circles. Although circles do not make decisions, their involvement in generating the solution is likely to enhance commitment. Management support of circles is critical because of the costs in time and training.

Once a group is established, various procedures for running meetings are available (Barker et al., 1987; Klopf, 1985; Scheidel & Crowell, 1979). One of the most familiar techniques is Robert's Rules of Order (Robert & Robert, 1981). This provides a way for groups to manage turn taking and the task as well. It is especially applicable to large groups (Brilhart & Galanes, 1992; Ross, 1989). One procedure for generating and prioritizing ideas, the *Delphi* (Dalkey, 1967), is designed to overcome geographic barriers to participation (Cragan & Wright, 1986; Klopf, 1985).

Internally, an extant group might wish to increase the involvement of members who may be on the periphery of events. *Buzz groups* (Phillips, 1948) divide the large group into smaller groups that discuss the same issue and can be used in any phase of the problem-solving model (Barker et al., 1987; Brilhart & Galanes, 1992; Cragan & Wright, 1986; Klopf, 1985; Scheidel & Crowell, 1979; Wilson & Hanna, 1990). Finally, there are strategies to deal with conflict when the group is facing challenging disagreements, such as *System 4T* (Likert & Likert, 1976) or *integrative decision making* (Filley, 1975).

Procedures for building involvement are not exclusively social in intent; some also have a clear, task-related function. Their design, however, has as one of its major goals to expand participation in the group. The assumption behind involving people is that involvement increases the amount of information available to the group, increases commitment to the decision, improves dissemination of that decision, and enhances commitment to group problem solving, thereby increasing the likelihood of quality thought throughout the process. Furthermore, if satisfaction is enhanced, members may be more enthusiastic the next time they participate in problem solving in that or other groups, but outsiders might be more trusting of problem solvers.

The Role of Communicative Behavior in Group Problem Solving

In specific problem-solving models and devices, the role of communication may or may not be identified. When it is addressed, it may be through a general guideline for behavior or it can take the form of a very crisp rule. When examined in research, it can be measured specifically, globally, or not at all. The differences in how communication is conceived theoretically and operationalized pragmatically is one of the barriers to effective research on communication and group procedures.

EXPLICIT RULES FOR COMMUNICATIVE BEHAVIOR

One of the ways communication is a variable is by its sheer presence or absence. For example, the first step of the NGT has silent, individual brainstorming as opposed to out loud group brainstorming. Intended to prevent such ills as social loafing and the focus effect, such a phase "leads to more total, more non-overlapping, and higher quality proposals than group generation" (Pavitt, 1993, p. 227). The incubation/gestation phase in several creative models described earlier is another example of a noninteractive step. The presence or absence of communication in the problem-solving process is reminiscent of the early studies on group versus individual decision making (see Shaw, 1981, for review), but instead of a dichotomous question it presents a more sophisticated issue: At what points in the problem-solving process should there be "time-outs" for individual thought? What it is about communication that renders its presence or absence effective (or not) at these times?

A second conception of communication is essentially topical, with or without a sequential factor. Most models consist of a list of issues the group should address to make an effective stab at the problem. *Reflective thinking* illustrates this: There are no guidelines for *how* the issues should be discussed, but merely that they *should* be; and in a particular order as well, such as "problem analysis" before "solution generation." Inappropriate topics may also be sanctioned, such as "No criticism of ideas" in brainstorming. As noted earlier, the functional approach questions whether it is the sequence of topics or the mere fact they have been discussed (presumably adequately) that makes a difference in effectiveness.

Although the topical conception of communication mandates the content of the act, there are other communication guidelines for how an act might be performed. For example, in brainstorming, there is the very specific suggestion, "Piggyback to create new ideas." Occasionally communication is seen as a sequence of speakers, such as the "round-robin" listing in the NGT. Other guidelines are more general. For example, the discussion phase of the NGT is oriented to clarifying ideas, rather than advocating them. Some models seem solely attitudinal or relational; Hall and Watson's (1970) *rules for consensus* are more like a philosophy of human relations than a problem-solving procedure.

IMPLICIT RULES FOR COMMUNICATIVE BEHAVIOR

Although models and devices vary in the degree to which the substance and style of communication is regulated, communication scholars have attempted to define the behaviors and skills associated with effective problem solving in general. These tactics can be associated with specific phases of group problem solving, or they can be generic, used in almost any kind of discussion. Ross (1989) provided examples of procedural functions such as starting the meeting, creating an agenda, and ending the meeting; Scheidel and Crowell (1979) extensively described these activities. Jensen and Chilberg (1991) outlined nine different communicative behaviors that focus on procedures: goal setting, orientation, focusing, tooling, clarifying or modifying procedures, regulating interaction, referencing the record, reporting on process, and modifying group process. Scheidel and Crowell (1979) specified communicative tactics for divergence phases: description, explication, and list making. For convergence, they suggested classification, evaluation, comparison, and synthesis.

Yet overall, the recommendations for communicative behavior are not associated with any problem-solving model or device, but rather from what we understand or believe about human interaction. As a general orientation, Ross (1989) reminded us of our roots when he cited Ewbank and Auer's (1941) notions of communication in the small group: that discussion was associated with problem solving, and decision making was associated with debate. Under rubrics such as *guidelines for productive participation* (Wood et al., 1986), *followership communication behaviors* (Cragan & Wright, 1986), *rules for relating* (Ross, 1989), *keys to effective participation* (Baird & Weinberg, 1981), *interaction roles* (Tubbs, 1992), or *increasing verbal effectiveness* (Wilson & Hanna, 1990), scholars mix prescriptions of proactive attitudes, task-related behaviors, and socially appropriate behaviors. Although Ellis and Fisher (1994) warned that effective communication is not solely a set of skills, this caution does not inhibit us from attempting to expand the behavioral repertoire of discussants.

Research on Procedures: An Agenda

1. DEVELOP AND PRIORITIZE DIMENSIONAL CRITERIA FOR SELECTION OF MODELS AND DEVICES

In reviewing the research on macro-level models, it is unclear exactly what leads scholars to select a particular procedure for study. One criterion seems to be simple dissemination. For example, the reflective thinking model and its variations had been widely distributed throughout our literature before the early research took place. Brainstorming follows a similar pattern in applied psychology. Another trend is from "real-world" events. The *groupthink* phenomenon led to vigilant decision making that spawned research on critical functions. Similarly, organizations are using creative and strategic models and thus research occurs. As anecdotal evidence and popularity increase, a threshold is reached at which scholars finally say, "Let's take a look, because it's there."

Studying a phenomenon because it exists is not necessarily a bad criterion; it has clearly driven solid research in a variety of disciplines. However, the problem of selection is exacerbated by the plethora of models and devices presently available, and new ones are appearing daily. For example, *Kaizen* (Imai, 1990; Stratton, 1990), in spite of its Japanese origins, is an incremental problem-solving technique applied in a group context, although Ross (1989) portrays it as a quality circle. The *Crawford slip* (Krone & Clark, 1990) is a focused Delphi. *Visioning* (Holder, 1988) involves group members focusing their energy on the desired end state, a common phase in many rational models, analogous to the single-question form. The *lion's den* (Bookman, 1988) is an American version of quality circles. The *lotus blossom* (Tatsuno, 1990) is a visual brainstorming; it requires a central theme to be written in the center of a lotus blossom diagram, and group members to generate related ideas. The *stepladder* (Rogelberg, Barnes-Farrell, & Lowe, 1992) regulates involvement by introducing prepared members into the group one by one. Separating management fads from procedures that will stand the test of time is a risky prospect for the scholar.

But whatever drives the selection, one essential research requirement is to ensure, when models are tested against each other, that they are operating at the same level of abstraction in the problem-solving process. To compare a device like brainstorming to a model like reflective thinking is comparing fruits and vegetables. Similarly, comparing an idea-generation device like brainstorming with a problem-analysis device like synectics would also be unsuitable. It is particularly troublesome to observe how often consensus is inappropriately tested; it should not be compared with idea-generation devices like the NGT, but rather to decision schemes and interaction rule systems.

Returning to the terminology issue, we need some way to classify and sort models and devices along underlying dimensions that may account for their effectiveness. Then, when comparing models (or devices) against each other, some dimensions would be similar or controllable while others vary. But small group scholars perpetuate differences in terminology, precluding a useful typology of procedures. For example, Cragan and Wright (1986) called reflective thinking a "problem-solving agenda system" and the nominal group technique a "specific discussion technique." Klopf (1985) referred to the former in its incarnation as the standard agenda, and in a section titled "Other Methods of Interaction" he included group performance system, brainstorming, nominal group technique, Delphi, problem census, role-playing, buzz group, panel, symposium, dialogue, and interview (the last five with the adjective *public*). Although it probably makes sense to keep reflective thinking and its variations in a "rational" class by themselves, the phrases *specific discussion techniques* and *other methods of interaction* are useless for practical or theoretical purposes.

Poole (1991) presented a typology that offers five dimensions for sorting procedures. *Scope* is analogous to the macro- and micro-level headings described here; it refers to the number of activities the procedure is intended to achieve. *Restrictiveness* refers to the degree to which the model or device prescribes communicative conduct; as we have seen, it runs the gamut from "not at all" to "almost scripted." *Comprehensiveness* refers to the specificity of the rules. *Group control* refers to whether the group needs outside assistance, such as a facilitator or mediator. This is an important factor because many creative models work best with outside facilitation, and many bona fide groups are not leaderless. *Member involvement* is the degree of participation available to group members. Although this may not be a complete list of dimensions, it is a useful framework from which to manipulate or control procedural elements at the macro- or micro-levels. Jensen and Chilberg's (1991) criteria for choosing a procedure suggest some other factors to be considered: task focus, time cost, conflict potential, social needs, promotion of cohesion, and pressure to conform. Another dimension might be ease of use or complexity (March & Shapira, 1992).

At the micro level, the most popular devices to study have been for idea generation, such as brainstorming and the NGT; and ways to evaluate and weigh solutions, such as DA and DI. The central question is similar to that asked of the functional model of decision making: "At what point can one be sure all critically relevant functions have been examined?" (Gouran, Hirokawa, Julian, & Leatham, 1993, p. 591). The subsequent question is, "What specific devices enhance what particular function?" Creative models, for example, consider "incubation" to be relevant to innovative solutions, yet we do not have research manipulating that variable alone, nor do we (yet) have a micro-level heading on "Procedures to create silence."

2. CONTROL, MANIPULATE, AND/OR MEASURE RELEVANT INDIVIDUAL DIFFERENCE VARIABLES

There are any number of individual difference variables that can have an impact on group performance (see Shaw, 1981, for review). Although research cannot take every conceivable factor into account, research on models and devices cannot afford to neglect relevant variables altogether. One important line of research relates to characteristic thinking modes used by group members during problem-solving interaction (Pyron, 1964). Members rated high in performance in problem-solving groups had greater reflective thinking ability, but the least useful group members scored in the lower one third of their group (Pyron & Sharp, 1963). When groups were formed on the basis of high, medium, or low reflective thinking ability, the high-scoring groups performed better on creative problem-solving tasks (Sharp & Milliken, 1964). Groups constructed on the basis of individual brainstorming ability were more effective when composed of highly creative members (Graham & Dillon, 1974). Comadena (1984), in a study of brainstorming groups, discovered that individuals who were higher in idea production had a greater tolerance for ambiguity than participants who were lower in idea production. One's "preference for procedural order" (Hirokawa, Ice, & Cook, 1988) can interact with the degree of procedural structure to affect decision performance, but a "preference for ideation" (Basadur & Finkbeiner, 1985) can affect idea generation behavior. Measuring creative tendencies (Kirton, 1976) is also relevant to problem solving.

It may not always be possible to construct groups to manipulate or balance the relevant abilities of the members, but even so, the role of these characteristics should be assessed as a potential confound; for example, Priem and Price (1991) discovered that participants have initial task and social expectations about DA, DI, and consensus, which could result in a self-fulfilling prophecy. Furthermore, various kinds of participant satisfaction, as outcome measures, should also be assessed. Given the reluctance to use new procedures, whether because of their difficulty, internalized group norms, or general resistance to change, how participants react to the process remains important data that should always be gathered whether or not it is the outcome of interest.

3. USE METHODOLOGY APPROPRIATE TO THE STUDY OF PROCEDURES

Aside from potentially confounding effects of group composition, Pavitt and Curtis (1994) argued strongly that the groups must be trained in procedures for an adequate test of models and devices. In applied research, training of bona fide groups goes without saying, but in laboratory research, giving instructions to the sample may constitute the only "training" received. Ironically, the college laboratory setting is ideal for quality research on procedures because training in models and devices can be readily incorporated into a course syllabus.

A second requirement is that group members must be motivated to do well. Aside from arousing member interest in the task, motivation can affect group interaction, as with free-riding tendencies (Albanese & Van Fleet, 1985). Varying perceptions of accountability can affect the incidence of groupthink (Kroon, 't Hart, & van Kreveld, 1991). Again, bona fide groups are more likely to be motivated, either internally or externally, whereas ad hoc laboratory groups can walk away from their decisions without a second thought.

Finally, attention must be given to the manipulation of the problem stimulus. The task is always problematic in small group research, partially because of the lack of a "problems typology" (see McGrath, 1984). Much has been written about the trade-off between unrealistic tasks with objective, correct answers, more characteristic of laboratory research, and realistic tasks the solutions of which are more difficult to evaluate, often seen in applied research. Whatever route is chosen, participants should have, or be provided with, a reasonable amount of information and time to solve the problems. Although there are interesting questions about the appropriateness of various models and devices on different kinds of tasks, until we have demonstrated prototypes of particular genres of tasks, two tasks representing the same genre should be used; otherwise results may be confounded by unintended task effects.

4. RETHINK OUR ASSUMPTIONS ABOUT COMMUNICATIVE BEHAVIOR

Communication as a Process Variable. This chapter has described the way communication has been conceptualized in research on procedures: as present or absent; as topical and/or sequential; as rules for individual behavior. However it is manifested in a model or device, in communication research it is often studied in an input-process-output framework of group discussion; that is, that procedures produce communicative behavior that produces outcomes, although other paths are entirely possible. Hewes (1986) articulated a difficulty with making appropriate attributions about effects of procedures:

> Do trained groups perform well with these agendas because their discussions are organized, because their members individually think about problems more rigorously, or some combination of the two? We do not know. If the first case is true, communication does have an impact on decision-making quality; in the second case, input factors operating at the individual level explain improvements in decision-making. (p. 268)

There are two issues embedded in Hewes's caution. The first is the extent to which we are studying problem-solving behavior and the extent to which we are studying communication. Many procedures, such as the rational, creative, and planning macro models, simultaneously provide goal paths and enhance the quality of individual, and hence group, thought; but just because thought is manifested orally in discussion does not make it a communication variable. Furthermore, individuals vary in their initial set of prediscussion skills, and they respond variously to training. To sort out individual inputs might be accomplished by pretraining all experimental participants in problem-solving skills such as critical and creative thinking; then the procedures themselves, and not the quality of thinking they engender in participants, would be the variable.

But even if this were done, to characterize the effect of communication as "organized discussion" is troublesome. It reflects the topical-sequential function of communication and neglects the relational function. For example, in research on decision-making functions, the communication variable is the extent to which the group has met the requirements of that particular function, often measured by a global rating by "expert" judges. One can imagine two groups arriving at exactly the same set of consequences, yet one discussion might be marked by sarcastic tones and rigidity whereas another group presents its ideas supportively and tentatively. One group may build on each others' ideas to identify the consequences, but in the other group the final list is merely an aggregation of individual contributions. And one group may disband with relief while the other looks forward to the next meeting. The sheer presence of an idea is one thing; the way it is presented is another; and its impact on group process is also another. Particularly when a procedure under inquiry speaks to the social dimension of the group, that quality of communication must surely be considered.

Communication as an Output Variable. Outcome measures in group problem solving are often associated with primary task activity such as the quality of solutions, the number of ideas, or the uniqueness of ideas. Although these are the most practical ways to assess outcomes in laboratory research, "there is little doubt that the value of a decision depends on the confluence of subsequent events" (Reagan & Rohrbaugh, 1990, p. 21). Case studies and action research can yield those subsequent events, but even so, their limited generalizabilty precludes a systematic test of models and devices. Reagan and Rohrbaugh (1990) offer a direction that should be popular with communication theorists: "Any assessment of the effectiveness of a group decision process requires directing primary attention to the process itself, not to subsequent outcomes" (p. 21). Again, this kind of assessment is seen in research on critical functions, where judges evaluate the degree to which the groups achieve a particular goal. This is a useful approach for assessing specific problem-solving devices. At the macro level, for strategies with more scope, Reagan and Rohrbaugh (1990) studied eight effectiveness criteria that emerge from different value systems. From the rational perspective, was the process goal-centered and the decision efficient? From the political perspective, was the process adaptable and the decision legitimate? From the consensual perspective, was the process participatory and the decision supportable? From the empirical perspective, was the process data-based and the decision accountable? An instrument to answer these questions appears promising in terms of convergent validity of a variety of observers on a variety of groups.

Communication as an Input Variable. The fact that individual-level factors could account for improved group problem solving, and the idea that communication has relational components, lead inevitably to the third role of communication. There is a basic irony to research on procedures as performed by communication scholars. With all our "guidelines," "followership," and "keys" for communicative behavior, we seldom see these as variables in our research on procedures. Yet they are as ever-present in texts and applied literature as any problem-solving model or device. If procedures intended to improve thought are confounded by abilities at the individual level (either as precursors or consequents), so are procedures that manipulate interaction confounded by abilities at the individual level (again, as precursors or consequents). Groups of socially skilled individuals might cooperate more naturally and adapt more readily and, hence, implement a procedure more effectively. Thus the more interesting question is what communicative behaviors promote satisfactory completion of which problem-solving requirements. In other words, "Do groups trained in Communication Skill Set A (or B or C) utilize Model (or Device) X (or Y or Z) more effectively than groups without Skill Set A (or B or C)?"

This course is not without peril. First, skills would have to be sorted into coherent sets; one tactic at a time would be an unwieldy and unproductive approach. It is beyond the scope of this chapter to identify and prioritize the ABCs of communication skills; our texts are full of them and there are probably more skills than procedures. Making these choices is, again, exacerbated by the abundance of labels and typologies for roles, behaviors, attitudes, and skills, leading to overlapping and multiple concepts. There are task and social skills; skills for any discussion and skills for specific phases; skills for paraphrasing. They vary in specificity from Scheidel and Crowell's (1979) prescription of "Say 'we,' 'our,' and 'us' " to general guidelines such as "Help others" (Klopf, 1985). Probably the most difficult skill to develop is the judgment to know when a particular tactic is necessary. "If a group is stalled in evaluation, ask for opinions" is not necessary if opinions are forthcoming from all. As Albrecht (1987) put it,

> The number one factor in the success of team creativity is the simple but profoundly important skill of process awareness. One of the keys to a

team's creative success is how effectively its members manage their own
interaction processes instead of becoming preoccupied about the "content," that is the subject at hand or the problem they are dealing with.
(p. 177)

Conclusion

At present, research on procedures crosses the domains of decision
theory, information processing, group dynamics, and human relations.
It is conducted by psychologists, sociologists, management scientists,
and speech communication theorists. This eclecticism is enriching if not
altogether programmatic. But from a disciplinary perspective, there is
a disturbing trend: other disciplines design procedures, then we look at
their effect on communication. Some scholars would deem this an
appalling way to approach the central questions of a discipline. It is
second-order research and although it makes a contribution, it is certainly not proactive. If we have any sense that communication is not
just a series of topics, not just a channel for transmitting ideas, then we
should ask what communication contributes to effective problem solving and its subordinate tasks; not communication as derived from the
mandate of some model or device, but communication as we, the
experts, independently consider it. And this returns us to where we
began—the need for a typology of procedures, but this time a typology
based on communicative behavior. Then we should ask what procedures can be designed to enhance communication in problem solving,
procedures that can maximize the interactive potential as well as the
cognitive abilities of human beings. Currently in small group communication research, procedures are driving our questions about communication, when communication should be driving our questions about
procedures.

References

Albanese, R., & Van Fleet, D. D. (1985). Rational behavior in groups: The free-riding
    tendency. *Academy of Management Review, 10,* 244-255.
Albrecht, K. (1987). *The creative corporation.* Homewood, IL: Dow Jones-Irwin.
Ang, S., & O'Connor, M. (1991). The effect of group interaction processes on performance
    in time series extrapolation. *International Journal of Forecasting, 7,* 141-149.
Ansoff, H. I. (1980). Strategic issue management. *Strategic Management Journal, 1,* 131-148.

Baird, J. E., Jr., & Weinberg, S. B. (1981). *Group communication: The essence of synergy* (2nd ed.). Dubuque, IA: William C. Brown.

Barker, L. L., Wahlers, K. J., Watson, K. W., & Kibler, R. J. (1987). *Groups in process: An introduction to small group communication* (3rd ed.). Englewood Cliffs, NJ: Prentice Hall.

Bartunek, J. M., & Murninghan, J. K. (1984). The nominal group technique: Expanding the basic procedure and underlying assumptions. *Group & Organizational Studies, 9,* 417-432.

Basadur, M., & Finkbeiner, C. T. (1985). Measuring preference for ideation in creative problem-solving training. *Journal of Applied Behavioral Science, 21,* 37-49.

Basadur, M., Graen, G. B., & Green, S. G. (1982). Training in creative problem solving: Effects on ideation and problem finding and solving in an industrial research organization. *Organizational Behavior and Human Performance, 30,* 41-70.

Basadur, M., & Thompson, R. (1986). Usefulness of the ideation principle of extended effort in real world professional and managerial creative problem solving. *Journal of Creative Behavior, 20,* 23-34.

Bookman, R. (1988). Rousing the creative spirit. *Training and Development Journal, 42,* 67-71.

Bormann, E. G., & Bormann, N. C. (1988). *Effective small group communication* (4th ed.). Edina, MN: Burgess.

Braybrooke, D., & Lindblom, C. E. (1970). *A strategy of decision.* New York: Free Press.

Brilhart, J. K. (1974). *Effective group discussion* (2nd ed.). Dubuque, IA: William C. Brown.

Brilhart, J. K., & Galanes, G. J. (1992). *Effective group discussion* (7th ed.). Dubuque, IA: William C. Brown.

Brilhart, J. K., & Jochem, L. M. (1964). Effects of different patterns on outcomes of problem-solving discussion. *Journal of Applied Psychology, 48,* 175-179.

Chakravarthy, B. S., & Lorange, P. (1991). *Managing the strategy process: A framework for a multibusiness firm.* Englewood Cliffs, NJ: Prentice Hall.

Chung, K. H., & Ferris, M. J. (1971). An inquiry of the nominal group process. *Academy of Management Journal, 14,* 520-524.

Collaros, P. A., & Anderson, L. R. (1969). The effect of perceived expertness upon creativity of members of brainstorming groups. *Journal of Applied Psychology, 53,* 159-163.

Comadena, M. E. (1984). Brainstorming groups: Ambiguity tolerance, communication apprehension, task attraction, and individual productivity. *Small Group Behavior, 15,* 251-264.

Cosier, R. A. (1978). The effects of three potential aids for making strategic decisions on predictive accuracy. *Organizational Behavior and Human Performance, 22,* 295-306.

Cosier, R. A., & Aplin, J. C. (1980). A critical view of dialectical inquiry as a tool in strategic planning. *Strategic Management Journal, 1,* 343-356.

Cosier, R. A., Ruble, T. L., & Aplin, J. C. (1978). An evaluation of the effectiveness of dialectical inquiry systems. *Management Science, 24,* 1483-1490.

Cragan, J. F., & Wright, D. W. (1986). *Communication in group discussions: An integrated approach* (2nd ed.). St. Paul, MN: West.

Dalkey, N. C. (1967). *Delphi.* Santa Monica, CA: RAND Corporation.

de Bono, E. (1967). *New think.* New York: Basic Books.

Delbecq, A. L., & Van de Ven, A. H. (1971). A group process model for problem identification and program planning. *Journal of Applied Behavioral Science, 7,* 466-491.

Delbecq, A. L., Van de Ven, A. H., & Gustafson, D. H. (1975). *Group techniques for program planning: A guide to nominal group and delphi processes.* Glenview, IL: Scott, Foresman.

Dewey, J. (1910). *How we think*. Boston: D. C. Heath.

Diehl, M., & Stroebe, W. (1987). Productivity loss in brainstorming groups: Toward the solution of a riddle. *Journal of Personality and Social Psychology, 53,* 497-509.

Dunnette, M. D., Campbell, J., & Jaastad, R. (1963). The effect of group participation on brainstorming effectiveness for two industrial samples. *Journal of Applied Psychology, 47,* 30-37.

Eden, C., Jones, S., & Sims, D. (1983). *Messing about in problems*. Elmsford, NY: Pergamon.

Eils, L. C., III, & John, R. S. (1980). A criterion validation of multiattribute utility analysis and of group communication strategy. *Organizational Behavior and Human Performance, 25,* 268-288.

Ellis, D. G., & Fisher, B. A. (1994). *Small group decision making: Communication and the group process* (4th ed.). New York: McGraw-Hill.

Erffmeyer, R. C., & Lane, I. M. (1984). Quality and acceptance of an evaluative task: The effects of four group decision-making formats. *Group & Organization Studies, 9,* 509-529.

Etzioni, A. (1968). *The active society: A theory of societal and political processes*. New York: Free Press.

Etzioni, A. (1992). Normative-affective factors: Toward a new decision-making model. In M. Zey (Ed.), *Decision making: Alternatives to rational choice models* (pp. 89-111). Newbury Park, CA: Sage.

Ewbank, H. L., & Auer, J. J. (1941). *Discussion and debate: Tools of a democracy*. New York: F. S. Crofts.

Filley, A. C. (1975). *Interpersonal conflict resolution*. Glenview, IL: Scott, Foresman.

Firestien, R. L. (1990). Effects of creative problem-solving training on communication behaviors in small groups. *Small Group Research, 21,* 507-521.

Fox, W. M. (1989). The improved nominal group technique. *Journal of Management Development, 8,* 20-27.

Frankel, S. (1987). NGT + MDS: An adaptation of the nominal group technique for ill-structured problems. *Journal of Applied Behavioral Science, 23,* 543-551.

Gamache, R. D., & Gagliano, C. C. (1988). Toolbox for practical creativity. In R. L. Kuhn (Ed.), *Handbook for creative and innovative managers* (pp. 101-112). New York: McGraw-Hill.

Geschka, H., Schaude, G. R., & Schlicksupp, H. (1975). Modern techniques for solving problems. In M. M. Baldwin (Ed.), *Portraits of complexity: Applications of systems methodologies to societal problems* (pp. 1-7). Columbus, OH: Battelle Memorial Institute.

Gordon, W. J. J. (1961). *Synectics: The development of creative capacity*. New York: Harper & Row.

Gouran, D. S. (1991). Rational approaches to decision-making and problem-solving discussion. *Quarterly Journal of Speech, 77,* 343-384.

Gouran, D. S., Hirokawa, R. Y., Julian, K. M., & Leatham, G. B. (1993). The evolution and current status of the functional perspective on communication in decision-making and problem-solving groups: A critical analysis. In S. A. Deetz (Ed.), *Communication yearbook 16* (pp. 573-600). Newbury Park, CA: Sage.

Graham, W. K., & Dillon, P. C. (1974). Creative supergroups: Group performance as a function of individual performance on brainstorming tasks. *Journal of Social Psychology, 93,* 101-105.

Green, S. G., & Taber, T. D. (1980). The effects of three social decision schemes on decision group process. *Organizational Behavior and Human Performance, 25,* 97-106.

Green, T. B. (1975). An empirical analysis of nominal and interacting groups. *Academy of Management Journal, 18*, 63-73.

Greene, R. J. (1986). Applying the creative process to circles. *Quality Circles Journal, 9*, 25-30.

Gryskiewicz, S. S. (1987). Predictable creativity. In S. G. Isaksen (Ed.), *Frontiers of creativity research: Beyond the basics* (pp. 305-313). New York: Bearly Limited.

Gulley, H. E., & Leathers, D. G. (1977). *Communication and the group process* (3rd ed.). New York: Holt, Rinehart & Winston.

Hall, J., & Watson, W. H. (1970). The effects of a normative intervention on group decision making performance. *Human Relations, 23*, 299-317.

Hare, A. P. (1992). *Groups, teams, and social interaction.* New York: Praeger.

Harkins, S. G., & Jackson, J. M. (1985). The role of evaluation in eliminating social loafing. *Personality and Social Psychology Bulletin, 11*, 457-465.

Hart, S., Boroush, M., Enk, G., & Hornick, W. (1985). Managing complexity through consensus mapping: Technology for the structuring of group decisions. *Academy of Management Review, 10*, 587-600.

Hegedus, D. M., & Rasmussen, R. V. (1986). Task effectiveness and interaction process of a modified nominal group technique in solving an evaluation problem. *Journal of Management, 12*, 545-560.

Herbert, T. T., & Yost, E. B. (1979). A comparison of decision quality under nominal and interacting consensus group formats: The case of the structured problem. *Decision Sciences, 10*, 358-370.

Hewes, D. E. (1986). A socio-egocentric model of group decision-making. In R. Y. Hirokawa & M. S. Poole (Eds.), *Communication and group decision-making* (1st ed., pp. 265-291). *Beverly Hills, CA: Sage.*

Hirokawa, R. Y., Ice, R., & Cook, J. (1988). Preference for procedural order, discussion structure, and group decision performance. *Communication Quarterly, 36*, 217-226.

Holder, R. J. (1988). Visioning: An energizing tool. *Journal for Quality and Participation, 11*, 18-22.

Hurst, D. K., Rush, J. C., & White, R. E. (1989). Top management teams and organizational renewal. *Strategic Management Journal, 10*, 87-105.

Imai, M. (1990). Kaizen wave circles the globe. *Tokyo Business Today, 58*, 44-48.

Isaksen, S. G. (1988a). Human factors for innovative problem solving. In R. L. Kuhn (Ed.), *Handbook for creative and innovative managers* (pp. 139-146). New York: McGraw-Hill.

Isaksen, S. G. (1988b). Innovative problem solving in groups. In Y. Ijiri & R. L. Kuhn (Eds.), *New directions in creative and innovative management: Bridging theory and practice* (pp. 145-168). Cambridge, MA: Ballinger.

Jablin, F. M., Seibold, D. R., & Sorenson, R. L. (1977). Potential inhibitory effects of group participation on brainstorming performance. *Central States Speech Journal, 28*, 113-121.

Janis, I. L., & Mann, L. (1977). *Decision making: A psychological analysis of conflict, choice, and commitment.* New York: Free Press.

Jarboe, S. (1988). A comparison of input-output, process-output, and input-process-output models of small group problem-solving effectiveness. *Communication Monographs, 55*, 121-142.

Jensen, A. D., & Chilberg, J. C. (1991). *Small group communication: Theory and application.* Belmont, CA: Wadsworth.

Johnson, D. W., & Johnson, F. P. (1987). *Joining together: Group theory and group skills* (3rd ed.). Englewood Cliffs, NJ: Prentice Hall.

Kao, J. J. (1991). *Managing creativity.* Englewood Cliffs, NJ: Prentice Hall.

Kelly, J. R., & Karau, S. J. (1993). Entrainment of creativity in small groups. *Small Group Research, 24,* 179-198.

Kepner, C. H., & Tregoe, B. B. (1965). *The rational manager: A systematic approach to problem solving and decision making.* New York: McGraw-Hill.

Kirton, M. J. (1976). Adaptors and innovators: A description and measure. *Journal of Applied Psychology, 61,* 622-629.

Klopf, D. W. (1985). *Interacting in groups: Theory and practice* (2nd ed.). Englewood, CO: Morton.

Krone, R. M., & Clark, C. H. (1990). Improving brainpower productivity. *Journal for Quality and Participation, 13,* 80-85.

Kroon, M. B. R., 't Hart, P., & van Kreveld, D. (1991). Managing group decision making processes: Individual versus collective accountability and groupthink. *The International Journal of Conflict Management, 2,* 91-115.

Kuhn, R. L. (Ed.). (1988). *Handbook for creative and innovative managers.* New York: McGraw-Hill.

Larson, C. E. (1969). Forms of analysis and small group problem solving. *Speech Monographs, 36,* 452-455.

Likert, R., & Likert, J. G. (1976). *New ways of managing conflict.* New York: McGraw-Hill.

Lorange, P. (1982). *Implementation of strategic planning.* Englewood Cliffs, NJ: Prentice Hall.

MacCrimmon, K. R. (1974). Managerial decision-making. In J. W. McGuire (Ed.), *Contemporary management: Issues and viewpoints* (pp. 445-495). Englewood Cliffs, NJ: Prentice Hall.

Maier, N. R. F. (1952). *Principles of human relations.* New York: John Wiley.

Maier, N. R. F. (1963). *Problem-solving discussions and conferences: Leadership methods and skills.* New York: McGraw-Hill.

Maier, N. R. F., & Hoffman, L. R. (1960). Using trained developmental leaders to improve further the quality of group decisions. *Journal of Applied Psychology, 44,* 247-251.

Maier, N. R. F., & Maier, R. A. (1957). An experimental test of the effects of "developmental" vs. "free" discussions on the quality of group decisions. *Journal of Applied Psychology, 41,* 320-323.

Maier, N. R. F., & Solem, A. R. (1962). Improving solutions by turning choice situations into problems. *Personnel Psychology, 15,* 151-157.

Maier, N. R. F., Solem, A., & Maier, A. (1957). *Supervisory and executive development: A manual for role playing.* New York: John Wiley.

Maier, N. R. F., & Thurber, J. A. (1969). The contribution of a discussion leader to the quality of group thinking: The effective use of minority opinions. *Human Relations, 5,* 277-288.

March, J. G., & Shapira, Z. (1992). Behavioral decision theory and organizational decision theory. In M. Zey (Ed.), *Decision making: Alternatives to rational choice models* (pp. 273-303). Newbury Park, CA: Sage.

Mason, R. O. (1969). A dialectical approach to strategic planning. *Management Science, 15,* B403-B414.

McBurney, J. H., & Hance, K. G. (1939). *The principles and methods of discussion.* New York: Harper & Brothers.

McGrath, J. E. (1984). *Groups: Interaction and performance.* Englewood Cliffs, NJ: Prentice Hall.

Miner, F. C., Jr. (1979). A comparative analysis of three diverse group decision making approaches. *Academy of Management Journal, 22,* 81-93.

Mintzberg, H., Raisinghani, D., & Theoret, A. (1976). The structure of "unstructured" decision processes. *Administrative Science Quarterly, 21,* 246-275.

Mortensen, C. D. (1970). The status of small group research. *Quarterly Journal of Speech, 56,* 304-309.

Nadler, G. (1970). *Work design: A systems concept* (Rev. ed.). Homewood, IL: Richard D. Irwin.

Napier, R. W., & Gershenfeld, M. K. (1973). *Groups: Theory and experience.* Boston: Houghton Mifflin.

Nemeth, C. (1977). Interactions between jurors as a function of majority vs. unanimity decision rules. *Journal of Applied Psychology, 7,* 38-56.

Nemeth, C. J., & Kwan, J. L. (1987). Minority influence, divergent thinking, and the detection of correct solutions. *Journal of Applied Social Psychology, 17,* 788-799.

Nemiroff, P. M., & King, D. C. (1975). Group decision-making performance as influenced by consensus and self-orientation. *Human Relations, 28,* 1-21.

Nemiroff, P. M., Pasmore, W. A., & Ford, D. L., Jr. (1976). The effects of two normative structural interventions on established and *ad hoc* groups: Implications for improving decision making effectiveness. *Decision Sciences, 7,* 841-855.

Nutt, P. C. (1984). *Planning methods for health and related organizations.* New York: John Wiley.

Osborn, A. (1957). *Applied imagination.* New York: Scribner.

Pavitt, C. (1993). What (little) we know about formal group discussion procedures: A review of relevant research. *Small Group Research, 24,* 217-235.

Pavitt, C., & Curtis, E. (1994). *Small group discussion: A theoretical approach* (2nd ed.). Scottsdale, AZ: Gorsuch Scarisbrick.

Phillips, G. M. (1966). *Communication and the small group.* Indianapolis, IN: Bobbs-Merrill.

Phillips, J. D. (1948). Report on discussion 66. *Adult Education Journal, 7,* 181-182.

Poole, M. S. (1991). Procedures for managing meetings: Social and technological innovation. In R. A. Swanson & B. O. Knapp (Eds.), *Innovative meeting management* (pp. 53-109). Austin TX: 3M Meeting Management Institute.

Priem, R. L., & Price, K. H. (1991). Process and outcome expectations for the dialectical inquiry, devil's advocacy, and consensus techniques of strategic decision making. *Group & Organization Studies, 16,* 206-225.

Pyron, H. C. (1964). An experimental study of the role of reflective thinking in business and professional conferences and discussions. *Speech Monographs, 31,* 157-161.

Pyron, H. C., & Sharp, H., Jr. (1963). A quantitative study of reflective thinking and performance in problem-solving discussion. *Journal of Communication, 21,* 46-53.

Rajagopalan, N., Rasheed, A. M. A., & Datta, D. K. (1993). Strategic decision processes: An integrative framework and future directions. In P. Lorange, B. Chakravarthy, J. Roos, & A. Van de Ven (Eds.), *Implementing strategic processes: Change, learning, and co-operation* (pp. 274-312). Oxford, UK: Basil Blackwell.

Rawlinson, J. G. (1981). *Creative thinking and brainstorming.* New York: John Wiley.

Reagan, P., & Rohrbaugh, J. (1990). Group decision process effectiveness: A competing values approach. *Group & Organization Studies, 15,* 20-43.

Robert, H. M., & Robert, S. C. (1981). *Robert's rules of order newly revised.* Glenview, IL: Scott, Foresman.

Rogelberg, S. G., Barnes-Farrell, J. L., & Lowe, C. A. (1992). The stepladder technique: An alternative group structure facilitating effective group decision making. *Journal of Applied Psychology, 77,* 730-737.

Ross, R. S. (1974). *Speech communication: Fundamentals and practice* (3rd ed.). New York: McGraw-Hill.

Ross, R. S. (1989). *Small groups in organizational settings.* Englewood Cliffs, NJ: Prentice Hall.

Rothwell, J. D. (1992). *In mixed company: Small group communication.* New York: Harcourt Brace Jovanovich.

Scheidel, T. M. (1986). Divergent and convergent thinking in group decision-making. In R. Y. Hirokawa & M. S. Poole (Eds.), *Communication and group decision-making* (1st ed., pp. 113-130). Beverly Hills, CA: Sage.

Scheidel, T. M., & Crowell, L. (1979). *Discussing and deciding.* New York: Macmillan.

Schweiger, D. M., & Finger, P. A. (1984). The comparative effectiveness of dialectical inquiry and devil's advocacy: The impact of task biases on previous research findings. *Strategic Management Journal, 5,* 335-350.

Schweiger, D. M., & Sandberg, W. R. (1989). The utilization of individual capabilities in group approaches to strategic decision-making. *Strategic Management Journal, 10,* 31-43.

Schweiger, D. M., Sandberg, W. R., & Ragan, J. W. (1986). Group approaches for improving strategic decision-making: A comparative analysis of dialectical inquiry, devil's advocacy, and consensus. *Academy of Management Journal, 29,* 51-57.

Schweiger, D. M., Sandberg, W. R., & Rechner, P. L. (1989). Experiential effects of dialectical inquiry, devil's advocacy, and consensus approaches to strategic decision-making. *Academy of Management Journal, 32,* 745-772.

Schwenk, C. R. (1990). Effects of devil's advocacy and dialectical inquiry on decision making: A meta-analysis. *Organizational Behavior and Human Decision Processes, 47,* 161-176.

Seibold, D. R. (1992). Making meetings more successful: Plans, formats, and procedures for group problem solving. In R. S. Cathcart & L. A. Samovar (Eds.), *Small group communication: A reader* (6th ed., pp. 178-191). Dubuque, IA: William C. Brown.

Sharp, H., Jr., & Milliken, J. (1964). The reflective thinking ability and the product of problem-solving discussion. *Speech Monographs, 31,* 124-127.

Shaw, M. E. (1981). *Group dynamics: The psychology of small group behavior* (3rd ed.). New York: McGraw-Hill.

Simon, H. A., & Associates. (1992). Decision making and problem solving. In M. Zey, (Ed.), *Decision making: Alternatives to rational choice models* (pp. 32-53). Newbury Park, CA: Sage.

Smart, C., & Vertinsky, I. (1977). Designs for crisis decision units. *Administrative Science Quarterly, 22,* 640-657.

Stewart, D. W., & Shamdasani, P. N. (1990). *Focus groups: Theory and practice.* Newbury Park, CA: Sage.

Stratton, A. D. (1990). Kaizen and variability. *Quality Progress, 23,* 44-45.

Tatsuno, S. M. (1990). Creating breakthroughs the Japanese way. *Research and Development, 32,* 336-142.

Taylor, D. W., Berry, P. C., & Block, C. H. (1958). Does group participation when using brainstorming facilitate or inhibit creative thinking. *Administrative Science Quarterly, 3,* 23-47.

Thomas, J. B., McDaniel, R. R., Jr., & Dooris, M. J. (1989). Strategic issue analysis: NGT + decision analysis for resolving strategic issues. *Journal of Applied Behavioral Science, 25,* 189-200.

Thompson, L. L., Mannix, E. A., & Bazerman, M. H. (1988). Group negotiation: Effects of decision rule, agenda, and aspiration. *Journal of Personality and Social Psychology, 54,* 86-95.

Thompson, P. C. (1982). *Quality circles: How to make them work in America.* New York: Amacom.

Torrance, E. P. (1957). Group decision making and disagreement. *Social Forces, 35,* 314-318.

Tubbs, S. L. (1992). *A systems approach to small group interaction* (4th ed.). New York: McGraw-Hill.

Van de Ven, A. H., & Delbecq, A. L. (1974). The effectiveness of nominal, delphi, and interacting group processes. *Academy of Management Journal, 17,* 605-621.

VanGundy, A. B., Jr. (1988). *Techniques of structured problem solving* (2nd. ed.). New York: Van Nostrand Reinhold.

Vroom, V. H., & Yetton, P. W. (1973). *Leadership and decision-making.* Pittsburgh, PA: University of Pittsburgh Press.

White, S. E., Dittrich, J. E., & Lang, J. R. (1980). The effects of group decision-making process and problem-situation complexity on implementation attempts. *Administrative Science Quarterly, 25,* 428-440.

Whitfield, P. R. (1975). *Creativity in industry.* Baltimore, MD: Penguin Books.

Wilson, G. L., & Hanna, M. S. (1990). *Groups in context: Leadership and participation in small groups* (2nd ed.). New York: McGraw-Hill.

Wright, D. W. (1975). *Small group communication: An introduction.* Dubuque, IA: Kendall/Hunt.

Wood, J. T. (1984). Alternative methods of group decision-making: A comparative examination of consensus, negotiation, and voting. In G. M. Phillips & J. T. Wood (Eds.), *Emergent issues in human decision making* (pp. 3-18). Carbondale: Southern Illinois University Press.

Wood, J. T., Phillips, G. M., & Pedersen, D. J. (1986). *Group discussion: A practical guide to participation and leadership* (2nd ed.). New York: Harper & Row.

Zander, A. (1982). *Making groups effective.* San Francisco: Jossey-Bass.

Zey, M. (1992). Criticisms of rational choice models. In M. Zey (Ed.), *Decision making: Alternatives to rational choice models* (pp. 9-31). Newbury Park, CA: Sage.

Procedural Influence on Group Decision Making

The Case of Straw Polls— Observation and Simulation

JAMES H. DAVIS
LORNE HULBERT
WING TUNG AU

Organizations and institutions of various kinds routinely assign groups of a dozen or fewer persons a major role in making decisions, ranging from filling an advisory role to making final determinations. Frequently, such groups are informal ad hoc collections, often with little special expertise pertinent to the task. Nonetheless, the ubiquitousness of such groups implies widespread confidence in consensual, relative to individual, decision making. Juries, panels, committees, and boards are among the many labels for groups of people who must agree on a solution, category, opinion, or other response, although they may have begun discussion with highly disparate preferences. Such disparate opinions may lead to conflict and confrontation

AUTHORS' NOTE: Portions of the research were supported by National Science Foundation grant NSF SBR 93-09405 to the first author.

in the process of establishing consensus, but the overall atmosphere is one of collaboration, if not cooperation.

Initial and developing disagreement must be resolved through discussion, sometimes through rather extended deliberation. Consequently, the promotion, management, and regulation of such discussion is important to the consensus process. Our attention here will focus on selected procedures for interaction management—in particular those techniques designed to foster or in some sense improve interpersonal communication. More precisely, we will be primarily concerned with *procedural mechanisms* (PMs) designed to manage communication, interaction, and collective action—especially how such PMs may themselves influence consensus outcomes. Following a short discussion of PMs in general (types, purposes, etc.), we will summarize in subsequent sections some results of research on selected PMs. Finally, we will elaborate on these results through computer simulations of the effects of PMs in interpersonal interaction situations that are unlikely to be studied empirically because of expense, ethical constraints, or general inaccessibility.

Procedural Mechanisms

The behavior of colleagues serving on committees is a routine source of coffee-room anecdotes, and the teller often displays a long-suffering attitude toward the confusion and disagreements marking the most recent meeting. Yet human interaction is not truly chaotic, and for all the frustration one can sometimes experience, task-oriented groups are generally characterized by some orderliness in pursuing consensus (i.e., sufficient agreement on a collective response). Sometimes this orderliness is the result of explicit rules governing interaction, as in the case of groups possessing a formal, written constitution. Other well-known examples are *standard operating procedures,* a familiar military phrase that gave rise to the post-World War II slang of "SOP" for explicit, situation-appropriate behavior. At other times, generally shared social norms and values regulate interpersonal exchanges in informal groups that otherwise possess no specified behavioral code. Most task-oriented groups are probably a mixture of the two extremes, and the important point is that whatever the source, it is generally possible to identify specific procedural mechanisms that may be responsible for guiding interaction and collective performance. For example, a panel may elect to regulate discussion by requiring speakers to be formally recognized in a certain way, or to meet criteria specified by a preexisting set of rules (e.g., Robert's Rules of Order; De Vries, 1990), perhaps modified for the special context and based on relevant experience. On the other hand, a criminal jury has no assigned procedures for managing discussion, and the foreperson must rely on shared cultural norms to define acceptable procedural mechanisms (e.g., hand-raising for floor recognition, person-by-person straw polls, etc.) for equitably publicizing member guilt preferences. Such PMs are familiar and are generally regarded as sound methods for promoting desirable aims. However, conventional wisdom may not always be correct, and it is reasonable to ask if PMs themselves may sometimes have unanticipated side effects or impact social actions in ways different from what is typically presumed.

One of the best known initial efforts to characterize and study procedural phenomena programmatically was due to Thibaut and Walker (1975). Their experimental investigation of the general procedures associated with the courtroom trial was an early example of what was to become a research trend of some magnitude, namely, the empirical study of *procedural justice* (see also the review of procedural models research by Walker & Lind, 1984). Much of this, and later, research was motivated by the question: Does a procedure mandated by law or custom do what it is assumed to do? Legal philosophy, popular opinion, and so on, establish what is fair and just. Legislation and judicial interpretation codify such notions and construct specific procedures designed to attain those ends. The courtroom, with its conspicuous emphasis on legal procedure for managing the behavior of participants, was an ideal candidate for study—and of considerable practical importance in its own right. Similarly, subsequent studies of the petit jury often addressed procedural issues (e.g., see Davis, 1980, 1984).

Parenthetically, it is worth noting that PMs in general have long occupied the attention of communication researchers (see Jarboe, Chapter 12 in this volume, for a general survey and discussion), not only to achieve basic understanding of the process involved, but with the aim of improving communication and collective performance. Political scientists and economists have in particular studied the logical properties of formal rules and procedures designed to translate individual opinion into collective action, an area sometimes called *social choice* or *public choice* (see Black, 1958; Fishburn, 1973; Mirkin, 1979; Mueller, 1989, to name only a few), including unintended side effects, biases, and procedural paradoxes (e.g., Balinski & Young, 1982; Brams, 1976). However, our interest in procedural rules or mechanisms is restricted to their *effects* on the actual *behavior* of consensus-seeking small groups. More precisely, we address the effects of selected PMs on *interpersonal behavior* and *cognitive processes* in the individual group member, emphasizing unintended side effects and subtle influences not evident from conventional wisdom or perhaps anticipated by "rules-makers."

Among the procedural mechanisms studied to date are techniques for selecting members; managing discussion; establishing consensus; structuring the task or agenda; publicizing opinions and voting; and enacting the group decision rule. We will discuss only a few examples of these PMs below (see Jarboe, Chapter 12 in this volume, for a wider-ranging discussion).

AGENDA INFLUENCE

One of the first studies to capture attention about the power of mere procedure to influence group outcomes was due to Plott and Levine (1978; Levine & Plott, 1977) who showed how aircraft purchase decisions of a flying club could be influenced by the mere organization of decision items on the slate from which choices were to be made. In other words, one who has agenda-setting authority can potentially bias the group decision.

However, it is not necessary that a sly chair or a crafty subcommittee surreptitiously manipulate agenda structure to produce bias. Happenstance or an intuitively attractive order of events, ostensibly evident and acceptable to all, can serve a similar function. For example, when faced with multiple charges, there are a number of reasons for trying a defendant on all of them at the same time, including economy and speed of resolution. (Criteria exist for severing charges and trying a defendant on each separately, but these issues are not relevant here.) However, the jury can only *decide* charges sequentially, and this raises the question of whether or not the verdict might be influenced by the mere *order* in which charges are deliberated and decided. This question of charge order has been addressed by a study (Davis, Tindale, Nagao, Hinsz, & Robertson, 1984) in which mock juries took up each of three charges (logically and legally independent) in either an ascending or a descending order of seriousness. (Other mock juries, free to choose any of the six possible sequences, showed an overwhelming preference for the two orders of charges, ascending or descending seriousness sequences, and chose each about equally often.) Results revealed that conviction on the middle charge (the same in both orders) was significantly more probable in a descending than ascending order. The proposed explanation suggested a comparison process to be responsible. We will not discuss such cognitive processes further, because our primary interest here is in the result as confirmation that agenda structure can significantly influence decisional outcome, apparently without participants' awareness (see Davis [1984] for a general discussion of order effects in courtroom trials).

COMMUNICATION MECHANISMS

If the mere order of agenda items can influence the consensual outcome, perhaps other sequential phenomena, such as the order of discussants mandated by the PMs adopted, might similarly impact consensus processes. Unlike agenda structure, which can be fashioned prior to actual group discussion, many communication-related procedural mechanisms (at least those considered here) are embedded in the social dynamics (e.g., a roll call vote) of the group, and take place in "real" time.

Individual members' personal positions, preferences, solutions, and more, are the stuff on which discussion operates to achieve consensus on a group position, solution, etc. The stimulation of interpersonal communication has long been a goal in the service of promoting everything from mutual understanding and equitable discussion input to improved collective performance (i.e., increased efficiency, enhanced creativity, etc.). For example, one colorful procedural intervention that sought essentially to increase members' idea output and foster interpersonal communication is that familiar set of prescriptions known as "brainstorming" (Osborn, 1957). Despite remarkably consistent negative empirical evaluations from the beginning (e.g., Dunnette, Campbell, & Jaastad, 1963; Taylor, Berry, & Block, 1958), and more recent meta-analyses that reveal an accumulated research literature of overwhelmingly negative results (Mullen, Johnson, & Salas, 1991), the popularity of brainstorming procedures continues to the present time. According to Diehl and Stroebe (1987, 1990), brainstorming prescriptions do not overcome "blocking" (the productivity-lowering consequences of "the convention that only one person can speak at a time"). In other words, the brainstorming procedure does *not* compensate for the typical group productivity loss generally observed in such group performance contexts (Davis, 1969; Steiner, 1972), but the notion is so compelling (and its practice perhaps such fun) that it persists in "popular" and institutional cultures as conventional wisdom.

Recently, Gallupe, Bastianutti, and Cooper (1991) have suggested that electronic decision aids may reduce or eliminate the typical performance inefficiencies generally found in task-oriented, face-to-face groups working under brainstorming procedures. It is notable, however, that the apparently facilitating procedural intervention (computer-mediated interaction) reduced the extent of interpersonal contact and exchange.

Next, consider a rather different PM; one common to diverse group performance environments and designed to publicize opinions efficiently and accurately, usually as an aid to reaching consensus: *polling*. We turn next to research on some features of the polling process, our primary concern in this chapter.

VOTING AND POLLING

Experts sometimes make exquisite distinctions between *polling* and *voting*. The general public typically uses the two terms interchangeably, although "polling" seems to be used more often to label member-by-member opinion expression, and "voting" is the more general term. We will not make a technical distinction between the two, but the actual procedural operations will be evident from the context. Within the context of the ubiquitous group decision-making process, it is not unusual for protracted discussion to be punctuated by efforts to "take stock" and publicize member or faction positions in the pursuit of consensus.

For example, member polling is commonplace during petit jury deliberations (e.g., see the discussion by Hastie, Penrod, & Pennington, 1983). It is thus not surprising that researchers have targeted such groups in evaluating the effects of different polling procedures (see

Hawkins [1960], and especially Stasser, Kerr, & Bray [1982], for general discussions of jury polling procedures). For example, Kerr and MacCoun (1985) found that private, in contrast to public, polling increased the rate of hung juries in a mock criminal trial. Focusing on public, member-by-member polling, it is evident that the procedural events can proceed in various ways. For one thing, there is the *timing* of such a poll to be considered, and for another, there is the particular *sequence* of votes that is created by choosing one of the r group members with which to begin, followed by selecting either of the two directions along which adjacent members respond in order. (Other member-by-member voting plans are conceivable but we will not discuss these possibilities here.) If either of these two factors systematically affects one or more members' vote, it is plausible in principle that through the selection of such apparently innocuous variables a crafty chair or mere happenstance could spuriously influence the group decision.

Again using the mock jury vehicle, recent research (Davis, Stasson, Ono, & Zimmerman, 1988) has demonstrated empirically that an individual juror's guilt preference can indeed be influenced by both *when* the poll is taken during deliberation, and the *particular sequence* of votes preceding the targeted individual voter. More precisely, six-person mock juries contained members who were evenly divided between those who preferred guilty and those who favored not guilty verdicts. Public polls were taken such that either all three guilty or all three not guilty sayers came first in the voting, and the straw poll was taken either early or late in deliberation. Attention focused on the fourth voter, because that person was the first to hold a contrary position; and, the 3:1 ratio was "Asch-sufficient" to induce opinion change with a reasonably high probability[1]. Results showed that the fourth voter's preference changed at a significant rate in contrast to those in a simultaneous public polling condition, *and* the change rate was higher for those confronted with an initial segment of not-guilty than guilty sayers. The latter finding is, of course, consistent with the notion that acquitting the guilty is a less serious error than convicting the innocent, a cultural value well represented in legal philosophy, trial procedure, and explicit judicial instructions. Not only was this asymmetry in influence observed in sequential responding, but it was evident in the vote timing results of Davis et al. (1988): Not-guilty sayers were more easily converted to a guilty preference by an *early* poll than a *later* one. Apparently discussion increased the salience of the relevant social norms. Such results are quite consistent, of course, with earlier findings of a general asymmetry in the power of majorities to convince minorities in determining the final verdict. Not-guilty majorities are generally more powerful in determining the final decision than guilty-favoring majorities— that is, the former prevails with a higher relative frequency. This asymmetry in the power of majorities to determine the final outcome has been called a "leniency bias" by MacCoun and Kerr (1988), and attributed to a "defendant protection norm" by Davis, Stasser, Spitzer, and Holt (1976) (see Tindale, Davis, Vollrath, Nagao, & Hinsz, [1990] for a detailed discussion of such majority influence asymmetries, along with other factional phenomena, and an evaluation of several relevant theoretical notions concerning the cognitive processes that might underlie such phenomena).

Observe that the social influence attributable to straw polling is not precisely what is usually meant by a majority group decision rule, because the two factions in Davis et al. (1988) were initially equal in size. That is, $r_G = r_{NG} = 3$, where $r_G + r_{NG} = r$, group size, r_G represents the overall number of guilty-sayers, and r_{NG} is similarly the subgroup of all those not inclined to a guilty decision. Consequently, the idea of a *local majority* was proposed, to emphasize that a *non-majority* can prevail, under certain conditions—namely, where the procedure creates a local (at that point in the sequence) imbalance in the opinion distribution. In Asch's studies, as well as in the many other studies in that general research paradigm, the unanimously erroneous confederates responded first in the sequence. Thus the majority of three or more existed in the "group" as a whole, (3, 1), (4, 1), (5, 1), . . . , for groups of 4, 5, 6, . . . , respectively, as well as at that point in the response sequence—E, E, E, X; E, E, E, E, X; E, E, E, E, E, X; . . . ; where E represents the experimenter's confederate, and X is the naive subject.

The notion of a local majority effect is useful for emphasizing and noting how the selection of polling sequences (especially in groups with minority factions larger than 1) may constitute procedural manipulation. Imagine that a six-person group ($r = 6$) is seated about a table, and members are unaware that guilt preferences are evenly divided (r_G, r_{NG}) = (3, 3) between those inclined to guilty and those who prefer not guilty. Results from a secret ballot or simultaneously raised hands would reveal this tie. However, a person-by-person poll (and many rationales or social circumstances come to mind for such a procedure) is quite different, because it must take place in one sequence or another. Suppose we arbitrarily label the jurors seated about a table 1, 2, 3, 4, 5, 6, and imagine that they are initially inclined to Guilty or Not Guilty, respectively: G, G, N, N, N, G. There are only six sequences, under the constraint that the voting is left to right and the array around the table is fixed. (There are 12 possible sequences, if the possibility of right to left polling is allowed, but we will not consider that now.) If polling proceeds 6, 1, 2, 3, 4, 5, the resulting G, G, G, N, N, N creates a 3:1 Asch-sufficient guilty-inclined "majority" (what we have called a "local majority") for member 3, now in the fourth position. However, under the same restrictions, if polling had begun with member 3, we have member sequence 3, 4, 5, 6, 1, 2, and the resulting N, N, N, G, G, G sequence would have presented the person in the fourth position with an opposite-inclined (Not Guilty) local majority. And, as discussed above, it has been observed (Davis et al., 1988) that the critical member (fourth position) often changes opinion in accordance with the local majority. Thus, at least for the group in which change occurs in this way, the "balance of power" is altered, with obvious implications for group-level actions.

However, the subsequent *group level* verdict distribution actually observed was not significantly affected by sequence in the study just described (Davis et al., 1988), despite the strong local majority effect that had been observed at the level of the *individual* voter. On the face of it, such a result was puzzling in the extreme. Note that local majorities in this case also created group-level majorities, $(r_G, r_{NG}) = (4, 2)$ or $(2, 4)$. Majorities have generally been observed to establish guilty or not guilty verdicts with high probability, according to experiments on mock juries (e.g., Davis, 1980) and post-trial interviews of ex-jurors (Kalven & Zeisel, 1966) alike. The puzzle was "solved" by computer simulations (see the discussion of "thought experiments" by Davis & Kerr, 1986), using the social decision scheme Model (Appendix; Davis, 1973, 1982; Stasser, Kerr, & Davis, 1989) together with the opinion change rates observed in the polling study. The simulation results (probability of conviction, P_G) for juries split (3, 3) at all levels of individual input (probability of a guilty vote, p_G), are given in Figure 13.1, for a two-thirds majority ("idealized," in the sense that events "happen" with probability near 1.00 or .00) and a social decision scheme actually

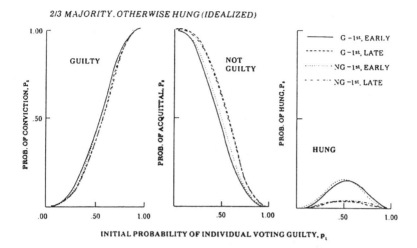

2/3 MAJORITY. OTHERWISE HUNG (IDEALIZED)

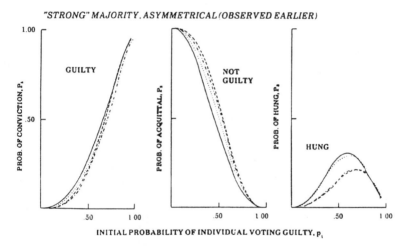

"STRONG" MAJORITY. ASYMMETRICAL (OBSERVED EARLIER)

Figure 13.1. Simulations showing the probability of an outcome (conviction, acquittal, and hung) as a function of the probability that an individual votes for guilty, presented for the idealized two-thirds majority decision rule (top panels) and for the estimated decision rule.
Reprinted from Davis et al. (1989), with permission of the American Psychological Association.

observed in earlier research ("estimated," in the sense that the relative frequencies tallied were taken as parameter values), and which includes the leniency bias.[2] These simulations clearly showed that the verdicts of six-person juries, under the stated conditions, *cannot* differ much, as a function of local majority effects. In other words, the effects of polling sequence that were pronounced at the *individual level* were not efficacious at the *group level*—demonstrating once more that simple individual member-to-group extrapolations can be perilous. However, Figure 13.1 does show some of the effects of early-late polling, especially pronounced in the panels in the third column that display graphs of P_H, the probability of a hung jury outcome as a function of the probability, p_G, of an individual preferring guilty.[3] In other words, Figure 13.1 shows that the absence of an observed difference in jury *verdicts* due to whether a guilty or not guilty triplet votes first, is thus not surprising, even though individual juror preferences had been rather strongly influenced.

The local majority effect was subsequently replicated in a second study (Davis, Kameda, Parks, Stasson, & Zimmerman, 1989), using the same mock trial, method, and member-by-member polling procedure, but additional distinguishable distributions of member guilt preferences were included, namely, $(r_G, r_{NG}) = (4, 2)$. Again, experimental results showed that votes in these straw polls were not independent; members critically positioned were significantly influenced by preceding opinions, for the three sequences investigated in the two studies: (3, 3)—G, G, G, N, N, N and N, N, N, G, G, G—and (4, 2)—G, G, G, G, N, N; but not for N, N, G, G, G, G. Again, computer simulations using the SDS model, parameter estimates from the two studies reported above, and assuming effects from only the four sequences as described showed that the *group-level* probability of conviction was not much influenced by the fairly strong sequence effects observed at the *individual level*. (The simulation, shown in Figure 13.2, did not include poll timing, as was discussed above and shown in Figure 13.1.)

And again, one is tempted to take comfort that procedurally induced biases at the individual level are apparently *not* manifest at the group level, and plausible extrapolations from this empirical result suggest that notion holds across the entire range of the probability of a guilty vote, $0.00 < p_G < 1.00$. Conventional wisdom has generally implied that group discussion generates prudence through error-catching, opinion-balancing, and so on, despite the accumulated contrary evidence from decades of empirical research (see the discussion by Davis, 1992). Now, at long last, we may have some evidence of group-mediated bias

2/3 MAJORITY. OTHERWISE HUNG (IDEALIZED)

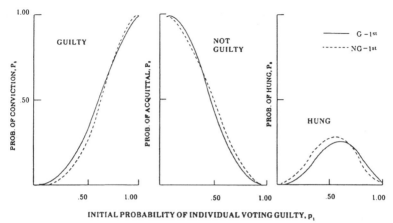

INITIAL PROBABILITY OF INDIVIDUAL VOTING GUILTY, p₁

"STRONG" MAJORITY, ASYMMETRICAL (OBSERVED EARLIER)

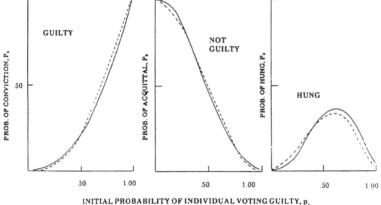

INITIAL PROBABILITY OF INDIVIDUAL VOTING GUILTY, p₁

Figure 13.2. Simulations showing the probability of an outcome (conviction, acquittal, and hung) as a function of the probability that an individual votes for guilty, presented for the idealized two-thirds majority decision rule (top panels) and for the estimated decision rule.
Reprinted from Davis et al. (1989), with permission of the American Psychological Association.

reduction. Yet such a conclusion may be premature. First, observe that only four sequences (those studied empirically in Davis et al., 1988, 1989) were investigated, out of the $2^6 = 64$ sequences of voters that are possible. In addition, there are other group sizes, other parameter values (individual position change rates), and other decision rules (or other social decision schemes) yet to be investigated. It is this complex of issues that will be considered later.

SUMMARY

By this point it is clear that some rather subtle changes in a group's internal distribution of opinion can be induced not only by such procedures as the structure of the agenda items to be decided, but merely by the timing and sequence structure of a straw poll. Although a straw poll is generally regarded as a "good thing" because it facilitates communication, it would seem now that consensus outcomes in practice may be biased either by the strategically motivated or by accident—PM side effects that are not generally regarded as desirable. On the other hand, the empirical effects due to the sequence structure of polls described above were fairly weak at the group level. Indeed, computer simulations using social decision scheme theory seem to confirm that only small effects due to vote sequence are likely to show up in the group decision, although timing emerges as a robust group-level influence (the further consequences of which we do not pursue here). Recall, however, that only a very limited number of initial opinion distributions and thus few actual sequences were considered—even in the computer simulations. The obvious next step is to pursue these questions under a wider variety of conditions (sequences not studied heretofore) that can and do actually arise in groups seeking consensus. Unfortunately, the huge number of subjects that would be required to establish a systematic empirical record is prohibitive. Empirical study is obviously a strategy to be exploited only for critical demonstrations and parameter estimates. Consequently, we pursued additional simulations, and these results will be discussed below.

Simulation 1: Polling Sequence Effects

Continuing with the criminal jury scenario, imagine r jurors seated about a table, each of whom has a verdict preference, G(uilty) or N(ot Guilty). There are r possible starting points for a poll, and the polling may proceed either to the left or right of that person, yielding $2r$

sequences from which pollster or fate may choose (hereafter just "poll-ster"). Ignore for now the possibility that some positions might them-selves be "natural locations" for beginning due to environmental fea-tures.[4]

As indicated in the Appendix, there are m possible distinguishable distributions of preferences when there are n mutually exclusive and exhaustive decision alternatives and r indistinguishable group mem-bers. These m arrays can be calculated from

$$m = \binom{n+r-1}{r} = \frac{(n+r-1)!}{r!(n-1)!}. \tag{13.1}$$

In the current application, $n = 2$, and the number of possible *sequences* for *each* such distinguishable distribution is thus given by the familiar binomial coefficient,

$$\binom{r}{r_1, r_2} = \frac{r!}{r_1! r_2!}, \tag{13.2}$$

where $r_1 = r_G$ = the number of guilty sayers, and $r_2 = r_{NG}$ = the number of not guilty sayers in a group of $r = r_1 + r_2$ people. If votes are independent events, and we know (or can accurately estimate) the probability of the array (r_1, r_2) by the familiar binomial (multinomial if $n > 2$) expression,

$$\binom{r}{r_1, r_2} p_1^{r_1} p_2^{r_2}, \tag{13.3}$$

then we can proceed as outlined in the Appendix to calculate the probability of each array occurring. Finally, the overall distribution, using a known (or estimated) social decision scheme matrix, may be computed as described in the Appendix. Unfortunately, as we have just demonstrated, sequential votes are *not* independent events in the decision environment that includes sequential polling. Thus, *each* of the 2^r possible sequences (the sum of all m binomial coefficients) must be inspected for those patterns that have significance for influencing some voters in the chain of events. In other words, for a six-person group, it is necessary to calculate the probability of each of the

$$2^6 = \sum_{\forall(r_1, r_2)} \binom{6}{r_1, r_2} = 64 \tag{13.4}$$

possible sequences. Fortunately, modern computing power makes it easy to calculate these probabilities for the $2^4 + 2^5 + \cdots + 2^{12} = 8{,}196$ relevant sequences necessary to simulate polling effects over even a few group sizes, namely, $r = 4, 5, \ldots, 12$.

To simulate the effects of polling, we supposed that under certain conditions the known or estimated individual probability of a guilty vote, p_G, would vary in the direction of the local majority. Specifically, three or more consistent votes in uninterrupted sequence—G, G, G or N, N, N—would add probability weight Δ_G, or subtract probability weight Δ_{NG}, respectively, from p_G. Thus the probability of each vote in each sequence, p_i, was determined according to the following algorithm:

Under the condition that,

the preceding three votes were not consistent and,
  the vote was G, $p_i = p_G$,
  or the vote was N, $p_i = p_{NG}$; or
the preceding three votes were all G and,
  the vote was G, $p_i = p_G + \Delta_G$,
  or the vote was N, $p_i = p_{NG} - \Delta_G$; or
the preceding three votes were all N and,
  the vote was G, $p_i = p_G - \Delta_{NG}$;
  or the vote was N, $p_i = p_{NG} + \Delta_{NG}$.

Given p_i, the probability of the sequence, p_{seq}, was calculated as

$$p_{seq} = \prod_{i=1}^{r} p_i \ .$$

Next, it was necessary to determine to which of the distinguishable distributions, (r_1, r_2), each of the 2^r sequences applied. Thus, if $r = 11$, the sequence, G, N, G, N, N, N, N, N, G, N, N, belongs in the distinguishable distribution, (3, 8), for which there are 165 sequences in all. Finally, the probability of each distinguishable distribution could be computed by summing the probabilities of each sequence included. From this point, the application of the social decision scheme model is straightforward and P_G, the probability of conviction (group decision) as a function of p_G, Δ_G and Δ_{NG} can be determined as before (see Appendix).

We calculated these probabilities under various levels of several factors:

1. Group size: $r = 4, \ldots, 12$;
2. Decision rule: Majority, simple majority, and rules induced from data and extrapolated to various group sizes (see Vollrath & Davis, 1980; and Note 2);
3. Probability of individual guilty preference, $p_G = .00, .05, \ldots, 1.00$;
4. Effect of polling on p_G, with increments, $\Delta_G = .00, .05, \ldots, 1.00$;
5. Effect of polling on p_{NG}, with increments, $\Delta_{NG} = .00, .05, \ldots, 1.00$.

In familiar analysis of variance terms, the above plan would constitute a 9 * 3 * 20 * 20 * 20 factorial design, with 216,000 *conditions* or cells.

GROUP SIZE

The three verdict distributions (one each for guilty, not guilty, and hung) were calculated as a function of p_G, under three different social decision schemes (see Note 2): (a) Simple majority, if it exists, otherwise hung; (b) the scheme estimated from earlier data, generalized to larger groups as well; and (c) a two-thirds majority, hung otherwise. The current simulation extended previous simulation results regarding jury size (Vollrath & Davis, 1980). Figure 13.3 presents the probability of guilty verdicts, P_G, for groups of size 9, 10, 11, and 12 plotted against the probability of an individual guilty preference. (Remember, we have not yet introduced a polling sequence factor, so there is of course no polling effect displayed in Figure 13.3.) Figure 13.3 shows the very substantial effect of group size on a guilty verdict, a much-discussed

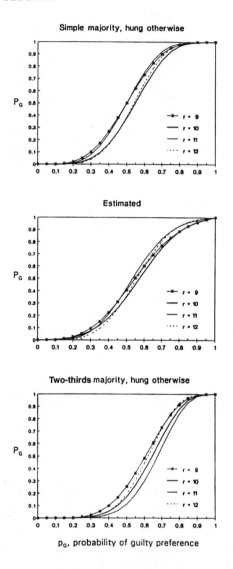

Figure 13.3. Plots of simulations of the probability of a guilty verdict as a function of the probability that an individual prefers guilty, presented for four group sizes (9-12) within each subgraph. The top subgraph uses the idealized simple majority decision rule, the middle subgraph uses the estimated decision rule, and the bottom subgraph uses the idealized two-thirds majority decision rule.

phenomenon. Unlike previous simulations, however, several larger group sizes (r = 9, 10, 11, and 12) were included here. Moreover, Figure 13.3 shows how group size interacts with the decision scheme that maps individual preference into a group decision. It is worth emphasizing again (see Note 3) that these and subsequent figures are not plots of data, but represent theoretical outcomes or logical consequences of assumptions about states of (social) nature. Hence differences between or among curves are "real," though often small in magnitude, especially because we have chosen plotting dimensions for efficiency and economy of presentation.

Finally, Figure 13.3 shows clearly the variation in group decision making that is dependent on whether the group size is simply odd or even, for the idealized majority, hung otherwise decision rule, and for the estimated decision rule (at middle levels of p_G). As we would expect, an even group size allows the possibility of factions of equal size, and thus there is a correspondingly greater proportion of hung jury outcomes. In Figure 13.3 this is represented by the generally larger conviction probability, P_G, for odd-sized groups (although this effect could have been shown in plots for hung verdicts as well).

In this simulation then, we have demonstrated that even-sized groups have more hung verdicts, and thus fewer decisions in general. Note that this effect is dependent on the decision rule *subscheme*—the secondary rule that is used to determine group outcome when the primary rule cannot be satisfied. Consider the social decision scheme estimated from the actual results of experiments on mock juries (see Note 2). It is clear from examination of the estimated decision rule that mock juries in this case would not incline to hung verdicts—and thus is apparently consistent with actual juries (Kalven & Zeisel, 1966). The even-odd effect decreases for the estimated decision rule, because mock juries do not often fail to decide (hang).

Within the confines of this relatively large effect for even- and odd-sized groups is the effect of small versus large group size. In general, a larger group size enhances any response tendency present in the population from which the group is sampled. That is, under the majority social decision schemes described earlier, any perturbations in the individual *distribution* will be *exaggerated* in the *distribution* of groups sampled from such a population, and this effect is exacerbated by group size increases. In other words, when $p_G > p_{NG}$, groups (operating on a majority rule) result in $P_G \gg P_{NG}$, and a guilty verdict is even more strongly preferred by larger juries. Thus consensus transforms individual opinions into relatively more consistent verdicts as group size increases.

In summary, any trends already present in the population of individual preferences (i.e., perturbations in the individual distribution) will be enhanced or exaggerated as group size increases for groups operating under majority rule. (Plurality rules, including majorities, have the general effect of exaggerating those perturbations evident in the individuals, producing a group distribution that is an exaggeration of the individual distribution; see Davis, 1982; Stasser et al., 1989.) Interestingly, such aggregation effects sometimes lead researchers to conclude that group members (relative to isolated individuals) are subject to various personal changes during interaction, and it is these changed individual members who in turn produce changes in group-level actions. Research on the "risky shift" may well have suffered from such misperceptions (see Davis, 1992). It is clear that the group-individual differences in decisions evident in the simulation results here could not be due to some kind of interaction influence on individual members; no such influences were included in the simulation. Social aggregation effects thus often represent a more parsimonious explanation for individual-group differences than conceptions that imply personal change in members. (Of course, individual members may sometimes change preferences as well, rather than just acquiesce in the consensus position, but it is almost always difficult in practice to determine whether member change is cause or effect of the group level action.)

The foregoing examples demonstrate how ostensibly fair, reasonable, and socially acceptable techniques for integrating group members' opinions can have unanticipated, and often unrecognized, consequences. Apparently simple communication and aggregation procedures can have complex effects on group outcomes.[5]

POLLING EFFECTS

Group size and decision rule, whether implicit or explicit, are basic structural features of group problem solving and decision making. The ways in which each influences the aggregation of member information and opinion have been demonstrated in various decision environments (e.g., Davis, 1982, 1992). These influences tend to be quite subtle because they are ostensibly part of the background and not conspicuously relevant to the exchange of information that is the chief basis for group action. But what is perhaps even more treacherous is the unintended, latent influence of a procedure designed in fact to *enhance* the open exchange of information, such as the straw poll discussed earlier. Figure 13.4 presents results of a computer simulation designed to assess how group size and decision rule interact with straw polling to affect consensus decisions.

Because no irregularities were observed over the closed interval 0.00 $\leq \Delta_G, \Delta_{NG} \leq 1.00$, only the values $\Delta_G, \Delta_{NG} = .25, .50, .75$, were plotted for simplicity. (The increments Δ_G and Δ_{NG} have the same meaning here as in earlier discussions.) Although not particularly obvious from Figure 13.4, increasing Δ_G uniformly increases P_G. Interestingly, the panels of Figure 13.4 reveal that the effect of increasing Δ_G is to *mitigate* the effect of group size (the plots for different group sizes come together). It may be that the effect of Δ_G is strong enough to wash out differences due to group sizes, although in general, Δ_G influences smaller-sized groups more than it does larger-sized groups. Also, the mitigation of the group size effect occurs to a greater extent for the two-thirds majority rule, and to a lesser extent for the simple majority rule. At this point, this is simply an observation. No underlying explanation is obvious at this time.

In Figure 13.5, jury conviction rates, P_G, for groups of 12, for all levels of Δ_G are plotted in the same subgraphs. Each subgraph shows a different decision rule. Inspection of Figure 13.5 shows that the effect of Δ_G is strongest for the two-thirds majority rule and weakest for the simple majority rule. Based on these results, we conclude that the more stringent the majority rule required for consensus, the greater the effect of polling of the sort studied here, a consequence that is not intuitively obvious.

As previously noted, petit juries display a decision bias (largely attributable to philosophical tenets associated with the English Common Law) that has been called the "leniency bias." The leniency bias is apparent in the asymmetry of the estimated decision rule; that is, consensus criteria for guilty verdicts are more demanding than for not guilty verdicts (see Note 2). Moreover, leniency was identified as a normative bias in experimental studies of polling effects (discussed

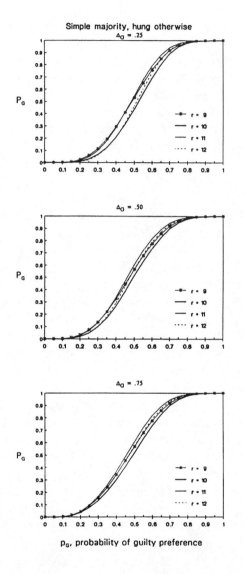

Figure 13.4a. Each of the three panels of Figure 13.4 (13.4a presents the simple majority rule, 13.4b presents the estimated rule, and 13.4c presents the two-thirds majority rule) plots the simulation of the probability of guilty verdict as a function of the probability that an individual prefers guilty, for four group sizes (9-12) within each subgraph. The topmost subgraph always shows the simulation of $\Delta_G = .25$; $\Delta_G = .75$ in the bottom-most subgraph, and $\Delta_G = .50$ in the middle subgraph.

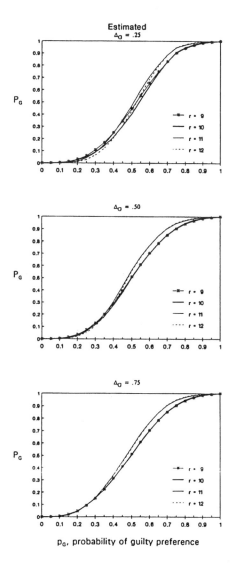

Figure 13.4b.

earlier, Davis et al., 1988; Davis et al., 1989), and was modeled in the simulations reported here by *asymmetric increments*—that is, $\Delta_G < \Delta_{NG}$, when appropriate.

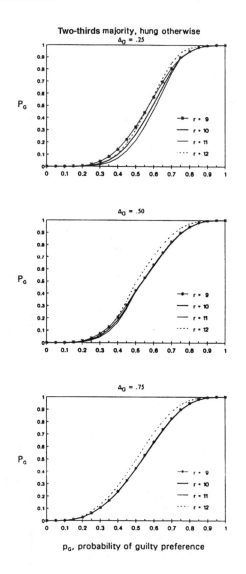

Figure 13.4c.

Consider Figure 13.6, where results are displayed for all three possible group outcomes (guilty, not guilty, and hung) for groups of 12, for increasing Δ_{NG}, and for the simple majority, hung otherwise (panel A);

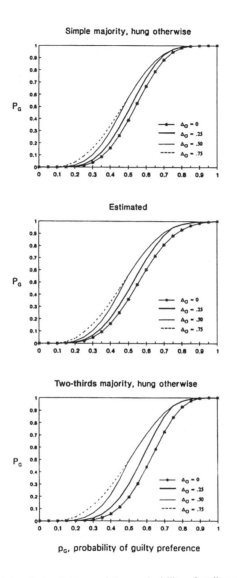

Figure 13.5. Plots of simulations of the probability of guilty verdict in a group of 12 as a function of the probability that an individual prefers guilty, presented for four levels of polling effect (Δ_G = .00, .25, .50, .75) within each subgraph. The top subgraph simulates the idealized simple majority decision rule, the middle subgraph simulates the estimated decision rule, and the bottom subgraph simulates the idealized two-thirds majority decision rule.

estimated (panel B); and two-thirds majority, hung otherwise (panel C) decision rules. Figure 13.6 reveals the effects of the normative bias at work, especially as it interacts with decision rule. Of course, as the leniency bias increases (Δ_{NG} becomes larger relative to Δ_G), not guilty verdicts are more probable. But, consider especially the panels for two-thirds majority, hung otherwise. In this case, although acquittal is more probable, conviction rates barely vary. It is evident from Figure 13.6c that under these conditions, normative bias reduces instances wherein the group is unable to decide—the not guilty verdict increase has been at the expense of the hung outcome. Because, in practice, a hung verdict allows the defendant to go free (at least for the moment) just as does acquittal, the polling procedure modeled with a normative bias has no substantive effect; that is, the same number of people would be convicted.

The above generalization, however, is dependent on the *subscheme* of the decision rule. Recall that the decision processes of mock juries (as captured by the estimated decision scheme) rarely result in hung verdicts. In this case, there are fewer hung verdicts available to be changed; there is a closer relationship between conviction and acquittal. Thus increasing the increment Δ_{NG} not only increases the probability of a not guilty verdict, but also decreases the probability of a guilty verdict. Obviously, the overall verdict consequences of the leniency bias in polling juries depends on the decision rule governing consensus.

Parenthetically, we might reemphasize that we have used three social decision schemes or group decision rules throughout our discussion to provide some appreciation of the role different consensus criteria play in the final outcome. Two of these are majorities, and correspond to widely accepted principles from conventional wisdom. The third, a majority of sorts, is highly irregular and asymmetrical; taken from actual six-person mock jury decisions observed earlier in experimental studies, it has been generalized to different group sizes. Obviously, there are many different social decision schemes that are associated with various kinds of groups and decision environments. We have not begun to exhaust the possibilities here.

We might also observe at this point that our evaluation of the various procedural effects is clearly a function of the decision task and context. Not only are different environments likely to give rise to different social decision schemes than those studied here, but the kind of normative

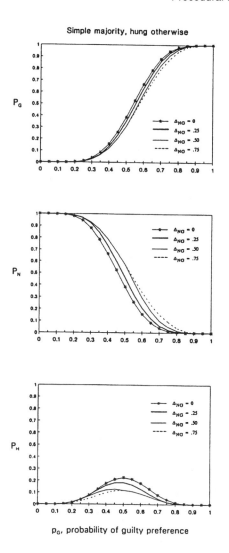

Figure 13.6a. Each of the three panels of Figure 13.6 (13.6a presents the simple majority rule; 13.6b the estimated rule; and 13.6c the two-thirds majority rule) plots the simulation of the probability of three different types of verdicts in a group of 12 as a function of the probability that an individual prefers guilty. Four levels of the effect of a not guilty local majority in a sequential poll (Δ_{NG} = .00, .25, .50, .75) are presented within each subgraph. The topmost subgraph always shows the probability of conviction; the probability of acquittal is in the middle subgraph; and the probability of a hung outcome is presented in the bottom subgraph.

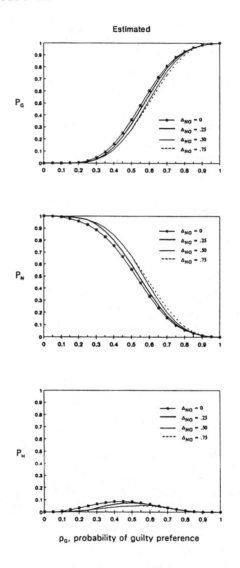

Figure 13.6b.

influences may be different as well. Indeed, there are numerous plausible scenarios. For example, yes/no hiring decisions confronting a personnel committee that is discussing professional credentials may also involve gender, race, and ethnicity of candidates in subtle ways. The

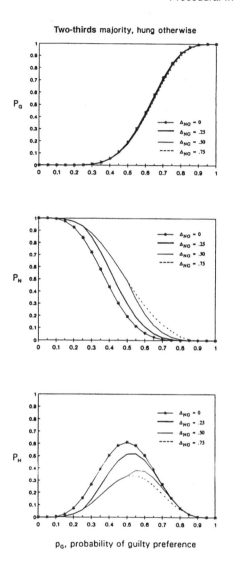

Figure 13.6c.

effects of straw polling in this case may be complicated not only by the sequence effects noted previously or by painfully familiar conventional prejudices, but by newer normative biases associated with affirmative action policies, acting after the fashion of the now familiar leniency bias. Whatever the bias, it is the subtlety and veiled character of its action that makes it so difficult to detect and characterize. Simulations, however sophisticated and detailed, require guiding parameter estimates from empirical research, and this in turn presupposes a sufficiently explicit theory.

Simulation 2: The "Sly Chair"

The discussion until now has generally explored some potential effects of procedural influence associated with sequential polling of members. The implicit emphasis has largely been on the hazards of a subtle and typically unrecognized source of influence, inflicted by happenstance rather than design. We now consider the possibility of sophisticated manipulation of procedural mechanisms by the crafty. Imagine a pollster with extensive knowledge of member opinions who wishes to influence the group outcome in a particular way. We will call a committee chairperson who possesses such sinister motives a "sly chair." The "sly chair simulation" to be reported is particularly relevant to a portion of the experimental procedure described earlier (Davis et al., 1988; Davis et al., 1989). Recall that in those studies, experimental conditions were manipulated so that "Asch-sufficient" factions of guilty- or not guilty-sayers communicated their preferences first in the polling sequence. We now assume that the sly chair "controls" three votes. That is, the sly chair in some fashion can rely with certainty on two allies among the members of the committee, jury, panel, etc.

Assume further that the sly chair has "locating power"; that is, through some artifice or other manipulation (e.g., courteous invitations to a seat on arrival), the sly chair can place allies in selected positions around a table. Estimates from Davis et al. (1988; Davis et al., 1989) were used to model opinion change effects of these arrangements on the fourth voting member and the outcome of deliberation of a six-person group. Because the presence alone of the allies influences the group's decision, an appropriate comparison for the sly chair with locating power simulation is a condition wherein the allies are distributed in all possible ways among the remaining $r - 3$ group members. Thus there are different numbers of sequences for different levels of locating power.

When the chair can place allies at the very beginning of the sequence, there are 2^{r-3} possible sequences. There are

$$\binom{r}{3, r-3} 2^{r-3}$$

possible sequences, when the chair does not have this power.

The calculation of p_{seq} proceeds in the same fashion as before, except the probability of the sly chair and allies selecting a given alternative (in the simulation, guilty preference) was set to unity, regardless of the surrounding pattern. As before, once all p_{seq} are determined, the sequences are grouped into the appropriate distinguishable distribution array and the probability, π_i of each such array is the sum of the p_{seq}. Then the social decision scheme is applied as described in the Appendix.

Again, using an experimental design framework, the sly chair simulation encompassed the levels of the following factors:

1. Group size: $r = 9, 12$;
2. Decision rule: as before, two-thirds majority, simple majority, and estimated rules induced from data and extrapolated to various group sizes;
3. Probability of individual guilty preference, $p_G = .00, .05, .10, . . ., 1.00$;
4. Effect of polling on p_G, with increments this time, $\Delta_G = .00, .25, . . ., 1.00$;
5. Effect of polling on p_{NG}, with increments this time, $\Delta_{NG} = .00, .25, . . ., 1.00$;
6. Locating power (the sly chair's ability to place allies at the beginning of a sequential poll): Level 1, the chair has locating power; level 2, the chair has no locating power, and the three allies are distributed at random (i.e., all possible distributions are equally probable).

RESULTS OF THE SLY CHAIR SIMULATION

The sly chair's preference was arbitrarily set to "guilty," largely for dramatic effect, because the particular preference is irrelevant. The effect of setting $p_G = 1.00$ for three positions in the sequential poll is regular and does not interact with any of the other factors. This procedure, of course, increases considerably the probability of a guilty verdict. All previously outlined effects are present in the current simulation, although they are enhanced or diminished according to conditions.

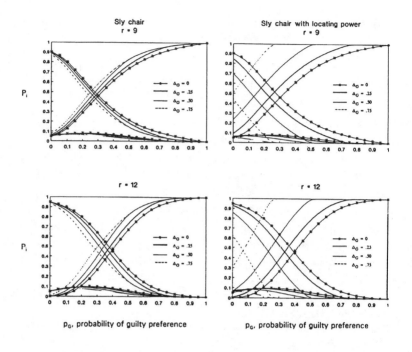

Figure 13.7. Plots of all three verdict outcomes (conviction, acquittal, and hung) for four levels of effect of a guilty-inclined local majority in a sequential poll (Δ_G = .00, .25, .50, .75). The leftmost subgraphs present the simple "sly chair" simulation (see text) and the rightmost subgraphs present the "sly chair with locating power" simulation (see text). The top row of subgraphs are for 9-person groups, and 12-person groups are presented in the bottom row.

Particularly interesting were the effects of positioning the sly chair's alliance at the beginning of the sequence, or at random (in all possible) positions in the sequence. Figure 13.7 shows the effect of increasing Δ_G (namely, Δ_G = .00, .25, .50, .75) for the two group sizes (r = 9, 12), for the estimated social decision scheme. (Each subgraph presents the probability of guilty, not guilty, and hung verdicts, unlike earlier graphs that separated the three outcomes. Note too that *guilty* and *convict*, and *acquit* and *not guilty* are often used interchangeably herein.) In the leftmost half of the figure are the subgraphs for the sly chair without the ability to order the sequence of voters (i.e., place the alliance at the beginning of a polling sequence). In the second column are the subgraphs for the simulation results wherein the sly chair arranges for the alliance to vote first.

The most striking aspect of Figure 13.7 is the substantial enhancement of the polling effect when the sly chair has some authority to manipulate, even slightly, the polling sequence. This simulation shows even more dramatically than those discussed earlier how group procedure can interact with member opinion and motivation to create large distortions in the mapping of member preference into group decision. (Such an effect does not interact with the decision rules studied here.)

An interesting question concerns the effect of group size in this simulation. Recall that in the previous simulation, the effect of increasing group size depended on the social decision scheme. In general, increases in group size for a stringent rule like two-thirds majority served to decrease slightly the probability of a guilty verdict. For the less stringent simple majority rule, however, increasing group size magnified the probability of a guilty verdict. When three votes are fixed, as they are in the present simulation, increasing group size uniformly *decreases* the probability of a guilty verdict. This can be seen in Figure 13.7 for the estimated decision rule, by comparing upper and lower panels. (Note that P_G, P_{NG}, and P_H are plotted on the same graph, unlike earlier practice, and thus P_i is the label on the ordinate.)

There are two reasons for this group size effect. First, an increase in group size will minimize proportionally the three preset votes, making additional guilty votes necessary for consensus. Also, an increase in group size increases the probability of not guilty local majorities (although this effect is to some extent offset by a similar increase for guilty local majorities). It should be noted that the effect of group size only *mitigates* the effect of the sly chair's alliance—this latter effect easily overwhelms the former. However, increasing group size constitutes a rational, though difficult-to-execute, counterstrategy for dissenters.

In Figure 13.8, we plot the same panels for the estimated decision rule for the two group sizes. This time, however, we show the effect in each panel of increasing the increment to the not guilty vote (Δ_{NG} = .00, .25, .50, .75); Δ_G in Figure 13.8 is arbitrarily set at .25. Figure 13.8 shows the situation wherein the chair prefers a counter-normative option, in the sense that not guilty local majorities enhance the tendency to vote not guilty, but guilty local majorities have a comparatively smaller effect. Figure 13.8 clearly shows the chair's preferred option: To mitigate the

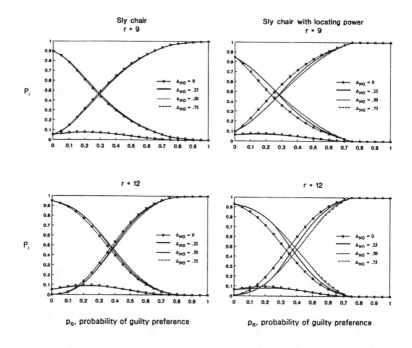

Figure 13.8. Plots of conviction, acquittal, and hung verdict outcomes for four levels of a not guilty-inclined local majority in a sequential poll, where $\Delta_{NG} =$ .00, .25, .50, .75. The leftmost subgraphs present the simple "sly chair" simulation (see text) and the rightmost subgraphs, the "sly chair with locating power" simulation (see text). The top row of subgraphs present the case of 9-person groups, and 12-person groups are presented in the bottom row.

effect of the not guilty local majority, the three votes controlled by the chair should be scattered in the polling sequence. This can be seen by examining the curves showing the probability of a not guilty preference in each panel of both columns of Figure 13.8. Note that as Δ_{NG} increases, the resultant increase in probability of a not guilty verdict is substantial when the chair arrays the three guilty votes at the beginning of the sequence (column 1). However, the same effect is severely hampered when the three votes are scattered in all possible spots in the sequence (column 2), a pattern that serves to "break up" Asch-sufficient coalitions of not guilty-sayers. The latter implies a counterstrategy to be pursued, when possible, against the strategic efforts of a sly chair to influence outcome by such manipulations of voting procedure. Of course, such a process is reminiscent of traffic police (radar) speed detectors, countered by motorists' radar detector detectors, answered by the recent development of radar detector detector detectors; and so on. . . .

Discussion

Procedural mechanisms, ostensibly employed to address some feature of group interaction/action management, are not always the benevolent agents generally assumed. Whether regarded as an undesirable side effect or as a necessary cost of reaching consensus, the effects associated with particular PMs deserve separate study and evaluation. Unfortunately, the subtlety with which procedural effects are manifest has apparently tended to shield them from research attention. Only now is an empirical research literature beginning to accumulate. Another problem is that PM influence on group decision making has not yet been conceptually related to cognitive processes in the individual group member, at least not to any appreciable extent. We have tended in this chapter to focus on the interpersonal aggregation-consensus processes, and the consequences for the group-level outcome. Obviously, both member reactions to interpersonal events, and consensus processes whereby member preferences are combined, concatenated or otherwise aggregated into the group action, underlie group decision making. Understanding the joint action of these two classes of factors is essential for a comprehensive theoretical account of group decision making.

One reason that we have organized this chapter around the criminal jury scenario is to illustrate vividly the importance of exposing verdict biases, intentional or accidental, in terms likely to be widely appreciated. Issues associated with just and fair criminal jury decisions invariably stimulate interest, among professionals and laity alike. The simulation results, of course, do not depend strictly on a jury format, but are in principle applicable to a wide range of decision-making groups. Our major point is that the seemingly innocuous poll as a member-by-member vote can, depending on the specific procedure, influence the overall outcome—and not in necessarily obvious ways. The original empirical research showed that timing as well as sequence influenced at least some members to change their opinion. The simulations reported here extended those results, focusing in particular on sequence. Not only did they show that the modest group-level effects observed earlier were probably due to the small group size, together with so few of the many possible within-group arrays of opinion, used in the initial experiments but illustrated as well that those early results were merely the "tip of the iceberg."

We also showed in passing that computer simulations could be a powerful tool for making inferences about consensus decisions. We extrapolated empirical findings to larger groups and over ranges of parameter values that we could not reasonably expect to investigate empirically. The cost in subjects, time, and other resources make such projects completely unrealistic in practice. However, the potential value of obtaining some information on PMs in important decision environments (such as petit jury decision making) motivate the use of such tools as computer simulation—not only to target the most critical areas for empirical investigation, but potentially to assist in policy making as well.

Our various conclusions, of course, must be constrained by a few words of caution. For example, straw polls are not, in principle, binding. The estimates of individual juror change rates, taken from Davis et al. (1988; Davis et al., 1989), may take different values, if the poll (as sometimes happens) were to be represented as decisive; that is, the group decision would be determined by the outcome of the poll. Also, juries (even mock juries) are typically taken seriously by their members (even college student subjects), but less solemn task environments may foster higher opinion change rates. Clearly, these and many other task/context issues that might interact with PMs, remain to be investigated—especially in ways that would offer some guidance for theory revision and the conduct of relevant simulations.

Finally, it is perhaps worth noting that one of the most promising task/context issues for further study is group decision making about *quantities*. The research referent we have addressed here is the group that confronts a polychotomy, most usually a dichotomy, and a consensus choice is required. Continuing the petit jury metaphor, imagine a *civil* jury that awards damages. Upon retiring for deliberation, a civil juror can have an award preference that falls anywhere along a continuum, in contrast to the member of a criminal jury who must prefer guilty beyond a reasonable doubt, otherwise not guilty. In the continuous case, faction development, compromise, and even the notion of majority take a different form and may be contrasted with their counterparts in the criminal jury. For example, how close (magnitude differences) must members of a majority-size faction be to each other before the faction members (and perhaps others) regard that subgroup as a (majority) faction? Such questions are among many yet to be addressed.

Recent studies (Davis et al., 1993) of mock jury decisions that are quantities (civil damage awards) have reported biases from sequential polls that are similar to those discussed at length in this chapter for the discrete (convict/acquit/hang) decision outcomes of criminal juries. However, theory addressing quantitative decisions that would support the simulations necessary for orderly extrapolations, like those considered here, is only now under development.

Notes

1. The classic studies by Asch (1956) first demonstrated that (at least) three consistent public judgments preceding a naive subject tended to bias the next (focal subject's) response in the advocated direction. Of course, confederates and subject did not interact, and were in no sense working to reach a collective consensus. Relevant literature reviews and discussions by Kiesler and Kiesler (1969) and Allen (1965, 1975) recount results of numerous variations on Asch's basic paradigm, and document that, despite some exceptions, little influence can generally be expected with less than a 3:1 pattern; similarly, little additional increment can be expected with larger majorities. Yet despite the voluminous literature, largely created some years ago, little research has addressed similar influence issues within *interacting* groups, especially those in which inter-faction dynamics, subgroup size distribution, or other structural features are at issue (see Tindale, Davis, Vollrath, Nagao, & Hinsz [1990] for an exception and a discussion of related social influence theories in such contexts).

2. The conventional phrase *majority rules* implies certainty in that, given a majority, it dominates. Yet as discussed earlier, majorities do not always "win." Under given conditions, a majority of some order may prevail only with some probability, and a majority favoring one alternative (e.g., not guilty) may consistently be more powerful than one favoring another (e.g., guilty). Thus these simulations used two different kinds of majority social decision scheme, one *idealized*, perfect and symmetrical, and a second that had been empirically *estimated* from earlier research data (Nagao & Davis, 1980), imperfect and asymmetrical. (A 2/3 idealized majority social decision scheme was also used in some simulations; but for the six-person case, a simple and 2/3 majority are the same.) Observe also that the social decision scheme matrix is comprehensive in that it provides for the case where the primary scheme (e.g., simple majority) does not exist. Thus a majority (guilty or not guilty) prevails with probability near 1.00, otherwise (e.g., a [3, 3] division), the outcome is hung, with probability near 1.00. The social decision scheme matrices in Figure 13.1 are respectively a simple majority (idealized) and an asymmetrical scheme observed (i.e., "estimated") earlier.

$$
\begin{array}{c}
 \\
(6,0) \\
(5,0) \\
(4,2) \\
(3,3) \\
(2,4) \\
(1,5) \\
(0,6)
\end{array}
\begin{array}{ccc}
G & NG & H \\
\left[\begin{array}{ccc}
1.00 & 0.00 & 0.00 \\
1.00 & 0.00 & 0.00 \\
1.00 & 0.00 & 0.00 \\
0.00 & 0.00 & 1.00 \\
0.00 & 1.00 & 0.00 \\
0.00 & 1.00 & 0.00 \\
0.00 & 1.00 & 0.00
\end{array}\right]
\end{array}
\quad
\begin{array}{c}
 \\
(6,0) \\
(5,0) \\
(4,2) \\
(3,3) \\
(2,4) \\
(1,5) \\
(0,6)
\end{array}
\begin{array}{ccc}
G & NG & H \\
\left[\begin{array}{ccc}
1.00 & 0.00 & 0.00 \\
0.93 & 0.07 & 0.00 \\
0.84 & 0.16 & 0.00 \\
0.16 & 0.68 & 0.16 \\
0.06 & 0.94 & 0.00 \\
0.00 & 1.00 & 0.00 \\
0.00 & 1.00 & 0.00
\end{array}\right]
\end{array}
$$

3. It is important to emphasize that the graphs of Figure 13.1, and graphs throughout the remainder of the chapter are *not representations of data*, although empirical observations may have guided the selection of numerical values for theoretical parameters. The graphs *represent logical consequences*, given the theory and parameter values. Thus all differences are "real," and even small numerical discrepancies are potentially of considerable importance—especially in view of the large number of cases that might in practice go through a system (in this instance the court system).

4. In passing, it is worth noting that even seemingly innocuous environmental features, such as table corners and ends, have been found to confer prominence (see Hawkins [1960] and Stasser, Kerr, & Bray [1982] for more comprehensive discussions). For this reason, small group researchers typically use rather featureless and symmetrical surrounds (e.g., Davis et al. [1988] and Davis et al. [1989] gathered data from subjects seated about hexagonal tables).

5. Other simulations (Davis, 1973; Ono, Tindale, Hulin, & Davis, 1988) have demonstrated an illusory level of consensus as a function not only of the social decision scheme used to achieve agreement, but the number of organizational levels along which the decision is transmitted, where groups decide at each level. This aggregation/levels effect was discovered independently in the study of hierarchically structured physical systems (Galam, 1991).

Appendix

The applications of this chapter require groups and individuals to make binary choices, that is, a selection among $n = 2$ response alternatives. However, the following brief description of the social decision scheme (SDS) model (Davis, 1973, 1982) takes the more general approach for the r-person group reaching a consensus choice on one of the $A_1, A_2, \ldots, A_n$ mutually exclusive and exhaustive alternatives defined by the task.

There are $m = C(n + r - 1; r) = (n + r - 1)!/[r!(n - 1)!]$ ways that r people can array themselves over n decision alternatives, if alternatives, but not people, are distinguishable. (If both people and alternatives are distinguishable, $m = n^r$, a larger number, but a case that is less common in empirical research.)

The faction structure (particular distinguishable distributions) is important not only because sheer numbers or subgroup size has been found to be a dominant force in determining decision in both formal and informal settings, but also because the weight of available information or number of "persuasive arguments" are necessarily confounded with the set of members that are their source. For example, a familiar decision rule that often governs a group is "majority rules," but a comprehensive model requires the specification of both the *order* of the majority (plurality) and the *sub-rule* that controls the consensus outcome when no majority exists. In practice, even though a group decision rule has been assigned, the final scheme that actually governs consensus may be different—a function of task and shared social or organizational norms. The empirical record shows that different schemes predominate in different decision environments, and in a generally orderly way depend upon task features.

Next, we need to know the probability of a distinguishable distribution, and given a particular distribution, what the probability is of the group choosing A_j, $j = 1, 2, \ldots, n$. The latter is controlled by the social decision scheme governing discussion and will be addressed below. The probability, π_i, of the ith distinguishable distribution, $(r_{i1}, r_{i2}, \ldots, r_{in})$, can sometimes be estimated directly, as when members' prediscussion positions are known. That is, in a suitably large sample of groups, π_i can be estimated directly by counting pre-discussion preferences. In other cases, members' prediscussion preferences may not be assessable, and the estimates, $\hat{\pi}_i$, $i = 1, 2, \ldots, m$, must be obtained indirectly. The probabilities, $\mathbf{p} = (p_1, p_2, \ldots, p_n)$, with which individuals prefer the decision alternatives, A_j, can be estimated from a suitable sample of individuals, and the estimates substituted in the multinomial term,

$$\pi_i = \begin{pmatrix} r \\ r_{i1}, r_{i2}, \ldots, r_{in} \end{pmatrix} p_1^{r_{i1}} p_2^{r_{i2}} \cdots p_n^{r_{in}} \qquad (13.5)$$

Whether $\pi = (\pi_1, \pi_2, \ldots, \pi_m)$ is directly or indirectly estimated (or theoretically defined—a rarity), our ultimate goal is to use this information together with a social decision scheme (a statement of how each faction structure resolves into a consensus) to predict the group decision distribution. That is, using information about individual preference probabilities, $\mathbf{p} = (p_1, p_2, \ldots, p_n)$, and/or the distinguishable distribution probabilities, $\pi = (\pi_1, \pi_2, \ldots, \pi_m)$, we seek to predict the group decision probabilities, $\mathbf{P} = (P_1, P_2, \ldots, P_{n'})$, and without loss of generality, let $n = n'$. Thus, we next define an $m \times n$ matrix, $\mathbf{D}$, of conditional probabilities, where $[d_{ij}]$ is the probability of a group with the ith distinguishable distribution choosing the jth decision alternative. The distribution, $\mathbf{P}$, is given by

$$\mathbf{P} = \pi \mathbf{D}$$

$$= (\pi_1, \pi_2, \cdots, \pi_n) \begin{bmatrix} d_{i1} & d_{12} & \cdots & d_{1n} \\ d_{21} & d_{22} & \cdots & d_{2n} \\ \vdots & & \cdots & \vdots \\ d_{m1} & d_{m2} & \cdots & d_{mn} \end{bmatrix} \qquad (13.6)$$

$$= (P_1, P_2, \cdots, P_n)$$

The importance of the SDS matrix is due to the mechanism it offers for encoding different theoretical notions of the consensus process for various special cases and applications that can be tested by contrasting point predictions with observed data, and in other cases for succinctly summarizing observed consensus decisions (see Kerr, Stasser, & Davis [1979] for a discussion of these "model testing" and "model fitting" strategies). Finally, the SDS model admits of useful simulations, especially within the context of organizational decision making or other environments where direct empirical observation is difficult, expensive, or even unethical (see Davis & Kerr, 1986).

Among the several extensions of the SDS model, we might mention briefly some special case models for addressing member opinion change and interfactional dynamics over time as particularly important developments (Davis et al., 1976; Kerr, 1982), especially because the preceding discussion may seem to imply a static input-output emphasis that is not appropriate for many group decision environments. One extension (Stasser & Davis, 1981) captures the dynamics of member position movements occasioned by social interaction processes, procedural mechanisms, and other influences. In brief, the vector π is operated on by a transition matrix, $\mathbf{S}$, the entries of which, $[s_{ij}]$, are conditional probabilities describing interfaction traffic. Thus, after T trials or occasions, $\pi \mathbf{S}^T \mathbf{D} = \mathbf{P}$; the model even provides for how the $[s_{ij}]$ themselves might *change* over time. Another special case has been proposed for the group decision that is not a single choice but a group *preference order* (Ono, 1986); and for accommodating individual differences (Kirchler & Davis, 1986), particular group compositions are hypothesized to act differently, depending on task structure.

References

Allen, V. L. (1965). Situational factors in conformity. In L. Berkowitz (Ed.), *Advances in experimental social psychology* (Vol. 2, pp. 133-176). New York: Academic Press.

Allen, V. L. (1975). Social support for nonconformity. In L. Berkowitz (Ed.), *Advances in experimental social psychology* (Vol. 8, pp. 2-46). New York: Academic Press.

Asch, S. E. (1956). Studies of independence and conformity: A minority of one against a unanimous majority. *Psychological Monographs, 70*(Whole No. 416).

Balinski, M. L., & Young, H. P. (1982). *Fair representation: Meeting the ideal of one man, one vote.* New Haven, CT: Yale University Press.

Black, D. (1958). *The theory of committees and elections.* New York: Cambridge University Press.

Brams, S. J. (1976). *Paradox in politics: An introduction to the non-obvious in political science.* New York: Free Press.

Davis, J. H. (1969). *Group performance.* Reading, MA: Addison-Wesley.

Davis, J. H. (1973). Group decision and social interaction: A theory of social decision schemes. *Psychological Review, 80,* 97-125.

Davis, J. H. (1980). Group decision and procedural justice. In M. Fishbein (Ed.), *Progress in social psychology* (Vol. 1, pp. 157-229). Hillsdale, NJ: Lawrence Erlbaum.

Davis, J. H. (1982). Social interaction as a combinatorial process in group decision. In H. Brandstatter, J. H. Davis, & G. Stocker-Kreichgauer (Eds.), *Group decision making* (pp. 27-58). London: Academic Press.

Davis, J. H. (1984). Order in the courtroom. In D. J. Muller, D. G. Blackman, & A. J. Chapman (Eds.), *Psychology and law* (pp. 251-266). London: John Wiley.

Davis, J. H. (1992). Some compelling intuitions about group consensus decisions, theoretical and empirical research, and interpersonal/internal aggregation phenomena: Selected examples, 1950-1990. *Organizational Behavior and Human Decision Processes, Special Issue: Group Decision Making, 52,* 3-38.

Davis, J. H., Kameda, T., Parks, C., Stasson, M., & Zimmerman, S. (1989). Some social mechanics of group decision making: The distribution of opinion, polling sequence, and implications for consensus. *Journal of Personality and Social Psychology, 57,* 100-114.

Davis, J. H., & Kerr, N. L. (1986). Thought experiments and the problem of sparse data in small group research. In P. Goodman (Ed.), *Designing effective work groups* (pp. 305-349). San Francisco: Jossey-Bass.

Davis, J. H., Stasser, G., Spitzer, C. E., & Holt, R. W. (1976). Changes in group members' decision preferences during discussion: An illustration with mock juries. *Journal of Personality and Social Psychology, 34,* 1177-1187.

Davis, J. H., Stasson, M., Ono, K., & Zimmerman, S. (1988). Effects of straw polls on group decision making: Sequential voting pattern, timing, and local majorities. *Journal of Personality and Social Psychology, 55,* 918-926.

Davis, J. H., Stasson, M. F., Parks, C. D., Hulbert, L., Kameda, T., Zimmerman, S. K., & Ono, K. (1993). Quantitative decisions by groups and individuals: Voting procedures and monetary awards by mock civil juries. *Journal of Experimental Social Psychology, 29,* 326-346.

Davis, J. H., Tindale, R. S., Nagao, D. H., Hinsz, V. B., & Robertson, B. (1984). Order effects in multiple decisions by groups: A demonstration with mock juries and trial procedures. *Journal of Personality and Social Psychology, 47,* 1003-1012.

De Vries, M. A. (1990). *The new Robert's rules of order.* New York: New American Library.

Diehl, M., & Stroebe, W. (1987). Productivity loss in brainstorming groups: Toward the solution of a riddle. *Journal of Personality and Social Psychology, 53,* 497-509.

Diehl, M., & Stroebe, W. (1990). *Productivity loss in idea-generating groups: Tracking down the blocking-effect* (Report). Psychological Institute, University of Tübingen.

Dunnette, M. D., Campbell, J., & Jaastad, R. K. (1963). The effect of group participation on brainstorming effectiveness for two industrial samples. *Journal of Applied Psychology, 47,* 30-37.

Fishburn, P. C. (1973). *The theory of social choice.* Princeton, NJ: Princeton University Press.

Galam, S. (1991). Political paradoxes of majority rule voting and hierarchical systems. *International Journal of General Systems, 18,* 191-200.

Gallupe, R. B., Bastianutti, L. M., & Cooper, W. H. (1991). Unblocking brainstorms. *Journal of Applied Psychology, 76,* 137-142.

Hastie, R., Penrod, S., & Pennington, N. (1983). *Inside the jury.* Cambridge, MA: Harvard University Press.

Hawkins, C. H. (1960). *Interaction and coalition realignments in consensus-seeking groups: A study of experimental jury deliberations.* Unpublished doctoral dissertation, University of Chicago.

Kalven, H., & Zeisel, H. (1966). *The American jury.* Boston: Little, Brown.

Kerr, N. L. (1982). Social transition schemes: Model, method, and applications. In H. Brandstatter, J. H. Davis, & G. Stocker-Kreichgauer (Eds.), *Group decision making* (pp. 59-80). London: Academic Press.

Kerr, N. L., & MacCoun, R. J. (1985). The effects of jury size and polling method on the process and product of jury deliberations. *Journal of Personality and Social Psychology, 48,* 349-363.

Kerr, N. L., Stasser, G., & Davis, J. H. (1979). Model testing, model fitting, and social decision schemes. *Organizational Behavior and Human Performance, 23,* 399-410.

Kiesler, C. A., & Kiesler, S. B. (1969). *Conformity.* Reading, MA: Addison-Wesley.

Kirchler, E., & Davis, J. H. (1986). The influence of member status differences and task type on group consensus and member position change. *Journal of Personality and Social Psychology, 51,* 83-91.

Levine, M. E., & Plott, C. R. (1977). Agenda influence and its implications. *Virginia Law Review, 63,* 561-604.

MacCoun, R., & Kerr, N. L. (1988). Asymmetric influence in mock jury deliberations: Jurors' bias for leniency. *Journal of Personality and Social Psychology, 54,* 21-33.

Mirkin, B. G. (1979). *Group choice.* New York: Winston/Wiley.

Mueller, D. C. (1989). *Public choice II.* Cambridge, UK: Cambridge University Press.

Mullen, B., Johnson, C., & Salas, E. (1991). Productivity loss in brainstorming groups: A meta-analytic integration. *Basic and Applied Social Psychology, 12,* 3-23.

Nagao, D. J., & Davis, J. H. (1980). Some implications of temporal drift in social parameters. *Journal of Experimental Social Psychology, 16,* 479-496.

Ono, K. (1986). *Group decision making and strategic position change.* Unpublished doctoral dissertation, University of Illinois.

Ono, K., Tindale, R. S., Hulin, C. L., & Davis, J. H. (1988). Intuition vs. deduction: Some thought experiments concerning Likert's linking-pin theory of organizations. *Organizational Behavior and Human Decision Processes, 42,* 135-154.

Osborn, A. F. (1957). *Applied imagination.* New York: Scribner.

Plott, C. R., & Levine, M. E. (1978). A model of agenda influence on committee decisions. *American Economic Review, 68,* 146-160.

Stasser, G., & Davis, J. H. (1981). Group decision making and social influence: A social interaction sequence model. *Psychological Review, 88,* 523-551.

Stasser, G., Kerr, N. L., & Bray, R. M. (1982). The social psychology of jury deliberation: Structure, process, and product. In N. L. Kerr & R. M. Bray (Eds.), *The social psychology of the courtroom.* New York: Academic Press.

Stasser, G., Kerr, N. L., & Davis, J. H. (1989). Influence processes and consensus models in decision-making groups. In P. Paulus (Ed.), *Psychology of group influence* (2nd ed., pp. 431-477). Hillsdale, NJ: Lawrence Erlbaum.

Steiner, I. D. (1972). *Group process and productivity.* New York: Academic Press.

Taylor, D. W., Berry, P. C., & Block, C. H. (1958). Does group participation when using brainstorming facilitate or inhibit creative thinking? *Administrative Science Quarterly, 3,* 23-47.

Thibaut, J., & Walker, L. (1975). *Procedural justice: A psychological analysis.* Hillsdale, NJ: Lawrence Erlbaum.

Tindale, R. S., Davis, J. H., Vollrath, D. A., Nagao, D. H., & Hinsz, V. (1990). Asymmetrical social influence in freely interacting groups. *Journal of Personality and Social Psychology, 58,* 438-449.

Vollrath, D. A., & Davis, J. H. (1980). Jury size and decision rule. In R. R. Simon (Ed.), *The jury: Its role in American society* (pp. 73-106). Lexington, MA: Lexington Books.

Walker, L., & Lind, E. A. (1984). Psychological studies of procedural models. In G. M. Stephenson & J. H. Davis (Eds.), *Progress in applied social psychology* (Vol. 2, pp. 293-313). Chichester, England: John Wiley.

New Communication Technologies for Group Decision Making

Toward an Integrative Framework

POPPY LAURETTA McLEOD

An important development in the research on technological support for group communication and decision making is the serious attention to developing the field's theoretical foundations. A variety of theoretical frameworks, designed to integrate past research findings and stimulate inquiry into new areas, have been proposed (e.g., Clapper & Prasad, 1993; Contractor & Seibold, 1993; DeSanctis, 1993; DeSanctis & Gallupe, 1987; Fulk, Schmitz, & Steinfield, 1990; Kydd & Ferry, 1991; Hollingshead & McGrath, 1995; Lyytinen & Ngwenyama, 1992; Ngwenyama & Lyytinen, in press; Poole & DeSanctis, 1992; Poole & Jackson, 1993). However, analogous to the empirical work, where individual researchers have tended to use one specific technology configuration combined with a specific task type and a specific research paradigm (Hollingshead & McGrath, 1995), theory building in this area has

AUTHOR'S NOTE: I would like to thank Scott E. Elston for research assistance in the preparation of this chapter, and Scott Poole and Randy Hirokawa for helpful comments and editorial guidance.

been similarly fragmented. Many of the theoretical developments have concentrated on a specific aspect of this research area, such as consensus development (e.g., Ngwenyama, Bryson, & Mobolurin, in press), or the match between technology features and task types (e.g., Straus & McGrath, 1994). Like the blind men in the famous legend, individual research programs have progressed as if they were studying different beasts. Fortunately, examples of bridges among these individual research streams have begun to appear (e.g., Dufner, Hiltz, Johnson, & Czech, 1995; Gallupe, Dennis, Cooper, Valacich, Bastianutti, & Nunamaker, 1992; Hiltz & Turoff, 1992).

In an excellent review of theoretical approaches that have been applied to research in computer-supported group decision making, DeSanctis (1993) recently described a dichotomy between individualist and collectivist approaches, having historical roots in the general literature on groups and organizations. In the individualist view, the purpose of groups and organizations is to maximize individual gain. Technology is thus a tool to help groups increase efficiency and effectiveness. The collectivist approach views groups and organizations as entities that evolve from social and cultural interaction. From this perspective, technology is a product of social evolution, and it takes on different meanings according to the cultural context. DeSanctis argued that individualist approaches have dominated group support system (GSS) research, and called for increased research based on collectivist approaches.

In this chapter, I propose an alternative view of DeSanctis's description. Rather than forming a dichotomy, the collectivist and individualist perspectives exist as a paradox (Quinn, 1989; Smith & Berg, 1987a, 1987b). That is, these approaches represent incompatible yet simultaneously "true" views of groups. Groups are at once instruments of rationality and stages upon which human dramas are acted. They foster both the worst and the best in human decision making and communication. But whether groups are treated as a means of goal attainment or as products of the social environment, we can nevertheless articulate a general set of communication processes common to all groups (Krone, Jablin, & Putnam, 1987). This chapter offers a basic model of the group communication process that can serve to integrate many of these theories and to suggest potential points of articulation among them. If researchers, operating under different paradigms, are nevertheless able to refer to a common overarching model, systematic accumulation of research findings across different laboratories and groups of scholars can proceed effectively, and perhaps avoid "cross-fertilization in a Tower of Babel" (Grudin, 1991). This model will be used to organize a review and critique of the literature on computer support for group communication and decision making, with the purpose of suggesting directions for future research.

The central assumption of this model is that no matter the specific theoretical orientation, the process of communication in decision-making groups consists of five basic elements. At the heart of the process is *exchange of information* among individuals, and *aggregation* of these exchanges over the total number of group members and over time. This exchange of information and aggregation are governed by a set of *constraining and enabling conditions*, and the exchange of information produces several types of *results*. Finally, through two *feedback* loops, (a) the exchange of information eventually produces changes in the constraining and enabling conditions, and (b) the results alter the information exchange process. The model is presented in Figure 14.1.

I will discuss the first parts of the model in terms of the general mechanism of information exchange, the types of information that are exchanged, and the aggregated patterns of information exchange. The remainder of the chapter will be focused more specifically on the role of technology in creating the constraining and enabling conditions for information exchange, and the results of the exchanges. It is beyond the scope of the chapter to present an exhaustive discussion of each section of the model. Rather, examples of relevant research will be discussed to demonstrate the possibilities of integrating across different findings. The chapter will conclude with propositions for future research.

NEW COMMUNICATION TECHNOLOGIES

The communication technologies discussed here can be described broadly as systems "which combine communication, computer and decision technologies to support problem formulation and solution in group meetings" (DeSanctis & Gallupe, 1987). I present here a brief description of these systems. More detailed accounts may be found in Wagner, Wynne, and Mennecke (1993), Johansen (1988), Dennis,

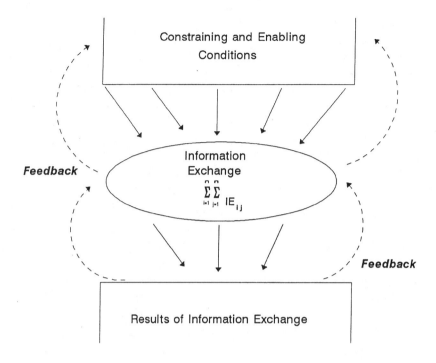

Figure 14.1. Comprehensive model of group communication.

George, Jessup, Nunamaker, and Vogel (1988), McLeod and Liker (1992), and DeSanctis and Gallupe (1987). The label *group support systems* (GSS) will be used throughout this chapter to refer to these technologies in general. The term *computer-mediated communication* will refer to the activity supported by these technologies.

One classifying system that has proven useful in describing these systems is in terms of their ability to support groups whose physical proximity varies along continua of time and space (Johansen, 1988). First are technologies that support face-to-face groups meeting at the same time in the same place. Technology support for this configuration is in the form of electronic decision rooms—typically equipped with a conference table, and computer workstations or keypads installed for individual participants. Central to these systems is software that links individual workstations through a network that enables group members to contribute to joint work, and in some cases to communicate directly with each other. Some of these software tools offer structured decision-making processes, such as the nominal group technique (Delbecq, Van de Ven, & Gustafson, 1975) or stakeholder analysis. In other cases, shareable word processing is also available. These rooms usually have available large screens for the display of group information.

Specific examples of these systems are GroupSystems, developed at the University of Arizona (Dennis et al., 1988; Nunamaker, Dennis, Valacich, Vogel, & George, 1993); Software Aided Meeting Management (SAMM), developed at the University of Minnesota (Poole, Holmes, Watson, & DeSanctis, 1993; Watson, DeSanctis, & Poole, 1988; Zigurs, Poole, & DeSanctis, 1988); VisionQuest, developed by Collaboration Technologies Corporation (Wagner et al., 1993); ShrEdit, developed at the University of Michigan (Olson, Olson, Storrøsten, & Carter, 1992); and the Capture Lab at Electronic Data Systems (Mantei, 1988).

In principle, any of these systems can also be used to support groups that are physically dispersed by simply locating the individual workstations in different rooms (e.g., Gallupe & McKeen, 1990). However, electronic mail and computer conferencing have been used more frequently in research on physically dispersed groups that communicate synchronously (e.g., Kiesler, Siegel, & McGuire, 1984; Straus & McGrath, 1994; Turoff & Hiltz, 1982).

Communication that is asynchronous—whether the participants "meet" at the same or a different place—requires record-keeping capabilities and shared accessibility to the records for all group members. Group members should be able to sign on to an ongoing session devoted to their work, observe the group's progress, see the contributions made by other group members, and make their own contributions. Electronic mail and computer conferencing, again, have been most commonly used to support asynchronous communication (e.g., Dufner et al., 1995; Walther & Burgoon, 1992). VisionQuest can also be used to support asynchronous group work, because it is structured around a set of "dialogues" that authorized group members can join and contribute to at any time, from any workstation located on the network.

Information Exchange and Aggregation

The information exchange process in the model is based on the classic communication theory view (e.g., Shannon & Weaver, 1949), involving a message encoded by a sender, sent through some channel to be decoded by a receiver. Common to many approaches to information exchange is the notion that information can be divided into different types. Although numerous schemes for classifying information types have appeared in the literature, I believe these variations represent different ways researchers have carved up the same pie.

One of the earliest and most fundamental divisions is task-oriented versus socioemotional information (Bales, 1953; Walther, 1992, 1994). These two types of information have been subdivided by different researchers into more specific types of messages, as represented, for example, by the Interaction Process Analysis categories (Bales, 1950; see also McLeod & Liker, 1992), the Decision Function Coding System (Poole et al., 1993; Poole & Roth, 1989), and other more ad hoc schemes (e.g., Hiltz, Turoff, & Johnson, 1989; Siegel, Dubrovsky, Kiesler, & McGuire, 1986; Walther & Burgoon, 1992; Zigurs, 1989).

A third information type that has been suggested as basic is symbolic information (Clapper & Prasad, 1993; Daft & Lengel, 1986; DeSanctis, 1993; Ngwenyama & Lyytinen, in press; Trevino, Lengel, & Daft, 1987). From a symbolic interactionist perspective, each message carries with it information not only about the group's task or the emotional state of its members, but also information on the legitimacy of particular ac-tions, the meaning of actions for the organization, or the nature of relationships among organizational actors, for example. These latter types of information are carried in symbols such as the communication medium chosen or the specific source of a message.

Another notion fundamental to the information exchange process is that the messages exchanged accumulate. Two basic approaches to the aggregation of information exchange have appeared in the literature— *additive* and *emergent*. In the additive approach, aggregation is repre-sented by counts of the messages sent during discussion. This would include, for example, the proportion of remarks falling into particular categories of information types (e.g., Dubrovsky, Kiesler, & Sethna, 1991; Hiltz et al., 1989; Kiesler, Zubrow, Moses, & Geller, 1985; McLeod & Liker, 1992; Weisband, 1992; Weisband, Schneider, & Connolly, 1995;

Zigurs et al., 1988), the proportion of time that groups spend on particular activities (e.g., Olson et al., 1992), and the relative number of remarks contributed by each group member (e.g., Dubrovsky et al., 1991; Gallupe, Cooper, Grisé, & Bastianutti, 1994; Siegel et al., 1986; Turoff & Hiltz, 1982; Valacich, Dennis, & Connolly, in press; Weisband et al., 1995).

The emergent perspective on aggregation places the focus on the patterns and structures that develop over time through the information exchange process, such as the temporal sequence of information exchange activities (e.g., Poole et al., 1993), the nature of cycling among various types of discussion activities (e.g., Olson et al., 1992; Poole et al., 1993), the functions of different information types for task accomplishment (e.g., Hirokawa, 1985; Hirokawa & McLeod, 1993; McLeod & Elston, 1994a), or the emergence of networks (e.g., Rice, 1982).

The additive approach might be likened to Hewes's (1986) description of group interaction as a "collective monologue." Drawing on Piaget's (1926) analysis of children's egocentric speech, Hewes argues that the need for interacting individuals to coordinate their behaviors with others while simultaneously planning their own actions poses a cognitive strain. As a result, the appearance of coordinated action is superficial; the contents of individual messages are not genuinely connected.

Poole and Jackson (1993) note, however, that many groups do indeed engage in true joint action, and that group interaction may be more accurately characterized as cycling between independence and convergence among group members. They propose that the theory of adaptive structuration (Gopal, Bostrom, & Chin, 1993; Poole & DeSanctis, 1990, 1992; see also Poole, Seibold, & McPhee, Chapter 5, this volume) can be used to articulate the process of moving from a baseline of unconnected parallel message sending to collective interaction from which discernable structures and patterns emerge.

According to adaptive structuration theory (AST), the aggregate pattern of information exchange among group members forms a system of rules and resources that enables and constrains interaction. At the same time, interaction itself produces the rules and resources, or structure. Structure thus has a dual nature—it both governs the patterns of information exchange, and is the thing produced by information exchange. The aggregation of information exchange, therefore, occurs according to a pattern that emerges from the information exchanges themselves.

Constraining and Enabling Conditions

Many factors affect the exchange of information in decision-making groups. The one of greatest interest here is technology. The fundamental question addressed in this section is, What are the ways that technology can facilitate and constrain the exchange of information in decision-making groups. I will discuss the factors that have been generally acknowledged to be the most important, though these factors have not necessarily received a corresponding amount of research attention. The following specific factors will be addressed: the fit between technology features and the group task, the direct effect of technology features, the proximity of group members in time and space, group size, and individual group member characteristics.

Task-Technology Fit. Task-technology fit is universally recognized as a central influence on information exchange in GSS-supported groups. Despite this, the relatively low amount of empirical work explicitly designed to examine this factor is a glaring gap in the GSS literature (Hollingshead & McGrath, 1995; McGrath & Hollingshead, 1993). In a critical review of the GSS literature that is the most extensive to date (including some 50 studies), Hollingshead and McGrath (1995) show that this is partly explained by a common method variance problem characterizing this literature as a whole. That is, each particular set of investigators is attached to a particular task-technology configuration, with few studies that vary task type and technology configuration together (for exceptions see Easton, George, Nunamaker, & Pendergast, 1990; Gallupe, DeSanctis, & Dickson, 1988; Jarvenpaa, Rao, & Huber, 1988; McLeod & Liker, 1992; Sambamurthy, Poole, & Kelly, 1993).

The work that has focused directly on the fit between features of GSS and the nature of the group task shares in common the view that tasks differ in the information processing and interaction demands placed on groups (Hirokawa & McLeod, 1993; Hirokawa & Pace, 1983; Poole & Roth, 1989). Task characteristics can be divided into objective characteristics that would not vary among groups, such as the degree of divisibility, and group task characteristics that depend on the group itself, such as novelty (Hirokawa & McLeod, 1993; Poole & Roth, 1989). Technology can similarly be conceived of in both fixed and variable terms. The objective or fixed characteristics would include features such as the availability of structured decision-making tools or the availability of shared views of group work. The variability lies in the meaning that group members attach to technology (Fulk & Boyd, 1991) and the choices that individual groups make in how they actually use these features (Poole & DeSanctis, 1990, 1992). Thus understanding the nature of task-technology fit and its effects on information exchange involves picking through a complex tangle of group characteristics, technology capabilities and use habits, group member beliefs and attitudes, and the environment external to the group.

The theory of media richness and media choice (Daft & Lengel, 1986; Trevino et al., 1987) has been the most frequently applied model in the theoretical attempts to match task types with technology types (Hollingshead, McGrath, & O'Connor, 1993; Kydd & Ferry, 1991; McGrath & Hollingshead, 1993; Poole et al., 1993; Valacich, Paranka, George, & Nunamaker, 1993). The general prediction based on this model is that tasks marked by high equivocality and ambiguity require "rich" media that are capable of carrying many different types of messages. Media can be arrayed along a continuum from rich (e.g., face-to-face) to lean (e.g., numeric symbols), with electronic communication considered to be relatively lean (McGrath & Hollingshead, 1993).

McGrath and Hollingshead (1993) and Hollingshead et al. (1993) have proposed an integration of the media richness model with McGrath's (1984) task circumplex, also widely cited in the GSS literature (e.g., DeSanctis & Gallupe, 1987; Hiltz & Turoff, 1992; McGrath, Arrow, Gruenfeld, Hollingshead, & O'Connor, 1993; Morrison, Morrison, & Vogel, 1992; Nunamaker, Vogel, & Konsynski, 1989; Raman & Wei, 1993). The four task types in the cognitive hemisphere of the task circumplex—generating ideas, choosing a demonstrably correct alternative, choosing a consensually preferred alternative, and negotiating conflicts of interest—range from low to high, respectively, in the level of interdependence among group members and the role of social context information. They hypothesized that computer-mediated communication, a lean medium, would better support idea generating and discrete choice tasks than consensus and negotiation tasks. Face-to-face communication would be the best choice for these latter two task types.

Fulk and Boyd (1991), among others, have argued that this theory does not adequately capture the complexities of new communication media. For example, an assumption underlying this theory is that the characteristics of the various media are fixed. Yet because of individual differences in perceptions of media, the characteristics are, in reality, variable. Further, the theory of media richness does not take into account the influence of the social environment. Fulk and Boyd (1991) cite evidence, for example, that patterns of technology use in groups are affected more by characteristics of the group itself than by characteristics of the technology.

Technology Features. In addition to the effects moderated through task characteristics, technology features exert direct influence over information exchange. Chief among these features are parallel input devices, availability of common views of group information, structured decision-making and record-keeping tools, support of anonymity, and support of dispersed communication. Three broad areas of direct effects of technology on information exchange will be discussed here: the types of information exchanged, participation rates, and the communication mechanism.

Let us consider first the differential effects of technology on communicating different information types. The general view is that computer-mediated communication increases task-oriented communication while decreasing relational information (Walther, 1992, 1994a, 1994b; Walther, Anderson, & Park, 1994). What is the evidence in support of this view?

GSS use is thought to increase task focus through structured decision-making and record-keeping tools and through providing groups with a common view of their work (McLeod, 1992). The actual empirical support for this expectation has been equivocal. The main obstacle to reconciling differences across studies is the inconsistency in operationalizing this construct. What can be taken for definitions of task focus include proportion of task-oriented comments (e.g., McLeod & Liker, 1992; Siegel et al., 1986), reciprocal of nontask behavior (e.g., Sambamurthy et al., 1993), depth of analysis (e.g., Steeb & Johnston, 1981), and number of alternatives generated (McLeod, 1992; Pinsonneault & Kraemer, 1989). Counting the number of alternatives generated is particularly problematic because it is also a task performance measure. But even among studies that do count task-oriented comments, the results have been mixed. For example, McLeod and Liker (1992) and Siegel et al. (1986) found lower and higher proportions, respectively, of task-oriented comments in GSS-supported than face-to-face groups, whereas Poole et al. (1993) found no differences. The search for an explanation of these differences in results is further complicated by the differences in technology and tasks used in these studies. Thus the empirical evidence that computer use increases decision-making groups' task focus is at best equivocal.

What about the evidence that computer-mediated communication decreases the exchange of socioemotional information? The work bearing on this question has been cast in a framework of the tone rather than the degree of socioemotional communication. More specifically, the extent to which computer support increases the negativity in the tone of information exchanged has been of keen interest. Quite a few studies have found computer-mediated communication to be more uninhibited and negative than face-to-face communication (Connolly, Jessup, & Valacich, 1990; Dubrovsky et al., 1991; Jessup, Connolly, & Galegher, 1990; Jessup, Connolly, & Tansik, 1990; Jessup & Tansik 1991; Kiesler et al., 1984; Kiesler et al., 1985; Siegel et al., 1986; Weisband, 1992). The basis for these findings, it is argued, is that anonymity and the absence of nonverbal cues lead to less attention to others, less social feedback, and lower self-awareness. The resulting deindividuation is responsible for the uninhibited and negative communication (Valacich, Jessup, Dennis, & Nunamaker, 1992).

Recently, however, a serious challenge to these findings and the theoretical basis for them has been mounted (Walther, 1992, 1994a, 1994b; Walther et al., 1994). Walther and his colleagues contend that the appearance of less positive relational information exchange via computer is an artifact stemming from the time limits imposed in these lab studies. It is not that the computer medium is incapable of conveying relational information, but rather that it has a narrower bandwidth than face-to-face and relational information and therefore takes longer to get across. According to Walther and Burgoon (1992) and Walther et al. (1994), when time constraints are removed, the amount of relational information conveyed by computer-mediated and face-to-face groups converges. In fact, in Walther and Burgoon's (1992) longitudinal study, computer-supported subjects showed higher relational communication than face-to-face subjects at all time periods, in stark contrast to findings from other studies. Walther (1994a, 1994b) argues that the anticipation of future interaction, rather than media, accounts for the level of relational communication in groups. People who know they will have a continued relationship in the future are prompted to exchange relational information as early as possible. One implication of Walther's work is that the motivations of the group members to communicate particular types of information may overshadow the effects of technology, especially over time.

The exchange of symbolic information through electronic media is of increasing interest (Clapper & Prasad, 1993; DeSanctis, 1993; McLeod, 1991; Ngwenyama & Lyytinen, in press). The symbolic function of information exchange imbues fundamentally ambiguous situations with meaning (Berger & Luckmann, 1967). Parties to an information exchange look beyond the manifest content of messages to take in also the packaging of the message, its source, or the timing of its delivery. These paralinguistic features of messages indicate, for example, legitimacy of the message or the social status of the interacting parties. One effect of computer-mediated communication is the reduction of this information through the removal of nonverbal cues. However, a great deal of symbolic information can still be conveyed if the identities of the communicating parties are maintained.

This distinction between the effects of anonymity and the absence of nonverbal cues is one that should receive more attention. Currently these two characteristics of GSS-supported communication are treated synonymously in both theoretical and empirical work because much of the empirical work has been conducted in settings where making the distinction does not matter—zero-history groups meeting for a single session. Knowing the author of specific comments does not convey much symbolic information (e.g., Siegel et al., 1986). But in groups whose members know each other, the preservation of identities in computer-mediated communication can add a tremendous amount of symbolic information. Even among unacquainted people, the simple knowledge of significant social characteristics can carry large amounts of information. Weisband et al. (1995), for example, demonstrated that among unacquainted groups of students who interacted via e-mail, the knowledge of only the different social status rankings of the group's members led to differential amounts of influence being afforded to the members occupying the various social ranks.

Dennis, Easton, Easton, George, and Nunamaker (1990) reported results of a study in which ad hoc groups were compared to established groups working on a business case task in a single-session lab study. The groups communicated only electronically, but their comments were not anonymous. Dennis et al. found less equal participation in the preacquainted groups than in the ad hoc groups. In contrast, Hiltz and colleagues (1989) reported no difference in uninhibited behavior or deindividuation between anonymous and identified computer groups of preacquainted managers from the same company. But they speculated that the strong conservative culture of the company may have masked any differences due to the experimental manipulations. These findings generally would suggest that as research in GSS moves into the field and becomes longitudinal, consideration of the differential effects of removing nonverbal cues and anonymity should increase.

Distribution of Participation. In addition to the types of information, technology use affects the overall amount and distribution of information exchange among group members. More specifically, the ability for parallel and anonymous input are thought to equalize participation rates across group members (Benbasat & Lim, 1993; Dennis et al., 1988; Hollingshead & McGrath, 1995; McLeod, 1992; Pinsonneault & Kraemer, 1989; Rao & Jarvenpaa, 1991). With respect to overall amount of participation, technology has been predicted both to increase (Dennis et al., 1988) and to decrease it (Hollingshead & McGrath, 1995). Several points suggest that the issue of participation be examined more closely.

One consideration is that participation and influence have generally been lumped together. Nearly all of the studies have examined *participation*, operationalized by counting remarks. On the other hand, *influence*, defined in terms of changes in group behavior or opinions resulting from the actions of individual group members, has not been studied to any great extent, nor has it received much empirical support. Zigurs et al. (1988) counted behaviors coded as influence attempts and the frequency of the success of those attempts. They found more equal distribution in face-to-face computer-supported than in noncomputer groups for one kind of influence behavior, but no difference for a second kind of influence behavior. Dubrovsky et al. (1991) measured influence as the distance between individual opinions and the group average opinion following discussion, and found some evidence for more equalized influence in groups supported by electronic mail than in face-to-face groups. However, Watson et al. (1988), Ho and Raman (1991), and Weisband et al. (1995) used measures of influence, and found no effect. McLeod and Liker (1992) counted behaviors rated as dominant and found no difference in the distribution of dominance between face-to-face computer and noncomputer groups.

On the other hand, the studies that count remarks do find more equal distribution within computer-supported than face-to-face groups (e.g., George, Easton, Nunamaker, & Northcraft, 1990; Hiltz et al., 1989; Siegel et al., 1986). But what are the effects of this participation equality on group process and outcome? It has been assumed but not demonstrated that participation equality translates into influence equality in GSS-supported groups. Although it is well known that participation and influence are correlated in face-to-face communication, this may not be true in computer-mediated communication. For example, the author of statements that receive favorable reactions from other group members, reinforced by these reactions, may be led to make other similar statements. This can eventually produce an unequal distribution of influence, even though rates of participation are equivalent.

A second issue to consider is the equating of participating with message sending. Electronic communication changes the communication mechanism by decoupling message sending from message receiving. This decoupling is particularly relevant when task type is taken into account. Those studies reporting increased overall "participation" in computer-supported groups are nearly all studies of brainstorming tasks that define participation by counting the number of ideas generated (e.g., Dennis & Valacich, in press-a; Gallupe, Bastianutti, & Cooper, 1991; Gallupe et al., 1992; Gallupe et al., 1994; George et al., 1990; Valacich et al., in press). In contrast, the studies in which groups are required to reach consensus have found computer support to lower the overall rate of participation, also measured by counting the number of remarks (e.g., Dubrovsky et al., 1991; Hiltz et al., 1989; Siegel et al., 1986; Straus & McGrath, 1994).

The overall increase in participation rates in brainstorming is a direct function of the decoupling of message sending and receiving. No coordination among members is required; members can "participate" and accomplish the task without responding to comments of other members. Thus there stand few encumbrances to message sending. In contrast, consensus tasks require participants to pay attention to messages sent by others, where the decoupling of message sending and receiving may actually add to the burden of coordination. As a consequence, in GSS-supported groups faced with a consensus task, the overall rates of message sending may be lower than in groups working on brainstorming tasks. Further, for consensus tasks the distribution of influence rather than participation may be a more relevant consideration.

Asynchronous Communication. McGrath and Hollingshead (1993) raise concerns that the absence of both verbal and nonverbal feedback in asynchronous communication may present coordination difficulties, and they predict that tasks involving consensus and negotiation would be more harmed by asynchrony than would tasks involving idea generation. In contrast, Hiltz and Turoff (1992) contend that efforts to remove the putative negative effects of asynchronous communication, making it seem more like face-to-face communication for the user, are misdirected. More appropriate would be attention to exploring the unique benefits of asynchronous communication. For example, the lack of immediacy may give people time for reflection, thorough digestion of the other group members' comments, and more thoughtfulness in composing contributions to the discussion. The work of Hiltz and Turoff and their colleagues suggests that these potential benefits depend on the techniques that groups use to structure their discussion and work processes (Dufner et al., 1995; Fjermestad et al., 1994).

Group Size. The average amount of participation per person in electronically supported groups appears to remain constant over group size (Dennis et al., 1990; Valacich, Jessup, et al., 1992). However, the benefits of GSS for brainstorming tasks are greater for large groups because the technology reduces production blocking more in large than small groups (Dennis & Valacich, 1994; Dennis, Valacich, & Nunamaker, 1990; Valacich, Dennis, & Nunamaker, 1992; Valacich et al., 1994). Group size has been investigated almost exclusively using brainstorming groups, and there is virtually no empirical evidence for other kinds of tasks. Dennis and Valacich (1994) have suggested that for tasks involving discussion GSS will also benefit larger groups more than smaller groups. As group size increases, they argue, the connectedness among individual member comments decreases. GSS may help group members to follow these independent communication streams. A final consideration is that group size may not be a fixed number (Nunamaker et al., 1989). The "logical" size of a group may vary as a function of the degree of knowledge overlap among the members, the nature of the task, and may change over time.

Individual Member Characteristics. The characteristics of the group members influence the type and amount of information that is available for exchange, and group members' willingness and ability to participate in information exchange. Proficiency with technology (e.g., Austin, Liker, & McLeod, 1993; Elwart-Keys, Halonen, Horton, Kass, & Scott, 1990; Gallupe, 1992; Mantei, 1988), personality traits (e.g., Rao, Desroches, & Trapnell, 1993) and attitudes toward technology use (DeSanctis, Poole, Dickson, & Jackson, in press) have been shown to affect patterns of information exchange in electronic settings.

FEEDBACK

We have examined the effect on information exchange of a number of factors. The constraining and enabling conditions produced by these factors are in turn affected by the exchange of information as it aggregates over time. This recursivity is the nucleus of adaptive structuration theory (DeSanctis & Poole, 1994; Poole & DeSanctis, 1990, 1992) and an extension proposed by Contractor and Seibold (1993), labeled self-organizing systems theory. The constraining and enabling conditions form a structure that governs social and task interaction among group members. Contractor and Seibold describe the process through which group member characteristics and actions generate the social structures that then govern those actions. Social structures are thus produced and reproduced through individuals' actions. Technologies present particular structures to groups, which only acquire meaning through the actions of group members' appropriations.

According to Poole and DeSanctis (1990, 1992), technologies can be described in terms of their *spirit*—the philosophy, values, and goals on which a set of structural features are based—and appropriations of technology structures may be consistent or inconsistent with the technology's spirit. In an analysis of GSS-supported groups engaged in a resource allocation task, DeSanctis and Poole (1991) reported that those groups whose appropriations of the GSS were consistent with its spirit were more likely to reach consensus than were groups showing appropriations inconsistent with the technology's spirit.

McLeod and Liker (1992) proposed that one property of structuration is the preponderance of influence that GSS and groups exert on each other. Those systems whose spirit is characterized by the imposition of structured discussion and task processes will change preexisting group structures more than they will be changed by group members' appropriations. A system whose spirit reflects a low level of structure impositions, such as a group editor (e.g., Olson et al., 1992), will be more reflective of a group's preexisting structure through its appropriations, than it will change that group's preexisting structure.

Research consistent with this idea is reported by Poole and DeSanctis (1992) and Austin et al. (1993). Poole and DeSanctis (1992) reported that when groups used a GSS that presented a high amount of restrictiveness on their process, group members were more likely to accept the structures offered by the technology, making fewer attempts to control the technology than when the GSS presented low restrictiveness. Austin et al. (1993) found that in groups supported by a low structure GSS, the appropriations of the technology reflected preexisting social status structures in the groups. Gallupe (1992) reports research suggesting that the preponderance of influence changes over time. He reported that even for systems high in the imposition of structures, groups over time adapted the technology more to themselves than vice versa.

Results of Information Exchange

The results of accumulated information exchange include task accomplishment and changes in the knowledge and opinions of group members. Here I examine the specific results pertaining to task performance quality, decision consensus and member opinion change.

Task Quality. There are few generalizations that can be made about the effect of technology use on the quality of group decision making (George, 1992). The most consistent finding is that, for brainstorming tasks, electronic support increases the volume of ideas, and in some cases the quality, over the ideas produced by interacting and nominal groups (Gallupe et al., 1991; Gallupe et al., 1992; Gallupe et al., 1994; Hymes & Olson, 1992), and these effects appear to increase with group size (Dennis & Valacich, 1993, 1994; Valacich et al., in press). However, in most of these studies the groups were not making actual decisions, only generating alternatives. In one study in which subjects both generated solution ideas and chose the best solution, George et al. (1990) reported no difference between face-to-face and electronic groups in the quantity or quality of the solutions chosen.

Hollingshead et al. (1993) and Straus and McGrath (1994), in contrast to most of these other brainstorming studies, found no differences in idea quantity between face-to-face groups and groups supported by computer conferencing. One possible explanation for the inconsistency in these findings is differences in the characteristics of the technology used. The electronic brainstorming program in the University of Arizona's GroupSystems, used by most of the brainstorming studies, is structured around a set of discrete files. Each of these files is sent to randomly chosen individual group members who can read previously entered comments and then enter their own comments. In computer conferencing, used by Hollingshead et al. and Straus and McGrath, the ideas are simply listed with no other structuring. Perhaps the chunking of the ideas in the files in GroupSystems enabled group members to read and absorb a comparably sized list of ideas faster than if the ideas were presented as an unstructured list as in the computer conferencing system. Consistent with this reasoning, Hymes and Olson (1992) reported evidence that as lists of ideas become unwieldy during brainstorming, the average rate of idea production per member decreases.

The results reported for other kinds of tasks are highly variable, due to differences in both the specific task characteristics and technology configurations. The effect of technology on decision quality for tasks with a demonstrably correct answer ("intellective" in the task circumplex), or for which quality is based on judgment (decision tasks) are somewhat mixed, but the modal finding is actually that technology makes no difference.

Comparing GSS-supported to face-to-face groups on decision quality for intellective tasks, Hiltz et al. (1989) and Zigurs et al. (1988) reported no difference, McLeod and Liker (1992) and Gallupe et al. (1988) reported higher quality among GSS groups, and Hollingshead et al.

(1993) reported lower quality among GSS groups. Each of these studies used a different task and, with the exception of the Zigurs et al. and Gallupe et al. studies, completely different technologies. The pattern of results for decision/judgment tasks is similar. George et al. (1990), Hollingshead et al. (1993), Galegher and Kraut (1990), Horton, Rogers, Austin, Brimm, and McCormick (1991), and Ocker et al. (1994) reported no effect. Olson et al. (1992) reported higher quality among GSS groups, and McLeod and Liker (1992) reported lower quality among GSS groups. Again, the overlap in specific tasks and technology is low.

Explanations for the inconsistencies in these findings are not readily apparent because of the wide differences in the experimental materials used. But, one place to begin searching is in the way that tasks are classified. Different tasks may be grouped into the same category by one set of criteria, but land in different categories using another set. For example, although I placed the business case analysis task used by Gallupe et al. (1988) in the task circumplex category "intellective," these researchers themselves actually used Guzzo's (1979) and Simon's (1964) task categorization systems to define the properties of their task. According to these schemes, the task can be described as problem finding, technical/factual, crisis, and business marketing. In the task circumplex the Gallupe et al. task would be placed in the same category as an item-ranking task such as the one used by Hiltz et al. (1989), but these two tasks clearly differ significantly on other dimensions as captured by the other schemes just described. Thus the predominance of the task circumplex in the GSS literature may be obscuring differences between tasks such as these.

Further, the specific integration with the media richness model proposed by McGrath and Hollingshead (1993) may only be adding to this problem. The primary point of articulation between the task circumplex and the media richness model is the degree of interdependence and coordination required by the task. Tasks requiring low coordination, like idea generation, would not be greatly affected by social context cues and could be carried out with a lean communication medium. Tasks characterized by high interdependence among group members, like negotiating conflicts of interest, are highly dependent on social context cues and would require the use of a rich communication medium. Yet the nature of interdependence among group members is more complex than is implied by this reasoning. In the classic organizational theory view, interdependence can be pooled, sequential, or reciprocal (Thomas, 1976), and these three different types of interdependence vary in the degree to which social context is important. Nominal group brainstorming would be the quintessential example of a task characterized by pooled interdependence, where independent actions contribute to the whole, but the actors do not depend on each other to get their part of the task done. Reciprocal interdependence, at the other extreme, is exemplified by conflict negotiation tasks in which individual actors are mutually dependent. Sequential interdependence falls between these two ends. But complex tasks can be characterized by all three types of interdependence. For example, a complex task such as zero-based budgeting, based on clearly defined accounting procedures, can be effectively executed with only pooled interdependence (see Hiltz & Turoff, 1992, for an example). In this case, interdependence could be high, but the role of social context cues would be minimal.

Another issue masked by the integration of the task circumplex with media richness is the variation in interdependence over time. A task may require a high degree of interdependence at an early stage of work or in a newly formed group, whereas the same task would require less or a different type of interdependence in an established group.

The quality of negotiation task outcomes is based both on the judged quality of the solution and on consensus among group members. Based on the combined task circumplex and media richness models, face-to-face groups should produce higher-quality solutions than GSS groups on negotiating tasks. In a longitudinal study, Hollingshead et al. (1993) did find this general result, but the difference disappeared over time. In addition, two major reviews of the literature on electronic support of negotiation (Lim & Benbasat, 1992; Poole, Shannon, & DeSanctis, 1992) challenge the media richness perspective, suggesting that electronic media are superior to face-to-face along a number of dimensions. For instance, the anonymous communication afforded by some electronic media can focus negotiating parties' attention on argument content rather than authorship, allowing the case that is strongest on its own merits to win (Poole et al., 1992). Further, the availability of external memory and decision-structuring tools can help participants overcome limits to human information processing, which can thus bring parties closer to optimal solutions (Lim & Benbasat, 1992).

Consensus. Consensus has been operationalized in lab studies variously as strength of individual agreement with the group decision, the number of group members whose individual opinions agree with the group decision, and the degree of change in individual decision following discussion. Although the empirical findings tend to be mixed (Dennis & Gallupe, 1993), two meta-analyses of lab studies have concluded that the effect of GSS use on consensus is generally negative (Benbasat & Lim, 1993; McLeod, 1992). GSS-supported groups take longer to reach consensus, and the degree of consensus achieved is lower than in face-to-face groups. It has been suggested that under conditions of equal participation, the absence of a dominant individual who advocates a particular position is one explanation for the difficulty in reaching consensus in GSS groups (George et al., 1990; Turoff & Hiltz, 1982). The conclusion that consensus is less likely with computer support may be overgeneral in that it does not take into account the effects of time or of variation in technology.

Hollingshead et al. (1993) found that over time, computer-supported groups eventually took the same amount of time to reach consensus as face-to-face groups. Sambamurthy et al. (1993) present evidence that GSS of higher levels of sophistication (DeSanctis & Gallupe, 1987) may enhance consensus development, and DeSanctis and Poole (1991) reported that appropriate uses of technology more likely lead to consensus than does inappropriate use. The way that consensus is operationalized in many studies has also been criticized for resting on faulty assumptions about the scaling of group member preferences and judgments (Bryson, Ngwenyama, & Mobolurin, in press; Hong & Vogel, 1993; Ngwenyama et al., in press). These authors have proposed new mathematical procedures for calculating consensus that address these problems.

Opinion Change. Change in individual and group opinion is a result of information exchange that is of particular relevance for consensus. Rarely do group members have total agreement on an issue at the outset of discussion, thus some change is required for consensus to be reached. The main question of interest here is, What is the role played by technology in opinion change in groups?

Siegel et al. (1986) and Kiesler et al. (1984) report that groups supported by computer conferencing and electronic mail exhibit significantly more choice shift than face-to-face groups after discussion of choice-dilemma tasks. Their tentative explanation for these findings was that the deindividuating effects of computer-mediated communication reduced awareness of the social context, which reduced reluctance to abandon positions held earlier. However, their analysis of the group discussion procedures did not reveal any differences in the processes that were related to this difference. Further, Dubrovsky et al. (1991) also reported no effect of communication medium on group choice shift. Hiltz et al. (1989), following the same line of reasoning and task, did not find any significant effects of computer conferencing on choice shift.

Taken together, the studies on consensus and opinion change suggest that, despite the apparent willingness of group members communicating electronically to change their positions, the effect of technology on consensus formation is weak or negative. One approach to seeking an explanation for these findings is to examine the actual degree of opinion change among group members—in terms of both frequency and size of change. Based on the arguments presented by Siegel et al. (1986), Kiesler et al. (1984), and Hiltz et al. (1989), we would expect more change activity in electronic than face-to-face groups. However, the absence of nonverbal cues may present coordination difficulty, which would offset the greater opinion change activity. The net result would be the weak or negative impact of technology that has been found in some studies. This type of explanation would be consistent with the recent evidence (DeSanctis & Poole, 1991; Hollingshead et al., 1993; Sambamurthy et al., 1993) that consensus improves with increasing sophistication and experience with technology.

The role of technology in mediating the influence of minority opinions has very recently begun to receive research attention (McLeod & Elston, 1994a, 1994b; Melone et al., 1993; Rao & Jarvenpaa, 1991). Rao and Jarvenpaa (1991) theorized that parallel input and, especially, anonymity of electronic communication would increase the likelihood that people whose opinions were very different from those of the majority of group members would express those opinions. The well-established minority influence effect (Nemeth, 1986) would lead to the prediction of improved decision quality, because exposure to dissenting opinions forces more thorough consideration of the problem and solution alternatives. Further, more private opinion change on the part of majority opinion holders would also be expected.

McLeod and Elston (1994b), using a jury decision task, reported higher private opinion change toward the minority opinion in computer-supported than face-to-face groups, and the change was smaller among anonymous than identified computer groups. Melone et al. (1993) found also that computer-supported groups exhibited greater shift toward the minority position on an ethics decision-making task. Neither of these studies examined decision quality or the probability of the emergence of minority opinions in discussion. The results of these studies are consistent with the arguments made in the group choice shift studies that electronic communication is associated with greater willingness following group discussion to abandon earlier held positions to reach consensus.

FEEDBACK

The accumulated results of information exchange eventually alter the nature of the information exchange itself. This feedback loop can be best understood by examining use of technology longitudinally. By *longitudinally* I mean both the spanning of multiple time periods and the temporal development of decisions within single sessions. Studies that take this perspective have demonstrated the variety of ways that use of technology changes as the results of information exchange accumulate. I will present just a few examples.

Gallupe (1992) and Chidambaram, Bostrom, and Wynne (1990) demonstrated that as information exchange resulted in increased familiarity and comfort with technology use, group members adapted the technology to fit their own style and increased their ability to resolve conflict. DeSanctis, Poole, Dickson, and Jackson (1993) demonstrated that the accumulation of information on the impacts of technology affected group member attitudes toward the technology that, in turn, affected their use patterns. Zack (1993) found that as the amount of shared information about a group's task accumulates, groups choose different media to use for information exchange. Poole et al. (1993) and McLeod and Elston (1994a) showed that the accumulated information about task accomplishment altered the types of messages exchanged over the course of decision development. Finally, Walther and Burgoon (1992) and Walther (1994a, 1994b) showed that as group members learned more about each other, the distribution of message types changed.

Viewed from the perspective of the comprehensive model, it is clear that the effects of technology on information exchange and the results from that exchange are dynamic. The role of time in computer-mediated communication is a promising area of research, and the growing interest in examining it is well placed (e.g., Chidambaram et al., 1990).

Future Research Considerations

The main result from this review of GSS literature is that few generalizations can be made about the effects of technology on information exchange, outcomes, attitudes toward technology, or usage patterns. The complexity of this field—considering the many alternatives for technology, tasks, group characteristics, and research methods—can lead one to the exasperating conclusion that "everything depends." The alternative extreme is to seek refuge in examining tiny bits of the problem, and generalizing from there. In fact, we have by now accumulated a good deal of knowledge about technology use for group communication and decision making. The challenge is in plotting a course through this literature that avoids the Scylla of entanglement in an overgrown thicket of contingencies, on one side, and the Charybdis of stumbling into a chasm of overgeneralization, on the other. This review, by placing the literature in a common framework, can be used to illuminate potential points for reconciling differences in research findings.

The suggestions for future research directions will be discussed in two levels. The first level is addressed toward research questions about which a fairly significant amount of knowledge has been accumulated. Directions for future research can be stated in terms of specific propositions that suggest the probable nature of relationships among a number of key variables. The second level is addressed toward questions that have received little attention or are characterized by results that are scattered and widely inconsistent. At this level, I will suggest general research questions that would provide promising avenues for future research.

RESEARCH PROPOSITIONS

The bulk of the research questions addressed in this literature have focused on technology as part of the constraining and enabling conditions for information exchange and its effects on task accomplishment. Inconsistent results have been reported in all of these areas. In this review I have suggested a number of specific factors that could provide reconciliation of some of the conflicting research findings. These included looking at the effects of anonymity separately from the effects of lack of nonverbal cues, separating participation in information exchange from influence on information exchange and decision outcomes, expanding the task classification schemes used in this research, examining the uses of electronic communication longitudinally, looking at message sending separately from message receiving, and comparing the effects of high-structure to low-structure communication technologies. I will restate here as formal research propositions the general suggestions relevant to each of these areas.

Anonymity and Nonverbal Behavior. This review has noted that the research literature has treated technology's support of anonymous communication and its removal of nonverbal cues synonymously, and I have suggested that under some conditions, these two characteristics may exert different effects.

Proposition 1a: In initially anonymous computer-mediated groups, the level of anonymity decreases over time as members exchange information.

Proposition 1b: In initially anonymous computer-mediated groups whose members anticipate future interaction, group members will proactively attempt to reduce the level of anonymity.

Proposition 1c: In previously acquainted computer-mediated groups, the addition of identity information will have a larger effect on information exchange than will the addition of this information in zero-history groups.

Proposition 1d: In zero-history groups, anonymity and the absence of nonverbal cues have similar effects; in previously acquainted groups, anonymity has a larger effect on information exchange than does the absence of nonverbal cues.

Proposition 1e: Over time, the effect of anonymity increases relative to the effect of having no nonverbal cues.

Participation. Participation has been implicitly equated both with influence and with message sending. GSS use may increase participation in tasks that do not require coordination of messages, and influence may be a more important measure than participation in tasks that do require coordination.

Proposition 2a: In GSS-supported groups, the rate of participation will be lower in consensus tasks than in idea generation tasks.

Proposition 2b: In GSS-supported groups, the rate of participation will be correlated with degree of influence for consensus tasks but not for brainstorming tasks.

Proposition 2c: In GSS-supported groups, the rate of participation will be lower in consensus tasks than in brainstorming tasks.

Technology Structures. One important difference in electronic communication technologies is the degree of structuring they impose on group decision-making and communication processes. This difference in structuring affects use of technology and the nature of group outcomes.

Proposition 3a: Computer-supported groups using a high-structure system will reach consensus more easily than will groups using a low-structure system.

Proposition 3b: The higher the structure inherent in the spirit of a GSS, the more will appropriations of the technology be consistent with its spirit.

Proposition 3c: The lower the structure inherent in the spirit of a GSS, the more will appropriations of the technology reflect preexisting structures in a group.

Task Characteristics. The GSS literature has relied heavily on the task circumplex, which may mask differences in tasks along dimensions that are captured by other classification approaches. One example is the degree of interdependence among group members that is required for task accomplishment. Interdependence differs in kind as well as degree, and thus the type of task interdependence should be considered when examining GSS effects.

> Proposition 4a: For complex tasks requiring pooled interdependence, computer-supported communication will enhance information exchange and increase decision quality.

> Proposition 4b: For complex tasks requiring reciprocal interdependence, synchronous computer-supported communication will inhibit information exchange and decrease decision quality.

> Proposition 4c: For complex tasks requiring reciprocal interdependence, asynchronous communication will enhance information exchange and increase decision quality.

Time Effects. The moderating effects of time include longitudinal changes and differences between synchronous and asynchronous communication. The changes over time to be considered are the accumulation of information, changes in group member states, and progress toward task completion. These changes are recursive, and the feedback causes further changes in the types and pattern of information exchanged and patterns of technology use.

> Proposition 5a: In electronically supported groups, the rate of exchange of relational and symbolic information increases over time; the rate of increase is greater than in face-to-face groups.

> Proposition 5b: During early stages of group development, with low experience with GSS, technology will have weak or negative effects on consensus formation; over time, and with increased experience, technology will have a positive effect on consensus formation.

Much of the research on asynchronous electronic communication is at an early stage, but some testable propositions have nevertheless emerged from this work. Part of the philosophy guiding the leading research program on asynchronous communication at NJIT (Hiltz & Turoff, 1992) is that asynchronous and synchronous communication each be used for the kinds of tasks they can most effectively support.

Important task characteristics to consider are the degree of divisibility and the ratio of independent to joint work required.

Proposition 6a: Tasks characterized by high divisibility and a high ratio of independent to joint work would be more effectively accomplished under asynchronous than synchronous communication.

Proposition 6b: Tasks characterized by low divisibility and a low ratio of independent to joint work would be more effectively accomplished under synchronous than asynchronous communication.

Another aspect of asynchronous communication to consider is the complete decoupling of message sending from message receiving. Parallel input allows an increase in messages sent, but not necessarily a concomitant increase in message processing capacity. Asynchronous communication may thus benefit some groups by providing ample time to process messages.

Proposition 7a: In synchronous computer-supported communication, the rate of message sending will be negatively correlated with the degree of message processing.

Proposition 7b: In asynchronous computer-supported communication, the rate of message sending will be uncorrelated with the degree of message processing.

GENERAL RESEARCH DIRECTIONS

The comprehensive model has served as an organizing framework for examining primarily lab research on GSS. This framework proved useful for indicating potentially fruitful areas in need of future research attention. To conclude the chapter, I will raise additional questions about issues not explicitly covered in this chapter, but that would also be important areas for future work.

One is the need to pay systematic attention to the "side effects" of everyday GSS use within organizations. Many of these unanticipated consequences may stem from the more symbolic, and the time-dependent facets of group decision making. How should organizations decide what kind and what magnitude of decisions should be approached with GSS? Because GSS can enable increased numbers of people to attend meetings, what happens to the signaling function of inclusion or exclusion from particular meetings? What happens to people's psychological feelings of consensus and commitment to a decision that was made through an anonymous process? Field research that can address some of these questions is just beginning to appear.

The need for more research and theorizing on time-dependent processes is evident from this review. Hollingshead and McGrath (1995) point out that certain processes, such as group formation or the emergence of leadership, can only be studied over time. The few longitudinal studies of GSS available have already presented challenges to what we thought we knew about GSS effects. For example, the "well-known" finding that lab-based GSS groups take longer to reach decisions than unsupported groups was shown by Hollingshead et al. (1993) to hold only for early stages of group development.

The implicit and explicit sentiments in nearly all of the reviews of the GSS literature seem to be that, although they may not be appropriate for every circumstance, GSS are generally good for groups and good for organizations. The practical benefits of technologies such as electronic mail and computer conferencing for general communication are well established. But the use of these technologies for more sophisticated group decision making, or the adoption of newer technologies designed specifically for this, are concepts that still need to be sold in many organizations. This review has shown that these new technologies benefit large brainstorming groups, but the benefits for accomplishing other kinds of tasks is less clear. Although there is evidence that higher levels of decision structuring may be of benefit for decision tasks, what is the increase in benefit over a well facilitated face-to-face meeting? Reports from field studies have indicated significant benefits in effectiveness and efficiency (Nunamaker et al., 1993), but these studies rely on retrospective self-reports from users. One area potentially of clear benefit is in the support of groups dispersed in time and space, that might not otherwise be able to "meet." Most of the research on this type of support is at an early stage, and thus it is perhaps too soon to assess the benefits. The focus of this chapter has been on research aimed toward theory building, but one conclusion that can be drawn is that more systematic attention to demonstrating convincingly the practical benefits of the various communication technologies should be an increasing priority.

References

Austin, L. C., Liker, J. K., & McLeod, P. L. (1993). Who controls the technology in group support systems? Determinants and consequences. *Human-Computer Interaction, 8,* 217-236.

Bales, R. F. (1950). *Interaction process analysis: A method for the study of small groups.* Reading, MA: Addison-Wesley.

Bales, R. F. (1953). The equilibrium problem in small groups. In T. Parsons, E. A. Shils, & R. F. Bales (Eds.), *Working papers in the theory of action.* New York: Free Press.

Benbasat, I., & Lim, L. (1993). The effects of group, task, context, and technology variables on the usefulness of group support systems: A meta-analysis of experimental studies [Special issue: Group support systems]. *Small Group Research, 24,* 430-462.

Berger, P., & Luckmann, T. (1967). *The social construction of reality.* Garden City, NY: Anchor.

Bryson, N., Ngwenyama, O. K., & Mobolurin, A. (in press). A qualitative discriminant process for scoring and ranking in group support systems. *Information Processing and Management.*

Chidambaram, L., Bostrom, R. P., & Wynne, B. E. (1990). A longitudinal study of the impact of group decision support systems on group development. *Journal of Management Information Systems, 7,* 7-25.

Clapper, D., & Prasad, P. (1993). *The rationalization of the organizational meeting: Implications of group support systems for power, symbolism, and face work.* Unpublished working paper, Clarkson University.

Connolly, T., Jessup, L. M., & Valacich, J. S. (1990). Effects of anonymity and evaluative tone on idea generation in computer-mediated groups. *Management Science, 36,* 689-703.

Contractor, N. S., & Seibold, D. R. (1993). Theoretical frameworks for the study of structuring processes in group decision support systems: Adaptive structuration theory and self-organizing systems theory. *Human Communication Research, 19,* 528-563.

Daft, R. L., & Lengel, R. (1986). Organizational information requirements, media richness, and structural design. *Management Science, 32,* 554-571.

Delbecq, A. L., Van de Ven, A. H., & Gustafson, D. H. (1975). *Group techniques for program planning: A guide to nominal group and Delphi processes.* Glenview, IL: Scott, Foresman.

Dennis, A. R., Easton, A. C., Easton, G. K., George, J. F., & Nunamaker, J. F. (1990). Ad hoc versus established groups in an electronic meeting system environment. In *Proceedings of the Twenty-Third Annual Hawaii International Conference on System Sciences* (pp. 23-29). Los Alamitos, CA: IEEE Computer Society Press.

Dennis, A. R., & Gallupe, R. B. (1993). A history of group support systems empirical research: Lessons learned and future directions. In L. Jessup & J. Valacich (Eds.), *Group support systems: New perspectives* (pp. 59-77). New York: Macmillan.

Dennis, A. R., George, J. F., Jessup, L. M., Nunamaker, J. F., & Vogel, D. R. (1988). Information technology to support electronic meetings. *MIS Quarterly, 12,* 591-624.

Dennis, A. R., & Valacich, J. S. (1993). Computer brainstorms: More heads are better than one. *Journal of Applied Psychology, 78,* 531-537.

Dennis, A. R., & Valacich, J. S. (1994). Group, sub-group, and nominal group in idea generation: New rules for a new media? *Journal of Management, 20,* 723-736.

Dennis, A. R., Valacich, J. S., & Nunamaker, J. F. (1990). An experimental investigation of the effects of group size in an electronic meeting environment. *IEEE Transactions on Systems, Man, & Cybernetics, 20,* 1049-1057.

DeSanctis, G. (1993). Shifting foundations in group support system research. In L. M. Jessup & J. S. Valacich (Eds.), *Group support systems: New perspectives* (pp. 97-111). New York: Macmillan.

DeSanctis, G., & Gallupe, R. B. (1987). A foundation for the study of group decision support systems. *Management Science, 33,* 589-609.

DeSanctis, G., & Poole, M. S. (1991). Understanding the differences in collaborative system use through appropriation analysis. In J. F. Nunamaker (Ed.), *Proceedings of the Twenty-Fourth Annual Hawaii International Conference on Systems Science, 3.* Los Alamitos, CA: IEEE Computer Society Press.

DeSanctis, G., & Poole, M. C. (1994). Capturing the complexity in advanced technology use: Adaptive structuration theory. *Organization Science, 5,* 121-147.

DeSanctis, G., Poole, M. S., Dickson, G. W., & Jackson, B. (1993). An interpretive analysis of team use of group technologies. *Journal of Organizational Computing, 3,* 1-29.

Dubrovsky, V. J., Kiesler, S., & Sethna, B. (1991). The equalization phenomenon: Status effects in computer-mediated and face-to-face decision-making groups. *Human-Computer Interaction, 6,* 119-146.

Dufner, D., Hiltz, S. R., Johnson, K., & Czech, R. (1995). Distributed group support: The effects of voting tools on group perceptions of media richness. *Group Decision and Negotiation, 4,* 235-250.

Easton, G. K., George, J. F., Nunamaker, J. F., & Pendergast, M. O. (1990). Using two different electronic meeting system tools for the same task: An experimental comparison. *Journal of Management Information Systems, 7,* 85-100.

Elwart-Keys, M., Halonen, D., Horton, M., Kass, R., & Scott, P. (1990). User interface requirements for face to face groupware. In *Proceedings of the Conference on Human Factors in Computer Systems* (CHI'90, Seattle, WA) (pp. 295-301). New York: Association for Computing Machinery.

Fjermestad, J., Hiltz, S. R., Ferront, F., Turoff, M., Ford, C., Johnson, K., Ocker, R., & Czech, R. M. (1994). *Distributed computer supported cooperative strategic decision making using structured conflict and consensus approaches.* Unpublished manuscript, School of Industrial Management, New Jersey Institute of Technology, Newark.

Fulk, J., & Boyd, B. (1991). Emerging theories of communication in organizations. *Journal of Management, 17,* 407-446.

Fulk, J., Schmitz, J., & Steinfield, C. (1990). A social influence model of technology use. In J. Fulk & C. Steinfield (Eds.), *Organizations and communication technology* (pp. 117-140). Newbury Park, CA: Sage.

Galegher, J., & Kraut, R. (1990). Computer-mediated communication for intellectual teamwork: A field experiment in group writing. In *Proceedings of the Third Conference on Computer-Supported Cooperative Work* (pp. 65-78). New York: ACM.

Gallupe, R. B. (1992). The executive decision centre. In R. P. Bostrom, R. T. Watson, & S. T. Kinney (Eds.), *Computer augmented teamwork: A guided tour* (pp. 268-284). New York: Van Nostrand Reinhold.

Gallupe, R. B., Bastianutti, L. M., & Cooper, W. H. (1991). Unblocking brainstorms. *Journal of Applied Psychology, 76,* 137-142.

Gallupe, R. B., Cooper, W. H., Grisé, M., & Bastianutti, L. M. (1994). Blocking electronic brainstorms. *Journal of Applied Psychology, 79,* 77-86.

Gallupe, R. B., Dennis, A. R., Cooper, W. H., Valacich, J. S., Bastianutti, L. M., & Nunamaker, J. F. (1992). Electronic brainstorming and group size. *Academy of Management Journal, 35*, 350-369.

Gallupe, R. B., DeSanctis, G., & Dickson, G. W. (1988). Computer-based support for group problem finding: An experimental investigation. *MIS Quarterly, 12*, 277-296.

Gallupe, R. B., & McKeen, J. D. (1990). Enhancing computer-mediated communication: An experimental investigation into the use of a group decision support system for face-to-face versus remote meetings. *Information & Management, 18*, 1-13.

George, J. F. (1992). An examination of four GDSS experiments. *Journal of Information Sciences, 18*, 149-158.

George, J. F., Easton, G., Nunamaker, J. F., & Northcraft, G. (1990). A study of collaborative group work with and without computer-based support. *Information Systems Research, 1*, 394-415.

Gopal, A., Bostrom, R. P., & Chin, W. W. (1993). Applying adaptive structuration theory to investigate the process of group support systems use. *Journal of Management Information Systems, 9*, 45-69.

Grudin, J. (1991). CSCW introduction. *Communications of the ACM, 34*, 31-34.

Guzzo, R. A. (1979). *The decision making quality of managerial groups.* Unpublished doctoral dissertation, Yale University.

Hewes, D. E. (1986). A socio-egocentric model of group decision-making. In R. Y. Hirokawa & M. S. Poole (Eds.), *Communication and group decision making* (1st ed., pp. 265-291). Beverly Hills, CA: Sage.

Hiltz, S. R., & Turoff, M. (1992). Virtual meetings: Computer conferencing and distributed group support. In R. P. Bostrom, R. T. Watson, & S. T. Kinney (Eds.), *Computer augmented teamwork: A guided tour* (pp. 67-85). New York: Van Nostrand Reinhold.

Hiltz, S. R., Turoff, M., & Johnson, K. (1989). Experiments in group decision making, 3: Disinhibition, deindividuation, and group process in pen name and real name computer conferences. *Decision Support Systems, 5*, 217-232.

Hirokawa, R. Y. (1985). Discussion procedures and decision-making performance: A test of a functional perspective. *Human Communication Research, 12*, 203-224.

Hirokawa, R. Y., & McLeod, P. L. (1993, November). *Communication, decision development, and decision quality in small groups: An integration of two approaches.* Paper presented at the annual meeting of the Speech Communication Association, Miami Beach.

Hirokawa, R. Y., & Pace, R. (1983). A descriptive investigation of the possible communication-based reasons for effective and ineffective group decision-making. *Communication Monographs, 50*, 363-379.

Ho, T. H., & Raman, K. S. (1991). The effects of GDSS and elected leadership on small group meetings. *Journal of Management Information Systems, 8*, 109-134.

Hollingshead, A. B., & McGrath, J. E. (1995). The whole is less than the sum of its parts: A critical review of research on computer-assisted groups. In R. A. Guzzo & E. Salas (Eds.), *Team decisions and team performance in organizations* (pp. 46-78). San Francisco: Jossey-Bass.

Hollingshead, A. B., McGrath, J. E., & O'Connor, K. M. (1993). Group task performance and communication technology. *Small Group Research, 24*, 307-333.

Hong, I. B., & Vogel, D. R. (1993). *Preference aggregation and consensus analysis for MCDM GDSS: A social-choice approach.* Unpublished manuscript, College of Business Administration, Western Kentucky University, Bowling Green.

Horton, M., Rogers, P., Austin, L., Brimm, D., & McCormick, M. (1991). The impact of face-to-face collaborative technology on group writing. In J. F. Nunamaker (Ed.),

Proceedings of the Twenty-Fourth Hawaii International Conference on System Sciences. Los Alamitos, CA: IEEE Computer Society Press.

Hymes, C. M., & Olson, G. M. (1992). Unblocking brainstorming through the use of a simple group editor. *Proceedings of the 1992 Conference on Computer Supported Cooperative Work* (Vol. 6). Toronto: Association for Computing Machinery.

Jarvenpaa, S. L., Rao, V. S., & Huber, G. P. (1988). Computer support for meetings of groups working on unstructured problems: A field experiment. *MIS Quarterly, 12,* 645-666.

Jessup, L. M., Connolly, T., & Galegher, J. (1990). The effects of anonymity on GDSS group process with an idea-generating task. *MIS Quarterly, 14,* 313-321.

Jessup, L. M., Connolly, T., & Tansik, D. (1990). Toward a theory of automated group work: The deindividuating effects of anonymity. *Small Group Research, 21,* 333-348.

Jessup, L. M., & Tansik, D. A. (1991). Decision making in an automated environment: The effects of anonymity and proximity on group process and outcome with a group decision support system. *Decision Sciences, 22,* 266-279.

Johansen, R. (1988). *Groupware: Computer support for business teams.* New York: Free Press.

Kiesler, S., Siegel, J., & McGuire, T. W. (1984). Social psychological aspects of computer-mediated communication. *American Psychologist, 39,* 1123-1134.

Kiesler, S., Zubrow, D., Moses, A. M., & Geller, V. (1985). Affect in computer-mediated communication: An experiment in synchronous terminal-to-terminal discussion. *Human-Computer Interaction, 1,* 77-104.

Krone, R. M., Jablin, F. M., & Putnam, L. L. (1987). Communication theory and organizational communication: Multiple perspectives. In F. M. Jablin, L. L. Putnam, K. H. Roberts, & L. W. Porter (Eds.), *Handbook of organizational communication* (pp. 18-40). Newbury Park, CA: Sage.

Kydd, C. T., & Ferry, D. L. (1991). A behavioral view of computer supported cooperative work tools. *Journal of Management Systems, 3,* 55-67.

Lim, L., & Benbasat, I. (1992). A theoretical perspective of negotiation support systems. *Journal of Management Information Systems, 9,* 27-44.

Lyytinen, K. J., & Ngwenyama, O. K. (1992). What does computer support for cooperative work mean? A structurational analysis of computer supported cooperative work. *Accounting, Management & Information Technology, 2,* 19-37.

Mantei, M. M. (1988). Capturing the capture lab concepts: A case study in the design of computer supported meeting environments. In I. Greif (Ed.), *Proceedings of the Second Conference on Computer Supported Cooperative Work* (Vol. 3, pp. 257-270). Portland, OR: Association for Computing Machinery.

McGrath, J. E. (1984). *Groups: Interaction and performance.* Englewood Cliffs, NJ: Prentice Hall.

McGrath, J. E., Arrow, H., Gruenfeld, D. H., & Hollingshead, A. B. (1993). Groups, tasks, and technology: The effects of experience and change [Special issue: Time, task, and technology in work groups: The JEMCO Workshop study]. *Small Group Research, 24,* 406-420.

McGrath, J. E., Arrow, H., Gruenfeld, D. H., Hollingshead, A. B., & O'Connor, K. M. (1993). Groups, tasks, and technology: The effects of experience and change. *Small Group Research, 24,* 406-420.

McGrath, J. E., & Hollingshead, A. B. (1993). Putting the "group" back in group support systems: Some theoretical issues about dynamic processes in group with technological enhancements. In L. M. Jessup & J. S. Valacich (Eds.), *Group support systems: New perspectives* (pp. 78-96). New York: Macmillan.

McLeod, P. L. (1991, August). *What if Jesus had communicated with his Apostles using a computer? Technology use by some famous groups.* Paper presented at the 51st Annual Meeting of the Academy of Management, Miami Beach.

McLeod, P. L. (1992). An assessment of the experimental literature on electronic support of group work: Results of a meta-analysis. *Human-Computer Interaction, 7,* 257-280.

McLeod, P. L., & Elston, S. E. (1994a). *Anonymity in GSS communication: A study of the search for identity.* Unpublished manuscript, University of Iowa, College of Business Administration.

McLeod, P. L., & Elston, S. E. (1994b, August). *Minority opinion and private opinion change: Moderating effects of GSS use and anonymity.* Paper presented at the 54th Annual Meeting of the Academy of Management, Dallas, TX.

McLeod, P. L., & Liker, J. K. (1992). Electronic meeting systems: Evidence from a low structure environment. *Information Systems Research, 3,* 195-223.

Melone N. P., McGuire, T. W., King, R., Hartman, A., Hartzel, K. S., Papageorgiou, E., & Gerwing, T. (1993). *The effects of computer-mediation on majority-minority influence and social responsibility in group decisions* (Unpublished Working Paper, #1993-16). Carnegie-Mellon University, Graduate School of Industrial Administration.

Morrison, J., Morrison, M., & Vogel, D. (1992). Software to support business teams. *Group Decision and Negotiation, 2,* 91-115.

Nemeth, C. J. (1986). Differential contributions of majority and minority influence. *Psychological Review, 93,* 23-32.

Ngwenyama, O. K., Bryson, N., & Mobolurin, A. (in press). Supporting consensus building in group decision making: Techniques for analyzing consensus relevant data in GSS. *Decision Support Systems.*

Ngwenyama, O. K., & Lyytinen, K. J. (in press). Group work as coordinated social action: A theoretical framework for groupware research. *ACM Transactions on Information Systems.*

Nunamaker, J. F., Dennis, A. R., Valacich, J. S., Vogel, D. R., & George, J. F. (1993). Group support systems research: Experiences from the lab and field. In L. M. Jessup & J. S. Valacich (Eds.), *Group support systems: New perspectives* (pp. 123-145). New York: Macmillan.

Nunamaker, J. F., Vogel, D., & Konsynski, B. (1989). Interaction of task and technology to support large groups. *Decision Support Systems, 5,* 139-152.

Ocker, R., Hiltz, S. R., Turoff, M., & Fjermestad, J. (1994). *Computer support for distributed software design teams: Preliminary experimental results.* Unpublished manuscript, School of Industrial Management, New Jersey Institute of Technology.

Olson, J. S., Olson, G., Storrøsten, M., & Carter, M. (1992). How a group editor changes the character of a design meeting as well as its outcome. *Proceedings of the Conference on Computer Supported Cooperative Work.* Toronto: The Association of Computer Machinery.

Piaget, J. (1926). *The language and thought of the child.* New York: Harcourt Brace.

Pinsonneault, A., & Kraemer, K. L. (1989). The impact of technological support on groups: An assessment of the empirical research. *Decision Support Systems, 5,* 197-216.

Poole, M. S., & DeSanctis, G. (1990). Understanding the use of group decision support systems: The theory of adaptive structuration. In J. Fulk & C. Steinfield (Eds.), *Organizations and communication technology* (pp. 173-195). Newbury Park, CA: Sage.

Poole, M. S., & DeSanctis, G. (1992). Microlevel structuration processes in computer-supported group decision making. *Human Communication Research, 19,* 5-49.

Poole, M. S., Holmes, M., Watson, R., & DeSanctis, G. (1993). Group decision support systems and group communication: A comparison of decision-making processes in computer-supported and nonsupported groups. *Communication Research, 20*, 176-213.

Poole, M. S., & Jackson, M. H. (1993). Communication theory and group support systems. In L. M. Jessup & J. S. Valacich (Eds.), *Group support systems: New perspectives* (pp. 281-293). New York: Macmillan.

Poole, M. S., & Roth, J. (1989). Decision development in small groups V: Test of a contingency model. *Human Communication Research, 15*, 549-589.

Poole, M. S., Seibold, D. R., & McPhee, R. D. (1985). Group decision-making as a structurational process. *Quarterly Journal of Speech, 71*, 74-102.

Poole, M. S., Shannon, D. L., & DeSanctis, G. (1992). Communication media and negotiation processes. In L. L. Putnam & M. E. Roloff (Eds.), *Communication and negotiation* (pp. 46-66). Newbury Park, CA: Sage.

Quinn, R. E. (1989). *Beyond rational management*. San Francisco: Jossey-Bass.

Raman, K. S., & Wei, K. K. (1993). The GDSS research project. In R. P. Bostrom, R. T. Watson, & S. T. Kinney (Eds.), *Computer augmented teamwork: A guided tour* (pp. 210-220). New York: Van Nostrand Reinhold.

Rao, V. S., Desroches, V. M., & Trapnell, P. (1993). *The effect of workplace reticence on preference for meeting type: An empirical study.* Unpublished manuscript, University of British Columbia, Vancouver.

Rao, V. S., & Jarvenpaa, S. L. (1991). Computer support for GDSS research. *Management Science, 37*, 1347-1362.

Rice, R. E. (1982). Communication networking in computer-conferencing systems: A longitudinal study of group roles and system structure. In M. Burgoon (Ed.), *Communication yearbook, 6* (pp. 925-944). Beverly Hills, CA: Sage.

Sambamurthy, V., Poole, M. S., & Kelly, J. (1993). The effects of variations in GDSS capabilities on decision-making processes in groups. *Small Group Research, 24*, 523-546.

Shannon, C., & Weaver, W. (1949). *The mathematical theory of communication*. Urbana-Champaign: University of Illinois Press.

Siegel, J., Dubrovsky, V. J., Kiesler, S., & McGuire, T. (1986). Group process in computer-mediated communication. *Organizational Behavior and Human Decision Processes, 37*, 157-187.

Simon, H. (1964). The architecture of complexity. *General Systems Yearbook, 10*, 63-76.

Smith, K. K., & Berg, D. N. (1987a). A paradoxical conception of group dynamics. *Human Relations, 40*, 633-657.

Smith, K. K., & Berg, D. N. (1987b). *Paradoxes of group life*. San Francisco: Jossey-Bass.

Steeb, R., & Johnston, S. C. (1981). A computer-based interactive system for group decision making. *IEEE Transactions on Systems, Man, and Cybernetics, SMC-11*, 544-552.

Straus, S. G., & McGrath, J. E. (1994). Does the medium matter? The interaction of task type and technology on group performance and member reactions. *Journal of Applied Psychology, 79*, 87-97.

Thomas, K. (1976). Conflict and conflict management. In M. Dunnette (Ed.), *Handbook of industrial and organizational psychology* (pp. 889-936). Chicago: Rand McNally.

Trevino, L., Lengel, R., & Daft, R. (1987). Media symbolism, media richness, and media choice in organizations: A symbolic interactionist perspective. *Communication Research, 14*, 553-575.

Turoff, M., & Hiltz, S. R. (1982). Computer support for group versus individual decisions. *IEEE Transactions on Communications, 30*, 82-91.

Valacich, J. S., Dennis, A. R., & Connolly, T. (1994). Idea generation in computer-based groups: A new ending to an old story. *Organizational Behavior and Human Decision Processes, 57*, 448-467.

Valacich, J. S., Dennis, A. R., & Nunamaker, J. F. (1992). Group size and anonymity effects on computer-mediated idea generation. *Small Group Research, 23*, 49-73.

Valacich, J. S., Jessup, L. M., Dennis, A. R., & Nunamaker, J. F. (1992). A conceptual framework of anonymity in group support systems. *Group Decision and Negotiation, 1*, 219-241.

Valacich, J. S., Paranka, D., George, J. F., & Nunamaker, J. F. (1993). Communication concurrency in the new media: A new dimension for media richness. *Communication Research, 20*, 249-276.

Wagner, G. R., Wynne, B. E., & Mennecke, B. E. (1993). Group support systems facilities and software. In L. M. Jessup & J. S. Valacich (Eds.), *Group support systems: New perspectives* (pp. 8-55). New York: Macmillan.

Walther, J. B. (1992). Interpersonal effects in computer-mediated interaction: A relational perspective. *Communication Research, 19*, 52-90.

Walther, J. B. (1994a). *Computer-mediated communication: Impersonal, interpersonal and hyperpersonal interaction.* Unpublished manuscript, Department of Communication Studies, Northwestern University, Evanston, IL.

Walther, J. B. (1994b). Anticipated on-going interaction versus channel effects on relational communication in computer-mediated interaction. *Human Communication Research, 20*, 473-501.

Walther, J. B., Anderson, J. F., & Park, D. W. (1994). Interpersonal effects in computer-mediated interaction: A meta-analysis of social and antisocial communication. *Communication Research, 21*, 460-487.

Walther, J. B., & Burgoon, J. K. (1992). Relational communication in computer-mediated interaction. *Human Communication Research, 19*, 50-88.

Watson, R. T., DeSanctis, G., & Poole, M. S. (1988). Using a GDSS to facilitate group consensus: Some intended and unintended consequences. *MIS Quarterly, 12*, 463-478.

Weisband, S. P. (1992). Group discussion and first advocacy effects in computer-mediated and face-to-face decision making groups. *Organizational Behavior and Human Decision Processes, 53*, 352-380.

Weisband, S. P., Schneider, S. K., & Connolly, T. (1995). Computer-mediated communication and social information: Status salience and status differences. *Academy of Management Journal, 38*, 1124-1151.

Wynne, B. E., Anson, R., Heminger, A. R., & Valacich, J. S. (1992). Support for organizational workgroups: An applied research program of theory building and field testing. In R. P. Bostrom, R. T. Watson, & S. T. Kinney (Eds.), *Computer augmented teamwork: A guided tour* (pp. 197-209). New York: Van Nostrand Reinhold.

Zack, M. H. (1993). Electronic messaging and shared context in an ongoing work group. In *Proceedings of the Twenty-Sixth Hawaii Conference on Systems Science.* Los Alamitos, CA: IEEE Computer Society Press.

Zigurs, I. (1989). Interaction analysis in GDSS research: Description of an experience and some recommendations. *Decision Support Systems, 5*, 233-241.

Zigurs, I., Poole, M. S., & DeSanctis, G. (1988). A study of influence in computer-mediated group decision making. *MIS Quarterly, 12*, 625-644.

Index

Abric, J., 238
Adaptive structuration theory (AST), 129, 432-433, 441. *See also* Structuration theory
Adkins, M., 42
Ager, J., 15
Albrecht, K., 375-376
Alderfer, C., 156-157
Alderton, S., 37, 259, 308
Alliger, G., 305
Altman, I., 215
Ambiguity moderated model (AMM), 260
AMM. *See* Ambiguity moderated model
Ancona, D., 164-165, 315-316, 330-331
Anderson, L., 15, 308
Andrews, P., 308
Appropriation, 122-123, 132-137, 139, 140-141
Argumentation theory:
and structuration theory, 35, 127-129, 140
persuasive (PAT), 37, 130, 246, 248, 249-252, 254, 259-260, 261
Asch, S., 64, 390, 391
Ashby, W., 319

Askling, L., 278
AST. *See* Adaptive structuration theory
Attribution theory, 37, 89-90
Auer, J., 100, 368
Austin, L., 442, 444

Bacon, C., 312
Baird, A., 100
Bales, R., 11, 12, 24, 25, 37-38, 41, 91, 98, 217, 218, 231
Ball, M., 36, 106
Banks, S., 126
Barge, J., 40, 320, 321, 329, 333
Barker, J., 163-164
Barker, L., 348
Barley, S., 126
Barnlund, D., 285
Bartunek, J., 360
Basadur, M., 352, 358-359
Baseline model. *See* Socio-egocentric theory
Bastianutti, L., 389
Beard, J., 306, 314
Beatty, M., 37
Becker, S., 27

Bell, D., 257
Bell, M., 30
Berg, D., 124
Berteotti, C., 162
Billingsley, J., 135
Black, E., 26
Bochner, A., 27
Boethius, S., 38
Bona fide group theory:
  boundaries in, 148, 149-152,
    154-155, 156, 161, 172-175
  characteristics of, 149-155
  coordinated group action in, 153,
    154-155, 156, 165
  development of, 40, 147-148
  external communication in,
    161-166
  group identity in, 150, 151-152,
    154-155, 166, 167, 169
  interdependence in, 149, 152-155,
    172-175
  intergroup communication in,
    153, 154-155, 156
  internal communication in,
    158-161
  interpretative frames in, 154-155,
    156
  jurisdiction/autonomy in,
    153-155, 156, 167
  membership fluctuation in, 150,
    151, 154-155
  representative roles in, 150, 151,
    154-155, 156
  research agenda for, 174-175
  vs. decision emergence model,
    167-168, 169, 170-171, 174
  vs. embedded intergroup
    relations theory, 156-157
  vs. normative/functional theory,
    166-167, 169-170, 174
  vs. organizational anarchy
    theory, 156-157
  vs. structuration theory, 168-169,
    171-174

See also Functional theory; Group
    communication history;
    Socio-egocentric theory;
    Structuration theory; Symbolic
    convergence theory
Bormann, E., 27, 36, 99, 152, 233, 293
Boster, F., 259, 260
Bostrom, R., 448
Bottger, P., 330
Boyd, B., 435
Bradley, P., 255, 308
Brainstorming, 353, 358-359, 366,
    367, 368, 369, 371
  and communication technology,
    182-183, 439-441, 443, 445, 451,
    454
  brainwriting, 358
  procedural influence of, 388-389
Brainwriting, 358. See also
    Brainstorming
Brashers, D., 42
Braybrooke, D., 351, 360
Brett, J., 162
Brewer, J., 122, 125
Brilhart, J., 348, 357
Brimm, D., 444
Brooke, M., 257
Brossman, B., 37, 128
Brown, R., 248
Bunyi, J., 308
Burgoon, J., 436-437, 449
Burnstein, E., 246, 250
Buzz groups, 365-366

Caldwell, D., 162, 315-316
Campbell, D., 152
Canary, D., 37, 127, 128, 130, 133
Cappella, J., 12
Capture Lab (Electronic Data
    Systems), 430. See also
    Communication technology
Carr, L., 21
Carter, L., 11

Chakravarthy, B., 354
Challenger (NASA), 270-271, 281, 282
Chandler, T., 37, 159, 230
Charettes, 365
Cheney, G., 37
Chidambaram, L., 448
Chilberg, J., 368, 370
Choice shifts:
    communicative influence of, 25,
        37, 246, 247-249, 250-251,
        258-260, 261
    in interaction theory, 25
Christie, S., 256-257
Cicourel, A., 122
Cline, R., 28, 37
Cline, T., 28, 37
Clinton, Bill, 58-59, 66
Coding schemes:
    Decision Proposal Coding
        System, 217
    flexible phase mapping, 224,
        238-239
    Interaction Process Analysis (IPA),
        24, 25
    observational, 21-22, 24, 25, 29
    research agenda for, 39
Cohen, S., 37-38
Colloquies, 364
Comadena, M., 371
Communication behavior:
    and communication technology,
        437-438, 450-451
    and decision performance,
        277-278
    and leadership, 310-313
    and procedures, 366-368, 373-376
    anonymous/nonverbal, 437-438,
        450-451
    influence of, 257
    See also Communicative influence
Communication technology:
    additive information aggregation
        in, 431, 432

aggregate information exchange
    in, 428, 429 (figure), 431-433
and adaptive structuration
    theory (AST), 432-433, 441
and brainstorming, 182-183,
    439-441, 443, 445, 451, 454
and decision performance, 294
and group consensus, 446
and group member
    characteristics, 441
and group size, 440-441
and individual opinion change,
    446-448
and information exchange
    results, 428, 429 (figure),
    442-449
and interdependence, 444-446,
    451-452
and leadership, 301
and relational information,
    435-437, 452
and socioemotional information,
    311-312, 314-315, 431, 436
and symbolic information, 431,
    437, 452
and task characteristics, 433-435,
    451-452
and task-oriented information,
    431, 435-436
and task performance quality,
    443-446
anonymity/nonverbal behavior
    in, 437-438, 450-451
asynchronous communication in,
    430, 440, 452-453
computer conferencing, 430, 439,
    443, 447
constraining/enabling conditions
    of, 428, 429 (figure), 433-442
emergent information
    aggregation in, 431, 432
features of, 132, 138-139, 435-438
for decision development,
    234-235, 238-239

group decision support systems
(GDSSs) in, 42, 131-132,
134-138, 139, 182-183, 234-235,
294
in structuration theory, 126, 129,
130-132, 133, 134-138, 139,
432-433, 435-438, 441, 442, 451
model for, 427-428, 429 (figure)
participation in, 438-440, 451
research agenda for, 449-454
spirit in, 132, 139, 442, 451
theoretical approaches to,
426-427
types of, 428-430
See also Group communication
history; Procedural influence;
Procedures
Communicative influence:
and ambiguity moderated model
(AMM), 260
and choice shifts, 25, 37, 246,
247-249, 250-251, 258-260, 261
and communication behavior,
257
and distribution valence model
(DVM), 261
and gender, 41, 255
and group consensus, 260-261
and group polarization, 246, 250,
251, 252-254
and individual characteristics,
255-256
and input factors, 255-258
and minority members, 246-247,
258, 259
and output factors, 258-261
and participation factors, 257-258
and persuasive arguments theory
(PAT), 37, 130, 246, 248,
249-252, 254, 259-260, 261
and task information, 256-257
problematics of, 243-247, 262
research on, 242-243

social comparison theory (SCT)
on, 246, 248-249, 250, 251-252,
254, 259
social identity theory (SIT) on,
246, 248, 249, 252-254, 259
theories on, 246, 247-254, 259
See also Decision development;
Decision performance; Group
communication history;
Leadership
Computer-mediated
communication. See
Communication technology
Conflict resolution, 325-327, 328
(figure), 331, 332, 333, 334,
335, 336
Constitutive analysis:
and decision performance, 6, 8-9,
286-287, 293-294
in structuration theory, 129
Contingency model
for decision development, 131,
222-224, 225-226, 227-228, 229,
237-238
for decision performance, 290-291
for group communication, 13-14
Continuous model, 221-224, 229,
230-231, 237-238
Contractor, N., 441
Contradiction, 124, 138-140
Cooper, J., 253
Cooper, W., 389
Courtright, J., 28
Cragan, J., 4, 27, 29, 38, 370
Craig, R., 82
Crawford slip, 369
Critical event model, 219-221, 229,
231-233, 237-238
Cronshaw, S., 306
Crowell, L., 25, 101, 167, 222, 232,
352, 355, 358, 368, 375
Curtis, E., 372

DA. *See* Devil's advocate
Dansereau, F., 15
Darley, J., 249
Darwin, C., 88
Dashiell, J., 20
Data-splitting, 323-324, 328 (figure),
    331, 332, 333, 334, 335, 336
Davis, J., 114, 130, 184, 185, 186,
    187-188, 244-246, 272, 390, 412,
    418
Dawes, R., 68
Decision development:
    and outcome, 235-237
    communication technology for,
        234-235, 238-239
    contingency model for, 131,
        222-224, 225-226, 227-228, 229,
        237-238
    continuous model for, 221-224,
        229, 230-231, 237-238
    critical event model for, 219-221,
        229, 231-233, 237-238
    deep structure model for,
        220-221, 229, 237-238
    delays/disruptions in, 223
    factors influencing, 9-11, 233-235
    flexible phase mapping for, 224,
        238-239
    group interaction in, 24-25,
        215-216
    group structural variables in, 224,
        235
    group task characteristics in, 224,
        233-234, 238
    multiple sequence model for, 35,
        203, 208n5, 217-218, 229-230,
        237-238
    normal breakpoints in, 223, 224,
        225-226, 227, 231-232
    objective task characteristics in,
        224, 233-234, 238
    path types in, 229-231
    phase model for, 24-25, 216-219,
        229, 237-238
    punctuated equilibrium model
        for, 220-221, 229, 237-238
    revolutionary period model for,
        220-221, 229, 237-238
    social construction model for,
        225-229, 237-238
    task perplexity in, 233, 234-235,
        238
    unitary sequence model for,
        217-218, 229-230, 235, 236,
        237-238
    See also Communicative
        influence; Decision
        performance; Group
        communication history;
        Leadership
Decision emergence model, 167-168,
    169, 170-171, 174
Decision performance:
    analytical/evaluative influences
        on, 289-291
    and *Challenger* (NASA), 270-271,
        281, 282
    and communication behavior,
        277-278
    and communication modalities,
        275, 289
    and communication procedures,
        275-277
    and communication quality,
        272-273, 277-278
    and communication role
        confusion, 284-287
    and communication structures,
        273-274
    and communication technology,
        294
    and decision correctness, 279-280,
        281-282
    and decision logic, 271
    and decision quality, 280-282
    and decision utility, 281-282
    and effort quality, 270

and information distribution, 287-288, 290-291
and information processing, 288-289, 290-291, 295n2
and information resources, 279
and integrative theory absence, 283-284
and mediation, 6-7, 8-9, 285-287, 293
and reflective thinking model, 276
and thinking quality, 270-271
appropriateness in, 283
constitutive view of, 6, 8-9, 286-287, 293-294
contingency model for, 290-291
importance of, 269-270, 295n1
imprecise measures of, 279-283
influences on, 270-271, 276, 287-291
research agenda for, 291-295
research limitations on, 279-291
social decision scheme (SDS) for, 272-273
task factors influence on, 276, 287-291
See also Communicative influence; Decision development; Group communication history; Leadership
Decision Proposal Coding System, 217. See also Coding schemes
Deep structure model, 220-221, 229, 237-238
Delbecq, A., 353
Delphi technique, 359, 365, 369
and socio-egocentric theory, 204, 208n6
Dennis, A., 428-429, 438, 441
DeSanctis, G., 42, 125, 126, 129, 131-132, 133, 134, 135, 136, 137, 138, 139, 227, 228, 238, 239, 427, 428-429, 442, 446, 448
DeStephen, R., 260

De Vader, C., 305
Devil's advocate (DA), 361
Dewey, J., 21, 102, 182-183, 276, 350
DI. See Dialectical inquiry
Dialectical inquiry (DI), 361
DICE simulation model, 186
Dickens, M., 20, 21, 22
Diehl, M., 359, 389
Discussion: Method of Democracy (Crowell), 101
Discussion and Debate (Ewbank/Auer), 100
Distribution valence model (DVM):
and communicative influence, 261
for socio-egocentric theory, 186-189
for structuration theory, 130
Dobbins, G., 306
Doelger, J., 226, 228, 238
Donnellon, A., 159-160, 161
Donohue, W., 37
Drecksel, D., 312, 313
Driskell, J., 310
Dubrovsky, V., 439, 447
DVM. See Distribution valence model

Eagly, A., 307-308, 309, 310, 313
Earle, W., 251
Easton, A., 438
Easton, E., 438
Elliott, H., 100
Ellis, D., 30, 191, 312, 368
Ellis, R., 306
Elston, S., 448, 449
Embedded intergroup relations theory, 156-157
Environment:
and leadership, 301-303, 315-317, 322-324, 328 (figure), 329-337
in structuration theory, 138
procedural influence of, 397, 408, 410-412, 420n4

Equilibrium theory, 24, 231
   punctuated, 220-221, 229, 237-238
Etzioni, A., 351
Ewbank, H., 100, 368
Excursion, 358
Eyo, B., 108

Fantasy. *See* Symbolic convergence
   theory
Fiedler, F., 304
Field theory:
   communication networks in, 23
   development of, 22-24
   group cohesion in, 23
   leadership in, 23-24
Fifth Discipline, The (Senge), 271
Finger, P., 361
Firestien, R., 352
Fisher, A., 318, 368
Fisher, B., 5, 25, 27, 28, 29, 30,
   202-203, 217, 225, 229, 231-232
Flexible phase mapping, 224,
   238-239. *See also* Coding
   schemes
Focus groups, 364
Ford, Gerald, 60
Forums, 364
Fox, W., 359
Frey, L., 32, 37, 39, 40, 259
Frost, P., 317
Fulk, J., 435
Functional theory:
   accommodation in, 64
   affiliative constraints in, 61-62,
      63-64, 66-68, 70-72, 74-77
   camaraderie in, 64
   cognitive constraints in, 60, 61-63,
      66-70, 74-77
   communication role in, 11-12,
      65-68
   current status of, 56-57
   decision quality in, 33-34
   defensiveness in, 64

deficiencies of, 57-60
development of, 32-34, 55-56
direct/indirect acknowledgment
   in, 62
egocentric constraints in, 61-62,
   64-65, 66-68, 72-77
leadership in, 24
majority sentiment in, 63
modifications for, 59, 74-77
pluralistic ignorance in, 61
proposal types in, 63
self-importance in, 65
sense of urgency in, 62
uneven interaction in, 63
vs. bona fide group theory,
   166-167, 169-170, 174
win-lose orientation in, 64
See also Bona fide group theory;
   Group communication
   history; Socio-egocentric
   theory; Structuration theory;
   Symbolic convergence theory

Gagliano, C., 357
Galanes, G., 348
Galegher, J., 444
Gallupe, R., 389, 428-429, 442, 444,
   448
Gamache, R., 357
Garland, H., 306, 314
Garlick, R., 259
GDSSs. *See* Group decision support
   systems
Geier, J., 313
Geist, P., 37, 42, 159
Gender:
   and leadership, 306, 307-310, 313
   in group communication, 41, 255
George, J., 428-429, 438, 443, 444
Gersick, C., 158, 220-221, 232, 233, 234,
   239
Giddens, A., 34, 117, 121, 122, 124,
   125, 126, 133, 141, 142

Gladstein, D., 14, 159, 162
Goethals, G., 249
Gouran, D., 5, 25, 27, 29, 30, 36, 56, 57, 136-137, 278, 279, 280-281, 282, 283, 294, 351
Graen, G., 352
Green, S., 352
Green, T., 359
Grounded theory, 28
Group communication history:
    coding schemes in, 21-22, 24, 25, 29, 39
    communication technology in, 42
    cultural issues in, 42
    current issues in, 38-43
    equilibrium theory in, 24
    field theory in, 22-24
    functional theory in, 24, 32-34, 37
    grounded theory in, 28
    group discussion superiority in, 21
    groupthink in, 28
    importance of, 19-20, 43
    input-output model in, 37
    Interaction Process Analysis (IPA) in, 24, 25
    interaction theory in, 24-26
    interact system model in, 28, 30
    leadership theory in, 23-24
    1920-1945, 20-22
    1945-1970, 22-26
    1970-1980, 26-32
    1980-1990, 32-38
    outcome-oriented research in, 15-16, 29, 30-31
    procedural development in, 31-32, 39-40
    process-oriented research in, 21-22, 24, 25, 29-30, 31
    reflective thinking model in, 21
    research content in, 29-31
    responsibility theory in, 37
    social behavior theory in, 37
    structuration theory in, 34-36, 37
    symbolic convergence theory in, 36
    System for the Multiple Level Observation of Groups (SYMLOG) in, 37-38
    theory role in, 3-9, 27-28
Group consensus:
    and communication technology, 446
    as communicative influence, 260-261
    in interaction theory, 25
    in outcome-oriented research, 30
    procedures for, 359, 361, 362-363, 369
    social decision scheme (SDS) for, 392-394, 397-402, 408, 413, 414, 415, 419n2, 420-422
    See also Group size; Majority rule decision
Group control, 370
    in structuration theory, 137-138
Group decision support systems (GDSSs):
    development of, 42, 182-183
    for decision development, 234-235
    for decision performance, 294
    in structuration theory, 131-132, 134-138, 139
    See also Communication technology
Group member characteristics, 255-256, 441
Group polarization, 246, 250, 251, 252-254
Group size:
    and communication technology, 440-441
    and social decision scheme (SDS), 392-394, 397-402, 408, 413, 414, 415
    See also Group consensus; Majority rule decision

Group support systems (GSS). *See* Communication technology
GroupSystems (University of Arizona), 430, 443. *See also* Communication technology
Group tasks:
   and communication technology, 431, 433-436, 443-446, 451-452
   and decision development, 224, 233-235, 238
   and decision performance, 276, 287-291, 443-446
   and information, 256-257, 431, 435-436
   and leadership, 306, 311-312, 314-315, 329-330, 333-334, 336-337
   characteristics of, 224, 233-234, 238, 433-435, 451-452
   communicative influence of, 256-257
   complexity of, 233, 234-235, 238, 306, 329-330, 336-337
   in structuration theory, 137, 226-228
   perplexity of, 233, 234-235, 238
Groupthink:
   and decision making, 160-161, 175, 369
   development of, 28
GSS (Group support systems). *See* Communication technology
Guetzkow, H., 72, 274
Gulley, H., 347-348, 357
Guzzo, R., 444
Gyr, J., 72

Hackman, J., 14, 283, 293, 295
Hale, J., 260
Hall, J., 367
Hance, K., 350
Hansen, C., 260-261
Harkins, S., 358

Harper, N., 278
Harré, R., 37
Harvey, J., 61
Haslam, S., 255-256
Hawes, L., 27, 28, 29, 30, 37
Hawkins, K., 307
Haythorn, W., 11
Heffernan, M., 20, 21, 22
Hegedus, D., 359-360
Heinecke, C., 217
Heller, M., 135
Hernes, G., 116
Hewes, D., 41-42, 130, 196, 202, 203, 244, 279, 291-292, 373, 432
Hiltz, S., 438, 440, 444, 447
Hirokawa, R., 5, 14, 29, 33, 56, 57, 191, 192, 235-236, 278, 286, 288, 289, 290, 292, 320, 321, 329, 333
Hirota, K., 274
Ho, T., 439
Hoffer, J., 234
Hoffman, L., 186
Hoffman, R., 261
Holdridge, W., 304
Hollingshead, A., 433, 434, 440, 443, 444, 445, 446, 454
Holmes, M., 131, 163, 224, 235, 236, 238-239
Holstein, J., 134
Holt, R., 391
Homans, G., 114
Honeycutt, J., 231
Horton, M., 444
House, R., 304
Howell, J., 317
How We Think (Dewey), 102
Hutchinson, K., 255-256
Hymes, C., 443
Hymes, J., 260-261

Input-output model. *See* Socio-egocentric theory

Interaction Process Analysis (IPA), 24, 25. *See also* Coding schemes
Interaction theory:
  choice shifts in, 25
  developmental processes in, 24-25
  development of, 24-26
  discussion breakdown in, 25-26
  equilibrium theory in, 24
  group consensus in, 25
  Interaction Process Analysis (IPA) in, 24, 25
  linear models in, 24-25
  naturally occurring phases in, 24-25
  rhetorical perspective in, 26
  spiral models in, 25
Interact system model, 28, 30
Interdependence:
  and communication technology, 444-446, 451-452
  in bona fide group theory, 149, 152-155, 172-175
IPA. *See* Interaction Process Analysis
Isaksen, S., 349-350, 352
Isenberg, D., 251

Jackson, J., 114, 358
Jackson, M., 42, 432
Jackson, S., 127, 128
Jacobs, S., 127, 128
Jago, A., 304-305
Janis, I., 28, 56, 60, 63, 65-66, 67, 71, 270, 329, 331, 333, 355
Jarboe, S., 37, 244, 351
Jarvenpaa, S., 447-448
Jensen, A., 368, 370
Jessup, L., 428-429
Johansen, R., 428-429
Johnson, A., 21
Johnson, B., 307-308
Johnson, Lyndon, 71-72
Julian, K., 56, 292
Junctures, 136, 140

Jurma, W., 308

Kano, S., 274
Kaplan, M., 251
Karau, S., 308, 309, 310, 313, 359
Kelley, H., 114
Kelly, J., 359
Kennedy, John, 36
Kenny, D., 305
Keough, C., 132, 134, 138-139
Kepner, C., 358
Kerr, N., 260-261, 390, 391
Ketrow, S., 311-312
Keyton, J., 40
Kiesler, S., 447
Kirkpatrick, S., 305
Kirsch, L., 42
Kitayama, S., 246
Kline, J., 30
Klonsky, B., 308
Klopf, D., 348, 370
Knutson, T., 30, 304
Koomen, W., 257
Kraut, R., 444
Kuhn, R., 352
Kushell, E., 308

Lacoursiere, R., 216
Lage, E., 258
Lake, R., 132, 134, 138-139
Lamm, H., 250
Landsberger, H., 217
Lanzetta, J., 11
Larson, C., 27
Lateral thinking, 357
Lawson, E., 274
Leadership:
  action mediation in, 319, 324-328
  and communication technology, 301
  and gender, 306, 307-310, 313
  and group climate, 331

and group/environment
   boundaries, 301-303, 315-317,
   322-324, 328 (figure), 329-337
and role relationships, 330-331
as mediation, 317-337
as medium, 6-7, 8-9, 318-319
charismatic, 317
communication behavior in,
   310-313
communication skills in, 320-336
communication traits of, 305-310,
   313
conflict resolution in, 325-327,
   328 (figure), 331, 332, 333, 334,
   335, 336
data-splitting in, 323-324, 328
   (figure), 331, 332, 333, 334, 335,
   336
defined, 303-304
development of, 23-24
discourse quality in, 311
in decision making, 324-325, 328
   (figure), 329-330, 331, 333, 334,
   335, 336
in field theory, 23-24
informing in, 316
in functional theory, 24
in structuration theory, 120-121,
   122-124
internal-external approach to,
   302-303, 313-318
motivation in, 327, 328 (figure),
   331, 333, 334, 336
networking in, 322-323, 328
   (figure), 331, 332, 334, 335, 336
object mediation in, 319, 322-324,
   332
parading in, 316
participation rate in, 310-311, 313
probing in, 316
problem centered, 359
procedural, 312
relational, 324, 325-326, 328
   (figure), 333-334, 335-336

self-monitoring in, 306, 313
socioemotional, 311-312, 314-315
task complexity in, 306, 329-330,
   336-337
task-oriented, 311-312, 314-315,
   333-334
universal-situational approach to,
   302, 304-313, 317-318, 320-321,
   329-337
   See also Communicative
   influence; Decision
   development; Decision
   performance; Group
   communication history
Leatham, G., 56, 292
Leathers, D., 5, 26, 30, 277, 347-348,
   357
Leavitt, H., 274
Lecuyer, X., 254, 262
Leistner, C., 26
Leniency bias, 391, 392-393, 403-408,
   410-412
Levine, M., 387
Lewin, K., 22-23
Lewis, L., 138
Liker, J., 428-429, 436, 439, 442, 444
Lind, R., 131
Lindblom, C., 351, 360
Linear model, 24-25
Lion's den, 369
Locating power, 412-417
Locke, E., 305
Lorange, P., 354
Lord, R., 305
Lorge, I., 184, 185, 272
Lotus blossom, 369
Luus, C., 256-257

Mabee, T., 37
Mabry, E., 12, 217
MacCoun, R., 260-261, 390, 391
MacKenzie, K., 219
Mackie, D., 253, 254

Maier, N., 261
Majority rule decision, 391-396
    and social decision scheme (SDS),
        392-394, 397-402, 408, 413, 414,
        415, 419n2, 420-422
    intentional bias effects on, 412-417
    polling sequence effects on,
        396-412
    See also Group consensus; Group
        size
Makhijani, M., 308
Mann, L., 28, 63, 270, 355
Mann, R., 219
March, J., 11
Markham, S., 15
Mason, R., 361
Mayer, M., 259
McBurney, J., 350
McCormick, M., 444
McGarty, C., 255-256
McGee, M., 29, 56
McGrath, J., 14, 215, 433, 434, 440,
    443, 444, 454
McLeod, P., 292, 428-429, 436, 439,
    442, 444, 448, 449
McPhee, R., 8, 127, 129, 130, 244,
    261
Mediation:
    action, 319, 324-328
    and environment, 328 (figure),
        329-337
    and group climate, 331
    and motivation, 327, 328 (figure),
        331, 333, 334, 336
    and relational management, 324,
        325-326, 328 (figure), 333-334,
        335-336
    and task complexity, 306, 329-330,
        336-337
    as medium, 6-7, 8-9, 318-319
    communication skills for,
        320-336

conflict resolution in, 325-327,
    328 (figure), 331, 332, 333, 334,
    335, 336
data-splitting in, 323-324, 328
    (figure), 331, 332, 333, 334,
    335, 336
in decision making, 324-325, 328
    (figure), 329-330, 332, 333, 334,
    335, 336
in decision performance, 6-7, 8-9,
    285-287, 293
in structuration theory, 124,
    130-131, 138-140
object, 319, 322-324, 332
role relationships in, 330-331
See also Leadership
Medium. *See* Mediation
Meeting, The (Schwartzman), 225
Meirowitz, B., 11
Melone, N., 448
Melville, C., 163-164
Mennecke, B., 234, 428-429
Meyer, A., 238
Meyers, R., 35, 42, 126, 127, 128, 130,
    132
Miller, D., 22
Miller, L., 29, 56
Mintzberg, H., 230, 233, 235,
    354
Mixed scanning, 364
Mongeau, P., 259
Monroe, C., 30
Morris, C., 217, 283, 295
Mortensen, C., 27, 346
Moscovici, S., 254, 258, 262
Motivation, 327, 328 (figure), 331,
    333, 334, 336
Mullen, B., 310
Multi-attribute utility model, 360
Multidimensional scaling, 360
Multiple sequence model:
    for decision development, 35,
        203, 208n5, 217-218, 229-230,
        237-238

in socio-egocentric theory, 203,
208n5
in structuration theory, 35
Murninghan, J., 360
Myers, D., 250, 251

Naffrechoux, M., 258
Nelson, W., 30
Nemeth, C., 258
Nesting, 128, 141
Newton, Isaac, 86-87
Newton, R., 308
Ng, S., 257
NGT. *See* Nominal group technique
Nixon, Richard, 61, 281
Nominal group technique (NGT),
351, 358, 359-360, 362-363, 366,
367, 369, 370
in socio-egocentric theory, 182-183
Normative model, 166-167, 169-170,
174. *See also* Functional theory
Nunamaker, J., 428-429, 438
Nutt, P., 230, 237, 353

O'Keefe, D., 37
Olbrechts-Tyteca, L., 127
Olsen, J., 11, 163
Olson, G., 443
Olson, J., 444
Organizational anarchy theory,
156-157
Osborn, A., 358
Owen, W., 307

Pacanowsky, M., 163-164
Panels, 364
Parson, T., 217
Pavitt, C., 345-346, 347, 349, 372
Perelman, C., 127, 128

Persuasive arguments theory (PAT),
246, 248, 249-252, 254, 259-260,
261
and structuration theory, 130
development of, 37
See also Argumentation theory
PERT. *See* Program
evaluation/review technique
Petelle, J., 30
Phase model, 24-25, 216-219, 229,
237-238
Piaget, J., 193-194, 432
Plott, C., 387
Pluralistic ignorance, 61
PMs (Procedural mechanisms). *See*
Procedural influence
Poole, M., 5, 8, 10, 14, 35, 42, 124,
125, 126, 127, 129, 130,
131-132, 133, 134, 135, 136,
137, 138, 139, 141, 186-187,
188, 203, 217-218, 219, 222-223,
224, 225, 226-227, 228, 230,
231, 233-234, 235, 236, 238-239,
244, 261, 282-283, 292, 347,
350, 370, 432, 436, 442, 446, 449
Price, K., 371
Priem, R., 371
Prince, G., 111
Problem census, 356
Problem-solving model, 347-348,
349-354, 368-370
Procedural influence:
and procedural justice, 386
and social decision scheme (SDS),
392-394, 397-402, 408, 413, 414,
415, 419n2, 420-422
and standard operating
procedures, 385
of agenda structure, 387-388
of communication process,
388-389
of defendant protection norm, 391
of discussion, 384-387, 417

of environmental factors, 397,
    408, 410-412, 420n4
of group size, 399-419, 440-441
of intentional bias, 387, 412-417
of leniency bias, 391, 392-393,
    403-408, 410-412
of locating power, 412-417
of majority rule decision, 391-396,
    399-417, 420-422
of polling process, 389-396
of polling sequence, 390-394,
    396-419, 420-422
of polling timing, 390-391, 393
    (figure), 394, 417
on civil damage awards, 418-419
types of, 387-397
See also Communication
    technology; Group
    communication history;
    Procedures
Procedural justice, 386
Procedural mechanisms (PMs). See
    Procedural influence
Procedures:
    and communication behavior,
        366-368, 373-376
    and comprehensiveness, 370
    and group consensus, 359, 361,
        362-363, 369
    and group control, 137-138, 370
    and member involvement, 370
    and restrictiveness, 370
    and scope, 370
    as agendas, 275-277, 346
    as decision making processes, 347
    brainwriting, 358
    building involvement, 365-366
    buzz groups, 365-366
    charettes, 365
    colloquies, 364
    Crawford slip, 369
    creative, 349-350, 352-353, 354,
        357, 366-367, 371
    criteria setting, 357-358

critical functions, 355
critical thinking, 349-350, 357
decision making schemes, 362-363
defined, 346-349
Delphi technique, 204, 208n6,
    359, 365, 369
development of, 31-32, 39-40
devil's advocate (DA), 361
dialectical inquiry (DI), 361
excursion, 358
focus groups, 364
formal discussion, 347
formats, 275-277, 346-347
forums, 364
goal identification/problem
    prioritization, 355-356
groupthink, 28, 160-161, 175, 369
idea generation, 358-360
ideals method, 360, 363-364
incrementalism, 360
integrative decision making, 366
interaction rules for, 349, 364-366
intervention, 354
Kaizen, 369
lateral thinking, 357
lion's den, 369
lotus blossom, 369
mixed scanning, 364
multi-attribute utility model, 360
multidimensional scaling, 360
outsider interfacing, 364-365
panels, 364
planning, 353-354
problem analysis, 356-357
problem census, 356
problem management sequence,
    352
problem-solving devices,
    347-348, 354-364, 370-371
problem-solving model, 347-348,
    349-354, 368-370
problem-solving strategy, 348
program evaluation/review
    technique (PERT), 363

program planning model, 353
quality circles, 355, 365, 369
range of, 345-346
rational model, 350-351, 354, 355, 369
research agenda for, 368-376
RISK, 361
Robert's Rules of Order, 365
role playing, 357
single question form, 356, 369
solution design/evaluation, 360-361
solution implementation/evaluation, 363-364
standard agenda performance system, 363
stepladder, 369
strategic planning model, 353-354, 356
symposiums, 364
synectics, 357, 369
System 4T, 366
visioning, 369
See also Brainstorming; Communication technology; Group communication history; Nominal group technique (NGT); Procedural influence
Process of Group Thinking, The (Elliott), 100
Program evaluation/review technique (PERT), 363
Program planning model, 353
Propp, G., 292
Public discussion:
background for, 99-100
colloquies, 364
discussional attitude in, 103
features of, 101-104
forums, 364
in symbolic convergence theory, 99-104

panels, 364
symposiums, 364
Public Discussion and Debate (Baird), 100
Punctuated equilibrium model, 220-221, 229, 237-238
Putnam, L., 40, 150, 155

Quality circles, 355, 365, 369

Raisinghani, D., 354
Raman, K., 439
Rao, V., 447-448
Rasmussen, R., 359-360
Rational model, 350-351, 354, 355, 369
Rawlinson, J., 352
Reagan, P., 374
Reflective thinking model, 182-183, 350-351, 359, 367, 368, 369, 370
and decision performance, 276
development of, 21
Reilly, N., 159
Reinking, K., 309
Relational information, 435-437, 452
Relational leadership, 324, 325-326, 328 (figure), 333-334, 335-336
Responsibility theory, 37, 259
Restrictiveness:
in structuration theory, 137
of procedures, 370
Revolutionary period model, 220-221, 229, 237-238
Riley, P., 126
Robert's Rules of Order, 365
Rogers, P., 444
Rognes, J., 162
Rohrbaugh, J., 374
Roles:
and leadership, 330-331
in bona fide group theory, 150, 151, 154-155, 156

in decision performance, 284-287
in functional theory, 65-68
of group communication theory, 27-28
playing of, 357
Ross, R., 346-347, 350, 367-368, 369
Rost, K., 33
Roth, J., 14, 35, 131, 137, 141, 222-223, 224, 230, 231, 233-234, 235, 292
Rothwell, J., 362

Sabourin, T., 159
Salas, E., 310
Salazar, A., 203-204, 292
Sambamurthy, V., 236, 446
SAMM. See Software Aided Meeting Management
Savage, G., 314
Sayles, L., 303, 334
Schantz, D., 37-38
Scheerhorn, D., 42
Scheidel, T., 25, 111, 167, 222, 232, 352, 355, 358, 368, 375
Schultz, B., 311, 312
Schwartzman, H., 225
Schweiger, D., 361
Schwenk, C., 361
Scope, 370
SCT. See Social comparison theory
SDS. See Social decision scheme
Secord, P., 37
Segal, U., 230, 233
Seibold, D., 35, 37, 126, 127, 128, 130, 132, 138, 162, 244, 261, 347, 441
Senge, P., 271
Severson, M., 312
Shaw, M., 14, 274, 304
Shields, D., 4
Shotter, J., 118
Siegel, J., 436, 447
Simon, H., 10, 274, 356, 444

Single question form, 356, 369
SIT. See Social identity theory
Small Group Research (Frey), 39
Smith, C., 120, 125, 134
Smith, K., 124
Social behavior theory, 37
Social comparison theory (SCT), 246, 248-249, 250, 251-252, 254, 259
Social construction model, 225-229, 237-238
Social decision scheme (SDS):
in decision performance, 272-273
in group consensus, 392-394, 397-402, 408, 413, 414, 415, 419n2, 420-422
in socio-egocentric theory, 185-189, 244
in structuration theory, 130
Social identity theory (SIT), 246, 248, 249, 252-254, 259
Socio-egocentric theory:
and communication influence, 179-193, 201-207, 243-244
and Delphi technique, 204, 208n6
and distribution valence model (DVM), 186-189
and Markov chains, 189
and multiple sequence model, 203, 208n5
characteristics of, 193-198
development of, 37, 41-42
falsification of, 198-202, 208n4
input defined in, 181
input-output evidence in, 180-189, 192-193
limitations of, 205-207, 208n8
nominal group technique (NGT) in, 182-183
output defined in, 181
plausibility of, 202-203
process defined in, 181
process evidence in, 180-182, 189-193

process-output evidence in,
180-182, 189-193
social decision scheme (SDS) for,
185-189, 244
value of, 203-205
See also Bona fide group theory;
Functional theory; Group
communication history;
Structuration theory; Symbolic
convergence theory
Socioemotional information,
311-312, 314-315, 431, 436
Socioemotional leadership, 311-312,
314-315
Software Aided Meeting
Management (SAMM)
(University of Minnesota),
430. *See also* Communication
technology
Solomon, H., 184, 185, 272
Sorenson, J., 235
Sorenson, R., 314
Spillman, B., 309, 310, 313
Spillman, R., 309
Spiral model, 25
Spirit (in communication
technology), 132, 139, 442, 451
Spitzer, C., 391
Stageberg, N., 26
Standard agenda performance
system, 363
Stasser, G., 256, 391
Steiner, I., 272
Stepladder, 369
Stogdill, R., 305
Stohl, C., 40, 150, 155, 163
Stoner, J., 25, 247
Strategic planning model, 353-354,
356
Straus, S., 443
Strauss, A., 136
Street, R., 12
Strodtbeck, F., 217, 218
Stroebe, W., 359, 389

Structuration theory:
adaptive, 129, 432-433, 441
analysis of, 124-126, 141-142
and persuasive arguments theory
(PAT), 130
appropriation in, 122-123,
132-137, 139, 140-141
argumentation in, 35, 127-129, 140
coherent discourse in, 226-228
communication technology in,
126, 129, 130-132, 133, 134-138,
139, 432-433, 435-438, 441, 442,
451
contradiction in, 124, 138-140
defined, 116-118
development of, 34-36
distribution valence model
(DVM) for, 130
environmental influences in, 138
functional/constitutive analysis
in, 129
group control in, 137-138
group development in, 35
group interaction in, 114-115,
118-121, 124-126, 130-137
group task in, 137, 226-228
influence on group decisions,
126-142
institutional influences on, 115,
116-117, 121-123, 124-126, 140,
141
junctures in, 136, 140
leadership in, 120-121, 122-124
mediation in, 124, 130-131,
138-140
modalities of, 133-135, 140-141
multiple sequence model in, 35
nesting in, 128, 141
patterns of group use in, 134-135
restrictiveness in, 137
social decision scheme (SDS) for,
130
stability/change in, 115-116, 118,
142n1

structural interaction in, 123-124
structuring moves in, 132-137,
    138-139, 140-141, 239
vs. bona fide group theory,
    168-169, 171-174
See also Bona fide group theory;
    Functional theory; Group
    communication history;
    Socio-egocentric theory;
    Symbolic convergence theory
Structuring moves, 132-137, 138-139,
    140-141, 239
Stutman, R., 225, 229, 231-232
Style theory, 23-24
Symbolic convergence theory:
    and general communication
        theories, 86-87
    and special communication
        theories, 83-86
    and theory defined, 82-83
    convergence defined in, 90
    development of, 36
    dramatizing messages in, 91-95,
        98, 99
    fantasy chains in, 93, 94, 233, 293
    fantasy defined in, 88-89
    fantasy sharing documentation
        in, 95-97
    fantasy sharing in, 36, 90-95
    fantasy sharing influences in,
        104-112
    fantasy sharing reasons in, 97-99
    fantasy theme in, 93, 95
    fantasy types in, 36, 96-97
    function of, 89-90
    group fantasy in, 93, 94, 95
    public discussion in, 99-104
    rhetorical vision in, 36, 100
    structure of, 87-89
    See also Bona fide group theory;
        Functional theory; Group
        communication history;
        Socio-egocentric theory;
        Structuration theory

Symbolic information, 431, 437, 452
SYMLOG. See System for the
    Multiple Level Observation of
    Groups
Symposiums, 364
Synectics, 357, 369
System for the Multiple Level
    Observation of Groups
    (SYMLOG), 37-38
System 4T, 366

Tanita, N., 127
Tasks. See Group tasks
Taylor, D., 184
Teboul, J., 42
Theoret, A., 354
Thibaut, J., 114, 386
Thompson, R., 358-359
Tompkins, P., 37
Toulmin, S., 127-128
Tregoe, B., 358
Tubbs, S., 347
Turner, T., 253-254, 255-256
Turoff, M., 440, 444

Unitary sequence model, 217-218,
    229-230, 235, 236, 237-238

Valacich, J., 441
Van de Ven, A., 353
VanGundy, A., 355
Van Lear, C., 239
Vinokur, A., 249
Visioning, 369
VisionQuest (University of
    Michigan), 430. See also
    Communication technology
Vogel, D., 428-429
Vroom, V., 304-305, 363
Vygotsky, L., 194

Wagner, G., 428-429
Walker, L., 386
Wallas, G., 109
Walther, J., 436-437, 449
Watson, R., 131, 439
Watson, W., 367
Weick, K., 175, 316-317, 318, 319, 323
Weisband, S., 437-438, 439
Wentworth, D., 308
Wetherell, M., 253
Witteman, H., 312
Women. *See* Gender
Wood, J., 313, 350, 363
Wright, B., 308
Wright, D., 4, 27, 29, 38, 350, 370

Wright, E., 256-257
Wright, G., 93-94
Wyatt, N., 40
Wynne, B., 234, 428-429, 448

Yetton, P., 330, 363

Zaccaro, S., 305
Zack, M., 448-449
Zander, A., 348
Zey, M., 351
Zigurs, I., 438-439, 444

About the Contributors

Wing Tung Au is a doctoral candidate in the Department of Psychology at the University of Illinois, Urbana-Champaign. His research interests include small-group decision making, social dilemmas, and coalition formation.

Carolyn L. Baldwin (M.A., Purdue University) is a doctoral candidate at the University of Minnesota, Minneapolis, and is currently an assistant lecturer in the Department of Speech Communication at Texas A&M University, where she teaches courses in small group communication. Her research interests include computer-supported collaborative group processes, information technologies in the workplace, and the role of emergent networks in organizations.

J. Kevin Barge (Ph.D., University of Kansas) is Associate Professor of Communication Studies at Baylor University. His primary research interests are leadership, decision making, and university governance. He has published several book chapters, as well as research articles in *Management Communication Quarterly, Journal of Applied Communication Research, Communication Quarterly,* and *Western Journal of Speech Communication.* He has served on the editorial boards of *Management Communication Quarterly, Communication Monographs,* and *Communication Studies.* He currently serves as editor for *Communication Studies.*

Ernest G. Bormann (Ph.D., University of Iowa) is Professor Emeritus of Speech Communications at the University of Minnesota, Minneapolis. He has published numerous articles in such journals as *Communication Monographs, Quarterly Journal of Speech, Communication Theory,* and *Journal of Broadcasting.* He has also authored (or coauthored) books such as *Communication Theory; The Force of Fantasy: Restoring the American Dream; Discussion and Group Methods; Interpersonal Communication in the Modern Organization;* and *Effective Small Group Communication.* He received the Charles H. Woolbert Research Award for his work with symbolic convergence theory. He is also the recipient of the B. Aubrey Fisher Mentoring Award of the International Communication Association, and the Distinguished Service and Distinguished Scholar Awards of the Speech Communication Association.

James H. Davis received his Ph.D. from Michigan State University and is currently Professor of Psychology at the University of Illinois, Urbana-Champaign. In addition to numerous articles on small-group problem solving and group decision making, he is the author of *Group Performance* and coeditor of *Dynamics of Group Decisions* (with H. Brandstatter & H. Schuler), *Group Decision Making* (with H. Brandstatter & G. Stocker-Kreichgauer), and *Progress in Applied Social Psychology,* Volumes 1 and 2 (with G. Stephenson). His research has primarily been concerned with formal models of group performance, especially group decision making.

Larry Erbert (Ph.D., University of Iowa) is Assistant Professor of Communication at Baruch College in New York City. His research interests include dialectical aspects of marital conflicts, group conflicts, and interpersonal and small group communication.

Lawrence R. Frey (Ph.D., University of Kansas) is Professor of Communication at Loyola University Chicago. Author of 6 books and 40 chapters, articles, and reviews, his edited text, *Group Communication in Context: Studies of Natural Groups,* received both the 1995 Gerald R. Miller Book Award from the Interpersonal and Small Group Interaction Division and the 1994 Distinguished Book Award from the Applied Communication Division of the Speech Communication Association. Another edited text, *Innovations in Group Facilitation: Applications in*

Natural Settings, received honorable mention for the 1995 Applied Communication Distinguished Book Award. A forthcoming text, *The Fragile Community: Living Together With AIDS* (with M. Adelman), explores the 7-year relationship on communication and community in an AIDS residential facility. He is a recipient of the Outstanding Teacher Award from the Central States Communication Association and is President-Elect of that association.

Dennis S. Gouran (Ph.D., University of Iowa, 1968) is Professor and Head of the Department of Speech Communication at The Pennsylvania State University. Author of more than 120 books, chapters, articles, and reviews, he specializes in the study of decision making in groups. Current editor of *Communication Monographs* and past editor of *Central States Speech Journal,* he is a Speech Communication Association Distinguished Scholar and recipient of the Speech Communication Association Robert J. Kibler and Distinguished Service Awards. He is also recipient of The Pennsylvania State University Faculty Scholar's Medal for the Social and Behavioral Sciences. He was past president of both the Speech Communication Association and Central States Speech Association.

Dean E. Hewes is Professor in the Department of Speech-Communication, University of Minnesota, Minneapolis. He received his Ph.D. at Florida State University in 1974. He has published roughly 50 articles and book chapters, and one book, on topics including the development of social speech in children, the sequential analysis of social interaction, the effects of personality on communicative behavior, cognitive approaches to interpersonal communication, small group communication, and research methodology. He is currently involved in research on effects of gossip on individuals and personal relationships, small group theory, the concept of "emergence" and its implications for communication theory, and fly fishing for muskies.

Randy Y. Hirokawa (Ph.D., University of Washington) is Professor of Communication Studies and Adjunct Professor with the Health Sciences Center at the University of Iowa. His research interests include group decision-making effectiveness, organizational communication, and interdisciplinary health care team education. Professor Hirokawa's many articles on communication and group decision-making effectiveness have appeared in such journals as *Communication Monographs, Communication Quarterly, Communication Studies, Human Communication Research, Management Communication Quarterly,* and *Small Group Research.* He is the former editor of *Communication Studies* and has served on the editorial boards of *Communication Monographs, Organizational Science,* and *Small Group Research.*

Lorne Hulbert received his Ph.D. in Psychology from the University of Illinois, Urbana-Champaign. He is currently a lecturer in social psychology at the University of Kent in Canterbury, England.

Anthony Hurst (M.A., University of Montana) is a doctoral candidate in the Department of Communication Studies at the University of Iowa and Assistant Professor of Mass Media/Corporate Communication at Buena Vista University. His research interests include group decision making and organizational communication. His current research focuses on the role of narrativity in the genesis of organizations and organizational cultures.

Susan Jarboe (Ph.D., University of Wisconsin, Madison) is Assistant Professor of Speech Communication at The Pennsylvania State University, University Park. Her interests include communication in problem solving and decision making, conflict, and applications of communication theory. Her work has appeared in *Communication Monographs, Small Group Research,* and the *Journal of Applied Communication Research.*

Poppy Lauretta McLeod (Ph.D., Harvard University) is Associate Professor of Organizational Behavior in the College of Business at the University of Iowa. Her research interest include communication and decision-making effectiveness in groups, especially as affected by electronic group support systems. She is on the editorial board of *Small Group Research,* and her articles have appeared in *Information Systems Research, Human-Computer Interaction, Journal of Management Information Systems, Journal of Applied Behavioral Science, Small Group Research,* and *Academy of Management Journal.*

Robert D. McPhee is Associate Professor and Chair of the Department of Communication at the University of Wisconsin—Milwaukee. His focal interests include organizational communication and communication/social theory. He has recently served as Chair of the Organizational Communication Division of the Speech Communication Association, as book review editor of *Communication Theory*, and as Associate Editor (overseeing organizational communication manuscripts) of *Human Communication Research*. Two of his recent publications, in *Communication Monographs*, concern the evolution of climate themes in a governmental organization and the determinants of a communication network in a local church.

Renée A. Meyers (Ph.D., University of Illinois) is Associate Professor in the Department of Communication at the University of Wisconsin-Milwaukee. Her research interests include small-group decision making and argument. She is a former recipient of the SCA Distinguished Dissertation Award, and serves on the editorial boards of several journals.

Marshall Scott Poole (Ph.D., University of Wisconsin) is Professor of Speech-Communication at Texas A&M University. His research interests include group and organizational communication, information technology, conflict management, organizational innovation, and process research methods. He has published more than 70 articles and chapters, and his coauthored or edited books include *Communication and Group Decision-Making* (1st and 2nd ed.), *Working Through Conflict*, and *Research on the Management of Innovation*. Dr. Poole is one of the principal developers of the computerized meeting support system, *Software Aided Meeting Management* (SAMM) and is currently working on a Windows-based group support environment. He has consulted for 20 years on organizational communication, teamwork, conflict management, innovation, and computerized communication technologies.

Linda L. Putnam (Ph.D., University of Minnesota) is Professor and Head of the Department of Speech Communication at Texas A&M University. Her current research interests include groups in organizations, communication strategies in negotiation, organizational conflict, and language analysis in organizations. She has published more than

60 articles and book chapters in management and communication journals. She is the coeditor of *Communication and Negotiation* (1992), *Handbook of Organizational Communication* (1987), and *Communication and Organization: An Interpretive Approach* (1983). She is the 1993 winner of the Charles H. Woolbert Research Award for a seminal article in the field.

David R. Seibold (Ph.D., Michigan State University) is Professor of Communication at the University of California at Santa Barbara. His research interests include group decision making, interpersonal influence, and organizational change. He has published widely and received numerous research awards, including two Golden Anniversary Monograph Awards and the Charles H. Woolbert Research Award. He serves as editor of the *Journal of Applied Communication Research* and is a former Chair of the Interpersonal Communication Division of the International Communication Association and Vice Chair of the Organizational Communication division in that association.

Cynthia Stohl (Ph.D., Purdue University, 1982) is Professor of Communication at Purdue University. Her research and teaching focus on organizational and small group communication, with a primary emphasis on the dynamic relationship between worker participation, communication networks, and global integration. Her work has appeared in several journals, including *Human Communication Research, Communication Monographs, Management Communication Quarterly,* and *Journal of Applied Communication Research*. Her book, *Organizational Communication: Connectedness in Action* (1995), won the SCA Organizational Communication Division Outstanding Book Award in 1995.

Sunwolf (J.D., University of Denver College of Law) is a doctoral candidate/graduate student in the Department of Communication at the University of California at Santa Barbara. A former trial attorney, she serves on the faculties of the National Criminal Defense College, Mercer Law School, and the Institute for Criminal Defense Advocacy, California Western School of Law. Her research interests include interpersonal influence and small group decision making in the courtroom.